High and persistent unemployment has been experienced by most developed countries during the 1980s, and inflationary pressures have recently emerged at rates of unemployment far higher than those experienced in the 1960s and 1970s. This suggests that there has been an increase in the natural rate of unemployment. Many researchers have sought to explain this development in terms of 'mismatch', arguing that the economies that have suffered most from persistently high unemployment are those that been least flexible in matching their unemployed with the available employment opportunities.

This book reports the proceedings of a conference on 'Mismatch and Labour Mobility', sponsored jointly by the Centre for Economic Policy Research, the Centre for Economic Performance (formerly the Centre for Labour Economics) at the London School of Economics and the Centro Interuniversitario di Studi Teorici per la Politica Economica (STEP).

The contributors to this volume examine the evidence on sectoral wage differentials, labour mobility and the ratio of unemployment to job vacancies, in detailed studies of seven countries with a wide variety of labour market and macroeconomic structures: the United States and Japan, three North European economies (West Germany, Sweden, and the United Kingdom), and two in Southern Europe (Italy and Spain).

They analyse the variations in unemployment rates across regions, occupations and demographic groups, and investigate whether these help to explain the growth and persistence of unemployment. The volume also includes a cross-country study of skills mismatch in relation to the effectiveness of training programmes.

T0339927

Mismatch and labour mobility

Centre for Economic Performance

The Centre for Economic Performance is part of the London School of Economics. It studies the reasons for economic success among firms and nations.

The Centre's staff are drawn from a variety of disciplines and include, besides the staff at LSE, important groups from Sheffield and Oxford universities. The Centre incorporates the former Centre for Labour Economics at LSE.

It is an ESRC research centre but also receives income from other bodies. It currently has grants from the Esmée Fairbairn Trust and the Alfred P. Sloan Foundation, and research contracts with the Department of Employment, the Department of Trade and Industry, the Commission of the European Communities and London Buses.

The research programmes of the Centre for Economic Performance are corporate performance and work organisation; industrial relations; human resources; entrepreneurship; national economic performance; and post-Communist reform.

Director

Richard Layard   *30 June 1990*

STEP

STEP (Centro Interuniversitario di Studi Teorici per la Politica Economica) is a joint research centre of the economics departments of the universities of Bologna and Venezia and the institute of economics of Bocconi University, Milan. The centre promotes research in the area of economic policy and, through its collaboration with the Centre for Economic Policy Research, provides another STEP in furthering the Italian contribution to European economics.

Directors

Giorgio Basevi, Mario Monti, Gianni Toniolo

Scientific Advisory Board

Fiorella Padoa Schioppa, Richard Portes, Luigi Spaventa

30 June 1990

Centre for Economic Policy Research

The Centre for Economic Policy Research is a network of 140 Research Fellows, based primarily in European universities. The Centre coordinates its Fellows' research activities and communicates their results to the public and private sectors. CEPR is an entrepreneur, developing research initiatives with the producers, consumers and sponsors of research. Established in 1983, CEPR is already a European economics research organisation, with uniquely wide-ranging scope and activities.

CEPR is a registered educational charity. Grants from the Leverhulme Trust, the Esmée Fairbairn Charitable Trust, the Baring Foundation, the Bank of England and Citibank provide institutional finance. The ESRC supports the Centre's dissemination programme and, with the Nuffield Foundation, its programme of research workshops. None of these organisations gives prior review to the Centre's publications nor necessarily endorses the views expressed therein.

The Centre is pluralist and non-partisan, bringing economic research to bear on the analysis of medium- and long-run policy questions. CEPR research may include views on policy, but the Executive Committee of the Centre does not give prior review to its publications and the Centre takes no institutional policy positions. The opinions expressed in this volume are those of the authors and not those of the Centre for Economic Policy Research.

Mismatch and labour mobility

Edited by

FIORELLA PADOA SCHIOPPA

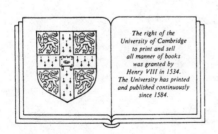

The right of the
University of Cambridge
to print and sell
all manner of books
was granted by
Henry VIII in 1534.
The University has printed
and published continuously
since 1584.

CAMBRIDGE UNIVERSITY PRESS

Cambridge

New York   Port Chester   Melbourne   Sydney

CAMBRIDGE UNIVERSITY PRESS
Cambridge, New York, Melbourne, Madrid, Cape Town, Singapore, São Paulo, Delhi

Cambridge University Press
The Edinburgh Building, Cambridge CB2 8RU, UK

Published in the United States of America by Cambridge University Press, New York

www.cambridge.org
Information on this title: www.cambridge.org/9780521402439

First published 1991
This digitally printed version 2008

A catalogue record for this publication is available from the British Library

Library of Congress Cataloguing in Publication data

Mismatch and labour mobility / edited by Fiorella Padoa Schioppa.
    p. cm.
Proceedings of a conference held in Venice on Jan. 4–6, 1990, sponsored by
the Centre for Economic Policy Research and others.
ISBN 0 521 40243 3
1. Labor market – Congresses. 2. Unemployment – Congresses.
3. Labor mobility – Congresses. I. Padoa-Schioppa, Fiorella, 1945–
II. Centre for Economic Policy Research (Great Britain)
HD5701.3.M57 1990
331.12′7 – dc20   90-2674

ISBN 978-0-521-40243-9 hardback
ISBN 978-0-521-10045-8 paperback

Contents

Figures

Tables

Preface

This volume contains the proceedings of a conference on 'Mismatch and Labour Mobility', held in Venice on 4–6 January 1990, sponsored jointly by the Centre for Economic Policy Research, the Centre for Labour Economics (now incorporated into the Centre for Economic Performance) at the London School of Economics, and the Centro Interuniversitario di Studi Teorici per la Politica Economica (STEP). Financial support for the conference was provided by Directorate General V (Employment, Social Affairs and Education) of the Commission of the European Communities, and the German Marshall Fund of the United States contributed to the travel costs entailed. Financial support for the production of the present volume was provided by the UK Department of Employment.

I am very grateful to Gianni Toniolo for co-organising the Conference and to the Economics Department of the University of Venice for their efficiency and warm hospitality during the Conference proceedings.

I thank Richard Portes, Stephen Yeo and Ann Shearlock for encouraging and enabling us to organise the Conference. Particular thanks go to Sarah Wellburn, CEPR Publications Officer, and to Barbara Docherty, Production Editor, for their outstanding professionalism.

I hope this book will acquaint the reader with the current state of debate on mismatch and connected labour-market problems: not all questions will find a ready-for-use answer, but we hope to have stimulated fresh debate, while providing some answers to the problems considered.

Fiorella Padoa Schioppa
15 June 1990

Acknowledgements

The editors and publisher wish to thank the following for permission to reproduce copyright material.

General Household Survey, for data in Tables 2.1 and 2.4 and Figure 2.1.
Employment and Earnings, for data in Tables 2.2, 2.4, 2.5, 2.8, 2.11, 2.13 and 2.15.
ILO, for data in Tables 2.3, 2.4 and 2.12 and Figure 2.1.
CPS, for data in Tables 8.1, 8.2, 8.3, 8.4 and 8.5.
Labour Force Survey, for data in Tables 2.5, 2.11, 2.17 and 2.19.
Department of Employment, for data in Tables 2.7, 2.10, 2.14, 2.17, 2.18, 7.1 and 7.3.
OECD, for data in Tables 1.2, 2.6, 2.9, 2.10 and 2.13, and Figure 1.2.
Employment and Training Report to the President, for data in Table 2.10.
US Bureau of Labor Statistics, for data in Tables 2.10, 8.2 and 8.3 and Figures 2.2 and 8.1.
HMSO, for data in Table 2.10 and Figure 2.2.
CSO, for data in Table 2.17 and Figure 2.1.
EUROSTAT, for data in Tables 1.2 and 2.16.
CBI, for data in Table 2.19 and Figure 7.2.
IFF Research Limited, for data in Table 2.19.
Sachverständigenrat zur Begutachtung der gesamtwirtschaftlichen Entwicklung, Jahresgutachten 1988/89, for data in Table 3.4.
Amtliche Nachrichten der Bundesanstalt für Arbeit, for data in Table 3.5.
Ministry of Labour (Japan), for data in Tables 4.1, 4.2, 4.7, 4.11, 4.12 and 4.13 and Figure 4.1.
Office of the Prime Minister (Japan), for data in Tables 4.3 and 4.4.
Fondazione Giacomo Brodolini and Centro Europa Ricerche, for data in Table 6N.3.
ISTAT, for data in Tables 6N.2 and 6N.4.
NBER Macroeconomics Annual 1989, for data in Table 7.5.

FIEF, for data in Table 10.2.
National Labour Market Board (Sweden), for data in Table 10.3.
Oxford Bulletin of Economics and Statistics, for data in Figure 2.1.
Historical Statistics of the United States, for data in Figure 2.2.
Jahrbuch für Regionalforschung, for data in Figure 3.7.
CEC, *Monthly Bulletin*, for data in Figure 1.2.
Isco-mondo Economica, *Monthly Bulletin*, for data in Figure 1.2.
Institut für Arbeitsmarkt und Berufsforschung, for data in Figure 3.9.
Brookings Institution, Washington, for data in Table 3.2.
Duncker and Humboldt, for data in Table 3.2.
Vandenhoeck and Ruprecht, Göttingen, Mannheim, for data in Figures 3.4–3.6.

Conference participants

Katharine Abraham, *University of Maryland*
Orazio Attanasio, *Stanford University and CEPR*
Charles Bean, *London School of Economics and CEPR*
Samuel Bentolila, *Banco de España*
Giuseppe Bertola, *Princeton University and CEPR*
Giorgio Bodo, *Banca d'Italia*
Giorgio Brunello, *Università di Venezia*
Renato Brunetta, *Fondazione Brodolini, Roma*
Michael Burda, *Institut Européen d'Administration des Affaires and CEPR*
Bruno Contini, *Università di Torino*
Per-Anders Edin, *Uppsala University*
Leonardo Felli, *Massachusetts Institute of Technology*
Wolfgang Franz, *Universität Konstanz*
Andrea Gavosto, *Banca d'Italia*
Bertil Holmlund, *Uppsala University*
Zmira Hornstein, *United Kingdom Department of Employment*
Richard Jackman, *London School of Economics*
Guy Laroque, *Institut National de la Statistique et des Etudes Econo-miques*
Richard Layard, *London School of Economics and CEPR*
John Martin, *OECD*
Karl Moene, *University of Oslo*
Anthony Murphy, *Nuffield College, Oxford*
Stephen Nickell, *Institute of Economics and Statistics, Oxford, and CEPR*
Fiorella Padoa-Schioppa, *Università di Roma 'La Sapienza', LUISS, and CEPR*
Makis Potamianos, *Commission of the European Communities*
Sherwin Rosen, *University of Chicago*
Nicola Rossi, *Università di Venezia*
Savvas Savouri, *London School of Economics*

Dennis Snower, *Birkbeck College, London, and CEPR*
David Soskice, *University College, Oxford*
Gianni Toniolo, *Università di Venezia and CEPR*
Ugo Trivellato, *Università di Padova*
Sushil Wadhwani, *London School of Economics and CEPR*
Stephen Yeo, *CEPR*

1 A Cross-country Comparison of Sectoral Mismatch in the 1980s[1]

FIORELLA PADOA SCHIOPPA

1 Foreword and summary

The idea on which the January 1990 Venice Conference on 'Mismatch and Labour Mobility' premised its proceedings was to verify whether the persistently high unemployment rates – observed in most countries since the first oil shock – could be explained by the growth of the frictional/structural component of unemployment, due to increasing mismatch.

Similar thoughts, inspiring many studies in this volume, have been widespread, especially in Europe, as indicated by the two following quotations. The 1990 *Annual Report* of the CEPS Macroeconomic Policy Group (Danthine *et al.*, 1990, 20) states: 'a common view is that Europe's unemployment problem is, to a significant degree, the result of a structural mismatch between the supply of, and the demand for, different skill types . . . Previous reports of this group have called attention to the need for greater differentials in labour costs, both regionally and across occupations if unemployment is to be kept at acceptable levels'. In turn, Burda and Wyplosz (1990, 1) add that 'high unemployment remains a highly visible feature of the European economic landscape. The conventional wisdom that has emerged over the past fifteen years is that high unemployment rates in Europe are symptomatic of insufficient economic activity or malfunctioning labor markets. Regardless of the cause, persistence or sluggish behavior of the stocks of unemployment and employment in European countries – in contrast to the United States, Canada and Japan – is taken as *prima facie* evidence of declining gross hiring and firing activity and deteriorating worker mobility'.

These being the presumptions on which this volume was based, it is only natural that it attempts to tackle the problem of sectoral imbalances under several different perspectives.

First of all, in an international perspective, the book compares the experiences of four main EC member states (two Northern – the United

1

Kingdom and Germany – and two Southern – Spain and Italy), of a non-EC European country (Sweden), and of two non-European countries (the United States and Japan).

Second, with regard to the content, the volume deals with at least four distinguished subjects. A first group of studies (Chapters 2, 3 and 4, respectively by Jackman, Layard and Savouri, by Franz and by Brunello) is devoted to exploring the nature of mismatch from different analytical and empirical viewpoints. A second group of studies (Chapters 5 and 6, respectively by Bentolila and Dolado and by Attanasio and Padoa Schioppa) aims at examining the connected problem of labour mobility and of interregional migration flows. Two contributions (Chapters 7 and 8, respectively by Bean and Pissarides and by Freeman) study the effect of technological shocks on employment and wage differentials of skilled vs. unskilled workers. A fourth set of studies (Chapters 9 and 10, respectively by Soskice and by Edin and Holmlund) attempts to assess whether private and public training and retraining programmes are effective in reducing the negative implications of sectoral shifts. The book ends with two excellent overview studies by Abraham and by Nickell (in Chapter 11), which makes any summary by me of each author's essential arguments superfluous. I will try only to highlight what I think to be the book's main achievements, as well as its main limitations.

The major result of this volume, in my opinion, consists in highlighting the looseness of the 'mismatch' concept – even though the term is frequently used both by experts and laymen – which explains why different mismatch definitions lead to such widely varying judgements on the same observable facts. This volume's lesson being as much destructive as constructive, one must state that the book also demonstrates its major limitation in failing to find a unified interpretation of the 'mismatch' phenomenon.

At least four approaches to mismatch emerge from the volume's studies. Approach (1) (described in section 2 below) associates mismatch with short-run sectoral shocks, which usually balance out at the aggregate level but temporarily raise both unemployment and vacancies: the turbulence index (in Lilien's, 1982, style) reveals this kind of mismatch. The remaining three approaches view mismatch as a more permanent phenomenon: the differences between them correspond to divergences on the concept of equilibrium unemployment relative to which mismatch is evaluated.

Approach (2) identifies mismatch within a disequilibrium (or rationing) model, under the basic assumption that the short side of each micro market determines its own employment level. At the aggregate level, given that the binding constraint is not the same in every micro market, unfilled vacancies in some sectors coexist with unemployment in others, and employment is lower than the minimum between aggregate labour demand and supply. In this framework, the equilibrium unemployment rate is the one which would arise if at the aggregate level the (notional) labour demand equalled supply: it is at the same time frictional and structural and, corresponding to the vacancy rate, is attributed to mismatch (section 3 below).

Approach (3) stems from the idea that frictional unemployment is unavoidable. It, then, defines mismatch as the distance of the unemployment rate from an optimal rate, proved to maximise aggregate hirings – under the conditions specified in section 4 below.

This optimal rate is obtained when the vacancy/unemployment rates ratio coincides across all micro markets. The corresponding mismatch indexes measure the intersectoral dispersion of the vacancy/unemployment rates ratios.

Approach (4) defines mismatch in terms of the NAIRU, as the distance of the unemployment rate from a minimum rate, compatible with price stability. This minimum is reached – under certain assumptions described in section 5 below – when all unemployment rates are identical in every micro market. The corresponding mismatch index measures the variance of the relative unemployment rates in the economic system.

Along with some elements of great interest, all these stands also present considerable shortcomings. This being the state of the mismatch theory, it is for the moment perhaps advisable to take up a cautious, rather eclectic approach, trying to combine the most relevant suggestions of the analyses undertaken (section 6 below).

In my view, the existence of the frictional/structural unemployment rate should be detected by the coexistence, at the aggregate level, of both unemployment and vacancies, even when aggregate labour demand equals labour supply: the benchmark equilibrium unemployment rate should therefore be equal to the vacancy rate (as in approach (2)). One would then say that a rise in frictional/structural unemployment relative to the observed unemployment rate requires a mounting vacancy/unemployment ratio. But the observed increase in this ratio might stem, ceteris paribus, from three causes: a reduction in the labour market aggregate disequilibrium (an upward movement along a 'Beveridge curve') or an outward shift of the 'Beveridge curve', the latter due to misplacement, either because frictions are growing within each micro market or – as a third possibility – because larger intersectoral discrepancies of unemployment and vacancies (and hence mismatch) are arising.

The growth of the vacancy/unemployment ratio at the aggregate level is thus a necessary, but not a sufficient, condition to make us suspect that the increasing mismatch is responsible for the rising unemployment rate. To identify whether, *ceteris paribus*, the growth in the vacancy/ unemployment ratio depends on higher misplacements or on falling aggregate disequilibria, one has to observe the unemployment rate: it has to increase in the former case and decrease in the latter. Finally, to distinguish whether higher misplacements are due to mismatch or to other reasons, one has to verify the existence of a growing intersectoral dispersion in the vacancy/unemployment ratios (accepting, on this point, the most important message contained in approaches (3) and (4)).

I therefore propose to adopt a threefold criterion to assess whether a growing mismatch uniquely explains a worsening in the unemployment rate dynamics: the vacancy/unemployment rate ratio, the unemployment rate, and finally the intersectoral dispersion of the vacancy/unemployment rates ratios have all to increase. There are other cases in which a growing mismatch can partly contribute to explaining the unemployment dynamics. In these cases – which arise when shifts of the 'Beveridge curve' are combined with movements along the 'Beveridge curve' – the intersectoral dispersion of the vacancy/unemployment ratios has to grow, with or without a parallel rise in the observed unemployment rate or in the vacancy/unemployment ratio.

Through this methodology, I analyse (in section 7 below) the industrial mismatch in the 1980s of 8 European countries for which data on 19 sectors, homogeneously defined across countries, have been regularly collected through EC business surveys ever since 1980. It then appears that, almost everywhere, the vacancy/unemployment ratio declined from 1980 to 1982–3, presented a cyclical positive trend up to 1987 and a sharp rise thereafter. In the meanwhile, almost everywhere, the dispersion index of the 19 sectors' vacancy/unemployment ratios was cyclically fluctuating, showing a general, year by year, negative correlation with the rate of change of the vacancy/unemployment ratio and a mildly negative trend after 1983.

It therefore seems most unlikely that industrial mismatch and structural imbalances supply a unique, or even an important, explanation of the European unemployment in the 1980s: the information contained in the country studies in this volume – concerning both the EC countries I have examined through the business survey data and other European and non-European countries – confirm (through different indicators) that nowhere in the 1980s has the industrial dispersion index been positively trended.

I should also point out that everywhere in Europe, in Japan and in the United States the unemployment performance has not been globally unsatisfactory in the 1980s. Reporting standardised cross-country data, I suggest (in section 8 below) that, though long-term comparisons between the *average* unemployment rates in the 1980s and in the 1970s (and *a fortiori* in the 1960s) reveal a worsening in all countries, almost everywhere the rate of change of unemployment rates *within* the 1980s has been positive only up to the mid-1980s, while becoming continuously negative thereafter. The 1980s clearly trace a downturn in all countries' unemployment rates, in a time interval running from 1983 (Belgium, Luxemburg, the Netherlands, the United States and Sweden) to 1985 (Germany, Spain, Ireland, Portugal, the United Kingdom) and 1986 (Italy and Japan), with no subsequent uptrend. Exceptions are France, showing a late downturn in 1987 and Denmark, whose unemployment rate turned down in 1982 but has moved up again since 1987.

Looking at all this empirical evidence, one therefore gets the impression that there exists a consistent story for the 1980s' unemployment rates. Contrary to the layman's opinion, unemployment steadily increased only up to the mid-1980s and then decreased almost everywhere. In the meantime, the vacancy/unemployment rates ratio declined almost everywhere up to about 1983 and then rose again: consequently, misplacements are not likely to explain the unemployment dynamics of the 1980s. As the intersectoral dispersion of the vacancy/unemployment ratios has been cyclical and has grown nowhere in the second half of the 1980s, one may apparently conclude that neither frictional nor structural changes – due to industrial mismatch – are important components of the initial rise and the subsequent fall in unemployment rates. Industrial mismatch possibly played a downward minor role in the second half of the 1980s, when it was slightly falling while unemployment rates were also decreasing.

Aggregate disequilibria (due to lack of aggregate labour demand relative to labour supply) probably bear the major responsibility for the unemployment rate increase of the first half of the 1980s and its reduction in the second half. Similar reasoning seems to apply both to the countries included in the EC business survey data set and to the others under consideration in this volume (Spain, Sweden, Japan and the United States).

Though no study in this volume apparently contradicts these conclusions, most authors would suggest that industrial mismatch is not really relevant, because geographical location more than other components has contributed to labour mismatch. To test this hypothesis, I have utilised the EC business survey information, not to measure the intersectoral dispersion within each country but to evaluate the 'regional' dispersion between the 8 European countries (the national states being 'regions' of *EUR*8), sector by sector and in industry as a whole. In fact, my data indicate that 'regional' mismatch in Europe has been positively correlated to the vacancy/unemployment ratios of *EUR*8 and has been positively trended after 1982 in most intermediate and consumer good sectors and in industry as a whole. One should state here with regard to the European unemployment in the 1980s that aggregate disequilibria have brought about a rise and then a fall in unemployment, while 'regional' imbalances within Europe have first decreased and then grown, increasingly explaining the declining rate of aggregate unemployment.

This suggests the value of few policy interventions, perhaps at a supernational level, particularly through training, retraining and manpower programmes; through some sort of deregulation in the labour market so as to enable it better to signal the relative labour scarcities while increasing the proper wage differentials; through a wise mix of subsidies and taxation in order to favour labour and capital mobility, whenever there emerge clear externalities or whenever market adjustments appear too slow.

2   Short-run and long-run sectoral shocks

As recalled in section 1, there are essentially two (implicit or explicit) assumptions in the studies in this volume:

1.   that there is a high and persistent unemployment rate to be explained;
2.   and that this rate possibly – and at least partly – depends on structural imbalances or labour mismatch (by skill, by occupation, by region or by sector).

While I shall return to the first aspect in section 8 below, I will devote the next few pages to a problem connected with the second aspect, notably the definition of 'mismatch'.

There are four main discrepancies emerging in the various mismatch concepts (hereafter labelled (1)–(4)) utilised by the authors and the discussants of the studies in this volume. The first regards the short- or long-term nature of the phenomenon analysed, as is outlined by Nickell (Chapter 11 in this volume: hereafter, the citation of an author, if not otherwise stated, will refer to his or her contribution to this book). According to approach (1), mismatch is associated with short-run sectoral shocks which (usually) balance out at the aggregate level and raise both unemployment in the contracting sectors and vacancies in the expanding ones, given that it takes time to reach the steady-state adjustment obtained through wage–price flexibility and factors' mobility.

This approach is apparently the one adopted by Freeman in his study (Chapter 8) on American labour market tightness, when he says: 'The simplest interpretation of a mismatch is in terms of shifts in the supply and demand schedules that in the long run induce offsetting long-term changes in labour supply'. This is also Brunello's point of view, expressed in his analysis of mismatch in Japan (Chapter 4): 'Let [the] economy be displaced from its long-run equilibrium by (temporary) sector-specific shocks that do not alter the aggregate relation between the demand and supply. In a frictionless economy the long-run equilibrium is instantaneously recovered. With frictions, however, the original displacement persists over time as the economy goes through a sequence of short-run equilibria. Because of relative wage rigidities, incomplete information and costly labour mobility, the sectoral distribution of unemployment (and vacancies) is altered and aggregate unemployment could be reduced by reallocating labour among different sectors. There is mismatch'.

It is certainly no accident that the only two studies exclusively embracing this approach in the present volume concern the only two non-European economies examined. Indeed, as Nickell states, the short-run stand, endorsed by many American economists,[2] 'is not taken to be very important by most European economists who are searching for explanations of the secular rise in unemployment over the last two decades'. The short-run approach emerges, however, as a minor ingredient also in other studies in the book, when looking at the industrial or the regional turbulence index (as in Lilien, 1982). In no country of our concern (EC, Sweden, the United States and Japan) do the regional and industrial turbulence indexes, reported for 7 countries by Jackman, Layard and Savouri (Chapter 2, hereafter JLS), by Bentolila and Dolado (Chapter 5) and by Brunello, rise in the 1980s as against the previous decades: a mild exception is found in the United Kingdom and Sweden (for the regional turbulence) and in the United Kingdom and the Netherlands (for the industrial turbulence).

The three other approaches to mismatch adopted in this volume, sometimes as an alternative to, sometimes in combination with, the first approach (and often in combination with each other) concern long-term phenomena: the difference between them essentially depends on the different definitions of equilibrium unemployment.

3 Equilibrium and disequilibrium unemployment

In approach (2), followed by Franz (Chapter 3) for Germany and by Bentolila and Dolado for Spain, mismatch is identified within the disequilibrium (or equilibrium with rationing) model, developed in the European Project on Unemployment (see Drèze and Bean, 1990). This model is based on the assumption that the short side of each micro market i

determines the level of transacted labour in i: the existence of rationing thus implies that there exists, in each i, either unfilled vacancies or unemployment. At the aggregate level, however, given that not all micro markets are rationed on the same side (for some markets, the binding constraint is labour demand, while for others it is labour supply), vacancies and unemployment coexist and aggregate employment is lower than the minimum between aggregate labour demand and supply. The larger the variance between micro markets, the smaller is aggregate employment relative to the minimum between aggregate labour demand and supply, and the more spread is mismatch said to be.

This simple idea is conveyed by the following aggregate employment equation, utilised within the European Project on Unemployment and here adopted by Franz and Bentolila and Dolado,

$$N = (LD^{-\rho} + LS^{-\rho})^{-1/\rho} : \tag{1}$$

N = aggregate employment; LD = aggregate (notional) labour demand, being

$$LD = N + V \tag{2}$$

with V = unfilled vacancies; LS = aggregate labour supply, being

$$LS = N + U \tag{3}$$

with U = aggregate unemployment; $1/\rho \geq 0$, indicating the variance between micro markets, represents the mismatch index. Indeed, if $1/\rho = 0$ and equation (1) is transformed into $N = \min(LD, LS)$, mismatch is said to be non-existent; the larger is $1/\rho$, the higher is the equilibrium (or structural) unemployment rate arising at full employment, defined (Beveridge, 1955, 77) 'as a state of affairs in which the number of unfilled vacancies is not appreciably below the number of unemployed persons'.

In fact, substituting equations (2) and (3) into equation (1), the latter is transformed into the following 'Beveridge curve'

$$1 = (1 + v)^{-\rho} + (1 + u)^{-\rho}, \tag{4}$$

where $v \equiv V/N$ is the aggregate vacancy rate and $u \equiv U/N$ is the aggregate unemployment rate. Therefore, if the equilibrium rate of unemployment, u^*, is defined, as before, at the full employment level where $u = v$,

$$u^* = v \tag{5}$$

i.e., in equation (4),

$$u^* = 2^{1/\rho} - 1, \tag{5'}$$

which increases when the mismatch parameter, $1/\rho$, rises.

Obviously, the observed aggregate unemployment rate, u, is bigger than u^* if and only if there is aggregate disequilibrium – i.e., if $LD < LS$. The ideal decomposition of u is therefore

$$u \equiv \frac{U}{N} = \left(\frac{LS - LD}{N}\right) + \left(\frac{LD - N}{N}\right) = \left(\frac{U - V}{N}\right) + \left(\frac{V}{N}\right)$$

$$= (u - v) + v$$

(5″)

The last component of the unemployment rate in the RHS of equation (5″), (v), is the equilibrium or structural or mismatch component of the unemployment rate; the first component, ($u - v$), is the disequilibrium component of the unemployment rate, due to insufficient aggregate labour demand relative to aggregate labour supply and is labelled u_s:

$$u_s = u - v$$

(5‴)

Both Franz for Germany and Bentolila and Dolado for Spain refer to the fact that the estimation of $1/\rho$ shows an outward shifting of the 'Beveridge curve' through time. Generally speaking, $1/\rho$ seems to be upward trended in *all* the countries where the same model[3] as in equations (1)–(5) has been estimated within the European Project on Unemployment – i.e., Austria, Belgium, Denmark, France, Italy and the Netherlands, the United States – while other forms of 'Beveridge curve' also show an outward shifting in the United Kingdom (see Jackman, Layard and Pissarides, 1984) and in Japan (Brunello), but not in Sweden (according to Edin and Holmlund in Chapter 10).

Approach (2) deserves four comments:

(a) First, the min condition at the micro market level rules out by definition the coexistence of unemployment and vacancies in each micro market. This is a very specific assumption: even in the absence of rationing (see, among others, Pissarides, 1985, 1986 and Blanchard and Diamond, 1990), the matching within each sector is a time-consuming process which is longer the more scattered is the information, the more limited is the search intensity, the higher is the choosiness on the part of employers and employees. Thus u_i and v_i coexist in each micro market, i, along a sectoral 'Beveridge curve'. Geographical, occupational and sectoral differences between idle workers and available jobs, which in this more general model are properly responsible for mismatch account for only a part of what might be generally called misplacement (following Dow and Dicks-Mireaux, 1958).

Only a fraction of the unemployment rate, u^*, existing at full employment, depends on mismatch and should be labelled structural unemployment, while the other portion, corresponding to frictional unemployment, depends on other causes of misplacement. In what follows we will adopt the definition given by Jackman and Roper (1987, hereafter JR, 10): 'it is customary to attribute the co-existence of unemployment and unfilled vacancies within a sector to labour market "frictions" (time taken over job search or recruitment due to imperfect information), while if there is unemployment (in excess of frictional) in some sectors of the economy and vacancies (in excess of frictional) in others, there is said to be structural imbalance and this category of unemployment is described as structural'.[4]

As suggested by Hansen's (1970) pioneering study, even within a disequilibrium model it is possible to relax the assumption that, at the micro market level, v_i and u_i cannot coexist and still come out with the equilibrium concept of unemployment, u^*, now redefined as frictional/structural.

In this case, however, the growth of $1/\rho$, observed through time, may not be caused by rising mismatch, and the corresponding increase in u^* cannot be said to depend exclusively on increasing structural imbalances, even though this does remain a correct formulation within the model of the European Project on Unemployment.

(b)   Though Franz and Bentolila and Dolado do not discuss this point anaytically, their estimates, aimed at explaining the growth in $1/\rho$, shed light on this element at an empirical level. Indeed, Franz states that the fact that the 'higher degree of fixity of labour due to legislative employment protection ... and higher investments in firm-specific human capital undertaken by the firm ... [has a] positive impact ... on the rise of the [so-called] structural rate of unemployment supports our suspicion of a shift in hiring patterns in the sense that employers appear to have become choosier': we know by now that this kind of rise in u^* is due to frictions within micro markets rather than to mismatch and structural imbalances between micro markets. A similar comment is partially appropriate for Bentolila and Dolado when, in replicating an econometric exercise produced in Padoa Schioppa (1990) within the disequilibrium model adopted in the European Project on Unemployment, they declare that they have 'successfully explained ... the trend of $1/\rho$ through ... the unweighted standard deviation of regional unemployment rates, ... the gross interregional migration as a proportion of total population ... the proportion of long-term unemployed (one year or more) in the labour force ... [and] ... finally, the turbulence index for total employment'.

(c)   There is furthermore, a considerable difference between showing the growth in the frictional/structural unemployment rate, u^*, and explaining through this increase the observed rise in the aggregate unemployment rate, u: the fact that u^* rises through time does not necessarily imply that the share of the observed unemployment due to frictional/structural reasons (u^*/u) also grows through time. To this end, it is interesting – and indeed illuminating – to verify from the data reported by Drèze and Bean (1990) concerning u^* and u that, though u^* increases between the early 1960s and the mid-1980s in all the ten countries analysed, only in Italy and France is u^*/u higher in 1986 compared to the beginning of the period.

(d)   Finally, even though the determination of the equilibrium rate of unemployment, u^* at $u = v$, is very common and appears in models close to Drèze and Bean (as Hansen, 1970 or Malinvaud, 1986) and in completely different models (such as Abraham, 1983 or Edin and Holmlund), it is also questioned by many people. For example, Jackman, Layard and Pissarides (1984, 4) propose to 'replace the commonly used criterion of $u = v$, which has no theoretical basis' (without explaining why this is so) and Abraham (1983, 722) states that it is not necessarily optimal to have 'the same number of jobs vacant as there are persons unemployed . . . The optimal vacancy rate/unemployment rate combination (along a 'Beveridge curve') will depend upon the marginal social costs associated with unemployment and with job vacancies'.

4   Equilibrium unemployment and maximum aggregate hirings

The critical comments about approach (2), referred to above, lay the basis for the third approach to the mismatch problem, which is largely adopted in the studies in this volume. The basic idea is that mismatch should be measured in terms of the distance from an equilibrium unemployment rate, u^{**}, different from u^* because it assumes that frictional unemployment is unavoidable within each micro market i. As JR (1987, 11) put it, 'it is thus necessary to measure the extent of sectoral imbalances relative to the existing aggregate levels of unemployment and vacancies in the economy, rather than to some hypothetical, but probably unattainable, state where the unemployment rate equalled the vacancy rate in each sector'. This equilibrium rate can be proved to be

$$u^{**} = v\,(u_i/v_i) \qquad \forall\, i : \tag{6}$$

The equilibrium aggregate rate of unemployment has the property that its ratio to the aggregate vacancy rate equals the unemployment/vacancy rate ratio in each micro market i.

The intuition behind this result is simple. Given the frictions within each i, a sectoral 'Beveridge curve' – supposed identical everywhere – arises. Hence, the aggregate 'Beveridge curve' has the same shape: its convexity implies that the minimum unemployment rate is reached when the sectoral (u_i/v_i) ratios are equalised. The demonstration produced by JR (1987) goes along the following lines. Let the hiring function in each micro market be H_i and assume that it is a linear homogeneous function of U_i and V_i. Then $\hat{h}_i = H_i/N_i$ is a linear homogeneous function of u_i and v_i and can be written as

$$\hat{h}_i = v_i h_i(u_i/v_i). \tag{7}$$

The maximum of aggregate hirings (ΣH_i), subject to $\Sigma U_i = U$ and to a given pattern of vacancy rates, is obtained at

$$h'(u_i/v_i) = \text{constant, if and only if } h_i = h \quad \forall i \tag{8}$$

Let us stress that the optimum unemployment/vacancy rate ratio, identified in equation (8) as the one which is equalised across micro markets, *requires* as a strong assumption that the hiring functions (h_i) be the *same* (equal to h) in each micro market. Indeed, if h_i were different in different i, the maximum of ΣH_i would not be reached by equalising (u_i/v_i) across micro markets, and thus the unemployment rate, u^{**}, as defined in equation (6), would no longer be optimal.

Though the necessary assumptions to obtain the result in equation (6) are strong, all the mismatch synthetical indexes utilised in approach (3) are based on them. They inevitably show that mismatch is higher the higher the intersectoral dispersion of the unemployment/vacancy rate ratios. The two most commonly used indicators,[5] as noted by Abraham, are:

$$M_1 = \tfrac{1}{2} \Sigma |\hat{u}_i - \hat{v}_i|,$$

where $\hat{u}_i$ is the share of unemployment in i, relative to aggregate unemployment, and $\hat{v}_i$ is the share of vacancies in i, relative to aggregate vacancies; and

$$M_2 = 1 - \Sigma (\hat{u}_i \hat{v}_i)^{1/2}.$$

M_1 measures (JR, 1987, 13) 'the number of unemployed workers who need to be moved from one sector to another in order to achieve structural balance – i.e., u^{**}; M_2 identifies (JR, 1987, 14) the 'contribution of structural imbalances to overall unemployment' (i.e., $M_2 = (u - u^{**})/u$), provided some further assumption on $h_i = h$ is added, namely that the hiring function is a Cobb–Douglas with equal elasticity (of $\tfrac{1}{2}$), relative to vacancies and unemployment.

Looking at the evidence on regional and occupational mismatch produced by the indexes M_1 and M_2, computed in the studies in this volume and in JR (1987), one would conclude that no country shows a positive trend in the occupational mismatch, while the regional one appears to increase in Germany and in Japan but not in the United Kingdom and in Sweden: these results are synthesised in Abraham's Tables 11.1 and 11.2.

5   Equilibrium unemployment and the minimum NAIRU

Approach (4) measures mismatch in terms of the NAIRU, as the distance between the unemployment rate and an equilibrium unemployment rate, u^{***}, which would be the minimum compatible with price stability. JLS, who first introduce this concept, followed by many authors in this volume, show that the minimum unemployment rate, u^{***}, is obtained when all unemployment rates are equalised across micro markets, i:

$$u^{***} = u_i \qquad \forall i. \tag{9}$$

The corresponding mismatch indicator is proved to be

$$M_3 = \tfrac{1}{2} \operatorname{var}(u_i/u).$$

The latter has three nice features. First, it is a frequently used dispersion index in descriptive statistics (being nothing but half of the squared coefficient of variation of unemployment rates, u_i). Second, it requires no knowledge of the vacancy rates by sectors – a piece of information which is unavailable for some countries (like Italy and Ireland) and is usually biased when officially available. Finally, it has the appealing property in the JLS model of being equal to $\log(u/u^{***})$, thus indicating the percentage of aggregate unemployment due to structural imbalances.

The latter property, however, is based on three strong assumptions which may or may not be verified in different countries and in different disaggregations of each country's labour market. These are: (a) the convexity of the sectoral wage function; (b) the dependence of every sector's wage-setting on the unemployment rate of that sector; (c) the equality of the wage-setting functions across micro markets, apart from a sectoral fixed effect, appearing in the constant of the equations.

For a better understanding of these three hypotheses, their analytical implications and their empirical validity, let us recall the functional form used by JLS for their wage equation in each micro market, w_i:

$$\log w_i = \beta_i - \gamma \log u_i, \tag{10}$$

where (a) holds true because $d^2 w_i/du_i^2 > 0$; condition (b) is self-evident; and assumption (c) is verified because γ is not sector-specific.

Combining the price function[6]

$$\log p = \delta_i \Sigma \log w_i + \text{constant} \tag{11}$$

with equation (10), the latter implies, at stable prices, p, a convex relation between the unemployment rates of the various sectors i.

This convexity is crucial to reach the result that the minimum aggregate unemployment rate, u^{***}, requires the equalisation of all u_i across micro markets.

Whether or not the assumptions contained in equation (10) are correct is merely an empirical matter.[7] JLS supply some evidence that equation (10) is not contradicted by few English and American data.

Freeman's study (Chapter 8) provides further support to the idea that there is an 'inverse relation between area unemployment and the earnings of young less-educated men. No relation [however, exists] between area unemployment and the earnings of young more-educated men'.

Bean and Pissarides (Chapter 7), in examining the determinants of industrial wages, look in particular for the 'role played by firm-/industry-specific factors *vis-à-vis* general economic factors'. Their econometric results show that both manual and non-manual wages (in log) depend on an industry-specific labour tightness variable (in log), but the latter is not unemployment.[8] More than that, aggregate unemployment appears to have a strong influence on industrial wages, albeit with a positive sign. Hence, 'both manual and non-manual wages are influenced by firm-/industry-specific factors as well as economy-wide developments . . . The skill shortage variable appears to be a better indicator of labour market pressures than the unemployment rate'. Therefore, following Bean and Pissarides and Freeman, we should conclude that in the United Kingdom and the United States an index like M_3 would not be the most appropriate to measure skill mismatch.

The suspicion that the assumptions embodied in equation (10) have a rather weak empirical foundation is even stronger for all the countries for which a sectoral regional wage equation has been analysed in the studies in this volume, or, as far as I know, elsewhere.[9]

Let us refer to our volume's results on regional wage-settings. As for Spain, Bentolila and Dolado state that 'the common view is that local supply and demand conditions play only a limited role in the determination of regional wages . . . In our estimates there is a well defined (albeit small) positive relationship between a region's relative wage and its unemployment differential'. But their estimated wage equation (being in *semi-log* form) does *not* lead to the convex relation between regional unemployment rates that is necessary to assign to M_3 the meaning of a mismatch index.

In Italy, as reported by Attanasio and Padoa Schioppa, regional wages do not seem to react negatively to regional unemployment rates. This occurs because contractual wages are determined at the national level, regional effective wages mostly depend on the leading sector's (North-Centre) unemployment rate (as shown by Bodo and Sestito, 1989) and the local net real wage dynamics seems to *compensate* the path of local unemployment, so that expected returns tend to equalise across regions (in a Harris–Todaro, 1970-style model).

The estimation of regional wage equations for Japan leads Brunello to conclude in Chapter 4 that 'regional unemployment rates do not significantly affect regional hourly real wages. Notice that the irrelevance of regional unemployment is quite robust to variations in the specification of [the] equation . . ., including the JLS regional wage equation. Overall, this evidence points to the stabilising role of Japanese local wages'.

The empirical evidence on regional wage-setting provided for Spain, Italy and Japan in this volume leads one to object to the general validity of equation (10), thus leading one to reject the idea that the minimum unemployment rate, u^{***}, is obtained in these countries where all u_i are equalised across regions. Consequently, M_3 loses its ability to measure geographical mismatch, though it remains a useful dispersion index of relative unemployment rates. As such, it has to be interpreted when it is used, among others, by Bentolila and Dolado, Attanasio and Padoa Schioppa and Brunello.

There is a final reason to believe that equation (10), with its three fundamental assumptions, is not generally confirmed by the data on most OECD countries, for which there exists a multiplicity of estimated aggregate wage equations. Notice that, if assumption (c) held true in each sectoral wage-setting – i.e., if γ were constant across micro markets – the wage function estimated at the aggregate level should also have the same form as equation (10) – a double log form. Indeed, if we call w the average wage rate (calculated as a geometric mean of sectoral w_i) and u the aggregate unemployment rate (calculated as a geometric mean of sectoral u_i), provided γ is constant, equation (10) is transformed into

$$\log w \equiv \Sigma \alpha_i \log w_i = \Sigma \beta_i \alpha_i - \gamma \Sigma \alpha_i \log u_i \equiv \text{constant} - \gamma \log u \quad (12)$$

Apparently, there exists overwhelming OECD empirical evidence contradicting equation (12) at the aggregate level. I will refer to three experiments, carried out by Grubb (1985), Bean, Layard and Nickell (1986) and Drèze and Bean (1990).

Grubb estimates in various pooled regressions the wage equation for 15 OECD countries, and shows that the best estimation implies in the long run the semi-log form

$$\log w = \text{constant} - \gamma u + \text{other push factors} \quad (13)$$

Grubb does not forget to try other types of wage equations – called Phillips curves – with steady implications different from equation (13), particularly with regard to the linear effect of u on log w. He concludes, however (17), that 'a simple test for non-linearity in the response to unemployment is to include log u in the Phillips curve . . . [in which case the estimates] show a tendency for u to be more significant than log u in the Phillips curve, so that the average response to unemployment is not strongly non-linear'.

Bean, Layard and Nickell (1986) tried a similar experiment and estimated the wage-setting equation of about 20 OECD countries, with the following long-term properties

$$\log w = \text{constant} + \frac{\gamma_2}{\gamma_1} \log(1 - u) + \text{other push factors} \qquad (13')$$

Although the estimates are quite sensible for most aspects, they are not very successful in terms of the parameters $\gamma_1\,\gamma_2$, that should be of equal sign to confirm the double-log form of equation (12) – necessary but not sufficient for the validity of equation (10). Extracting from the group of countries they analyse all those belonging to the EC, plus the three other countries involved in this volume (the United States, Japan and Sweden), the estimation of Bean, Layard and Nickell (1986) show that only Denmark and France present an equal *and* significant sign for γ_1 and γ_2.

The estimations carried out in ten countries within the European Project on Unemployment supply our third test on the greater empirical robustness at the aggregate level of equation (13) than (12): Drèze and Bean (1990) survey the estimated wage equations – presumably the preferred ones at each country level – and indicate that, though these equations are different from many points of view, they all have a long-run solution similar to equation (13), with the exception of France (where u appears linearly in a $\Delta \log w$ equation without a steady state[10]), and the Netherlands (where unemployment does not appear as a regressor).

If the semi-log form for the wage-setting were preferred even at the sectoral level – a subject still to be studied in depth – then the convexity in the u_i function would be lost and the minimum variance in relative unemployment rates would no longer represent the identifying condition of the equilibrium unemployment rate u^{***}; M_3 could still be calculated, but should not be interpreted as a mismatch index.

All this empirical evidence leads me to consider the index M_3 as a useful piece of information on the dispersion of unemployment rates across micro markets, rather than as a mismatch indicator; Nickell, too, seems to share this assessment. If that is so, there is no presumption that M_3 should provide indications similar to those of M_1 or M_2 on the mismatch path in the various countries. This is why Abraham is, in my opinion, only partly correct when, referring to M_1, M_2 and M_3, she states that '[t]he disturbing feature of the results . . . is that trends in measured skill mismatch within individual countries appear to be quite sensitive both to the measure used and to the occupational groupings employed in their construction . . . [while] the geographic mismatch measures . . . appear to be somewhat more robust, in the sense that the movements in different mismatch measures for a particular country seem generally to be similar': there is no reason to be disturbed when two indicators of two different phenomena are uncorrelated.

But Abraham is right when she stresses that the comparisons between various mismatch indexes are affected by spurious discrepancies in occupational or regional groupings; she is also right when she states that the meaning of these indicators is weakened by the presence of quite different hiring functions in different micro markets, and by the absence of sufficiently disaggregated data, truly corresponding to distinct labour markets.

With all these *caveats*, it is finally interesting to look at the indexes M_3, as computed in the studies in this volume, because the dispersion of unemployment rates by occupation seems to have increased wherever it has been calculated (in Sweden, in Germany and probably in Spain and in the United States – up to 1983); only in the United Kingdom has it not been trended. The regional dispersion of unemployment rates has grown in Italy, in the United States and probably in Japan, while it has decreased (up to 1985) in the United Kingdom and in Spain, and has shown no definite trend in Sweden.

6   A more eclectic approach to mismatch

What has been stated so far on the various definitions of the equilibrium unemployment rate – u^*, u^{**}, u^{***} – and on the corresponding mismatch indicators, brings us to the conclusion that all these concepts present, along with interesting aspects, considerable shortcomings. This being the state of the theory, it is worth adopting a rather eclectic approach to mismatch. My own, which I will use in providing some further cross-country comparison of the sectoral mismatch dynamics, is as follows.

The identification of the presence of the frictional/structural unemployment rate should be based on the coexistence, at the aggregate level, of both unemployment and vacancies, even when aggregate labour demand equals labour supply: the benchmark equilibrium unemployment rate should therefore remain $u^* = v$. One would then say that a rise in fric-

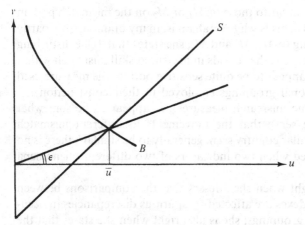

Figure 1.1 The aggregate disequilibrium (S) and the Beveridge curve (B)

tional/structural unemployment *relative* to the observed unemployment rate requires a mounting (v/u) ratio. But the observed increase in (v/u) might derive, *ceteris paribus*, from three causes: a reduction in the labour market aggregate disequilibrium (an upward movement along a 'Beveridge curve') or an outward shift of the 'Beveridge curve' (for given aggregate disequilibrium in the labour market), the latter due either to growing frictions within each micro market (lower search intensity, higher choosiness) or – as a third possibility – to larger intersectoral discrepancies of unemployment and vacancies, that is to mismatch.

My reasoning is very simple and, closely following Malinvaud (1986), may be graphically expressed on the $u - v$ plane (Figure 1.1). The aggregate disequilibrium, recalling equations (2) and (3), is described by the straight line S, which draws relation (5''') – i.e., $v = u - u_s$: S coincides with the diagonal when the disequilibrium unemployment, u_s, is zero. Curve B (standing for the 'Beveridge curve') indicates all possible combinations of the aggregate unemployment and vacancy rates compatible with steady conditions in the labour market ($\hat{h}_i$ = given in equation (7)). The intersection between B and S identifies the observed unemployment rate, $\bar{u}$, and the (v/u) ratio (equal to the tangent of angle ε). A reduction in the labour market aggregate disequilibrium leads, *ceteris paribus*, to a parallel upward shift in S, hence to a rise in the (v/u) ratio: if aggregate disequilibrium does not exist, the intersection between B and the 45° line S implies that the observed unemployment rate ($\bar{u}$) equals the equilibrium one (v). Also an outward shift of the B curve, *for given S*, increases the (v/u) ratio, and hence the misplacement percentage of the unemployment rate. Obviously, what distinguishes one case from the other is that in the

Table 1.1. *Criteria identifying when mounting mismatch is uniquely responsible for the unemployment rate increase*

Ceteris paribus causes of change	Outward shift of *B*:		Upward shift of *S*:
Indexes	Higher mismatch	Higher frictions	Lower aggregate disequilibrium
(v/u)	+	+	+
M_4	+	/	/
u	+	+	−

former the observed unemployment rate declines, while in the latter it rises. But not all outward shifts of the 'Beveridge curve' are due to mismatch – i.e., to a growing dispersion of the vacancy/unemployment rates ratios across micro markets.

In this approach, dispersion is measured in a rather standard way, by half of the weighted variation coefficient of the (v_i/u_i) ratios, where the weights, η_i, should be equal[11] to the share of unemployment in i relative to aggregate unemployment, $\hat{u}_i$. This dispersion index, labelled as M_4,[12] is therefore

$$M_4 = \tfrac{1}{2} \sqrt{\frac{\sum \left(\frac{v_i}{u_i}\right)^2 \eta_i}{\left(\sum \frac{v_i}{u_i} \eta_i\right)^2} - 1} = \tfrac{1}{2} \sqrt{\sum \left(\frac{\hat{v}_i}{\hat{u}_i}\right)^2 \eta_i - 1}$$

In synthesis, my rather eclectic approach to assessing whether a growing mismatch uniquely explains the worsening in the unemployment rate dynamics is based on three building blocks: the (v/u) growth at the aggregate level is a necessary, but not a sufficient, condition to make one suspect that mismatch is rising relative to the overall unemployment; an increasing degree of mismatch also requires a higher dispersion index, M_4 and, under the *ceteris paribus* condition, a higher level of the unemployment rate. Table 1.1 summarises the criteria identifying the presence, *ceteris paribus*, of a mounting mismatch responsible for the unemployment rate increase: (+) implies a growth; (−) a decrease; (/) shows a constant index.

Of course, there are other cases in which a growing mismatch can partly contribute to explaining the unemployment dynamics. In all these cases – which arise when both the *B* and the *S* curves move together – the dispersion index, M_4, has to rise.

7   Empirical evidence on industrial mismatch in Europe

I use this methodology in a European data set concerning 8 countries[13] and 19 industrial sectors,[14] homogeneously defined across countries, for the period 1980–9. The empirical evidence consists of yearly averages of quarterly data gathered through EC business surveys, which report (by country and by sector) the percentage of firms whose production plans are hindered by insufficient demand, by lack of equipment or by shortage of labour force. In the wake of what has been done within the European Project on Unemployment, the $(v_i/u_i)^j$ ratio (i.e., the ratio between vacancies and unemployment in sector i and country j) is proxied by the ratio of firms constrained by lack of labour force relative to all other constrained firms in sector i and country j; the $(v/u)^j$ ratio – i.e., the vacancy/unemployment rate ratio of industry as a whole in country j – is constructed similarly.

The single and basic idea underlying this approximation – a more elaborate version of which may be found in Bean and Gavosto (1989), while some implications are derived in Bean and Pissarides – is the following: for each i and j there is a one-to-one correspondence between the number of firms declaring themselves to be constrained by shortage of labour force and the number of their unfilled vacancies; there exists a similar correspondence between the number of firms declaring themselves to be hindered by lack of demand or lack of equipment and the number of the 'effective' unemployed in i and j.

This procedure does not contain the shortcomings typical of data sets on job vacancies where, as Abraham notes 'the numbers reported are derived from administrative records rather than from surveys designed for statistical purposes'; neither is it affected by the usual bias on unemployment data by sector, when job searchers are classified according to their latest job, as it is well known that 'individuals cannot easily be assigned to a single occupational or even a single [individual] geographic category. Any one individual's previous experience might have prepared him or her for employment in a number of occupations. Indeed, . . . a substantial number of job changers also report changes in occupation'. My approximations, however, present another limitation: I assume that the 'effective' labour supply in each sector i consists, apart from the employed in i, only of those workers the firms in sector i would be ready to hire, if there were no productive capacity or final demand constraints (the lack of labour force being excluded by assumption). The unemployment pool does not therefore include those who would never get an offer from the existing firms: 'effective' unemployment refers only to the firms' point of view.

Although this strong assumption has been already successfully adopted within the European Project on Unemployment, I have tried to verify its validity through a control solution provided by the OECD official data on unemployment and vacancies – knowing, however, that this control solution is itself imperfect, for the reasons pointed out by Abraham.[15] I have drawn a comparison on the $(v/u)^j$ industrial ratios for the years and for the countries for which I had both the EC business survey observations and the more traditional OECD empirical evidence: the corresponding plots[16] (see Figures 1.2a–i) indicate that, with the exception of Denmark, whose official data on vacancies are obviously downward biased, the paths of the two $(v/u)^j$ series are rather well correlated. According to these sources, almost everywhere in Europe, in the United States and in Japan the (v/u) ratio first decreases in the beginning of the 1980s, and then rises.

I have consequently computed the $(v_i/u_i)^j$ ratios for each of the 19 sectors and for industry as a whole, of every European country, j, belonging to $EUR8$: notably, Belgium (B), Germany (D), Denmark (DK), France (F), Ireland (IRL), Italy (IT), the Netherlands (NL), the United Kingdom (UK).

The computation was tedious because these EC data, being used here for the very first time – unlike the corresponding national data which have been analysed many times before – contained inconsistencies and mistakes which I have patiently (and provisionally) tried to overcome.

With regard to the existing inconsistencies, an indicator was offered whenever the observed $(v/u)^j$ ratio in industry as a whole of the j country in a given year did not correspond to the weighted average of the 19 sectors' $(v_i/u_i)^j$ ratios of the same country in the same year.[17] In these cases, I was confronted with a threefold choice. (a) If I could resort to the national statistical sources from which the EC data originated, the correction was immediate.[18] When that was impossible (notably for all countries except for Italy), I looked for outliers, quarter by quarter and sector by sector. Then, (b) if there emerged a blatant outlier in a specific quarter and sector, in computing the yearly average I abandoned that observation so as to eliminate the relevant discrepancy.[19] (c) If no blatant outlier was specifically found, I preferred to avoid 'discretional interventions'.[20] This is why Figure 1.2 shows few persisting differences between the observed $(v/u)^j$ and the constructed weighted average of the 19 sectors' $(v_i/u_i)^j$: they are small but disturbing and hopefully in the future the EC DG2, which is responsible for these data, will introduce the necessary corrections with the collaboration of the corresponding National Statistical Institutes.

After some data excavation work on the European business survey information, I suspect that other errors remain in my graphs. They are difficult to discover, however, because they are not revealed by inconsist-

(a)

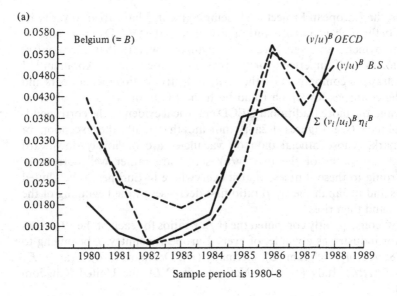

(b)

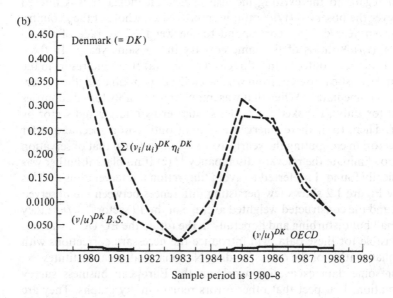

Figure 1.2 (see p. 26)

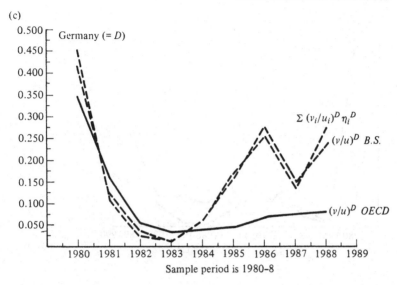

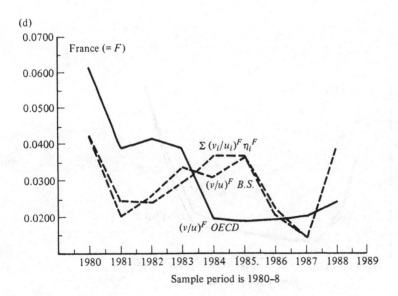

Figure 1.2 (see p. 26)

(e)

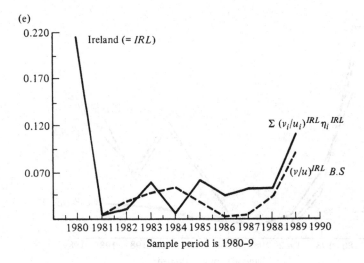

Sample period is 1980–9

(f)

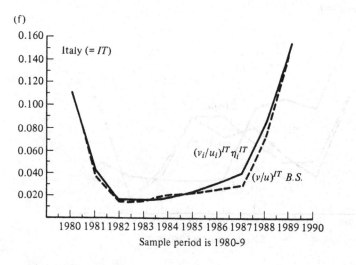

Sample period is 1980–9

Figure 1.2   (see p. 26)

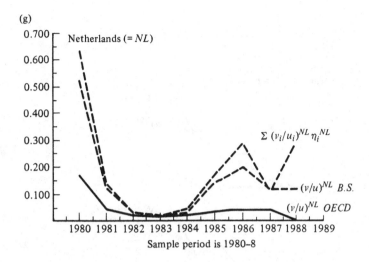

Sample period is 1980-8

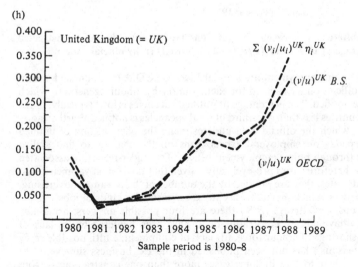

Sample period is 1980-8

Figure 1.2 (see p. 26)

(i)

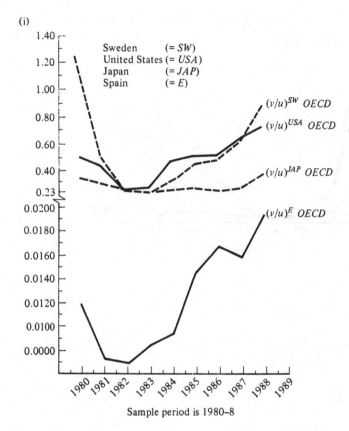

Sample period is 1980–8

Figure 1.2 Differences between the EC observed $(v/u)^j$, the EC constructed weighted average of 19 sectors' $(v_i/u_i)^j$ and the OECD $(v/u)^j$ official data
Notes:
OECD data on unemployment are standardised. OECD data on unfilled vacancies are the official ones provided for each country by labour agencies to which vacancies are notified. The percentage of notified vacancies is low: typically, in the European countries less than one-third of total vacancies is notified. Furthermore, the extent to which the official data underestimate the phenomenon of unfilled vacancies depends on employers' expectations on the chances to find skilled labour force through public employment offices. The under-reporting associated to these data therefore varies pro-cyclically. Given that no data on vacancies exist in the United States, they are proxied by the number of 'help-wanted advertising' in the newspapers, which inevitably lay stress on particular kinds of jobs.

In the EC business surveys (*B.S.*) there are four possible answers: firms may declare (a) to have met no constraints or to have been hindered by (b) lack of demand, (c) shortage of labour force, (d) lack of equipment; a fifth possible reply (i.e., 'other reasons') has not been published in the EC business surveys up to 1988. Firms appear to give in some cases more than one constraining reason. France and the United Kingdom are particular cases, as the answer 'no constraint'

Figure 1.2 (*cont.*)

is not envisaged in the national surveys. EC business surveys for the United Kingdom include the reply 'other reasons' in the 'no constraint' group. This is immaterial for the results which are reported here because, for comparative purposes, data have been reproportioned fixing equal to 100 the sum of the firms answering to be hindered either by lack of labour force, or by insufficient demand or by lack of capacity. The *B.S.* $(v/u)^j$ ratio indicates for every country, j, the 'observed' vacancy/unemployment ratio in industry as a whole, as it appears in the EC publications.

$$\Sigma (v_i/u_i)^j \eta_i^j$$

is the corresponding vacancy/unemployment ratio in industry as a whole reconstructed as a weighted average of 19 industrial sectors with weights equalling the value added shares of each country's sector i on its overall industry. These are the weights utilised by EC.

Sources: OECD, *Main Economic Indicators. Historical Statistics* (various years); Commission of the European Communities, 'Results of the Business Surveys', *Monthly Bulletin* (various years); Isco-Mondo Economico, 'Congiuntura Italiana', *Monthly Bulletin* (various years) for the Italian 1984 and 1988 data.

encies within the EC data set. To correct these mistakes, one should compare the national and the European empirical evidence for all quarters and all sectors. Having accomplished this task only for Italy, I could correct the 1984 datum, where both the (v/u) ratio and the corresponding average of the 19 sectors' (v_i/u_i) ratios coincided, presenting an unexplained and non-existing peak. I strongly believe, however, that this kind of bias also affects, for instance, the 1983 Danish and Irish data. All in all, I would stress that of the 8 countries analysed here, those showing the most reliable data are the larger ones (United Kingdom, France, Germany, Italy); with regard to years, the least reliable are probably 1983 and 1988–9.

Figure 1.3 reports, country by country, the computed average of the $(v/u)^j$ ratio in industry as a whole and the 19 sectors' dispersion index, M_4^j. It is interesting to note that, while the absolute values of $(v/u)^j$ and M_4^j vary greatly[20] across countries and within the same country in different years, the temporal paths of $(v/u)^j$ and M_4^j are very similar for most countries j.

As far as the (v/u) ratios are concerned, the most common path consists of a fall from 1980 to 1982–3, followed by a (modestly cyclical) rise, with a peak in 1989. Exceptions to such dynamics are found in the United Kingdom, whose trend has been uninterruptedly positive since 1981 and in Denmark, France and Ireland, which present a cyclical pattern of (v/u) without a definite trend. The *EUR8* vacancy/unemployment rates ratio traces the same dynamics, with a minimum in 1982–3, a mildly cyclical positive trend between 1983 and 1988, a sharp rise thereafter.

(a)

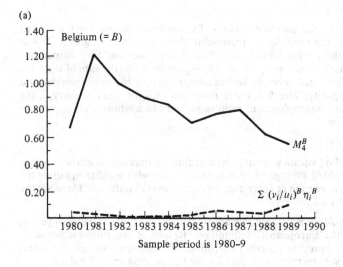

Sample period is 1980–9

(b)

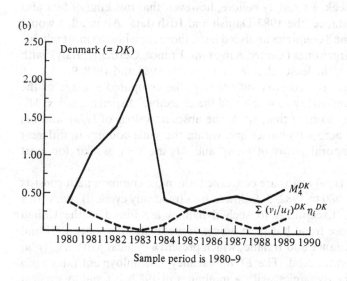

Sample period is 1980–9

Figure 1.3   (see p. 32)

(c)

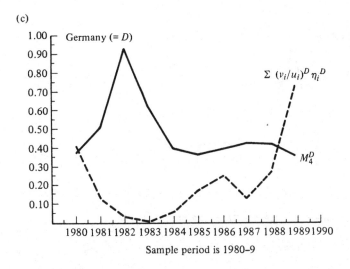

$$\text{Germany } (= D)$$

$$\Sigma \ (v_i/u_i)^D \eta_i^D$$

$$M_4^D$$

Sample period is 1980–9

(d)

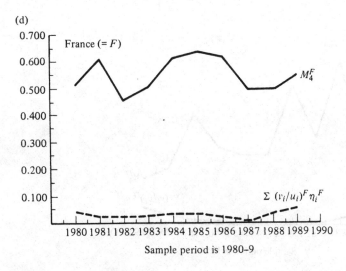

$$\text{France } (= F)$$

$$M_4^F$$

$$\Sigma \ (v_i/u_i)^F \eta_i^F$$

Sample period is 1980–9

Figure 1.3   (see p. 32)

(e)

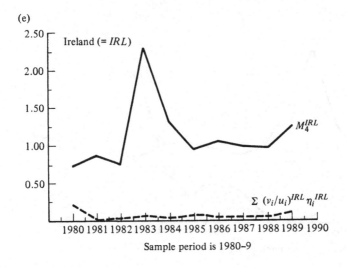

Sample period is 1980–9

(f)

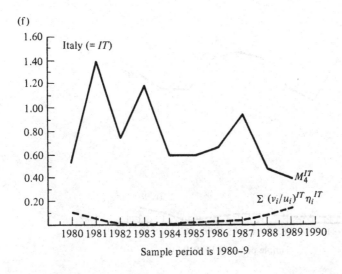

Sample period is 1980–9

Figure 1.3   (see p. 32)

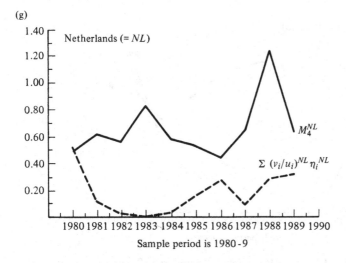

(g)

Netherlands (= NL)

M_4^{NL}

$\Sigma \ (v_i/u_i)^{NL} \eta_i^{NL}$

Sample period is 1980 - 9

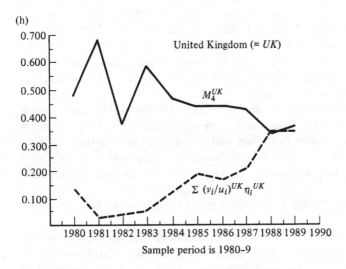

(h)

United Kingdom (= UK)

M_4^{UK}

$\Sigma \ (v_i/u_i)^{UK} \eta_i^{UK}$

Sample period is 1980–9

Figure 1.3   (see p. 32)

(i)

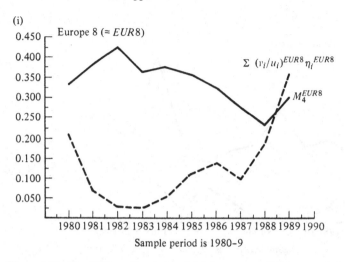

Figure 1.3   **The EC constructed weighted average of 19 sectors' $(v_i/u_i)^j$ and the industrial dispersion index $(M_4)^j$**

The intersectoral dispersion index, M_4, calculated in each country on the same 19 sectors homogeneously defined, deserves two comments: (a) almost everywhere this variable is clearly cyclical and its variation year by year, country by country, is usually *negatively* correlated to the sign of the corresponding (v/u) yearly rate of change;[22] (b) after a global peak, reached in almost all countries between 1981 and 1983, M_4 shows a *negative* trend everywhere, with the exception of the Netherlands[23] and France, where it is not trended at all. Again, at the *EUR8* level, the intersectoral dispersion index, M_4, follows the same path common to the majority of European countries, rising from 1980 to 1982 and declining thereafter with moderate cycles.

The information contained in the country studies in this volume, concerning both the EC countries I have examined through the business survey data and other European and non-European countries, confirm that *nowhere* in the 1980s has the industrial dispersion index M_3 been positively trended, whereas in many countries it has decreased cyclically (see M_3 by industry computed for Spain – by Bentolilla and Dolado – and for Sweden, the United States, the United Kingdom and Germany – by JLS).

In this situation, there is no reason to believe that the increase in the vacancy/unemployment rates ratio, observed almost everywhere in Europe after 1982–3, depends on a mounting intersectoral dispersion of vacancies and unemployment: the potential explanatory power of mismatch and structural imbalances by industry, relative to unemployment, seems to be very modest.

8   Is unemployment in Europe really high and persistent?

In more general terms the growth in the (v/u) ratio observed in most European and non European countries in the second half of the 1980s might have nothing to do with misplacement – that is, with an outward shift of the 'Beveridge curve'. We already know from Figure 1.1 and Table 1.1 that to identify the reasons for the rise in the vacancy/unemployment ratio and to see whether its origin lies, *ceteris paribus*, in an outward shift of the B curve or in an upward shift of the S curve, it is necessary to observe the temporal path of the unemployment rate.

Standardised cross-country data on this variable[24] are provided by Table 1.2, which shows two very important aspects. Though long-term comparisons on the average unemployment rates in the 1980s mark a worsening relative to the 1970s and to the second half of the 1960s in all European and non-European countries analysed in this volume, in the 1980s unemployment rates have clearly started to fall in all countries since 1983 (Belgium, Luxemburg, the Netherlands, the United States and Sweden), since 1985 (Germany, Spain, Ireland, Portugal, the United Kingdom) and since 1986 (Italy and Japan), with no subsequent uptrend. The only exceptions were France, registering a late downturn in 1987 and Denmark, whose unemployment rate turned down in 1982 but has moved up again since 1987. Perhaps it is no coincidence that the latter are two of the only three EC countries I have examined through the business survey data, without a positive trend in the (v/u) ratio since 1983. Also *EUR9* reaches its unemployment rate peak between 1984 and 1986 and then falls uninterruptedly. From this empirical evidence, one therefore gets the impression[25] that there exists a consistent story for the 1980s unemployment rates. Contrary to the common opinion, unemployment steadily increased only up to the mid-1980s and then decreased almost everywhere. In the meantime, the vacancy/unemployment rates ratio declined almost everywhere up to about 1983 and then soared again: consequently, misplacements have a limited explanatory power for unemployment dynamics in the 1980s. As the intersectoral dispersion has been cyclical, without a positive correlation, year by year, with the (v/u) ratio, and has grown nowhere in the second half of the 1980s, one may apparently conclude that neither frictional nor structural changes – due to industrial mismatch – are important components of the initial rise and the subsequent fall in the unemployment rates. Industrial mismatch possibly played a downward minor role in the second half of the 1980s, when it was

Table 1.2. *Unemployment rate, percentage of civilian labour force*

	B	DK	D	GR	E	F	IRL	IT
1964–70	2.1	1.2	0.9	5.0	2.7	2.0	5.1	5.4
1971–80	4.9	4.6	2.7	2.2	5.4	4.3	7.1	6.6
1980	7.9	6.6	3.3	2.8	11.6	6.4	7.4	7.7
1981	10.2	10.4	4.7	4.0	14.4	7.6	10.0	8.0
1982	11.9	11.1	6.8	5.8	16.3	8.3	11.6	8.7
1983	12.6	9.5	6.9	9.0	17.8	8.2	15.2	9.0
1984	12.6	9.1	7.1	9.3	20.6	9.9	17.0	9.5
1985	11.7	7.6	7.3	8.7	21.9	10.3	18.4	9.4
1986	11.9	5.8	6.5	8.2	21.2	10.4	18.3	10.6
1987	11.5	5.8	6.4	8.0	20.5	10.5	18.0	10.1
1988	10.4	6.4	6.4	8.5	19.6	10.2	17.8	10.6
1989	9.4	7.4	5.6	8.5	17.6	9.5	16.7	10.5
1990**	8.8	7.6	5.4	8.5	16.5	9.1	16.2	10.6
1981–90	11.1	8.1	6.3	7.9	18.6	9.4	15.9	9.7

Notes:
   * The unemployment rate of Sweden is the percentage of the *total* and not only
   the civilian labour force.
  ** EC forecast.
*** The average excludes the years 1989–90.

slightly declining while unemployment rates were also decreasing. It seems very probable that aggregate disequilibria (due to lack of aggregate labour demand relative to labour supply) bear the major responsibility for the unemployment rate increase of the first half of the 1980s and its reduction in the second half.

The observed variations in (v/u), M_4 and u have not precisely corresponded to those stylised in Table 1.1 because Table 1.1 is oversimplified, for one major reason. There, I presume that curves S and B could move *one at a time*, as if explanations in terms of frictions, sectoral imbalances and aggregate disequilibria were alternative to each other: reality does not accept the *ceteris paribus* condition on which theoretical analysis is based. Probably both curves S and B moved together and in the second half of the 1980s the S curve was likely to shift upward while the B curve was possibly moving downward: these combined shifts would be consistent with the facts which show a decrease in the unemployment rates and in the industrial dispersion index, M_4, together with an increase in the vacancy/unemployment ratio.

Up to now, I have been concentrating my attention on labour market imbalances between industrial sectors only, so as to start exploiting an important European data set, rich in homogenous cross-country data.

Table 1.2. (*cont.*)

L	NL	P	UK	EUR9	EUR12	USA	JAP	SW*
0.0	1.0	2.6	1.7	2.3	2.4	4.1	1.2	1.7
0.3	4.2	5.2	3.9	4.3	4.4	6.3	1.8	2.1
0.7	6.2	7.8	5.7	5.8	6.4	7.0	2.0	2.0
1.0	8.6	7.6	9.1	7.6	8.1	7.5	2.2	2.5
1.3	11.6	7.5	10.5	8.9	9.5	9.5	2.4	3.2
3.6	12.5	7.7	11.2	9.2	10.0	9.5	2.6	3.5
3.0	12.5	8.4	11.4	9.8	10.8	7.4	2.7	3.1
3.0	10.4	8.5	11.5	9.7	10.9	7.1	2.6	2.9
2.7	10.3	8.3	11.5	9.8	10.8	6.9	2.8	2.7
2.7	10.2	6.8	10.6	9.4	10.4	6.1	2.8	1.9
2.2	10.3	5.6	8.7	9.0	10.0	5.4	2.5	1.6
1.8	9.9	5.2	6.8	8.2	9.0	5.1	2.5	—
1.7	9.6	5.2	6.5	8.0	8.7	5.2	2.6	—
2.3	10.6	7.1	9.8	9.0	9.8	7.0	2.6	2.7***

Sources:
EUROSTAT for the EC countries: from 1964 onwards these data are based on the EUROSTAT new definition and are therefore different from those published by the same source in previous issues; OECD for the United States (*USA*), Japan (*JAP*) and Sweden (*SW*).
These figures are published (with the exclusion of those concerning Sweden) by the Commission of the European Communities, *Annual Report 1989–90* (1989); for Sweden, OECD, *Main Economic Indicators. Historical Statistics, 1960–1979* and *1969–1988*.

Perhaps if I had used M_4 to measure the imbalances on other labour market components (skill, location), I could have attained different results.

The country studies contained in this volume hint at the possibility that location contributed more than other elements to labour mismatch. The European business survey empirical evidence allows us to verify whether geographical mismatch has worsened in the 1980s within the *EUR8* aggregate, once it is assumed that the 8 European National States under observation constitute different 'regions' of Europe. Stating that Europe as such is not an optimal mobility area cannot be a reason to reject this kind of exercise: indeed, it is worth measuring mismatch precisely within areas where mobility *exists* but is *imperfect*. Moreover, many National States in Europe, such as Spain and Italy, have shown over the 1980s a very limited interregional mobility, their gross internal migration flows having come to an end by the mid-1970s (see Bentolila and Dolado and Attanaasio and Padoa Schioppa). In any case, the imminent 1992 completion of the internal market leads us to consider Europe more and more as an institutional labour market.

For all these reasons, I decided to compute, sector by sector, and for industry as a whole, the $EUR8$ (v/u) ratios and the corresponding dispersion index, M_4, emerging between the 8 different European countries.[26] Figure 1.4 reports the results for industry as a whole and for three large

(a)

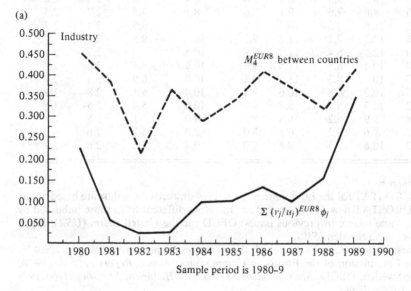

(b)

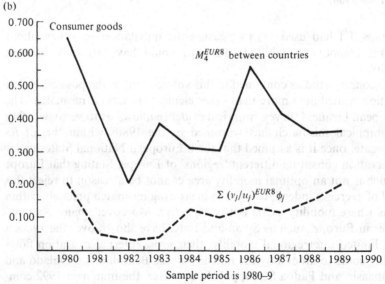

Figure 1.4 (see p. 37)

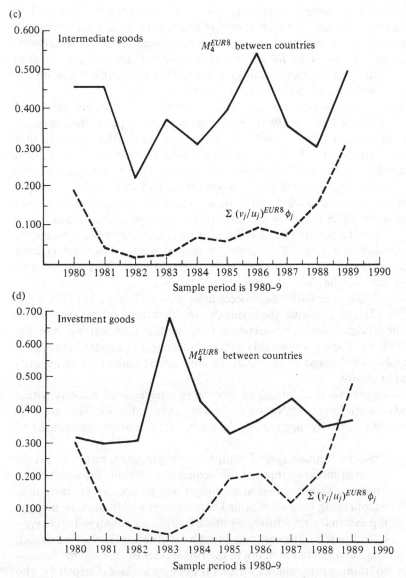

Figure 1.4 The *EUR8* (*v/u*) ratios and the intercountry dispersion index (*M₄*) in 4 sectors

sub-sectors – those of consumer goods, of intermediate goods and of investment goods.[27] In fact, there are grounds to believe that 'regional' mismatch in Europe has been positively correlated to the vacancy/unemployment ratios of $EUR8$ and has been positively trended after 1982 in most intermediate and consumer good sectors (generally not in investment goods[28]) and in the overall industry.

Not even in this case, however, can the growing 'regional' imbalances of the second half of the 1980s be said uniquely to 'explain' the European unemployment rate dynamics of that period, as this has followed in a downward trend a direction opposite to what would have been required according to Table 1.1. Most probably, shifts in the B and S curves have contemporaneously emerged, in a combination of structural and disequilibrium phenomena which led to those outcomes. Indeed, if in the second half of the 1980s both indicators, (v/u) and the 'regional' dispersion index, M_4, showed a positive trend and positively correlated cycles, whereas the unemployment rate fell, this means that aggregate disequilibria have decreased while, at the same time, the unemployment share explained by 'regional' mismatch has increased.

As noted by the CEPS Macroeconomic Policy Group (Danthine *et al.*, 1990, 33), this confirms 'the layman's view that there are unquestionable static efficiency gains to be expected from an increased degree of mobility in Europe. These gains would result from an improved match between the supply and demand of labour at the continental scale, both in quantity and in quality'.

Policy interventions aimed at promoting interregional mobility within and between European National States are, then, called for. They might be threefold, as partly suggested by the studies in this volume, and consist of:

(a)   Training, retraining and manpower programmes, meant to favour regional mobility through the acquisition of skills (in Europe also linguistic skills in foreign languages will be necessary), more than encouraging long-term skilled employment within firms or improving external competitiveness of each firm and country. This is typically a public objective, possibly at a supernational level, and as such it is not analysed in depth in the two studies of this volume devoted to training programmes (neither the one by Soskice (Chapter 9), who is more interested in the internal-to-firm training systems, nor the one by Edin and Holmlund (Chapter 10), analysing the Swedish public programmes only).

(b)   The interregional widening of net real wage differentials (more common in the United States – as explained by Freeman – than in Europe and in Japan – as suggested by Brunello and Bean and

Pissarides): this would permit dealing with sectoral imbalances through factors' mobility (shifting labour demand and supply) rather than through rising unemployment and vacancies. The basic policy idea (implicit in Attanasio and Padoa Schioppa and Nickell) leads to some sort of deregulation, so as to give the market back its capacity to signal the relative labour scarcities.

(c) The subsidisation of workers' mobility towards regions with higher vacancies and of capital mobility in the opposite direction. According to JLS, this policy of '(1) shifting the jobs towards the workers (e.g., by cutting employers' taxes in those sectors where unemployment is high), and (2) shifting the workers towards the jobs (e.g., by subsidies to migration or training)' is not always appropriate. Indeed, they demonstrate that this is never appropriate unless 'there are externalities (other than simply unemployment itself) . . . This argues for increased taxes in regions which are congested (typically low-unemployment regions) and subsidies to skill-formation, where there is an external benefit that is not privately appropriated . . . [Moreover, if] there is a leading sector whose employment rate pushes up wages elsewhere, that sector generates external disbenefits which make it a candidate for extra taxation'.

A second reason for combining taxes and subsidies in order to raise factors' mobility is justified by the willingness to speed up a process of resource reallocation across regions that the market might reach, albeit at an excessively low pace. 'We find', Bentolila and Dolado conclude, 'that interregional migration responds significantly to economic variables such as real wage and unemployment differentials, but . . . the convergence of the process to a long-run equilibrum with compensating wage differentials is very slow. We infer that a regional policy targeted at moving jobs to people – in contrast to relying on the movement of people to jobs – could save a sizeable amount of unemployment during the short and medium run, specially starting from a high national unemployment rate.'

NOTES

1 I thank Michel Biart of the EC Commission (DG2) and Andrea Gavosto and Guido Pellegrino of the Bank of Italy for help and suggestions. I am also grateful to my research assistants, Paola Felli, Federica Ribechi, Luca Rizzuto and Chiara Rossi for their patient work.
2 See also the Discussion of Chapter 2 by Rosen in this volume and Lilien (1982), Abraham and Katz (1986), Davis (1987).
3 The European Project on Unemployment model distinguishes the part of labour demand determined by output demand from the part determined by profitability. Hence, a rise in $1/\rho$ could be due to an increase in output misplacement as well as to an increase in labour misplacement.

4 This definition corresponds to the one given by Turvey (1977).

5 But others are available, such as, for example, the one proposed by Evans (1988), which is 'neutral' to shifts in the aggregate demand.

6 This function is derived from a Cobb–Douglas technology. Such a technological assumption is not 'heavy' and could easily be substituted by others, more general, without affecting the overall results, as indicated by JLS.

7 Without loss of generality for my conclusions, all the empirical tests on the relation between wage-settings and unemployment rates are carried out measuring the unemployment rate as the number of unemployed relative to the labour supply rather than to the employment level.

8 This variable originates from business survey data on skilled labour shortages by industry: this kind of information is the one I use in section 7.

9 Coe (1990), reporting OECD sectoral data, shows that the level of sectoral real wages depends on the growth rate of sectoral employment, but the level of sectoral real wages (in log) depends on the level of aggregate unemployment (in log).

10 Coe and Gagliardi (1985) also estimate a Phillips curve for 10 OECD countries where a steady-state behavioural equation for the wage rate does not exist. It is worth noticing, however, that according to these authors, in the short-run $\Delta \log w$ is non-linearly related to u.

11 Nevertheless, the weights adopted here are shares of the value added because they have to be consistent with those preferred by EC statistical sources.

12 As with the other dispersion indexes – M_1, M_2, $M_3 - M_4$, too, has a minimum value of 0, but it might present a weakness that the other indicators do not show, if the percentage of unemployment in some sector i relative to the overall unemployment were 0 (i.e., $\hat{u}_i = 0$). This case, however, never shows up in the EC business survey data.

13 Data have existed ever since 1976 for the following countries: Italy, Germany, the Netherlands, Belgium, Luxemburg (L), Ireland. Since 1977, information for the United Kingdom and France are also provided, though they are initally scattered. Since 1980, we have data for Denmark as well. Since 1985 data on Greece (GR) are added and, finally, data on Spain and Portugal started in 1989. Surveys are carried out four times a year up to 1981 and have become quarterly since 1982. About 20,000 firms are interviewed in each period. Their distribution in the member countries is mainly a function of the number of their firms in the different sectors. This number is so low in Luxemburg that its data are hardly meaningful; that is why Luxemburg is eliminated from the $EUR9$ group for which there exist business survey data ever since 1980: the aggregate I am analysing is therefore formed by 8 countries and is called $EUR8$.

14 The sectors are: textiles; footwear and clothing; timber and wooden furniture; manufacture of paper products, printing and publishing; leather and leather goods; processing of plastics; mineral oil refining; production and preliminary processing of metals; manufacture of non-metallic mineral products; chemicals; man-made fibres; manufacture of metal articles; mechanical engineering; manufacture of office machinery and data-processing machinery; electrical engineering; manufacture of motor vehicles and motor vehicle parts and accessories; manufacture of other means of transportation; manufacture of rubber products; precision engineering, optics and the like.

15 An example of the extent to which official OECD data on the (v/u) ratios are

biased may be supplied by Germany: it is sufficient to use the German data corrected by Franz to verify that, since 1983, the (v/u) ratio with corrected data on vacancies has sharply risen in a way which is closer to that identified through the EC business surveys than to that shown by OECD official data.

16 There are no official data on vacancies in Italy and Ireland, which are instead included in the EC business surveys. By contrast, there exist OECD (v/u) ratios for Spain, Sweden, Japan and the United States, which do not have business survey data comparable to those collected at the *EUR*9 level. For thoroughness sake, Figure 1.2 reports (from one statistical source, only) the (v/u) ratio of Italy, Ireland, Spain, Sweden, Japan and the United States.

17 That happened for Italy in 1988, Germany in 1984, the Netherlands in 1986 and 1988, Ireland in 1988–9, the United Kingdom in 1989 and France in 1983.

18 Admittedly, there has been a simple, easy-to-eliminate mistake in handing over information from national statistical sources to readers of EC publications.

19 I have eliminated the inconsistency between $(v/u)'$ and the weighted average of the 19 sectors' $(v_i/u_i)'$ in the following cases: Germany in 1984 (excluding the third quarter for the construction of motor vehicles and motor vehicles parts and accessories); France in 1983 (excluding the second quarter for the construction of motor vehicles and motor vehicles parts and accessories); Ireland in 1988 (excluding the second and fourth quarters for the textiles sector and the third for timber and wooden goods manufacture) and in 1989 (excluding the third and fourth quarters for the textiles sector).

20 From this viewpoint, a case apparently deserving particular attention is that of the Netherlands in the second half of the 1980s and particularly in 1988–9. The EC data are probably biased and I strongly suspect that the bias-creating sectors are those of cars and electric machinery, experiencing in 1988–9 not only a drastic fall in the absolute number of firms constrained by lack of demand, but also a quick reversing of their ratio relative to firms constrained by other reasons. Regarding the whole data series as 'suspect' and finding no single data outlier, I have decided not to intervene: the 1988–9 Dutch data contain a possible mistake and the M_4 index constructed for these years looks strange.

21 The 1989 reconstructed values of (v/u) reach peaks of 75% in Germany, 33% in the Netherlands, 35% in the United Kingdom, 20% in Denmark, 15% in Italy, 11% in Ireland, 10% in Belgium and 6.6% in France.

22 The notable exception to this general rule is France, where the signs of the rate of change of (v/u) and M_4 coincide in five out of nine years under observation.

23 In the case of the Netherlands, the observed data indeed show an increase in M_4 between 1986 and 1988, but for the reasons described in n. 18 above, I feel that those data are not completely reliable.

24 The unemployment rates reported in Table 1.2 measure the ratio between unemployment and labour force. In this study I usually label as 'unemployment rate' the ratio between unemployment and employment. The distinction between the two concepts is immaterial for the conclusions reached here, because if the former (U/LS) rises (declines), the latter (U/N) rises (declines) too.

25 In few cases, unlike my general conclusion, the mismatch story would be consistent. This happens when the rates of change of all three indicators – (v/u), M_4 and u – are identically signed, either all positive (rising structural imbalances to 'explain' the increasing unemployment rates through growing industrial mismatch) or negative (decreasing structural imbalances to 'explain'

the decreasing unemployment rates through declining industrial mismatch). These few cases are observed in my data in the following situations: Belgium (1985–6: + + + ; 1987–8: – – –); France (1983–4: + + +); Ireland (1982–3: + + +); the Netherlands (1987–8: + + +); the United Kingdom (1982–3: + + +); EUR8 (1983–4: + + + ; 1986–7: – – –). Out of 81 observations, less than 10% show three-data groups with identical signs, which makes this noise negligible.

26 The country's weight, different in different sectors, being labelled ϕ_j

27 Consumer goods include: footwear products; timber and wooden furniture (partially); paper and paper products, printing and publishing (partially); metal articles (partially); electrical engineering (partially); other means of transportation (partially); leather and leather goods; precision engineering, optics and the like; motor vehicles and their parts and accessories (partially). Intermediate goods comprise: textiles, timber and wooden furniture (partially); paper and paper products, printing and publishing (partially); plastics; metal production and preliminary processing; mineral oil refining; metal articles (partially); non-metallic mineral products (partially); chemicals (partially); man-made fibres; motor vehicles and their parts and accessories (partially); and rubber products. Investment goods include: mechanical engineering; office and data-processing machinery; electrical engineering (partially); motor vehicles and their parts and accessories (partially); other means of transportation (partially).

28 The main exception to this general rule concerns electrical engineering (in investment goods) showing a positive correlation between the 'interregional' dispersion index and the corresponding vacancy/unemployment ratio.

REFERENCES

Abraham, K. G. (1983). Structural/Frictional vs. Deficient Demand Unemployment: Some New Evidence', The American Economic Review, 73(4), 708–24.

Abraham, K. G. and L.F. Katz (1986). 'Cyclical Unemployment: Sectoral Shifts or Aggregate Disturbances', Journal of Political Economy, 94, 507–22.

Bean, C. R. and A. Gavosto (1989). 'Outsiders, Capacity Shortages and Unemployment in the United Kingdom', London School of Economics, Centre for Labour Economics, discussion paper, 332.

Bean, C. R., P. R. G. Layard and S. J. Nickell (1986). 'The Rise in Unemployment: A Multi-Country Study', Economica, 53 (Supplement) S1–S22.

Beveridge, W. (1955). 'Full Employment in a Free Society', in M. W. Ebenstein (ed.), Modern Political Thought, New York: Rinehart & Co, 575–88.

Blanchard, O. J. and P. Diamond (1990). 'The Beveridge Curve', Brookings Papers on Economic Activity, 1, 1–74.

Bodo, G. and P. Sestito (1989). 'Disoccupazione e dualismo Territoriale', Temi di Discussione, 123 (August) Servizio Studi Banca d'Italia.

Burda, M. and C. Wyplosz (1990). 'Gross Labor Market Flows in Europe: Some Stylized Facts' (mimeo).

Coe, D. T. (1990). 'Insider–Outsider Influences on Industry Wages', Empirical Economics, 15, 163–83.

Coe, D. T. and F. Gagliardi (1985). 'Nominal Wage Determination in Ten OECD Economies', OECD, working paper, 19.

Commission of the European Communities (various years). 'Results of the Business Survey', Monthly Bulletin.

Commission of the European Communities (1989). 'Annual Economic Report 1989–90', *European Economy*, **42**.

Danthine, J. P., C. R. Bean, P. Bernholz and E. Malinvaud (1990). 'European Labour Markets: A Long Run View', Commission of the European Communities, Directorate-General for Economic and Financial Affairs, economic paper, **78**.

Davis, S. J. (1987). 'Fluctuations in the Pace of Labor Reallocation', Carnegie-Rochester Conference Series on Public Policy, **27**, 335–402.

Dow, J. C. R. and L. A. Dicks-Mireaux (1958). 'The Excess Demand for Labour. A Study of Conditions in Great Britain, 1946–56', *Oxford Economic Papers*, **10**, 1–33.

Drèze, J. H. and C. R. Bean (1990). 'Europe's Employment Problem: Introduction and Synthesis', in J. H. Drèze and C. R. Bean (eds), *European Unemployment: Lessons from a Multi-Country Econometric Study*, Cambridge: MIT Press, **forthcoming**.

Evans, G. (1988). 'Sectoral Imbalance and Unemployment in the United Kingdom', London School of Economics, Centre for Labour Economics, discussion paper, **300**.

Grubb, D. (1985). 'Topics in the OECD Phillips Curve', London School of Economics, Centre for Labour Economics, discussion paper, **231**.

Hansen, B. (1970). 'Excess Demand, Unemployment, Vacancies and Wages', *The Quarterly Journal of Economics*, **LXXXIV**(1), 1–23.

Harris, J. R. and M. P. Todaro (1970). 'Migration, Unemployment and Development: A Two-Sector Analysis', *American Economic Review*, **60**(1), 126–42.

Isco-Mondo Economico (various years). 'Congiuntura Italiana', *Monthly Bulletin*.

Jackman, R., P. R. G. Layard and C. A. Pissarides (1984). 'On Vacancies', London School of Economics, Centre for Labour Economics, discussion paper, **165** (revised).

Jackman, R. and S. Roper (1987). 'Structural Unemployment', *Oxford Bulletin of Economics and Statistics*, **49**(1), 9–37.

Lilien, D. M. (1982). 'Sectoral Shifts and Cyclical Unemployment', *Journal of Political Economy*, **90**(4), 777–93.

Malinvaud, E. (1986). 'La Courbe de Beveridge', in Association Française de Science Economique (ed.), *Colloque Annuel de l'AFSE: Flexibilité, Mobilité et Stimulants Economiques*, Paris: Nathan Editions, 1–19.

OECD (various years). *Main Economic Indicators. Historical Statistics*.

Padoa Schioppa, F. (1990). 'Classical, Keynesian and Mismatch Unemployment in Italy', *European Economic Review*, **34**(2/3), 434–42.

Pissarides, C. A. (1985). 'Short-Run Equilibrium Dynamics of Unemployment, Vacancies, and Real Wages', *American Economic Journal*, **75**(4), 676–90.

Pissarides, C. A. (1986). 'Unemployment and Vacancies in Britain', *Economic Policy*, **1**(3), 500–59.

Turvey, R. (1977). 'Changement et Chomage Structurels', *Revue Internationale du Travail*, **116**(2), 229–36.

2   Mismatch: A Framework for Thought[1]

R. JACKMAN, R. LAYARD AND
S. SAVOURI

As everybody knows, unemployment rates differ widely between occupations and between regions, as well as across age, race and (sometimes) sex groups. The striking thing is how stable these differences are. In all countries unskilled people have much higher unemployment rates than skilled people. Similarly, youths have higher rates than adults. In addition in most countries (though not the United States) regional differences are highly persistent – with unemployment always above average, for example, in the North of England and the South of Italy.

The first task is to document these differences (in section 1) and then to explain them (in section 2). An obvious question is why occupational and geographical mobility does not eliminate the differences between unemployment rates in different occupations and different regions. We attempt to answer this question. Our main focus is thus on the *persistent* imbalance between the supply and demand for labour across skill groups, regions and age groups. But there are additional imbalances which are *temporary*. Suppose, for example, that there are two occupations which have the same average unemployment rate over time but in one year demand shifts from one occupation to the other; this will produce a temporary imbalance until corrected.[2] Such 'one-off' structural shocks have aroused great interest in relation to the issue of real business cycles (see Lilien, 1982). They are also clearly of interest to the unemployed themselves. But they account for a fairly small fraction of the inequality among unemployment rates observed in the average year. In any event our framework encompasses both kinds of phenomena (since both reflect imbalances between the demand and supply of labour) and we shall refer to both by the generic title 'mismatch'.

The next question is how the *structure* of unemployment rates is related to the *average* level of unemployment. Many people in Europe attribute the rise in unemployment to increased imbalances between the pattern of labour demand and supply – in other words, to greater mismatch. The question is: have exogenous forces raised average unemployment by changing the structure of unemployment rates? To answer this question we need to develop a relevant measure of mismatch, consistent with our overall framework of explanation. We develop the theory in section 3, while in section 4 we offer empirical evidence in support of our framework. The general conclusion is that, while mismatch is a serious problem, it has not in most countries increased over time.

Since the structure of unemployment is related to the average level of unemployment, what (if anything) should be done to alter the structure? The standard recipes are to shift demand towards the sectors with high unemployment rates, and to shift supply away from them. As we show in section 5, this must be right when supply is effectively exogenous. However, the more elastic supply becomes, the less strong is the case for intervention – except where standard externality arguments apply. These externality arguments may indeed be important, so that jobs should be shifted towards less-congested regions and people should be shifted into high-skilled occupations.

Thus far the discussion of mismatch has been entirely in terms of differences in employment rates – i.e., in the ratio between total labour demand and total labour supply. But it is also instructive to look at intergroup difference in the ratio of vacancies to unemployment – i.e., in the ratio of *excess* labour demand to *excess* labour supply. We explore this in section 6 and ask how a mismatch of this kind affects the location of the aggregate u/v curve.

We ought at this point to issue a health warning. Despite its obvious importance, the topic of mismatch has so far been subject to remarkably little rigorous analysis.[3] The propositions of this study are therefore particularly exploratory.

1 The structure of unemployment: some facts

1.1 Occupational differences

The most striking difference in unemployment rates is between skill groups. In Britain and the United States the unemployment rate of semi-skilled and unskilled workers is over four times that of professional and managerial workers (see Tables 2.1 and 2.2). A simple measure of the dispersion of the unemployment rates is the coefficient of variation (using relative labour forces as weights). For reasons given in section 3 we use as our fundamental measure of mismatch the square of this – in other words the *variance of relative unemployment rates* (var u_i/u). In Britain the variance across occupations was 22% in 1985, much the same as in the United States.

Table 2.1. *Unemployment by occupation: Britain, 1985*

	Rates (%)			% of unemployed		
	Men	Women	All	Men	Women	All
Professional and managerial	2.9	4.8	3.3	7	6	7
Other non-manual	5.9	6.8	6.7	10	48	23
Skilled manual	11.3	8.0	10.9	41	8	29
Semi-skilled manual (incl. personal services)	19.1	11.5	15.0	28	36	31
Unskilled manual	28.5	3.2	17.0	14	2	10
All	11.2	8.8	10.2	100	100	100
$\text{var}\left(\dfrac{u_i}{u}\right)$	44%	10%	22%			

Notes:
1. Unemployment is classified by occupation in last job.
2. The unemployment rate in an occupation is the number unemployed who were previously in an occupation relative to the numbers employed plus unemployed. Since many of the unemployed have never worked or do not record previous occupation, the national unemployment rate ('all') exceeds the mean of the occupational unemployment rates.
3. In calculating var(u_i/u), u is the mean of the occupation-specific unemployment rates.

Source: General Household Survey.

In Table 2.3 we provide data for other countries (but with no skill breakdown of manual workers). Focusing on the ratio between manual and non-manual employment rates, the striking thing is how low this is in Germany (a result of their training system?).

Over time the pattern of occupational unemployment rates is remarkably stable, as revealed by the correlation between the rates in the mid-1970s and mid-1980s (see Table 2.4). But has the *spread* altered? The answer is that in no country except Sweden is there any evidence of increased mismatch since the late 1970s, though in the United States there is some evidence of increased occupational imbalance since the early 1970s.

The next question is: where do the occupational differences in unemployment rates come from? Are they due to differences in duration or in inflow rates? As a broad generalisation, mismatch stems more from differences in inflow rates than in duration. This is certainly true of

Table 2.2. *Unemployment by occupation: United States, 1987*

	Rates (%)			% of unemployed		
	Men	Women	All	Men	Women	All
Professional and managerial	2.2	2.4	2.3	10	11	10
Other non-manual	3.7	4.7	4.3	13	40	25
Skilled manual	6.0	6.4	6.1	22	3	14
Personal services	7.5	7.8	7.7	13	28	19
Semi- and unskilled manual	9.3	9.9	9.4	43	19	32
All	6.2	6.2	6.2	100	100	100
var(u_i/u)	24%	19%	21%			

Notes: See Table 2.1.

Source: Employment and Earnings (January 1988) p. 170.

occupational differences (see Table 2.5). Unemployment is highest in those occupations which have high general turnover.

Closely related to difference in occupational unemployment rates are differences in educational unemployment rates. Since education (unlike occupation) is a characteristic of a person, these rates are in many ways more meaningful. However, except in the United States and Britain, it is difficult to find time series data on these rates, so we confine ourselves here to the snapshot of Table 2.6. This confirms the much greater problems experienced in most countries by people without good academic or vocational qualifications.

1.2 Region

Unemployment rates also differ greatly between and within regions. But the regional differences are much less than the occupational differences (see Tables 2.7 and 2.8). For example in Britain the variance of relative unemployment rate across 10 regions is only about 6%, compared with a variance of 21% across 5 occupations. Only when one gets down to travel-to-work areas do major geographical differences emerge. Across Britain's 322 travel-to-work areas the variance of relative unemployment rates is 24%. But in the United States, even when we go to the 51 'states', the variance is still only about 8%.

Table 2.3. *Unemployment rate by occupation: various countries, 1987*

	United States	Australia[1]	Austria	Canada	Finland	Germany[2]	Ireland	New Zealand	Norway	Spain	Sweden
Professional and technical[3]	2.2	2.0	2.7	4.7	1.8	6.5	3.2	1.7	0.7	6.1	1.2
Administrative and managerial	2.6	2.1	0.9	4.5	—	4.3	3.7	1.0	0.2	2.9	—
Clerical and related	4.2	3.3	3.8	7.4	2.5	—	6.0	2.8	1.2	8.2	1.0
Sales	4.9	5.0	4.5	6.7	4.0	8.6	8.6	3.6	1.3	7.5	1.8
Service	7.7	6.1	8.4	11.6	4.1	6.6	9.7	3.9	1.6	13.0	3.2
Agriculture	7.1	3.8	1.7	10.0	2.7	3.2	2.54	5.0	0.7	13.2	2.8
Other manual	8.0	6.2	6.2	10.9	7.1	10.2	18.2	5.3	2.3	13.7	2.1
Average of above	5.4	4.5	4.8	8.2	4.0	7.4	9.3	3.7	1.4	11.4	1.7
All	6.2	8.0	4.7	8.9	5.0	7.5	17.7	4.1	1.5	20.5	1.9
Ratio of manual to non-manual unemployment rate	2.27	1.94	1.82	1.88	2.29	1.49	2.26	2.01	2.19	1.88	2.03
var(u_i/u) (%)	18.5	15.0	19.9	11.2	28.1	11.4	45.1	14.9	25.3	7.2	16.7

Notes:
1. Australia 1986.
2. Germany 1985.
3. Occupational classifications according to International Standard Occupational Classification. The first 4 categories are treated as non-manual.
   See notes to Table 2.1.

Source: ILO, *Year Book* (1988).

Table 2.4. *Dispersion of occupational unemployment rates,*
1973–87   var(u$_i$/u) (%)

	United Kingdom (5)[1]	United States (7)	Australia (7)	Canada (7)	Germany (6)	Spain (7)	Sweden (8)
1973		13.1					9.0
1974	23.3	15.1					9.6
1975	14.0	20.2		12.3			7.6
1976	20.5	14.0		9.2	8.8	15.2	12.1
1977	21.0	12.3	13.8	10.7		15.7	12.5
1978	16.2	12.4	18.4	9.5	9.1	16.4	12.4
1979	24.4	15.2	14.3	10.9		19.7	12.8
1980	20.4	22.7	15.1	12.4	9.1	20.6	12.4
1981	21.2	21.1	17.2	13.3		20.0	15.9
1982	21.4	25.1	17.4	15.1	16.9	21.4	17.4
1983	22.8	21.5	25.7	13.6		21.1	15.9
1984	20.5	19.9	22.2	11.2	14.1	16.7	12.1
1985	22.3	20.6	19.7	11.3	11.4	12.9	13.3
1986		20.6	15.0	10.8		11.1	16.6
1987		18.5		11.2		7.2	16.7
Correlation between first and last years	0.87	—	0.92	0.95	0.86	1.00	0.83

Ratio of manual to non-manual unemployment rates

	United Kingdom (5)[1]	United States (7)	Australia (7)	Canada (7)	Germany (6)	Spain (7)	Sweden (8)
1973		1.80					1.74
1974	1.76	1.93					1.78
1975	1.74	2.18		1.89			1.65
1976	2.13	1.94		1.71	1.04	2.08	1.91
1977	2.12	1.85	1.68	1.78		2.14	1.93
1978	1.78	1.85	2.16	1.70	1.18	1.95	2.04
1979	2.27	2.04	1.97	1.80		1.99	2.02
1980	2.34	2.46	1.97	1.92	1.27	2.04	1.96
1981	2.41	2.39	1.86	1.97		1.98	2.25
1982	2.53	2.58	2.14	2.04	1.69	1.86	2.34
1983	2.57	2.46	2.36	1.97		1.75	2.22
1984	2.20	2.38	2.46	1.86	1.60	1.99	1.95
1985	2.45	2.42	2.14	1.87	1.49	1.91	1.85
1986		2.41	1.93	1.86		2.00	1.98
1987		2.27		1.88		1.88	2.02

Notes: 1. Numbers in brackets are numbers of categories.
See Table 2.1.

Sources:
United Kingdom: *General Household Survey* (breakdown as in Table 2.1).
Others: ILO, *Year Book* (1988) (breakdown as in Table 2.3, which amalgamates skilled and non-skilled manual workers).
United Statse: *Employment and Earnings* uses even more different classifications before and after 1983, but the trend in each sub-period is as shown above.

Table 2.5. *Unemployment by occupation: inflow and duration, 1984 and 1987*

	Britain (1984)			United States (1987)		
	Inflow rate (% per month) (S/N)	Average duration (months) (U/S)	Unemployment rate (%) (U/L)	Inflow rate (% per month) (S/N)	Average duration (months) (U/S)	Unemployment rate (%) (U/L)
Professional and managerial	0.50	11.2	5.3	0.74	3.0	2.3
Clerical	0.88	10.1	8.0	1.58	2.6	4.3
Other non-manual	1.14	11.8	12.2	1.97	2.9	6.1
Skilled manual	1.02	14.2	12.6	2.96	2.4	7.7
Personal services						
Other manual	1.32	14.1	15.5	2.84	3.0	9.4
All	0.94	12.8	10.8	2.23	2.6	6.2

Note: The sources listed below provide data on L, N, U and S (inflow). These are then used to produce 'steady-state' estimates of duration. However the estimate of monthly inflow is an underestimate, comprising all those unemployed at a point in time who became unemployed in the previous month (it thus excludes those who enter and leave within a month). In Britain the numbers in the category on the *Labour Force Survey* (LFS) definition of unemployment are only 70% of those in their first month of benefit receipt. The *General Household Survey* is broadly consistent with the LFS.

Sources:
Britain: *Labour Force Survey* tapes. This records only previous occupation and industry for those unemployed under 3 years. The unemployment rate in each occupation is computed by taking the numbers unemployed less than 3 years who were previously employed in the stated occupation and raising it by the ratio of total unemployed to numbers of unemployed reporting their previous occupation. A similar procedure is done for those unemployed for under one month.
United States: *Employment and Earnings* (January 1988) p. 185.

Table 2.6. *Unemployment rate by highest educational level, 1988, %*

	Australia		Austria		Belgium		Canada		Finland		Germany		Greece	
	M	F	M	F	M	F	M	F	M	F	M	F	M	F
Degree	2.6	5.5	0.8	2.4	3.2	7.7	3.4	5.5	1.2	0.7	3.0	6.9	4.2	12.7
Sub-degree	4.2	6.8	—	—	—	—	6.3	7.2	—	—	3.0	8.8	8.1	14.1
Vocational	4.7	—	3.1	3.1	—	—	—	—	—	—	5.9	8.2	—	—
Upper secondary	6.4	7.7	3.4	2.9	4.6	15.9	8.5	9.8	4.0	3.2	5.5	8.1	7.3	18.7
Other	9.5	7.8	5.5	4.9	9.0	22.4	11.2	12.7	9.2	5.6	14.4	12.9	3.9	6.2
All	6.3	7.3	3.5	3.7	6.9	17.4	7.9	9.0	7.4	4.6	6.9	9.4	4.8	9.9

	Italy		Netherlands		Norway		Spain		Sweden		United Kingdom		United States	
	M	F	M	F	M	F	M	F	M	F	M	F	M	F
Degree	3.3	9.3	4.4	11.4	0.4	1.1	9.9	27.4	0.8	0.8	3.7	4.7	1.8	2.1
Sub-degree	—	—	4.3	10.7	—	—	11.3	21.8	1.4	0.8	—	—	4.3	3.6
Vocational	—	—	—	—	—	—	—	—	2.2	2.1	8.1	10.1	—	—
Upper secondary	9.2	20.0	4.8	10.3	1.1	2.4	18.8	33.7	1.4	1.5	7.7	7.0	6.7	5.4
Other	6.2	15.3	10.9	16.5	2.2	2.2	14.7	17.9	2.1	2.2	14.8	11.3	10.7	9.6
All	6.7	16.3	7.5	13.2	1.5	2.1	15.5	24.4	1.8	1.8	10.4	9.7	5.6	4.8

Note: 'Sub-degree' is some post-secondary education but not a degree (identified only in some countries). 'Vocational' includes any vocational qualification below a degree (identified only in some countries).

Source: OECD, *Employment outlook* (July 1989) pp. 85–6.

Table 2.7. *Unemployment by region: Britain, Summer 1988*

	Inflow rate (% per month) (Inflow/N)	Average duration (months) (U/Outflow)	Unemployment rate (%) (U/L)
South East	0.80	5.7	5.3
East Anglia	0.83	4.7	4.9
South West	1.03	5.0	6.2
West Midlands	0.97	7.6	9.0
East Midlands	0.97	6.4	7.5
Yorkshire and Humberside	1.20	6.8	9.7
North West	1.30	7.2	10.9
North	1.47	7.0	12.2
Wales	1.40	6.2	10.6
Scotland	1.50	6.9	11.7
Total	1.07	6.4	8.0
var(X_i/X)	5.7%	2.0%	10.6%

Source: Department of Employment *Gazette* (October 1988) Table 2.23. The data do not relate to a steady state; the data relate to benefit recipients.

Table 2.8. *Unemployment by region: United States, 1988*

	Unemployment rate (%)
New England (1) [1]	3.1
New York and New Jersey (2)	4.1
Middle Atlantic (3)	4.9
South East (4)	5.6
Central: North East (5)	6.0
Central: South West (6)	7.8
Central: North West (7)	4.9
Mountain (8)	5.8
Pacific (9)	5.3
North West (10)	6.2
Total	5.4
var(u_i/u)	4.1%

Note:
1. Numbers in brackets are standard numbers for each region.

Source: Employment and Earnings (May 1989) Table 3.

Table 2.9. Dispersion of regional unemployment rates, 1974–87 $var(u_l/u)$, %

	Australia (8)[1]	Canada (10)	France (22)	Germany (11)	Finland (12)	Italy (20)	Japan (20)	Sweden (24)	Britain (10)	United States (51)
1974	3.5	—	7.1	—	39.0	—	7.6	—	14.3	—
1975	3.1	7.1	3.9	—	26.4	—	4.1	—	7.2	—
1976	2.1	7.9	3.8	3.6	15.8	—	4.3	17.1	4.5	5.3
1977	1.5	8.5	3.5	5.0	16.6	14.3	7.2	14.6	4.9	4.4
1978	1.4	8.3	3.9	6.6	13.8	12.4	7.4	15.5	6.7	3.7
1979	2.0	9.3	4.0	6.3	13.1	12.5	7.1	11.7	8.8	3.9
1980	1.4	8.7	3.7	4.9	19.2	18.1	6.9	15.6	9.2	5.0
1981	2.9	10.4	3.2	4.3	22.4	13.1	5.9	16.4	6.6	5.6
1982	1.6	4.9	3.0	4.2	20.0	11.5	5.0	13.7	5.6	5.5
1983	0.8	3.2	3.1	5.9	16.9	9.3	5.9	10.4	5.4	5.2
1984	2.0	5.1	3.2	7.3	22.1	7.9	6.4	11.0	5.1	6.0
1985	2.6	7.1	2.8	8.3	23.5	9.7	6.6	11.6	5.0	5.1
1986	1.8	8.2	2.8	—	20.5	13.6	5.8	14.8	5.1	6.6
1987	2.8	9.5	2.8		18.8	19.6	5.4	14.5	6.3	7.8
Correlation between first and last years	−0.11	0.67	0.50	0.83	0.91	0.84	0.91	0.69	0.92	−0.33

Note: Numbers in brackets are number of regions in the country.

Source: OECD, Regional Database on unemployment and labour force except for United Kingdom, which is based on Savouri (1989). UK data for 1967–73 are 12.8, 13.3, 14.9, 13.7, 14.3, 15.2, 17.5.

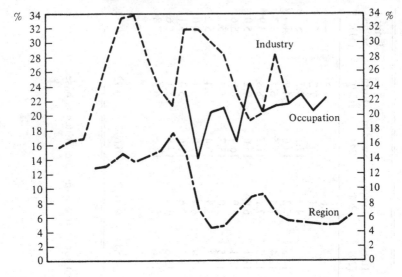

(a)   var u_i/u

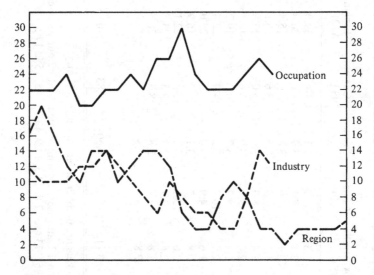

(b) u/v mismatch (see section 6)

Figure 2.1   (see p. 55)

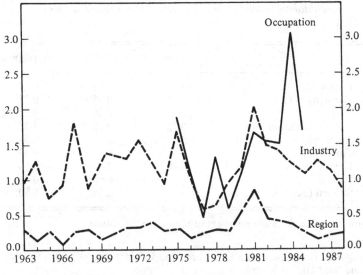

(c)   Turbulence $_2^1 \Sigma \left| \Delta(N_i/N) \right|$

Figure 2.1   Fluctuations in mismatch and turbulence: Britain, 1963–87 (shaded area = downturn)

Sources:
(a)   Industry – ILO *Yearbook of Labour Statistics* (various issues).
      Regional – CSO, *Regional Trends and Regional Statistics* (various issues).
      Occupation – *General Household Survey* tapes.
(b)   Jackman and Roper (1987) Table 2, updated using Department of Employment *Gazette*.
(c)   Industry – See Figure 2.2.
      Regional – See Table 2.10.
      Occupation – *General Household Survey* tapes.

Turning to the variance in other countries, we provide comparable data in Table 2.9. These show the high persistence of regional differences in some countries (Italy, the United Kingdom, Japan, Germany) and the total absence of persistence in the United States and Australia. Thus, while the correlation coefficient of the mid-1970s and the mid-1980s, unemployment rates across British regions is 0.92, across the US states it is – 0.33.

How has dispersion altered? In no country is there any important increase since the mid-1970s, and in Britain it is now markedly lower than in the early 1970s. As regards the cyclical pattern of mismatch, we have investigated this only for Britain. The figures are plotted in Figure 2.1a and show a clear tendency for regional mismatch to fall in downturns and

Table 2.10. *Regional turbulence indices (averages of annual values)*
$\frac{1}{2}\Sigma|\Delta(N_i/N)|$

		1960s	1970s	1980s
(E)EC	France (22)[1]	—	0.93	0.99
	Germany (11)	0.52	0.45	0.38
	Italy (20)	0.73	0.46	0.71
	United Kingdom (10)	0.23	0.28	0.37
	Australia (8)	0.49	0.48	0.51
	Canada (10)	0.51	0.46	0.53
	United States (10)	0.40	0.61	0.54
EFTA	Finland (12)	—	0.66	0.51
	Sweden (24)	—	0.35	0.50

Note: Numbers in brackets are numbers of regions in the country.

Sources:
OECD, Regional Database on Labour Force and Unemployment except for the United States and United Kingdom.
United States: 1952–75: *Employment and Training Report to the President* (1982) Table D-1.
United Kingdom: 1975–88: US Bureau of Labour Statistics, *Employment and Earnings* (various issues).
    1951–68: Department of Employment and Productivity, *British Labour Statistics, Historical Abstract, 1886–1968* (London: HMSO, 1971) Table 131.
    1969–70: Central Statistical Office, *Regional Statistics*, 12 (London: HMSO, 1976) Table 8.1.
    1971–89: Department of Employment *Gazette, Historical Supplement No. 2*, 97 (11) (November 1989) Table 1.5.
Annual data available on request.

rise in upturns. In other words in a downturn unemployment rises proportionately more in the low-unemployment regions. Even so *employment* falls more *slowly* in the low-unemployment regions, bringing about substantial changes in the pattern of employment. To look at the degree of 'turbulence' in the pattern of regional employment we can compute $\frac{1}{2}\Sigma|\Delta(N_i/N)|$ indicating what fraction of all jobs in the economy have 'changed region'. This is plotted in Figure 2.1c, and shows a marked redistribution of employment during the 1979–81 downturn.

One naturally asks whether the problems of the 1980s can be attributed in general to a greater pace of change in the pattern of employment between regions. To answer this, we compute the regional turbulence index, $\frac{1}{2}\Sigma|\Delta(N_i/N)|$, for a number of countries. Table 2.10 gives averages of this for different decades. Only in Britain and the United States is the degree of turbulence any higher in the recent past then in the 1960s, and in Britain this turbulence was concentrated in the early 1980s.

1.3   Industrial differences

We can turn now to differences in industrial unemployment rates. These are a less well defined concept, for when industrial rates are computed, unemployed people are attributed to the industry in which they were last employed, and many eventually find employment elsewhere. As Table 2.11 shows, unemployment is well above average in construction, and in bad times manufacturing, too, gets hit. But durations are remarkably similar in all industries, with unemployment differences being due to difference turnover rates.

The pattern of industrial unemployment rates is remarkably constant, as is shown in the correlations in Table 2.12. And there is no sign, except perhaps in Australia, that the dispersions have increased over time.

This does not mean that the process of industrial restructuring is not an important source of unemployment. As Table 2.13 shows, about 1% of jobs 'change industry' each year. But, contrary to popular belief, there is no evidence that this process has been accelerating. People seem constantly to forget the massive restructurings of the past, such as the huge exodus from European agriculture in the 1950s and 1960s, which was accompanied by so little unemployment.

In fact in most countries except the United States the rate of structural shift has been slowing down. And in Britain there is no difference between the level now and the mid-1960s, as Figure 2.1 shows. Both turbulence and industrial mismatch increase in downturns,[4] but in the late 1930s were at normal levels. Where there is a remarkable difference in both Britain and the United States is between the 1930s and the postwar period. As Figure 2.2 shows, there is every reason to think of 1930s unemployment as being due significantly to the 'problems of the declining industries'.

1.4   Age, race and sex

Unemployment is, of course, almost everywhere more common among young people than among adults (see Table 2.11). As so often, the difference results from higher inflow rates – and certainly not from unusual duration. The youth unemployment problem was accentuated in the 1980s by a big rise in the relative number of youths, reflecting the baby boom of the late 1950s and 1960s. In consequence, much more attention

Table 2.11. *Unemployment by industry, age, race and sex, 1984 and 1987*

	Britain (1984)			United States (1987)		
	Inflow rate (% per month) (S/N)	Average duration (months) (U/S)	Unemployment rate (%) (U/L)	Inflow rate (% per month) (S/N)	Average duration (months) (U/S)	Unemployment rate (%) (U/L)
Industry						
Agriculture	0.82	10.6	8.0	4.88	2.4	10.5
Manufacturing	0.88	16.6	12.7	2.06	3.1	6.0
Construction	1.57	12.7	16.6	4.52	2.9	11.6
Energy	0.76	10.1	7.1			
Services	0.90	11.6	9.4			
Transportation and public utilities				1.57	3.0	4.5
Distribution				2.96	2.5	6.9
Finance and service industries				2.08	2.5	4.9
Age						
16–19	3.33	8.5	22.1	10.15	2.0	16.9
20–24	1.33	15.3	16.9	4.46	2.4	9.7
25–54	0.74	13.1	8.8	1.76	3.0	5.0
55–64	0.47	19.2	8.3	0.97	3.7	3.5
Race						
White	0.92	12.6	10.4	2.15	2.6	5.3
Other	1.43	17.6	20.1	5.14	2.9	13.0
Sex						
Male	0.78	16.1	11.2	2.28	2.9	6.2
Female	1.17	9.7	10.2	2.87	2.3	6.2
All	0.94	12.8	10.8	2.54	2.6	6.2

Note: See Table 2.5

Source:
Britain: *Labour Force Survey* tapes, see Table 2.5
United States: *Employment and Earnings* (January 1988) pp. 160, 166, 169, 170, 174, 175.

Table 2.12. *Dispersion of industrial unemployment rates, 1973–87* $var(u_i/u)$ *(%)*

	United Kingdom (9)[1]	United States (9)	Australia (7)	Canada (9)	Germany (9)	Spain (9)	Sweden (7)
1973	21.2	7.3					
1974	31.8	9.3	4.1				8.7
1975	31.8	15.3	5.7		17.6		5.1
1976	29.9	8.1	8.1	7.6	13.0	59.0	7.6
1977	28.3	6.1	8.9	9.8	12.0	60.3	2.7
1978	22.9	5.8	11.9	10.6	11.1	54.4	7.5
1979	19.1	5.8	8.3	8.9	11.3	57.2	3.7
1980	20.1	10.6	8.6	10.6	10.0	53.6	3.2
1981	28.2	9.4	9.6	8.3	9.5	48.6	6.2
1982	21.8	13.9	11.1	12.5	11.7	41.2	5.7
1983		11.0	24.3	12.7	10.4	37.2	4.7
1984		8.7	10.4	10.9	11.1	34.7	3.8
1985	8.8	5.9	9.2	12.3	26.5	3.6	
1986		9.9	9.1	8.3	11.7	19.9	5.2
1987		9.0	9.9	7.1	10.0	11.9	4.0
Correlation between first and last years	0.86	0.89	—	0.95	0.80	0.96	0.81

Note:
1. Numbers of industrial sectors in brackets. Bars indicate breaks in the series. Correlations are not calculated cross breaks.

Source: ILO, *Year Book* (1988).

has been devoted to youth unemployment than to any other aspect (see, for example, successive issues of the OECD *Employment Outlook*). For this reason we shall concentrate mainly on other dimensions of mismatch. We shall also say little about race differences (which are acute and reflect mainly inflow differences), nor about sex differences (which in most, but not all, countries are fairly small).

2   How the structure of unemployment is determined

Why do unemployment rates differ across groups? In thinking about this, it is essential to distinguish between situations according to whether the labour force structure is exogenous or endogenous. In the short run the labour force is already allocated between groups; but in the long run migration is possible between skill groups and regions, though not normally between sexes and races. There *is* migration between age groups, but it is unfortunately exogenous. We shall begin with the case where the labour force is taken as given, and then turn to the case where migration occurs and a long-run equilibrium has been established.

Table 2.13. *Industrial turbulence indices (averages of annual values)* $\frac{1}{2}\Sigma|\Delta(N_i/N)|$

		1950s	1960s	1970s	1980s
(E)EC	Belgium (8)[1]	0.94	0.94	0.96	0.89
	France (8)	1.04	0.96	0.68	0.65
	Germany (8)	1.35	1.15	0.92	0.64
	Italy (8)	2.18	1.43	1.11	1.29
	Netherlands (8)	0.74	0.89	0.96	1.14
	Spain (8)	1.55	1.19	1.53	1.36
	United Kingdom (24/25)	0.91	1.12	1.17	1.27
	Australia (8)	—	1.76	1.21	1.40
	Canada (8)	—	—	0.83	0.90
	USA (8)	0.93	0.67	0.89	0.96
EFTA	Austria (8)	—	—	1.10	1.08
	Sweden (8)	—	1.45	1.52	0.67
	Switzerland (8)	—	0.90	0.99	0.50

Note: Numbers of industrial sectors in brackets.

Source: OECD, *Labour Force Statistics* (various years) except for the United States and the United Kingdom. See also sources to Figure 2.2.

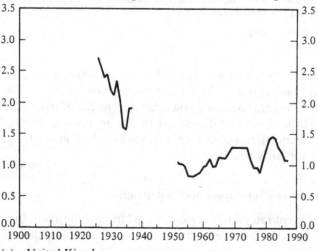

(a)　United Kingdom
Figure 2.2　(see p. 61)

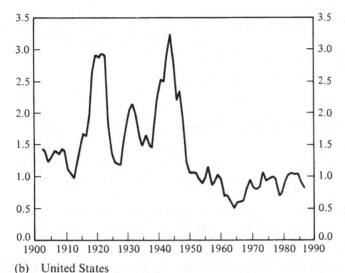

(b)   United States

Figure 2.2   Industrial   turbulence   index,   5-year   moving   average,   1900–90
$\frac{1}{2}\Sigma|\Delta(N_i/N)|$
Sources:
UK Industrial Employment Statistics
1924–39   Department of Employment and Productivity, *British Labour Statistics, Historical Abstract, 1886–1968* (London: HMSO, 1971) Table 114.
1948–68   Department of Employment and Productivity, *British Labour Statistics, Historical Abstract, 1886–1968* (London: HMSO, 1971) Table 132.
1969–70   Department of Employment and Productivity, *British Labour Statistics
Yearbook, 1972* (London: HMSO, 1972) Table 63.
1971–89   Department of Employment, *Gazette, Historical Supplement No. 2*, 97
(11) (November 1989) Table 1.2.

Note: For the years 1948–70, the data represents 24 industry orders, the 1948–59
data for 1948 SIC, and the 1959–70 data for 1958 SIC. The data for 1971–89 are
for 25 industry orders from 1980 SIC. For the lists of the respective industries, see
the above sources.
US Industrial Employment Statistics
1901–55   *Historical Statistics of the United States: Colonial Times to 1970: Part I.*
D.127–41.
1955–88   US Department of Labor, Bureau of Labor Statistics, *Employment and
Earnings* (May 1989) Table B1.

Note: Index is for 8 divisions: Mining; Construction; Manufacturing; Transportation and Public Utilities; Wholesale and Retail Trade; Finance, Insurance,
and Real Estate; Services; Government.

2.1   Labour force given (e.g., by age)

In the short run, the disposition of the labour force (between $L_i s$) is given.
Employment is determined by the pattern of labour demand and the

process of wage formation. For simplicity we can suppose that output (Y) is produced by a CES production function that is homogeneous of degree one in the different types of labour (N_i):

$$Y\rho = \varphi \Sigma \alpha_i N_i \rho \qquad (\rho \leqslant 1, \ \Sigma \alpha_i = 1)$$

where $\rho - 1 = -1/\sigma$.

Ignoring imperfect competition, the *labour demand* for the ith type of labour is then given by

$$W_i = \alpha_i \varphi \left(\frac{N_i}{Y}\right)^{-(1/\sigma)} = -\alpha_i \left(\frac{N_i}{L_i} \frac{L_i}{L}\right)^{-(1/\sigma)} X \qquad (i = 1, \ldots, n) \ (1)$$

where W_i is the real wage, L_i the labour force in the ith sector, and X the productivity factor $\varphi(Y/L)^{1/\sigma}$. The coefficient α_i is an indicator of productivity of labour of type i.

Wages in each sector are determined by the *wage function*, which we shall write as

$$W_i = \beta_i f \left(\frac{N_i}{L_i}\right) X \qquad (f' > 0)(i = 1, \ldots, n) \tag{2}$$

where the coefficient β_i is an indicator of 'wage push'.

The evidence for this formulation will be discussed later. Its theoretical basis is a mixture of bargaining outcomes, efficiency wages and pure labour supply (Jackman *et al.*, 1991).[5]

Both the demand function and the wage function are drawn in Figure 2.3. Taken together, they determine the unemployment rate of each group as an increasing function of its wage push relative to productivity (β_i/α_i) and also its relative size (L_i/L):[6]

$$u_i = g^1 \left(\underset{+}{\frac{\beta_i}{\alpha_i}}, \underset{+}{\frac{L_i}{L}}\right)$$

$$W_i = g^2 \left(\underset{+}{\alpha_i}, \underset{+}{\beta_i}, \underset{-}{\frac{L_i}{L}}, \underset{+}{X}\right)$$

Thus, if an age group increases in relative size, its unemployment rate will go up and its wage down. (The demand curve as drawn shifts left, since a given N_i corresponds to a lower N_i/L_i.) This is exactly what happened to youths in the United States as a result of the baby boom (see Freeman and Bloom, 1986).

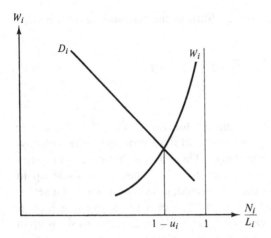

Figure 2.3   Employment and wages in a single sector: labour force given

Equally, the unemployment rate of a group will be affected by its turnover rate. Wage push develops if it is easy for unemployed people to find work. At a given unemployment rate, the chances of finding work are proportional to the rate at which jobs are being left; thus the wage push variable (β_i) is higher the higher is turnover. This helps to explain why unemployment is higher for young people.

2.2   *Labour force endogenous* (i.e., by occupation or region)

The same analysis cannot be applied to occupational/educational unemployment rates nor to differences in unemployment across regions, except in the very short run, for in the longer run the number of people in each occupation or region itself depends on wages and job opportunities. Migration can change the share of the total labour force in each sector. Migration into a sector (M_i) depends on the extent to which expected income in the sector exceeds that elsewhere; it also depends on the costs of belonging to the sector (e.g., the associated training cost or the climatic discomfort).[7] Thus the net inmigration rate (M_i/L_i) is given by

$$\frac{M_i}{L_i} = \text{h}\left(W_i \frac{N_i}{L_i} \middle/ (1 + c_i)\lambda X \right) \qquad (i = 1, \ldots, h - 1) \qquad (3)$$

where c_i reflects the differential costs of belonging to the sector.

Suppose initially that we define the long-run equilibrium as a condition of zero net migration. Then in equilibrium the *zero-migration condition* gives

$$W_i \frac{N_i}{L_i} = (1 + c_i)\zeta X \qquad (i = 1, \ldots, h - 1) \tag{3'}$$

where $\zeta = h^{-1}(0)$.

This is the long-run supply condition for the choice of sectors. The equalisation of net advantage requires that if a sector has higher employment, it will have to have lower wages. This relationship reflects long-run migration behaviour, and could therefore be expected to show up in cross-sectional evidence. On the other hand, once workers are in a sector they will press for the setting of higher wages if employment is higher. This relationship repeated year after year could be expected to show up in time series evidence.

To understand why unemployment rates differ between sectors, we combine equations (3') and (2) to obtain

$$u_i = j^1 \left(\frac{\beta_i}{1 + c_i} \right)$$

$$W_i = j^2(\beta_i, c_i, c_i, x)$$
$$+ \quad + \quad +$$

This says that wage differentials between sectors must reflect cost differences, except that wages in a sector can be lower if its employment rate is unusually high. We note that relative unemployment rate and wage rates in the long run are determined by supply factors alone; demand conditions determine only the absolute magnitude of employment and of the labour force in each sector.

There are $(h - 1)$ zero-migration conditions. These, taken together with the wage-setting equations and the price equation (linking the set of feasible real wages), determine the real wages (W_i) and employment rates (N_i/L_i) in each group.

The partial equilibrium for a sector is illustrated in Figure 2.4. As before, the wage-setting relation shows that wages rise as higher employment creates wage push. This reflects the way in which workers behave once they are in a sector. On the other hand, their migration decisions imply that higher wages must be associated with lower employment to equalise the net advantages of the different sectors. So long as the differential wage push in a sector is in proportion to its cost differential, it will have the same unemployment as elsewhere. But if the wage push is excessive, higher unemployment must result – otherwise the sector would continue to attract labour.

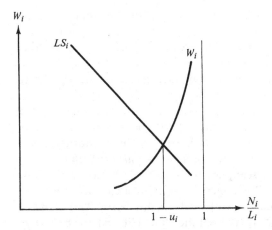

Figure 2.4   Employment and wages in a single sector: labour force endogenous, zero migration

Consider, for example, the standard human capital model, where occupation 1 requires one more year of schooling than occupation 2. Under full unemployment

$$\frac{W_1}{W_2} = 1 + r = \text{(here)} \frac{1 + c_1}{1 + c_2}$$

Allowing for unemployment

$$\frac{W_1(N_1/L_1)}{W_2(N_2/L_2)} = \frac{1 + c_1}{1 + c_2}$$

as indicated by equation (3′). So long as $W_1/W_2 = 1 + r$ the unemployment rates will be equal. But suppose the differential is squeezed (because $\beta_1/\beta_2 < 1 + r$). Then the uptake of schooling will fall until the unskilled unemployment rate has risen sufficiently relative to the skilled rate.

A similar model was used by Harris and Todaro (1970) to explain urban unemployment in poor countries. If the urban wage gap (W_1/W_2) is excessive relative to any cost differences, people will pile into the towns until there is sufficient urban unemployment ($N_1/L_1 < 1$). Thinking along similar lines Hall (1970) showed that unemployment differences between US cities was positively correlated with their wage rates. A similar model was used earlier to explain the unemployment of educated people in India by excessive wages for the educated (Blaug, Layard and Woodhall, 1969).

So let us ask: how well does the notion that unemployment depends on $\beta_i(1 + c_i)$ explain the pattern of unemployment rates? There is strong evidence in Tables 2.5 and 2.11 that those occupations and industries with high turnover rates (and thus high β_i) have high unemployment rates. Wage pressure will also be higher the greater is union strength. Other things being equal, union power in an occupation or industry will thus increase its unemployment rate, as will factors increasing the firms' incentive to pay efficiency wages.

As regards training costs (c_i), occupations where these are high do tend to have low unemployment rates. This is partly because, for reasons of compensating differentials, their wages have to be high, with the result that they are kept well above the level of unemployment benefits.

Across regions, as we have seen, unemployment is also higher in those which have high turnover. But typically unemployment differences are greater than can be adequately explained on this basis. And in many countries, like Britain and Italy (but not the United States), the pattern of regional unemployment differences is highly persistent. The outmigration of labour from the high unemployment areas is only just sufficient to keep pace with the transfer of jobs. There is thus a *steady-state* migration of jobs *and* workers, with relative unemployment rates and relative wages very stable. Regions like the North of England or the South of Italy provide a steadily decreasing share of total employment, and this down-ward drift in employment share is matched by a downward drift in the share of the labour force. Matters are often made worse by the fact that the 'natural' growth rate of population (due to the difference between new entrants and retirements) is higher in the regions that are losing jobs. We also need to allow for this.

2.3   Labour force endogenous with steady-state migration

We can easily handle those long-run steady-state patterns with two small modifications of our earlier framework. First, employment is changing at a steady state rate $\hat{N}_i$ (which differs across sectors). This arises due to exogenous shifts in demand (e.g., due to changes in its industrial mix) – with relative wages unchanged. Since the employment rate (N_i/L_i) is constant, in this dynamic steady state it follows that

$$\hat{L}_i = \hat{N}_i = (\text{say}) \; \hat{\alpha}_i$$

In addition there is (as between regions) a differential 'natural' growth of working population (corresponding to the difference between new entries and exits from the population of working age).[8] If the total labour force is growing at $\hat{L}$, this is the average rate of 'natural' population growth. But a region has problems if its natural population growth Π_i exceeds that level.

To see this, we can now extend our equation (3) to show how the labour force changes due not only to net migration, $h(.)$, but to natural population growth (Π_i). This gives

$$\hat{L}_i = h\left(W_i \frac{N_i}{L_i} \middle/ (1 + c_i)\lambda X\right) + \Pi_i$$

Since the unemployment rates are constant in the steady state, with $\hat{L}_i = \hat{N}_i$, it follows that

$$h\left(W_i \frac{N_i}{L_i} - (1 + c_i)\lambda X\right) + \Pi_i - \hat{N}_i = 0$$

At given W_i a region will thus have a lower employment rate (N_i/L_i) if its rate of population growth exceeds its rate of job creation.

Turning to Figure 2.4, in such a region the long-run labour supply relation (LS_i) is shifted down – raising unemployment and lowering wages. This helps to explain persistent high unemployment, as in Southern Italy and Northern Ireland. People have constantly wondered why one-off injections of jobs into such areas have had no enduring effect on their unemployment rates; our story shows why. It also helps to explain low unemployment in skilled occupations; if skilled jobs are always increasing faster than unskilled, this will tend to lower steady-state unemployment in the skilled occupations.[9]

The analysis in this section is out of line with traditional analyses of structural unemployment, which emphasise the role of one-off demand shifts. However, as we showed in section 1, there are such striking persistent differences in unemployment rates that we feel these deserve the primary attention.

3   How mismatch is related to the NAIRU

The preceding analysis provides in principle a complete account of the unemployment rate for each separate group, and thus also of the aggregate unemployment rate. In principle our theory could thus stop at this point. However, many people are interested in explaining aggregate unemployment without going through the daunting task of explaining each of the individual rates. In particular, people ask: does increased structural imbalance help us to understand the recent high unemployment in Europe?

So is there some simple index by which one could assess how the structure of unemployment is related to its average level (both, of course, being endogenous)? The answer is: yes. The basic idea goes back to Lipsey (1960). It is worth beginning with an analogous framework to his, before modifying it in the direction of greater rigour. Figure 2.5 sets out

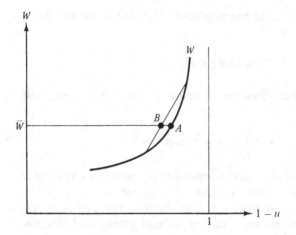

Figure 2.5   Introductory presentation of mismatch and the NAIRU

the wage function, assumed to be the same for each of two equal-sized groups. $\bar{W}$ is the feasible average wage. If both unemployment rates are equal, aggregate unemployment is at A. If the two unemployment rates differ but the average wage remains at $\bar{W}$, the average unemployment will have to be at B. Overall unemployment is thus higher. The further apart the unemployment rates, the higher the average unemployment.

This result depends entirely on the convexity of the wage function, for which there is much evidence (see below). But the formulation is un-rigorous. In particular, it relies on identical wage functions for each group, which on reasonable assumptions turn out to be unnecessary.

To see this, and to derive the relevant mismatch index, we begin with the feasible set of real wages, given by the price function. For simplicity we shall assume constant returns to scale in the different types of labour. If we also initially assume a Cobb–Douglas production function, the nominal price is given by

$$P = \Pi W_i^{\alpha i} e^{-A} \quad (\Sigma \alpha_i = 1)$$

where A is a combined index of technical progress and of product market competition.

Setting the price level at unity and taking logs, the *price function* gives a feasible real wage frontier.

$$A = \Sigma \alpha_i \log W_i \tag{4}$$

In addition we shall assume double logarithmic wage functions (evidence

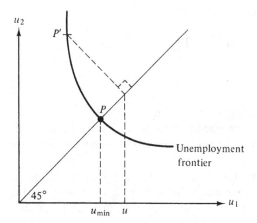

Figure 2.6 The unemployment frontier: wages responding to own-sector unemployment

for the United Kingdom follows, for other countries see, for example, Grubb, 1986). The *wage functions* are thus:

$$\log W_i = \beta_i - \gamma \log u_i \tag{5}$$

Substituting the wage functions into the price functions gives an *unemployment frontier*

$$A = \Sigma \alpha_i \beta_i - \gamma \Sigma \alpha_i \log u_i \tag{6}$$

This shows the locus of all combinations of sectoral unemployment rates which are consistent with the absence of inflationary pressure, given the behaviour of wage setters.

This frontier is illustrated in Figure 2.6 for the case of two sectors of equal size ($\alpha_1 = \alpha_2 = \frac{1}{2}$). Since the function is convex to the origin, the lowest possible *average* level of unemployment (u_{min}) is where unemployment is the same in both sectors.[10] This occur at point P in Figure 2.6. If, instead, the unemployment rates differ, as at P', average unemployment is higher – in this case it is u'. The further apart the different unemployment rates, the higher their average level.

We can readily derive an expression that shows how average unemployment is related to the dispersion of the unemployment rates across sectors. We start from equation (6) and add $\gamma \log u$ to both sides and divide both sides by γ. This gives

$$\log u = \text{const} - \Sigma \alpha_i \frac{\log u_i}{\log u}$$

Since $\Sigma \alpha_i = 1$, expanding $\log u_i/u$ around 1 gives[11]

$$\log u \simeq \text{const} - \Sigma \alpha_i \left(-\tfrac{1}{2} \right) \left(\frac{u_i}{u} - 1 \right)^2$$

$$= \text{const} + \tfrac{1}{2} \text{var} \, \frac{u_i}{u} \tag{7}$$

The minimum level of log unemployment is now given by the constant, $(\Sigma \alpha_i \beta_i - A)/\gamma$, and occurs when unemployment rates have been equalised. But, if unemployment rates are unequal, unemployment rises by the proportion $\tfrac{1}{2}$ var(u_i/u).

Given equation (7), the natural index of the structure of unemployment, viewed as a 'cause' of the average unemployment rate, is $\tfrac{1}{2}$ var(u_i/u); this measures the proportional excess of unemployment over its minimum. Since it is zero if labour demand and supply have the same structure, it is natural to give it the name 'mismatch' (*MM*).[12] Thus

$$MM = \tfrac{1}{2} \text{var} \, \frac{u_i}{u} = \log u - \log u_{\min}$$

As the data in section 1 showed, mismatch on this definition has not increased. In other words, we cannot use changes in the structure of unemployment as an explanation of the higher average level of unemployment rates.

At this point we need to deal with a misconception. We do *not* mean that the *number* of unemployed people who are 'mismatched' has failed to rise, for it unemployment rises for some *other* reason and the proportional mismatch is constant, the absolute numbers mismatched will rise. This corresponds well with the feeling of many Europeans that there are now more people who are structurally unemployed than used to be the case. The point is that it is possible *both* for this to be true *and* for structural factors as a *cause* of unemployment to have been constant.

Clearly this need not mean that mismatch is unimportant. In fact the figures we gave earlier for Britain show precisely how important it is. In 1985 the variances of relative unemployment rates were

'Across'

7 occupations	0.22
322 travel-to-work areas	0.24
10 industries	0.14
10 age groups	0.22
2 race groups	0.03
2 sex groups	0.01
	0.86

Assuming these imbalances to be approximately orthogonal, we can add them together and conclude that the degree of mismatch equals approximately half their sum – i.e., 0.4. Mismatch thus would account for roughly one-third of total unemployment – a serious matter.

3.1   Qualifications

Clearly the measure of mismatch that we have developed is very model-specific. It depends on our assumptions about

1.   the curvature of the price function
2.   the curvature of the wage function, and
3.   the assumption that wages depend on unemployment in the sector in question and not in some leading sector.

how much do things change if we vary these assumptions?

The first assumption is not that important. Suppose, for example, that the production function is CES with an elasticity of substitution σ between each type of labour. Then we show (in Appendix 1) that the appropriate measure of mismatch is

$$MM = \tfrac{1}{2}(1 - \gamma(\sigma - 1)) \operatorname{var} \frac{u_i}{u}$$

In general the elasticity of substitution between skill groups, age groups, sex groups and regional products exceeds unity (e.g., Hamermesh, 1986; Layard, 1982). But γ is quite small – of the order of 0.1 (see below). Thus $\gamma(\sigma - 1)$ will not be large. However, it is true, as one would expect, that for a given dispersion of u_i/u mismatch declines as types of labour become more substitutable. It is also true (given $\sigma > 1$) that mismatch declines as wage flexibility (γ) increases. Since $\sigma > 1$, mismatch may equal somewhat less than half $\operatorname{var}(u_i/u)$.

But many people object to the notion that mismatch should be measured by relative unemployment differentials. They feel that *absolute* differences are what matter – so that for constant $\operatorname{var}(u_i/u)$ mismatch will have risen if average unemployment is higher; they are wrong: this is true whatever the curvature of the wage function.

To see this, we can assume quite generally that

$$\log W_i = \beta_i - \gamma \frac{u^\alpha - 1}{\alpha} \qquad (-\infty < \alpha \leq 1; \alpha \neq 0)$$

where the parameter α determines the curvature of the wage function.

With $\alpha - 1$, the function is linear and as α falls the curvature increases (with wages tending to $\beta_i - \gamma \log u$ as α tends to zero). The level of unemployment is now determined by[13]

$$\frac{u\alpha - 1}{\alpha} = \frac{\Sigma \alpha_i \beta_i - A}{\gamma} + \frac{(1 - \alpha)u^\alpha}{2} \operatorname{var}\left(\frac{u_i}{u}\right)$$

As $\alpha \to 0$, this tends to

$$\log u = \Sigma \alpha_i \beta_i - A + \tfrac{1}{2} \operatorname{var}\left(\frac{u_i}{u}\right)$$

but whatever α, u is increasing in $\operatorname{var}(u_i/u)$. Only relative unemployment matters, whatever the curvature of the wage function. Needless to say if there is no curvature ($\alpha = 1$) there is no problem of mismatch whatever the variance. However all the evidence supports the notion of curvature, and we shall in the next section provide evidence in support of the log formulation.

3.2   Leading sector issue

All the analysis so far is postulated on the basis that wages in a sector depend only on the unemployment rate in the same sector. This is not how many analysts of mismatch think. Suppose instead that wages depend only on unemployment in some leading sector (like the South of England or electrical engineering) whose unemployment rate is denoted u_L. Then

$$\log W_i = \beta_i - \delta \log u_L$$

and the unemployment function is

$$A = \Sigma \alpha_i \beta_i - \delta \log u_L$$

This tells us the minimum unemployment we can have in the leading sector before general overheating emerges in the economy. There is no point in having unemployment higher than u_L anywhere else since it would have no effect on wage pressure. On the other hand presumably unemployment elsewhere cannot be lower than in the leading sector (since the leading sector is likely to be the tightest market). Thus[14]

$$MM = \log u - \log u_L$$

This is much greater than mismatch as measured on the assumption that wages respond to unemployment in each sector (rather than in the leading sector only) for, with a given set of unemployment rates, the minimum level of unemployment is much higher in the 'own-sector' case than the unemployment rate in the 'leading-sector' case. In the own-sector case

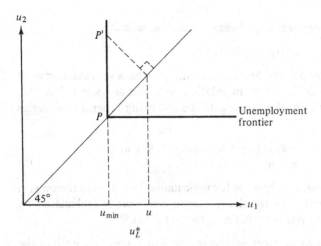

Figure 2.7 The unemployment frontier: wages responding to leading-sector unemployment

equation (6) shows that the same wage pressure is generated by $\Sigma \alpha_i \log u_i$ as by $\Sigma \alpha_i \log u_{\min}$ (with all rates equal). Thus, since $\Sigma \alpha_i = 1$,

$$\log u_{\min} = \Sigma \alpha_i \log u_i$$

In other words the minimum level of unemployment ($u_{\min}$) is then the *geometric mean* of all the actual unemployment rates. But in the 'leading-sector' case, it is given by u_L which is the *lowest* of all the rates. The gap between u and $u_{\min}$ is thus greater in the leading-sector wage model than it is when wages respond to own-sector unemployment.

The point is illustrated in Figure 2.7. Assuming that the leading sector is the one with the lowest unemployment rate, the unemployment frontier becomes a right-angle. As we have drawn the actual pattern of unemployment at P', sector 1 is the leading sector and actual unemployment greatly exceeds $u_{\min}$.

So have we grossly underestimated mismatch by ignoring the leading sector issue? This depends on whether the leading-sector theory of wages is right. Before addressing this question, we should consider one further possibility: that wages in one group depend simply on the aggregate unemployment rate:

$$W_i = f'(u)$$

In this case there is no mismatch, as we have defined it, since the NAIRU is independent of the distribution of unemployment and depends only on its average.

4   Evidence on sectoral wage behaviour and on mobility

4.1   Regional wage behaviour (Britain)

To check on our model, the first issue to study is the wage determination equation (2). We do this first in relation to regional wage behaviour, beginning with Britain. We investigate the following general time–series wage equation

$$w_i = a_1 \log u_i + a_2 \log u_L + a_3 \log u + a_4 X + a_{5i} t \\ + a_6 w_{i,-1} + a_{0i} \tag{8}$$

Here w_i is the log real hourly wage for male manual workers in region i (in units of GDP), and X is trend log output per worker (calculated by interpolating log output per worker between peaks).[15]

There is a regional fixed effect a_{0i} and regional time trend for each of the 10 regions of Britain. The equation was fitted to annual data for 1967 to 1987, and the results are shown in Table 2.14.

In row 1 we include as possible influences own-region unemployment (u_i), leading-region (South-East) unemployment (u_L), and national unemployment (u). We find that own-sector unemployment is insignificant and the national unemployment rate is significant but wrongly signed. Because of the collinearity between these measures we tried dropping first national unemployment (row 2) and then leading-sector unemployment (row 3). In both cases, own-sector unemployment remained significant and correctly signed, whereas leading-sector or national unemployment (respectively) too significant but wrongly signed coefficients.

This finding has parallels in other studies. The perverse sign on, say, national unemployment may arise from the fact that it stands as a proxy variable for unobserved aggregate supply shocks. An adverse supply shock will tend to raise unemployment in the nation as a whole and at the same time tend to raise wages at any given local unemployment rate in each region; hence it takes a positive sign in a regression equation. One may avoid this problem simply by dropping the national unemployment term in the equation (as we do in rows 4–7) but the coefficient on own-sector unemployment is then biased towards zero (given that own-sector unemployment will also be correlated with supply shocks).

It is nonetheless interesting, using this formulation, to check the effect of the level of long-term unemployment in the region. In row 5 this comes in with the correct (positive) sign. Alternatively the change in unemployment, which is negatively correlated with long-term unemployment, comes in with a negative sign (row 6). As row 7 shows, when both

Table 2.14. *Determinants of regional wage rates, Britain; dependent variables: w_i; other independent variables: x, t, allowing region-specific time trends*

Regression	Independent variables						s.e.	LM auto-correlation statistic
	$\log u_i$	$\log u_L$	$\log u$	$\left(\dfrac{LTU}{U}\right)_i$	$\Delta \log u_i$	$w_{i,-1}$		
1	−0.074 (6.0)	−0.015 (1.1)	0.046 (2.7)	—	—	0.12 (2.2)	0.0123	5.7
2	−0.062 (5.2)	0.042 (3.9)	—	—	—	0.079 (1.5)	0.0125	13.3
3	−0.069 (6.0)	—	0.058 (4.7)	—	—	0.14 (2.7)	0.0123	3.8
4	−0.020 (3.9)	—	—	—	—	0.14 (2.7)	0.0130	7.6
5	−0.019 (3.6)	—	—	0.02 (0.9)	—	0.17 (2.7)	0.0131	9.5
6	−0.020 (3.2)	—	—	—	−0.0006 (0.1)	0.14 (2.3)	0.0131	11.4
7	−0.025 (3.5)	—	—	0.057 (1.5)	−0.013 (1.3)	0.16 (2.6)	0.0130	7.6

Note:
Estimation by pooled time-series OLS for the 10 standard regions of Great Britain, 1967–87.
u is the national unemployment rate excluding regions i and L.
The small sample bias tends to bias the coefficients towards zero by a factor $\frac{1}{20}$ (Nickell, 1981). The constraints that the coefficients on u_i, w_{i-1} and R_i in equation (5) are the same in each region are jointly satisfied, with a test statistic of 1.7 against a critical 5% value of $F_{27,(49),0.05} = 1.7$. The constraints on u_i and w_{i-1} in equation (4) are similarly accepted at the 5% level with a test statistic of 0.8 against a 5% critical value of $F_{(18,159),0.05} = 1.6$. The LM autocorrelation statistic is constructed by retrieving the residuals $\hat{u}_i$ from our estimated equation regressing $\hat{u}$ on X and $\hat{u}_{-1}$, then retrieving R^2 from this later equation. Under the (null hypothesis) H_0: serially independent disturbances the statistic TR^2 is $\sim \chi^2(1)$. $\chi^2(1)$, 0.05 = 3.8.
Our results are shown to be robust to possible endogeneity between u_i and w_i when we estimate by instrumental variables using lagged unemployment and lagged real national income as instruments. Our results are also unaffected by replacing regional trends and trend log output by year time dummies.

Source: Department of Employment *Gazette*; for details see Savouri (1989).

variables are included, both are (marginally) significant and correctly signed. Given other evidence on the effects of long-term unemployment, our preference is for row 5. (When hysteresis variables are allowed for in the 'horse-race' of rows 1–3 the signs on the hysteresis terms are always wrong for leading-sector unemployment and aggregate unemployment, in the same way as reported in rows 1–3 for u_L and u.)

We may use the simplest of the own-sector unemployment wage equations (row 4) to test whether the unemployment coefficients are significantly different across regions. An F-test on constraining the coefficient values across regions to be the same is satisfied. This means that one can obtain more precise estimates of the regional wage equation by looking simply at relative wage movements. This procedure is not subject to biases coming from unobservable supply shocks. This we can take equation (8) and insert national average values and then subtract the averaged equation from equation (8). This gives[16]

$$w_i - w = a_1(\log u_i - \log u) + a_2(w_{i,-1} - w_{-1}) + (a_{0i} - a_0) + a_{3i}t$$

This procedure is more accurate since the estimates of the coefficients on local unemployment do not now depend at all on how the influences of any common national variables is modelled. The results of this analysis, comparable with rows 4 and 5 of Table 2.14, are

$$(w_i - w)_t = -0.049(\log u_i - \log u)_t + 0.63(w_i - w_t - 1) + (a_{i0} - a_0) + a_{3i}t$$
$$\quad\quad\quad (5.8) \quad\quad\quad\quad\quad\quad\quad (11.7)$$

(s.e. = 0.0074)   LM = 5.1 $\chi^2(1), 0.05 = 3.8$)

and

$$(w_i - w)_t = -0.045(\log u_i - \log u)_t + 0.68(w_i - w_t - 1)$$
$$\quad\quad\quad (5.6) \quad\quad\quad\quad\quad\quad\quad (12.9)$$
$$+ 0.16\left(\frac{LTU_i}{U_i} - \frac{LTU}{U}\right) + (a_{i0} - a_0) + a_{3i}t$$
$$\quad (4.2)$$

(s.e. = 0.0070   LM = 4.0 $\chi^2(1), 0.05 = 3.8$)

On this basis we find that regional wages respond to local unemployment with a long-run elasticity of 0.13. This is greater than the value of 0.02 implied by row 4 of Table 2.14 and closer to elasticities of around 0.10 found at many other levels of disaggregation (Layard and Nickell, 1986; Nickell and Wadhwani, 1989; Oswald, 1986). But the key point is that we have confirmed the strong effect of the local labour market upon regional wages.

The next question is whether our use of the double-log-linear wage function is justified. Indeed is the wage function convex (downward) *at all* – or is it *more* convex than the double-log-linear formulation implies?

To investigate this in a reasonably general way we replace $\log u$ by a quadratic in the level of unemployment (the cubed term being found completely insignificant). The result is

$$(w_i - w)_t = -0.91(u_i - u)_t + 0.84(u_i^2 - u^2)_t + 0.59(w_i - w)_{t-1}$$
$$ (3.7) \qquad\qquad (1.02) \qquad\qquad (9.5)$$
$$+ a_{3i}t + (a_{0i} - a_0)$$
$$(\text{s.e.} = 0.0075)$$

While a t-statistic of 1.02 suggests a degree of additional curvature, it is insufficiently well defined to justify abandoning the double logarithm form.

We should briefly contrast these estimates with the 'wage curves' estimated from cross-section data by Blanchflower and Oswald (1989). When estimated across British regions, these show $\partial w / \partial u$ becoming positive at high levels of unemployment. This is because the cross-sectional data capture a mixture of the wage equation and the long-run supply equation – the latter having the opposite slope to the former (see Figure 2.4).

4.2 Regional wage behaviour (United States)

Similar analyses have been made for wage determination at the level of US states, using annual data for 1975–88. Given the lack of stability in unemployment rankings across US states, there is no plausible leading sector. But it is interesting to compare the effects of state-level unemployment and national unemployment. This is done in Table 2.15. Again the powerful influence of local unemployment is apparent. This is even more so when we run the equation for relative wages:

$$w_i - w = -0.0280(\log u_{i,-1} - \log u_{-1}) + 0.676(W_{i,-1} - W_{-1})$$
$$ (5.1) \qquad\qquad\qquad (23.0)$$
$$+ (a_{0i} - a_0)$$
$$(\text{s.e.} = 0.02599 \qquad \text{LM} = 21.4$$

This gives an unemployment elasticity for wages of 0.09. We then tested for the constancy of this elasticity by running a quadratic in u (u^3 being again insignificant). The implied elasticities ($u\,\partial w / \partial u$) were

u	$u\,\partial w / \partial u$
0.02	– 0.019
0.04	– 0.030
0.06	– 0.032
0.08	– 0.027
0.10	– 0.013

Table 2.15. *Determinants of regional wage rates, United States; dependent variables:* w_i*; other independent variables:* x, t

| Regression | Independent variables | | | s.e. | LM auto-correlation statistic |
	$\log u_i$	$\log u$	$w_{i,-1}$		
1	− 0.023	0.032	0.82	0.0197	9.8
	(5.5)	(5.02)	(36.5)		
2	− 0.010	—	0.83	0.0201	11.8
	(2.9)		(36.3)		
3	—	0.009	0.82	0.0202	15.5
		(1.8)	(35.8)		

Note:
Both the terms $\Delta\log u_i$ and $\Delta\log u$ were not significant.
Wages are hourly wages of production workers.

Sources:
Employment and Earnings.
Prices are GDP deflator.
Productivity is trend output per worker (peak to peak).

This again lends reasonable support to the constant elasticity approach over the most relevant parts of the range.

4.3   Regional labour mobility

As regards the regional model, the next relationship to be investigated is the inmigration function, equation (3). The equation is

$$\frac{M_i}{L_i} = b_1 \log\left(\frac{N_i/L_i}{N/L}\right) + b_2 \log\left(\frac{W_i}{W}\right) + b_3 \log\left(\frac{P}{P_i}\right) + b_{4i}$$

or, for estimation purposes

$$\frac{M_i}{L_i} = b_1(u - u_i) + b_2(w_i - w) + b_3(p - p_i)$$

Here P refers to house prices, there being for Britain no time series on other cost of living differences between regions (which are in any case small).

The equation was fitted to annual data for 1968–86 (see Savouri, 1989), and the results were

$$\frac{M_i}{L_i} = 0.081(u - u_i) + 0.058(w_i - w) + 0.010(p - p_i) + b_{4i}$$
$$\quad\;(2.7) \qquad\qquad (3.9) \qquad\qquad (1.6)$$
$$(\text{s.e.} = 0.0031) \qquad (\text{LM} = 37.3)$$

Interestingly the equation is consistent with the idea that the real wages and the employment rates have the same proportional effect on migration. Pissarides and Wadsworth (1989) have argued that the absolute rate of migration falls when the general level of unemployment is high but we were unable to find such an effect.

For the United States we estimated the following equation for 1975–88:

$$\frac{\Delta L_i}{L_i} - \frac{\Delta L}{L} = 0.546(u - u_i) + 0.013(w_i - w) + b_i$$
$$\phantom{\frac{\Delta L_i}{L_i} - \frac{\Delta L}{L} = 0.546}(7.8) (0.5)$$

For the United States we do not (yet) have data on local price levels. This may be one reason why we find no significant effect of local wages, though this problem is common in US studies (Greenwood, 1985). But local unemployment has a much more powerful effect than in Britain.

4.4 Occupational wages and mobility

In due course we shall be able to report a similar analysis of the dynamics of the market for skills. At this stage we shall simply note that, in Britain at least, occupational unemployment has a strong effect on occupational wages, with an elasticity well above 0.1. In consequence the relative wages of manual workers have fallen sharply in the 1980s.

We have not been able to undertake any similar analysis for other European countries yet, due to lack of data on unemployment by occupation. But we are struck by the fact that in no other European country except Denmark have wage differentials increased during the 1980s as they have in Britain (see Table 2.16). And in France and Belgium they have narrowed. Can this be a partial clue to high European unemployment?

Turning to skill formation, there is a strong effect of wages on the choice of skill. Thus if we interpret M_i as the excess of entrants to departures in a skill group, the number of entrants is highly sensitive to expected earnings. In the United States the earnings elasticity of entrants has been variously estimated in the range 1–4 (Freeman, 1986), while in the United Kingdom Pissarides (1981, 1982) gives figures of $\frac{1}{2}$–$1\frac{1}{2}$. Relative unemployment effects on educational choice are less well determined.

Taking a unit elasticity and a working life of 50 years, we can thus infer that if wages in a skill group are higher by 1% numbers in the skill group will rise by some 0.02% per annum above what they would otherwise do. This is of the same order as the effect on a region's labour force if wages in the region are higher by 1% (see above).

Table 2.16. *Non-manual wages relative to manual wages, 1970–86   index 1980 = 100*

	Belgium	Denmark	France	Germany	Holland	Italy	United Kingdom
1970	—	—	—	—	—	—	—
1971	—	—	—	—	—	—	—
1972	—	—	1.19	0.96	—	1.27	—
1973	—	—	1.15	0.97	—	1.23	0.95
1974	—	—	1.11	0.97	—	1.17	0.97
1975	1.03	1.10	1.09	0.97	0.99	1.12	0.96
1976	1.01	1.09	1.04	0.98	1.01	1.05	0.95
1977	1.01	1.08	1.02	0.99	0.99	1.01	0.96
1978	1.01	1.03	1.02	0.99	1.00	1.02	0.97
1979	1.01	1.02	1.01	1.00	1.00	1.04	0.98
1980	1.00	1.00	1.00	1.00	1.00	1.00	1.00
1981	0.99	1.00	0.98	1.00	1.01	0.98	1.01
1982	0.98	1.01	0.95	1.00	1.01	0.95	1.00
1983	0.97	1.03	0.93	1.01	1.02	0.95	1.06
1984	0.97	1.04	0.94	1.02	1.00	0.98	—
1985	0.97	1.06	0.94	1.02	0.98	1.01	1.04
1986	0.97	1.08	—	1.02	—	—	1.07

Source: Eurostat Review (1970–1980), (1977–1986).

Manual: Gross hourly earnings, all industries, nominal. Table 3.6.1.
Non-manual: Gross monthly earnings, all industries, nominal. Table 3.6.12.

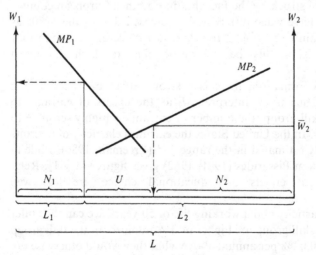

Figure 2.8   Skilled and unskilled labour markets: L_1, L_2 fixed (W_1 flexible, W_2 rigid)

5 Policy implications

So are there any policies which can improve things when there is mismatch? Policies commonly advocated include:

1. shifting the jobs towards the workers (e.g., by cutting employers' taxes in those sectors where unemployment is high), and
2. shifting the workers towards the jobs (e.g., by subsidies to migration or training).

Frequently both are advocated (e.g., by Johnson and Layard, 1986). But is the analysis correct?

5.1 An illustrative case (W_2 totally rigid)

We shall begin with the highly simplified case of two skill groups, with the skilled wage (W_1) perfectly flexible and the unskilled wage (W_2) perfectly rigid. There is then full employment in the skilled labour market, and unemployment in the unskilled one. If unemployed leisure is of zero value (as we shall assume throughout), this outcome is clearly inefficient.

What is the appropriate policy response? We shall begin with the case where the labour forces (L_1 and L_2) are given. This is illustrated in Figure 2.8. In this situation two things are clear

1. An employment subsidy to employers hiring unskilled workers would increase unskilled employment. This would have to be financed. Since it is unrealistic to posit lump-sum taxation, we shall assume that any employment subsidies have to be financed by other employment taxes. In the present case this implies a tax on skilled labour; since wages of skilled labour are perfectly flexible and labour supply inelastic, this tax involves no efficiency costs. Skilled workers remain fully employed, and the increased employment of unskilled workers raised employment and thus output.
2. Equally if we could turn unskilled workers into skilled workers; this would increase (gross) output, for suppose we transfer one individual from group 2 to group 1: employment in the skilled sector will rise, since W_1 is flexible, and (to the first approximation) employment in the unskilled sector will be unaffected, since W_2 is fixed. To find the output effects we shall assume that $Y = F(e_1 L_1, e_2 L_2)$ where e_i is the employment rate. If we have one more skilled worker, output rises by approximately F_1. This is the net social return to training. By contrast, the net expected private return is $(F_1 - e_2 F_2)$ which is much lower. This appears to suggest a case for subsidies to training and migration.

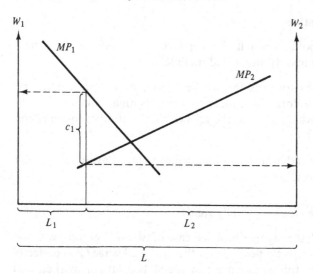

Figure 2.9 Skilled and unskilled labour markets: L_1, L_2 variable (W_1, W_2 flexible)

On the line of reasoning so far, we should then be willing to subsidise employment in group 2 *and* migration into group 1. These are the arguments commonly heard. But they will not really stand up. For subsidies to migration can be evaluated only within a general theory of migration behaviour. Once we do this, we realise that the employment *tax* on skilled workers (proposal 1) will reduce skilled wages and thus discourage migration. The migration subsidy (proposal 2), when amortised, would be equivalent to an employment *subsidy* to skilled workers, partially or wholly offsetting the initial tax. Is there any sense in such a combined operation? The answer is that employment taxes and migration subsidies cannot be thought of as distinct entities. The only question is: what should be the net taxes paid by each group of workers?

Let us pursue this issue in the context of our simple example, and ask: 'suppose there were initially no taxes on either group and W_2 is rigid; is there any subsidy to one group, paid for by a tax on the other, that would increase output?'

Net output is

$$Y = F(e_1 L_1, e_2 L_2) - c_1 L_1$$

where c_1 is the amortised cost of training.

We want to maximise this subject to the constraints, including those coming from migration behaviour. In the steady state this implies the *zero-migration condition*, which for simplicity can be written in the additive form

$$W_1 e_1 = W_2 e_2 + c_1$$

In other words, net expected income in sector 1 $(W_1 e_1 - c_1)$ equals expected income in sector 2, the private and social costs of training (c_1) being for the present assumed to be the same.

If all wages were fully flexible, we should have full employment in both sectors $(e_1 = e_2 = 1)$. This would maximise net output, as illustrated in Figure 2.9.

If, however, W_2 is rigid, output is reduced. The migration condition becomes (with $e_1 = 1$)

$$W_1 = \bar{W}_2 e_2 + c_1$$

The question is: if we start from zero taxes, is there any self-financing scheme of taxes and subsidies which would increase net output?

The answer is 'no', for given that $L_2 = L - L_1$, the change in net welfare when policy changes is

$$(F_1 - e_2 F_2 - c_1) dL_1 + F_1 L_2 de_2$$

But private choice has already set the first term to zero. So policy action can improve welfare only if it can alter the employment rate of the unskilled.

But this it cannot do (even though it *can* change L_1 and L_2); for, if $\bar{W}_2$ is fixed, so is W_1. Hence, by the zero-migration condition, e_2 is fixed.

To see why W_1 cannot change, note that (under perfect competition in product markets)

$$dW_1 = dF_1 - dt_1$$

The real wage frontier implies

$$dF_1 = -\frac{N_2}{N_1} dF_2$$

while the government budget constraint implies

$$-dt_1 = \frac{N_2}{N_1} dt_2 + s$$

But since W_2 is fixed, $dF_2 - dt_2$ is zero and hence $dF_1 - dt_1$ is also zero. There is no scope for improving things; the best taxes and subsidies are no taxes and subsidies. Though unemployment involves an externality, it is not an externality that can be offset by these kinds of taxes and subsidies.

There are two basic qualifications to this. First, if there is an external social cost or benefit, this must be corrected by taxation or subsidy. And second, if individuals differ in their costs, there may well be a case for taxing the costly sector. But to investigate these issues, let us proceed to the more general case where both wages are flexible, and taxes are non-zero, though differentially so.

We begin with the case where the labour forces are exogenous and observe the potent role of policy. Then we proceed to the case where the labour force are endogenous and policy analysis is more complex.

5.2   Labour force given

To find the ideal tax structure, we maximise net outut subject to a revenue requirement and to the wage functions and labour demand functions. The problem is

$$\max_{t_i, W_i, e_i} Y = F(e_1 L_1, e_2 L_2)$$
$$+ \varphi(t_1 e_1 L_1 + t_2 e_2 L_2 - R)$$
$$+ \psi_1(W_1 - f^1(e_1)) + \varphi_2(W_2 - f^2(e_2))$$
$$+ \theta_1(W_1 + t_1 - F_1) + \theta_2(W_2 + t_2 - F_2)$$

where R is a revenue requirement, W_i is take-home pay and t_i is a per-worker tax levied on employers. This requires

$$\frac{\partial Y}{\partial t_i} = \varphi e_i L_i + \theta_i = 0$$

$$\frac{\partial Y}{\partial W_i} = \psi_i + \theta_i = 0$$

which imply $\psi_i = \varphi e_i L_i = -\theta_i$, and in addition

$$\frac{\partial Y}{\partial e_i} = F_i L_i + \varphi t_i L_i + \psi_i \frac{\partial W_i}{\partial e_i} - \theta_i F_{ii} L_i$$

$$= \left(W_i + t_i + \varphi t_i - \varphi e_i \frac{\partial W_i}{\partial e_i} + \varphi e_i L_i F_{ii} \right) = 0$$

Hence the standard Ramsey-like condition that[17]

$$\frac{t_i}{W_i} = \frac{\varphi}{1 + \varphi} \left(\frac{1}{\eta_S} + \frac{1}{\eta_D} \right) - \frac{1}{1 + \varphi} \tag{9}$$

where η_S is the wage elasticity of employment (in the wage function) and η_D is the wage elasticity of employment (in demand).

The tax rate should be higher the more flexible are wages and the less elastic demand. In general, unskilled labour markets are likely to have relatively inflexible wages and relatively elastic demand.

Concentrating on wage flexibility, if the wage function is double-log, then $\partial \log W_i / \partial \log u_i$ will be similar (e.g., $-\alpha$) in all groups and

$$\frac{\partial \log W_i}{\partial \log e_i} = \frac{\partial \log W_i}{\partial \log u_i} \frac{e_i}{u_i} = \alpha \frac{(1 - u_i)}{u_i}$$

Hence wage flexibility will be inversely proportional to unemployment. Taxing flexible markets means taxing those with low unemployment; so long as t_1/W_1 is too low, output could be increased by raising t_1 and lowering t_2, thus stimulating employment where wages are inflexible and reducing it where they are flexible.

This argument has been used to justify subsidies to less skilled labour financed by taxes on skilled labour; it is a standard conclusion in much of the theory of manpower policy.

5.3 Labour force endogenous

But it is valid only if the labour force is exogenous (e.g., by age, race or sex). If the labour force is endogenous, everything changes. We shall show that, if there are no externalities, efficiency requires that the absolute level of the net tax (after netting out any subsidy) should be roughly equal for all groups. More precisely, the 'expected' net tax burden should be equal: that is, groups with lower employment rates should pay proportionally higher taxes.

The problem now is to maximise net output, $F(e_1 L_1, E_2 L_2) - c_1 L_1$, subject to the budget constraint, the two wage functions, the two demand functions, and the *zero-migration condition*. The policy instruments are t_1 and t_2, but to examine the properties of the optimum we again choose the full set of variables (L_1, t_1, t_2, W_2, e_1 and e_2) to maximise net output. Thus

$$\begin{aligned}
\max_{t_i, W_i, e_i, L_i} Y^* = {} & F(e_1 L_1, e_2 L_2) - c_1 L_1 \\
& + \varphi(t_1 e_1 L_1 + t_2 e_2 L_2 - R) \\
& + \psi_1(W_1 - f^1(e_1)) + \psi_2(W_2 - f^2(e_2)) \\
& + \theta_1(W_1 + t_1 - F_1) + \theta_2(W_2 + t_2 - F_2) \\
& + \lambda(W_1 e_1 - W_2 e_2 - c_1)
\end{aligned}$$

where the last (and additional) constraint is the zero-migration constraint, enabling us to determine L_1.

Adding this zero-migration constraint changes everything. The focus of the analysis shifts to the first-order condition for L_1. This

$$\begin{aligned}
\frac{\partial Y^*}{\partial L_1} &= F_1 e_1 \\
&= W_1 e_1 - W_2 e_2 - c_1 + t_1 e_1 - t_2 e_2 + \varphi(t_1 e_1 - t_2 e_2) = 0 \quad (10)
\end{aligned}$$

The zero-migration condition ensures that the first three terms sum to zero, so that optimality requires that

$$t_1 e_1 = t_2 e_2 \tag{11}$$

Expected taxes should be equal in each sector.[18] The Ramsey-type equation (9) is no longer valid since if fails to take into account the migration condition. Thus, even in the presence of wage rigidity and differential unemployment, the classic principles of public finance apply and there is no case for differential taxation unless there are externalities (other than simply unemployment itself).

However, there may well be externalities; the most obvious are the congestion externalities from regional migration. Suppose that net output is not $Y - c_1 L_1$ but $Y - c_1 L_1 - c_s L_1$, where the costs c_1 are privately borne but the remaining social costs c_s are not. Then the optimality condition becomes

$$t_1 e_1 + B(1 - e_1) = t_2 e_2 + B(1 - e_2) + \frac{c_s}{1 + \varphi}$$

The congested sector should pay higher taxes in the standard Pigovian manner in order to equate the private and social returns to migration. This argues for increased taxes in regions which are congested (typically low-unemployment regions) and subsidies to skill-formation, where there is an external benefit that is not privately appropriated.

There is, however, a more subtle form of externality. We have so far allowed only for one type of 'original' labour, which can then be allocated between two sectors. In fact there may be different types of original labour – say, of different ability or taste – for whom there are different costs (c_i) of entry to sector 1. The average cost (c_1) per sector 1 worker is thus an increasing function of L_1. If $C(L_1)$ is the total cost of L_1, the migration condition is thus

$$W_1 e_1 - W_2 e_2 - C' = 0 \qquad (C', C'' > 0)$$

Optimality now requires

$$\frac{\partial Y^*}{\partial L_1} = (W_1 + t_1)e_1 - (W_2 + t_2)e_2 - C'$$
$$+ \varphi(t_1 + e_1 - t_2 + e_2) - \lambda C'' = 0$$

where λ is the multiplier on the supply condition $e_1 + W_1 - e_2 + W_2 - C' = 0$.

Hence

$$t_1 e_1 = t_2 e_2 + \frac{\lambda C''}{1 + \varphi} \tag{12}$$

The extent of the expected tax differential $(t_1 e_1 - t_2 e_2)$ is higher the less responsive migration is to changes in financial incentives. For λ and φ are positive,[20] and C'' is the inverse of the supply response dL_1/dW_1, suitably discounted.

As we have seen, both regional and occupational labour forces respond very slowly to wage differentials which could make the last term in equation (12) quite important (even after multiplication by the discount rate). (Even without standard externality arguments) there is thus certainly some efficiency case for lower absolute tax rates on occupations and regions with low-employment rates. But the standard externality arguments differ sharply between occupations and regions, favouring tax concessions for high-skilled groups and tax penalities for congested regions.

Of course, the whole discussion has as premise the assumption that unemployment of a group affects only the wage of that group. If there is a leading sector whose employment rate pushes up wages elsewhere, that sector generates external disbenefits which make it a candidate for extra taxation. The reader will find it easy to modify our framework to deal with that case.

What we have said in this section is not the last word on tax progressivity, for there are well-known equity arguments in its favour, which we have not considered. There is also the case for progressive taxes to discourage wage pressure (Jackman et al., 1991). In that context we recommend a linear tax structure $(tW - S)$ with quite high t and a high flat rate subsidy S. But the implication of the present study is that, if it is possible to have different subsidies, S_i, for different groups, the optimal tax structure (in the absence of externalities) involves $(tW_i - S_i)e_i$ being equated between groups.

6   Mismatch and the unemployment/vacancy relationship

We have not so far referred to vacancies at all in discussing mismatch. This is because we believe that the main issue is the mismatch between the total labour force of each type (L_i) and the employment (N_i). Hence our index MM.

It is helpful to use the shift of the aggregate u/v curve to isolate changes over time in the effectiveness of the unemployed. One cannot do this without first isolating the effect of mismatch on the location of the u/v curve. Hence we need an index of mismatch between u and v, which we shall call mm.

6.1   Theory

We need to see how differences in the ratio u_i/v_i across different groups affect the location of the aggregate u/v curve. Suppose, first, that each group had the same u/v curve based on the hiring function

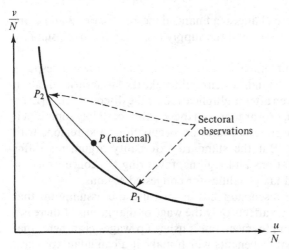

Figure 2.10   The u/v curve of a group

$$H_i = A v_i^\alpha u_i^{1-\alpha}$$

If the entry to unemployment in each sector is $S_i = sN_i$, where s is the entry rate (assumed common to all groups), then in the steady state (with $H_i = sN_i$) the u/v curve is

$$s = A \left(\frac{v_i}{N_i}\right)^\alpha \left(\frac{u_i}{N_i}\right)^{1-\alpha} \tag{13}$$

This is shown in Figure 2.10.

If u/N and v/N were always the same for each group, then the national aggregate u/v curve would be identical to that shown in Figure 2.10. But if group 1 was at P_1 and group 2 at P_2 (and the two groups were of equal size) the aggregate national observation would be at P. This follows from the convexity of the relationship, and implies that inequalities in u_i/v_i always increase u/N at given v/N.

The same is true even if the hiring functions differ, as they do (see below). To see the quantitative effect of variations in the u_i/v_i ratios, we can begin by modifying the hiring function, equation (13), for each group to obtain

$$\frac{S_i}{A_i} = v_i^\alpha u_i^{1-\alpha}$$

where $u_i = u_i/N_i$ and $v_i = v_i/N_i$.

We then multiply and divide the right-hand side by $v^\alpha u^{1-\alpha}$ and take a weighted average of all the equations. This gives

$$\Sigma f_i \frac{s_i}{A_i} = \left[\Sigma f_i \left(\frac{v_i}{v}\right)^\alpha \left(\frac{u_i}{u}\right)^{1-\alpha}\right] v^\alpha u^{1-\alpha}$$

where $f_i = N_i/N$.

The term in brackets is a matching index, which has a maximum value of unity when the u_i/v_i ratio is the same in all groups.[20] At this point the aggregate unemployment rate is as low as it can be, for a given level of vacancies. But, as the u_i/v_i ratios diverge, the aggregate u/v curve shifts out.

If it natural to measure mismatch by the proportion to which unemployment is higher than it could be at given vacancies. u/v mismatch is thus measured by

$$mm = \log u - \log u_{\min} = -\frac{1}{1-\alpha} \log\left[\Sigma f_i \left(\frac{v_i}{v}\right)^\alpha \left(\frac{u_i}{u}\right)^{1-\alpha}\right]$$

This is approximately[21]

$$mm \simeq \tfrac{1}{2}\alpha(\sigma^2_{v_i/v} + \sigma^2_{u_i/u} - 2\rho_{u_i v_i}\sigma_{u_i/u}\sigma_{v_i/v})$$

where σ is the standard deviation and ρ the correlation coefficient (positive or negative).

6.2   Evidence

Let us examine the size of this mismatch index and its movements over time. Table 2.17 shows relative vacancy rates and relative unemployment rates by occupation, region and industry in Britain in 1982. To obtain the mismatch index we need a value of α, which can be taken as approximately $\tfrac{1}{2}$ (Pissarides, 1986; Jackman, Layard and Savouri, 1987; Blanchard and Diamond, 1989).[22] Using this value for α, Table 2.18 shows the movement of the mismatch index over time. The striking thing is the very small magnitude of the mismatch index, and the fact that it has not risen over time. In other words, any shift that has occurred in the aggregate u/v curve has also been a shift in the average u/v curve for each sector.

Jackman and Roper (1987) present similar evidence for France, Germany, the Netherlands, Austria, Finland, Norway and Sweden. Except in Sweden there is no evidence of increased mismatch.

As regards the cyclical behaviour of mismatch, this was illustrated in Figure 2.1 using the index mm'. It shows a tendency for regional mismatch to fall in downturns and for industrial mismatch to rise.

Much has been made of the latter phenomenon by Lilien (1982). He has argued that fluctuations in unemployment are often *caused* by exogenous shifts in labour demand between industries, producing mismatch and hence changes in unemployment. But can we reasonably think of these

Table 2.17. *Unemployment rates and registered vacancy rates by occupation, region and industry: Britain, 1982 (relative to national average)*

	u_i/u	v_i/v
Occupation		
Managerial and professional	0.32	0.49
Clerical and related	0.80	1.05
Other non-manual	0.84	1.93
Skilled manual	0.87	0.84
Other manual	1.87	1.31
Region		
South East	0.73	1.10
South West	0.89	1.30
East Midlands	0.92	0.92
West Midlands	1.24	0.67
Yorkshire and Humberside	1.11	0.74
North West	1.24	0.77
North	1.39	0.85
Wales	1.30	1.22
Scotland	1.17	1.24
Industry		
Agriculture	0.94	0.31
Mining and quarrying	0.88	0.12
Manufacturing	1.03	0.66
Construction	2.13	1.03
Gas, electricity and water	0.33	0.31
Transport	0.68	0.48
Distribution	0.86	1.31
Services	0.53	1.36
Public administration	0.68	1.31

Notes:
Unemployment data relate to previous occupation and industry of unemployed registered at Job Centres.
Vacancy rates relate to vacancies registered at Job Centres.

Sources:
Occupation
Department of Employment *Gazette* (June 1982) Tables 2.11 and 3.4 (Employment figures from Labour Force Survey).

Region
Vacancies: Department of Employment *Gazette* (December 1985) Table 3.3.
Employment: *Regional Trends* (1985) Table 7.1.
Unemployment: Department of Employment *Gazette* (June 1982) Table 2.3 (made consistent with unpublished Department of Employment continuous series).

Industry
Department of Employment *Gazette* (June 1982) Table 3.3 and (July 1982) Table 2.9.

Table 2.18. *u/v mismatch: time series, Britain, 1963–88*

Mismatch index (%)

$$2\left[1 - \sum \frac{N_i}{N}\left(\frac{u_i}{u}\frac{v_i}{v}\right)^{1/2}\right]$$

Year	Regional (9 groups) (1)	Industrial (24 groups) (2)	Occupational (24/18 groups) (3)
1963	16	12	22
1964	20	10	22
1965	16	10	22
1966	12	10	24
1967	10	12	20
1968	14	12	20
1969	14	14	22
1970	10	12	22
1971	12	10	24
1972	14	8	22
1973	14	6	26
1974	12	10	26
1975	6	8	30
1976	4	6	24
1977	4	6	22
1978	8	4	22
1979	10	4	22
1980	8	8	24
1981	4	14	26
1982	4	12	24
1983	2	—	—
1984	4	—	—
1985	4	—	—
1986	4	—	—
1987	4	—	—
1988	5	—	—

Source: Author's calculations based on data published in successive issues of the Department of Employment *Gazette*.

cyclical shifts in mismatch as exogenous? If they were, we should expect the resulting mismatch to increase not only unemployment but vacancies. As Abraham and Katz (1986) show, this is not what happens when we see a short-run rise in the turbulence index. Instead unemployment rises and vacancies fall. Thus the notion that business downturns are typically initiated by structural demand shifts is implausible.

Table 2.19. *Differences between occupations in vacancy flows and stocks: Britain, 1988*

	Unemployment (1984)				Vacancies (1988)			% of firms reporting shortage of labour (January 1988) (7)
	Inflow rate (% per month) (1)	Average duration (months) (2)	Unemployment rate (%) (3)		Engagement rate (% per month) (4)	Duration of vacancies (months) (5)	Vacancy rate (%) (January) (6)	
Managerial and professional	0.50	11.2	5.3	Managerial and professional	1.0	2.2	2.2	
Clerical	0.88	10.1	8.0	Clerical	2.3	1.5	3.4	
Other non-manual	1.14	11.8	12.2	Skilled and semi-skilled manual	2.8	1.2	3.4	Skilled 20
Skilled manual	1.02	14.2	12.6	Retail and catering, personal services	5.8	0.9	5.1	
Semi- and unskilled manual	1.32	14.1	15.5	Unskilled manual	3.8	0.6	2.1	Other 4
All	0.94	12.8	10.8		2.8	1.0	2.9	

Sources:

Unemployment:
See Table 2.5.

Vacancies:
IFF Research Ltd, *Vacancies and Recruitment Study* (May 1988) 12 Argyll Street, London W1V 1AB.
Col. (4) = Engagements ÷ Employed (Table 4.3).
Col. (5) = Col. (6) ÷ Col. (4).
Col. (6) = Vacancies ÷ Employed (Appendix 9).

Labour shortages: CBI Industrial Trends Survey.

However over the longer term the degree of turbulence in industrial structure *is* clearly an important factor affecting unemployment. But for this purpose we need to take a moving average of the index. If we do this, as we have said, we find that industrial turbulence in the 1930s was double its postwar average in both Britain and the United States, and the same was true of Britain in the 1920s. Thus it is quite appropriate to blame a part of interwar unemployment on the 'problems of the declining industries'.

6.3 Further evidence on occupations

Finally, we present some evidence on the duration of occupational vacancies in Britain. This is given in Table 2.19. The first point concerns the vacancy rates. These are based on a national survey which included all vacancies rather than adjusted data based on vacancies registered at Job Centres. It shows no clear tendency for higher vacancy rates in more skilled occupations, but the turnover rate is very much lower in the more skilled occupations; from this it follows that the duration of vacancies is very much longer in the skilled occupations. (The situation was very similar in 1977, the year of the only other national survey of vacancies: Jackman, Layard and Pissarides, 1984, p. 45.)

All of this raises obvious questions about which occupations are facing labour shortages. When employers in manufacturing were asked 'Do you expect your output to be limited by shortages of (a) skilled labour and (b) other labour', only 4% replied Yes for 'other labour' compared with 20% for 'skilled labour'. These replies coincide with the view that, from the employers' side, the proper pressure of demand variable is the *duration* of vacancies, rather than the vacancy rate. We must, however, note that from the point of view of workers the comparable duration (of unemployment) is similar in all groups, and it is the unemployment *rates* which differ. We have not yet found a satisfactory way of interpreting these fascinating data.

7 Conclusions

It may now be helpful to bring together in summary form some of the main arguments of this study.

1. There are huge differences in unemployment rates between occupations, regions, age groups and races. These differences are for the most part very persistent and do not reflect the legacy of structural shocks. They are however quite closely related to differences in

turnover rates (i.e., in the rate of entry to unemployment), with differences in unemployment durations playing a minor role.

2. Unemployment rate differences between age groups are affected by demographic factors. But unemployment differences between occupations and regions can be explained only jointly with mobility between groups. In each case high unemployment is associated with low costs of entry and high levels of wage push. Where (as in Britain but not the United States) regional unemployment differences are highly persistent, these importantly reflect steady-state differences in job growth relative to the natural growth of population.

3. One naturally asks whether the rise in European unemployment can be explained by increased mismatch. To investigate this we assume (and later check) that wage behaviour in a sector is primarily caused by unemployment in that sector, rather than by unemployment in some leading sector. Given this assumption, the relevant index of mismatch is a half the variance of the relative unemployment rates; on this basis mismatch has incresed in no country we studied except Sweden, but the *level* of mismatch still in Britain explains at least one-third of all unemployment.

4. As regards policy, if the members in each group are exogenous (e.g., as in each age group), then it pays to subsidise employment where it is low and to tax employment where it is high. But where workers choose their sectors (as with occupations and regions) the matter is more complex. If there are no standard 'externalities' (other than unemployment), no leading sector in wage determination, and all workers are identical, there is no efficiency case for any tax/subsidy scheme to improve the structure of unemployment rates. Contrary to the standard notions of 'manpower policy', expected taxes should be equal for all groups.

   But tax/subsidy arrangements should be used to discourage bad externalities (e.g., congestion in low unemployment regions), to promote good externalities (e.g., skill training), and to discourage overheating in any leading sectors. In addition where workers vary (upward-sloping supply curves) it may be right to subsidise employment in high unemployment groups.

5. Finally we examine the mismatch between unemployment and vacancies. We show that this mismatch has not worsened either, and cannot be used to explain the outward shift of the u/v curve that has occurred in many countries.

APPENDIX: MISMATCH AND SUBSTITUTION BETWEEN TYPES OF LABOUR

The curvature of the real wage frontier depends on the elasticity of substitution in demand between different types of labour.[23] Using a CES production function of the form

$$Y\rho = \varphi\Sigma\alpha_i N_i\rho \qquad (\Sigma\alpha_i = 1,\ \rho - 1 = -1/\sigma,\ \sigma \geq 0,\ \sigma \neq 1)$$

we obtain a price function[24]

$$P = \Sigma\alpha_i\sigma W_i^{-(\sigma-1)}/A'$$

where A' is again a combined index of technical progress and product market competition.

Setting the price level at unity, the *price function* gives us a feasible real wage frontier

$$A' = \Sigma\alpha_i\sigma W_i^{-(\sigma-1)}$$

If the *wage functions* are

$$W_i = \beta_i u_i^{-\gamma}$$

the *unemployment frontier* is now

$$A' = \Sigma\alpha_i\sigma\beta_i^{-(\sigma-1)}u_i^{\gamma(\sigma-1)}$$

Using empirically relevant magnitudes such as $\gamma \simeq 0.1$ (see below), and $0 < \sigma < 10$, this is a concave function in the u_is.

To find the aggregate unemployment rate, we multiply by $u^{-\gamma(\sigma-1)}/A'$ to obtain

$$u^{-\gamma(\sigma-1)} = \frac{1}{A'}\Sigma\alpha_i\alpha_i^{\sigma-1}\beta_i^{-(\sigma-1)}\left(\frac{u_i}{u}\right)^{\gamma(\sigma-1)}$$

If α_i, β_i, u_i/u and L_i/L are approximately independent,[25] then

$$\log u \simeq \tfrac{1}{2}(1 - \gamma(\sigma - 1))\, \text{var}\,\frac{u_i}{u} + \text{const}$$

Mismatch is now

$$MM = \tfrac{1}{2}(1 - \gamma(\sigma - 1))\, \text{var}\,\frac{u_i}{u}$$

NOTES

1 We are grateful to George Johnson for comments and discussions and for goading us to collect data; we are grateful to J. Hassan, B. Kan, U. Lee, R. Moghadam, M. Sadler and J. Schmitt for helping collect them. We also thank O. Blanchard, P. Diamond, S. Nickell and K. Roberts for helpful discussions and Joanne Putterford for wonderful typing.

2 Note that a temporary shock in favour of a high unemployment group will actually *reduce* the total imbalance.

3 Honourable exceptions are Lipsey (1960), Archibald (1967), Baily and Tobin (1977), Johnson and Blakemore (1979) and hopefully the chapters in this

volume arising out of the CEPR/CLE/STEP conference, Venice (4–6 January 1990).

4 This is not because turbulence creates mismatch which creates aggregate unemployment (Lilien, 1982) – see Abraham and Katz (1986); it is because aggregate shocks are highly sectorally unbalanced – and thus create both aggregate unemployment *and* more turbulence and more mismatch. Such shocks particularly affect high sectors (e.g., construction).

5 Neither bargaining theory nor efficiency wage theory have so far made much progress in explaining the wages of one group out of many groups employed. This is a key area for research. Honourable exceptions to this remark include Lazear (1989) who showed how envy could lead employers to prefer more egalitarian wage structures than otherwise. A related argument is developed in Akerlof and Yellen (1987).

6 X is not of course exogenous but can be solved for by substituting N_i ($= (1 - u_i)L_i$) into the production function.

7 It is best to think of W_i as measuring the wage in terms of its power to purchase market bundles of goods.

8 This arises from differential age structures and differential change in participation rates.

9 The 'natural' population growth in *each* occupation (i.e., the growth in the absence of net migration) is $\hat{L}$.

10 This assumes $\alpha_i \doteq L_i/L$, for the minimisation of u requires

$$\min_{u_i} \Sigma \frac{L_i}{L} u_i - \varphi(\Sigma \alpha_i \log u_i - \text{const})$$

that is,

$$\frac{L_i}{L} - \varphi \frac{\alpha_i}{u_i} = 0$$

If $\alpha_i = L_i/L$, this requires $u_i = \varphi$ (all i).

11 This assumes that the weights α_i (which are shares of the wage bill) are either equal to L_i/L (which are shares of the labour force), or that $(\alpha_i - L_i/L)$ is independent of u_i/u.

12 Note that mismatch is the proportional excess of actual unemployment over the unemployment needed to yield the same inflationary pressure if all unemployment rates were equal. Readers familiar with the Atkinson (1970) index of inequality will note the close correspondence between his measure and our mismatch measure. Atkinson measured inequality as the proportion by which actual output exceeded the output needed to yield the same social welfare is individual incomes were equal.

13 Let

$$\gamma \frac{u_i^{\alpha - 1}}{a} = f(u_i)$$

$$f(u_i) \doteq f(u) + f'(u)(u_i - u) + \tfrac{1}{2} f''(u)(u_i - u)^2$$

So

$$A = \Sigma \alpha_i \beta_i - \Sigma \alpha_i f(u_i)$$
$$= \Sigma \alpha_i \beta_i - \gamma \left[\frac{u^{\alpha - 1}}{\alpha} + 0 + \tfrac{1}{2}(1 - \alpha) u^{\alpha - 2} \Sigma \alpha_i (u_i - u)^2 \right]$$

This gives

$$u = \left(\frac{1 + \alpha(\Sigma \alpha_i \beta_i - A)/\gamma}{1 - \frac{\alpha(1 + \alpha)}{2} \text{var} \frac{u_i}{u}} \right)$$

Since $0 < u < 1$, $\Sigma \alpha_i \beta_i - A < 0$ and u is increasing in var(u_i/u) for all values of α.

14 Of course wages could depend on both one-sector unemployment (u_i) and leading-sector unemployment (u_L):

$$\log u = \frac{\Sigma \alpha_i \beta_i - A}{\gamma + \delta} + \frac{\gamma}{\gamma + \delta} \tfrac{1}{2} \text{var} \left(\frac{u_i}{u} \right) + \frac{\delta}{\gamma + \delta} \log \left(\frac{u}{u_L} \right)$$

15 We also did estimates in which X took the fitted values from regressing output per worker on a quintic in time. The coefficients in the corresponding wage equations were almost identical to those in Table 2.14.

16 No serious bias exists from letting W and u be the log of the averages, rather than the average of the logs.

17

$$\frac{1}{\eta_S} = \frac{e_i}{W_i} \frac{\partial W_i}{\partial e_i} \quad \text{and} \quad \frac{1}{\eta_D} = \frac{e_i L_i}{W_i} \frac{\partial F_i}{\partial (e_i L_i)}$$

Strictly, the latter is $1/\eta_D$ only if t_i is small.

18 There are two further terms which sum to zero. These are

$$- \theta_1(F_{11}e_1 - F_{12}e_2) - \theta_2(F_{21}e_1 - F_{22}e_2)$$
$$= \varphi e_1(e_1 L_1 F_{11} + e_2 L_2 F_{21}) - \varphi e_2(e_1 L_1 F_{12} + e_2 L_2 F_{22})$$
$$= \varphi e_1(0) - \varphi e_2(0) \quad \text{(by Euler's Theorem)}$$

19 In the case of a migration subsidy of s paid to workers who get trained and employed in sector 1, we arrive at exactly the same conclusion. The tax condition is

$$(t_1 - s)e_1 L_1 + t_2 e_2(L - L_1) - R = 0$$

The migration condition is

$$e_1(E_1 + s) - e_2 W_2 - c_1 = 0$$

Hence $\dfrac{\partial Y^*}{\partial L_1} = 0$ implies

$$(t_1 - s)e_1 - t_2 e_2 = 0$$

20 The conclusion would be unaffected if costs were a proportion of $W_2 e_2$. φ is positive, because a reduction in R raises Y. As regards λ, if the zero-migration constraint did not hold and people could be physically allocated to sectors, the optimum allocation would be given by equation (10), with c_1 replaced by C'. We can assume that in this situation $t_1 e_1 - t_2 e_2 > 0$: in other words we should want to have a smallish number of unskilled people and then subsidise their employment to keep them in work. But we cannot do this since by equation (10) this would reduce incentives to migrate below the acceptable level. It follows that if there is a supply equilibrium constraint, an additional incentive to move would raise welfare. Hence $\partial Y^*/\partial$ net return $= \lambda > 0$.

21 We seek to

$$\max_{u_i, v_i} \sum \left(\frac{v_i}{v}\right)^\alpha \left(\frac{u_i}{u}\right)^{1-\alpha} + \lambda(\Sigma v_i - v) + \varphi(\Sigma u_i - u)$$

This requires

$$\alpha \left(\frac{v_i}{u_i}\right)^{\alpha-1} \left(\frac{1}{v}\right)^\alpha \left(\frac{1}{u}\right)^{1-\alpha} + \lambda = 0 \qquad \text{(all } i)$$

If

$$v_i = \theta u_i \quad \text{(all } i), \quad \sum \left(\frac{v_i}{v}\right)^\alpha \left(\frac{u_i}{u}\right)^{1-\alpha} = \sum \left(\frac{\theta u_i}{u}\right)^\alpha \left(\frac{u_i}{u}\right)^{1-\alpha} = \frac{\Sigma u_i}{u} = 1$$

22 Expanding $\left(\frac{v_i}{v}\right)^\alpha \left(\frac{u_i}{u}\right)^{1-\alpha}$ around $\frac{v_i}{v} = \frac{u_i}{u} = 1$,

we have

$$\left(\frac{v_i}{v}\right)^\alpha \left(\frac{u_i}{u}\right)^{1-\alpha} \simeq 1 + \alpha \left(\frac{v_i}{v} - 1\right) + (1 - \alpha) \left(\frac{u_i}{u} - 1\right)$$

$$+ \tfrac{1}{2} \alpha(\alpha - 1) \left(\frac{v_i}{v} - 1\right)^2 + \tfrac{1}{2} (1 - \alpha)(-\alpha) \left(\frac{u_i}{u} - 1\right)^2$$

$$+ (1 - \alpha)\alpha \left(\frac{v_i}{v} - 1\right)\left(\frac{u_i}{u} - 1\right)$$

Hence

$$\sum \frac{N_i}{N} \left(\frac{v_i}{v}\right)^\alpha \left(\frac{u_i}{u}\right)^{1-\alpha} \simeq 1 - \tfrac{1}{2} \alpha(1 - \alpha)[\sigma^2_{v_i/v} + \sigma^2_{u_i/u} - 2\mathrm{cov}_{v_i/v, u_i/u}]$$

Note also that this equals

$$1 - \tfrac{1}{2} \alpha(1 - \alpha) \sum \frac{N_i}{N} \left[\left(\frac{v_i}{v} - 1\right) - \left(\frac{u_i}{u} - 1\right)\right]^2$$

$$= 1 - \tfrac{1}{2} \alpha(1 - \alpha) \sum \frac{N_i}{N} \left(\frac{v_i}{v} - \frac{u_i}{u}\right)^2$$

Thus it is closely related to the index

$$\sum \frac{N_i}{N} \left|\frac{v_i}{v} - \frac{u_i}{u}\right| = \sum \left|\frac{V_i}{V} - \frac{U_i}{U}\right|$$

used in Jackman and Roper (1987).

23 See Jackman *et al.* (1991, Chapter 5). The British studies find α about 0.3, while the US studies find a value nearly twice as high. For reasons given there the true value probably lies in between, and this is confirmed for British data in Jackman *et al.*, Chapter 5, Annex 2 which suggests a coefficient around $0.29/(0.46 + 0.29)$.

24 This reflects the elasticity of substitution in production or the elasticity of substitution in consumption between different products.

25 Under monopolistic competition with demand elasticity η,

$$W_i = \frac{\partial Y}{\partial N_i} (1 - 1/\eta) + A' \alpha_i \left(\frac{N_i}{Y}\right)^{-(1/\sigma)} (1 - 1/\eta)$$

By Euler's Theorem

$$1 = \sum_i \frac{\partial Y}{\partial N_i} \frac{N_i}{Y} = (1 - 1/\eta)^{-1+\sigma} A^\sigma \sum_i W_i \left(\frac{W_i}{\alpha_i}\right)^{-\sigma}$$

26 If $\sum \alpha_i = 1$ and α_i, x_i, y_i and z_i are independent, then $\sum \alpha_i x_i y_i z_i = \bar{x}\,\bar{y}\,\bar{z}$. Hence if α_i, β_i and u_i are independent, equation (5) implies

$$u^{-\gamma(\sigma-1)} = \frac{1}{A'} \sum \alpha_i \alpha_i^{\sigma-1} \sum \alpha_i \beta_i^{-(\sigma-1)} \sum \alpha_i \left(\frac{u_i}{u}\right)^{\gamma(\sigma-1)}$$

or

$$u^{-\gamma(\sigma-1)} = \sum \alpha_i \left(\frac{u_i}{u}\right)^{\gamma(\sigma-1)} \times \text{const}$$

Going on, if we assume $(\alpha_i - L_i/L)$ independent of u_i/u, we obtain

$$u^{-\gamma(\sigma-1)} = \sum \frac{L_i}{L} \left(\frac{u_i}{u}\right)^{\gamma(\sigma-1)} \times \text{const}$$

Since

$$\sum \frac{L_i}{L} \left(\frac{u_i}{u}\right)^{\gamma(\sigma-1)} \simeq 1 + \tfrac{1}{2}(\gamma(\sigma-1) - 1)\gamma(\sigma-1)\,\text{var}\,\frac{u_i}{u},$$

$$- \gamma(\sigma-1)\log u \simeq \tfrac{1}{2}(1 - \gamma(\sigma-1))\gamma(\sigma-1)\,\text{var}\,\frac{u_i}{u} + \text{const}.$$

REFERENCES

Abowd, J. and O. Ashenfelter (1981). 'Anticipated Unemployment, Temporary Layoffs and Compensating Differentials', in S. Rosen (ed.), *Studies in Labor Markets*, Chicago: University of Chicago Press.

Akerlof, G. A. and J. L. Yellen (1987). 'The Fair Wage/Effort Hypothesis and Unemployment', Berkeley: University of California (mimeo).

Abraham, K. and L. Katz (1986). 'Cyclical Unemployment: Sectoral Shifts or Aggregate Disturbances?', *Journal of Political Economy*, **94**, 507–22.

Archibald, G. (1967). 'Regional Multiplier Effects in the UK', *Oxford Economic Papers*, **19(1)**.

(1969). 'The Phillips Curve and the Distribution of Unemployment', *American Economic Review*, **LIX(2)**.

Atkinson, A. (1970). 'On the Measurement of Inequality', *Journal of Economic Theory*, **2**, 244–63.

Baily, M. and J. M. Tobin (1977). 'Macroeconomic Effects of Selective Public Employment and Wage Subsidies', *Brookings Papers on Economic Activity*, **2**, 511–41.

Blanchard, O. and P. Diamond (1989). 'Beveridge and Phillips Curves', Cambridge, MA: MIT (mimeo).

Blanchflower, D. and A. Oswald (1989). 'The Wage Curve', London School of Economics, Centre for Labour Economics, discussion paper, **340**.

Blaug, M., R. Layard and M. Woodhall (1969). *The Causes of Graduate Unemployment in India*, London: Allen Lane.

Freeman, R. (1986). 'Demand for Education', in O. Ashenfelter and R. Layard (eds), *The Handbook of Labor Economics*, vol. 1, Amsterdam: North-Holland, 357–86.

Freeman, R. and D. Bloom (1986). 'The Youth Labour Market Problem: Age or Generational Crowding', OECD *Employment Outlook* (September), 106–28.

Greenwood, M. (1985). 'Human Migration: Theory, Models and Empirical Studies', *Journal of Regional Sciences*, **25**, 521–44.

Grubb, D. (1986). 'Topics in the OECD Phillips Curve', *The Economic Journal*, **96**, 55–79.

Hall, R. (1970). 'Why is the Unemployment Rate so High at Full Employment?', *Brookings Papers on Economic Activity*, **3**, 369–402.

Hamermesh, D. (1986). 'The Demand for Labor in the Long Run', in O. Ashenfelter and R. Layard (eds), *The Handbook of Labor Economics*, vol. 1, Amsterdam: North-Holland, 429–71.

Harris, J. and M. Todaro (1970). 'Migration, Unemployment and Development: A Two-Sector Analysis', *American Economic Review*, **60**, 126–42.

Jackman, R., R. Layard and C. Pissarides (1984). 'On Vacancies', London School for Economics, Centre for Labour Economics, discussion paper, **165** (revised).

Jackman, R. and S. Roper (1987). 'Structural Unemployment', *Oxford Bulletin of Economics and Statistics*, **49(1)**, 9–37.

Jackman, R., R. Layard and S. Savouri (1987). 'Labour Market Mismatch and the "Equilibrium" Level of Unemployment', London School of Economics, Centre for Labour Economics, working paper, **1009**.

Jackman, R., R. Layard, S. Nickell and S. Wadhwani (1991). *Unemployment*, Oxford: Oxford University Press.

Johnson, G. and A. Blakemore (1979). 'The Potential Impact of Employment Policy for Reducing the Unemployment Rate Consistent with Non-Accelerating Inflation', *American Economic Review*, **69** (Papers and Proceedings), 119–30.

Johnson, G. and R. Layard (1986). 'The Natural Rate of Unemployment: Explanation and Policy', O. Ashenfelter and R. Layard (eds), *The Handbook of Labor Economics*, vol. 2, Amsterdam: North-Holland, 921–99.

Layard, R. (1982). 'Youth Unemployment in Britain and the United States Compared', in R. B. Freeman and D. A. Wise (eds), *The Youth Labor Market Problem: Its Nature, Causes and Consequences*, Chicago: University of Chicago Press.

Layard, R. and S. Nickell (1986). 'Unemployment in Britain', *Economica*, **53** (Supplement), S121–S169.

(1987). 'The Performance of the British Labour Market', in R. Dornbusch and R. Layard (eds), *The Performance of the British Economy*, Oxford: Oxford University Press.

Lazear, E. (1989). 'Pay Equality and Industrial Policies', *Journal of Political Economy*, **97(3)**, 561–80.

Lilien, D. (1982). 'Sectoral Shifts and Cyclical Unemployment', *Journal of Political Economy*, **90**, 777–93.

Lipsey, R. (1960). 'The Relation Between Unemployment and the Rate of Change of Money Wage Rates in the United Kingdom, 1862–1957: A Further Analysis', *Economica*, **27(1)**, 1–31.

Nickell, S. (1981). 'Biases in Dynamic Models with Fixed Effects', *Econometrica*, **49(6)**, 1417–26.

Nickel, S. and S. Wadhwani (1989). 'Insider Forces and Wage Determination', London School of Economics, Centre for Labour Economics, discussion paper, **334**.

Oswald, A. (1986). 'Wage Determination and Recession: A Report on Recent Work', London School of Economics, Centre for Labour Economics, discussion paper, **243**.

Pissarides, C. (1981). 'Staying-on at School in England and Wales', *Economica* **48(192)**, 345–64.

(1982). 'From School to University: The Demand for Post-Compulsory Education in Britain', *the Economic Journal*, **92(367)**, 654–67.

(1986). 'Unemployment and Vacancies in Britain', *Economic Policy*, **3**, 489–560.

Pissarides, C. and J. Wadsworth (1989). 'Unemployment and the Inter-Regional Mobility of Labour', *Economic Journal*, **99**, 739–55.

Savouri, S. (1989). 'Regional Data', London School of Economics, Centre for Labour Economics, working paper, **1135**.

Discussion

SHERWIN ROSEN

Relatively high growth rates have made it difficult to explain the recent high European unemployment rates within the usual business cycle framework. Mismatch is an interesting alternative hypothesis. This study sets forth an inclusive definition of mismatch unemployment, estimates its importance from historical data, and examines its public policy implications. The authors conclude that mismatch may account for a large share of total unemployment, but not for the recent increase in the unemployment rate.

Most economists probably would define 'mismatch' as a state in which jobs and workers are located in different places; such conditions rise from unanticipated shifts in the composition of demand or in technology due to such things as trade liberalisation, deregulation and privatisation. Permanent changes set up a disequilibrium which cause labour and other resources to move higher-valued uses. Historical evidence suggests that these adjustments occur over lengthy periods of time: not only are there large marginal costs of adjustment, but substantial fixed costs imply that mobility decisions are conditioned on permanent rather than on temporary changes. It may take a long time for people to understand that the changes are indeed permanent; nonetheless, mobility works to move the economy towards an equilibrium allocation of resources.

Jackman, Layard and Savouri (hereafter JLS) take a rather different approach. They define mismatch, without reference to equilibrium or disequilibrium, as the variance in relative unemployment rates among occupational, education, industry and regional categories. However, the fact is that unemployment rates systematically differ among these categories on a more or less permanent basis. Skilled workers always have smaller unemployment rates than unskilled workers, independent of the state of the market. Employment and output variability are always greater in construction and in durable goods manufactures than in services and non-durables manufacturing, and urban–rural and North–South regional differences can persist for generations. Many of these differences arise in a stationary equilibrium and are fully factored into the decisions of workers and firms. After all, part of the known return to acquiring more skill is a lower incidence of unemployment as well as a higher wage; and part of the risk of working in the construction trades is known to be a higher incidence of unemployment. Should these permanent, fully anticipated, differences among categories be counted as mismatch? If structural changes alter the efficient skill, industry or occupational mix, the implied changes in weights might well be counted as mismatch. Yet this could go in either direction, in principle – from skilled to unskilled (say) as well as the other way around. In that case 'solving' the mismatch problem might require a permanent increase in (structural) unemployment!

With only one exception JLS show that there is a declining trend in the variance of relative unemployment in most EC countries: mismatch by this measure has fallen even though unemployment levels have increased. A reader is left wondering what other factors are left to explain the increasing aggregate unemployment rates. What has become of the dislocations caused by economic integration, privatisation and the rest? Have these gone so smoothly as not to show up in unemployment and vacancy statistics? Is the variance of relative unemployment rates sufficiently sensitive to measure these things?

The theory underlying the JLS measure is based on a stable relationship between the real wage rate and the unemployment rate. This relationship replaced the Phillips curve in an earlier generation of models, and follows recent theorising on efficiency wages, insider–outsider theory and yet other theories of real wage rigidity. I am not convinced that the weight of empirical evidence supports this change in emphasis and structure. To be sure, simple Phillips curves did not survive the inflationary environment of the 1960s, because they did not make the proper distinctions between anticipated and unanticipated changes in prices. Yet viewed in terms of unanticipated changes, the Phillips curve has hardly disappeared. In fact, there is more *direct* evidence for it than for the efficiency wage as a principle cause of unemployment.

One can take the idea of efficiency wages seriously, as I do, and at the same time remain agnostic or even sceptical about its importance for aggregate unemployment. As a theoretical matter, current models simply restrict many other contractual mechanisms that would ameliorate the unemployment effects. And empirical support for the JLS measure rests on indirect evidence: mainly that there are unaccounted industry wage differentials in cross-section data that is notoriously weak in measures of productivity, specific human capital investment and industry working conditions. But even granting the point for the sake of argument, what factors caused efficiency wages to increase in the 1980s in Europe? Why are they ever so small in Japan and apparently decreasing in the United States during this period? And if increased trade union militancy is the answer in Europe, how did the unions allow so much trade liberalisation and economic integration in the EC? What about the decline of US unions and the worldwide trend toward market economies? I cannot fault JLS for not answering these questions, but at the same time they naturally weigh heavily in my assessment of the subjective likelihood of their theory.

The subtle change from rates of change of wages in the Phillips curve to rigid real wage *levels* in efficiency wage and related models naturally alters the focus from more transient disequilibrium notions of unemployment to the more permanent concept used here. As JLS so clearly show, combining the real wage–unemployment relationship with labour demand functions and the factor price frontier yields an unemployment frontier, from which their mismatch index follows. Convexity of the unemployment frontier implies that greater variance of unemployment across sectors results in a larger average unemployment rate, by Schwartz's inequality. Two specific comments arise in this connection:

First, the calculation attributing one-third of total unemployment to mismatch uses an inappropriate decomposition of the variance of unemployment across occupations, industries, ages, races and sex. These classifications are not orthogonal. Instead, they overlap each other, so variances are double counted when they are just added together as JLS do. This means that one-third is a generous upper bound estimate of their mismatch-induced unemployment.

Second, their theory requires a causal chain running from high real wages to high unemployment, yet there is precedent for thinking that the reverse causation is also important. The prospective risk of unemployment can cause a positive association with wages from the theory of equalising differences. Seasonal employment among fisherman and service workers in tourist trades are familiar examples, but the point obviously generalises. It would be helpful if JLS had sketched how their interpretation of the structural wage–unemployment locus was identified in their empirical work.

The policy analysis in this study is elegant and useful in stressing how behavioural supply relationships and individual incentives interact with policy instruments. These issues are very important, yet I think they survive a much broader set of alternative views of mismatch. Specifically, the JLS theory requires an enormous amount of allocation information embodied in the wage at any moment of time, compared with an older paradigm of matching and mismatching. In the alternative, matching involves specific capital through costly search or through direct investment. Rents implied by the employment relationship are firm-specific (as well as embodying occupation, industry and regional specificity) and cause matches to endure for long periods of time. The observed wage divides and allocates these rents between worker and employer. However, at any moment in time this division is somewhat arbitrary because it must be distributed over the expected life of the match. In this sense, the wage is partly an instalment payment on the worker's share of the investment and introduces a wedge between current wages and current market conditions that the JLS theory requires. In fact, the causes of unemployment rate differences by skill, occupation and education are probably best explained in this alternative fashion. Taking account of these alternative views seems to argue for a less inclusive and more disequilibrium-oriented definition of mismatch, and a broadening of its measure to include such things as personal income as well as unemployment.

3 Match and Mismatch on the German Labour Market[1]

WOLFGANG FRANZ

1 Introduction

In the past fifteen years unemployment in the Federal Republic of
Germany (FRG), as well as in other countries, has experienced a tre-
mendous increase, in many cases to a postwar high. At present it
seems to be stuck at the levels reached in the mid-1980s. The focus
of explanation for the causes of this rise of unemployment, and its
persistence, has shifted towards structural factors. More specifically,
it is claimed that among other determinants of structural unemployment, growing labour market imperfections and maladjustments such
as a regional or qualitative mismatch between labour demand and
supply and/or a reduced search intensity, partly supported by generous unemployment benefits, are important factors which can be
blamed.

This study aims to take stock of the empirical evidence for and
against these arguments. The prerequisite for an informed discussion
of these issues is a theoretical framework which offers a clear-cut and
empirically tractable definition of structural unemployment. The study
uses two theoretical tools, namely the unemployment/vacancy
relationship (u/v curve), often christened the 'Beveridge curve', and a
macroeconometric disequilibrium model, in order to provide a basis
for the empirical investigation. The study is organised as follows. In
section 2 the Beveridge curve and in section 3 the rationing model are
employed to check whether there are structural imbalances on the
German labour market, and whether they have increased; as it turns
out, there is some reason to accept both premises. Hence, in section 4
the study goes on to try to identify the causes of these growing
maladjustments. In section 5 the importance of some possible causes
is tested, using the two tools discussed. Section 6 presents some concluding remarks.

105

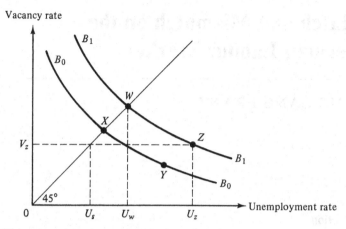

Figure 3.1   Stylised Beveridge curve

2 u/v Analysis

In this section the u/v curve – i.e., the relationship between unemployment and vacancies – is used as an analytical instrument to identify the extent, and the causes, of a possible increase in structural unemployment.

2.1   Theoretical Considerations

As it is well known, the basic idea of the u/v curve is that for any given structure of the labour market, vacancies and unemployed persons may be related in a manner indicated by the stylized curve B_0B_0 presented in Figure 3.1. Locations on the 45° ray represent situations in which the number of unemployed equals the number of vacancies; this means that unemployment is due to labour maladjustment since, in principle, there is a job for each person unemployed. All positions on the Beveridge curve at which the number of unemployed exceeds the number of vacancies (i.e., all positions to the right of the 45° ray) indicate that there is demand deficiency or that inflexible wages are too high, whereas in the opposite case employers are rationed in the sense that the number of unemployed is not great enough to fill the existing vacancies. A movement on the Beveridge curve from, say, X to Y thus means that the increase in unemployment is mainly due to classical and/or Keynesian determinants. A worsening of the functioning of the labour market causes an outward shift of the Beveridge curve to, say, B_1B_1. A movement from X to W indicates, therefore, that the higher unemployment associated with this shift is the result of greater labour maladjustment rather than demand deficiency or classical factors. As has been mentioned already, locations on the ray from the origin represent situations in which the number of unemployed equals the number of vacancies; in the present context, this amount of unemployment (such as $\overline{OU}_w$ for $B_1 B_1$) is one approximate measure of structural/frictional unemployment. This is due to the notion that the labour market is not able to match the unemployed to the existing unfilled job openings. It should be pointed out that combinations on the 45° ray are not necessarily optimal. This is due to the following consideration: if policymakers are free to choose any point on the Beveridge curve, the optimal vacancy/unemployment relation is where the marginal costs associated with another unemployed person (such as the output losses) equal those associated with another unfilled job (such as the costs of waiting in a longer queue or some inflationary pressure).[2]

While the u/v relation presented so far seems intuitively plausible, it is necessary to base it on a sound theoretical foundation in order to exploit its implications for the functioning of the labour market. Such a theory is developed in more detail in another paper[3] and is sketched here very briefly. The theory consists of three elements:

1. *The search process seen from the viewpoint of the firm with a vacancy*: Leaving aside standard aspects of an optimal level of production and employment, the firm faces the following problem. It is uncertain about the abilities of each applicant (which determine the worker's efficiency) but it knows the density function of these abilities prevailing on a suitably defined labour market. Moreover, there is a minimum hiring standard to be met by the applicant due to specific requirements or legal restrictions for the job under consideration. The firm is allowed to train workers, but it has to incur training costs; in screening workers, the firm sets its minimum hiring standard endogenously, then evaluates expected training costs, and finally makes a wage offer. From this viewpoint, two aspects are important for the matching process: first, the minimum hiring standard which may or may not be met by the job seeker and, second, the wage offer made by the firm which may or may not be accepted by the applicant.

2. *The search process seen from the viewpoint of the job seeker*: The applicant's decision is based on a conventional job search model. The job seeker maximises expected wealth by accepting a wage offer which is not lower than the reservation wage. The individual contacts several employers submitting wage offers. The distribution of wage offers is the source of uncertainty: although its parameters are known to the searcher, each offer is a realisation of a random variable. Determinants of the reservation wage are the search costs, the

unemployment benefits, the density function of wage offers, and the discount rate.

3. *The matching technology governing the labour market*: The probability that a vacancy will be filled can be decomposed into two probabilities – that an unemployed person contacts an employer with a vacancy, and that a match is formed conditional on a contract between both searchers (*contact* and *contract* probability, respectively). Factors influencing the contact probability are the number of unemployed persons and vacancies and the availability of information about both groups; the probability that a match is formed depends on the probability that the applicant meets the minimum hiring standard and that the reservation wage does not exceed the wage offered by the firm.

The Beveridge curve can then be derived by making use of the identity that the change in the number of unemployed persons equals the difference between (exogenous)[4] inflows into and outflows from unemployment. The foregoing analysis concerns the outflows from unemployment to employment, which is the number of vacancies times the probability that a vacancy is filled with an unemployed applicant. These relationships constitute the Beveridge curve and various sources for possible shifts of the u/v curve can be identified:

1. The Beveridge curve shifts unambiguously outwards if the probability that a contact is made decreases; this may be due to a lower search intensity of the job seeker induced by higher unemployment benefits.[5]
2. On the other hand, persons with a long duration of unemployment many run out of unemployment benefits and, therefore, intensify their search (the *contact* probability increases) and lower their reservation wage (the *contract* probability increases). From this one would conclude that a higher share of long-term unemployed causes an inward shift of the u/v curve. Long-term unemployment may, however, discourage people from searching any longer. Moreover, if firms use unemployment as a screening device in order to identify the unknown productivity of the applicant, then a higher share of long-term unemployed lowers the *contract* probability – i.e., we face an outward shift of the Beveridge curve. The total effect of the variable: share of long-term unemployed on the u/v curve is therefore ambiguous.[6]
3. The *contact* probability decreases when the regional dispersion between unemployed persons and vacancies increases because the concomitantly larger information gap causes a malfunctioning of the matching process. On the other hand, the effect of such higher

imbalances on the *contract* probability may be ambiguous. Consider the following example with two regions ('south' and 'north' for short) where south is a nice region with high standards of living and north is just the opposite. If the unemployed are located in the north and vacancies are now also opened in the south rather than only in the north this may *ceteris paribus* facilitate matching because the 'attractiveness' can be viewed as a higher wage offer. Of course, the opposite may hold for the unemployed who are in the south.[7] Moreover, a greater regional dispersion may imply higher (non-pecuniary) costs of changing location for the unemployed person which lowers his or her willingness to accept a wage offer from a firm in a distant location.

4. An existing vacancy may not be filled even if an applicant shows up. First, the job seeker may not meet the minimum hiring standard due to several imperfections; he or she may not have the professional qualifications required for the job in question, his or her work experience may be too short or have been evaluated badly by former employer(s). This is called a 'qualifications mismatch', in the sense that a vacancy is not filled by an (unemployed) applicant because his or her qualifications are inadequate compared to the requirements for the work-place under consideration. Leaving aside a qualifications mismatch, higher qualifications (acquired, for example, by some training programmes organised by the labour office do not necessarily mean a higher *contract* probability: on the other hand, they increase the probability that the applicant will meet the requirements set by the firm but, on the other, they raise the applicant's reservation wage.

2.2 *Empirical analysis*

The empirical investigation starts with a data analysis concerning the u/v relationship. Official figures of vacancies include only those vacancies reported to the labour office. In the absence of other reliable data we attempt to adjust these data by dividing them by the fraction of new hires managed by the labour office; a correct measure of this ratio is also not available. We therefore approximate it with the ratio of cumulated inflows of vacancies during one year to the sum of new hires during the same year. The time series of this variable varies procyclically, with a decreasing trend since 1969. The shortcomings of this approximation are obvious. Among other problems it assumes an equal duration of all vacancies regardless of whether they are registered at the labour office or not. Figures 3.2 and 3.3 display, for 1962–88, the u/v curve using official and corrected vacancy data, respectively.[8] A rough inspection of Figures

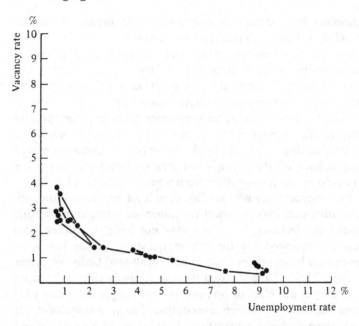

Figure 3.2   Beveridge curve: official data for vacancies

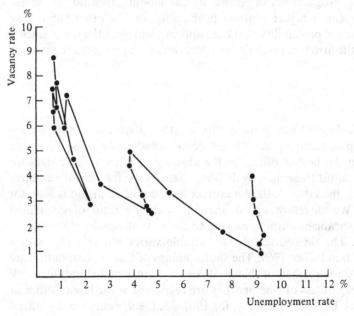

Figure 3.3   Beveridge curve: corrected data for vacancies

3.2 and 3.3 reveals that a possible shift of the Beveridge curve is more obvious for corrected vacancy data. It has been shown elsewhere, however, that the u/v curve based on official data also exhibits shifts.[9]

When estimating the u/v curve we used both OLS and instrumental variables estimation because unemployment and vacancies are determined jointly so that vacancies as the explanatory variable may not be truly exogenous. The results, however, differ only negligibly; we therefore chose to use OLS estimates. Moreover, we experimented with different linear and non-linear relationships. Most explanatory power (in terms of the square of the correlation coefficient and the sum of squared residuals) was obtained by using a log-linear form:

$$ln\, u_t = \alpha_0 + \alpha_1\, ln\, v_t + \varepsilon_t \tag{1}$$

where u_t = official unemployment rate
    v_t = corrected vacancy rate
    ε_t = residual.

Table 3.1 displays the results of this data analysis. Possible shifts of the Beveridge curve are taken into account by intercept and slope dummies: $D74$ ($D82$) is unity since 1974 (1982) but zero before these years. We also introduced either the lagged endogenous variable or the first difference of $ln\, v$ in order to allow for partial adjustment and cyclical variations (not reported in Table 3.1). While $\Delta ln\, v$ turned out to be insignificant, $ln\, u_{t-1}$ did not always lack significance. In any case, however, the dummies retained their significance and approximate values displayed in Table 3.1.

Although the dummies are in accordance with the hypothesis of an outward shift of the Beveridge curve, these results should be viewed with some care. For example, since 1982 the sum of the coefficients associated with $ln\, v$ is not significantly different from zero. An inspection of Figure 3.3 suggests that this zero slope may reflect the outward-shifting Beveridge curve in those years. Alternative explanations, however, cannot be ruled out for certain – such as that either a Beveridge curve simply does not exist any longer, or that we are moving on an anti-clockwise loop not adequately modelled (despite several efforts, as mentioned above).

Summing up, several data deficiencies and methodological problems cloud the issue; there is weak evidence for outward shifts of the Beveridge curve. The next relevant question is: what has caused these shifts?

3   Lessons from a rationing model

In this section we make use of the evidence for or against higher structural unemployment provided by a macroeconometric rationing model. Since a

Table 3.1. *Estimates of the Beveridge curve, 1967–88[a]*

Explanatory variables	Dependent variable $\ln u_t$			u_t
	(1)	(2)	(3)	(4)
constant	2.89	2.14	1.58	0.26
	(11.0)	(21.5)	(8.1)	(0.8)
$\ln v_t$	−1.32	−1.12	−1.04	
	(6.8)	(18.0)	(17.7)	
$1/v_t$				2.08
				(2.4)
$\ln SLU$			0.18	
			(3.1)	
SLU				0.06
				(2.6)
$D74$				2.45
				(7.0)
$D82$				3.00
				(5.0)
$D74*\ln v_t$		0.55	0.52	
		(9.0)	(10.1)	
$D82*\ln v_t$		0.62	0.47	
		(7.2)	(5.5)	
$\bar{R}^2$	0.68	0.97	0.97	0.97
DW	0.33	2.37	2.25	2.17
SER	0.50	0.16	0.13	0.57
SSR	5.00	0.44	0.28	5.44

Note:
[a] See text for explanation; *t*-values in brackets; *SLU* denotes the share of long-term unemployed; *SER* is the standard error of regression and *SSR* the sum of squared residuals.

more detailed description of the model and its results is presented elsewhere,[10] we very briefly outline the central idea of this approach.

3.1   Basic structure of the model

When wages and prices are not adjusting fast enough to clear markets at any instant of time, some form of rationing is observed. On each micro market for goods transacted quantities can be constrained by demand YD, productive capacity YC, or by available labour YS. Rationing on each of N micro markets can therefore be described by:

$$Y_i = \min(YD_i, YC_i, YS_i), \qquad i = 1, \ldots, N \qquad (2)$$

In the absence of labour hoarding transacted labour (L) is the minimum of labour (LD) needed to produce YD, of labour that can be employed by existing capital (LC) and of labour supply (LS):

$$L_i = \min(LD_i, LC_i, LS_i), \qquad i = 1, \ldots, N \qquad (3)$$

These min-conditions hold for micro markets. If the statistical distribution of demand and supply on the micro markets follows a joint log-normal distribution, aggregate transaction can be approximated by a CES-type function of the aggregate concepts of demand and supply denoted by:

$$L = [LD^{-\rho} + LS^{-\rho} + LC^{-\rho}]^{-1/\rho} \qquad (4)$$

with $L \leq \min(LD, LC, LS)$ where the inequality sign holds for all finite values of ρ.

The parameter ρ reflects the mismatch between demand and supply components on micro markets. For $\rho \to \infty$, the equation tends to the usual min-condition – i.e., the aggregate economy is subject to only one of the constraints.

   The variables YC and LC are explained on the basis of a technology which can be characterised by *ex ante* substitution possibilities but *ex post* limitationality. More specifically, we assume an *ex ante* CES production function with constant returns to scale (K denotes the capital stock and γ stands for technical progress).

$$YC = \gamma \quad [\delta(e^{\gamma l(t)} \cdot LC)^{(\sigma-1)/\sigma} + (1-\delta)(e^{\gamma k(t)} \cdot K)^{(\sigma-1)/\sigma}]^{\sigma/(\sigma-1)} \qquad (5)$$

When prices (P) are set as a constant mark-up on average production costs (such as wages W and user cost of capital Q) in the long run, firms can maximise profits by minimising their input costs, which gives the following first-order conditions:

$$A^* := (yc - lc)^* = \mathrm{const} + \sigma(w - p) + (1 - \sigma)\gamma_l(t) \qquad (6)$$

$$B^* := (yc - k)^* = \mathrm{const} + \sigma(q - p) + (1 - \sigma)\gamma_k(t) \qquad (7)$$

Lower-case letters denote logs of the variables. Optimal factor productivities are determined by the respective factor–product–price ratios and an efficiency term reflecting technical progress. Ex post productive capacity is determined by fixed factor productivities and the stock of capital:

$$yc = B^* + k \qquad (8)$$

$$lc = yc - A^* \qquad (9)$$

A disadvantage of the specifications (2)–(4) may be seen in the inability to distinguish between a capacity mismatch – i.e., the inadequacy of installed capital to match the composition of the demand for goods – and a mismatch between labour supplied and demanded due to differences in qualification profiles, regional immobility and other labour market inflexibilities. Since these different types of mismatch require different types of corrective policies, it is more appropriate to assume a two-stage process of firms' employment decisions.[11] For the goods market we assume:

$$Y_i = \min(YG_i, YS_i), \qquad \text{with} \quad YG_i = \min(YD_i, YC_i) \qquad (10)$$

and, correspondingly, for the labour market

$$L_i = \min(LG_i, LS_i), \qquad \text{with} \quad LG_i = \min(LD_i, LC_i). \qquad (11)$$

This means that the individual firm in a first step determines its labour demand in accordance with the restrictions of the goods markets and compares in a second step its labour demand with available labour supply. If the minimum of log-normally distributed variables is itself approximately distributed log-normally, smoothing by aggregation results in a nested employment function:

$$L = [(LD^{-\rho_1} + LC^{-\rho_1})^{\rho_2/\rho_1} + LS^{-\rho_2}]^{-1/\rho_2} \qquad (12)$$

The parameter ρ_2 describes a labour market mismatch, whereas ρ_1 captures a capacity mismatch. Turning to the treatment of aggregate demand YD, private consumption, investment, exports and imports are endogenous variables, whereas government expenditures and housing investment are treated exogenously. Consumption depends on disposable income, the interest rate, and on a labour market indicator; the investment equation is based on the accelerator principle. Rationing is introduced in the following way. Excess demand for domestic goods will lead to additional imports to bypass the constraint while, on the other hand, excess demand on the world market will restrain German imports. The opposite may hold for exports: domestic constraints will hinder foreign demand, while supply constraints on the foreign market may induce additional German exports. Rationing of the demand components other than exports and imports will be observed only in the case of simultaneous constraints on the domestic and the world markets. No significance of those effects was found; therefore they may be regarded as rather small. Demands for exports (XD) and imports (MD) are calculated for a situation with no rationing on the domestic market. This gives the following identities for goods demand:

$$YD = C + I + G + XD - MD + \text{housing investment} \tag{13}$$

and for labour demand:

$$ld = yd - A^* \tag{14}$$

There are two central features of this model. First, the model distinguishes proportions of firms being constrained by the demand for goods π_K, by existing capacities π_C or by available labour π_S, where

$$\pi_K = [(LC^{-\rho_1} + LD^{-\rho_1})^{(\rho_2 - \rho_1)/\rho_1} \cdot LD^{-\rho_1}]/L^{-\rho_2} \tag{15}$$

$$\pi_C = [(LC^{-\rho_1} + LD^{-\rho_1})^{(\rho_2 - \rho_1)/\rho_1} \cdot LC^{-\rho_1}]/L^{-\rho_2} \tag{16}$$

$$\pi_S = (LS/L)^{-\rho_2} \tag{17}$$

Second, and more important for our considerations is the calculation of a so-called 'structural rate of unemployment at equilibrium' ($SURE$) – i.e., a situation of labour market equilibrium for which $LG = LS$:[12]

$$SURE = 1 - 2^{-1/\rho_2} \tag{18}$$

In an analogous way a 'structural rate of unused capacity at equilibrium' ($SUCE$) can be evaluated:[13]

$$SUCE = 1 - 2^{-1/\rho_1} \tag{19}$$

$SUCE$ is calculated for an hypothetical situation of equilibrium (i.e., $LG = LS$) and absence of a mismatch on the labour market (i.e., $\rho_2 \to \infty$). Hence, $SUCE$ characterises excess capacities exclusively due to rigidities and frictions on the goods market. In the presence of a labour market mismatch, however, one can calculate an analogous expression for $SUCE$ ($SUCEL$) which also takes into account inflexibilities on the labour market.[14]

It is defined as:

$$SUCEL = 1 - 2^{-[(1/\rho_2) + (1/\rho_1)]} \tag{20}$$

The difference between $SUCEL$ and $SUCE$ therefore indicates to what extent excess capacities, if any, are due to labour market imperfections.

3.2 Empirical results

Referring to equations (15)–(17), Figure 3.4 displays the shares of firms being constrained by goods demand (π_K), existing capacities (π_C) or available labour (π_S). While the periods 1960–6 and 1969–74 are characterised by the preponderance of capacity and labour supply constraints, rationing from the demand side becomes dominant in recession periods

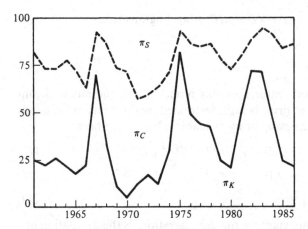

Figure 3.4   Share of firms being in different regimes, 1961–86
Source: König and Entorf (1990) 122.

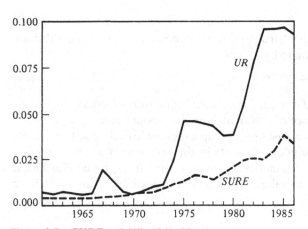

Figure 3.5   *SURE* and *UR*, 1961–85
Source: König and Entorf (1990) 133.

with peaks in 1967, 1975, and 1982–3. In the course of a restrictive monetary and fiscal policy at the beginning of the 1980s an investment squeeze took place, and hence to a growing extent existing capacities gained importance as a limiting factor. Turning to structural unemployment, Figures 3.5 and 3.6 reveal the time pattern of *SURE*, *SUCE* and *SUCEL*, together with the unemployment rate (*UR*) and the degree of capacity utilisation (*UC*). We observe an increasing value of *SURE*, indicating a greater importance of structural unemployment. This is confirmed by an inspection of the difference between *SUCEL* and *SUCE*.

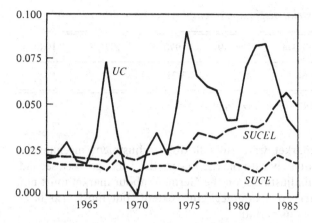

Figure 3.6   *SURE, SUCEL* and *UC*, 1961–85
Source: König and Entorf (1990) 132.

While *SUCE* remains, by and large, constant during the time period under consideration, this does not hold for *SUCEL*. The growing difference between both rates highlights possible spillovers from labour market imperfections to the underutilisation of capacities.

Like the Beveridge curve and its possible shifts, the concept of the *SURE* and its estimation is anything but unambiguous or immune to attack. On the other hand, while the estimated values are subject to some imprecision the general outcome of an increase of the *SURE* holds regardless of which specification is used. Structural unemployment may therefore in fact have gained importance. If so, what are the reasons?

4   An examination of possible causes

Section 4 aims to provide an empirical assessment of various explanations for the increased maladjustments highlighted in sections 2–3. As has been emphasised already, economic theory offers a variety of reasons, but an empirical treatment is limited by the availability of adequate data.

The hypothesis that structural unemployment rose in the late 1970s and early 1980s rests on two distinctive, but not mutually exclusive, empirical assertions:[15]

1.   There has taken place a more rapid structural change in these years than was previously the case. Put differently, a permanent increase in the pace of structural change has tended to raise the flows of people both into and out of unemployment, and to enlarge the pool of those being unemployed between jobs.

Table 3.2. *Interindustrial dispersion of employment growth, 1960–83*

Time period	1960–4	1965–9	1970–4	1975–9	1980–3
ED	2.64	3.21	3.21	2.29	1.85

Sources: Flanagan (1987) 81; Franz (1989) 333.

2. If the labour market were fully flexible, adjustment mechanisms would cope adequately with the rise in structural change. As a second proposition, maladjustment on the German labour market must not only have existed to a non-negligible extent, but must also have worsened during this period.

It is well documented that premise 1 does not hold. Aggregate indexes of structural change do not support the hypothesis of a speed-up in the pace of structural change. For example, Table 3.2 in a summary fashion displays an index which captures industrial variations in employment growth. The index (*ED*) is developed by Lilien (1982) and is defined as

$$ED = \left[\sum_i (\Delta ln\, E_{it} - \Delta ln\, E_t)^2 \cdot (E_{it}/E_t) \right]^{1/2} \tag{21}$$

where E denotes employees and i refers to 8 industries of the manufacturing sector.

The declining trend of *ED* since 1975 is at variance with the proposition of a speed-up in structural change. Therefore we turn to assertion 2, namely the failure of labour supply to adjust to new patterns of labour demand.

4.1   Labour mobility

Labour heterogeneity may be due to regional dispersions in the sense that jobs are located in other regions than those in which the unemployed are found. These imbalances are, however, of minor importance if the unemployed are prepared to move. Therefore, we have to check two aspects:

1. Have regional dispersions between the unemployed and the vacancies increased during the past 15 years?
2. Has regional mobility of the unemployed decreased during the same time period?

Table 3.3. *Mismatch indicators, 1976–88*

Year	Regional dispersion	Professional dispersion	Share of unskilled unemployed	Share of unskilled employed	Share of vacancies	(3)–(5)
	(1)	(2)	(3)	(4)	(5)	(6)
1976	0.359	0.730	52.3	34.4	47.3	5.0
1977	0.381	0.701	53.2	32.9	45.5	7.7
1978	0.443	0.707	54.4	30.7	44.0	10.4
1979	0.457	0.705	53.3	29.3	46.1	7.2
1980	0.438	0.721	54.0	28.2	41.3	12.7
1981	0.455	0.713	54.8	28.7	34.3	20.5
1982	0.456	0.703	51.8	29.3	29.8	22.0
1983	0.422	0.610	50.8	28.6	30.4	20.4
1984	0.476	0.592	49.4	27.6	30.5	18.9
1985	0.492	0.628	49.7	26.5	29.0	20.7
1986	0.462	0.625	50.8	25.7	36.5	14.3
1987	0.461	0.591	50.5	24.7	27.7	22.8
1988	0.444	0.573	50.8	—	27.4	23.4

Note: See text for definitions and sources.

To begin with, regional dispersion is measured by:[16]

$$M = \sum_i |u_i - v_i| \qquad (22)$$

where u_i denotes the proportion of the unemployed who were located in region i and v_i refers to the proportion of vacancies in region i.

If $u_i = v_i$ for all i, M equals zero and therefore indicates that the coexistence of unemployed persons and vacancies is *not* associated with a *regional* dispersion between them but is due to a qualifications mismatch (for example). Due to a lack of data this series can be calculated only since 1976 for all 141 regional labour market districts ('Arbeitsamtsbezirke').[17]

Column (1) of Table 3.3 displays an increase of this measure of 37% between 1976 and 1985, with the major shift between 1976 and 1979 (27%). Despite some variation of this measure in the 1980s, no clear-cut positive or negative trend can be identified. Therefore – in contrast to the 1970s – regional mismatch does not seem to be able to contribute much to the outward shift of the Beveridge curve or the *SURE* in that decade.[18] To some extent this regional mismatch may have been supported by an insufficient interregional wage flexibility; based on his calculations on the regional pattern of wages Paqué (1990) shows that it is quite uniform and stable over time. He therefore claims that this wage structure does not

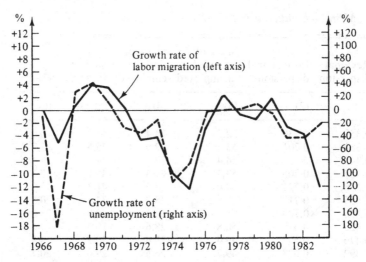

Figure 3.7   Migration and unemployment, 1966–83
Source: Birg (1985); calculations by the author.

adequately reflect the changes of regional labour market situations such as the emerging north–south divide in West Germany. This may be true, but doubts remain whether more regional wage flexibility simply cures regional unemployment by migration, thus creating unwarranted desert regions.

Turning to regional mobility, Figure 3.7 displays two time series, namely the growth rate of labour migration within the FRG and the growth rate of unemployment.[19] As can be seen, there is a sharp decline of migration between 1973 and 1976, and from 1980 on. A visual inspection of both series suggests that the growth rate of unemployment is highly correlated with the growth rate of migration, and is the leading variable.[20] More specifically, to a major extent variations of labour migration seem to be a cyclical phenomenon.[21]

On the other hand there is a negative trend since 1970. Considering entries into states of the FRG, Karr *et al.* (1987) have shown that an index of these entries of members of the labour force declined from 1970 = 100 to 1984 = 44. At the beginning of the 1970s this rapid slow-down may have been due to an immigration stop for non-EC guestworkers enacted in 1973.[22] But even if we restrict the analysis to the period between 1975 and 1984 a more than 20 percentage points decrease of the index is observed (1975 = 67).

While several empirical studies conclude that regional mobility of unemployed persons is higher compared with employees,[23] it is unknown whether the time pattern of the regional mobility of the unemployed looks similar to the one outlined above. In follow-up studies of the unemployed undertaken in 1975 and 1983, respectively, there was a slight increase of the proportion of long-term unemployed who answered that they would (perhaps) be prepared to move to a different area (1975: 28%; 1983: 32%).[24] This is, of course, only very scattered evidence which does not allow firm general conclusions. It points, however, to the possibility that regional labour mobility of the (long-term) unemployed may not possess as sharp and negative a trend as is the case for employees.

What, if anything, can be learnt from these observations? There is evidence for an increased regional mismatch, especially in the late 1970s. Regional labour mobility did decline, although it is less obvious whether this holds for the unemployed, too. In summary, labour mobility may be able to account for the rise in structural unemployment, but the extent of this contribution does not seem to be overwhelming.

4.2 Qualifications mismatch

As a first attempt to measure a qualifications mismatch a corresponding measure to equation (22) is calculated where the regional classification is replaced by 327 professions. As column (2) of Table 3.3 indicates, this series, by and large, remains constant between 1976 and 1982 and drops sharply afterwards. This stands in marked contrast to the increasingly popular argument that the unemployed, to a growing extent, do not meet the requirements concerning qualifications.

One reason for this discrepancy may be that 'professions' do not suffi-ciently proxy 'qualifications': the unemployed person may be a toolmaker – a profession many firms are looking for – but he may not be acquainted with computer-aided machines – a requirement becoming increasingly widespread – to quote only one popular example.

In the absence of sufficient time series about the qualifications of unemployed persons and vacancies, we try to capture at least a possible mismatch between skilled and unskilled unemployed and vacancies, respectively. More specifically, we first calculate the share of unskilled unemployed among all unemployed and, second, the corresponding series for employed people and vacancies, respectively, where unskilled employ-ment may mirror the respective situation concerning job opportunities. As can be seen from columns (3) and (4) of Table 3.3, the share of unskilled unemployed remains roughly constant at about 50% during 1976–87, whereas the share of unskilled employees declines from one-third to one-quarter.[25] The corresponding development of unskilled vacancies is even more rapid. Crude as they are, all skill indicators point

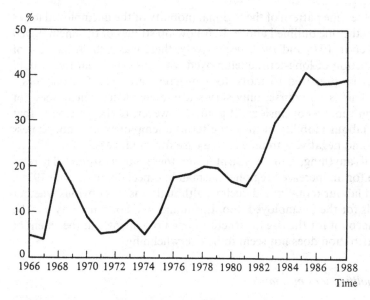

Figure 3.8   Share of long-term unemployment, 1966–88
Note: See text for definition and sources.

to an emerging wedge between supply of and demand for unskilled labour
(such as column (6) in Table 3.3). As has been shown elsewhere, this
possible qualifications mismatch is probably not due to a *more* com-
pressed wage structure.[26] The wage structure – measured by various
coefficients of variation – has remained fairly constant. It is another
question – which cannot be answered here – whether a *more* flexible wage
structure would have mitigated the problem.

As has been outlined in the theoretical section 'long-term unemployment' may also refer to some qualifications mismatch if firms use
unemployment experience as a screening device. It has been stressed,
however, that long-term unemployment may also facilitate the matching
process if the long-term unemployed reduce their reservation wage.
Figure 3.8 displays the share of the unemployed with an unemployment
duration of one year and more among all the unemployed.[27] This share
shows a rapid rise until 1985 and remains roughly constant at the high
level of about 35%. Between 1975 and 1983 this share triples while the
unemployment rate doubles.

What are the reasons for this development? In the process of job
matching over time a cohort of unemployed will develop which consists
mainly of unemployed people with less favourable qualifications.[28] The
longer and the more severe the unemployment period, the more often are

these people rejected by firms. If the exit probability from unemployment decreases with the duration of unemployment, then a vicious circle of long-term unemployment is easily established.

We very briefly check these premises in turn:

1. In order to gain insight into the dynamic structure of how previous unemployment rates (UR) determine the present share of long-term unemployment (SLU) the following simple regression is estimated using the Almon technique for distributed lag estimation:

$$SLU_t = a_0 + \sum_{i=0}^{s} \lambda_i UR_{t-i} + \epsilon_t \qquad (23)$$

As a result more than 90% of the variance of SLU can be explained by this crude specification. The pattern of the weights follows an inverted U with the maximum in $t-4$ and $t-5$ ($\lambda_4 = \lambda_5 = 0.87$; $\Sigma \lambda = 3.3$).[29] SLU is thus positively influenced by the history and severeness of unemployment. It should be needless to emphasise that equation (23) simply exhibits the dynamic structure of how long-term unemployment is created rather than attempting to 'explain' unemployment.

2. It is also well documented that exit probabilities decline with unemployment duration. Controlling for heterogeneity it can be shown that the shape of the hazard function for unemployed youths is log-normal and that state dependence rather than occurrence dependence is the problem.[30] Wurzel (1988) finds evidence for a Weibull distribution for the hazard function, thus indicating that escaping from unemployment becomes more unlikely the longer the duration of unemployment. Note that this conclusion holds, too, when the age of the unemployed is taken into account. This point will be considered again below.

3. In an empirical study based on Austrian individual data Ebmer (1989) investigates the recruitment behaviour of firms. Using a bivariate logit model for the employer's and the job seeker's decision he finds evidence (for Austria) that recruitment possibilities are largely reduced by long-term unemployment and recurrent unemployment spells as well as by various 'unfavourable' characteristics such as age, physical disability, and the like. There is thus reason to suspect that firms in fact use unemployment as a screening device.

Summing up, it should be stressed that in the absence of adequate data it is difficult to find evidence for or against a qualifiactions mismatch; there seems to be a qualifications mismatch in the sense that persons with a long duration of unemployment are viewed as less qualified candidates due to a

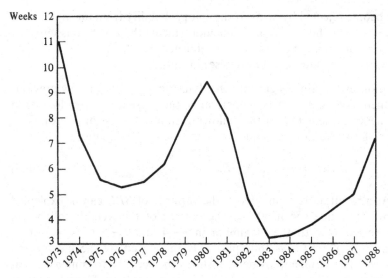

Figure 3.9   Duration of vacancies, weeks, 1973–88
Source: Ermann (1988).

high depreciation of (specific) human capital. Moreover, in contrast to the
constant share of unskilled unemployed the corresponding share of
unskilled employed has been declining, and the unskilled unemployed
thus face greater difficulties in leaving the unemployed register.

4.3   Employer 'choosiness'

Another argument for explaining the speed-up in structural unemployment widely voiced in the media is that employers have become more
'choosy' in selecting workers and/or unemployed persons for available
jobs. In the theoretical section this proposition was discussed within the
context of the qualifications requirements determined by the firm and the
reservation wage of the unemployed. With respect to employer 'choosiness' it is especially claimed that the extension of legislative protection
against dismissal has lead to a more intensive screening of job applicants.

If increased employer choosiness was the reason for the observed
outward shift of the Beveridge curve, the duration of vacancies (cyclically
adjusted) should have risen. Figure 3.9 shows the time series of the
average duration of vacancies (DV) 1973–87. The following regression is a
crude attempt to disentangle cyclical and trend movements of this series:

$$DV_t = 4.88 - 1.43 \cdot UR_t + 0.499 \cdot TIME$$
$$(2.4) \quad (4.8) \qquad (2.8) \qquad\qquad\qquad (24)$$
$$\bar{R}^2 = 0.091; \quad DW = 2.20; \quad \rho = 0.420$$
$$(1.6)$$

where ρ denotes the first-order autocorrelation coefficient and UR is instrumented by lagged values of UR and vacancy rates.

In contrast to other countries such as the United Kingdom the average duration of vacancies increases over time. Without putting too much emphasis on this result, the significant positive time trend does not conflict with the 'employer choosiness' explanation.

Moreover, the high and increasing duration of unemployment of older workers is often viewed as another piece of evidence. In order to get some more insight, Table 3.4 compares some characteristics of stocks and flows of unemployment. Although incomplete vocational training, by and large, does not differ tremendously between stocks and flows (except flows in employment) this observation is at variance with the importance of age and physical disability. While some 5% of all inflows into the unemployment pool are more than 54 years old, this number quadruples for the stock of long-term unemployed and is slightly more than one-half for flows into employment.[31] Moreover, unemployed persons with health deficiencies are overrepresented in the stock of unemployed compared with the flows. With respect to age, these figures confirm the well known result that for the elderly the risk of becoming unemployed is much lower compared with that for young people. The reverse holds, however, for the

Table 3.4. *Structure of unemployment, 1987*

Group of unemployed (1)	More than 54 years old (2)	With health deficiencies (3)	Without complete vocational training (4)
All unemployed	13.5	20.0	50.5
Long-term unemployed	21.8	22.2	46.4
Inflows	5.2	11.9	44.1
Outflows	5.0	11.1	41.9
Outflows into employment	2.9	9.2	38.2

Sources: H.-U. Bach and F. Egle, Die öffentliche Arbeitsvermittlung, Mannheim: 8, 1989, 34 (mimeo); *Sachverständigenrat zur Begutachtung der gesamtwirtschaftlichen Entwicklung, Jahresgutachten 1988–89*, Tables 10 and 11; calculations by the author.

duration of unemployment.[32] It is argued that this phenomenon is due to institutional regulations which make it difficult, if not impossible, to lay off older workers; the same laws which protect the elderly prevent firms from hiring them. Recent experience in the FRG with fixed-term contracts casts some doubts on this argument, however; in an empirical study it has been shown that only a very limited number of new hires were initiated by those non-standard forms of employment and, more importantly, virtually no (older) unemployed persons benefited from those fixed-term contracts.[33] A better explanation of the high share of elderly people among all long-term unemployed may therefore be that firms view them as incapable of coping with new technical developments and/or that the fixed costs of training are seen to be too high to justify hiring such persons. Indeed, König and Entorf (1990) argue that labour has increasingly become a fixed factor, and they claim that the rise of the $SURE$, to be discussed in section 5 below, can to a considerable extent be explained by this fixity.

Summing up, while there might be increased employer choosiness it seems that it is less due to effects of dismissal protection and more due to fixed costs of labour due to training and absence from work[34] which leads firms to intensify search and screening efforts. Parenthetically we note that some of the persons with unfavourable characteristics are (or have been) employed due only to social reasons: firms may be reluctant to fire those employees (such as alcoholics), bowing to social norms saying that it is an improper and/or unsocial thing to do so or because other employees largely do the work of these people in order to protect them. In the case of bankruptcy or more serious dismissals these persons find themselves in the unemployment pool, of course, with virtually no chance to escape from unemployment.

4.4   Search

As has been outlined in the theoretical section, reduced search intensity supported by generous unemployment benefits is another candidate frequently put forward in public discussion concerning the causes of unemployment. In order to be capable of explaining the outward shift of the Beveridge curve and the increase of the $SURE$, search intensity must have decreased during the past fifteen years. If so, we have to check whether the eligibility and/or the replacement ratio of unemployment benefits have changed and facilitated a longer search process.

To begin with unemployment benefits, several pieces of evidence are offered which give rise to the presumption that unemployment benefits are probably not a good candidate to explain search behaviour:

1.   The share of unemployed receiving unemployment benefits ('Arbeitslosengeld') declined substantially from 65.8% to 42.2% between

Table 3.5. *Duration of unemployment by sex and receipt of unemployment benefits, months, 1980 and 1988*

		1980	1988
Incomplete duration			
Recipients:	Males	5.3	8.0
	Females	5.4	8.0
Non-recipients:	Males	12.0	10.5
	Females	12.3	14.4
Complete duration[a]			
Recipients:		5.5[b]	4.9
Non-recipients:		8.9[b]	9.1

Notes:
a Taken from unemployed learning the unemployment register.
b 1982.

Sources: Amtliche Nachrichten der Bundesanstalt für Arbeit (1989) 347; (1981) 176 (incomplete duration); (1988) 1563; (1983) 1397 (complete duration); calculation by the author: for the last duration interval ('2 years and more') 36 months have been assumed.

1975 and 1988. The respective figures for unemployment assistance ('Arbeitslosenhilfe') – which is lower and the entitlement to which is restricted – are 10.3% and 23.6%.[35] Even if both types of unemployment compensation are taken together, a decrease of the share of 10 percentage points is observed.

2. Though not very conclusive, the most commonly calculated aggregate replacement ratio – i.e., unemployment benefits per unemployed recipients divided by net income per employee – decreased from 54% to 48% between 1975 and 1988.[36] These figures are in accordance with figures obtained by others such as Bruche and Reissert (1985) or Burtless (1987) which exhibit stability through the early 1980s and a slight decline thereafter. It is also hard to see why much of the spurt in unemployment in 1975 and 1981 can be accounted for by a system of unemployment insurance which remained virtually unchanged for two decades.

3. Data on unemployment duration which distinguish between persons who receive unemployment benefits and those who do not, do not support the assertion that the duration is longer for the first group. Table 3.5 gives rise to the suspicion that just the opposite is the case.

4. The econometric evidence of the effect of unemployment benefits on the duration of unemployment is mixed. Using panel data Wurzel

(1988) finds no indication that receipts of unemployment benefits exert a negative influence on the re-employment probability. Hujer and Schneider (1989), in a study based also on panel data, conclude that the entitlement to unemployment benefits does not affect exit probabilities. Franz (1982a) evaluates in an econometric analysis based on individual data that the reservation wage of unemployed persons increases only marginally if the person is entitled to unemployment benefits. Finally, Franz and König (1986) calculate complete spell durations using a Markov approach to estimate the transition probabilities. For males until 1981 the complete spell length is slightly higher for those entitled to benefits. Since 1982, however, there is a duration reversal, so that the duration of unemployment is lower for those males entitled to benefits; this reversal has been valid for females throughout the period since 1974. The same authors conclude from an aggregate time series study that there might be a positive effect of benefits and entitlement on unemployment, but the regression results are anything but robust with respect to differing variable definitions, time period under consideration, and the like (König and Franz, 1978).

Summing up, given this mixture of results it is extremely difficult to draw firm conclusions. At best, unemployment benefits exert a small positive effect on unemployment duration. Unemployment benefits do not therefore seem to be the most promising candidate for explaining more than a negligible part of the development of structural unemployment.

In the absence of time series data about search behaviour of unemployed persons, it is impossible to check whether search intensity has fallen during the past fifteen years. There is, however, empirical evidence which indicates that the long-term unemployed may reduce search or even give up looking for a job due to discouragement.[37] The increasing share of long-term unemployed may therefore be negatively correlated with search intensity.

5   The *SURE* and the Beveridge curve reconsidered

In section 4 several causes of a possible increase of mismatch were investigated empirically. The results are, however, partly inconclusive and somewhat speculative. The obvious question is whether more insight can be gained by an econometric analysis of the Beveridge curve and of the *SURE* discussed in section 3. More specifically, to what extent can the aforementioned candidates for a mismatch account for the outward shift of the Beveridge curve and/or the increase of the *SURE*?

Unfortunately, such an econometric examination must be narrowed down to a very scattered treatment. Reliable data for most of the mismatch variables in question are available only through the mid-1970s. Even a modest estimation thus winds up with some 10 degrees of freedom which is insufficient by all conventional standards. Only a few econometric studies can therefore be discussed which are not (so greatly) plagued by this problem.

To begin with the development of the *SURE*, König and Entorf (1990, 14) obtain the following regression result for the parameters ρ_1 and ρ_2 (see equation (12)):

$$\rho_1 = 51.3 - 4.89 \cdot MM$$
$$ (6.3)\ \ (2.5)$$
$$\rho_2 = 538.3 - 840.7 \cdot NWC - 50.4 \cdot RR$$
$$ (3.2)\ \ \ \ \ (3.4)\ \ \ \ \ \ \ \ \ \ (2.5)$$

$$\bar{R}^2 = 0.997; \qquad DW = 1.64; \qquad \text{Sample period: 1961–86}$$

where *MM* stands for a mismatch indicator of the goods market, *NWC* is the share of non-wage labour costs among all labour costs and *RR* denotes the replacement ratio of unemployment benefit.

The latter two variables and their influence on the labour market mismatch indicator ρ_2 deserve some comment.

NWC is, in the (1990) study by König and Entorf, designed to approximate the higher degree of fixity of labour due to legislative employment protection (see section 4.3 above) and higher investments in firm-specific human capital undertaken by the firm, to mention only two examples. While the *NWC* variable exhibits a strong positive trend, the *RR* variable is, by construction, subject to cyclical variations.[38] The explanatory power of *NWC* depends, of course, on the suitability of this variable as a proxy for fixity of labour, which is difficult to infer. But if so, the significant positive impact of *NWC* on the rise of the *SURE*[39] supports our suspicion of a shift in hiring patterns in the sense that employers appear to have become choosier. Turning to unemployment benefits, a simulation experiment[40] which fixes *RR* on its average value $\overline{RR} = 35.8\%$ leaves the *SURE* virtually unchanged until 1978. From 1979 to 1983 the simulated *SURE* is slightly lower than the *SURE* estimated with actual values of *RR*. Afterwards, however, since $RR < \overline{RR}$, the simulated *SURE* exceeds its actual value by a considerable magnitude. In other words, while the development of *RR* does not contribute greatly to an explanation of the rise of *SURE* in periods other than after 1983: the *SURE* of that time period would have been much higher had there not been a declining *RR*.

Turning to the outward shift of the Beveridge curve, several attempts have been undertaken to replace the dummies reported in Table 3.1 by economic variables. These efforts are plagued by the scarcity of sufficient time series. In the absence of other reliable data, we experimented with the replacement ratio, various regional mismatch indicators, and the share of long-term unemployed among all unemployed. As a result, both the replacement ratio and the regional mismatch indicator yielded insignificant and incorrectly signed parameters.

On the other hand, as can be seen from columns (3) and (4) of Table 3.1, the share of long-term unemployment is highly significant and indicates that the effect of a possible deterioration of human capital and the screening hypothesis outweigh the impact stemming from a reduced reservation wage. Of course, this variable does not explain everything as the dummy variables are still significant.

6   Concluding remarks

A popular view widely voiced in the media and in the economists' profession says that the most convincing explanation of the spurt in unemployment, and/or its persistence, is that labour market imperfections have increased. Germany is seen as a good example for what is termed 'Eurosclerosis'. It is argued that a myriad of regulations, protections, and generous benefits prevent labour market forces from working. More specifically, various kinds of inflexibilities such as reduced labour mobility, a higher qualifications mismatch between labour supplied and demanded, and the increased choosiness of employers and job seekers are viewed as factors which share most of the responsibility for the greater maladjustment.

Based on a theoretical foundation this study tries to marshall the empirical evidence for or against the mismatch hypotheses. The outcome of this analysis is fairly mixed, the adverse shifts of both the Beveridge curve and of the structural rate of unemployment at macroeconomic equilibrium suggest higher labour market imperfections. The reasons are, however, less clear. Due to a fragility of the empirical foundations of some explanations it is extremely difficult to identify the sources and the nature of a possible mismatch, let alone to make a quantitive assessment of the extent to which these factors can account for the outward shift of the Beveridge curve. Given this unsatisfactory empirical basis it is impossible to end up with firm conclusions. It seems safe to say that the probable increased malfunctioning of the labour market does not stem from an accelerated pace of structural change; while there exists a mismatch between jobs and the unemployed in terms of regions and skills –

and, moreover, some choosiness on both sides of the labour market may be present – it is less obvious whether the importance of these explanations has increased. At best, one can guess that some higher imbalances in terms of qualifications and a greater choosiness on the part of employers may have interfered with the smooth balancing of labour demanded and supplied. In order to keep pace with technical progress firms need willing and qualified workers who will stay with the job because employers invest in their training. Screening is costly, and even when done is imperfect; firms are therefore reluctant to hire apparently less qualified workers such as the long-term unemployed, whose share among all unemployed has increased considerably. If this is so, structural unemployment feeds on itself – i.e., the Beveridge curve is plagued by the hysteresis phenomenon. This view discounts the notion that, although increasingly present, rigidities did not hit the German labour market in prosperous times (until, say, the early 1970s) but served as a a ratchet or threshold for labour market clearing afterwards. The hysteresis explanation purports to show that the events after prosperity in fact caused these problems, rather than simply revealing their existence; while this does not seem to be a totally unconvincing diagnosis, it still remains to be proven.

NOTES

1 I am grateful for able research assistance and helpful comments to W. Scheremet, G. Heidbrink, K. Siebeck, W. Smolny, H. Entorf, U. Cramer and F. Padoa Schioppa.
2 See Abraham (1983), Hamermesh and Rees (1988), and Jackman, Layard and Pissarides (1989).
3 See Franz and Siebeck (1990).
4 See Akerlof, Rose, and Yellen (1988) for an analysis of separations.
5 These results are also obtained by Jackman, Layard and Pissarides (1989) and Jackman and Roper (1985).
6 See also Budd, Levine and Smith (1987) for this argument.
7 Note that this example does not refer to a concept of equilibrium unemployment due to, say, a situation of differential amenities, as in G. Brunello's study (Chapter 4 in this volume).
8 One might wish to correct data on unemployed persons, too, because official data contain only those unemployed who register as such at the labour office; they therefore do not include discouraged workers, for example. It is not clear, however, to what extent those people are really looking for a job as required by the theoretical underpinning of the Beveridge curve; we therefore stay with the official unemployment data in this study. See Franz (1987a) for an analysis with corrected unemployment data.
9 See Franz (1987a) for details.
10 For more details the reader is referred to Entorf, Franz, König and Smolny (1990), on which the following discussion draws.

11 See Gagey, Lambert and Ottenwaelter (1988), Lambert (1988), Franz and König (1990) and Entorf, König and Pohlmeier (1989).
12 As with points X and W in Figure 3.1, the $SURE$ is not an optimal unemployment rate. See Sneessens and Drèze (1986) for a general description of this concept (which differs, however, from that employed by König and Entorf, 1989).
13 König and Entorf (1990) 122.
14 König and Entorf (1990) 122.
15 See the paper by Flanagan (1987) and its discussion by J. P. Martin.
16 See also Jackman, Layard and Pissarides (1989), Jackman and Roper (1986) and Franz and König (1986).
17 These calculations are based on official unemployment and vacancy data. *Source*: Franz and König (1986), calculations by the author based on data from *Amtliche Nachrichten der Bundesanstalt für Arbeit*, various issues.
18 A similar time pattern of M is obtained when u_i and v_i enter the dispersion measure with weights such as the share of employment and the like.
19 'Labour migration' refers to the migration of members of the labour force between the 11 states of the FRG. Unfortunately, data after 1983 are not comparable with previous data due to an important change of definitions. Moreover, a time series of migration of unemployed persons is not available.
20 See Franz (1989) for a more detailed analysis including causality tests.
21 Karr *et al.* (1987) estimate that a 1% decline of the utilisation of labour leads to a 3–4% decrease of regional labour mobility.
22 See Franz (1981) for a theoretical and econometric analysis of in- and outflows of foreign workers.
23 See the studies quoted in Karr *et al.* (1987).
24 Brinkmann (1987) 295.
25 'Unskilled' is defined as the absence of a complete vocational education (including technical college or university degree). Calculations are based on data in Tessaring (1988) and *Amtliche Nachrichten der Bundesanstalt für Arbeit, Arbeitstatistik 1988 – Jahreszahlen 1988*. The data for unskilled vacancies are taken from so called 'structural analyses' also contained in the *Amtliche Nachrichten der Bundesanstalt für Arbeit*, various issues.
26 See Franz (1989) pp. 309–15.
27 *Sources*: Institut für Arbeitsmarkt- und Berufsforschung; *Amtliche Nachrichten der Bundesanstalt für Arbeit*; calculations by the author. These data differ slightly from those officially published because we have corrected for the structural break in 1981.
28 See also Budd, Levine and Smith (1987).
29 See Franz (1987b) pp. 113–14 for more details. The regression covers the time period 1961–86 and is based on annual data.
30 See Franz (1982b).
31 In 1987 nearly 9% of total labour force was in the age group 55–65.
32 See Evans, Franz and Martin (1984) for an international comparison.
33 See Büchtemann and Höland (1989) for more details.
34 Due to maternity leave or educational leave, for example.
35 *Source*: *Amtliche Nachrichten der Bundesanstalt für Arbeit – Jahreszahlen 1988*, 34–5, 238–9, 242–3; calculations by the author.
36 *Sources*: Institut der deutschen Wirtschaft, Zahlen zur wirtschaftlichen Entwicklung in der Bundesrepublik Deutschland, 1989 (Table 30); *Amtliche Nach-*

richten der Bundesanstalt für Arbeit – Jahreszahlen 1975 and 1988. Unemployment benefits per worker are calculated as the ratio: expenditures of the Federal Labour Office for 'Arbeitslosengeld' (except contributions to health insurance and to old age pensions) divided by the number of recipients to net monthly income per employee.

37 See Noll (1985) 294.

38 The reason is that new entrants in the unemployment pool are to a larger extent entitled to unemployment compensation.

39 Recall that the $SURE$ increases with ρ_2 falling.

40 I am grateful to Horst Entorf for carrying out this simulation for me.

REFERENCES

Abraham, K. G. (1983). 'Structural/Frictional vs. Deficit Demand Unemployment: Some New Evidence', *American Economic Review*, **73**, 708–24.

Akerlof, G., A. Rose and J. Yellen (1988). 'Job Switching and Job Satisfaction in the U.S. Labor Market', *Brookings Papers on Economic Activity*, **2**, 495–594.

Birg, H. (1985). 'Der Bevölkerungstrend von den nördlichen nach den südlichen Bundesländern und der Bevölkerungsverlust von Berlin (W) an das Bundesgebiet', *Jahrbuch für Regionalforschung*, **6**, 5–27.

Brinkmann, C. (1987). 'Unemployment in the Federal Republic of Germany: Recent Empirical Evidence', in P. J. Pedersen and R. Lund (eds.), *Unemployment: Theory, Policy and Structure*, Berlin, de Gruyter, 285–304.

Bruche, G. and B. Reissert (1985). *Die Finanzierung der Arbeitsmarktpolitik: System, Effektivität, Reformansätze*, Frankfurt/M. and New York: Campus.

Büchtemann, C. F. and A. Höland (1989). *Befristete Arbeitsverträge nach dem Beschäftigungsförderungsgesetz 1985. Ergebnisse einer empirischen Untersuchung i.A. des Bundesministers für Arbeit und Sozialordnung*, Bonn: Bundesminister für Arbeit und Sozialordnung.

Budd, A., P. Levine and P. Smith (1987). 'Long-Term Unemployment and the Shifting U–V Curve: A Multi-Country study', *European Economic Review*, **31**, 296–305.

(1988). 'Unemployment, Vacancies and the Long-Term Unemployed. *The Economic Journal*, **98**, 1071–91.

Burtless, G. (1987). 'Jobless Pay and High European Unemployment', in R. Z. Lawrence and C. L. Schultze (eds), *Barriers to European Growth. A Transatlantic View*, Washington, DC: Brookings, 105–62.

Cramer, U. (1988). 'Gewinne und Verluste von Arbeitsplätzen in Betrieben – der "Job-Turnover" – Ansatz, Mitteilungen aus der Arbeitsmarkt- und Berufsforschung*, **21**, 361–77.

Ebmer, R. (1989). 'Some Micro Evidence on Unemployment Persistence, paper presented at the 4th Annual Congress of the European Economic Association (mimeo).

Entorf, H., W. Franz, H. König and W. Smolny (1990). 'The Development of German Employment and Unemployment: Estimation and Simulation of a Disequilibrium Macro Model' in C. Bean and J. Drèze (eds), *European Unemployment*, Cambridge, MA: MIT Press.

Entorf, H., H. König and W. Pohlmeier (1989). 'Labor Utilization and Non-Wage Labor Costs in a Disequilibrium Macro Framework', in R. A. Hart (ed.), *New*

134 Wolfgang Franz

Issues in Wages, Non-Wages and Employment. The Conference Proceedings, Luxembourg: Office for Official Publications of the European Communities.

Ermann, K. (1988). *Arbeitsmarktstatistische Zahlen in Zeitreihenform. Jahreszahlen für die Bundesrepublik Deutschland – Ausgabe 1988 – Beiträge aus der Arbeitsmarkt- und Berufsforschung*, 3.1, Nürnberg, 180–1.

Evans, J. M., W. Franz and J. P. Martin (1984). 'Youth Labour Market Dynamics and Unemployment: An Overview, in OECD (ed.), *The Nature of Youth Unemployment. An Analysis for Policy Makers*, Paris: OECD, 7–28.

Flanagan, R. J. (1987). 'Labor Market Behavior and European Economic Growth', in R. Z. Lawrence and C. L. Schultze (eds), *Barriers to European Growth. A Transatlantic View*, Washington, DC: Brookings, 175–211.

Franz, W. (1981). 'Employment Policy and Labor Supply of Foreign Workers in the Federal Republic of Germany: A Theoretical and Empirical Analysis', *Zeitschrift für die gesamte Staatswissenschaft*, 137, 590–611.

(1982a). 'The Reservation Wage of Unemployed Persons in the Federal Republic of Germany: Theory and Empirical Tests', *Zeitschrift für Wirtschafts- und Sozialwissenschaften*, 102, 29–51.

(1982b). *Youth Unemployment in the Federal Republic of Germany. Theory, Empirical Results, and Policy Implications. An Economic Analysis*, Tübingen: Mohr and Siebeck.

(1987a). 'Hysteresis, Persistence, and the NAIRU: An Empirical Analysis for the Federal Republic of Germany', in R. Layard and L. Calmfors (eds), *The Fight Against Unemployment*, Cambridge, MA: MIT Press, 91–122.

(1987b). 'Strukturelle und friktionelle Arbeitslosigkeit in der Bundesrepublik Deutschland: Eine theoretische und empirische Analyse der Beveridge-Kurve', in D. G. Bombach, B. Gahlen, and A. Ott (eds), *Arbeitsmärkte und Beschäftigung: Fakten, Analysen, Perspektiven*, Tübingen: Mohr and Siebeck, 301–23.

(1989). 'Beschäftigungsprobleme auf Grund von Inflexibilitäten auf Arbeitsmärkten?', in H. Scherf (ed.), *Beschäftigungsprobleme hochentwickelter Volkswirtschaften*, Berlin: Duncker and Humblot, 303–40.

Franz, W. and H. König (1986). 'The Nature and Causes of Unemployment in the Federal Republic of Germany since the 1970's: An Empirical Investigation', *Economica*, 53 (Supplement) S219–S244.

(1990). 'A Disequilibrium Approach to Unemployment in the Federal Republic of Germany', *European Economic Review*, 34, 413–22.

Franz, W. and K. Siebeck (1990). 'Theoretical Aspects of the Relation between Unemployment and Vacancies', University of Konstanz, discussion paper, 102, Konstanz.

Gagey, F., J. P. Lambert and B. Ottenwaelter (1988). 'A Disequilibrium Estimation of the French Labor Market Using Business Survey Information', paper presented at the May 1988 Meeting of European Unemployment Programme, Chelwood Gate.

Hamermesh, D. and A. Rees (1984). *The Economics of Work and Pay*, New York: Harper & Row, 3rd edn.

Hujer, R. and H. Schneider (1989). 'The Analysis of Labor Market Mobility Using Panel Data', *European Economic Review*, 33, 530–6.

Jackman, R., R. Layard and C. Pissarides (1989). 'On Vacancies', *Oxford Bulletin of Economics and Statistics*, 51, 377–94.

Jackman, R. and S. Roper (1985). 'Structural Unemployment', *London School of Economics*, Centre for Labour Economics, discussion paper, 233.

Karr, W., M. Koller, H. Kridde and H. Werner (1987). 'Regionale Mobilität am Arbeitsmarkt', *Mitteilungen aus der Arbeitsmarkt- und Berufsforschung*, **20**, 197–212.

König, H. and H. Entorf (1990). 'Strukturelle Arbeitslosigkeit und unausgelastete Kapazitäten: Ergebnisse eines makroökonomischen Rationierungsmodells', *Allg. Statistisches Archiv*, **74**, 117–36.

König, H. and W. Franz (1978). 'Unemployment Compensation and the Rate of Unemployment in the Federal Republic of Germany', in H. G. Grubel and M. A. Walker (eds), *Unemployment Insurance. Global Evidence of its Effects on Unemployment*, Vancouver: The Fraser Institute, 236–66.

Krugman, P. R. (1987). 'Slow Growth in Europe: Conceptual Issues', in R. Z. Lawrence and C. L. Schultze (eds), *Barriers to European Growth. A Transatlantic View*, Washington, DC: Brookings, 48–76.

Lambert, J. P. (1988). *Disequilibrium Macroeconomic Models. Theory and Estimation of Rationing Models Using Business Survey Data*, Cambridge: Cambridge University Press.

Lilien, D. M. (1982). 'Sectoral Shifts and Cyclical Unemployment', *Journal of Political Economy*, **90**, 777–93.

Noll, H.-H. (1985). 'Arbeitsplatzsuche und Stellenfindung', in H. Knepel and R. Hujer (eds), *Mobilitätsprozesse auf dem Arbeitsmarkt*, Frankfurt/M. and New York: Campus, 275–303.

Paqué, K.-H. (1990). 'Unemployment in West Germany. A Survey of Explanations and Policy Options', The Kiel Institute of World Economics, working paper, **407**, Kiel.

Sneessens, H. R. and J. H. Drèze (1986). 'A Discussion of Belgian Unemployment, Combining Traditional Concepts and Disequilibrium Econometrics', *Economica*, **53** (Supplement), pp. S89–S117.

Tessaring, M. (1988). *Arbeitslosigkeit, Beschäftigung und Qualifikation, Mitteilungen aus der Arbeitsmarkt- und Berufsforschung*, 1/1988.

Wurzel, E. (1988). 'Unemployment Duration in West Germany – An Analysis of Grouped Data', Universität Bonn, Institut für Stabilisierungs- und Strukturpolitik, discussion paper, **88/2**.

Discussion

RENATO BRUNETTA

It was a real pleasure for me to prepare this discussion, both for the quality and for the clarity and intellectual honesty of this study. In my discussion I will try, first, concisely to summarise the analytical structure of the study, commenting on its main results; then I will point out some issues which, in my view, the study could have considered in order to make it more complete.

1   Analytical structure

1. Professor Franz's study aims at giving an interesting empirical analysis of the causes, increase and persistence of unemployment in the Federal Republic of Germany, particularly in the last fifteen years (1975–90).

    The focus of the study are the structural factors which affected the German labour market in terms of imperfections and 'maladjustments' such as:

    (a) regional or qualitative mismatch;
    (b) reduced search intensity due to unemployment benefits.

    As a theoretical framework, the paper uses two tools:

    (a) the u/v (unemployment vacancy) relationship – that is, the well known 'Beveridge curve'; and
    (b) a macroeconomic disequilibrium model.
2. Following the theory of the Beveridge curve, unemployment is due to labour 'maladjustment', as in principle a job exists for each unemployed individual. All positions on the u/v curve where the number of unemployed exceeds the number of vacancies indicate 'demand deficiency' (Keynesian unemployment) *or* too high wages (classical unemployment).
3. The u/v curve shifts outwards if the probability that a *contract* may be signed decreases (i.e., if search intensity decreases in relation with unemployment benefits). In the case of long-term unemployment without unemployment benefits and low reservation wages, the *contract* probability increases, causing an inward shift of the u/v curve. On the firms' side, normally, long-term unemployment, lowers the *contract* probability, shifting the Beveridge curve outwards.

    The general effect of long-term unemployment is hence very difficult to define.
4. The *contract* probability decreases in the presence of regional dispersion between unemployment and vacancies.

    To evaluate the *contract* probability, it is necessary to consider the costs of the changing location in terms of reservation wages.
5. Qualification mismatch implies that a vacancy is not filled by an applicant because his or her qualifications are inadequate (either higher or lower), compared to the requirements for the job under consideration.

6. The empirical analysis in the study with the u/v method indicates an outward shifting of the curve. (*But*, what caused these shifts?)

7. The other tool utilised is the Rationing Model, when wages and prices are not adjusting fast enough to clear markets at any moment in time.

   The empirical model displays the shares of firms being either constrained by goods demand, by existing capacities, or by available labour.

   The empirical results show that the periods 1960–6 and 1969–74 are characterised by a preponderance of capacity and labour supply constraints; while rationing from the demand side becomes dominant in recession periods (1967, 1975, 1982 and 1983).

8. The model also provides some interesting indicators:

   - 'the structural rate of unemployment at equilibrium' (*SURE*).
   - 'the structural rate of unused capacity at equilibrium' (*SUCE*), that characterises excess capacities exclusively due to rigidities and frictions on the goods market.
   - With labour market mismatch we will have a corresponding expression for *SUCE*, which also takes into account inflexibilities on the labour market: *SUCEL*.
   - The difference between *SUCEL* and *SUCE* indicates to what extent excess capacities are due to labour market imperfections.

   The empirical results

   - Show an increasing value of *SURE* (increasing of structural unemployment).
   - Show *SUCE* remaining constant.
   - And show *SUCEL* increasing, indicating possible spillovers from labour market imperfections to the underutilisation of capacities. (*But*, what are the reasons of increasing structural unemployment?)

2   Causes of mismatch

Regional mismatch does not seem to contribute much to the outward shift of the Beveridge curve or the *SURE* in the decade examined, and labour mobility does not seem to be overwhelming.

   The *mismatch of qualifications* implies that persons with a long duration of unemployment are viewed as less qualified (depreciation of specific human capital).

   Another argument for explaining the speed-up in structural unemployment is the fixed cost of labour due to training and absence from work, which leads the firm to intensify search and screening efforts.

Unemployment benefits exert little positive effect on unemployment duration.

3   Concluding remarks

1. The study shows that an outward shift in the Beveridge curve occurred, as did an increase of structural mismatch indicators in the Federal Republic of Germany.

    What are the microeconomic causes at the base of these increasing imperfections of the German labour market? The study analyses four possible hypotheses:

    (a) a reduction of labour mobility;
    (b) an increase of mismatch between the demand and supply of qualifications;
    (c) intensified selection processes on the firms' side;
    (d) a decrease of job search intensity on the unemployed side;

    The study considers some *quantitative* indicators referring to these specific aspects of the labour market, but the results (as the author himself affirms) seem to be insufficient and ambiguous.

2. Nevertheless, the mismatch exists, both in regional, and qualifications terms; certainly, the phenomena of research and selection are present both on the supply and on the demand side. What is less clear is if the weight of these phenomena has increased over time.

    Once again, the changes in the labour market clash with a weak quantitative analysis (as the author himself states) which is unable to verify the theoretical hypothesis put forward. This situation is not new for those who study labour economics.

    The study seems well structured from the point of view of its conceptual framework and of its quantitative methodology, but it seems to overlook the variety of behaviours and phenomena in the German labour market. It comments well on individual behaviour (according to the theoretical framework), but it cannot interpret macrophenomena.

    Is the author aware of all this? There are many references to these problems in his study – from the flow concepts for the labour market to the role played by qualifications, from the discrimination aspects which affected some age segments of labour forces to the weight of institutional rules and to the microeconomic processes provoked by the duration of unemployment.

    These specific issues are not adequate to the theoretical framework utilised. The theoretical framework is not verified, and the result is a great deal of dissatisfaction (shared by the author himself). Neverthe-less, the analysis denotes the confirmation of an unconventional interpretative hypothesis in which, in our view, greater weight is given to the dynamic, demographic and generational processes both on the firms' side, and on the workers' choices. All this, however, is not sufficiently stressed.

3. If this interpretation is acceptable, we need an integration, especially with regard to the analysis of the labour market from the generational aspect.

Models of this kind underline the great relevance of labour market flows, by considering employment as a 'population'. Other useful issues to integrate the study could involve the following:

–   the impact of new technology in terms of technological unemploy-ment and declining sectors;
–   the changing of immigration policy: the Federal Republic of Germany has always selected its immigrant manpower since the end of the 1970s; this strategy has been more and more difficult both for the workers coming from outside the EC, and for the 'East Germans';
–   the effects on unemployment of the restraint of economic growth at the end of the 1970s and in the second half of the 1980s.
–   The dynamic mismatch between structural changes and the parallel reactions in the rule systems (school, labour market, welfare).

Is it possible to incorporate these additional elements in the theoreti-cal framework adopted by the author? Perhaps, but I will leave the answer to Professor Franz.

4 Mismatch in Japan[1]

GIORGIO BRUNELLO

Tokyo is the information center of the country, where both the service industry and the international functions are concentrated. A place that is not linked up with Tokyo is bound to decline (free translation from Haruo, Shimada, *Nihon Keizai Shinbun*, 22 May 1989).

1 Introduction

Since the end of the 1970s, high (10% and more) and persistent unemployment has been a major issue in Europe. During the same period, Japanese unemployment increased from a very low 2% level to a temporary peak of 3% in the first half of 1987 (after the 'endaka' shock). This very low unemployment rate, accompanied with some specific features of the Japanese labour market such as the bonus system and the large size of the secondary sector, has induced many observers to consider Japan as a 'no problem' country, at least as far as unemployment is concerned.

This emphasis on the low level of unemployment (and the possible measurement issues involved) overlooks the fact that Japan, despite wage flexibility, the bonus system and the procyclical labour supply, which have all helped reduce the impact of exogenous shocks on the unemployment rate, has witnessed during the past ten years or so a significant increase in the NAIRU (see Hamada and Kurosaka, 1986 and the references therein), with unemployment showing the same sort of persistency exhibited by the major European economies (see Brunello, 1989 and the references therein).

Economic theory offers two main explanations of the current increase in the NAIRU in most developed countries (for the United States see Summers, 1986 and Topel and Murphy, 1987). The first explanation is 'hysteresis' (see Blanchard and Summers, 1986). The idea here is that a high NAIRU today is the result of high unemployment yesterday. The second explanation focuses on an array of supply factors, ranging from union power to search intensities, from efficiency considerations and the wedge to mismatch (see Layard and Nickell, 1986 for Britain and Summers, 1986 for the United States).

Separating the 'hysteresis' explanation from the 'structural' explanation is rather artificial, and could misrepresent the thrust of current research, which usually blends the two explanations together (see for instance Jackman, Layard, Nickell and Wadhwani, 1991, hereafter JLNW). Such a separation is useful, however, for the purpose of this study, which is to investigate a specific structural factor – mismatch – in the context of the recent increase in Japanese equilibrium unemployment. We shall thus ignore hereafter both 'hysteresis' and a number of structural factors such as union behaviour and the equilibrium exchange rate. These factors are not crucial here and have been already explored elsewhere (see Brunello, 1989, 1990).

It is useful to begin with a definition of 'mismatch'. Consider the long-run equilibrium of an economy composed of n sectors (areas). Unemployment rates differ among areas because of compensating differentials; there is equilibrium heterogeneity; aggregate demand equals aggregate supply; the aggregate unemployment rate cannot be reduced by reallocating labour among different sectors. Let this economy be displaced from its long-run equilibrium by (temporary) sector-specific shocks that do not alter the aggregate relation between demand and supply. In a frictionless economy the long-run equilibrium is instantaneously recovered. With frictions, however, the original displacement persists over time as the economy goes through a sequence of short-run equilibria. Because of relative wage rigidities, incomplete information and costly labour mobility, the sectoral distribution of unemployment (and vacancies) is altered and aggregate unemployment could be reduced by reallocating labour among different sectors. There is mismatch.[2]

This definition of mismatch is more or less standard and assumes explicitly that temporary displacements do not affect the (stable) long-run equilibrium. An alternative definition, recently proposed by Jackman, Layard and Savouri (1990, hereafter JLS), considers as mismatch both the long-run equilibrium dispersion of unemployment rates and the temporary displacements from it. If equilibrium heterogeneity is substantial, these two definitions have remarkably different implications both for empirical measurement and for policy. According to the latter definition, policy should focus on unemployment dispersion *per se*. According to the former definition, policy should be aimed at temporary displacements without trying to affect compensating differentials.

So far, empirical measurement of mismatch has included equilibrium heterogeneity. Jackman and Roper (1987, hereafter, JR), for instance, assume that the n areas in the economy share the same matching technology. JLS, on the other hand, assumes that the dispersion of unemployment is zero in a 'no mismatch equilibrium'. Following the (standard) definition proposed in this study both these empirical measures are inadequate and should be revised accordingly.

The main purpose of this study is to implement this revision by using the Japanese labour market data. This exercise is useful *independently* of the chosen definition of mismatch because it clarifies the relative importance of equilibrium heterogeneity. As a by-product, we hope to be able to learn something about Japanese mismatch and its effects on the dynamics of the unemployment rate.

The study is organised as follows. Section 2 starts with some stylised facts on the distribution of unemployment and vacancies in Japan. Section 3 discusses the JLS approach and suggests a correction based on the concept of a stable spatial equilibrium. Section 4 takes up the JR approach and discusses Lilien's (1982) stigma. Section 5 explores the relation between mismatch and the macro u/v curve. Some conclusions follow in section 6.

2   Some stylised facts

This section presents some basic facts on the distribution of unemployment and vacancies in Japan by skill, industry, age, sex and region. We start with unemployment and vacancies by skill group (Table 4.1).[3] We stress two main points. First, the dispersion of unemployment by skill is higher among women, mainly because of the high unemployment rate among the unskilled. Notice that in Britain the opposite holds, with unemployment dispersion being higher among men (see JLNW, 1989, Chapter 5). Second, the unemployment rate of technical and managerial workers is relatively high in Japan when compared to Britain and the United States.

Table 4.2 shows the distribution of unemployment by age, sex, industry and region at a given point in time. The distribution of unemployment by age groups is two-peaked because of the relatively high unemployment rate of workers aged 55–64. It is well known that this second peak in the distribution is closely related to the practice of mandatory retirement at the age of 55 (changing recently to 60). This two-peaked distribution is not shared by the United States and Britain, where unemployment rates decline with age. Using some simple steady state accounting, Table 4.3 breaks down the distribution of unemployment into the distribution of monthly flows and the distribution of average duration. Table 4.3 shows

Table 4.1. *Unemployment and vacancies by skill, 1985*

Skill	Vacancy rates (V_i/E_i)		
	Men	Women	All
Technical and managerial	1.6	2.9	1.8
Clerical	0.5	0.7	0.6
Sales	2.8	3.2	2.9
Services	2.9	2.5	2.7
Transportation	1.5	0.8	1.5
Production			
Skilled	2.3	3.7	2.6
Unskilled	2.0	3.3	2.7
Skill	Unemployment rates (U_i/E_i)		
	Men	Women	All
Technical and managerial	1.6	2.4	2.1
Clerical	1.2	1.7	1.5
Sales	1.5	2.3	1.7
Services	1.6	1.8	1.7
Transportation	1.3	0.7	1.3
Production			
Skilled	1.1	1.6	1.2
Unskilled	2.5	6.9	4.0
All	2.6	2.7	2.6
var(u_i/u)	3.7%	57.6%	13.6%

Note: E_i is employment, V_i is vacancies and U_i is unemployment.

Sources:
Ministry of Labour, *Koyo Doko Chosa Hokoku* and Ministry of Labour, *Rodo Shijo Nenpo.*

that the second peak in the distribution of unemployment by age in Japan is due to a substantial increase in unemployment duration after age 55. Inflow rates are in general very small compared with the United States and smaller than British flows. Average duration is slightly higher in Japan than in United States but much smaller than in Britain.

Next, Table 4.4 presents some time series evidence on the dispersion of unemployment by age, sex and region. As explained in the Data Appendix, the definition of unemployment by industry changes too frequently and cannot be used as reliable time series evidence. The same holds for unemployment by skill. Table 4.4 suggests that the (weighted) dispersion

Table 4.2. *Unemployment by age, sex, industry and region, 1985*

Age groups	By age[a]
15–19	7.28
20–29	3.67
30–39	2.18
40–54	1.70
55–64	3.73
65 and over	1.66
	By sex[a]
Men	2.58
Women	2.66
	By industry (U/E) (1982)[a]
Construction	2.58
Manufacturing	1.74
Transportation	1.73
Sales	1.83
Services	1.40
	By region[b]
Hokkaido	4.5
Tohoku	2.7
Minami Kanto	2.5
Kita Kanto	1.6
Hokuriku	1.7
Tokai	1.9
Kinki	2.9
Chugoku	2.6
Shikoku	2.8
Kyushu	3.5

Note: Unemployment by industry excludes the unemployed without previous job experience.

Sources:
a Ministry of Labour, *Rodoryoku Chosa Tokubetsu Chosa.*
b Ministry of Labour, *Rodoryoku Chosa Nenpo.*

Table 4.3. *Unemployment average duration, months, by age, sex and industry, 1985*

Age group	S/N By age	U/S	U/N
15–24	1.61	3.18	5.11
25–44	0.42	5.58	2.34
45–54	0.31	6.50	2.01
55 and over	0.40	12.33	3.65
	By sex		
Males	0.42	6.20	2.82
Females	0.57	4.73	2.75
	By industry		
Construction	0.57	5	2.80
Manufacturing	0.19	8	1.50
Transportation	0.28	8	2.20
Sales	0.38	5	1.90
Services	0.17	8.5	1.44

Notes:
S = Monthly inflow in the unemployment pool (= numbers unemployed less than 1 month).
N = Labour force.
U = Numbers unemployed.

Source: Office of the Prime Minister, *Rodoryoku Chosa Tokubetsu Chosa.*

of unemployment by region does not exhibit any significant trend. It also suggests a slight increase in the dispersion of unemployment by age in the last few years. Contrary to the evidence for Britain, there is no evidence of an upward trend in the dispersion of unemployment by sex.

3   The dispersion of local unemployment rates

As mentioned in the introduction, regional mismatch is usually explained by sluggish labour mobility and sluggish relative wage adjustment. Consider an economy composed on n local labour markets.[4] Workers and firms are homogeneous but areas differ in their amenities. The long-run equilibrium in this economy can be described by the following version of the Rosen–Marston model (see Rosen, 1979, Marston, 1985).

Table 4.4. *Dispersion of unemployment rates: Japan, 1972–87*

Year	By age	By sex	By region
1972	21.60		
1973	19.30		
1974	16.40		9.30
1975	11.80		4.80
1976	11.50		5.60
1977	15.30		10.90
1978	13.40		10.60
1979	16.70	0.30	9.30
1980	15.20	0.08	10.50
1981	17.80	0.17	7.70
1982	26.50	0.05	6.50
1983	14.80	0.01	8.50
1984	17.90	0.05	9.50
1985	20.10	0.04	9.40
1986	20.40	0.03	7.60
1987	22.10	0.01	8.00

Notes:
Age groups (8): 15–19; 20–24; 25–29; 30–34; 35–39; 40–54; 55–64; 65 and over.
Regions (10): Hokkaido; Tohoku; Minami Kanto; Kita Kanto; Hokuriku; Tokai;
Kinki; Chugoku; Shikoku; Kyushu.

Sources: Office of the Prime Minister, *Rodoryoku Chosa Nenpo*.
Rokoryoku Chosa Tokubetsu Chosa.
The weights are employment shares, as in Abrahams (1987).

$$V[W_i, U_i, A_i] = k \qquad (i = 1, \ldots, n-1) \tag{1}$$

$$C[W_i, U_i, A_i] = 1 \qquad (i = 1, \ldots, n) \tag{2}$$

$$\frac{dV/dW_i}{dV/dU_i} = \frac{dC/dW_i}{dC/dU_i} \qquad (i = 1, \ldots, n) \tag{3}$$

$$\sum_i^n N_i/(1 - U_i) = M \tag{4}$$

where V is the indirect utility function of a representative worker
W_i is the local real wage
U_i is the local unemployment rate
A_i is the local set of amenities
C is the minimum cost function of a representative firm using a
technology with constant returns to scale
k is a constant

M is total exogenous labour supply

N_i is local employment.

Equation (1) says that labour is perfectly mobile in the long run so that indirect utilities are equalised among areas. Equation (2) sets the allocation rule for firms. Firms move among areas up to the point where the zero profit condition holds in each local market. Higher unemployment leads to higher productivity for a given wage either because it reduces quits or because it improves the utilisation of labour within firms (see Hall, 1972 for details). Equation (3) is the allocation rule for workers, who choose among areas so as to maximise their indirect utility subject to equations (1) and (2). Equation (4) sets aggregate employment equal to the exogenously given aggregate labour supply minus aggregate unemployment.

The set of $3n$ equations include the $3n$ endogenous variables W_i, U_i, N_i, which can be implicitly solved as functions of the exogenous variables (amenities A_i). In the long-run equilibrium a given distribution of amenities thus leads univocally to an equilibrium distribution of wages and unemployment rates. Since amenities are slowly changing variables, the equilibrium describes a stable hedonic curve

$$U_i = G[W_i] \tag{5}$$

The slope of the hedonic curve depends on the shape of the utility and cost functions and on the sign of the correlation between shifts in amenities and shifts in productivities. Hall (1972) spells out the conditions under which the hedonic curve is positively sloped.[5]

Local demand and supply shocks displace local markets from their spatial equilibrium. If labour is perfectly mobile in the short run (as well as in the long run), no displacement can actually be observed since the economy returns immediately to its long run equilibrium. Local information plays no role (see Topel, 1986). If labour mobility is less than perfect, however, displacement is observable. Its size depends crucially on the responsiveness of local wages to local conditions. If wages are completely rigid, the adjustment to the (unchanged) long-run equilibrium is fully borne out by labour mobility. If wages are fully flexible and clear local labour markets continuously, the displacement is smaller and the adjustment quicker.

Given this framework, we define 'mismatch' as the process of adjustment to the spatial equilibrium under conditions of limited labour mobility and limited wage flexibility. The maintained hypothesis that the hedonic curve is stable over reasonably limited periods of time allows us to measure mismatch with the dispersion of the deviations of actual unemployment rates from their equilibrium values.

It is useful to relate this measure to the index of mismatch MM suggested by JLS. They measure mismatch as follows. Let U_{min} and U be respectively the minimum and the aggregate unemployment rates. Assume a Cobb–Douglas technology with the associated factor price frontier. Let the local wage be set according to a wage pressure equation that depends on local (and possibly aggregate) unemployment. Additional assumptions on the covariance between labour force shares and relative unemployment rates yield[6]

$$MM = \log U - \log U_{min} = \text{var}(U_i/U)/2 \tag{6}$$

where var is for variance and U_i is local unemployment.

The JLS definition implies that absence of mismatch is equivalent to a degenerate distribution of unemployment rates ($U_i = U_{min}$ for any i). According to our definition based upon the Rosen–Marston model, however, this is correct only if the distribution of amenities is degenerate. If amenities differ across areas (as they usually do), equilibrium unemployment also differs. In this case the JLS index MM of mismatch fails to discriminate between 'disequilibrium' (mismatch) and equilibrium unemployment dispersion. In more detail, the variance of relative unemployment can be decomposed as follows

$$\text{var}(U_i/U) = \text{var}(U_i^*/U) + \text{var}[(U_i - U_i^*)]/U$$
$$+ 2\text{cov}\{U_i^*, [U_i - U_i^*]\}/U \tag{7a}$$

where U_i^* is local equilibrium unemployment.

The first component in the RHS of equation (7a) is the variance of (relative) equilibrium unemployment. The second component corresponds closely to our definition of mismatch. The third component is the covariance element. Granted that this covariance is small enough, we suggest that a more adequate index of mismatch in presence of equilibrium heterogeneity is

$$MM_1 = \text{var}[(U_i - U_i^*)/U]/2 \tag{7b}$$

where $MM_1 < MM$.

Notice that MM could be smaller than MM_1 if the covariance between equilibrium unemployment and the deviations from it is negative and relatively large. An example of $MM < MM_1$ is when there is equilibrium heterogeneity but actual unemployment rates are all equal to the average rate.

In order to compute MM_1 we need first to estimate U_i^*. Following Marston (1985), we posit the following empirical model

Table 4.5. *Regional dispersion of unemployment: spatial equilibrium and mismatch, %, 1975–87*

Year	MM	MM_1 (1975–87)	MM_1 (1980–7)
1975	4.8	0.21	
1976	5.6	0.13	
1977	10.9	0.11	
1978	10.6	0.09	
1979	9.3	0.12	
1980	10.5	0.13	
1981	7.7	0.10	0.11
1982	6.5	0.04	0.04
1983	8.5	0.03	0.03
1984	9.5	0.05	0.04
1985	9.4	0.05	0.05
1986	7.6	0.02	0.02
1987	8.0	0.02	0.01

Number of regions		10 (1975–87)	10 (1980–7)
Serial correlation coefficient R		0.23 (2.58)	0.367 (3.32)
Test for equality of A_i $[LR(1)]$		75.06	51.01
Chow test for parameter stability $[F(11,108)]$		2.038 (critical value at 1%: 2.43)	
$\text{var}[A_i/U_i]$		8.02	8.33
$\text{var}[Z_i/U_i]/\text{var}[U_i/U]$		0.10	0.06
$\text{var}[A_i/U_i]/\text{var}[U_i/U]$		95.88	98.40
$2\,\text{cov}[A_i/U_i, Z_i/U_i/U]/\text{var}[U_i/U]$		4.00	1.50

Notes:
$Z_i = [U_i - U_i^*]$
t-values within parentheses.

$$U_{it} = A_i + B_i + E_{it} \tag{8a}$$

$$E_{it} = RE_{it,-1} + H_{it} \tag{8b}$$

where A_i is the time-invariant, area-specific factor
B_{it} is a common time-varying factor
E_{it} is a first-order autoregressive error
H_{it} is a white noise.

A_i and B_t are meant to capture respectively area-specific and common, time-varying equilibrium unemployment effects. E_{it} is meant to capture mismatch and R its degree of persistence.

Model (8a)–(8b) is estimated by pooling the available annual data (1975–87) for the 10 Japanese regions listed in Table 4.4. The stochastic component A_i is handled as an area specific parameter by using regional dummies (see Hsiao, 1986 for a discussion of this approach). Estimates are based on the Beach–McKinnon maximum likelihood procedure. Indexes MM and MM_1 are presented in Table 4.5. Table 4.5 clearly suggests that, on average, most of the variation in relative unemployment rates is *equilibrium variation*. Even including the *small* covariance between A_i and estimated residuals *disequilibrium variations* are only slightly over 4% of total variance. Equilibrium heterogeneity thus appears to be substantial.

The main implication of Table 4.5 is that the MM index suggested by JLS largely *overestimates* regional mismatch by including in it substantial variations in equilibrium unemployment. Table 4.5 suggests a number of other interesting points. First, the hypothesis that equilibrium local unemployment rates are equal ($A_i = K$ where K is a constant) is strongly rejected by a Likelihood Ratio test. Second, the Chow test for parameter stability cannot reject the null at the 1% level of confidence. Since rejection occurs if the level of confidence is 5%, we also present the estimates of model (8a)–(8b) for the sub-period 1980–7. These estimates confirm the results for the full period. Third, the estimated value of R, our measure of persistence of mismatch, is much larger in Japan than in the United States. Marston (1985) finds that R in the United States is not significantly different from zero. We find that parameter R in Japan is significantly different from zero and ranges between 0.2 and 0.4 depending on the time period. These results confirm recent evidence presented by the OECD (1989), which indicates that the regional pattern of unemployment is more persistent in Japan (and in Europe) than in the United States.

Finally, our evidence points both to a *slight decline* in the size of mismatch and to an increase in its persistency since the beginning of the 1980s. A smaller MM_1 could be explained with a reduction in the size of local shocks and/or with an *increase* in labour mobility (and wage flexibility). On the other hand, higher persistence could be explained with a *decline* in labour mobility (and wage flexibility). As documented in Figure 4.1, labour mobility among local markets has steadily declined since the early-middle 1970s.[7] Thus labour mobility cannot help in explaining the observed reduction in MM_1. On the other hand, the reduction in the size of local and industrial shocks is worth exploring as an alternative explanation because of the documented reduction in the size of Japanese business cycles after the first oil shock (see Horiye, Naniwa and Ishihara, 1987).

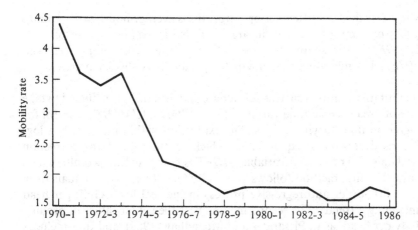

Figure 4.1   Mobility among regions, 1970–86
Source: Rodo Hakusho (1988) p. 107.

Persistency is also related to local wage flexibility. For a given degree of labour mobility, high local wage flexibility leads to less persistency as the economy moves rapidly back to its spatial equilibrium. If local wages are completely rigid, however, the brunt of adjustment must be borne by labour mobility and persistency is higher than in a situation of fully flexible local wages. The extent of local wage flexibility can be measured by studying the responsiveness of local wages of local shocks. Given the identifying assumption of costly labour mobility, it is easy to show that market clearing wages should be positively correlated with local demand or supply shifts (see Pissarides and Mogadhan, 1989, Topel, 1986). Without continuous market clearing, this correlation survives if one thinks of local wages as being determined by a Layard–Nickell wage pressure function. In this case, a negative local shock will increase local unemployment over its spatial equilibrium level. Higher local unemployment will lead to a decline in the real wage by reducing local wage pressure. On the other hand, the correlation between local wages and local shocks should be zero or close to zero if local wages are rigid.

The relation between local wage dynamics and local shocks can be investigated empirically with the following Error Correction Model:[8]

$$
\begin{aligned}
D\log W_{it} = {} & \text{constant} + aD\log W_{it,-1} + bDTEN_{it} \\
& + dDLARGE_{it} + fD\log SHIFT_{it} \\
& + g\log SHIFT_{it,-1} - h[\log W - k_0\log U \\
& - k_1 TEN - k_2 LARGE]_{it,-1} \\
& + mD\log U_{it} + TIME\ DUMMIES + e_{it} \qquad (9)
\end{aligned}
$$

where D is the first difference operator, W_{it} is average hourly real earnings (gross of bonuses) of men in area i, TEN_{it} is average tenure of men, $LARGE_{it}$ is the share of firms with more than 1000 employees, and $SHIFT_{it}$ is a measure of unanticipated productivity shocks in area i.

Qualititative controls such as sex, tenure and firm size are included to take care of area specific time varying effects. *TIME DUMMIES* control for aggregate time varying effects. The expression within brackets is a log-linearised version of equation (5) which captures the error correction mechanism. The crucial variable *SHIFT* is computed in two alternative ways. The first method follows Topel (1986) and uses the residuals from the a first-order autoregressive process in the real local GNP per head (including a trend). The second method uses the actual values of productivity per head, as in Pissarides and Mogadhan (1989), and thus includes also anticipated local shifts.

Equation (9) is preferred to the (by now standard) wage equation estimated by JLS because it models explicitly short-run wage dynamics as an adjustment process toward the long-run equilibrium. The data are a panel of 47 prefectures for the years 1974–86. The description of the data sources is left to the Data Appendix at the end of the study. The estimation method is the *GMM* version of the Anderson–Hsiao estimator proposed by Arellano and Bond (1988), which treats the lagged dependent variable as endogenous and differences out the fixed effect.[9] Results are shown in Table 4.6.

There are three main findings. First, changes in local information (*SHIFT*) significantly affect changes in local real wages. Second, the response of local wages to unexpected productivity shocks is larger than the response to actual productivity shifts (compare column (1) and (2) of Table 4.6). This result indicates that anticipated shocks trigger labour inflows into the areas where the wage is expected to increase and thus reduce wage pressure. Last but not least, regional unemployment rates do not significantly affect regional hourly real wages. Notice that the irrelevance of regional unemployment is quite robust to variations in the specification of equation (9), including the JLS regional wage equation.[10]

Overall, this evidence points to the stabilising role of Japanese local wages. Further evidence on the issue can be gained by looking at the correlation between local wages and local net labour inflows. Suppose once again that we start from a spatial equilibrium. A positive area-specific shock hits the nth local market and a symmetric negative shock hits the kth market. Unemployment initially increases in the kth market and falls in the nth market. If mobility is costless, workers will move from the kth to the nth market. Equilibrium will be restored without any change in local wages. In this case there is no correlation between net employment inflows and local wage changes. If mobility is costly but local wages are fully rigid, the disequilibrium will take time to fade away but still we will not be able to observe any correlation between wage changes and net labour inflows. Finally, if mobility is costly *and* local wages are responsive to local conditions, the nth area will see both an increase in the net labour inflow and an increase in the local wage. The opposite will be observed in the kth area. Thus a positive correlation between changes in local wages and net labour inflow will be observed over time. Figures 4.2 and 4.3 plot these two variables for the period 1975–85 in two selected areas. The first area, Tokyo, is a typical immigration region whereas the second area, Kagoshima, is a typical outflow region. Both figures suggest that local wage changes and net inflows are positively correlated.

We can summarise this section as follows. According to our measure MM_1, we found no evidence of a positive trend in Japanese regional mismatch. If any evidence exists, it points to a decline in the index during the last few years, accompanied with an increase in persistency.

4   The distribution of vacancies

4.1   Regional mismatch

So far, the analysis has completely ignored vacancies. Firms have been assumed to locate among areas and to be able to fill their demand for labour at the going price instantaneously and costlessly. In a world of imperfect information and frictions, however, filling available job slots

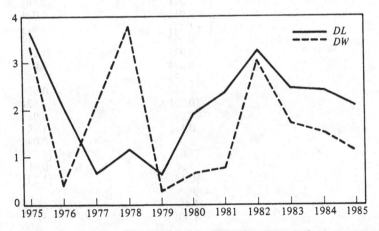

Figure 4.2   Real wage changes, %, and index of net labour inflow, Tokyo, 1975–85

Table 4.6. *Local wage dynamics, estimates, 47 Prefectures: 1977–86; Anderson–Hsiao instrumental variables*

	Dependent variable: $D \log W_{it}$	
	(1)	(2)
Constant	− 0.0002	− 0.011
	[− 0.02]	[− 1.38]
$D \log W_{it,-1}$	− 0.039	− 0.020
	[− 1.04]	[− 1.09]
$DTEN_{it}$	0.221	0.209
	[5.60]	[4.95]
$DLARGE_{it}$	0.321	0.313
	[5.36]	[6.02]
$D \log SHIFT_{it}$	0.153	0.071
	[5.36]	[2.55]
$\log SHIFT_{it,-1}$	0.279	0.157
	[4.24]	[4.39]
$D \log U_{it}$	− 0.022	0.019
	[− 0.30]	[0.51]
$\log U_{it,-1}$	− 0.047	0.044
	[− 1.21]	[− 1.26]
$\log W_{it,-1}$	− 0.758	− 0.777
	[− 8.72]	[− 14.26]
$TEN_{it,-1}$	0.159	0.133
	[3.18]	[2.51]
$LARGE_{it,-1}$	0.296	0.312
	[3.79]	[3.90]
D78	0.014	0.020
	[0.64]	[1.54]
D79	− 0.005	0.018
	[− 0.82]	[2.60]
D80	− 0.013	0.004
	[− 1.48]	[0.62]
D81	0.022	0.014
	[0.92]	[1.09]
D82	0.024	0.036
	[1.73]	[3.56]
D83	0.014	0.026
	[0.96]	[2.62]
D84	− 0.001	0.015
	[− 0.11]	[1.79]
D85	0.020	0.033
	[2.63]	[4.54]
D86	0.007	0.011
	[0.45]	[1.13]
TN	470	470
SC	11.46 (7)	16.58 (9)
M2	− 1.401	− 1.377

Table 4.6 (*cont.*)

Notes:

SHIFT in column (1) is defined as the residual from a first-order autoregressive with a deterministic trend of local GNP per head. *SHIFT* in column (2) is defined as real productivity per head. *t*-values within brackets.

Variables $D\log W_{it,-1}$, $\log W_{it,-1}$, $D\log U_{it}$, $\log U_{it,-1}$ in both columns and $D\log SHIFT_{it}$, $\log SHIFT_{it,-1}$ in column (2) are treated as endogenous.

Additional instruments include: $W_{it,-2}$, $TEN_{it,-1}$, $TEN_{it,-2}$, $LARGE_{it,-1}$, $LARGE_{it,-2}$, $MANUF_{it,-1}$, $MANUF_{it,-2}$, $U_{it,-2}$, $GNP_{it,-2}$, $VU_{it,-2}$ and $W_{it,-3}$, where VU_{it} is the local job offers/job seekers ratio (unadjusted).

SC is the Sargan criterion for instruments validity.

M_2 is the test for serial correlation of residuals proposed by Arellano and Bond (1988). The statistic has a standard normal distribution under the null. Serial correlation is rejected at the 5% level of confidence if M_2 is outside the interval $-1.96, 1.96$.

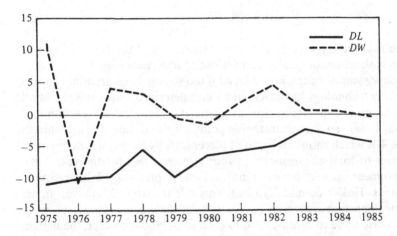

Figure 4.3 Real wage changes, %, and index of net labour inflow, Kagoshima (Kyushu), 1975–85

requires a costly search process on both the worker's and on the firm's side (see Hansen, 1970, Pissarides, 1985 and Blanchard and Diamond, 1990 for a detailed discussion). The definition of mismatch in this context is given by a comparison between the actual and the optimal allocation of vacancies and unemployment among areas. Assume, for instance, that all areas share the same job matching technology. Let this common technology imply that hirings in each area depend positively both on unemployment and on vacancies. Assume also that the technology is a convex, linear homogeneous function (see Jackman, Layard and Pissa-

Table 4.7. *Ratio of placements by public employment agencies to total engagements, four selected regions, 1987*

	Hokkaido	Kita Kanto (Tokyo)	Kyushu	Tokai (Nagoya)
1987	0.6209144	0.0656519	0.2056697	0.1187355

Sources: Ministry of Labour, *Koyo Doko Chosa* and Ministry of Labour, *Rodo Shijo Nenpo.*

rides, 1984). Given these assumptions, one can show that the optimal allocation of unemployment, given the configuration of vacancies, requires that the vacancy–unemployment ratio be the same among areas (see JR, 1987 for a proof). An index of mismatch is thus readily given by

$$MM_2 = 0.5* \sum_i |u(i) - v(i)| \tag{10}$$

where u_i is the share of local unemployment out of total unemployment and v_i is the share of local vacancies out of total vacancies.

These assumptions are, however, a bit too strong. Even granting that the matching technology has exactly the shape described above, it is clear that the assumption of a common hiring function is open to question (see Wood, 1988). To demonstrate this point, let us consider the evidence in Table 4.7, which shows the ratio of placements by the public employment agencies to total engagements in four selected areas for the year 1987. Government agencies have a significant role to play in net labour exporting areas (Hokkaido and Kyushu). This role is marginal however, in net labour importing areas such as Tokyo and Nagoya.

It is reasonable to assume that, in each local labour market, the matching technology associated with public government agencies differs from the matching technology associated with, say, private advertising.[11] The local hiring function is a weighted average of these different matching technologies, with weights given by their relative importance in the matching process. Since these weights vary among areas, composition effects are sufficient to generate heterogeneous hiring functions.[12] Heterogeneity suggests that we consider the following hiring function

$$H_{it} = B_{it}[U_{it}/V_{it}]^a V_{it} \tag{11}$$

where H_{it} is hirings in area i at time t, U_{it} is unemployment, V_{it} vacancies and a and B_{it} are parameters.

The optimal allocation of unemployment given total unemployment and the allocation of vacancies is obtained as in JR (1987) by solving the following problem

$$\max_{U_{it}} \sum_i H_{it} = \sum_i B_{it}[U_{it}/V_{it}]^a V_{it}. \tag{12}$$

subject to

$$\sum_i U_{it} = U = \text{constant}$$

and to

$$V_{it} \text{ taken as given.}$$

The log-linear version of the first-order condition is

$$\log[U_{it} - V_{it}] = \text{constant} - \log B_{it}/(a - 1) \tag{13}$$

Assume that B_{it} can be decomposed into common time-varying and fixed area-specific effects. An empirical version of equation (13) is then given by

$$\log[U_{it} - V_{it}] = \text{constant} + b(i)*LDUMS \\ + f*TIME + \text{errors} \tag{14}$$

where $LDUMS$ is a set of local dummies, $TIME$ is a time trend, b_i is the area-specific parameter and f is the parameter associated with the common aggregate effects.

The estimates of the parameters in equation (14) can be used to compute an adjusted version of equation (10), defined as follows

$$MM_3 = 0.5* \sum_i |u_i - v_i \tag{15}$$
$$*[\exp\{\text{constant} + b(i)LDUMS + f*TIME\}*v|$$

where v is the aggregate vacancy–unemployment ratio.

Table 4.8 presents the MM_2 and MM_3 indexes of regional mismatch. The standard JR (1987) index (MM_2) appears in three alternative versions, one based on unadjusted data and the other two based on two different adjustments of regional vacancies, each trying to account for the discrepancy between registered and total vacancies. A description of the adjustment technique is relegated to the Data Appendix. The MM_3 index is computed using vacancies adjusted as in column (2) of Table 4.8. Figure 4.4 plots the three versions of MM_2 whereas Figure 4.5 plots MM_2 and MM_3. Figure 4.4 confirms the common finding that regional mismatch is counter-cyclical. Figure 4.5 shows that correcting for equilibrium heterogeneity generates an index of regional mismatch that declines over time.

Table 4.8. *Regional mismatch, JR (1987) style, %, 10 regions, 1975–87*

	MM_2			MM_3
Year	(1)	(2)	(3)	(4)
1975	16.17	8.1	18.5	20.24
1976	16.92	11.99	18.01	16.82
1977	17.65	13.27	19.22	15.13
1978	18.11	14	19.72	11.83
1979	17.92	16.03	21.8	13.30
1980	17.16	14.82	22.16	13.16
1981	16.8	13.89	23.18	11.37
1982	17.48	15.74	22.72	9.40
1983	18.35	16.78	23.18	7.19
1984	18.57	17.61	22.72	6.55
1985	17.99	15.94	23.44	6.74
1986	16.92	16.58	22.14	5.63
1987	15.41	16.08	22.7	4.29

Notes:
Column (1) uses unadjusted vacancies.
Column (2) uses vacancies adjusted as in Layard, Jackman and Pissarides (1984).
Column (3) uses vacancies adjusted by a weighted ratio of engagements to placements.

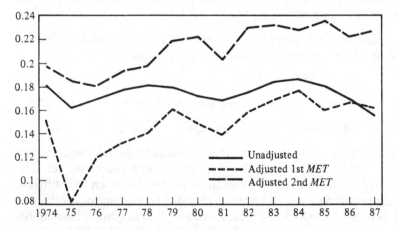

Figure 4.4   Mismatch: JR (1987) style, 1974–87

Figure 4.5 also highlights the remarkable difference between MM_2 and MM_3 and suggests that a good deal of the mismatch measured by JR (1987) could be explained with heterogeneous hiring technologies: notice the similarity of this conclusion with that concerning the indexes MM and MM_1 in the previous section of this study.

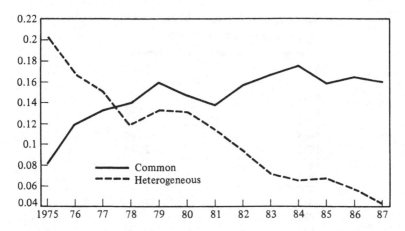

Figure 4.5 **Regional mismatch: common and heterogeneous hiring function, 1975–87**

4.2 Age and industrial mismatch

So far, we have focused only on regional mismatch. In this section we shall briefly consider age and industrial mismatch. Age mismatch is of potential interest because of both the distribution of unemployment by age (see Table 4.4 above) and the ageing of the Japanese labour force (see Figure 4.6). Moreover, in an economy characterised by long tenures and extensive on-the-job training, age mismatch is also a rough proxy of skill mismatch. The JR (1987) index of age mismatch (MM_2) based on eight

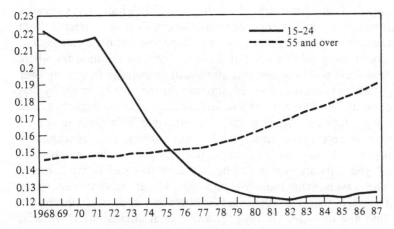

Figure 4.6 **Labour force share by age: the young and the old, 1968–87**

Table 4.9. *Age mismatch, JR (1987) style, 8 age groups, 1972–88*

Year	%
1972	19.80
1973	15.65
1974	15.82
1975	20.03
1976	20.14
1977	18.75
1978	19.20
1979	17.86
1980	16.83
1981	18.12
1982	19.30
1983	20.29
1984	19.89
1985	19.51
1986	19.92
1987	20.46
1988	17.66

age groups and on unadjusted vacancies is presented in Table 4.9. The index is slightly counter-cyclical, but has no positive trend. Further disaggregation by sex and age reveals little more (see Tachibanaki and Sakurai, 1988). This conclusion obviously depends on the hypothesis that the hiring function is homogeneous and that registered vacancies are a good measure of total vacancies.

Industrial mismatch is more difficult to grasp. While industrial vacancies are a well-defined concept, industrial unemployment presents both measurement and conceptual problems. Japanese industrial unemployment counts only job leavers and classifies them by the industry where they held their previous job; this classification changes frequently over time. Where concept is concerned, suppose for the sake of simplicity that the economy consists only of two industries, 'software engineers' and 'hamburger flippers'. Since it takes in principle little training for an unemployed software engineer to flip hamburgers, it is conceptually difficult to classify as mismatch unemployment the number of unemployed software engineers who could be allocated to flip hamburgers. The reason is that industrial and occupational mismatch is usually meant to imply that it takes substantial time and resources to convert old skills into new ones (see Oi, 1987 for a very clear discussion). Obviously, things are easier when we think of an excess of unemployed unskilled workers in the presence of unfilled skilled jobs.

A standard measure of industrial mismatch is Lilien's sigma (1982), which is given by the relative dispersion of employment growth rates among industries. This index is easy to compute because it does not require data on unemployment by industry. It is, however, difficult to interpret. The most obvious criticism has been raised by Abraham and Katz (1986), who show that Lilien's sigma is not in general independent of aggregate demand fluctuations, a substantial problem when one wishes to measure 'residual' or 'frictional' unemployment. Attempts to take care of this problem have been made, among others, by Evans (1988) and Neelin (1987). Another criticism is that the original index ignores the issues of persistency in the direction of employment changes, which could be captured by adding to the variance of current employment changes the covariances of sequential employment changes (see Davis, 1987). Last, but not least, Lilien's sigma takes mismatch as an exogenous factor, which basically means treating industrial employment shocks symmetrically and independently of the industry involved. As mentioned above, it makes a difference for the issue of mismatch whether unemployment inflows occur in the 'software engineers'' sector or in the 'hamburger flippers'' sector. It also makes a difference whether the reallocation of labour from a declining to an expanding industry is achieved mainly by quits or mainly by hiring new graduates. Since new entrants have little firm-specific human capital and could enter any sector, adjustment to the same size of industrial turbulence is bound to be quicker in an economy such as Japan, where interfirm mobility is low and hirings of new graduates very important (see Higuchi, 1988 and Oi, 1987).

These objections notwithstanding, the index has been used extensively in empirical work and we present it here for the sake of international comparison. Figure 4.7 shows Lilien's sigma for the period 1970–87 based on 9 and on 12 industries. Both versions of the index are counter-cyclical, as in Britain and in the United States, and stationary. If industrial turbulence *per se* affects unemployment, we would expect to find that Lilien's sigma enters significantly and positively in a regression of the unemployment rate which controls for aggregate demand shocks. Since industrial mismatch affects unemployment and vacancies in the same direction, we also would expect that Lilien's sigma would have a positive effect on the vacancy rate (see Abraham and Katz, 1986). The issue is explored in Table 4.10, which presents the results from fitting on quarterly data 69:3–87:4 unemployment and vacancy rates on their past values, trends, unanticipated money supply growth and Lilien' sigma.

The results clearly suggest that the predictions above are not borne out

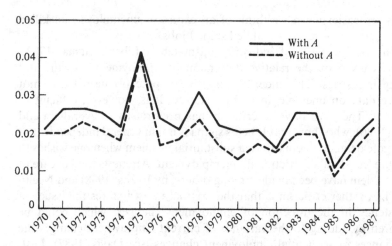

Figure 4.7   Lilien's sigma, with and without agriculture, 1970–87

by the data.[13] An increase in industrial turbulence *reduces* the vacancy rate, which suggests a movement along the u/v curve rather than a shift of it. The implication is that Lilien's sigma could be a proxy of aggregate demand rather than of mismatch. This might explain why industrial turbulence has no effect on unemployment once aggregate demand shocks have been controlled for. The findings in column (2) are not surprising from a mere statistical viewpoint. In Japan adjusted vacancies and Lilien's sigma are integrated of order zero whereas the unemployment rate is integrated of order one. If we regress a non-stationary variable on a stationary one, the theoretical value of the coefficient should be zero (see Granger, 1986). These findings could also be explained with a straightforward extension of Lilien's model which takes explicitly into account some institutional features of the Japanese labour market. The model can be conveniently summarised in the following five equations.

$$U_t - U_{t-1} = INF_t - OUT_t \tag{16}$$

$$INF_t = L_t + bQ_t + e_{1t} \tag{17}$$

$$L_t = c - d[DE_t + Q_t] + fS_t + e_{2t} \tag{18}$$

$$Q_t = g - hU_t + e_{3t} \tag{19}$$

$$OUT_t = iU_{t-1} + \Sigma jk(j)\,UDM_{t-j} + mS_t + e_{4t} \tag{20}$$

where U is unemployment
   INF is inflows in the unemployment pool
   OUT is outflows in the unemployment pool

Table 4.10. *The relation between Lilien's sigma, unemployment and vacancies, quarterly data, 69: 3–87: 4*

Dependent variable	(1) v (adjusted)		(2) u
s	− 0.100		0.005
	[− 1.91]		[0.22]
s[− 1]	0.062		− 0.019
	[− 1.18]		[0.45]
s[− 2]	0.703		0.109
	[− 1.35]		[0.45]
udm	− 0.024		− 0.007
	[− 0.61]		[− 0.39]
udm[− 1]	0.069		− 0.018
	[1.74]		[− 0.98]
udm[− 2]	0.093		− 0.004
	[2.29]		[− 0.20]
v[− 1]	0.681	u[− 1]	0.785
	[5.78]		[5.72]
v[− 2]	0.467	u[− 2]	− 0.309
	[3.46]		[0.23]
v[− 3]	− 0.352		—
	[− 1.35]		
R²	0.936		0.968
LM[4]	7.08		7.10

Notes:
s is the net Lilien's sigma.
udm is unanticipated money supply.
LM is the Lagrange multiplier test for serial correlation.
t-values within brackets.
Seasonal dummies included.
Method: OLS.

L is layoffs
Q is quits
DE is employment changes
S is Lilien's sigma
UDM is unanticipated money supply
e_{it} is a random term.

Equation (16) defines unemployment changes as the difference between inflows and outflows. Equation (17) defines inflows as a function of layoffs and $E − U$ quits. Equation (18) defines layoffs as a negative function of net hirings and a positive function of Lilien's sigma. Equation

Table 4.11. *Percentage of firms which have entered or are planning to enter new lines of business, sample of 4500 firms with more than 100 employees (multiple answers allowed)*

	Have entered between 1980 and August 1987	Will enter in the next five years
Product diversification within main line of business	61.3	53.8
Entry into a new line of business	15.2	12.7

Source: Japanese Ministry of Labour, *Sangyo Rodo Jiho Chosa*, 1988.

(19) defines pro-cyclical quits. Equation (20) finally expresses outflows from the unemployment pool (1/unemployment duration) as a function of previous unemployment, unanticipated monetary policy and Lilien's sigma.

Model (16)–(20) is equivalent to Lilien's original formulation apart from the inclusion of S_t in equation (20). This inclusion is meant to capture the fact that industrial turbulence increases both involuntary separations which end up in the unemployment pool and flows from the unemployment pool to the non-labour force (discouraged workers). As documented in Ono (1981) and Hayami, Higuchi and Seike (1985), the female participation ratio in Japan declined very sharply after the first oil shock. This decline corresponds to the peak in Lilien's sigma and points to a substantial discouraged worker effect. Some manipulation of the equations above yields

$$U_t = z_1 + z_1 U_{t-1} + \sum_{j=0}^{N} z_{2j} UDM_{t-j} + [f - m) S_t \qquad (21)$$

+ error terms

Equation (21) shows that the impact of Lilien's sigma on unemployment could be positive, negative or zero depending on the relative values of parameters f and m and that the results in Table 4.10 could be explained if parameters f and m had similar values. There is some evidence that parameter f in Japan is low by international standards as firms in dire straits respond first by moving workers around and then by laying off (see

Table 4.12. *Reasons for entry into new lines of business, sample of 4500 firms with more than 100 employees (multiple answers allowed)*

	Have entered between 1980 and August 1987	Will enter in the next five years
Demand in the current line of business is sluggish	52.3	66.5
Demand in the new line is brisk	47.8	41.8
Actual technology can be applied in new line	59.1	56.9
Labour surplus in the current line	25.1	26.9

Source: Japanese Ministry of Labour, *Sangyo Rodo Jiho Chosa*, 1988.

Brunello, 1988 and Ono, 1989).[14] There is also evidence of markedly pro-cyclical labour supply at least up to the beginning of the 1980s (see Brunello, 1989).

The fact that Japanese firms tend to 'internalise' mismatch and thus reduce the size of parameter f can be documented with the data in Tables 4.11–4.13. Table 4.11 shows the percentage of firms in a sample of 4500 that entered or plan to enter new lines of business. Table 4.12 shows that the need to place surplus labour is an important reason to open a new business line. Table 4.13 stresses that transfers of employees from the current to the new lines of business are of paramount importance as a method of filling new vacancies.[15]

To summarise this section, there is precious little evidence that either age or industrial mismatch in Japan have increased in the last fifteen years or so. Given the pitfalls associated with the standard measurement tools,

Table 4.13. *Methods of filling vacancies in the new lines of business, sample of 4500 firms with more than 100 employees (multiple answers allowed)*

Hirings from school graduates	32.1
Hirings from job changers	37.1
Transfers from current line of business, including dispatchments to subsidiaries	81.2
Temporary inflow of employees on loan from other firms or from employment agencies	12.8

Source: Japanese Ministry of Labour, *Sangyo Rodo Jiho Chosa*, 1988.

however, it is difficult to say whether the lack of trend results from underlying economic behaviour or from measurement errors. Lilien's sigma has no significant effect on the unemployment rate, both because it proxies aggregate demand shocks and because of institutional factors which lead firms to internalise mismatch and reduce its impact on the unemployment rate.

5   Mismatch and the macro u/v curve

Most OECD countries have witnessed during the 1970s and 1980s repeated shifts in their macro u/v curve (see JLNW, 1991 for Britain and Summers, 1986, Abraham, 1987 and Topel and Murphy, 1987 for the United States). A number of potential explanations for these shifts have been offered, including changes in the degree of imbalance between local unemployment and vacancies (mismatch once again). In this final section we shall look at the Japanese macro u/v curve and discuss whether mismatch has played any significant role in its eventual shifts.

Consider a steady-state economy where outflows from the unemployment pool are equal to inflows. Inflows are usually modelled as a fixed proportion of total employment. This makes sense in countries such as Britain and Japan where, contrary to the United States, 'the outs win' in the dynamics of unemployment. As in the case of Britain, the inflow rate in Japan is relatively small and exhibits little variation when compared with the outflow rate (see Ariga *et al.*, 1987). Outflow rates are modelled by assuming an aggregate hiring function which depends positively on aggregate unemployment and vacancies. Here we follow Holzer (1989) and model the equality between aggregate inflows and outflows as follows

$$tE = b(s_L U)^x (s_F V)^y \tag{22}$$

where E is employment, t is the exogenous separation rate, U is unemployment, V is vacancies, $s(L) \Rightarrow s_L$ and $s(F) \Rightarrow s_F$ express the search intensity of workers and firms respectively and b, x, y are parameters of the matching technology.

It is straightforward to derive from (22) the long run u/v curve

$$V/U = b/t^{1/y} s_L^{-x/y} s_F^{-1} U^{-(x+y)/y} \tag{23}$$

Shifts in the aggregate u/v curve can be explained in this framework with shifts in the search intensity of firms and employees, with shifts in the separation rate or, finally, with shifts in the parameters of the aggregate matching technology. It is clear that mismatch exerts its direct influence through the latter. An indirect influence on search intensities cannot be

Table 4.14. *IV estimate of the macro (u/v) curve, annual data, 1969–87*

| | Dependent variable: $\log(U/E)$ | |
	(1)	(2)
Constant	− 6.760	− 5.214
	(− 7.57)	(− 7.62)
$\log(V/E)$	− 0.924	− 0.472
	(− 6.06)	(− 6.45)
$\log(U/E)_{-1}$	0.021	0.103
	(0.15)	(0.77)
Trend	0.029	0.027
	(4.96)	(4.45)
SEE	0.045	0.047
SC	8.82 [5]	6.44 [5]
SSC	1.86 [2]	3.12 [2]
H	0.04 [1]	0.01 [1]

Notes:
Column (1) is based on unadjusted vacancies.
Column (2) is based on adjusted vacancies (first method).
SC is the Sargan test for instrument validity.
SCC is the Sargan test for serial correlation of residuals.
H is a score test for heteroscedasticity of residuals.
t-values within parentheses; degrees of freedom within brackets.

Additional instruments include the lags of U/E, the separation rate, real GNP, the share of insured unemployed, the share of women in the labour force and the share of services in total unemployment.

excluded *a priori* if the returns and costs of search depend both on the first and on the second moment of the distribution of unemployment and vacancies (see Appendix).

By focusing exclusively on off-the-job search, this framework excludes shifts originated by changes in the composition of total search between on-the-job and off-the-job search. As discussed in the Appendix, however, this exclusion is not likely to modify our results.

We start by fitting a macro u/v curve for Japan where we replace the shifting variables in (23) with a 'catch-all' time trend. Data on vacancies are both unadjusted and adjusted as in column (2) of Table 4.8. Table 4.14 presents our results for the period 1969–87. Notice that adjusting the data affects the slope of the u/v curve but has no influence whatsoever on the parameters of the time trend. Our results show that the unemployment curve in Japan, as elsewhere, has shifted outwards in the past twenty years or so.

Next, we try to capture these shifts with economic variables related to

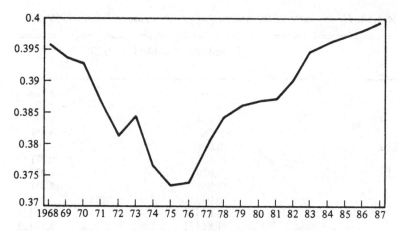

Figure 4.8   Employed women: share of total employment, 1968–87

search intensity, separations and the matching technology. Our variables are the percentage of women in the labour force (*FEM*), the percentage of labour force aged 55 years and more (*G2*), the percentage of total employment engaged in the service industry (*LSER*) and the percentage of insured unemployment (*BEN*). Variables *FEM*, *LSER* and *BEN* are plotted in Figures 4.8, 4.9 and 4.10. As for mismatch, we include the unadjusted index MM_2 of age mismatch and *S*, Lilien's sigma. Regional mismatch is excluded both because we have too few observations and because it appears to decline, not increase, over time.

It is instructive to look first at the statistical properties of these variables.

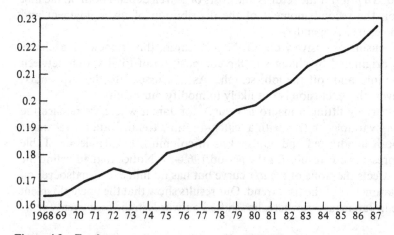

Figure 4.9   Employment share: service sector, 1968–87

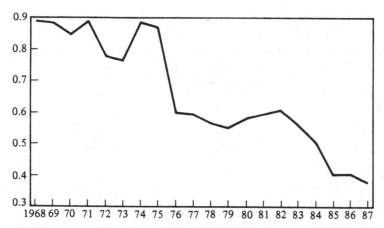

Figure 4.10   Unemployment insurance: share of insured unemployed, 1968–87

In particular, we want to know whether they are all integrated of the same order. This is a crucial statistical property that we require in order to explain the long-run comovements of unemployment and vacancy rates. If a variable is integrated of order one (non-stationary) whereas another variable is integrated of order zero (stationary), their dynamic behaviour should diverge over time rather than converge to some sort of 'equilibrium relationship' (see Granger, 1986). Table 4.15 presents the Augmented Dickey–Fuller (ADF) tests of all the variables of interest; small

Table 4.15. *Augmented Dickey–Fuller (ADF) tests, annual data, 1968–87*

Variable	Statistic
u	− 1.52
v unadjusted	− 5.97
v adjusted (as in Column (2) of Table 4.10)	− 4.77
s	− 3.19
v/u unadjusted	− 2.85
v/u adjusted	− 2.37
LSER	0.59
BEN	0.47
G55	0.17
FEM	− 2.87
Lilien sigma (9 sectors)	− 9.54
Lilien sigma (12 sectors)	− 6.84
Age mismatch	− 11.2

Note: All the regressions include two lags and a drift. The critical value at the 5% level of confidence is − 3.00.

Table 4.16. *Cointegrating vector and error correction model, macro (u/v) curve, annual data, 1969–87*

	Cointegrating vector Dependent variable: v/u	
Constant	− 3.565	(− 7.95)
LSER	0.900	(2.71)
FEM	1.01	(2.67)
u	− 1.792	(− 15.96)
R^2	0.993	
ADF test of residuals	− 13.65	

	Dynamic model Dependent variable: Dv/u			
$Dv/u(- 1)$	0.306	(0.79)		
Du	− 1.753	(− 11.30)		
$Du(- 1)$	0.796	(1.07)		
DMM_2	—		0.497	(1.99)
$DMM_2(- 1)$	—		− 0.297	(− 1.36)
$DMM_2(- 2)$	—		0.344	(1.29)
DS	2.045	(0.77)		
$DS(- 1)$	− 0.996	(− 0.40)		
$DS(- 2)$	0.311	(0.16)		
$RES(- 1)$	− 0.934	(− 2.62)	− 0.661	(− 2.20)
R^2	0.975		0.984	
LM(2)	1.93		1.13	

Note: The regressions include a constant. LM is the Lagrange multiplier test for serial correlation of residuals.

letters indicate logarithms. These tests are suggestive of the fact that the vacancy rate, the separation rate, MM_2 (age) and Lilien's sigma are stationary. Non-stationarity cannot be rejected for all the remaining variables.[16]

Since the v/u ratio is also non-stationary, it makes sense to look for a long-run 'equilibrium relationship' involving the vacancy/unemployment ratio and non-stationary variables such as *U, LSER, BEN, FEM* and *G55*. To use a fashionable expression, such a relationship requires that these variables should be cointegrated. It is plain, however, that it makes no sense at all to try to include mismatch, a stationary variable *according to our measures MM_2 and S*, in this cointegrating exercise. The main implication is that standard indexes of mismatch do not help explaining shifts in the long-run u/v relation.

Our preferred cointegrating regression is shown in Table 4.16. Variables *G*55 and *BEN* are excluded because they are not significant once *LSER* and *FEM* have been controlled for.[17] The shift in the Japanese u/v curve can thus be explained with the increasing share of services and women in the labour force.

The fact that our indexes of mismatch cannot explain shifts in the equilibrium u/v locus does not rule out the possibility that these indexes have a role to play in the dynamic adjustment from a steady state to the next. Given the close relationship between cointegration and error correction (see Granger and Engle, 1987), we investigate this possibility with the following equation

$$
\begin{aligned}
Dv/u = a_0 &+ a_1 Dv/u_{-1} + a_2 Du \\
&+ a_3 Du_{-1} + a_4 DS + a_5 DS_{-1} + a_6 S_{-2} \\
&+ a_7 RES_{-1} + e
\end{aligned}
\tag{24}
$$

where D is the first-difference operator, e is the error term and RES is the stationary residual from the cointegrating vector.

The results presented in the second part of Table 4.16 suggest that (changes in) age mismatch MM_2 influence (changes in) the vacancy/ unemployment ratio along the dynamic adjustment path from one steady-state equilibrium to the next.[18]

6   Conclusions

The main reason why macroeconomists are interested in mismatch is that theory suggests that it could affect the NAIRU. This study has reviewed some of the existing measures of mismatch in the context of the Japanese labour market during the period 1970–87. The main results can be summarised as follows.

1. The Japanese macro u/v curve has shifted outwards during the period under study.
2. There is no evidence that increases in *regional* mismatch helped this shift.
3. Our measure of regional mismatch (MM_1) points both to a slight reduction and to increased persistence in the last few years. The adjustment of local real hourly wages have helped reduce the impact of local shocks. This evidence can be explained only in part by the reduction in labour mobility among areas. The reduction in the size of local shocks, accompanied by the reduction in the size of macro business cycles since the first oil shock, is an important part of the whole story.

4. Regional mismatch according to JR (1987) does not exhibit any upward trend. This result could be driven, however, by equilibrium heterogeneity. If this heterogeneity is controlled for, regional mismatch shows a clear negative trend, which confirms point 3 above.
5. Age mismatch is stationary and cannot help explain the shifts in the steady-state u/v curve. Evidence suggests that it does help in explaining the dynamic process followed by unemployment and vacancies as they adjust from one long-run equilibrium to the next.
6. Lilien's sigma does not help explain the dynamics of aggregate unemployment but helps predict aggregate vacancies. An explanation of the poor performance of the index in the unemployment equation stresses the institutional features of the Japanese labour market, and in particular the importance of hirings from school pro-cyclical (female) labour supply and inter/intrafirm transfers.

Given all these results, how do we explain the current drift in the macro u/v curve? The evidence in this study (and in Hamada and Kurosaka, 1986) suggests that the increased share of the service sector and of women in the labour force are important factors. The first factor works mainly through the higher separation rate and (probably) the lower search intensity of firms, whereas the second factor is expected to lead both to a higher separation rate and a lower search intensity by workers.

As a final remark, it is important to stress that we have focused almost entirely on *regional* mismatch. As the discussant of this study rightly points out (see p. 180 below), the exclusion of skill mismatch could be crucial as shortages of skilled labour are, and have been, a major policy issue in Japan. Our omission of skill mismatch is justified only by the lack of adequate data on a time series basis. We have tried to proxy skill with age; this proxy makes sense only if skills can be acquired exclusively on the job and are entirely firm-specific. Obviously this is not very satisfactory even for Japan, a country with relatively long tenures and a high content of firm-specific human capital. Needless to say, a satisfactory analysis must await the development of an adequate data set.

APPENDIX

1. Here we follow closely Pissarides (1986, 552–3). Let the probability p of moving from unemployment to employment be defined as

$$p = h[c, V/U, \text{var}(V/U)] \tag{A1}$$

where c is search intensity, V/U is the unemployment/vacancy ratio and var is its variance across areas, industries or skills.

The function h is homogeneous of degree one in V and U.

Let the cost of search be

$$k = k[c, \text{var}(V/U)] \tag{A2}$$

The cost of search and the probability of finding a job are assumed to depend on the level and the dispersion of unemployment and vacancies. The asset value during unemployment is

$$rWu = b + p[We - Wu] \tag{A3}$$

where b is the income stream (unemployment benefits gross of the value of leisure and net of search costs), and $p[We - Wu]$ is the expected capital gain from changing status in a steady-state environment (see Pissarides, 1986 for the notation).

The asset value during employment is

$$rWe = w + s[Wu - We] \tag{A4}$$

where we assume that the wage rate w is constant and that flows out of employment end up in the unemployment pool. Substituting equation (A4) into equation (A3) and maximising with respect to c, we obtain the following implicit function

$$c^* = c[V/U, \text{var}(V/U), w, b, r \dots] \tag{A5}$$

so that the dispersion of unemployment and vacancies affects search intensity.

2. Assume that search can be either on-the-job (J) or off-the-job (U). Let the matching function be a nested Cobb–Douglas with constant returns to scale in the total number of job seekers

$$tE = b[(s_u U)^{ax}(s_j J)^{(1-a)x}](s_F V)^y \tag{A6}$$

where s_u and s_j are respectively the search intensity of unemployed and employed workers. Define

$$K = s_j J / s_u U \tag{A7}$$

and assume that K is time-invariant. Then equation (23) can be extended as follows

$$V/U = bt^{1/y} s^{-x/y} s^{-1} U^{-(x+y)/y} K^{-x/y} \tag{A8}$$

An increase in K reduces vacancies for each unemployment rate and shifts the u/v curve towards the origin. In Japan the unemployment rate between 1974 and 1987 increased from 1.4% to 2.9%, whereas the share of those searching on the job increased from 1.8% to 4.2% (see Ono, 1989, Table 10.7, p. 217). Given search intensities, these numbers suggest that K increased during the same period, with an implied inward shift of the u/v curve. Changes in the parameter K cannot therefore be responsible for the observed outward shift in the u/v curve.

DATA APPENDIX

1. *Unemployment and vacancies by skill*   Data on vacancies by skill group are from a special survey on vacancies carried out by the Ministry of Labour and published since 1981 as the Survey on Labour Mobility (*Koyo Doko Chosa Hokoku*). This is an establishment survey on firms with more than 5 employ-

ees. 'Vacancies' are defined as openings for regular employees for which the firm is actively searching.

Unemployment by previous occupation is available from the special spring issue of the Labour Force Survey (*Rodoryoku Chosa Hokoku*); this classification is hardly a classification by skill. A rough estimate of unemployment by skill at a given point of time can be obtained by using data on the stock of job seekers who are registered with the prefectural employment agencies. These data are available by skill from the Survey on the Labour Market (*Rodo Shijo Nenpo*). They include a small proportion of on the job searchers. Our estimate of U_i used in Table 4.1 is given by

$$U_i/E_i = \frac{[V_i/E_i]*0.94}{V_i/JS_i}$$

where JS_i is the stock of job seekers who have applied to the employment agencies, V_i is vacancies by skill, E_i employment by skill and 0.94 is the percentage of the annual flow of JS who are searching off the job.

2. *Data for equation* (9)   These come from the following sources:

W_{it}:   Ministry of Labour, Annual Survey on the Wage Structure (*Chingin Census*).
TEN_{it}:   as above.
$LARGE_{it}$:   as above.
$MANUF_{it}$:   as above.
W_{it}:   is deflated by the local retail price index, available from the Office of the Prime Minister, Annual Report on Price Indexes (*Shohisha Bukka Shisu Nenpo*).
GNP_{it}:   nominal local GNP is from the Economic Planning Agency, Annual Report on Economic Accounts by Prefecture (*Kenmin Keizai Keisan Nenpo*). Real GNP is obtained by deflating nominal GNP by the local retail price index.
U_{it}:   unemployment by region is from the Ministry of Labour, Survey on the Labour Force (*Rodoryoku Chocu Hokoku*).

3. *Registered vacancies*   The widely used job offers – job seekers ratio (*JOJS*) (see for instance Hamada and Kurosaka, 1986) is based on registered unfilled vacancies over registered applications. This index is riddled with problems, which makes one wonder why many Japanese economists are willing to use it so frequently as a measure of labour market tightness. One problem is double counting of applications, as one can register in more than one office. Another problem is that registered vacancies and placements underestimate actual turnover (see Table 4.7 in the text and Inoki, 1984 for a very instructive discussion of these data).

Adjustment of vacancies is an hazardous job, which often requires strong assumptions (see Roper, 1986). One method has been suggested by Jackman, Layard and Pissarides (1984) and consists of assuming that the average duration of registered and unregistered vacancies is the same. Since outflows and inflows are equal in the steady state, this corresponds to assuming that

$$Vr/Ir = Vt/S \tag{A9}$$

where Vr is registered vacancies, Ir is inflows in the pool of registered vacancies, Vt is total vacancies and S is total separations

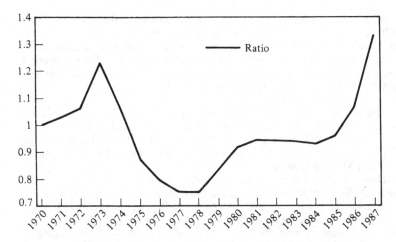

Figure 4N.1 Residential land price/gross wage, large cities, 1970–87

An alternative method exploits the fact that public employment agencies are far more effective in the countryside (Hokkaido, Kyushu) than in big metropolitan areas (especially Tokyo). This is equivalent to assuming that the duration of registered vacancies is lower than the duration of total vacancies in the countryside and higher in metropolitan areas. So we assume that

$$Vt = Vr * Engagements/Placements * w \qquad (A10)$$

where w is a weighting factor taking the (arbitrary) value of 4/3 in Hokkaido, 1/3 in Tokyo and 3/4 elsewhere.

In most of section 3 and in section 4 of the study we use the adjustment method shown in equation (A9).

4. *Variables used in Tables 4.18 and 4.19* These are from the following sources:

FEM   from Ministry of Labour, Annual Survey of the Labour Force.
G2   as above.
LSER   as above.
BEN   Ministry of Labour, Monthly Data on Unemployment Benefits (*Koyo Hoken Jigyo Geppo*).

NOTES

1 This study was written while I was with the Department of Economics, Osaka University, Japan. I wish to thank Fiorella Padoa Schioppa and Sushil Wadhwani for detailed comments and Richard Jackman for a useful conversation. I am also grateful to Kenn Ariga, Takenori Inoki, Kuramitsu Muramatsu, Fumio Ohtake and Toshiaki Tachibanaki for comments and suggestions when the original paper was presented at Kyoto University. The usual disclaimer applies.

2 This ignores frictional unemployment due to imbalances within each sector.

3 See the Data Appendix for a detailed explanation of the data.

4 In this section we shall focus on regional mismatch but the analysis can be readily extended to cover industrial and occupational mismatch.

5 These conditions include risk neutrality. Another important assumption is that no valuable leisure results from unemployment. JLS (1989) present a somewhat different version of spatial equilibrium; their major innovation is to replace equation (2) with a wage pressure equation.

6 See JLS (1989) for details.

7 This decline could be related to the increase in the residential land price/gross wage ratio in major metropolitan areas since the beginning of the 1980s and especially after 1984 (see Figure 4N.1). The impact of the house price/wage ratio on labour mobility and local wages has been studied by Bover, Muellbauer and Murphy (1989).

8 See Davidson et al. (1978) and Canning (1989).

9 The fixed effect includes the ratio of male to female employment and the share of manufacturing employment. The Arellano–Bond estimator (1988) takes explicitly into account heteroscedasticity.

10 Several experiments with the JLS wage equation yield significant aggregate effects (which include the aggregate unemployment rate). Regional unemployment is never significant if the dependent variable is the hourly real wage. It is often significant if the dependent variable includes hours. Results are available from the author on request.

11 Hiring through the public employment agency saves advertising and search costs but could lead to higher wages, especially for small firms. The law requires that each opening be screened by the prefectural agencies and rejected if pay and working conditions are significantly below average. (See Law no. 141, 30/11/1947, in *Roppo Zensho*, 1989.)

12 A simple model of heterogeneous matching functions is presented in Brunello (1990).

13 It is worth mentioning that the covariances of current and past employment changes à la Davis are usually significant in a regression similar to that presented in column (2) of Table 4.10; see Ohtake (1988).

14 Ono's evidence is based on OECD data that compare involuntary separation rates among developed countries. Conclusive international evidence that Japanese firms replace layoffs with transfers more than other firms do is hard to find. If we focus on intrafirm transfers, a rough comparison between Japan and the US suggests that the 1971–81 average of transferred employees was 3.25% in Japan and 1.25% in the United States. The Japanese number is from the Ministry of Labour *Koyo Doko Chosa* and the American number is an estimate based on the Bureau of Labor Statistics, *Employment and Earnings*. The estimate consists of assuming that 25% of the item 'other separations' are due to transfers; see Medoff (1979).

15 The degree of 'internalisation' of mismatch is probably related to the high degree of firm-specific human capital accumulated within large Japanese firms. This and the tendency to hire straight from school makes skilled labour readily available in the external labour market a relatively scarce commodity.

16 As it is well known, these tests have low power.

17 Since the correlation between $G55$ and $LSER$ is 0.97 in our sample, the results presented by Hamada and Kurosaka (1986), which suggest that only the latter variable is significant in a regression that includes both $G55$ and $LSER$, are hardly surprising.

18 Given the limited number of observations we restrict the dynamic process to exclude the changes in LSER, *FEM* and *BEN*. The main results are independent of this exclusion.

REFERENCES

Abraham, K. (1987). 'Help-Wanted Advertising, Job Vacancies and Unemployment', *Brookings Papers on Economic Activity*, **1**, 207–48.
Abraham, K. and L. Katz (1986). 'Cyclical Unemployment: Sectoral Shifts or Aggregate Disturbances?', *Journal of Political Economy*, **94**, 507–22.
Arellano, M. and S. Bond (1988). 'Some Tests of Specification for Panel Data: Monte Carlo Evidence and an Application to Employment Equations', Oxford (mimeo).
Ariga, Kenn *et al.* (1987). 'Labour Market Dynamics in Japan', *KIER Discussion Paper*, **245**, Kyoto University.
Blanchard, O. and L. Summers (1986). 'Hysteresis and the European Unemployment Problem', in S. Fischer (ed.), *NBER Macroeconomic Annual*, Cambridge: NBER.
Blanchard, O. and P. Diamond (1990). 'The Beveridge Curve', *Brookings Papers on Economic Activity*, **1**, 1–74.
Bover, O. J., Muellbauer and A. Murphy (1989). 'Housing, Wages and UK Labour Markets', *Oxford Bulletin of Economics and Statistics*, **51**, 97–162.
Brunello, G. (1988). 'Organisational Adjustment in the Japanese Labour Market: an Empirical Evaluation', *European Economic Review*, **32**, 841–60.
(1989). 'Hysteresis and "the Japanese Unemployment Problem"', *Oxford Economic Papers*, forthcoming.
(1990a). 'Real Exchange Rate Variability and Japanese Employment', *Journal of the Japanese and International Economies*, **4**, 121–38.
(1990b). 'Heterogeneous Matching, Mismatch and the Macro U–V Curve', *Economics Letters*, forthcoming.
Canning, D. (1989). 'Regional Unemployment and Wage Differentials in the UK', London: LSE (mimeo).
Davidson, J., D. Hendry, T. Srba and S. Yeo (1978). 'Econometric Modelling of the Aggregate Relationship between Consumer's Expenditure and Income in the UK', *Economic Journal*, **189**, 661–93.
Davis, S. (1987). 'Fluctuations in the Pace of Labor Reallocation', *Journal of Monetary Economics* (Supplement), **27**, 335–402.
Evans, G. (1988). 'A Cyclically Adjusted Index of Structural Imbalance', London School of Economics, Centre for Labour Economics, discussion paper, **300**.
Granger, C. (1986). 'Developments in the Study of Cointegrated Economic Variables', *Oxford Bulletin of Economics and Statistics*, **48**, 213–28.
Granger, C. and R. Engle (1987). 'Dynamics Specification with Equilibrium Constraints: Cointegration and Error Correction', *Econometrica*, **55**, 251–76.
Hall, R. (1972). 'Turnover in the Labor Force', *Brookings Papers on Economic Activity*, **3**, 709–64.
Hamada, K. and Y. Kurosaka (1986). 'Trends in Unemployment, Wages and Productivity: The Case of Japan', *Economica*, **53** (Supplement), S275–S296.
Hansen, B. (1970). 'Excess Demand, Unemployment, Vacancies and Wages', *Quarterly Journal of Economics*, **85**, 1–23.

Hayami, K., Y. Higuchi and A. Seike (1985). 'Rodo Shijo: Danjo Rodoryoku no Shugyo Kodo no Henka', in Y. Hamada (ed.), *Nihon Keizai no MacroBunseki*, Tokyo: Tokyo University Press.

Higuchi, Y. (1988). 'Senmonteki Shokugyo no Zoka to Rodo Ido', *Keizai Seminar*, **44–49**.

Holzer, H. (1989). 'Structural/Frictional and Demand Deficient Unemployment in Local Labor Markets', *NBER Working Papers*, **2652**, Cambridge: NBER.

Horiye, Y., S. Naniwa and S. Ishihara (1987). 'The Changes of Japanese Business Cycles', *Bank of Japan Monetary and Economic Studies*, 49–100.

Hsiao, C. (1986). *Analysis of Panel Data*, Cambridge: Cambridge University Press.

Inoki, T. (1984). 'Nyushoku Keiro to Rodo Shijo no Kozo – Kokyo Shokuan no Yakuwari', in K. Koike, *Gendai no Shitsugyo*,Tokyo: Domonkan, 33–53.

Jackman, R. and S. Roper (1987). 'Structural Unemployment', *Oxford Bulletin of Economics and Statistics*, **49**, 9–37.

Jackman, R., R. Layard and C. Pissarides (1984). 'On Vacancies', London School of Economics, Centre for Labour Economics, discussion paper, **165** (revised).

Jackman, R., R. Layard and S. Savouri (1990). 'Mismatch: A Framework for Thought' (Chapter 2 in this volume).

Jackman, R., R. Layard, S. Nickell and S. Wadhwani (1991). *Unemployment*, Oxford: Oxford University Press.

Japanese Ministry of Labour (1988). *Rodo Hakusho*, Tokyo.

Layard, R. and S. Nickell (1986). 'Unemployment in Britain', *Economica*, **53** (Supplement), S121–S169.

Lilien, D. (1982). 'Sectoral Shifts and Cyclical Unemployment', *Journal of Political Economy*, **90**, 777–93.

Marston, S. (1985). 'Two Views of the Geographic Distribution of Unemployment', *Quarterly Journal of Economics*, **100**, 57–79.

Medoff, J. (1979). 'Layoffs and Alternatives under Trade Unions in US Manufacturing', *American Economic Review*, **69**, 380–95.

Neelin, J. (1987). 'Sectoral Shifts and Canadian Unemployment', *Review of Economics and Statistics*, 718–23.

OECD (1989). *Employment Outlook*, Paris: OECD.

Ohtake, F. (1988). 'Sangyo Kozo no Henka to Shitsugyoritsu-Kokusai Hikaku', in K. Koike (ed.), *Kokusai Kankyoka ni okeru Koyo Mondai*, Ministry of Labour, 51–79.

Oi, W. (1987). 'Comment on the Relation between Unemployment and Sectoral Shifts', *Journal of Monetary Economics*, Supplement, **27**, 403–20.

Ono, A. (1981). *Nihon no Rodo Shijo*, Toyo Keizai.

(1989). *Nihonteki Koyo Kanko to Rodo Shijo*, Tokyo: Toyo Kenzai

Pissarides, C. (1984). 'Search Intensity, Job Advertising and Efficiency', *Journal of Labor Economics*, **2**, 128–43.

(1985). 'Short-run Equilibrium Dynamics of Unemployment, Vacancies and Real Wages', *American Economic Review*, **75**, 676–90.

(1986). 'Unemployment and Vacancies in Britain', *Economic Policy*, **3**, 489–560.

Pissarides, C. and R. Mogadhan (1989). 'Relative Wage Flexibility in Four Countries', London School of Economics, Centre for Labour Economics, discussion paper, **331**.

Roper, S. (1986). 'The Economics of Job Vacancies', London School of Economics, Centre for Labour Economics, discussion paper, **252**.

Rosen, S. (1979). 'Wage-Based Indexes of Urban Quality of Life', in P. Miesz-
kowski and M. Straszheim (eds), *Current Issues in Urban Economics*, Bal-
timore.
Summers, L. (1986). 'Why is the Rate of Unemployment so High at Full Employ-
ment?', *Brookings Papers on Economic Activity*, 2, 339–83.
Tachibanaki, T. and T. Sakurai (1988). 'Nihon no Rodo Shijo to Shitsugyo',
Keizai Keiei Kenkyu, Japan Development Bank, pp. 1–79.
Topel, R. (1986). 'Local Labor Markets', *Journal of Political Economy*, 94,
(Supplement), 111–43.
Topel, R. and K. Murphy (1987). 'The Evolution of Unemployment in the United
States: 1968–85', in S. Fischer (ed.), *NBER Macroeconomics Annual*, Cam-
bridge, MA: MIT Press, 11–68.
Wood, A. (1988). 'How Much Unemployment is Structural?', *Oxford Bulletin of
Economics and Statistics*, 50, 71–81.

Discussion

S. WADHWANI

This study is packed with information and provides a very interesting
read.

My main reservation, however, concerns the definition of 'mismatch'
that is adopted. On the study's definition, differences in unemployment
rates between regions that are *permanent* would not count, as they are said
to arise from differences in amenities. It is, however, by no means clear
that an amenities-based explanation of permanent unemployment differences is plausible. To make the point in a stark fashion, the unemployment rate in Northern Ireland has consistently exceeded that in South-
East England for at least 60 years: an amenities-based 'explanation' of
this fact would actually have to argue that Northern Ireland is more
congenial to live in, as compared to South-East England.

There are alternative theoretical models to account for relatively *persistent* unemployment differences. A labour market where 'insiders' are
powerful provides one such example. The model contained in Jackman *et
al.* (1990), is able to account for permanent differences in unemployment
rates in terms of differences in population and/or employment growth.
Since most of the dispersion in regional unemployment rates is relatively
permanent (on the author's estimates, in Japan 95% of the variation in

relative unemployment rates is permanent), it is important to study, and explain, them. The author might contend that 'mismatch' refers only to transitory differences. However, if we accept that definition then, given the relative insignificance of such transitory differences, 'mismatch' becomes a much less interesting subject of inquiry.

One can, in some models (see, for example, Jackman *et al.*, 1990), link an increase in the *dispersion* of unemployment rates (which they call mismatch) to an increase in the *level* of unemployment. For that reason alone, a time series of the dispersion is interesting, although I acknowledge that calling it 'mismatch' may cause confusion.

An intriguing fact reported in the study (but not commented on) is that in Japan, the land where wages are supposed to be highly flexible (see, for example, Grubb *et al.*, 1983), regional wages do not appear significantly to depend on regional unemployment (although they doubtless depend on aggregate unemployment). This is a new and surprising fact. Incidentally, to illustrate the difficulties in coming up with a unique definition of 'mismatch' which is always satisfactory, note that if regional wages in Japan really respond only to the national unemployment rate then, on the Jackman *et al.* (1990) definition, there is no mismatch. Yet the differences in unemployment rates might still be something of legitimate interest to economists.

No study on Japan would be complete without some reference to a practice which is unique to that country. The author's discussion of the 'internalisation' within the firm of job transfers between industrial sectors is fascinating; the fact that over a quarter of firms were considering entry into a new line of business because they had too many employees in the current line of business (Table 4.15) is strikingly different from how British managers think. The author's use of the existence of such attitudes as an explanation for the absence of any significant link between unemployment and Lilien's sigma (1982) would be more convincing if:

1. The author provided some *direct* evidence that the absence of such a link could not be explained by the *pattern* of demand shocks (cf. Abraham and Katz, 1986).
2. Is there any *direct* evidence that the discouraged worker effect rises when Lilien's sigma is high?
3. Can the author cite any evidence which shows that the effect of variations in Lilien's sigma on layoffs is lower in Japan, as compared to other countries?

This is already a rather long and fairly comprehensive study. Some evidence on regional mobility within Japan would nonetheless have been useful. Also, some discussion on the training system in Japan would have been valuable, especially in the light of Soskice (1990).

Finally, I must confess to a certain confusion as to whether I should read this study as implying that, ultimately, mismatch does not really play a significant role in explaining unemployment. Japan is widely held to be a 'miracle' country; it has managed to combine high growth rates and low unemployment rates with a relatively moderate average rate of inflation. Yet, as in many European countries, the unemployment–vacancies (u/v) relationship has shifted out. The measure of industrial turbulence, and other indices of dispersion across regions and occupations in Japan, are quite comparable with the numbers for many other OECD countries. Survey measures of the shortage of skilled labour suggest that, if anything, Japan suffers more than other OECD economies (see, for example, Wadhwani, 1987). So there is no reason to believe that Japan does especially well along the dimension of mismatch: is it, then, right to conclude that the factors that explain why European unemployment rose, but Japanese unemployment did not, are essentially orthogonal to mismatch?

REFERENCES

Abraham, K. and L. Katz (1986). 'Cyclical Unemployment: Sectoral Shifts or Aggregate Disturbances?', *Journal of Political Economy*, **94**, 507–22.

Grubb, D., R. Jackman and R. Layard (1983). 'Wage Rigidity and Unemployment in OECD Countries', *European Economic Review*, **21**, 11–39.

Jackman, R., R. Layard and S. Savouri (1990). 'Mismatch: A Framework for Thought' (Chapter 2 in this volume).

Lilien, D. (1982). 'Sectoral Shocks and Cyclical Unemployment', *Journal of Political Economy*, **90**, 777–93.

Soskice, D. (1990). 'Skills Mismatch, Training Systems and Equilibrium Unemployment: A Comparative Institutional Analysis' (Chapter 9 in this volume).

Wadhwani, S. (1987). 'The Macroeconomic Implications of Profit-Sharing: Some Empirical Evidence', *Economic Journal*, **97** (Supplement).

5 Mismatch and Internal Migration in Spain, 1962–86[1]

SAMUEL BENTOLILA and JUAN J. DOLADO

1 Introduction

High European equilibrium unemployment has been the most important economic development in the last fifteen years, and macroeconomists have put a lot of effort into trying to explain it. The studies made for the first Chelwood Gate conference, collected in *The Rise in Unemployment* (Bean *et al.*, 1986), analysed the roles of real wages and demand contraction in the increase of unemployment after 1973, but then the persistence of high unemployment over time became the main issue. This task was picked up by the second Chelwood Gate conference, which studied the role of capital constraints and insider wage-setting in generating persistence. Among the common findings across countries in the latter conference, as summarised by Drèze (1990), was that employment was consistently and significantly below the minimum of labour supply, classical and Keynesian employment.

Deficient matching between labour supply and demand became a natural suspect to explain this finding, and so the first steps are being taken, for example in Chapter 2 of this volume, to develop a theory of mismatch. It is also useful to provide empirical evidence on the various dimensions of mismatch, at the very least to find out which are more relevant for each country; this study is devoted to the latter task for the case of Spain.

Spain had very low unemployment – around 1% – in the 1960s but then experienced a sustained increase in the 1970s and the first half of the 1980s, reaching a 21.5% rate in 1985, by far the highest in the OECD. Since then, the unemployment rate has drifted downwards, reaching 17.2% in 1989. Spain is unfortunately thus an interesting country in which to study the persistence of unemployment, and of mismatch as a potential cause for it.

Bentolila and Blanchard (1990) analyse the causes of the rise in

182

unemployment in Spain and argue, in line with 'insider–outsider' theories, that one of these causes is that high unemployment induces changes in the labour market through which increases in actual unemployment can lead to rises in equilibrium unemployment – i.e., the so-called 'hysteresis' effect. In particular, they argue that the prolonged period of high unemployment in Spain has contributed to a reduction of the search intensity of the unemployed, above all of their willingness to look for work in regions other than their own – i.e., a source of mismatch from the labour supply side.

In order to examine the likelihood of mismatch being an important cause for the rise in Spanish unemployment, we follow an eclectic approach, analysing the issue from several angles. One view – Jackman, Layard and Savouri's in Chapter 2 of this volume – equates mismatch to relative unemployment rate dispersion. In the first part of section 2 we document the fact that unemployment rate imbalances in absolute terms have greatly widened in Spain as the national rate was rising; nevertheless, when we compute a relative unemployment rate dispersion measure we find that it has fallen over time according to most characteristics of the labour force, seemingly implying that mismatch has been falling, not rising, over time.

In the second part of section 2 we pursue a different strategy. Disequilibrium models interpret mismatch as arising from heterogeneity of regimes (classical, Keynesian, repressed inflation) across different sectors in the economy. In line with the second Chelwood Gate conference approach, we thus take the estimated measure of mismatch derived from the disequilibrium model fitted to the Spanish economy, and regress it on variables related to mismatch, such as the proportion of long-term unemployed in the labour force, regional unemployment rate dispersion, interregional migration flows, relative energy prices, or employment turbulence, finding a very good fit. This suggests that this measure might be a good proxy for overall mismatch in Spain. Unfortunately, it behaves exactly in the opposite way that the dispersion indices commented on above do: it rises steadily until the mid-1980s, and then falls a little: it clearly implies that mismatch is today at historically high levels in Spain. At the end of section 2 we list a number of reasons leading us to think that the latter index might give a more accurate view than the former.

Finally, the fact that regional variables play a key role in explaining the latter index of mismatch reinforces our previous belief that the geographical aspect of the labour market is important in understanding the rise in unemployment in Spain. There have always been genuine differences in languages, uses, etc. across Spanish regions, and this could easily lead to the segmentation of markets. Migration flows, which in the early

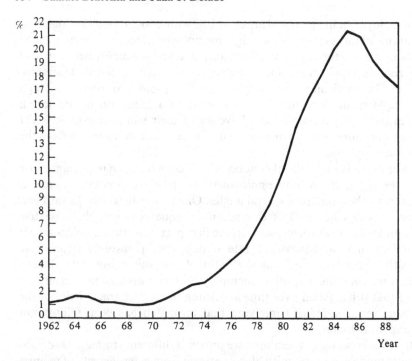

Figure 5.1   National unemployment rate, 1962–89

1960s were high both towards Europe and within Spain, have also fallen dramatically, coinciding with the rise in unemployment. Bentolila and Blanchard (1990) stress the rise in overall unemployment as the main factor inhibiting labour mobility in Spain. In section 3 we analyse this proposition by setting up an econometric model of internal migration in Spain. We find that net interregional migration flows respond to economic incentives – in particular to unemployment and wage differentials – but with low elasticities and long lags. The observed fall in these flows can therefore be partially explained by the reductions in such differentials that have taken place in Spain. We find also that migration flows are deterred by housing price differentials[2] and by the overall unemployment rate. In consequence, while labour mobility will increase as the overall unemployment rate continues to fall in the next few years, this process is bound to be slow, and there is a role for policy in speeding up the process. We dwell on such measures at the end of section 3.

Finally, section 4 draws some preliminary conclusions, and opens issues for future research.

2   Stylised facts of Spanish unemployment and mismatch indices

2.1   Evolution over time

In this sub-section we sketch an account of the evolution of Spanish unemployment over time, depicted in Figure 5.1. From 1960 to 1974 Spain made the transition from an agricultural to an industrial economy, and experienced high growth, low unemployment, moderate inflation and high productivity growth. In 1975 Franco died, and the two years it took to establish the new political institutions saw a wage explosion and the transmission of wage costs and the oil price shock into booming inflation (25% in 1977). The inflationary momentum was broken by a contractionary monetary policy and a series of nationwide agreements on wage growth, whereby wage moderation was progressively attained.

The reduction of inflation implied the cost of a sharp slowdown and a large increase in unemployment, which reached a staggering 21.5% in 1985. The causes of the increase have been extensively analysed (see Dolado *et al.*, 1986, Fina, 1987, Andrés *et al.*, 1990 or Bentolila and Blanchard, 1990). The initial rise in unemployment can be attributed to the large increases in real wages and the contractionary monetary policies that ensued; there is much less consensus about the continued rise in the 1980s. Bentolila and Blanchard (1990) single out three factors in explaining such a rise: a profit squeeze which led many firms to bankruptcy and the remaining ones to curtail investment, a productive reorganisation effort which caused massive labour shedding, and hysteresis effects, by which equilibrium unemployment rose with actual unemployment. In this study we are specially concerned with the last-mentioned.

The literature on hysteresis, which originally stressed the lack of concern of 'insider' wage-setters for the interests of unemployed 'outsiders', has recently shifted emphasis towards the determinants of the pressure from the unemployed on the wage-setting process (Layard and Nickell, 1987). Hysteresis arises if depressed labour markets lead to less downward wage pressure from outsiders: this may happen if, for instance, the long-term unemployed lose skills or get discouraged and stop searching.

As in most European countries, equilibrium unemployment – i.e., the rate compatible with steady inflation or the NAIRU – has risen in Spain, although not as much as actual unemployment, given that inflation has fallen since 1977; and it is a common finding that unemployment puts little downward pressure on wages in Spain (e.g., Dolado and Malo de Molina, 1985, Dolado *et al.*, 1986, or Andrés and García, 1989). Moreover, in 1986–8, a boom period in which output and employment grew respectively by 4.7% and 2.7% annually, unemployment fell by only

2 percentage points, from 21.5% in 1985 to 19.5% in 1988. In contrast, during 1989, unemployment fell more quickly, to 17.2%, but inflation accelerated by 2 percentage points, to 6.8%, an overheating typically arising near equilibrium unemployment.

The long period of high unemployment in Spain has almost certainly induced changes in the behaviour of the unemployed, towards reducing their search effort and so decreasing downward pressure on wage bargains. There are several features consistent with this: the stigma of being unemployed is mostly gone, the pool of the unemployed has been relatively stagnant until recently, unemployment falls mostly on spouses and youths – who can survive while being out of work – and, finally, migration flows, which were high in the early 1960s, are now quite small.

How much of the rise in equilibrium unemployment can be attributed to mismatch? We lack a fully worked-out model of the relationship between the NAIRU and mismatch, and do not develop one in this study. Instead, we follow an eclectic approach, by computing two sets of measures which, under two different models, proxy for mismatch. If we were to get similar answers from both measures, we would feel confident in having found a robust stylised fact. The two models we are referring to are the Jackman–Layard–Savouri (hereafter JLS) multisectoral model of determination of the NAIRU (see Chapter 2 in this volume), and the Sneesens–Drèze disequilibrium model. In the next two sub-sections we shall consider each in turn.

2.2   Mismatch as unemployment rate dispersion

In their Chapter 2 in this volume, JLS derive a relation between mismatch and the NAIRU in a multisectoral model, using two building blocks: the factor price frontier arising from a Cobb–Douglas production function, and a double-logarithmic wage function whereby sectoral wages depend on their own-unemployment rate. The combination of both elements gives rise to an unemployment frontier – i.e., the locus of all combinations of sectoral unemployment rates consistent with the absence of inflationary pressure. In this setup, the movement of unemployed workers from relatively high to relatively low unemployment-rate sectors can reduce the national unemployment rate without raising inflation. As a consequence, unemployment rate dispersion is a sign of mismatch, a natural measure of the latter turning out to be (half) the squared coefficient of variation of sectoral unemployment rates, i.e.:

$$MM = \tfrac{1}{2}\,\mathrm{var}(u_i/u_N) \tag{1}$$

where u_i denotes the unemployment rate of sector (group) i and u_N the

Table 5.1. *Composition of unemployment, fourth quarter, %, 1976, 1985 and 1989*

	Percentage structure			Unemployment rate		
	1976	1985	1989	1976	1985	1989
(a) *Age*						
16–19 years old	31.5	19.8	12.8	17.1	54.9	36.6
20–24 years old	19.6	28.3	27.7	10.6	42.5	32.3
25–54 years old	43.0	46.6	52.8	3.6	15.7	13.5
55 years old +	5.9	5.4	6.7	2.1	8.0	8.3
Total	100.0	100.0	100.0	4.9	21.2	16.9
(b) *Sex*						
Male	65.7	59.2	49.2	5.2	18.6	12.7
Female	34.3	40.8	50.8	6.8	27.6	24.8
Total	100.0	100.0	100.0	4.9	21.2	16.9
(c) *Skill*						
Professional and managerial	1.9	2.4	3.1	1.2	6.0	4.9
Clerical	4.8	5.2	6.3	2.4	11.0	9.3
Other non-manual	3.7	4.6	4.3	1.9	10.3	7.5
Unskilled	89.6	87.8	86.2	6.0	26.1	21.5
Total	100.0	100.0	100.0	4.9	21.2	16.9

Sources: See Appendix 2.

national rate (hereafter the sub-index N denotes the national value of a variable).

In the application of this model, before reporting computed MM indices, we document that, in fact, important unemployment rate imbalances have developed in Spain as unemployment was rising. We present, in Table 5.1, the breakdown of unemployment by age, sex and skill in (the fourth quarter of) three selected years. Its composition has shifted towards the 20–54-year-old group, and by 1989 more than half of the unemployed were in their prime age. Still, since the latter is the largest group in the labour force, their unemployment rate is always much lower than the youngest workers' rate, which reached 55% in 1985. Turning now to the sex composition of unemployment, women have gone from being a third to a half of the unemployed, with their unemployment rate almost doubling the male rate by 1989.

Table 5.2 shows the regional structure of unemployment. Unemployment rate divergence has greatly increased over time, as evidenced by Figure 5.2, which plots the sum of the absolute differences in unemployment rates across regions, weighted by their labour force share.

Table 5.2. *Regional unemployment rates, 1962, 1976, 1985 and 1989, annual averages, %*

	1962	1976	1985	1989
Andalucía	3.4	9.9	29.2	27.0
Aragón	0.2	2.5	17.2	12.1
Asturias	0.3	3.4	18.0	17.8
Baleares	0.4	3.9	13.5	10.7
Canarias	1.1	8.3	25.7	21.5
Cantabria	0.5	2.9	15.5	17.8
Castilla–La Mancha	0.5	4.5	15.5	14.1
Castilla–León	0.3	4.2	17.6	16.7
Cataluña	0.9	3.4	21.7	14.3
País Vasco	0.2	3.7	22.7	19.6
Extremadura	1.7	8.0	27.0	26.4
Galicia	0.4	1.7	13.1	12.1
Madrid	1.1	5.1	21.1	13.2
Murcia	1.4	4.8	18.9	16.2
Navarra	0.1	3.9	18.8	12.8
La Rioja	0.3	1.8	16.5	10.1
Valencia	1.2	3.6	19.9	15.4
National average	1.1	4.3	21.4	17.2

Sources: See Appendix 2.

Do these imbalances translate into growing mismatch, as measured by the *MM* index? Table 5.3 presents, and Figure 5.3 plots, the index from 1977 to 1989,[3] by sex, age, education, skill and sector.[4] The age, sector and education dimensions all show decreasing values over time; the sex and skill indices are stable up to 1985 and increase thereafter. The latter two are, therefore, the only ones consistent with the widespread perception of increasing mismatch in Spain in the last few years. The fall in the former three indices reveals that, although absolute differences in unemployment rates have increased over time, relative differences have fallen. For instance, in 1976:4 the difference between the prime-age and the 16–19-year-old unemployment rates was 15 percentage points, rising to 23 percentage points by 1989:4. However the former rate quadrupled from 1976 to 1989, while the latter *only* doubled.

The case of regions, for which we compute a series starting in 1962 and report the results in Table 5.4 and Figure 5.4. is quite striking. In 1962, when national unemployment was very low, geographical unemployment dispersion was very high; but it fell dramatically afterwards, bottoming out in 1985, when national unemployment reached its maximum. The

Table 5.3. *MM mismatch indices, %, 1977–89*

	Sex	Age	Education	Skill	Sector
1977	0.6	28.5	2.8	7.1	27.2
1978	1.3	32.6	4.9	6.6	24.8
1979	1.1	31.4	6.4	6.9	25.8
1980	1.0	30.9	5.1	7.0	24.2
1981	1.1	29.5	5.7	6.8	21.7
1982	1.4	27.2	5.8	6.5	18.1
1983	1.4	25.3	5.7	6.4	16.1
1984	1.4	23.3	4.9	7.0	15.7
1985	1.6	20.3	4.3	6.7	11.7
1986	2.2	19.2	3.5	7.6	8.4
1987	3.2	18.3	3.4	8.8	6.4
1988	4.6	25.0	3.5	8.6	2.9
1989	5.8	25.0	2.3	8.7	2.5

Note:
The level of disaggregation is:

(a) *Age*, 3 groups (16–24, 25–54 and 55 or more years old).
(b) *Education*, 5 groups (illiterate, primary school, high school, vocational training and university).
(c) *Skill*, 4 groups (as in Table 5.1).
(d) *Sector*, 4 groups (agriculture and fishing, manufacturing, construction and services.

Sources: See Appendix 2.

reason is the same as before: absolute differences in unemployment rates increased substantially, but the denominator of the *MM* index, the national rate, rose so much more than the numerator that it dwarfed the latter's increase. Since 1985 regional dispersion has been increasing again, as the national rate was falling.

2.3   Mismatch as micro market constraint heterogeneity

A different measure of mismatch results from the model common to all papers in the second Chelwood Gate conference. The model is explained in detail by Drèze (1990), so here we review only its main features. It is a disequilibrium model, in which rationing arises from wage and price stickiness as well as from short-run rigidity of technical coefficients of production. As is usual in these models, employment can be constrained by lack of demand (i.e., the Keynesian regime), lack of productive capacity (i.e., the classical regime), or lack of labour (i.e., the repressed

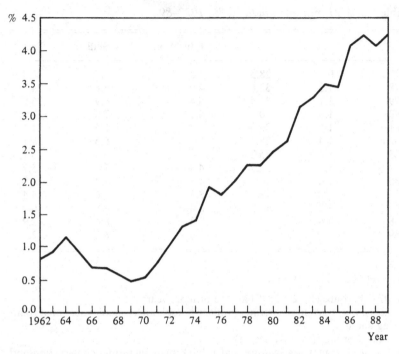

Figure 5.2   Regional unemployment inequality index, 1962–89

inflation regime). If every sector in the economy were constrained in an identical way, aggregate employment would equal the minimum of these three employment levels. Such a situation being highly unlikely, aggregation is performed in the model allowing for heterogeneity of constraints; in particular, aggregation is done via a constant elasticity of substitution (CES) function whose parameter, $1/\rho$, turns out to measure the degree of disparity in the rationing regime of different sectors: the latter goes to zero as ρ goes to infinity. Mismatch is in this way identified with regime disparity across sectors, and is revealed by actual employment being lower than the minimum of labour supply, classical and Keynesian employment.

The variable $1/\rho$ measures frictional (structural) unemployment. To understand why, we need to recall the CES equation giving aggregate employment, $\tilde{L}$:

$$\tilde{L} = (LK^{-\rho} + LP^{-\rho} + LS^{-\rho})^{1/\rho} \tag{2}$$

where LK and LP are Keynesian and classical employment and LS is labour supply.

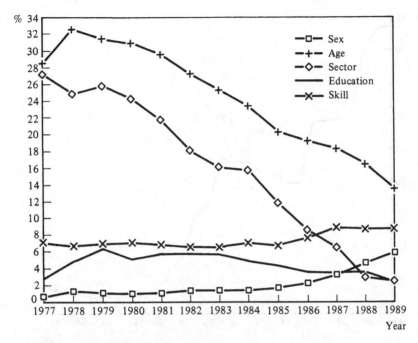

Figure 5.3 *MM* mismatch indices, 1977–89

Now if $LK = LP = LS$, then $\tilde{L} = 3^{-\rho}LS$, so that:

$$1/\rho = (\log 3)^{-1}\tilde{u} \tag{3}$$

where $\tilde{u} = 1 - (\tilde{L}/LS)$ is the frictional unemployment rate, and we have used the approximation $\log(1 + x) \approx x$.

Table 5.4. *MM regional mismatch indices, %, 1961–70*

1961	n.a.	1971	21.7	1981	3.1
1962	43.6	1972	21.7	1982	2.8
1963	43.3	1973	23.1	1983	2.5
1964	40.3	1974	23.0	1984	2.6
1965	29.8	1975	23.6	1985	2.4
1966	29.6	1976	16.8	1986	3.0
1967	29.3	1977	15.2	1987	3.6
1968	28.9	1978	9.2	1988	3.6
1969	19.8	1979	6.3	1989	4.4
1970	19.9	1980	4.1	1990	n.a.

Note: n.a. = not available.

Sources: See Appendix 2.

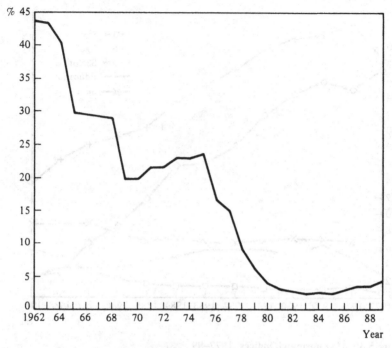

Figure 5.4   *MM regional mismatch index, 1962–89*

This expression also serves to show that $1/\rho$ is in the same (rescaled) units as the unemployment rate.

Figure 5.5 shows $1/\hat{\rho}$ as estimated for Spain, in Andrés *et al.* (1990), by one of us and other colleagues. It increases slowly up to 1973, quickly from 1974 to 1985, and falls slowly afterwards – i.e., it follows a path similar to that of the unemployment rate. Can we account for the behaviour of $1/\rho$ using economic variables related to mismatch? Andrés *et al.* regressed ρ on a trend (t), a proxy of mismatch (*PMM*), and (the logarithm of) an index of the relative price of energy inputs (LPRM). *PMM* is Layard and Nickell's (1986) turbulence index – i.e., the sum of absolute changes in sectoral shares of employment.[5] This variable should capture the need for relocation of labour across sectors as the composition of employment changes, being therefore positively correlated with mismatch; *LPRM* should also increase mismatch, by changing the relative price of inputs.

Estimating the equation for $1/\hat{\rho}$, instead of $\hat{\rho}$, for 1965–87, we get: (t-ratios in parenthesis)

$$1/\hat{\rho}_t = 0.031 + 0.002t + 0.059(PMM_t + PMM_{t-1}) \qquad (4)$$
$$(4.28) \quad (4.99) \quad (2.08)$$

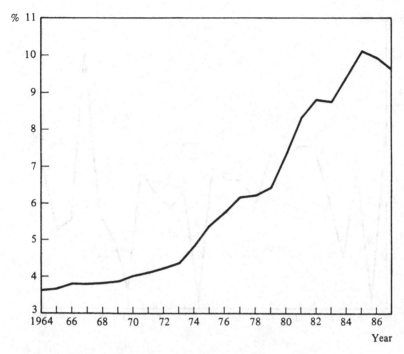

Figure 5.5   Estimated mismatch 1964–87: disequilibrium model $(1/\rho)$

$$+ \, 0.005 \, (LPRM_t + LPRM_{t-1})$$
$$(2.90)$$
$$R^2 = 0.95 \qquad DW = 0.22 \qquad \text{s.e.} = 0.005$$

The signs are as expected, but there is strong evidence of non-stationarity in the residuals. We would also like to know what explains the trend. To substitute for it, following Padoa Schioppa (1990), we chose the following variables: the unweighted standard deviation of regional unemployment rates (SDU),[6] gross interregional migration as a proportion of total population (GMI), and the proportion of long-term unemployed (1 year or more) in the labour force (LTU). The first and third variables should raise mismatch, the second should lower it. Finally, we use the turbulence index for total employment $(TURB)$, plotted in Figure 5.6, instead of PMM. The results are as follows:

$$1/\hat\rho_t = 0.054 + 0.007 \, SDU_{t-1} - 0.023 \, GMI_t \qquad (5)$$
$$(20.80) \quad (7.30) \qquad\qquad (5.38)$$
$$+ \, 0.002 \, LTU_t + 0.001 \, TURB_t + 0.006 \, LPRM_t$$
$$(8.72) \qquad\quad (2.41) \qquad\qquad (6.27)$$
$$R^2 = 0.99 \qquad DW = 1.93 \qquad \text{s.e.} = 0.0016$$

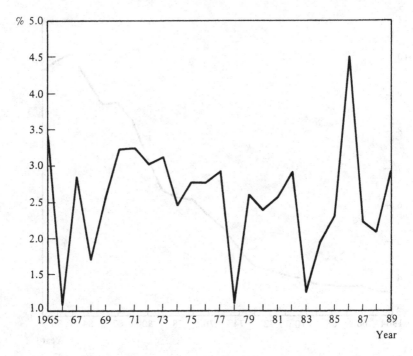

Figure 5.6   Turbulence, 1965–89

The fit is now much more satisfactory, with no sign of residual serial correlation. We tried quadratic terms of *LTU* and *TURB* but, contrary to Padoa Schioppa's (1990) finding for Italy, they were not significant at all. We also ran the regression reintroducing the trend term, but it was insignificant (*t*-ratio of 1.49), implying that we have successfully explained away the trend.

Can we account for the fall in mismatch, as measured by $1/\hat{\rho}$, in 1986–7? Three variables behaved positively: gross migration increased in those two years, the proportion of long-term unemployed fell, and so did the price of energy imports. They overcame the continued rise in regional unemployment rate dispersion and the 1986 turbulence blip.

This measure of mismatch does, unfortunately, give a different answer from JLS's *MM* index. The latter falls according to most characteristics of the labour force, while $1/\hat{\rho}$, which is an overall measure, steadily increases over time.

The units of measurement help explain the different behaviour of the two indices, *MM* is a squared coefficient of variation – i.e., a (squared) standard deviation divided by a (squared) mean; it is therefore dimensionless. But $1/\rho$ is in the same units as the unemployment rate (see equation (3)) – i.e., in the square root of the units of the numerator of MM. As we mentioned before, the latter *does* rise steadily over time (as does the index of absolute unemployment rate differences plotted in Figure 5.2), but its rise is dwarfed by that of the denominator, the national unemployment rate.

The matter thus boils down to the following question: is it *only* relative unemployment rate dispersion that matters, or do absolute unemployment rates and differentials also provide independently valuable information about mismatch? To put it more bluntly: suppose that an economy has two types of labour with equal size labour forces and with respective unemployment rates of 2% and 4%. Is mismatch the same if the latter are 10% and 20%? The MM index says so, but this is hard to accept. Higher unemployment is usually associated with a higher proportion of long-term unemployment, for example, which is itself likely to produce mismatch. The catch is that mismatch may be both a *cause* for the persistence of high unemployment and a *consequence* of it. In summary, we think the numerator of MM to be interesting on its own.

In the case of Spain, two reasons induce us to believe that $1/\hat{\rho}$ might be giving a more accurate picture, in the sense that mismatch is nowadays in Spain at historically high levels. First, we find no evidence in section 3 below of double-logarithmic wage (i.e., concave) equations at the regional level, a specification which is clearly rejected in favour of a semi-logarithmic form. Second, if mismatch had really been falling according to most dimensions (and dramatically in some of them), it would be very difficult to understand the overheating currently taking place in Spain.

We end this section by noting that two regional variables help explain $1/\hat{\rho}$: (unweighted) unemployment rate dispersion and migration flows. The latter have been falling steadily since the early 1960s, a fact which we would need to explain in order to improve our understanding of mismatch in Spain. Further insight, however, requires formal modelling of the role of unemployment rate disparities, and their interaction with wage setting, in the regional labour allocation process. We undertake this task in the following section.

3   Analysis of migration flows

In this section we analyse the behaviour of internal migration flows in Spain since 1962. We review a few stylised facts, set up a framework of analysis and comment on the time path of our explanatory variables.

Finally, we report our estimation results and derive policy implications from them.

3.1 Stylised facts

Even though Spain is a relatively small country, there are genuine differences between regions in terms of weather, language, traditions, etc. which have played an important role in Spanish history. The traditional administrative division is into 50 provinces, but these have always been grouped into regions, whose limits have changed over time. The current structure, dating from 1978, consists of 17 so-called 'Autonomous Communites', which have their own parliaments and governments, with wide-ranging political powers.

Spanish population has increased from 31 million in 1962 to 38.5 million in 1986.[7] Migration flows were very high in Spain in the 1960s and early 1970s. Gross outflows to other (mainly European) countries averaged 0.3% of the population in 1960–74; they then fell dramatically, to 0.06% over 1975–86, being overtaken by returns, so that net migration was negative until 1980, and positive but negligible afterwards.

Interprovincial migration flows, as a percentage of population, were very high in the early 1960s, but have been falling since: the 1962–9 average was 1.22%, it was 1.09% in 1970–5 and 0.92% over 1976–86. The decline is more marked for interregional flows (i.e., excluding within-region moves) which, for those three periods were, respectively, 0.65%, 0.50% and 0.36%. The reason is that intraregional flows have grown at the same rate as the population, while interregional flows have fallen in absolute terms; as a result the former went from representing 46% of total interprovincial migration in the 1960s to representing 61% over 1976–86. Figure 5.7 plots interregional flows since 1962, both the official series and the adjusted one we use in our regression analysis (see below).

Some information on the characteristics of migrants is available. As expected, younger people – under 25 years old – are more likely to move: over 1962–86 they represented almost half of all migrants, but just 42% of the population. In the 1960s the proportions of young people in both the population and migration were increasing, but the 1970s and 1980s show an ageing of both the population – 42% were young in 1970, 40% in 1986 – and migration – 51% of migrants were young in 1970, only 46% in 1986. In terms of sex, even though the participation of women in the population has increased (from 48.5% in 1960 to 49% in 1986), their share of migration has fallen (from 53% in 1962 to 51% in 1986). Finally, the available data on labour force status are quite useless. Most migrants (around 60%) are classified as 'non-active', but it is unclear if this

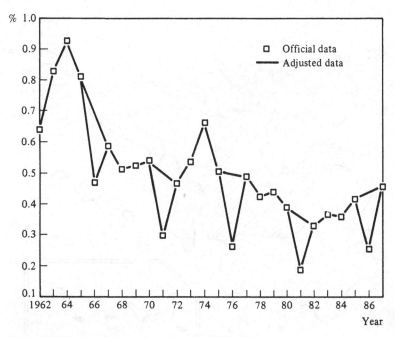

Figure 5.7 Interregional migration rate, 1962–87

considers only out-of-the-labour-force migrants or if some or all of the unemployed workers are counted in. Within those labelled as 'active', around three-quarters were manual workers in the 1960s, with the proportion declining in the 1970s and 1980s in favour of skilled non-manual workers, which amount to almost 40% of all migrants in 1986.

In order to highlight other features of migration, we have grouped – looking at *per capita* income and gross migration flows – the 17 administrative regions into more aggregate regions (in the spirit of Attanasio and Padoa Schioppa in Chapter 6 in this volume). We distinguish five super-regions; Big Cities (*BC*), North (*NO*), Northeast (*NE*), Centre (*CE*) and South (*SO*); Figure 5.8 and Appendix 1 provide information on the location of regions and their grouping. The *SO* is the most agricultural, less developed region, followed by the *CE*. The most advanced, with strong industrial and service sectors, is the *BC* region (the big cities are Madrid and Barcelona), followed by the *NO*, which specialised in basic industries but also kept important farming and fishing sectors. Figure 5.9 shows that, in terms of *per capita* GDP, the former are the poorest areas and the latter the richest. The *NE* region is in between, and it was joined by *NO* in the late 1970s. Figure 5.9 also reveals that, though slowly, disparities in *per capita* income have been closing.

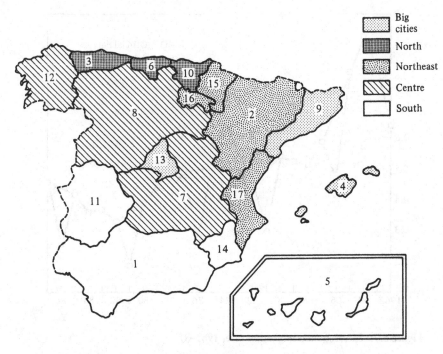

Figure 5.8 Regional structure and aggregate regions
Note: Region numbers correspond to those in Appendix 1.

It is interesting to look at the relative position of regions with respect to other variables. In the 1960s and 1970s, the *SO* and *CE* regions lost population in favour of *BC*, while in the 1980s population shares have stabilised. In Figure 5.10 we can see that unemployment is highest in *SO*, lowest in *CE*, and also a surprisingly bad unemployment performance for *BC*. These facts are the result of the behaviour of the labour force and employment over time. Since 1975 employment has fallen everywhere, while the labour force has been more or less stable in *NO*, *NE* and *SO*, has fallen in *CE* (accounting for its lower unemployment rate) and has risen in *BC* (accounting for its bad unemployment record).

Figures 5.11 and 5.12 portray gross outmigration and inmigration rates. They show a clear pattern until 1976: *SO* and *CE* had high gross outflows (the other regions had low ones); and *BC*, *NO* and *NE* had sizeable gross inflows. The result, in Figure 5.13, is immediate: high net inflows to the latter three regions mirroring high net outflows from the former two. The picture is much more muddled after 1976, when gross flows become low everywhere and the regions' roles reverse: *BC* and *NO* become net senders

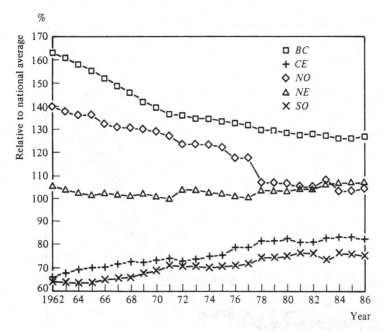

Figure 5.9   Relative *per capita* real GDP, 1962–86, 1980 pesetas

and *SO* becomes a net receiver (probably due to return migration), while *CE* ends up in balance.

Turning to wages and prices, the real (consumption) wages per employee follow a similar pattern as real *per capita* GDP (Figure 5.9), except that wages in *NO* remain closer to *BC*'s than to *NE*'s wages, while wages in *CE* are more similar to the latter than to those in *SO*. These disparities in the behaviour of wages and *per capita* income point to differences in the evolution of non-wage income across regions. Consumer prices have grown more in *BC* and *NO* than elsewhere. Finally, housing price indices show higher than average increases in *SO* and lower ones in *NO* and *CE*.

We now turn to a formal analysis of migration flows.

3.2   *Framework of analysis*

There is a vast literature on migration theory and its empirical applications.[8] The two leading, complementary approaches are the labour flow and the human capital models. The former is grounded on the idea that, in equilibrium, factors of production should receive the same return in every region, as long as factors are mobile. Migration is thus viewed as the response of labour to wage inequalities across regions. In the human

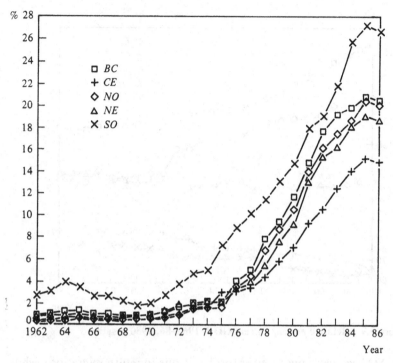

Figure 5.10   Regional unemployment rates, 1962–86

capital approach, people move to maximise their expected lifetime utility across regions, which takes into account all features of life in a given place, both economic and non-economic. The model we use is a generalisation of the well-known Harris–Todaro (1970) model, which has been adapted by Pissarides and Wadsworth (1987) to derive the probability that a person will migrate as a function of personal characteristics and market variables.

The approach we take adapts the previous models to a pooled regression context, along the lines of Pissarides and McMaster (1984) in their study of regional migration in the United Kingdom.[9] The basic idea is to compute the differential between expected returns and costs of moving, and examine which variables affect such a differential: the higher the differential, the higher will be the probability of migrating. Suppose that there are two regions, 1 and 2, and we want to model the net inflow of migrants to region 1. Each region has an unemployment rate u_i and a wage rate w_i ($i = 1, 2$), and there is an unemployment benefit, available to all the unemployed, which is a given proportion b of the wage rate. There are also costs of moving from one region to another, including travel

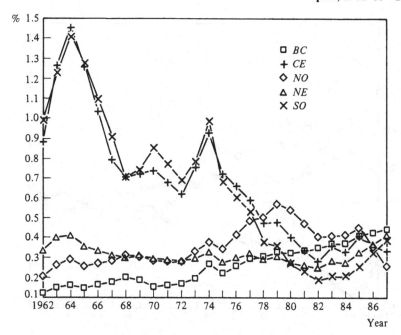

Figure 5.11   Gross outmigration rates, 1962–87

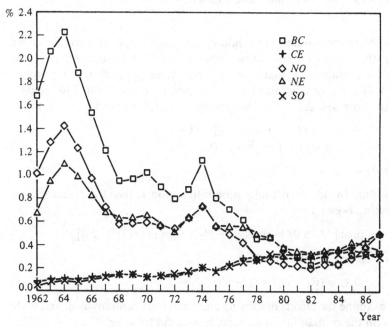

Figure 5.12   Gross inmigration rates, 1962–87

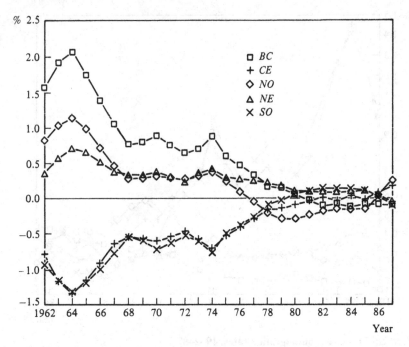

Figure 5.13   Net inmigration rates, 1962–87

fares, rental or purchase of a house, etc. For analytical convenience we write the costs of living in a given region as a proportion c_i of the respective wage, so that the relevant wage rate is the net wage, $\tilde{w}_i = w_i(1 - c_i)$. In this form the cost of moving from region 2 to region 1 can be expressed as $c_1 - c_2$. The expected return for a worker in region i is:

$$R_i = u_i b w_i(1 - c_i) + (1 - u_i)w_i(1 - c_i)$$
$$= \tilde{w}_i[1 - (1 - b)u_i] \quad (i = 1, 2) \tag{6}$$

where $0 < b, c_i < 1$.

Denoting by M_1 the net migration into region 1, then the probability of migrating is given by:

$$\text{prob}[M_1 \geq 0] = \text{prob}[R_1 - R_2 \geq 0] = \text{prob}[DR_1 \geq 0] \tag{7}$$

where the return differential is:

$$DR_1 = (\tilde{w}_1 - \tilde{w}_2) - (1 - b)(u_1 \tilde{w}_1 - u_2 \tilde{w}_2) \tag{8}$$

To examine the effects of moving costs and the unemployment and wage rates on the probability of moving, it is useful to write:

$$w_1 = w_2 + dw_1; \quad w_2 = w \tag{9a}$$

$$u_1 = u_2 + du_1; \quad u_2 = u \tag{9b}$$

$$c_1 = c_2 + dc_1; \quad c_2 = c \tag{9c}$$

where dj_1 ($j = w, u, c$) represents the respective differential, and w, u and c capture the respective overall levels effects.

Substituting [9a–c] into (8), we get:

$$
\begin{aligned}
DR_1 = {} & dw_1(1 - c) - wdc_1 - dw_1 dc_1 \\
& - (1 - b)[(u + du_1)(w + wd_1)(1 - c - dc_1) \\
& - uw(1 - c)]
\end{aligned}
\tag{10}
$$

which, by assuming that the cross-differential terms are of smaller order of magnitude, can be approximated by:

$$
\begin{aligned}
DR_1 \cong {} & dw_1(1 - c) - wdc_1 \\
& - (1 - b)[(udw_1)(1 - c) \\
& + du_1 w(1 - c) - uwdc]
\end{aligned}
\tag{11}
$$

The effects of the differentials on DR_1 are given by:

$$\partial DR_1/\partial dw_1 = (1 - c)[1 - [1 - b)u] > 0 \tag{12a}$$

$$\partial DR_1/\partial du_1 = -(1 - b)w(1 - c) < 0 \tag{12b}$$

$$\partial DR_1/\partial dc_1 = -w[1 - (1 - b)u] < 0 \tag{12c}$$

Therefore net migration into region 1, M_1, depends positively on the wage differential and negatively on the unemployment and moving cost differentials, all with respect to region 2.

It is also easy to derive the effects of the overall levels on DR_1:

$$\partial DR_1/\partial dw = -dc_1[1 - (1 - b)u] - (1 - b)du_1(1 - c) \tag{13a}$$

$$\partial DR_1/\partial du = -(1 - b)[dw_1(1 - c) - wdc_1] \tag{13b}$$

$$\partial DR_1/\partial dc = (1 - b)du_1 w - dw_1[1 - (1 - b)u] \tag{13c}$$

$$\partial DR_1/\partial db = (1 - c)[udw_1 + wdu_1] - uwdc_1 \tag{13d}$$

The sign of the four previous effects are, in general, ambiguous, but can be determined for particular cases. For example, equation (13a) implies that a higher overall wage reduces migration into regions with higher unemployment and higher cost of moving, and equation (13b) says that higher overall unemployment discourages inflows into regions with higher wages and lower costs of moving. In any event, the sign of all the level effects have to be determined empirically.

In summary, we can represent the probability of net inflows to region i by:

$$\text{prob}[M_i \geq 0] = f[dw_i, du_i, w, u, c, b, Z^i] \tag{14}$$

where f is a function satisfying $f_1 > 0, f_2 < 0$ and $f_3 < 0$, and the remaining signs are ambiguous.

We reserve c_i for the monetary costs of living in region i and Z^i for other relative characteristics, including the weather, public services like education or health care, and amenities.

3.3   Econometric analysis of migration

We now present the results of estimating a formal model of migration. We are concerned with three basic issues. First, we examine how regional migration rates respond to regional real wage and unemployment levels and differentials, and to moving costs. Second, we analyse the extent to which these differentials persist in the face of migration. Third, we draw some implications from these adjustment processes for regional economic policy. To deal with the first two issues we estimate two pooled cross-section time series regression equations, one for net interregional migration rates and another for regional wage differentials. We close the model by introducing a third equation in an *ad hoc* manner, linking the absolute variation in unemployment with net migration rates, which is derived as a 'pseudo-identity' and hence is not estimated. We consider each equation in turn.

3.3.1 Net migration equation

For estimation purposes we use an empirical specification of the probability of migration, similar to the one used by Pissarides and McMaster (1984) for the United Kingdom and also by the most relevant work on Spain we know of, Santillana (1978). The latter estimates several cross-section models of bilateral migration flows between Spanish provinces, for selected years between 1960 and 1973. This study finds a significant response of migration to economic variables, mainly to earnings differentials, as well as an important positive effect of the stock of migrants in the province of destination, which the author interprets as proxying for a reduction in informational and settling-down costs for new migrants. In contrast, we analyse the more aggregate interregional flows while substantially enlarging the period, and we use a pooling approach to estimation.

The ideal dependent variable would be the movements of workers between regions, but we have data only on population flows. Our dependent variable, m_{it}, is equal to the net flows into a region divided by the region's population in the previous year, which approximates the probability concept.[10] The alternative of estimating separate equations for gross flows was discarded because the unidirectionality of flows makes gross and net migration behave quite comparably for most of the period. As shown in Figure 5.7, the official data on gross migration present extremely low peaks every five years, coinciding with census years. We believe this anomaly is due to the collection of the new census in those years, and have proceeded to smooth out the peaks by linearly interpolating each region's gross flows, as in the adjusted series in Figure 5.7.[11]

The regressors, X_i, are wage and unemployment differentials with respect to nationwide levels – i.e., $du_i = u_i - u_N$ and $dw_i = w_i - w_N$ – and a set of extra variables, Z^i, proxying for costs of moving, risk aversion, employment structure, influence of external migration, etc. which we discuss below. In order to capture level effects of overall unemployment and wage rates, we allow for regression coefficients to depend inversely on such levels,[12] so that the estimated model is:

$$m_{it} = \alpha_i' X_{it} + \epsilon_{it} \qquad (i = 1, \ldots, N; t = 1, \ldots, T) \qquad (15)$$

where $\alpha_i = \alpha_{i0} + \alpha_{i1}(1/u_N) + \alpha_{i2}(1/w_N)$.

This implies, for example, the presence of absolute differences, du_i and dw_i, and relative differences, defined as $ru_i = u_i/u_N$ and $rw_i = w_i/w_N$, the latter approximated in logarithmic form by $\omega_i = \log(w_i/w_N)$, to be measured in percentage points, as well as cross-product terms – like, for example, ω_i/u_N. Lagged dependent variables are also included, since migration flows exhibit considerable inertia,[13] and because these variables might proxy for the stock of migrants from other regions.

As a first check on the chance that unemployment and wage differentials have in explaining the downward path of migration, we should recall that relative unemployment rates have in fact converged over time, as revealed by the regional mismatch index computed above. As stated before, the same is not true for absolute differentials of unemployment rates, as is evident from Table 5.5, which reports du_i for 1962–86 and two subsamples. As to real wage differentials, Table 5.5 also reports the values of ω_i. A synthetic answer about their evolution is given by the following index of wage inequality:

$$\sum_i (N_i/N)[\log(w_i/w_N)]^2 \qquad (16)$$

The larger the index, the more different are regional wages, and if all wages are the same the index is equal to zero. Figure 5.14 plots the index

Table 5.5. *Migration, wages and unemployment by region, averages in percentages, 1962–86, 1962–75 and 1976–86*

Region	Year	m_i	du_i	ru_i	ω_i
AND	1962–86	− 0.49	4.11	2.11	− 20.62
	1962–75	− 0.83	2.47	4.12	− 23.30
	1976–86	− 0.02	6.18	1.59	− 17.19
ARA	1962–86	− 0.13	− 1.88	0.62	− 2.57
	1962–75	− 0.26	− 0.76	0.89	− 1.06
	1976–86	0.03	− 3.31	0.73	− 4.49
AST	1962–86	− 0.07	− 1.47	0.69	11.22
	1962–75	− 0.07	− 0.64	1.01	14.35
	1976–86	− 0.07	− 2.53	0.81	7.24
BAL	1962–86	0.13	− 2.54	0.45	− 1.68
	1962–75	0.15	− 1.24	0.41	1.43
	1976–86	0.09	− 4.19	0.70	− 5.64
CAN	1962–86	0.13	1.11	1.03	− 11.14
	1962–75	0.12	− 0.32	1.33	− 9.42
	1976–86	0.15	2.93	1.31	− 13.34
CNT	1962–86	− 0.06	− 2.06	0.59	5.57
	1962–75	0.11	− 0.74	0.91	8.24
	1976–86	0.00	− 3.73	0.72	2.17
CLM	1962–86	− 0.82	− 1.33	0.67	− 25.55
	1962–75	− 1.33	− 0.65	1.00	− 24.62
	1976–86	− 0.16	− 2.19	0.88	− 26.73
CLE	1962–86	− 0.49	− 1.29	0.71	− 4.88
	1962–75	− 0.79	− 0.61	1.04	− 3.00
	1976–86	− 0.11	− 2.15	0.85	7.27
CAT	1962–86	0.72	0.00	0.86	6.17
	1962–75	1.32	− 0.52	1.13	6.53
	1976–86	− 0.04	0.67	1.01	5.73
PVA	1962–86	0.47	− 0.25	0.63	10.90
	1962–75	1.03	− 1.14	0.51	15.95
	1976–86	− 0.25	0.88	1.06	4.48
EXT	1962–86	− 0.90	1.88	1.36	− 30.32
	1962–75	− 1.58	0.57	2.22	− 33.07
	1976–86	− 0.05	3.56	1.36	− 26.83
GAL	1962–86	− 0.13	− 3.34	0.47	− 3.41
	1962–75	− 0.20	− 0.80	0.85	− 5.57
	1976–86	− 0.02	− 6.58	0.47	− 0.66
MAD	1962–86	0.52	0.21	1.05	16.32
	1962–75	0.83	0.05	1.70	17.94
	1976–86	0.13	0.42	1.09	14.26
	1962–86	− 0.05	0.10	1.37	− 18.44

Table 5.5. (*cont.*)

Region	Year	m_i	du_i	ru_i	ω_i
MUR	1962–75	− 0.21	1.17	2.82	− 19.83
	1976–86	0.13	− 1.25	0.93	− 16.67
	1962–86	0.22	− 1.26	0.60	− 4.55
NAV	1962–75	0.30	− 0.92	0.73	− 2.44
	1976–86	0.13	− 1.69	0.88	− 7.25
	1962–86	0.03	− 2.61	0.38	− 8.50
LRJ	1962–75	− 0.14	− 1.30	0.35	− 10.13
	1976–86	0.24	− 4.28	0.60	− 6.42
	1962–86	0.45	− 0.65	0.90	− 8.01
VAL	1962–75	0.69	− 0.20	1.46	− 9.00
	1976–86	0.14	− 1.23	0.89	− 6.77

Sources: See Appendix 2.

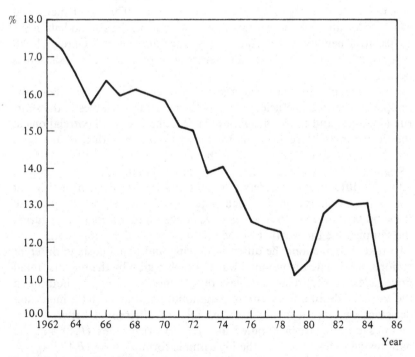

Figure 5.14   Real wage inequality index, 1962–86

Table 5.6. *Sample correlation coefficient, 1964–86*

Short run (changes)

Δm_i	$\Delta\omega_i$	$\Delta\omega_{i-1}$	Δdu_i	Δdu_{i-1}	Δru_i	Δru_{i-1}	Δpa_i
	0.04	-0.13	-0.04	-0.02	-0.09	-0.03	-0.00

$\Delta\omega_i$	$\Delta\omega_{i-1}$	Δdu_i	Δdu_{i-1}	Δpa_i
	0.05	0.01	0.13	-0.01

Long run (levels)

m_i	ω_i	ω_{i-1}	du_i	du_{i-1}	ru_i	ru_{i-1}	pa_i
	0.52	0.51	-0.13	-0.13	-0.26	-0.24	-0.10

ω_i	ω_{i-1}	du_i	du_{i-1}	pa_i
	0.98	0.04	0.10	0.15

across regions. Inequality was relatively high in the early 1960s, but has been coming down since, except for 1980–4. This is partly explained by a generalised fall in wage dispersion since the early 1970s – as Dolado and Malo de Molina (1985) stress for industry – due, in the second half of the 1970s, to a new system of nationwide wage agreements. García (1990) reports a 27% fall in dispersion across sectors and a 17% fall across occupations.[14]

In order to provide more descriptive measures, Table 5.6 contains the sample correlation coefficients among the previous variables in the short run (changes) and the long run (levels). We observe small correlations in the short run and larger ones in the long run, but in both cases the signs are the expected ones according to the model.

Regional dummy variables have been included in the set of regressors, to allow for different *fixed effects* on migration rates, introducing a different constant for each region. Through these variables we expect to capture all the subset of variables in Z^i which have not changed systematically during the sample, like the weather or the relative degree of urbanisation.

To take into account the different moving and living costs in different regions, we deflate the nominal wage in each region by the regional retail price index, so that relative wages are real ones. Since finding housing in the region of destination seems of paramount importance in the migration decision, we have also included the relative differential between each region's housing (own imputed and rental) price index (PA_i) and the nationwide index (PA_N), in the logarithmic form $pa_i = \log(PA_i/PA_N)$. A significant coefficient on this variable would signal that migrants give it an importance exceeding its share in the overall retail price index. We expect a negative effect of this variable.

To consider potential effects of the employment composition in the migration decision we included a variable measuring the proportion represented by the building sector in each region's total employment. It has been noted (e.g., Fina, 1987) that construction provided the transition for migrants from agricultural regions when they moved to the cities. A drop in this variable would make migration harder, so we expect a positive sign on this variable. Some researchers suggest that employment growth captures employment opportunities better than the unemployment rate, so we also tried to include in the regression the relative employment growth in a region.

The possibility of having a non-linear utility function in equation (6), such that $\tilde{w}_i$ and $b(1 - c_i)$ are substituted by $V[\tilde{w}_i]$ and $V[b(1 - c_i)]$, with $V' > 0$ and $V'' < 0$, has been considered by adding a 3-year moving average of the standard deviations of regional and unemployment rates, which would have a negative effect if risk aversion exists.

Finally, we have used two time dummy drift effects, to capture specific events. The first one, $DEUR$, taking on a zero value before 1976 and unity afterwards, tries to capture the effects of economic opportunities of migration to European countries. If internal migration was an intermediate step towards external migration, we would expect a negative sign on this variable. The second dummy variable, DPV, is defined as $DEUR$ but just for the Basque Country. It tries to capture political events in that region, which may have induced an outflow of migrants above that explained by purely economic factors.

Since the regressors are potentially endogenous we estimated both by instrumental variables – using two lags of each variable as instruments – and by three-stage least squares. The corresponding Hausman tests for endogeneity of the contemporaneous regressors were never significant and the results were very similar to ordinary least squares (OLS) estimates, so the latter are presented in order to simplify the computation of tests. Due to the use of two lags, the effective estimation period is 1964–86 and the corresponding number of observations is 391.

The selected specification of the pooled regression, whose encompassing test of the unrestricted equation (i.e., allowing for 3 coefficients per variable, plus cross-terms) is $F(30,341) = 0.98$ (5% critical value $= 1.46$), appears in the first block of Table 5.7. Only 10 of the 17 shift dummies were significant at the 10% level, the remaining were excluded from the final specification. The regression fits very well ($\bar{R}^2 = 0.98$ in the equivalent regression with m_{it} as the dependent variable) and the pooling restrictions (i.e. that all regions have the same

Table 5.7. Regressions: net migrations and wages (pooling)

1. Net migrations

$$\Delta m_{it} = 0.02 + 0.42\,\Delta m_{it-1} - 0.16\,m_{it-1} + 0.20\,\Delta\omega_{it-1} - 0.59\,\Delta\omega_{it-1} - 0.06\,\Delta ru_{it}$$
$$(3.07)(16.31)\quad (16.30)\quad (1.61)\quad (4.25)\quad (2.73)$$
$$[3.00][12.03]\quad [14.08]\quad [1.47]\quad [5.24]\quad [2.67]$$

$$-\,0.41\,ru_{it-1} + 0.04(\omega_{it}/u_{Nt})_{-1} - 0.02(pa_{it}/u_{Nt}) - 0.077\,DPV - 4.14\,AST$$
$$(10.04)\quad (4.46)\quad (2.33)\quad (2.90)\quad (2.05)$$
$$[15.86]\quad [4.07]\quad [2.40]\quad [3.46]\quad [3.01]$$

$$-\,4.98\,BAL + 2.34\,CAN - 3.06\,CNT - 5.83\,CLM - 6.61\,CLE - 2.60\,GAL$$
$$(2.48)\quad (1.16)\quad (1.60)\quad (2.90)\quad (3.35)\quad (1.35)$$
$$[2.61]\quad [1.43]\quad [2.00]\quad [2.40]\quad [2.81]\quad [2.57]$$

$$+\,3.20\,MUR + 3.50\,NAV + 3.77\,VAL$$
$$(1.65)\quad (1.90)\quad (1.83)$$
$$[2.25]\quad [1.68]\quad [2.87]$$

$N = 391$, $\bar{R}^2 = 0.72$, $DW = 1.96$, s.e. $= 0.083$, $SS = 2.58$, $SK(2) = 4.28$
$FP\,(134,237) = 0.96\,[1.20]$, $FHET\,(45,334) = 1.46\,[1.37]$

2. Wages

$$\Delta\omega_{it} = 0.03 + 0.14\,\Delta\omega_{it-1} + 0.28\,\Delta du_{it-1} + 0.06\,du_{it-1} - 0.23\,\Delta\omega_{it-1} + 0.02\,pa_{it-1}$$
$$(6.19)(4.62)\quad (2.72)\quad (12.21)\quad (10.18)\quad (2.26)$$
$$[6.80][4.40]\quad [2.68]\quad [9.44]\quad [9.43]\quad [2.36]$$

$$-8.32AND - 4.08ARA - 1.22AST - 3.19BAL - 5.85CAN - 2.10CNT - 9.49CLM$$
$$(8.32) \quad (5.94) \quad (2.30) \quad (4.32) \quad (6.65) \quad (3.61) \quad (8.52)$$
$$[7.83] \quad [6.33] \quad [2.37] \quad [4.09] \quad [6.51] \quad [3.65] \quad [8.25]$$

$$-4.62CLE - 1.78CAT - 0.96PVA - 11.06EXT - 3.55GAL - 7.69MUR - 4.90NAV$$
$$(6.24) \quad (3.00) \quad (1.76) \quad (9.11) \quad (4.86) \quad (7.90) \quad (6.86)$$
$$[6.50] \quad [4.10] \quad [2.44] \quad [8.74] \quad [5.13] \quad [7.93] \quad [7.08]$$

$$-5.05LRJ - 4.20VAL$$
$$(6.24) \quad (5.05)$$
$$[5.78] \quad [5.37]$$

$N = 391$, $\bar{R}^2 = 0.44$, $DW = 2.17$, s.e. $= 0.017$, $SS = 0.114$, $SK(2) = 24.57$
$FP(80,289) = 0.91$ [1.27], $FHET(15,359) = 1.61$ [1.67]

Notes:

N	no. of observations
$\bar{R}^2$	coefficient of multiple correlation (corrected by d.f.)
DW	Durbin–Watson statistic
s.e.	Standard deviation of the residuals
SS	Sum of squared residuals
SK	Jarque and Bera's test of normality (distributed as chi-square with 2 d.f.)
$FP(\ldots)$	F-pooling encompassing test (in brackets 5% c.v.)
$FHET(\ldots)$	White's (1982) F-heteroscedasticity test (in brackets 5% c.v.)

The ordinary t-ratios appear in parenthesis whilst White's heteroscedasticity consistent t-ratios appear in brackets.

coefficients) are accepted at conventional significance levels (*FP* test in Table 5.7).

However, some of the individual equations, reported in Appendix 3, do not fit very well (in particular, *AST* and *CAN*), or have wrong signs, revealing some heterogeneity across regions. However, most of the wrong signs are associated with insignificant variables and the low R^2s are associated with regions where few migration flows have occurred. Moreover, of the 51 level coefficients corresponding to relative unemployment and wages, and housing differentials (i.e., β_6, β_7 and β_8), 43 were correctly signed, so we feel reasonably confident about the homogeneity of the chosen specification across regions. There is no indication of first-order autocorrelation, and slight signs of heteroscedasticity, as evidenced by the value of White's (1982) test. We report both ordinary t-ratios (in parenthesis) and heteroscedasticity-consistent t-ratios (in brackets); although their levels vary, the implications of both sets of t-ratios are similar. We discuss below the possible origin of a nonconstant variance.

In order to avoid perfect collinearity with the constant term, the dummy variable corresponding to Madrid (*MAD*) has been excluded, so that the fixed effects are interpreted as deviations from the inflow rate in Madrid. There is some association between the dummy coefficients and the weather: regions with warm weather (*CAN*, *MUR*, *VAL*) tend to have significant positive constants above *MAD* (except *BAL*). A relationship with the degree of urbanisation is also present, capturing a marginally significant positive constant in the case of *NAV* and *VAL*, among the region with big cities, while *PVA* and *CAT* do not differ from *MAD*.

The response of net migration to changes in wage and unemployment differentials reveal some interesting patterns. Interregional migration rates respond significantly to wage and unemployment differentials in a permanent way, but the response is small, rather slow and affected by the general level of unemployment, the latter confirming the hypothesis advanced by Bentolila and Blanchard (1990). In particular, the (w_i/u_N) and (pa_i/u_N) terms completely dominated the w_i and pa_i terms, respectively. The estimated wage effect implies that if in a given region wages rise by 1% above the national average, annual migration into the region rises by 0.002 of 1% of the region's population in the short run,[15] and by $0.0025/u_N$ of 1% in the long run. The influence of changes in the region's relative wage thus depends in the long run on the overall level of unemployment, the response being larger in times of low than in times of high unemployment. So, for example, at 10% national unemployment, the inflow in response to a 1% favourable relative wage is in the long run 0.025 of 1% of the region's population, while at 20% national unemployment the effect is halved. The discouraging effect of the level of national unemployment in the long but not the short run may be interpreted as follows: when taking a migration decision agents consider only their region's relative wage, while in the long run, once they get information from their predecessors about the difficulties of getting a job in other regions when the nationwide unemployment rate is high, they discount the relative wage rate and their response is consequently lowered.

With respect to unemployment effects, we again find confirmation of the depressing effect of general unemployment, since both in the short and the long run it is relative unemployment that seems to matter. Since relative unemployment rates may be written as:

$$u_i/u_N = 1 + (1/u_N)(u_i - u_N) \tag{17}$$

having (u_i/u_N) as a regressor is equivalent to assuming that the coefficient on the difference $(u_i - u_N)$ is inversely proportional to u_N: when national unemployment rises, the response of net migration to unemployment differences falls. Numerically, at 10% national unemployment, a 1 percentage point rise in a region's unemployment rate leads to an outflow of 0.006 of 1% of the region's population while in the long run the effect is 0.09 of 1%. As in the effect of relative wages, when the national unemployment rises to 20%, the effect is halved. Comparing the long-run responses of net migration to wages and unemployment differentials, we find evidence that the response is (about four times) larger to unemployment, which has important implications for the design of a sensible regional policy, as discussed below.

As for the remaining explanatory variables, we were able to find only a small effect with respect to relative housing prices, scaled by u_N. A 1% increase in such a variable for a region leads to a net outflow of $0.0002/u_N$ of 1% of the region's population in the short run, and of $0.00125/u_N$ of 1% in the long run. None of the variables proxying for risk aversion, employment structure, employment growth or European opportunities were significant. Contemporaneous and lagged effects were tried, with the corresponding tests being non-significant in every case: $F(2,369) = 0.65$, 0.46, 0.83 for the variance of wages and employment, and the building sector variable, respectively, $F(3,368) = 0.38$ for (three lags of) relative employment growth, and $F(1,370) = 1.26$ for $DEUR$, all well below their respective 5% critical values. Only the DPV dummy was significant, accounting for a relative fall of 7.7% of annual migration in the Basque Country starting from 1976.

Since, as stated before, the behaviour of net migration changes after 1975, it is important to check the stability of the equation. We thus reestimate the equation for two sub-samples, 1964–75 and 1976–86, and

Table 5.8. *Migration, sub-samples, 1964–75 and 1976–86*

Variable	1964–75	1976–86	1976–86
const	0.02	0.03	0.02
	(2.00)	(2.78)	(2.72)
Δm_{it-1}	0.43	0.34	0.31
	(11.97)	(6.47)	(6.77)
m_{it-1}	− 0.17	− 0.21	− 0.20
	(12.61)	(7.38)	(8.26)
$\Delta\omega_{it}$	0.11	0.32	0.30
	(0.40)	(2.12)	(2.00)
$\Delta\omega_{it-1}$	− 0.58	− 0.58	− 0.55
	(2.15)	(3.80)	(3.73)
Δru_{it}	− 0.05	− 0.07	− 0.07
	(1.80)	(1.88)	(1.88)
ru_{it-1}	− 0.14	− 0.13	− 0.13
	(5.78)	(7.17)	(8.26)
ω_{it-1}/u_{Nt-1}	0.04	0.02	—
	(3.50)	(0.75)	
pa_{it}/u_{Nt}	− 0.02	− 0.07	− 0.07
	(1.74)	(1.70)	(1.84)
AST	− 6.62	− 3.00	− 2.11
	(1.86)	(1.19)	(0.94)
BAL	− 4.42	− 6.45	− 6.51
	(1.36)	(2.54)	(2.57)
CAN	1.23	4.64	4.34
	(0.38)	(2.03)	(1.92)
CNT	− 5.70	− 2.00	− 1.47
	(1.77)	(0.85)	(0.66)
CLM	− 10.08	− 3.00	− 3.37
	(3.05)	(1.27)	(1.46)
CLE	− 12.18	− 2.66	− 2.34
	(3.68)	(1.15)	(1.03)
PVA	− 0.97	− 9.67	− 8.99
	(0.30)	(3.73)	(3.75)
GAL	− 3.50	− 2.58	− 2.26
	(1.13)	(1.13)	(1.01)
MUR	(3.14)	4.11	3.51
	(1.09)	(1.70)	(1.55)
NAV	4.70	2.74	2.50
	(1.60)	(1.16)	(1.11)
VAL	7.57	1.02	0.67
	(2.10)	(0.44)	(0.30)

Table 5.8. (*cont.*)

Variable	1964–75	1976–86	1976–86
N	204	187	187
s.e.	0.094	0.068	0.068
$\bar{R}^2$	0.74	0.68	0.68
DW	0.85	2.07	2.05
$SK(2)$	3.86	3.02	2.99
$FHET$	1.36 [1.35]	1.16 [1.35]	

$FCH\ (22,351) = 1.24\ [1.57]$

Note: As in Table 5.7. *FCH*: Chow's *F*-Stability test.

test for coefficient instability. The two sub-sample regressions are reported in Table 5.8. The corresponding Chow test does not reject stability at the 5% level, though it is noticeable that two coefficients suffer shifts. The coefficient on (ω_i/u_N) is not significant in the second sub-sample, implying the absence of a permanent effect on net migrations after 1975, with unemployment taking the sole role as explanatory variable. This is in agreement with the diminishing role of relative wages as resource allocation mechanisms, as mentioned above. The pa_i coefficient also shifts, reflecting an increasing effect on migration of the widening housing price differentials. The last column in Table 5.8 presents the estimation of the migration equation without the lagged wage level, with the remaining coefficients hardly changing, which is used for simulation exercises below.

There are also strong downward shifts in the *CLM* and *VAL* dummies, and all excluded dummy variables were again not significant in either sub-sample. Since heteroscedasticity tests do not reveal any problems in either sub-sample we conclude that the heteroscedasticity present in the full sample is mostly due to the change in the wage and housing price coefficients.

3.3.2 Regional wage equation

The second question that we analyse is the extent to which regional wage and unemployment differentials persist. We want to emphasise from the start that we do not pretend to have a complete model of regional wage determination. The latter issue has been studied in depth by several authors (e.g., Cowling and Metcalf, 1967 for the UK and Rodríguez, 1988 and references therein for Spain). The common view is that local supply and demand conditions play only a limited role in the determination of regional wages. Our being able to explain just over 40% of the variance of changes in wages – conditioning only on shift dummies and unemployment and housing price differentials – seems to agree with that view. In particular, we do not control for employment composition across regions, while in his study Rodríguez (1988) concludes that interprovincial nominal wage differentials in Spain are to a large extent due to the specialisation of southern regions in low-wage sectors.

The OLS regression model results for the change in relative wages is reported in the second block of Table 5.7. Contrary to the case of migration, most shift dummies are very significant, with *AND*, *CLM*, *EXT* and *MUR* well below the relative growth in *MAD* and *AST*, *CNT* and *PVA* around the same growth as in *MAD*, which is the highest. This is possibly related to the composition of employment across regions: the regions corresponding to the first four dummies are all in the South of Spain, those associated to the latter three dummies are in the North. The pooling and the remaining parameter restrictions pass at the 5% level, and there are no signs of either first-order autocorrelation or heteroscedasticity in the residuals.

There are two non-competing hypotheses to test. The first is a short-run one, the *Phillips curve* view by which as desired employment increases employers raise wages to attract more labour – i.e., a negative relationship between unemployment and changes in wages, in our case between variables which are relative to the national mean. We were not able to capture this effect in either the full sample or the second sub-sample, with only small favourable evidence in the first sub-sample (see below). The positive coefficients on the level and the differences of relative unemployment seem to imply that the mere rise in actual employment, in spite of the fall in wages, is sufficient for employers in order to attract labour. Though the simple correlations in Table 5.6 point in the same direction, we believe this not to be a satisfactory feature but, since data on the many other variables which may influence regional wages were not available to us – and the statistical performance of the equation is fairly correct – we keep it as is.

The other hypothesis concerns expected wage equalisation. In the long run, with perfect labour mobility and in the absence of risk aversion or other variables, expected returns would equalise across regions – i.e., $R_i = R_N$, with R_i as in equation (6). Since $R_i/R_N = 1$, $ln(R_i/R_N) = 0$, and the long-run condition reads:

$$ln(w_i/w_N) + ln\{[1 - (1 - b)u_i]/[1 - (1 - b)u_N]\}$$
$$+ ln[(1 - c_i)/(1 - c_N)] = 0 \qquad (18)$$

Making use of the approximation $ln[1 - (1 - b)u_i] \cong - (1 - b)u_i$ and the functional assumption $(1 - c_i)/(1 - c_N) = (PA_i/PA_N)^{-\theta}$, we get:

$$ln(w_i/w_N) = (1 - b)(u_i - u_N) + \theta pa_i \qquad (19)$$

If there were no unemployment benefits, expected wages would equalise across regions, whereas if the unemployment compensation were 100% of the wage rate, then the expected return, apart from moving costs, would be equal to the wage rate, hence it would be wage rates that tend to be equal: $w_i = w_N$. In between there is a continuum of cases indexed by b, giving rise to a positive relation between the region's relative wage (w_i/w_N) and the relative unemployment level, $u_i - u_N$, with a coefficient possibly different from unity.

Another possibility of getting a coefficient different from unity arises if factors such as risk aversion play a role, causing some non-linearity in the expected returns from moving or staying. It is, however, possible to show under simple assumptions, like having a concave constant relative risk aversion (CRRA) utility function, that the trade-off between the unemployment differential $u_i - u_N$ on the relative wage $ln(w_i/w_N)$ would be larger than unity. In this sense, we expect to be able to discriminate between the linear utility *cum* replacement ratio hypothesis and the concave CRRA utility hypothesis, by examining the size of the estimated slope coefficient.

In our estimates there is a well defined (albeit small) positive relationship between a region's relative wage and its unemployment differential. Regions with above-average unemployment will tend to have, in the long run, above-average wages. So wages eventually compensate for differences in unemployment, but at the rate 0.3:1. The restriction that the coefficients of the two level terms are equal in absolute value is clearly rejected (t-ratio = 8.03). To be precise, we find that in a long-run steady state relative wages, in deviation of their drifts and their relative moving costs, are a fixed proportion of relative unemployment rates. Making all first-difference terms equal to zero, the long-run solution yields:

$$ln(w_i/w_N) = D_i + 0.09 pa_i + 0.3(u_i - u_N) \qquad (i = 1, \ldots, 17) \quad (20)$$

where D_i is the long-run value of the ith dummy and the same approximation as in equation (19) has been used.

Our estimates thus imply that in the short run wages do not respond to above-average unemployment (recall that the contemporaneous value of u_i does not appear in the regression) while in the long run, if a region has, on average, 1 percentage point of unemployment above the national level, its wage rate would be 0.3% above the average rate for the country as a whole. According to our discussion of equation (19), this implies an estimated replacement ratio of 0.7, which fits reasonably well with the scanty evidence we have about the sample average of this variable. For

Table 5.9. *Wages, sub-samples, 1964–75 and 1976–86*

Variable	1964–75	1976–86
const	0.04	0.05
	(4.68)	(5.16)
$\Delta\omega_{it-1}$	-0.25	-0.14
	(4.90)	(3.06)
Δdu_{it-1}	0.51	0.28
	(1.52)	(2.49)
ω_{it-1}	-0.27	-0.35
	(6.51)	(6.91)
du_{it-1}	0.05	0.07
	(6.75)	(8.16)
pa_{it-1}	0.03	0.01
	(1.60)	(1.15)
AND	-10.94	-10.74
	(5.84)	(5.92)
ARA	-4.98	-6.15
	(4.66)	(4.95)
AST	-1.08	-2.26
	(1.50)	(2.72)
BAL	-4.33	-5.43
	(3.95)	(4.00)
CAN	-7.11	9.42
	(4.80)	(6.02)
CNT	-2.78	-3.10
	(3.38)	(2.97)
CLM	-10.88	-14.37
	(5.47)	(6.49)
CLE	-5.58	-7.16
	(4.77)	(5.23)
CAT	-2.70	-2.65
	(3.11)	(2.84)
PVA	-0.83	-2.40
	(1.17)	(2.58)
EXT	-13.85	-14.73
	(6.05)	(6.49)
GAL	-5.43	-4.61
	(4.20)	(3.98)
MUR	-9.14	-11.00
	(4.91)	(6.22)
NAV	-5.68	-7.21
	(5.15)	(5.39)
LRJ	-6.74	-6.90
	(4.52)	(5.03)
VAL	-5.77	-6.73
	(3.88)	(4.93)

Table 5.9. (cont.

Variable	1964–75	1976–86
N	204	187
SS	0.053	0.052
s.e.	0.017	0.018
$\bar{R}^2$	0.42	0.48
DW	2.16	2.26
$FHET$	0.83 [1.83]	1.02 [1.83]

FCH (22,347) = 1.35 [1.55]

Note: As in Table 5.7 and Table 5.8.

example, Dolado et al. (1986) construct its time series for industrial workers, obtaining a sample mean of 0.67 for 1966–86, with a range going from 0.61 at the beginning of the sample to 0.75 at its end. To examine the hypothesis of risk aversion we included as extra regressors the standard deviations of regional wage and employment rates, but both were insignificant. This gives us some confidence that the replacement ratio hypothesis provides a better interpretation of the evidence.[16]

It should be noted that, as in the migration equation, convergence to the long-run equilibrium is slow. For example, if a given region's relative wage is 1% above the national average, ceteris paribus, this will lead, in the following year to an 0.28 of 1% decline in the region's relative wage rate, an 0.20 of 1% decline in the second year, an 0.17 of 1% decline in the third, and so on, until the original deviations are eliminated. Finally, we find a positive effect of relative rental housing prices on relative wages, such that in the short run, if a region's housing price index is 1% above the national average, its real wage rate would tend to be 0.02 of 1% above the nationwide average, whilst such effect is 0.1 of 1% in the long run.

As with the migration equation, we estimate the wage equation in the two sub-samples 1964–75 and 1976–86. The results are presented in Table 5.9. Apart from the coefficients on the lagged changes of wages and of unemployment differentials the remaining ones do not change much, and the Chow test of parameter stability is easily passed at the 5% level. The pooling restrictions are again not rejected, but we found that in the first sub-sample the contemporaneous value of the unemployment differential was negative with a t-ratio of 1.62 (not reported). This may point to a short-run Phillips curve effect being present in that sub-sample, an effect not found at all in the second subsample. The individual equations (see Appendix 3) show the same picture, with only AND and NAV showing some signs of a Phillips curve effect.

3.3.3 Regional unemployment equation

To close the model we need an equation for regional unemployment rates. We made several attempts using migration rates and wages, but all of them failed. At the end, in order to be operative at the simulation stage, we reached a compromise solution by which the equation was not estimated but was derived as a 'pseudo-identity', following the same approach as in Pissarides and McMaster (1984).

Just to see what is involved, assume that there are no outflows and all new immigrants, M_{it}, are unemployed during the first year of arrival. Then the absolute number of unemployed in region i would be $U_{it} = U_{it-1} + M_{it}$. Dividing by the population (POP) at $t-1$ and after some simple algebra we can express the unemployment rate as:

$$\frac{U_{it}}{L_{it}} = \frac{L_{it-1}}{L_{it}} \frac{U_{it-1}}{L_{it-1}} + \frac{POP_{it-1}}{L_{it}} \frac{M_{it}}{POP_{it-1}}$$

$$= \frac{L_{it-1}}{L_{it}} u_{it-1} + \frac{POP_{it-1}}{L_{it}} m_{it} \tag{21}$$

With a basically constant labour force – which one gets for Spain comparing 1986 with 1962 – and assuming a constant population–labour force ratio, this could approximately be written as:

$$\Delta u_{it} \cong \alpha m_{it} \tag{22}$$

where α^{-1} is the labour force–population ratio.

Guided by the sample value of this ratio, around 0.4, and realising that assuming full unemployment for the migrants is an extreme, we chose for α the value of 1.5 (in fact 0.015, recall that we use m_i in percentage terms but not u_i), which would correspond to 60% of migrants being unemployed during the first year in the simplified case above. Given that the wage changes in the simulations below are small, we feel some confidence about the order of magnitude chosen. Experimentation with values around 0.01 in the simulations below changed the results only slightly, giving in any case a stable path of the system towards the long-run compensating equilibrium between wages and unemployment rates. For example, taking the long-run coefficients derived from the estimated migration and wage equations for the total sample with $u_N = 15\%$ we would have, abstracting from constants and housing prices:

$$m_i = 1.67 w_i - 5.83 u_i \ (+ \text{ terms in } \Delta w_i, \Delta u_i, \Delta m_i) \tag{23a}$$

$$w_i = 0.21 u_i \ (+ \text{ terms in } \Delta w_i, \Delta u_i) \tag{23b}$$

$$\Delta u_i = 0.015 m_i \tag{23c}$$

Ignoring short-term changes and substituting the first two equations into the third the evolution of u_i is guided by an AR(1) process with a root of 0.92, whereas if the parameter in the unemployment equation was 0.01 the coefficient would be 0.95, also stable.[17] Notice that the process by which the regional unemployment rates tend to be equalised (in deviations from drifts and housing prices) is quicker the lower the level of overall unemployment. For instance, if u_N was 7.5%, then the root of the AR(1) process would be 0.89, greatly reducing the length of the adjustment. In order to analyse more precisely the pattern of adjustment, and the concomitant role of regional policy, we devote the next section to a properly dynamic simulation of the model.

3.4 Simulations and regional employment policy implications

Our previous empirical findings support the view that:

1. net regional migration rates respond non-linearly to wage and unemployment differentials, and
2. there is a tendency for regional unemployment and wage differentials to approach a long-run compensating equilibrium in terms of deviations of their respective drifts and housing prices.

If the process by which wage and unemployment differentials disappear was fast, and there were no differences in drifts and moving costs, these findings would cast doubt on the effectiveness of a regional employment policy; the latter could then be defined only in a neutral sense: moving jobs to people or the opposite.

This conclusion is certainly true in the long run. But according to our empirical findings there are significant drifts in wage differentials and also the adjustment of migration and wages is slow; regional employment policy might then be able to speed up the process of equalisation. We would advocate several types of policies.

First, measures could be taken to encourage jobs to move before people do. Some of these policies should give firms more incentives to hire more labour in depressed regions, like marginal employment subsidies or the lowering of payroll taxes.[18] This would apply to regions like the Northeast, with a relatively – in national terms – high unemployment rates and real wages. But labour is already cheapest in the South which reveals the lack of other conditions. In particular, to be effective, these policies should be complemented by higher investment in infrastructure in general, and communications in particular, which has been very low in Spain in the recent past (see Viñals *et al.* (1990)). In this way, less favoured areas could become an attractive alternative for the location of firms, which is not the case now.

Table 5.10. *Regional system dynamic adjustment path*

	Whole sample			First sub-sample			Second sub-sample		
Year	m	du	w	m	du	q	m	du	w
1	− 0.031	0.933	0.333	− 0.039	0.918	0.556	− 0.034	0.926	0.342
2	− 0.031	0.886	0.336	− 0.041	0.857	0.561	− 0.036	0.872	0.321
3	− 0.030	0.841	0.287	− 0.040	0.797	0.411	− 0.036	0.818	0.248
4	− 0.029	0.797	0.239	− 0.038	0.740	0.260	− 0.034	0.767	0.190
5	− 0.028	0.756	0.202	− 0.037	0.684	0.151	− 0.333	0.717	0.152
6	− 0.027	0.716	0.174	− 0.036	0.630	0.083	− 0.031	0.671	0.128
7	− 0.026	0.677	0.152	− 0.035	0.578	0.044	− 0.030	0.626	0.112
8	− 0.024	0.641	0.135	− 0.034	0.527	0.022	− 0.028	0.584	0.101
9	− 0.023	0.606	0.121	− 0.032	0.479	0.010	− 0.026	0.545	0.092
10	− 0.022	0.572	0.110	− 0.030	0.434	0.003	− 0.025	0.508	0.085
11	− 0.021	0.540	0.101	− 0.029	0.391	− 0.002	− 0.023	0.473	0.078
12	− 0.020	0.510	0.093	− 0.027	0.351	− 0.005	− 0.022	0.440	0.072
13	− 0.019	0.481	0.086	− 0.025	0.314	− 0.008	− 0.020	0.410	0.067
14	− 0.018	0.453	0.080	− 0.023	0.279	− 0.010	− 0.019	0.381	0.062
15	− 0.017	0.427	0.075	− 0.021	0.248	− 0.012	− 0.018	0.355	0.058
16	− 0.016	0.402	0.070	− 0.019	0.219	− 0.013	− 0.017	0.330	0.054
17	− 0.016	0.379	0.065	− 0.017	0.193	− 0.013	− 0.015	0.307	0.050
18	− 0.015	0.357	0.061	− 0.016	0.170	− 0.013	− 0.014	0.285	0.046
19	− 0.014	0.336	0.057	− 0.014	0.148	− 0.013	− 0.013	0.265	0.043
20	− 0.013	0.316	0.054	− 0.013	0.129	− 0.013	− 0.012	0.246	0.040
21	− 0.012	0.297	0.050	− 0.011	0.112	− 0.013	− 0.012	0.229	0.037
22	− 0.012	0.280	0.047	− 0.010	0.097	− 0.012	− 0.011	0.213	0.035
23	− 0.011	0.263	0.044	− 0.009	0.084	− 0.011	− 0.010	0.198	0.032
24	− 0.010	0.247	0.041	− 0.008	0.072	− 0.011	− 0.009	0.184	0.030
25	− 0.010	0.232	0.039	− 0.007	0.061	− 0.010	− 0.009	0.171	0.028

A second set of policies would make it economically more profitable for people to move, for instance by stepping up the programme of subsidies for migration established in 1986 and by temporarily subsidising housing in target areas, so that housing price differentials would have less of a deterrent effect on migration. Finally, a third type of policy should aim at variables which in our econometric model are the regional dummy variables – i.e., public goods and amenities which make it more pleasant to live in a given area: education, health care, cultural events, etc. The distribution of these public goods is also quite uneven in Spain, and its improvement could provide an important motivation for migration.

Because geographical disparities have always been sizeable, regional development policy is an old-age subject in Spain. The classic study is

Table 5.10. (*cont.*)

Year	Whole sample			First sub-sample			Second sub-sample		
	m	*du*	*w*	*m*	*du*	*q*	*m*	*du*	*w*
26	− 0.009	0.219	0.037	− 0.006	0.052	− 0.009	− 0.008	0.159	0.026
27	− 0.009	0.205	0.034	− 0.005	0.044	− 0.009	− 0.007	0.148	0.024
28	− 0.008	0.193	0.032	− 0.005	0.037	− 0.008	− 0.007	0.137	0.022
29	− 0.008	0.182	0.030	− 0.004	0.031	− 0.007	− 0.006	0.128	0.021
30	− 0.007	0.171	0.028	− 0.004	0.026	− 0.007	− 0.006	0.119	0.019
31	− 0.007	0.160	0.027	− 0.003	0.021	− 0.006	− 0.006	0.110	0.018
32	− 0.006	0.151	0.025	− 0.003	0.017	− 0.005	− 0.005	0.102	0.017
33	− 0.006	0.142	0.024	− 0.002	0.014	− 0.005	− 0.005	0.095	0.015
34	− 0.006	0.133	0.022	− 0.002	0.011	− 0.004	− 0.004	0.088	0.014
35	− 0.005	0.125	0.021	− 0.002	0.009	− 0.004	− 0.004	0.082	0.013
36	− 0.005	0.117	0.019	− 0.001	0.007	− 0.003	− 0.004	0.076	0.012
37	− 0.005	0.110	0.018	− 0.001	0.005	− 0.003	− 0.004	0.071	0.011
38	− 0.004	0.104	0.017	− 0.001	0.004	− 0.003	− 0.003	0.066	0.011
39	− 0.004	0.097	0.016	− 0.001	0.003	− 0.002	− 0.003	0.061	0.010
40	− 0.004	0.092	0.015	− 0.001	0.002	− 0.002	− 0.003	0.057	0.009
41	− 0.004	0.086	0.014	− 0.001	0.001	− 0.002	− 0.003	0.053	0.009
42	− 0.003	0.081	0.013	0.000	0.000	− 0.002	− 0.002	0.049	0.008
43	− 0.003	0.076	0.013	0.000	0.000	− 0.001	− 0.002	0.046	0.007
44	− 0.003	0.071	0.012	0.000	0.000	− 0.001	− 0.002	0.042	0.007
45	− 0.003	0.067	0.011	0.111	− 0.001	− 0.001	− 0.002	0.039	0.006
46	− 0.003	0.063	0.010	0.000	− 0.001	− 0.001	− 0.002	0.037	0.006
47	− 0.003	0.059	0.010	0.000	− 0.001	− 0.001	− 0.002	0.034	0.006
48	− 0.002	0.055	0.009	0.000	− 0.001	− 0.001	− 0.002	0.032	0.005
49	− 0.002	0.052	0.009	0.000	− 0.001	− 0.001	− 0.001	0.029	0.005
50	− 0.002	0.049	0.008	0.000	− 0.001	0.000	− 0.001	0.027	0.004

Richardson (1975), and a more recent survey is provided by Martín (1988). Regional policies have been implemented in the past, which helps account for the convergence of regional GDP per capita over time (as shown in Figure 5.9). However, the long period of recession, 1975–85, brought a large part of the official development policy to a halt. What is needed is to take advantage of the economic growth taking place today to divert a larger part of those resources into regional development policies. Some of the policies we advocate are considered in the medium-term regional development plan of the Spanish Government for 1989–93 (Ministerio de Economía y Hacienda, 1989a, 1989b), but it remains to be seen whether or not they will be implemented. One should be aware that on these issues there is a significant coordination problem between the

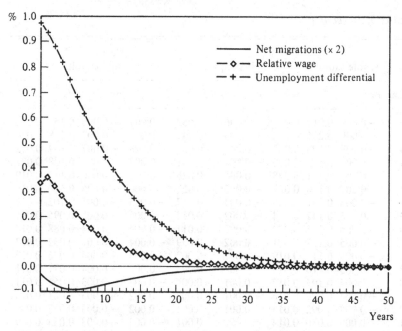

Figure 5.15 Regional system: adjustment path, total sample

central government and the 17 regional governments, which depends on a stable agreement on regional financing, which has still not been reached.

Can the efficiency of these policy proposals be defended analytically? JLS show that a rigorous case for expected tax differentials in favour of high unemployment groups can be made, and that such differentials should be higher the less responsive is the labour force to wage inequalities. Since we find low responsiveness and slow adjustment to economic incentives, our proposals would meet the conditions required by the theory.

In order to illustrate the role of these policies, we have used the estimates of the regional system formed by the migration and wage equations to compute the following simulation. We take as the initial state one in which a given region's unemployment rate is 1 percentage point above the national rate – which is kept unchanged at 15%, not an improbable figure for 1990 – assuming zero drifts and housing price differentials. This will encourage net outmigration until the differential is eliminated. The model is closed by using the proposed relation between changes in regional unemployment rates and net migration rates. Since the migration equation shows some signs of instability, we have performed the calculation for the total sample and the two sub-samples. The results are given in Table 5.10 and in Figures 5.15, 5.16 and 5.17.

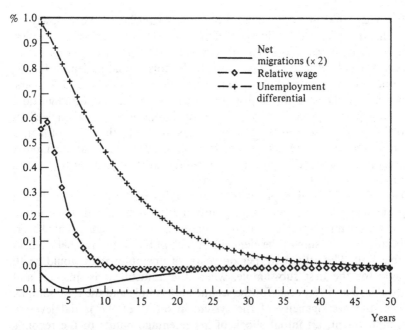

Figure 5.16 Regional system: adjustment path, first sub-sample

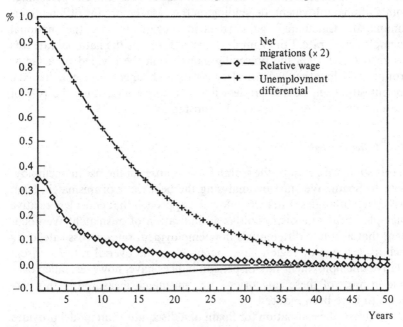

Figure 5.17 Regional system: adjustment path, second sample

It is clear that unemployment differentials vanish only very slowly, as roughly illustrated above by the high root that its autoregressive representation would have. In the first sub-sample, it takes 9 years after the initial shock for half of it to disappear, while the corresponding length for the second sub-sample and the total sample is between 11 and 9 years, respectively. During the adjustment there is continuous outmigration, which reaches a peak 5 or 6 years after the initial shock and then declines slowly. Wages also adjust, initially increasing due to the effect of lagged wages and larger unemployment, but falling afterwards, as unemployment falls. They reach a peak in the second year (first year for the second sub-sample) and then fall monotonically.

The role of regional employment policy in this example can be evaluated by the *saving* in unemployment points that would happen if the initial regional unemployment rate were increased by 1 percentage point. This is measured by the sum of the elements in each of the columns labelled *du* in Table 5.10. The estimated 'person-years' of unemployment would be 10 points for the first sub-sample, where the adjustment is quicker, and between 13 and 16 points for the second sub-sample and the total sample. Given the homogeneity of the system in terms of the initial level of unemployment, an initial shock of x percentage points to the regoin's unemployment differentials will be taken between $10x$ and $16x$ percentage points of unemployment, depending on the case, before the differential is eliminated. Calculated gains depend negatively on the national unemployment rate. For example, if instead of 15% the national rate was assumed to be 10% the preceding gains would be divided by a factor around 1.5. In other words, at times of high unemployment, like the present situation, people are less likely to move and, thus, the role of regional employment policy can be substantial.

4   Conclusions

In this study we continue the search for the causes of the rise in unemployment in Spain. We start by analysing the behaviour of mismatch, from two different angles. First we follow the approach that considers relative unemployment rate dispersion as an indication of mismatch. We document that absolute differentials in unemployment rates across categories such as sex, age or region have increased as the overall rate has risen; relative unemployment rate dispersion indices have, however, fallen over time in most of these categories – i.e., mismatch measured in this way seems to have been reduced.

In contrast, the estimation for Spain of a disequilibrium model provides a measure of mismatch, understood as the heterogeneity of constraints on firms in different markets, which steadily increases over time. We find we can statistically explain the path followed by this index by regressing it on a set of variables related to mismatch. On account of this and the casual evidence provided by the current overheating situation in Spain, we reluctantly conclude that the disequilibrium measure seems to provide a more accurate picture of the behaviour of mismatch in Spain.

Part of the rise in mismatch, as measured by the latter index, comes from the evolution of the regional distribution of economic variables. To gain a better understanding on this aspect of mismatch, and given that internal migration has steadily decreased in Spain since the early 1960s, we set up and estimate an econometric system modelling internal migration flows and regional wage differentials. We find, on the one hand, that interregional migration responds significantly to economic variables such as real wage and unemployment differentials, but with a relative small value and also with long lags. On the other hand, the overall unemployment rate and housing price differentials are also found to deter migration. We then simulate the dynamic response of the system to an exogenous increase in the unemployment rate of a region, finding that the convergence of the process to a long-run equilibrium with compensating wage differentials is very slow. We infer that a regional policy targeted at moving jobs to people – in contrast to relying on the movement of people to jobs – could save a sizeable amount of unemployment during the short and medium run, specially starting from a high national unemployment rate. Other policy recommendations, related to tax schemes and regional house price measures are also set out.

A lot remains to be done. Our econometric model can be improved further by including omitted variables, unavailable at this time, but which are probably important, like those approximating the availability of public goods and amenities, or the demographic characteristics of the population by region. Moreover, cross-section variation could be gained by repeating the exercise for provinces instead of the more aggregate regions.

This kind of dynamic system could similarly be estimated for the case of mobility across economic sectors. The issue of skill scarcity, the only interesting dimension where the unemployment dispersion mismatch index is increasing in the recent past, should also be expored. The construction sector, where shortages of manpower in general – and skilled manpower in particular – have been reported in the last few years, would be an extremely interesting sector to analyse. We have to leave these issues for further research.

APPENDIX 1: GROUPING OF REGIONS INTO 5 AGGREGATE REGIONS

1. Big Cities (*BC*):   4. Baleares (*BAL*)
                         9. Cataluña (*CAT*)
                         13. Madrid (*MAD*)
2. North (*NO*):   3. Asturias (*AST*)
                         6. Cantabria (*CNT*)
                         10. País Vasco (*PVA*)
3. Northeast (*NE*):   2. Aragón (*ARA*)
                         15. Navarra (*NAV*)
                         16. La Rioja (*LRJ*)
                         17. Valencia (*VAL*)
4. Centre (*CE*):   7. Castilla La Mancha (*CLM*)
                         8. Castilla León (*CLE*)
                         12. Galicia (*GAL*)
5. South (*SO*):   1. Andalucía (*AND*)
                         5. Canarias (*CAN*)
                         11. Extremadura (*EXT*)
                         14. Murcia (*MUR*)

APPENDIX 2: SOURCES AND DEFINITIONS

1. *Migration and population*
   The source is: Instituto Nacional de Estadística (INE), *Anuario Estadístico de España* (1960–87).
2. *Labour force, employment and unemployment data*
   For national data, the source is: INE, *Encuesta de Población Activa* (1964–89). In the available disaggregate classifications, we have used the homogeneisation of these data contained in Ministerio de Economía y Hacienda (MEH) (1987). For regional employment and unemployment the source is: Banco de Bilbao, *Renta Nacional de España y su Distribución Provincial* (1962–85, available every other year except for 1966). An interpolation to get annual data was done using the profile of the aggregate unemployment series from INE, *Encuesta de Población Activa*. The levels were rescaled to that of the homogeneised data in MEH (1990).
3. *Wages*
   The source is as for regional unemployment data. The series is nominal compensation for employees in the province divided by the number of wage earners. The interpolation to get annual data was done using the profile of the wage series in: INE, *Encuesta de Salarios* (1962–86).
   Nominal wages were deflated by the consumer price index for each province from: INE, *Indice de Precios al Consumo* (1962–86).
   All provincial CPI series were set to 100 in 1962. Housing and rental prices are taken from the appropriate item in the retail price index.
   Regional data were calculated by weighting each province's wages by its share of dependent employment in the region.
   The aggregation of provinces into regions is the official one, established in 1978, extended backwards to 1962.

APPENDIX 3: MIGRATION AND WAGE EQUATIONS

$$\Delta m_{it} = \beta_0 + \beta_1 \Delta m_{it-1} + \beta_2 m_{it-1} + \beta_3 \Delta\omega_{it} + \beta_4 \Delta\omega_{it-1} + \beta_5 \Delta ru_{it} + \beta_6 ru_{it-1} + \beta_7(\omega_{it}/u_{Nt})_{-1} + \beta_8(pa_{it}/u_{Nt})$$

Table 5.A1. *Migration equations*

Region	β_0	β_1	β_2	β_3	β_4	β_5	β_6	β_7	β_8	R^2	DW
AND	0.03 (0.77)	0.57 (2.69)	−0.11 (1.23)	0.10 (0.06)	0.42 (0.25)	−0.11 (0.57)	−0.20 (3.04)	−0.21 (0.25)	−1.30 (1.14)	0.36	2.06
ARA	0.09 (0.76)	−0.13 (0.63)	−0.02 (0.13)	−0.40 (0.80)	−1.12 (2.28)	−0.12 (0.95)	−0.67 (0.62)	0.97 (0.56)	0.12 (0.20)	0.16	2.28
AST	−0.13 (1.36)	0.00 (0.02)	−0.36 (1.29)	0.25 (0.52)	−0.47 (1.23)	0.08 (1.01)	1.24 (1.04)	0.24 (0.78)	−0.18 (0.80)	0.05	2.01
BAL	−0.06 (1.29)	0.76 (6.10)	−0.14 (1.13)	0.55 (1.36)	−0.56 (1.26)	−0.07 (0.47)	−0.16 (6.68)	0.24 (1.24)	−0.61 (1.53)	0.87	1.98
CAN	0.20 (1.27)	0.17 (0.40)	−0.51 (1.16)	0.57 (0.99)	−0.58 (1.10)	−0.08 (1.04)	−0.67 (0.91)	0.61 (1.05)	0.33 (0.70)	0.05	1.38
CNT	0.00 (0.01)	0.26 (0.90)	−0.55 (2.37)	0.18 (0.91)	−0.41 (0.47)	0.01 (0.13)	−0.15 (0.13)	0.63 (1.57)	−0.33 (0.69)	0.20	1.93
CLM	0.01 (0.15)	0.50 (4.64)	−0.18 (2.00)	0.11 (1.01)	−1.85 (1.82)	0.16 (1.10)	−0.09 (1.80)	0.98 (1.86)	−0.35 (0.25)	0.77	1.95
CLE	−0.29 (0.73)	0.50 (2.16)	−0.24 (2.40)	0.50 (0.72)	−1.23 (0.72)	−0.10 (0.26)	−0.27 (0.67)	0.54 (0.58)	−0.27 (0.09)	0.25	2.21

Table 5.A1. (cont.)

Region	β_0	β_1	β_2	β_3	β_4	β_5	β_6	β_7	β_8	R^2	DW
CAT	0.01	0.26	−0.10	0.37	−1.25	−0.27	−0.13	−0.20	−0.16	0.84	2.40
	(0.36)	(2.64)	(1.51)	(2.17)	(1.83)	(1.09)	(6.01)	(0.96)	(1.46)		
PVA	0.19	0.53	−0.34	0.38	−0.77	0.16	−0.22	0.47	−0.12	0.84	2.32
	(1.42)	(4.81)	(6.35)	(1.05)	(0.53)	(0.83)	(2.92)	(0.49)	(0.80)		
EXT	0.03	0.40	−0.15	0.18	−0.70	0.00	−0.14	−0.20	−0.15	0.89	2.37
	(0.70)	(5.72)	(4.30)	(0.92)	(1.07)	(0.06)	(10.8)	(0.44)	(1.00)		
GAL	0.05	0.16	−0.19	−0.02	−0.71	−0.20	−0.13	1.41	−0.95	0.46	2.49
	(1.34)	(0.72)	(2.17)	(0.04)	(1.42)	(2.49)	(1.69)	(2.47)	(2.03)		
MAD	0.03	0.40	−0.20	1.25	1.82	0.10	−0.15	0.56	0.10	0.74	2.43
	(0.92)	(3.32)	(2.66)	(2.67)	(2.17)	(1.05)	(3.52)	(1.06)	(0.82)		
MUR	0.05	0.11	−0.19	0.19	−0.73	−0.01	0.28	0.99	−0.65	0.27	1.84
	(1.04)	(0.51)	(2.10)	(0.53)	(2.06)	(0.22)	(0.72)	(2.20)	(1.40)		
NAV	0.40	−0.21	−0.35	0.45	0.10	−0.25	−2.16	0.63	−1.87	0.76	1.79
	(4.57)	(1.74)	(4.24)	(1.00)	(0.16)	(5.46)	(5.17)	(1.75)	(1.56)		
LRJ	0.03	−0.17	−0.17	0.42	−0.49	−0.29	−0.15	0.54	−0.16	0.55	1.88
	(0.83)	(0.92)	(1.33)	(1.44)	(1.62)	(1.51)	(3.77)	(1.13)	(0.38)		
VAL	0.02	0.71	−0.23	0.87	−0.72	−0.01	−0.12	0.19	−0.13	0.52	2.30
	(0.07)	(3.81)	(1.63)	(2.42)	(0.85)	(0.06)	(0.04)	(1.14)	(2.26)		

Note: The coefficients β_7 and β_8 are multiplied by 10.

$$\Delta\omega_{it} = \beta_0 + \beta_1\Delta\omega_{it-1} + \beta_2\Delta du_{it-1} + \beta_3 du_{it-1} + \beta_4\omega_{it-1} + \beta_5 pa_{it-1}$$

Table 5.A2. *Wage equations*

Region	β_0	β_1	β_2	β_3	β_4	β_5	R^2	DW
AND	− 0.39	0.36	− 0.64	0.20	− 0.43	0.11	0.44	2.15
	(4.24)	(1.51)	(1.79)	(3.88)	(4.27)	(1.90)		
ARA	− 0.01	0.18	0.52	− 0.42	− 0.07	0.10	0.04	2.00
	(1.56)	(0.71)	(0.93)	(0.68)	(0.27)	(1.20)		
AST	0.02	0.27	0.07	0.05	− 0.23	0.00	0.08	1.85
	(1.03)	(1.08)	(0.10)	(0.96)	(1.64)	(0.08)		
BAL	0.02	0.22	0.34	0.04	− 0.39	0.05	0.58	2.00
	(0.69)	(1.56)	(0.71)	(3.04)	(2.30)	(0.99)		
CAN	− 0.02	0.15	0.38	0.04	− 0.27	0.04	0.24	2.22
	(1.13)	(0.79)	(0.83)	(1.97)	(2.21)	(0.60)		
CNT	0.02	0.33	− 0.34	0.06	− 0.38	0.03	0.48	2.33
	(2.52)	(2.45)	(0.37)	(2.38)	(3.84)	(0.06)		
CLM	− 0.05	0.12	− 0.18	0.08	− 0.22	− 0.11	0.31	2.34
	(0.86)	(0.64)	(0.49)	(2.48)	(0.90)	(1.68)		
CLE	− 0.02	0.17	0.81	0.21	− 0.31	0.00	0.11	2.10
	(0.22)	(0.57)	(0.97)	(0.02)	(1.30)	(0.00)		
CAT	0.05	0.10	− 0.09	0.56	− 0.46	0.06	0.38	2.12
	(3.03)	(0.76)	(1.13)	(3.07)	(3.21)	(1.80)		
PVA	0.03	0.28	− 0.18	0.05	− 0.27	0.19	0.65	2.15
	(4.24)	(2.86)	(0.25)	(3.55)	(5.13)	(2.93)		
EXT	− 0.08	0.52	0.24	0.05	− 0.20	0.12	0.60	2.30
	(2.70)	(0.46)	(1.03)	(2.62)	(2.40)	(2.14)		
GAL	− 0.03	0.10	0.64	− 0.82	− 0.53	− 0.04	0.03	1.80
	(1.50)	(0.28)	(0.87)	(0.41)	(1.83)	(1.04)		
MAD	0.07	0.31	0.08	0.68	− 0.40	0.10	0.26	1.87
	(2.16)	(1.72)	(0.16)	(0.65)	(2.42)	(1.28)		
MUR	− 0.08	0.24	0.40	0.04	− 0.45	0.02	0.53	2.26
	(2.73)	(1.59)	(1.03)	(2.73)	(2.90)	(1.00)		
NAV	− 0.01	0.37	− 0.48	0.06	− 0.22	− 0.02	0.64	1.70
	(1.76)	(3.00)	(1.33)	(3.20)	(1.84)	(0.33)		
LRJ	0.00	0.05	0.85	0.06	− 0.16	0.11	0.70	1.78
	(0.10)	(0.58)	(2.00)	(5.47)	(1.70)	(1.90)		
VAL	0.00	0.09	0.26	0.07	− 0.12	0.02	0.17	1.52
	(0.00)	(0.44)	(0.45)	(2.15)	(1.63)	(0.18)		

NOTES

1 We are most grateful to César Alonso for his extremely capable help in collecting and organising the data and in estimating the model. We thank Florella Padoa Schioppa, our discussant Nicola Rossi, and the participants at the Venice conference (1990) and at a seminar at the Bank of Spain for their comments. We also thank Jaume García for providing us with some of the data. The responsibility for all the views expressed and all mistakes is ours.
2 Echoing the theme of Muellbauer and Murphy (1989).
3 The first complete year for which we have homogeneous data is 1977.
4 Not all characteristics are equally interesting: change of sex is (almost) impossible, change of age is exogeneous, and the sectoral classification is not very informative, since workers do not necessarily find jobs in the same sector where they worked last.
5 Formally:

$$PMM = \sum_i |\Delta(N_i/N)|$$

where N_i is employment in sector i and N is total employment.

The sectors are: agriculture, industry, construction and services.
6 SDU is the square root of the numerator of JLS's MM index, but unweighted.
7 Due to lack of data for most variables after 1986, in the remainder of the study we restrict ourselves to the period 1962–86.
8 See, for example, the survey by Shields and Shields (1989) and the references therein.
9 Although we were not aware of their paper when we wrote the first draft of our own study.
10 See Appendix 2 for sources and definitions of all variables.
11 When we did not make this correction the econometric results – available from us on request – were not very different from those reported below.
12 This procedure was suggested to us by Richard Layard and Stephen Nickell.
13 Probably exacerbated by our adjustment of the official data.
14 Fina (1987) remarks that these numbers should be taken with caution, due to a methodological break in the series.
15 In the estimation, m_{it} is in percentage terms while the unemployment and wage variables are proportions; we do this in order to write coefficients with two digits.
16 We decided against including the replacement ratio in the wage or the migration equation as a regressor, because we feel the quality of the constructed measure is too low.
17 If short-term differences were included we would get a more general $AR(p)$ process, whose gain at $L = 1$ would be identical to the previous values, giving a similar picture of the adjustment process; see Wickens and Breusch (1988).
18 Similar measures have been proposed for the UK by C. Huhne (1990).

REFERENCES

Andrés, J., J. Dolado, C. Molinas, M. Sebastián and A. Zabalza (1990). 'The Influence of Demand and Capital Constraints on Spanish Unemployment', in

J. Drèze et al. (eds), *Europe's Employment Problem*, Cambridge, MA: MIT Press.

Andrés, J. and J. García (1989). 'Main Features of the Spanish Labour Market Facing 1992', Universidad de Valencia (mimeo).

Attanasio, O. and F. Padoa Schioppa (1990). 'Regional Inequalities, Migrations and Mismatch in Italy, 1960–86' (Chapter 6 in this volume).

Banco de Bilbao, *Renta Nacional de España y su Distribución Provincial*, Madrid (various issues).

Bean, C. et al. (eds) (1986). *The Rise in Unemployment*, London: Basil Blackwell.

Bentolila, S. and O. Blanchard (1990). 'Spanish Unemployment', *Economic Policy*, **10**, 233–81.

Cowling, K. and D. Metcalf (1967). 'Wage–Unemployment Relationships: A Regional Analysis for the UK 1960–65', *Oxford Bulletin of Economics and Statistics*, **29**, 31–9.

Dolado, J. and J. Malo de Molina (1985). 'Desempleo y Rigidez del Mercado de Trabajo en España', Banco de España, *Boletín Económico* (September) 22–40.

Dolado, J., J. Malo de Molina and A. Zabalza (1986). 'Spanish Industrial Unemployment: Some Explanatory Factors', in C. Bean et al. (eds), *The Rise in Unemployment*, London: Basil Blackwell, 313–34.

Drèze, J. (1990). 'European Unemployment: Lessons from a Multi-country Econometric Exercise', in J. Drèze et al. (eds), *Europe's Employment Problem*, Cambridge, MA: MIT Press.

Fina, L. (1987). 'Unemployment in Spain. Its Causes and the Policy Response', *Labour*, **1(2)**, 29–69.

García, P. (1990). 'Evolución de la Estructura Salarial Española durante el Periodo 1963–1986', in S. Bentolila and L. Toharia (eds), *Estudios de Economía del Trabajo en España, III: El Problema del Paro*, Madrid: Ministerio de Trabajo y Seguridad Social.

Harris, J. and M. Todaro (1970). 'Migration, Unemployment and Development: a Two-Sector Analysis', *American Economic Review*, **60**, 126–42.

Huhne, C. (1990). 'Tackling Regional Gap Needs a Rethink', *Guardian* (January).

Jackman, R., R. Layard and S. Savouri (1990). 'Mismatch: A Framework for Thought' (Chapter 2 in this volume).

Layard, R. and S. Nickell (1986). 'Unemployment in Britain', in Bean et al. (1986) 121–70.

(1987). 'The Labour Market', in R. Layard and R. Dornbusch (eds), *The Performance of the British Economy*, Oxford: Clarendon Press, Chapter 5, 131–79.

Martín, M. (1988). 'Evolución de las Disparidades Regionales: Una Perspectiva Histórica', in J. García (ed.), *España, Economiía*, Madrid: Espasa-Calpe, S.A., 704–43.

Ministerio de Economía y Hacienda (1990). 'Nota sobre el Enlace Provisional de las Series de la Encuesta de Población Activa', in S. Bentolila and L. Toharia (eds), *Estudios de Economía del Trabajo en España, III: El Problema del Paro*, Madrid: Ministerio de Trabajo y Seguridad Social.

Ministerio de Economía y Hacienda (1989a). *Plan de Desarrollo Regional de España, 1989–1993*, Madrid: Secretaría de Estado de Hacienda.

(1989b). *Plan de Reconversión Regional y Social de España, 1989–1993*, Madrid, Secretaría de Estado de Hacienda.

Muellbauer, J. and A. Murphy (1989). 'Housing and Regional Migration to and from the South East' (mimeo).

Padoa Schioppa, F. (1990). 'Classical, Keynesian and Mismatch Unemployment in Italy', *European Economic Review*, **34**(1/2), forthcoming.
Pissarides, C. and I. McMaster (1984). 'Regional Migration, Wages and Unemployment: Empirical Evidence and Implications for Policy', London School of Economics, Centre for Labour Economics, discussion paper, **204**.
Pissarides, C. and J. Wadsworth (1987). 'Unemployment and the Inter-Regional Mobility of Labour', London School of Economics, Centre for Labour Economics, discussion paper, **296**. ((1989), *Economic Journal*, **99**, 739–55.)
Richardson, H. (1975). *Regional Development Policy and Planning in Spain*, London: D. C. Heath.
Rodríguez, C. (1988). *Los Determinantes de las Diferencias Interprovinciales de Salarios en España*, Universidad de Oviedo, Servicio de Publicaciones.
Santillana, I. (1978). 'The Economic Determinants of Internal Migration: A Case Study of Spain, 1960 to 1973', unpublished Ph.D. dissertation, Indiana University.
Shields, G. and M. Shields (1989). 'The Emergence of Migration Theory and a Suggested New Direction', *Journal of Economic Surveys*, **3**, 277–304.
Viñals, J. *et al.* (1990). 'The "EEC *cum* 1992" Shock: the Case of Spain', in C. Bliss and J. Braga de Macedo (eds), *Unity with Diversity in the European Economy: The Community's Southern Frontier*, Cambridge: Cambridge University Press.
White, H. (1982). 'A Heteroskedasticity-Consistent Covariance Matrix Estimator and a Direct Test for Heteroskedasticity', *Econometrica*, **48**, 817–38.
Wickens, M. and T. Breusch (1988). 'Dynamic Specification, the Long Run and the Estimation of Transformed Regression Models', *Economic Journal*, **98**, 189–205.

Discussion

NICOLA ROSSI

The study by Bentolila and Dolado is an important attempt to shed some light on the working of the Spanish labour market and to provide, eventually, a partial explanation for the dramatic rise in Spanish unemployment from 1% in 1960 to almost 22% in 1985 and for its persistence at those unprecedented levels thereafter. The authors explicitly refer, in the latter respect, to the study by Bentolila and Blanchard (1990) where it is suggested that high unemployment could have reduced the willingness to work in other regions, thereby inhibiting labour mobility and determining a regional mismatch from the labour supply side. Bentolila and Dolado deal, first, with the basic issue of measurement of mismatch and suggest that the usual indicator based on relative unemployment rate dispersion should give way to alternative measures of mismatch explicitly derived from disequilibrium models of the labour market. Having thus documented the rise of mismatch throughout the sample period, Bentolila and Dolado focus on its major determinants and set up an econometric model of internal migration in Spain. The main result appears to be that migration flows respond non-linearly to unemployment so that migration flows are lower the higher the unemployment rate, thereby providing support for Bentolila and Blanchard's case.

Bentolila and Dolado's study has certainly to be commended for its neat presentation of the Spanish case and for its painstaking collection and thorough analysis of regional Spanish data. The evidence presented in the study is well organised and the case for focusing on the deficient matching between labour supply and demand is definitely well augmented. However, as I will try to show in what follows, the study still leaves some questions unanswered.

To start with, the widely different performance of alternative indicators of mismatch is quite striking, and points up the fact that they are, in fact, measuring entirely different concepts. In this respect, I wonder whether the dispute on the appropriateness of alternative indicators could, and should, be resolved by means of the indirect evidence referred to in section 2. It is certainly rather unusual to use regression analysis, as in section 2, to assess the appropriateness of the *dependent* variable. More importantly, however, the real question is the following: to which theory – that is, to which indicator – do the variables which in section 2 are (rather vaguely) supposed to be related to mismatch actually refer?

Let us now revert to the theoretical analysis of migration flows. In the light of the crucial role played by non-linearities in the model, the study would have gained from a more detailed discussion of the issue of the specification of the net migration equation. In particular, it appears of paramount importance to understand under which conditions (say, on preferences) if any, differences or ratios in unemployment rates should actually appear as legitimate regressors. In the study however, this important issue is treated in a somewhat *ad hoc* manner and left mostly to the data to explain.

A second doubtful aspect of the theoretical section is given by the regional unemployment equation (or 'pseudo-identity'). The assumption that all new immigrants in a given region are unemployed during the first year of arrival is, needless to say, somewhat unrealistic. The authors do recognise this when they come actually to represent regional unemployment, but they still solve the model under the assumption that 6 out of 10 of all new immigrants spend the first year unemployed. I would tend to regard this figure as still quite high; looking at the Italian experience, it could be suggested that such figures might have been justified in the 1950s and 1960s, but certainly not nowadays.

Reverting now to the empirical application, the first issue to be dealt with is, I think, a measurement one. Basic data refer to population and not to workers; as such, they are likely to be generated by households' and not by individual decisions. Household characteristics such as family size and composition should therefore possibly also be taken into account.

Over and above measurement problems, the empirical application reflects, to some extent, the attitude of the authors toward the non-linearities of the migration equation. In this respect, it is not difficult to remain under the impression that the empirical results are not as robust as the study sometimes seems to imply. A quick look at Appendix 3 reveals that in a significant number of regions it would be difficult to reject the hypothesis that migration is generated by very simple autoregressive processes with no drifts, no role whatsoever being played by unemployment differences or ratios or by wage differentials. Undoubtedly, the cross-regional variability turns out to be a key factor in pinning down the pooled estimates; however, in the light of the previous remark not much weight should be given to the 'easily accepted' pooling restrictions. To put it differently, the evidence of Appendix 3 suggests some heterogeneity across regions, and casts some doubts on the basic specification of the internal migration model.

Summing up, Bentolila and Dolado have prepared an interesting piece of applied work which contains a number of important insights into the working and performance of the Spanish labour market. As with all good studies, though, Bentolila and Dolado bring out a number of interesting, and still unanswered, questions for future research.

REFERENCE

Bentolila S. and O. Blanchard (1990). 'Spanish Unemployment', *Economic Policy*, **10**.

6 Regional Inequalities, Migration and Mismatch in Italy, 1960–86[1]

ORAZIO P. ATTANASIO and FIORELLA
PADOA SCHIOPPA

Migration is an effect, not a remedy: it is the way Southern peasants have
found to subtract themselves from the evil, but it is not the solution to
the evil . . .

Admittedly, migration corrects some of those intertwining problems
out of which arises the so-called Southern Question (*la questione meridionale*): migration, for instance, forces peasants to go to school; it steps
up their mental development bringing them in contact with the more
civilised populations; it brings a considerable accumulation of capital
into the Mezzogiorno of Italy. But it does not reforest ruined land, it
does not eliminate malaria, it does not improve our suffocating tax and
customs' systems, it does not help our authorities to improve and indeed
it often worsens them, intensifying their perversion. On the other hand,
it is accompanied by a phenomenon which is far from being good, the
loosening of family ties . . .

Today, more than ever before, in the face of migration a serious,
intense and systematic programme is necessary to solve the Southern
problem; that is, to create in the South a moral and economic State
where migration becomes in turn a positive element meant to accelerate
the solution to the Southern problem (Salvemini, 1958).

Despite Italy's long tradition of mass migration to foreign lands, the
notion that large-scale internal migration may need to be accepted, and
even encouraged, as a way of evening-out inter-regional inequalities in
income levels has found few sponsors. Nonetheless, some commentators
on the events of the 'fifties' hold that migration of Southern workers –
partly abroad but mostly to the North of Italy – which actually took
place during that period, and which probably amounted to many hun-
dreds of thousands, made a bigger contribution towards improving the
living standards of persons originally resident in the South and of
members of their families who sometimes remained behind living on
remittances, than did the whole Southern policy. A policy which ought,
one might think, to be given more consideration in the future is that of
assisted migration, accompanied by measures for removing certain dis-
incentives – connected with the structure of taxation and of labour costs
(Lutz, 1960).

237

1   Introduction

Over the period from 1961 to 1969, male unemployment rates averaged 0.024 in Piemonte (Northern Italy) and 0.062 in Calabria (Southern Italy). Net migrations (defined as the difference between emigrants and immigrants) relative to the population of the region (defined as net migration rates) averaged − 12.39 and 12.30 in these two regions. From 1980 to 1986 male unemployment rates averaged 0.049 and 0.106 in the same regions, while the figures for net migration rates were 1.20 and 2.22. A similar picture emerges (as will be documented below) when we consider other regions from the North and the South.

This study is an attempt to understand why, in the presence of high (and

Figure 6.1   Italy: administrative regions, ISTAT partitions and geographical areas

Italian administrative regions

1. Piemonte (*PI*)
2. Valle d'Aosta (*VA*)
3. Lombardia (*LO*)
4. Trentino-Alto Adige (*TA*)
5. Veneto (*VE*)
6. Friuli-Venezia Giulia (*FV*)
7. Liguria (*LI*)
8. Emilia-Romagna (*ER*)
9. Toscana (*TO*)
10. Umbria (*UM*)
11. Marche (*MA*)
12. Lazio (*LZ*)
13. Abruzzo (*AB*)
14. Molise (*MO*)
15. Campania (*CA*)
16. Puglia (*PU*)
17. Basilicata (*BA*)
18. Calabria (*CL*)
19. Sicilia (*SI*)
20. Sardegna (*SA*)

Italian partitions according to ISTAT

1. Nord-occidentale (1, 2, 3, 7)
2. Nord-orientale (4, 5, 6, 8)
3. Centrale (9, 10, 11, 12)
4. Meridionale (13, 14, 15, 16, 17, 18)
5. Insulare (19, 20)

Italian geographical areas

1. Nord-Ovest (*NO*) = North-West (1, 2, 3, 7)
2. Nord-Est (*NE*) = North-East (4, 5, 6)
3. Centrale (*CE*) = Centre (8, 9, 10, 11)
4. Lazio (*LZ*) = Lazio (12)
5. Sud-Est (*SE*) = South-East (13, 14, 16)
6. Sud-Ovest (*SO*) = South-West (15, 17, 18, 19, 20)

sometimes increasing) differentials in unemployment, internal gross out-migration and net migration rates were dramatically reduced in Italy.

Our purpose is mainly a descriptive one. With the help of a newly-created data set, which is analysed here for the first time, we try to construct a consistent picture of the dynamics of migration behaviour within Italy in the years 1960–86. This could be considered as a first step towards a better understanding of the migration phenomenon and, in particular, how this phenomenon has changed in recent years.[2] Our explanation is primarily economic, even though we recognise the importance of social and political factors, underlying what has been called the 'cultural model hostile to the process of migration' (Sarcinelli, 1989, 132).

The study lacks any explicit normative implication. We try to understand why workers, unlike in the 1960s, do not migrate from the South to the North-Centre of Italy, even in the presence of strong and persistent regional imbalances. We do not mean to imply that workers should migrate; a companion paper could (and perhaps should) be written to try to understand why capital does not move from the North-Centre to the South, or does so incompletely.

Italy is divided into 20 administrative regions, as clarified by the map of Italy in Figure 6.1. We started our analysis at this level but we soon realised the necessity of somewhat synthesising the information presented. We therefore decided to aggregate the 20 regions in six larger geographical areas, described in the map. Of course, this choice is somewhat arbitrary but we believe that the exposition of the results is greatly simplified without losing too much in interesting economic information.

We think that our measure of migration (change in anagraphical residence from one town to another) has a different interpretation and meaning depending on whether the destination is the same area or a different one in Italy. For this reason we were careful in the definition of our areas, trying to delimit them so as to have economically and sociologically homogeneous environments. While the first criterion for aggregation was geographical contiguity (with the exception of the two big Islands), we also looked at a variety of economic and sociological indicators in making our choice. It should be remembered, though, that the aim of this study is not the explaining of regional differences in Italy, but rather how these differences (whose presence is documented below) interplay with the migration phenomenon.

Some of the divisions were obvious: the North-Western (*NO*) regions (Piemonte, Lombardia, Liguria and Valle D'Aosta), where industry was first developed in Italy and which were the destination of a large proportion of the big migration flows of the 1950s and 1960s, constituted an almost inevitable choice.

Another fairly homogeneous area is, in our opinion, the North-East (*NE*): these regions (Veneto, Friuli-Venezia Giulia, Trentino-Alto Adige) are characterised by an agricultural sector larger than in the North-West. Furthermore, their development in the late 1970s and early 1980s has been very rapid so that they turned from being areas with highly positive net migration to being areas with negative net migration rates.

Our third group, which will be denominated Centre (*CE*), is formed by extremely dynamic and wealthy regions in the centre of Italy (Emilia-Romagna, Toscana, Umbria and Marche). These regions are characterised by very high *per capita* income, small and technologically advanced industries, a fairly large but extremely modern agricultural sector, and a very rapid growth in recent years. As we will see, this area has been the largest net recipient of emigrants in the 1980s.

The fourth group is formed by Lazio (*LZ*), the administrative region which contains Rome. Given the size of the capital city and the importance of the public sector in that region, we felt that we could not aggregate Lazio to any other area.

This left us with the Southern regions and the Islands. These regions are those with the lowest *per capita* income, the largest percentage of GDP produced in agriculture, the lowest activity rates and so on; however, we think it important to try to differentiate between different regions of the

Mezzogiorno of Italy. Some regions have, for a plethora of reasons, experienced much faster growth in the 1980s than others, and one might hope that the gap with the Northern-Central regions had narrowed; obvious examples of this phenomenon are some South-Eastern regions (Abruzzo and Molise) which, in many respects, are becoming more and more similar to the dynamic Central regions which they border.

The most difficult decision to make was for the region Puglia (the 'heel' of the 'boot'). Looking at economic indicators, we had a hard time in deciding if Puglia was more similar to Abruzzo or to the other Southern regions. In the end we decided to aggregate Puglia with the South-Eastern regions for two related reasons: on the one hand, especially in more recent years, Puglia has been indicated as following the 'Adriatic model' of development and in some respects is similar to Abruzzo; on the other hand, looking at some sociological indicators, it is clear that Puglia is very different from the other Southern regions.

In particular, the presence of organised crime is much less important in Puglia than in regions like Calabria, Sicilia, Sardegna or Campania. In 1986 the number of murders per 100,000 inhabitants was 3.74 in the South West and 1.11 in the South East.[3] Even though, as we have already said, the aim of the study is not that of explaining the reasons for the persistence of regional imbalances, we do believe that the massive presence of organised crime imposes heavy negative externalities on the economic environment and development that cannot be ignored in the definition of 'homogeneous' areas. The last two groups were thefore formed by what we will refer to as the South-Western (SO – i.e., Campania, Calabria, Basilicata, Sicilia and Sardegna) and the South-Eastern (SE – i.e., Abruzzo, Molise and Puglia) regions.

In the study we will point to the existence of very strong inequalities between these six areas. One may wonder whether regional imbalances imply regional mismatch; the answer is difficult, due in part to the ambiguity of the mismatch concept. In a 'weak' sense, mismatch 'can be thought of as an empirical concept that measures the degree of heterogeneity. More formally, it can be represented by a shift parameter in the job matching function' (Pissarides, 1989, 22); 'Changes in this parameter are intended to capture such changes in geographic or other differences between jobs and workers – what is sometimes called mismatch – as well as differences in search behaviour' (Blanchard and Diamond, 1990, 10). According to this first approach, mismatch is almost a synonym of labour market heterogeneities and therefore the dispersion of regional unemployment rates might be sufficient to identify one reason for it.

In a 'strong' sense, by contrast, 'there is mismatch between vacant jobs and unemployed workers such that if the latter were available with different skill and/or in different places, the level of unemployment would fall' (Jackman and Roper, 1987, 11). The identification of mismatch in such a 'strong' sense presupposes the estimation of 'natural' unemployment rates at the regional level and testing the hypothesis that unemployment in excess of the natural rate differs across regions. In this sense mismatch is a fundamental determinant of structural unemployment.

The estimation of natural rates of unemployment at a regional level is beyond the scope of this study. We will, therefore, focus on the 'weaker' definition of mismatch[4] and concentrate on the relation between regional imbalances and migration rates.

According to the traditional model of migration, as proposed by Harris and Todaro (1970) and generalised, for instance, by Pissarides and Wadsworth (1987), the probability of interregional migration is higher, the greater the difference (for a given cost of migration) between the expected utility in the destination region compared to that of the region of origin.[5] This means that, given the aggregate level of unemployment and the level of reservation and net real wages in the two regions, the probability of migration tends to increase with unemployment differentials. This probability rises with the net real wage differential between the destination and the origin region and declines with the aggregate unemployment level, given the unemployment differentials, if and only if the difference between the net real wage and the reservation wage is higher at destination than at the origin.

The remainder of the study is organised as follows. In section 2 we document the existence of strong economic differences among the six geographical areas described above; this section is not an exhaustive report on regional imbalances, but provides a useful factual background against which the analysis of the following sections is developed.

Section 3 describes the behaviour of some key factors that should be relevant for labour demand or supply and for migration decisions, such as net real wages, productivity, unit labour costs and reservation wages in levels and differentials.

Section 4 looks at other variables which are likely to be important for migratory behaviour, such as the aggregate unemployment rate, the housing rentals' value, etc.

Section 5 considers the gross and net regional migration rates in detail, and stresses some links between the dynamic behaviour of these series and the ones described in the previous sections. For several reasons which will be discussed below, we do not present a formal econometric model but only a set of very preliminary regressions which should be interpreted as an attempt to measure some correlations between the relevant time series:

we believe that there is something to be learned from a careful analysis of the data and of these correlations.

Section 6 presents some evidence on migration rates disaggregated by sex, age and working condition groups. Unfortunately, the data prior to 1969 have been destroyed by ISTAT and are not available.

Section 7 concludes the study, and is followed by a detailed Data Appendix.

2   Regional imbalances: some basic facts

The divide between the South (Mezzogiorno) and the rest of the country is as old as the history of Italy. (Cafiero, 1989; Toniolo, 1988). It is not our aim to give an even partial account of the causes of such a division or of the voluminous literature on the topic.[6] In this section we want briefly to give some figures which may be helpful as a point of reference and provide some factual background to the analysis of the migration phenomenon which is the core of the study.

While the gap – or, better, as it has sometimes been called, the economic dualism – between the North-Centre and the South is a well known phenomenon in Italy, two related aspects – which we wish to stress in this section – are more controversial: the existence of wide differentials within the two main geographical areas and their dynamics in the 27 years under observation. Using some particularly relevant indicators, we will show that the economic performances of the six areas considered are so differentiated one from the other that we may even talk of different 'Mezzogiornos', or of more than one 'North of Italy'. We shall further consider to what extent the gap between poorer and richer areas has become narrower and, by contrast, to what extent it has remained remarkably large and has sometimes even grown.

Had one to choose a single welfare index for different areas, this would probably be the *per capita* value added at factor cost and constant prices, presented in Figure 6.2.

The graph in Figure 6.2 prompts various comments. In the more than 25 years observed, *NO* has always maintained pole position, while *SO* has always been the lame duck of the group, slightly preceded by *SE*, whose performance has become a little more satisfactory since the mid-1970s. During the period considered, the *per capita* value added at factor cost and constant prices of *NO* has been, and remains, twice that of *SO*. *NE*, which is often associated with *NO* in the regional analysis of Italy, was more similar to the Mezzogiorno in 1960 and only in the 1970s did the situation begin to improve so that it is now close to *NO*. The case of *LZ*, given the presence of Rome and the consequently widespread public

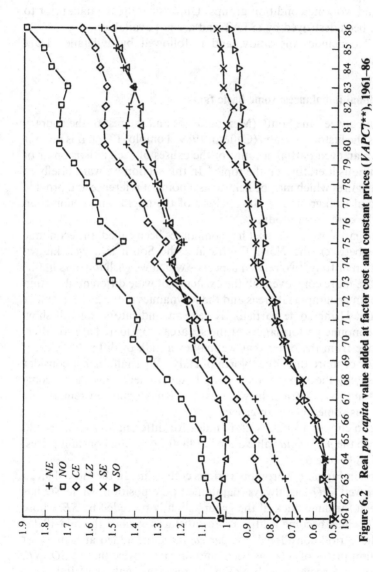

Figure 6.2 Real *per capita* value added at factor cost and constant prices (*VAPCT****), 1961–86

sector, is a special one. It has registered an overall population growth far beyond that of its native population. More recently, it has been affected by the introduction of the decentralised governments for the administrative regions, therefore passing since the 1970s from a top to an intermediate ranking position in *per capita* value added at factor cost and constant prices. The performance of *CE*, whose *per capita* value added at factor cost and constant prices runs parallel to that of *NO* over the entire period, moving closer to it in percentage terms, is also remarkable.

To sum up, the gap between the better off and the worse off has maintained a stable ratio of 2:1, though, generally speaking, the interregional inequality of the *per capita* value added at factor cost and constant prices is today slightly less than in the 1960s. Using the coefficient of variation shown in column 1 of Table 6.1 as an inequality index, however, we see that, while in the first 15 years important results have been attained in reducing the regional gap (the all-time minimum was reached in 1975), regional inequalities have widened again in the following years.

A partly similar judgement can be made on the interarea comparison of the employment and unemployment rates, which are perhaps more relevant variables for the study of the migration phenomenon. In fact, the interregional coefficient of variation of unemployment rates (see column (2), Table 6.1) ceased to diminish even before that for the *per capita* value added at factor cost and constant prices, notably in the mid-1960s. The lowest level of the coefficient of variation for unemployment rates was reached immediately after registering the peak of interregional migration rates, approximately when the aggregate unemployment rate was at a minimum and the postwar birth rate[7] was at a maximum. Nowadays such a coefficient of variation is much higher than in the 1960s, showing in the 1970s stable levels almost double those of 1965, and fluctuating in the 1980s with a rising trend since 1984.

Figures 6.3 and 6.4, referring to the male and female unemployment rates for each area,[8] indicate that, up to the first half of the 1960s, the interregional unemployment gap was small for both sexes, though wider for females than for males. Since the second half of the 1960s, the male differential has been growing due to the fact that in the three areas with lower male unemployment rates (*NO*, *NE*, *CE*), these rates began first further to decrease and then stabilised up to the beginning of the 1980s. In the meantime, the three areas with higher male unemployment rates (*LZ*, *SE*, *SO*) experienced a further increase. In the early 1980s, male unemployment rates grew everywhere, but faster in the two Southern areas than in the Northern-Central ones, while *LZ* remained more or less stationary at a high level. According to this indicator, again, one notes that the initial *NE* position is closer to that of the Mezzogiorno and only

Table 6.1. *Coefficients of variation, 1960–86*

	Real per capita value added (1)	Total unemployment rates (2)	Total employment rates (3)	Total agricultural employment rates (4)	Net real wages (5)
1960	n.a.	0.261939	0.122908	0.289755	n.a.
1961	0.290819	0.275878	0.125127	0.302649	0.197873
1962	0.293266	0.273960	0.121393	0.320356	0.171318
1963	0.272280	0.268302	0.131753	0.304846	0.163287
1964	0.278703	0.239838	0.129596	0.318067	0.142864
1965	0.260691	0.188968	0.121591	0.333171	0.139621
1966	0.262810	0.217899	0.116399	0.339511	0.147253
1967	0.246245	0.265816	0.117686	0.353311	0.123022
1968	0.251195	0.295702	0.120878	0.364557	0.119700
1969	0.245865	0.338446	0.131153	0.396135	0.110459
1970	0.253491	0.335024	0.129912	0.401243	0.092758
1971	0.232612	0.319686	0.123789	0.419349	0.074432
1972	0.236683	0.328751	0.116483	0.445902	0.071628
1973	0.230423	0.331552	0.117503	0.449815	0.066644
1974	0.236913	0.324067	0.115821	0.449651	0.059501
1975	0.218520	0.340655	0.120359	0.457793	0.053336
1976	0.239647	0.320550	0.120444	0.484181	0.063895
1977	0.236890	0.354150	0.122481	0.502608	0.062434
1978	0.242790	0.327943	0.119642	0.479156	0.069931
1979	0.234281	0.326951	0.115139	0.487710	0.071616
1980	0.237233	0.396811	0.122857	0.476875	0.069269
1981	0.238056	0.345580	0.124917	0.467556	0.067317
1982	0.242002	0.323784	0.116370	0.471373	0.071609
1983	0.227007	0.290957	0.106102	0.454062	0.070333
1984	0.241924	0.255283	0.110112	0.435836	0.073958
1985	0.243102	0.282364	0.107333	0.462079	0.059397
1986	0.252176	0.355655	0.114753	0.439480	0.059234

since the late 1960s has it moved nearer to *NO*, with a performance which, in some years, was even better.

The pattern of female unemployment rates is similar, apart from the fact that the trend is almost uninterruptedly increasing in all years and areas (with the exception of *LZ*, where it is high but steady). Here too the smallest values are registered in the three areas of the North-Centre and the highest figures in Southern areas. Again, as in the case of male unemployment, since the second half of the 1970s, female unemployment is lower in *SE* than in *SO*.

Table 6.1. (*cont*)

Nominal wages (6)	Net nominal wages (7)	Unit labour costs (8)	Real productivity at 1970 prices (9)	Disability pensions relative to value added (10)	Gross out-migration rates (11)
0.196850	n.a.	n.a.	n.a.	0.249943	0.382241
0.186646	0.192907	0.135213	0.127400	0.225491	0.459646
0.168411	0.182042	0.115848	0.136736	0.239868	0.365677
0.161411	0.163544	0.130074	0.108732	0.219294	0.336851
0.141856	0.156172	0.106531	0.112436	0.231497	0.238527
0.137350	0.135501	0.102833	0.106531	0.238814	0.145986
0.150226	0.130336	0.092684	0.108766	0.237483	0.179155
0.126365	0.143010	0.101056	0.100377	0.235561	0.292682
0.124985	0.119839	0.089385	0.097704	0.258822	0.353931
0.115493	0.118481	0.087905	0.090140	0.262288	0.360392
0.098450	0.108925	0.082932	0.090149	0.287626	0.366683
0.085669	0.092747	0.079044	0.074072	0.274124	0.345808
0.085646	0.079044	0.059537	0.092889	0.317215	0.301359
0.071641	0.078780	0.067578	0.085870	0.294419	0.333039
0.057927	0.062471	0.059276	0.089911	0.344337	0.305625
0.051163	0.054070	0.063080	0.070894	0.357339	0.281750
0.063848	0.046032	0.060816	0.097317	0.372714	0.275882
0.059841	0.057954	0.058136	0.097209	0.362014	0.278138
0.063967	0.051988	0.060151	0.099538	0.357916	0.279973
0.054504	0.056796	0.061226	0.091840	0.345057	0.279368
0.050435	0.047863	0.064983	0.093956	0.359122	0.264815
0.049273	0.042365	0.054665	0.098265	0.357352	0.257316
0.051564	0.040546	0.053324	0.106233	0.364007	0.231985
0.052407	0.043572	0.055619	0.090531	0.347089	0.219193
0.054127	0.042032	0.055369	0.100286	0.371784	0.214097
0.054828	0.044630	0.054352	0.099641	0.381641	0.230661
0.057616	0.042492	0.059055	0.101601	0.394035	0.245434

Turning to consider the regional employment rates (i.e., the percentage of employed relative to the resident population), we see that *CE* has a slight lead, followed by *NO*, and in turn by *NE*, whose employment rates are particularly close to those of the other two areas since the early 1970s. Again, it is no surprise that *SO* occupies the last position, preceded by *SE*, overtaken in turn, with a superiority gained mainly in the 1980s, by *LZ*.

All areas' employment rates registered an uninterrupted fall up to the late 1960s and then stabilised with no particular change in the coefficient of variation (see column (3), Table 6.1). This aggregate trend corresponds

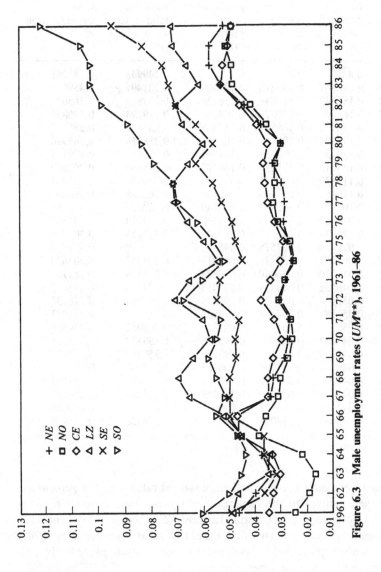

Figure 6.3 Male unemployment rates (UM^{**}), 1961–86

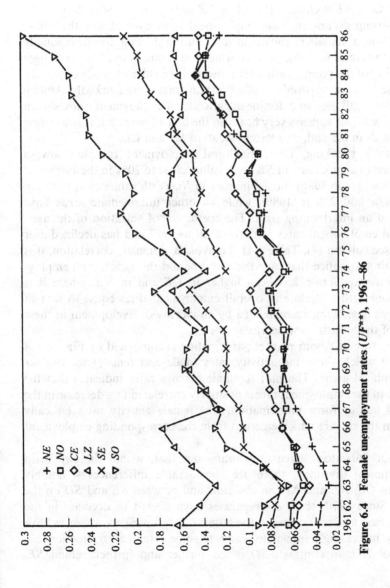

Figure 6.4 Female unemployment rates (UF**), 1961–86

to two diverging tendencies for males and females (see Figures 6.5 and 6.6). While the male employment rate keeps falling, particularly in *NO* and in *CE* – being more stable in other areas and even slightly increasing since 1975 – the female employment rate has a *U*-path, reaching everywhere its minimum in 1972. The recovery started in 1973, thus restoring in each area the 1980s' female employment rates close to those of the early 1960s. Once again the ranking between areas is extremely clear: *NO* and *CE* are first, *NE* is close, followed by *LZ* and SE, while *SO* is last.

The strong decline in male employment rates over almost the whole period and of female employment rates during the first decade is usually linked to several reasons, some of which are common to all areas (longer schooling of the young, earlier retirement of the elderly), while others are supposed (but not proved) to affect certain areas more markedly. Among them, we recall the rapid decline in agricultural employment rates, shown by Figure 6.7: it appears very heavy in the first 15 years but is still strong afterwards in *SE* and, to a lesser extent, in *SO* and *CE*.

Generally speaking, the agricultural employment rate has always remained at a maximum in *SE* (with values close to 20% in the 1960s and lower than 8% in 1986) and a minimum in *NO* (with values close to 8% in the 1960s and 2% in 1986), while all other intermediate areas have followed an intertwining path. The coefficient of variation of the agricultural employment rates has grown up to 1977 and has declined ever since (see column (4), Table 6.1). To avoid a simplistic correlation, it is interesting to notice that over the entire period the agricultural employment rates reduction has been higher in *CE* and in *NE*, where it is combined with a decline in overall employment rates equal to that of other regions, being accompanied by an increased development in these areas of the industry and service sectors.

Our picture of labour market participation is completed by Figures 6.8 and 6.9 which show the activity rates (male and female) for our six geographical areas. The plot for male activity rates indicates that the decline in the employment rate is positively correlated to a decrease in the rate of labour force participation. The female activity rates basically confirm the picture which emerged from the corresponding employment rates.

All our indicators agree in pointing out that, within the two main geographical divisions, there are considerable differences – notably between *CE*, *NE* and *NO* on one side, and between *SE* and *SO* on the other. Since 1970, these discrepancies have started to decrease in the former case and to increase in the latter: *CE* and *NE* performances have become increasingly similar to – and, to some extent, even superior to – those of *NO*; in contrast, *SO* is left further and further behind *SE*.

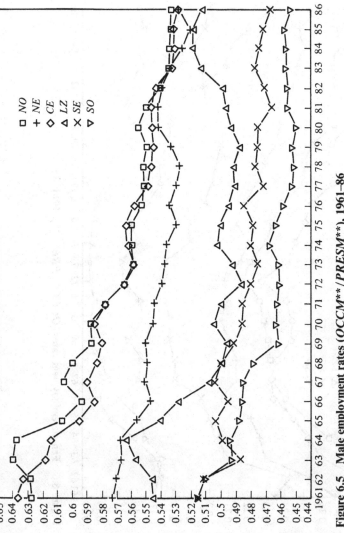

Figure 6.5 Male employment rates (*OCCM**/PRESM***), 1961–86

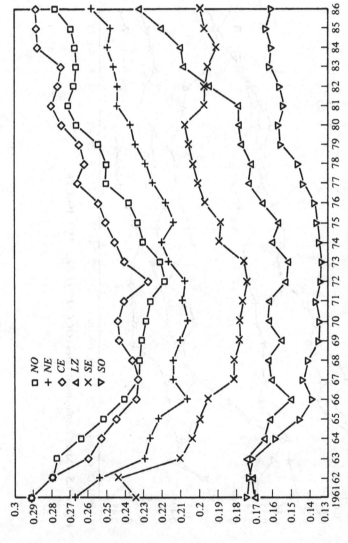

Figure 6.6 Female employment rates (*OCCF**/PRESF***), 1961–86

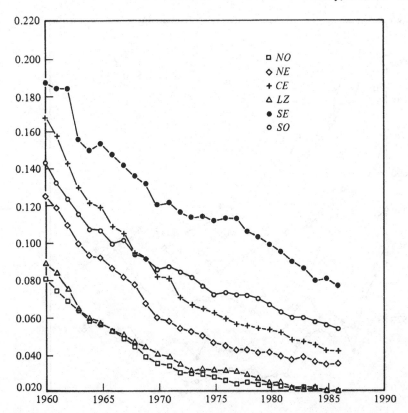

Figure 6.7 Agricultural employment rates (*OCCAGR**/PREST***), 1960–86

According to some indexes, today's regional inequalities are fewer than in the past while, according to others, they are greater. Many doubts remain, but two facts are clear: regional inequalities have increased over the last decade and the distance from *SO* has certainly grown, *SE* remaining poor but in a relatively improved position compared with that of the past and of the other Southern area. It seems appropriate to indicate with the term 'Adriatic' the 'winning' model of Italian regional development, since the most dynamic areas, in particular *NE* and *SE*, look out onto the Adriatic Sea and also four of the six administrative regions forming the CE area have a view over the Adriatic (see Fuà, 1983).

3 Reservation and net real wages; productivity and unit labour costs

After our discussion of regional imbalances, one might expect to find lower net real wages in the Southern regions; they would certainly consti-

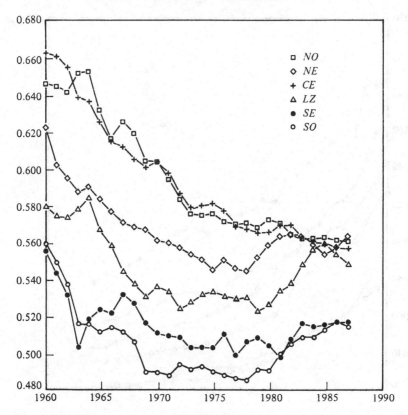

Figure 6.8   Male activity rates (*FLM**/PRESM***), 1960–86

tute an incentive to migrate from the Mezzogiorno. As we will see, however, this is not necessarily the case.

We consider several measures of wage. The first is the hourly wage paid to blue collar employees injured at work in the industrial and agricultural sectors. This series has some problems because it excludes the service sector which has been one of the most dynamic in recent years, especially in some regions. Furthermore, it includes data only for firms complying with the rules of the public insurance system: therefore, it probably overestimates the average wage for those areas (in the South) where 'black labour' (not only that acting in the totally underground economy) is more important. However, this is the first regional 'wage' series as such which is available from Italian data (until now, researchers relied upon labour cost data derived from national accounts statistics).

The second series considered are estimations of the effective wage rate in the private sector as a whole (including services) and in the public sector:

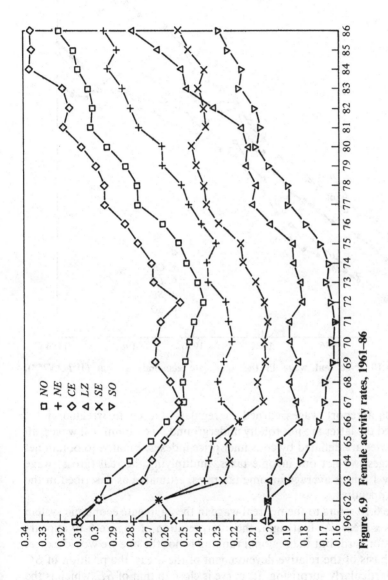

Figure 6.9 Female activity rates, 1961–86

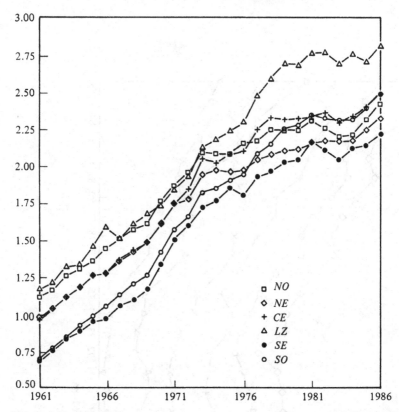

Figure 6.10   Net real wage in the aggregate economic system (*WTON7***), 1961–86

these data report wages earned in regular or even in irregular jobs, provided the latter are not totally underground.[9] To obtain real wages, all these series are deflated by consumer price indexes. Finally, to obtain net real wages, we net out income taxes, multiplying the real (gross) wage rates by 1 minus average income tax rates, estimated as described in the Data Appendix.

Figure 6.10 refers to the net real wage in the aggregate economic system of the six areas. At first sight, the interpretation of Figure 6.10 appears straightforward, but the regional ranking is not the one we would expect on the basis of the relative development of the areas, the position of *SO* being particularly surprising. Its curve is close to that of *SE*, which is the lowest in the period under consideration up to the mid-1970s, when the inequality between net real wages seems at a minimum (see the coefficient of variation in column (5), Table 6.1). Since 1976, the net real wage of *SO* has moved first closer to that of *NE*, then exceeded it and by the end of the 1970s it has overtaken that of *NO*, nearing the net real wage of *CE*.

On second thoughts, however, we may be led to doubt this interpretation of Figure 6.10: given that real wages were obtained using regional price indexes, their level across regions is not strictly comparable – that is, if the real wage in a given year in a given region is numerically higher than in another, we cannot say that the purchasing power of this wage was greater: the only valid comparison is for the rates of change.

From this point of view, we can state only that in Figure 6.10 – where we use price indexes with 1970 as a base year – we observe a dynamic behaviour of the net real wages particularly striking in the poorest regions: *SO* shows the strongest growth, followed by *SE*; the slowest increase is that of *NO* and *NE*, followed by *CE*; *LZ*, as usual, has its own story. Only if one is willing to assume that the 1970 prices were uniform across Italy, might one conclude from Figure 6.10 that the net real wage of *SO* goes, over our sample period, from being well below that of *NO* to being above it.

In an attempt to understand the reasons for these net real wage regional patterns, we considered three possible explanations: a different regional dynamics for nominal wages, fiscal pressure and consumer prices.

As far as nominal wages are concerned, we may recall that, since 1969,[10] with the abolition of what were known as 'wage cages' (*gabbie salariali*), unions have imposed the principle of equal minimum pay for every region. This has probably reduced nominal wage dispersion. As indicated in column (6), Table 6.1, the nominal wage inequality is indeed small – and, interestingly, did not increase markedly in the 1980s. The pattern of nominal regional wages is similar, if we consider average wages for the whole economy and for the private sector. But the data possibly overesti-mate the nominal wage growth in the Southern areas, where the totally underground economy is likely to be more important.

Another element which we think relevant is the behaviour of public sector wages, given the increased proportion of public sector employees, in the Mezzogiorno more than elsewhere: indeed, we observe in Figure 6.11 that the percentage of public sector employees is in *SO* now equal to that in *LZ*. The ratio of wages in the public and private sector is everywehre above unity and is particularly favourable in Southern areas (see Figure 6.12).

Looking at movements in income tax rates, we realise that income taxation differences cannot explain the striking dynamics of regional net real wage differentials mentioned above. Indeed, as one might expect in a progressive tax system,[11] the regional net nominal wage ranking is exactly the same as the regional nominal wage ranking, but the degree of inequal-

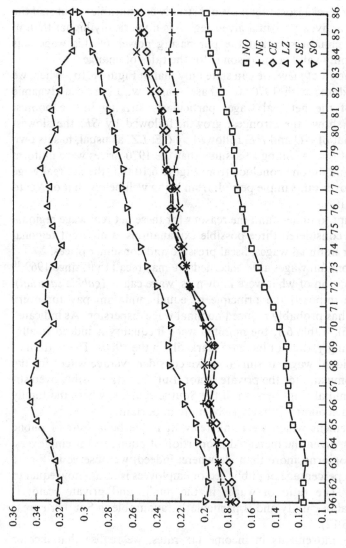

Figure 6.11 Proportion of public sector employees relative to total employees (*DIPPU***/*DIPTO***), 1961–86

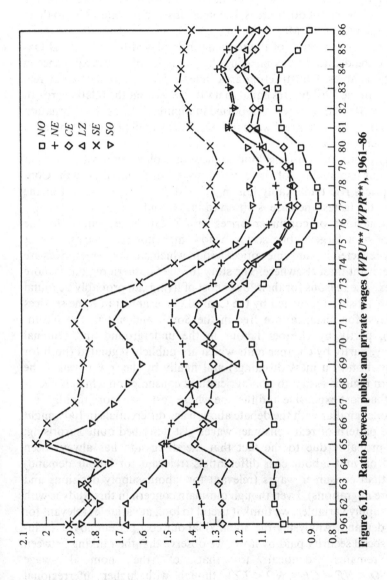

Figure 6.12 Ratio between public and private wages (WPU^{**}/WPR^{**}), 1961–86

ities between different areas is reduced due to progressivity; this is shown in the comparison between columns (7) and (6) in Table 6.1. The net nominal wage of *SO* is higher than that of *SE* and, though lower than the net nominal wages of other areas, becomes closer in the late 1970s to these than to the rest of the Mezzogiorno.

A further confirmation of the marginal role played by differential taxation can be deduced by comparing the dynamics of gross real wages in the various areas. Constructing area indexes for the private sector real wages, with the 1961 figures equal to unity, we see that the relative growth of *SE* and *SO* is impressive, as reported in Figure 6.13. A similar situation appears from the other real wage indexes. The overall picture is similar to that of net real wages.

The dynamics of consumer prices, therefore, play the most important role in our explanation of the net real wages' differential growth. Consumer prices rise remarkably less in *SO* and *LZ* than in the rest of the country; the fastest increase is observed in *NO* and *NE*.

The behaviour of consumer prices in *LZ* can be explained by the presence of a large public sector, whose high nominal wages are not directly reflected in consumer prices and in which administered prices are more relevant than elsewhere. The story for the Southern regions is more complex. The reasons for their lower cost of living can probably be found partly in subsidies provided by the Central Government in some services (highways, for instance, are free in the South and not in the North-Centre), partly by cheaper labour in the underground and criminal economy, partly by cheaper rents which are publicly regulated (both for residential and business dwellings) and finally by the lower weight the Southern regions assign to non-agricultural consumption which is everywhere the most expensive and the one whose cost rises more rapidly.[12]

Someone familiar with the debate about wage differentials in Italy might find the pattern of real consumer wages just described quite surprising; this is probably due to the fact that the discussion has always been focused on unit labour cost differentials (relevant for labour demand) rather than consumer wages (relevant for labour supply decisions and therefore migrations). Even though our main concern in this study is with labour supply variables, we think it useful to look at variables relevant for labour demand. Analysing the nominal labour cost per employee, inclusive of social security paid by firms, we observe that the ranking between areas remains identical to that of the nominal wage ($SE < SO < NE < CE < NO < LZ$), though with higher interregional differentials: this is due to the so-called social contribution detaxations, specially conceived for Southern regions and introduced since the end of 1968.[13] The picture is slightly changed when we look at real labour costs

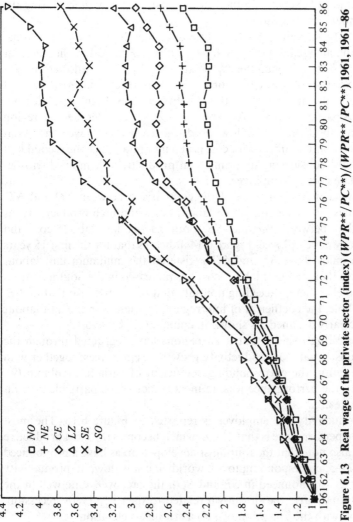

Figure 6.13 Real wage of the private sector (index) $(WPR^{**}/PC^{**})/(WPR^{**}/PC^{**})$ 1961, 1961–86

per employee (the deflation is obtained through the product price). The ranking is approximately the same ($SE < SO < NE < CE < LZ < NO$), but the six areas are now clearly divided in three groups: SE and SO being clearly the bottom ones, CE and NE moving closely together in the middle and NO and LZ exchanging the leading position a few times during the period under consideration.

Productivity (in value) per employee does not show an equal regional ranking and an equal interregional variability: CE has taken the lead ever since 1976 (NO occupying the top position up to 1975), followed by NE, LZ, SO, SE in stable decreasing order. It is therefore no surprise that unit labour costs are largely differentiated between areas. Figure 6.14 demonstrates this particular point. As expected, LZ is the leader, being a region with high labour cost and low productivity per employee; nor is it unexpected that CE unit labour cost is at a minimum since the second half of the 1970s, considering its primacy in productivity combined with an intermediate cost per employee.

Less obvious is the outcome of the comparison between NO and NE, because these show medium–high labour costs and high productivity, as well as that between SO and SE, both having low labour cost and productivity per employee. Figure 6.14 indicates that for the first 15 years up to the mid-1970s, SE and SO registered the minimum unit labour costs. Since then, the unit labour cost has increased in the Southern areas more than elsewhere, exceeding not only that of CE but also that of NE. On the whole, the coefficient of interregional variation in the unit labour cost has clearly declined, as shown in column (8), Table 6.1.

It is interesting to note that if all regions have registered through the years a substantial real productivity growth of employees, together with an initial fall in the corresponding coefficient of variation (column (9), Table 6.1), the performance was, in most recent years, particularly brilliant in some areas.

Real productivity per employee is reported in Figure 6.15. The most impressive performance is that of CE, which becomes the most productive area. We also note that the four most developed areas have a pronounced dip in 1974–5, corresponding to the worldwide slowdown in productivity (which is less pronounced in SE and SO); they recover quite well in the mid-1970s and, after the slowdown related to the early 1980s' recession, they show (with the exception of LZ) a strong acceleration.

From the picture described so far, one may appreciate that, since the mid-1970s, the regional pattern of nominal wages, consumer prices, income taxation, social contributions net of differentiated detaxations, product prices and labour productivity has been such as to discourage factor mobility. On the one hand, incentives to migrate from the Mezzo-

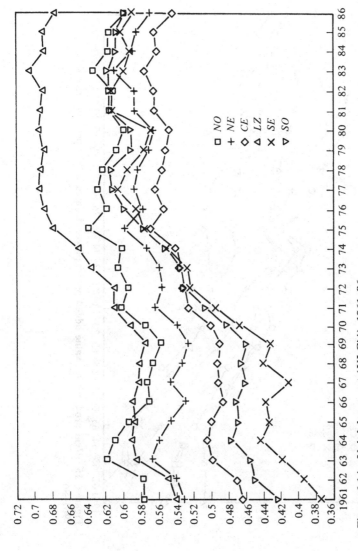

Figure 6.14 Unit labour cost (*ULC***), 1961–86

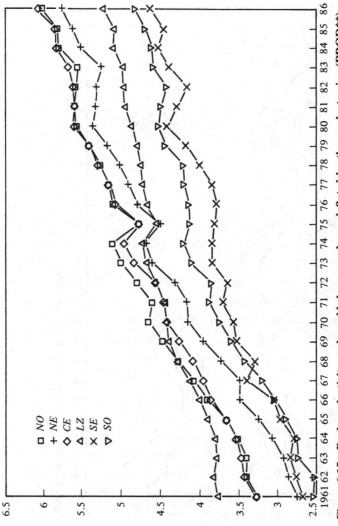

Figure 6.15 Real productivity: value added per employee deflated by the product price (PROD**), 1961–86

giorno, particularly from *SO* to the North-Centre, have been reduced by the decline in consumer wage differentials – and, in the case of *SO*, by a rise in the net real wage relative to that of the Northern areas. On the other hand, firms' migration inflow to the South from the North-Centre (particularly from *NO*), has been discouraged by the increased homogeneity of unit labour costs.

To conclude section 3, we should at least mention some of the variables that probably influence regional reservation wage differentials. A direct measurement of reservation wages is of course impossible: the evidence derived from some appropriate proxies is, however, extremely interesting. One of the most suitable indicators in this sense is offered by the regional distribution of disability pensions: indeed, in a country where there were no unemployment benefits until recently (except for the temporary layoffs subsidies supplied by the Wage Supplementation Fund – *Cassa Integrazione Guadagni*), these pensions have allowed the granting of public transfers to the unemployed (or, more generally) to entire weak sectors of the Southern society, independently of their real conditions of permanent (total or partial) disability.

Figure 6.16, showing the ratio between disability pensions and value added in each area,[14] indicates that pensions have accomplished their role of raising disposable income, particularly where produced income was low, with a regional ranking leading Southern areas to double the ratio of *NO* in the 1960s and more than double it afterwards, thus causing an uninterrupted growth of the relative variability index (column (10), Table 6.11.). Similar comments could be derived from the regional comparison of the number of people entitled to a disability pension relative to either the overall or the employed population.

A parallel argument could be made for the increase in the percentage of public sector employees. This tendency (together with the high level of public sector wages and with the fact that public sector jobs are usually tenured), has probably increased the incentives to 'wait unemployment' in Southern areas, as pointed out by Bodo and Sestito (1989). This is not inconsistent with the presence of low wages in the underground economy mentioned above: on the contrary, these help to explain why people might prefer to be unemployed or employed underground in the South for a longer period, queueing for a public job in the Mezzogiorno, rather than migrating to get a lower paid job more quickly in the Northern-Central private sector.

All this suggests that internal migrations to the North-Centre have been discouraged over the years by relatively higher Southern reservation wages and by an ever-increasing standard of living amongst the population of the South.[15]

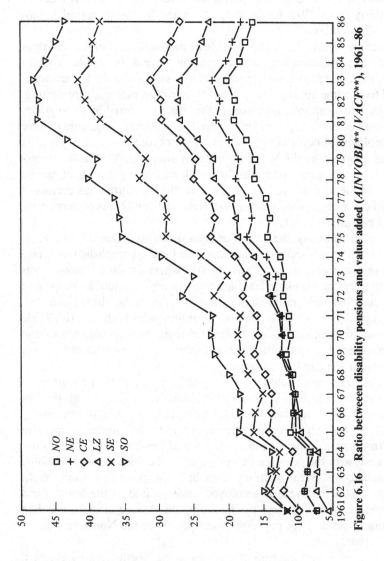

Figure 6.16 Ratio between disability pensions and value added (*AINVOBL**/VACF***), 1961–86

4   The aggregate unemployment level and other factors limiting migration flows

Until now we have listed a series of conflicting phenomena which have affected the incentives to migrate since the 1970s. Relative unemployment rates, as documented in section 2, have increased in the South of the country; on the other hand, as illustrated in section 3, *SO* has particularly benefited from a relative rise in net real wages and in public transfers supporting its disposable income more than elsewhere.

Other factors can also be important in determining the net migration flow and, in the case at hand, in explaining its reduction.

Mincer (1978), for instance, recalls that more than in the past, particularly in developed regions, women want to have a professional life within a dual-career family, which means that migrations are subject to a new, more binding constraint, it being in general more difficult to find a convenient working situation for a couple than for an individual male, when the female is less skilled. But one should not ignore that today women's desire to work encourages women, both single and married, to outmigrate, given the high interregional female unemployment rate differentials. This could change in a substantial way the nature of the incentives considered by both sexes in deciding whether or not to migrate. Data enabling us to evaluate the importance of these factors in the Italian framework are lacking, but some available evidence on the individual characteristics of emigrants – which will be discussed in section 6 – suggests that this idea has begun to apply in the Italian context as well.

Among the conditions boosting or halting the migration process, McCormik (1983) and Muellbauer and Murphy (1988) list those relative to the price of basic facilities, especially housing. Following the lead of these authors, we analyse relative housing prices, defined as the ratio between the housing rentals' value (the amount really paid by renters or self-imputed by owners and renters) and the blue collars wages in industry and agriculture. Given that the housing price is an index, the levels of housing prices, deflated by the nominal wages, are not comparable across regions. One striking feature nonetheless emerges from Figure 6.17. While relative housing prices in *NE* and *CE* are quite stable compared to those in *NO*, relative housing prices in *SO* and *SE* decrease dramatically compared to those of the other regions over our sample period. As usual *LZ* has its own story.

Rental costs are by no means the only relevant index for the Italian housing market, as this is also rationed by the regulation which protects renters, especially since the 1978 introduction of the Rent Control Act (*Equo Canone*, law of 27 July 1978, n. 392). This law has almost

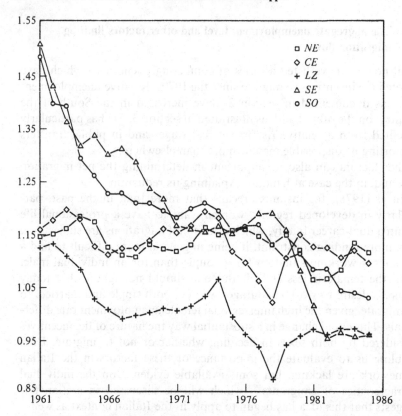

Figure 6.17 Relative housing price in each area compared to the relative housing price in $NO(PCAB**/INAIL**)/(PCAB\ NO/INAIL\ NO)$, 1961–85

completely eliminated the market for rented housing, and particularly so in the North-Centre of Italy and in the big metropolitan centres. Unfortunately, we do not have data on the availability of rented accommodation in the various regions, but we are convinced that this has been a major problem for people deciding to emigrate. We therefore suggest that if the existence at reasonable costs of basic facilities like housing is a relevant variable for migration, both the dynamics of housing prices and the crippling of the market for rentals have constituted a major disincentive to interregional mobililty.

Labour laws are themselves another obstacle to migration flows, which affect various countries in different ways, to the extent that they impose hiring and firing constraints or costs to mobility. Such laws can create threshold levels of minimum benefits or maximum costs and geographical mobility is decided only beyond these, as described in Bentolila and

Bertola (1990) and Bertola (1990). These rigidities, which became relevant in Italy in the 1970s following the imposition of a series of rules and regulations, the most important of which was the *Statuto dei Lavoratori* ('Workers' Act' of 20 May 1970, n. 300), have played a limiting role on migration flows, as discussed in Modigliani *et al.* (1986).

According to the modern approach to migration research, the most significant of all factors explaining mobility seems to be the general condition of the labour market in the aggregate and in the hosting regions. This idea lies at the basis of the study by Bentolila and Blanchard (1990, 2–15): 'with the Spanish economy in a bootstrap, high unemployment decreasing labour mobility and leading to little wage pressure and thus to further unemployment ... Low regional mobility is a new phenomenon in Spain ... Unemployment itself is the reason for low mobility ... Workers who become unemployed can rely on a family network to support them if they stay; when unemployment is high everywhere, moving means giving up this support in exchange for a low probability of finding work'.

This idea is also expressed by Pissarides and Wadsworth, (1987, 27) who, analysing British cross-section data, assert that 'at higher overall unemployment rates, migration propensities are reduced'. In a time series analysis on UK, Pissarides and McMaster (1988) state that 'aggregate unemployment may also affect the gains from migration ... If unemployment is higher everywhere, the employed feel more secure where they are ... The unemployed may also be discouraged from moving. With higher unemployment everywhere, the duration of unemployment is longer in all regions; if the unemployed are risk averse or face liquidity constraints, when durations are longer the marginal cost of moving is higher' (4).

With reference to the Greek situation, Katseli and Glytsos (1986) recall that migration flows are positively correlated to the probability of employment in the area of destination. With reference to Italy, Sestito (1989) confirms that 'from econometric estimates carried out on the inter-regional movements, it turns out that *pull* more than *push* factors play a leading role in explaining geographical mobility' (5), a subject also widely discussed in the survey on the American situation carried out by Greenwood (1975).

Though many of these arguments are not theoretically very strong and though our formula (note 5) shows that in a simple model the probability of migration is negatively correlated to the aggregate unemployment rate only under restrictive conditions, the inverse relation between migrations and the aggregate unemployment rate seems a fairly robust empirical fact. If this were the case, we would expect that a strong disincentive to interregional migration flows had been created in Italy since the mid-

1970s, when the aggregate unemployment rate began to increase sharply,[16] reaching unprecedented levels in 1987, with no slowdowns.

In addition to unemployment differentials and possibly to aggregate unemployment, other factors can be important in the explanation of the interregional migration. We think that the occurrence of a number of years with very low migration flows (perhaps because of low unemployment differentials or of high levels of aggregate unemployment) can make the migration decision in subsequent years more costly. The reason for this probably lies in the loosening of a series of links and familiar networks that can help the prospective emigrant, especially in a situation in which accommodation and search costs are substantial. We believe that this kind of hysteresis phenomenon may, at least in part, explain why in recent years the decrease of unemployment rates in Northern and Central regions, not matched in Southern regions, has not stimulated a rise in migration flows from the Mezzogiorno.

5   Interregional migration rates

Having examined some basic facts about regional differences in Italy, we now turn to the empirical evidence on interregional migrations. Our data consist of observations on changes in residence by region of origin and region of destination. For aggregate flows the data are available from 1960 to 1986. In the following section we will also discuss some of the data disaggregated by age, sex and working condition.

Changing residence is not compulsory when moving to a new region. Indeed, our observations are probably affected by substantial underreporting and lags in the change of residence, which are possibly more serious for the Southern regions. This was, however, the only source available – and one that has never been exploited before, to our knowledge; another major drawback of the data is that they do not allow any estimate of the 'stock' of emigrants in any region.

A detailed description of the data is presented in the Data Appendix. For each year we started from a 20×20 matrix representing the migration flows within Italy: the elements on the diagonal show the mobility within each region. Aggregating across regions we were able to construct $27 \times 6 \times 6$ matrices for our six geographical areas, one for each year. Figures 6.18 and 6.19 illustrate the ratios relative to the resident population of gross within-area movements and of gross migration outflows toward the rest of Italy, these ratios being referred to as migration rates.

Many interesting features emerge. First of all, migration rates within areas[17] are always larger than those between areas. In 1962, a peak year for the overall migration, 30–37 individuals out of 1,000 emigrated within

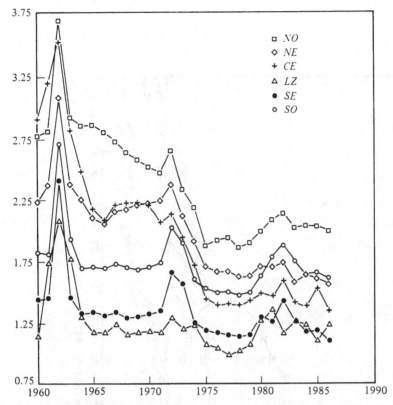

Figure 6.18 Within-area migration rates (*EMIN**/PREST***), 1960–86

NO, CE, NE and 20–25 within the other areas, while 6 from *NO*, 11 from *LZ* and *CE*, 13 from *NE*, 17 from *SO* and 21 from *SE* moved to the rest of Italy.

Even in the areas of maximum interregional movement, therefore, migration rates were more limited than the intraregional shift within any part of Italy. The areas of maximum intraregional mobility never coincided with those of maximum movement towards the rest of the country, the former being particularly high in the most developed areas. These distinctions are narrowed during our sample period, owing to the overall fall in the intraregional and interregional mobility, to the particularly strong decline in migrations within the areas of *NO* and *CE* (Figure 6.18) and to the particularly sharp reduction in the out-migrations from *SO* and *SE* (Figure 6.19). In the mid-1980s, in the Southern areas 5–6 individuals out of 1,000 migrated towards the rest of Italy, while 11–16 moved within the same areas. In the same period, intraregional shifts

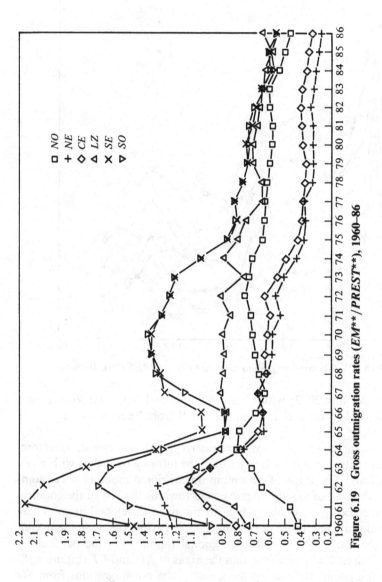

Figure 6.19 Gross outmigration rates (*EM***/*PREST***), 1960–86

involved 20 individuals out of 1,000 in *NO* and 12–15 in other areas; the interregional shifts consisted of 5 individuals out of 1,000 from *NO*, 6 from *LZ* and 3 from *CE* and *NE*.

If we divide migration flows within areas by those between areas, we note that this ratio grows through time, except in *NO* (where the ratio declines from 6.6 to 4.2), in *CE*, where it remains stable (equalling 3–4) and in *LZ* where the ratio is stationary (at 1.5–2); it is worth observing that the ratio in *SE* rises from 0.96 to 1.96, while in *SO* it increases from 1.8 to 2.8.

The fact that within-areas movements are higher in the most dynamic regions (and in the regions with a negative migration balance), while migrations toward the rest of Italy are higher in the poorest regions, leads us to believe that within-area migration rates measure a very different phenomenon from migration rates outside the area. Intraregional shifts are probably more a reflection of various demographic and economic factors and are not necessarily motivated by the difficulty in finding a job in the place of residence. Interregional movements, on the contrary, are probably mostly originated by a disequilibrium situation. For more or less the same reasons, we think that migrations out of regions with a positive migration balance probably reflect a different phenomenon than migrations out of areas with a negative migration balance. Figure 6.20 presents gross outmigration rates for *SE*, *SO* and *NE* and gross inmigration rates for *NO*, *CE* and *LZ*; as can be seen, the curves are basically specular.

Looking at the gross outmigration rates towards the rest of Italy in each area, after the 1962 peak, a sharp fall is observed up to 1965. This is followed by a slight, almost uninterrupted decline in all areas except in *SO* and *SE*, which again experienced a local maximum in 1969–70. In 1975, their migration rates reached 1965 levels and have declined since then. When gross outmigration rates decrease everywhere (1965, 1975 and following years), the outmigration rate differentials decline, because then the areas with higher outmigration rates register a higher reduction. The opposite happens when gross outmigration rates increase. This is why the coefficient of variation of interregional gross migration rates (column (11), Table 6.1) has a global maximum in 1961 and a local one in 1970, and has a minimum in 1965, declining without interruption in the 1970s and, with the exception of the two latest years, in the 1980s.

This explains why net migration rates, plotted in Figure 6.21, show the maximum gap in 1961–62, then in 1969–70, while the minimum values are reached in 1965, in 1975 and the following years.

Over the 25 years 1960–86, net mobility has fallen sharply everywhere. Of all four areas having a positive migration balance in 1960, two soon

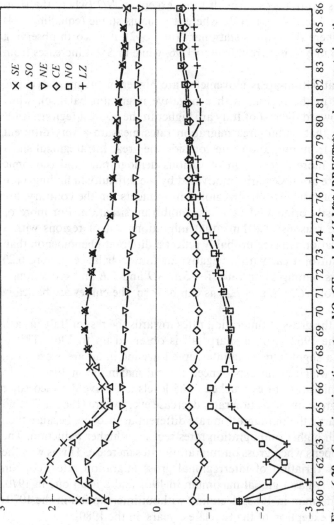

Figure 6.20 Gross immigration rates: *NO, CE* and *LZ* (*LM**/PREST***) and gross outmigration rates: *SE, SO* and *NE* (*EM**/PREST***), 1960–86

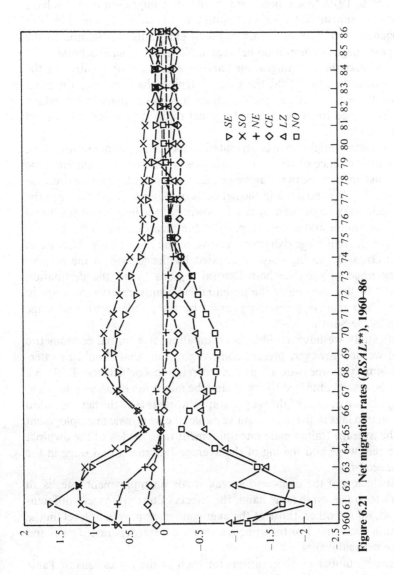

Figure 6.21 Net migration rates (*RSAL***), 1960–86

registered a negative net migration rate – *CE* in 1967 and *NE* in 1970. By contrast, *SE* and *SO* first registered a fall in 1965 and later a rise lasting up to 1970. Since then, their net positive migration balances have started to diminish, *SO* always remaining higher than *SE*, which in 1986 approached zero. The two main areas of emigrants' destination in the 1960s (with negative migration balances), *NO* and *LZ*, have definitely lost their role and the *NO* migration balance even became positive in the 1980s. Since the mid-1970s, the Central regions have become the main areas of destination. The major variations have taken place in *NE*, which has transformed from an area of large net outmigration into one of net inmigration.

Several factors might have contributed to the decline of migration rates, despite the presence of strong unemployment differentials. Among these we may list an increase in the aggregate level of unemployment, a decrease in the net benefits and a rise in the net costs of moving. The decrease in the net benefits may be proxied by the narrowing of the interregional net real wage differentials and in certain parts of the Mezzogiorno by the exceeding of the net real wage dynamics relative to the rest of Italy. The rise in the net costs of moving may be proxied by the growth in the relative housing price of the Northern-Central regions – i.e., the destination regions – or the increase of the potential emigrants' reservation wage in absolute and relative terms, as proxied by the public sector real wage growth in the South.

In this study we have avoided the estimation of a formal econometric model; we do, however, present some regressions that should be interpreted simply as measure of partial correlation coefficients. Table 6.2 shows the results obtained by regressing the migration balances relative to the population in each of the six geographical areas (i.e., the net migration rates) on two lags of the dependent variable, the own-male unemployment rate, the average Italian male unemployment rate, the log of the own-net private real wage and the log of the average Italian net real wage in the private sector.

The inclusion of the own- and average male unemployment rates is an attempt to grasp, on the one hand, the effects of unemployment differentials and, on the other, those of the aggregate unemployment level on the migration decisions. For the same reasons, we insert separately own- and average net real wages.

The small number of observations for each of the regressions in Table 6.2 limits the possibility of precisely estimating a large number of parameters. Partly to get around this problem, we decided to run a set of 'pooled' regressions for the migration flows from each area. These results are reported in Table 6.3. Each column represents the gross outmigration

Table 6.2. *Regressions on net migration rates in the six geographical areas*

Method of estimation: Ordinary Least Squares Dependent variable: *RSAL NO*

Regressors	Estimated coefficient	*t*-statistic	
Constant	1.96610	2.1488	R^2: 0.980663
RSAL NO(− 1)	0.90356	7.2850	s.e. of regression: 0.754043E–01
RSAL NO(− 2)	− 0.62046	− 7.2692	Durbin–H: − 0.544372
log(*WPRN7 NO*)	− 1.81660	− 1.8850	
log(*WPRN7 IT*)	2.32970	3.0116	
UM NO	21.38400	2.3000	
UM IT	− 14.67200	− 2.0434	

Method of estimation: Instrumental variables Dependent variable: *RSAL NO*
Instrumental variables: *RSAL NO*(− 1), *PROD NO*, *PROD IT*, *UM NO*,
UM IT, *PROD NO*(− 1), log(*WPRN7 IT*)(log(*WPRN7 NO*) (− 1),
LAMDA NO − LAMDA IT, *RSAL NO* (− 2), Constant

Regressors	Estimated coefficient	*t*-statistic	
Constant	0.75701	0.59844	R^2: 0.977552
RSAL NO(− 1)	0.90775	6.71570	s.e. of regression: 0.813188E–01
RSAL NO(− 2)	− 0.60695	− 6.57530	Sargan: 0.0235162
log(*WPRN7 NO*)	− 3.46710	− 2.44260	
log(*WPRN7 IT*)	3.62470	3.25200	
UM NO	23.12100	2.29470	
UM IT	− 17.72100	− 2.25290	

Table 6.2 (*Cont.*)

Method of estimation: Ordinary Least Squares Dependent variable: *RSAL NE*

Regressors	Estimated coefficient	*t*-statistic	
Constant	− 0.76070	− 1.28620	R^2: 0.929193
RSAL NE(− 1)	0.95775	5.70090	s.e. of regression: $0.465631E\text{--}01$
RSAL NE(− 2)	− 3.32834	− 2,03230	Durbin–H: $− 0.123413E\text{--}01$
log(*WPRN7 NE*)	− 0.51148	− 0.64256	
log(*WPRN7 IT*)	0.34680	0.48759	
UM NE	1.07030	0.34386	
UM IT	0.30384	$0.85157E\text{--}01$	

Method of estimation: Instrumental variables   Dependent variable: *RSAL NE*
Instrumental variables: *RSAL NE*(− 1), *PROD NE*, *PROD IT*, *UM NE*,
UM IT, *PROD NE*(− 1), log(*WPRN7 IT*)(log(*WPRN7 NE*) (− 1),
LAMDA NE − *LAMDA IT*, *RSAL NE* (− 2), Constant

Regressors	Estimated coefficient	*t*-statistic	
Constant	− 1.48010	− 1.48730	R^2: 0.915310
RSAL NE(− 1)	0.93675	5.04590	s.e. of regression: $0.510360E\text{--}01$
RSAL NE(− 2)	− 0.32806	− 1.85250	Sargan: 0.1136743
log(*WPRN7 NE*)	− 2.02650	− 1.17230	
log(*WPRN7 IT*)	1.69230	1.10620	
UM NE	0.93287	0.27040	
UM IT	− 0.30895	$− 0.78032E\text{--}01$	

Table 6.2 (*Cont.*)

Method of estimation: Ordinary Least Squares   Dependent variable: *RSAL CE*

Regressors	Estimated coefficient	*t*-statistic	
Constant	− 0.53818	− 0.78602	R^2: 0.909880
RSAL CE(− 1)	0.66571	3.20070	s.e. of regression: 0.453250E–01
log(*WPRN7 CE*)	0.11078	0.14118	Durbin–H: − 0.560536
log(*WPRN7 IT*)	− 0.21190	− 0.24041	
UM CE	1.27100	0.33325	
UM IT	0.35677	0.10275	

Method of estimation: Instrumental variables   Dependent variable: *RSAL CE*
Instrumental variables: *RSAL CE*(− 1), *PROD CE, PROD IT, UM CE,*
UM IT, PROD CE(− 1), log(*WPRN7 IT*) (− 1), log(*WPRN7 CE*) (− 1),
LAMDA CE − *LAMDA IT*, Constant

Regressors	Estimated coefficient	*t*-statistic	
Constant	− 1.28480	− 1.31330	R^2: 0.897460
RSAL CE(− 1)	0.46441	1.63970	s.e. of regression: 0.483972E–01
log(*WPRN7 CE*)	1.39010	0.95393	Sargan: 0.2406369
log(*WPRN7 IT*)	− 1.64450	− 1.01260	
UM CE	− 0.38136	− 0.88403E–01	
UM IT	3.06950	0.69781	

Table 6.2 (*Cont.*)

Method of estimation: Ordinary Least Squares Dependent variable: *RSAL LZ*

Regressors	Estimated coefficient	*t*-statistic	
Constant	0.53877	0.47773	R^2: 0.888857
RSAL LZ(− 1)	0.17838	1.26470	s.e. of regression: 0.130729
RSAL LZ(− 2)	0.41480	2.81980	Durbin–H: 0.356726
log(*WPRN7 LZ*)	0.42326	0.59505	
log(*WPRN7 IT*)	− 0.26233	− 0.34338	
UM LZ	− 0.56649	− 0.10117	
UM IT	0.34859	0.97572E–01	

Method of estimation: Instrumental variables   Dependent variable: *RSAL LZ*
Instrumental variables: *RSAL LZ*(− 1), *PROD LZ*, *PROD IT*, *UM LZ*,
UM IT, *PROD LZ*(− 1), log(*WPRN7 IT*) (− 1), log(*WPRN7 LZ*) (− 1),
LAMDA LZ − *LAMDA IT*, *RSAL LZ*(− 2), Constant

Regressors	Estimated coefficient	*t*-statistic	
Constant	0.63063	0.52802	R^2: 0.878703
RSAL LZ(− 1)	0.10381	0.67481	s.e. of regression: 0.878703
RSAL LZ(− 2)	0.35984	2.29170	Sargan: 2.86733
log(*WPRN7 LZ*)	1.33380	1.35420	
log(*WPRN7 IT*)	− 1.09590	− 1.07750	
UM LZ	2.35630	0.38348	
UM IT	2.08260	− 0.51383	

Table 6.2 (*Cont.*)

Method of estimation: Ordinary Least Squares Dependent variable: *RSAL SO*

Regressors	Estimated coefficient	*t*-statistic	
Constant	2.55490	1.5772	R^2: 0.941714
RSAL SO(− 1)	8.66990	4.8955	s.e. of regression: 0.891375E–01
RSAL SO(− 2)	− 0.60882	− 4.9316	Durbin–H: 0.996484
log(*WPRN7 SO*)	− 3.18580	− 2.2661	
log(*WPRN7 IT*)	3.80260	2.0645	
UM SO	7.44620	1.2225	
UM IT	− 14.03900	− 1.4122	

Method of estimation: Instrumental variables Dependent variable: *RSAL SO*
Instrumental variables: *RSAL SO*(− 1), *PROD SO*, *PROD IT*, *UM SO*,
UM IT, *PROD SO*(− 1), log(*WPRN7 IT*) (− 1), log(*WPRN7 SO*) (− 1),
LAMDA SO − LAMDA IT, *RSAL SO*(− 2), Constant

Regressors	Estimated coefficient	*t*-statistic	
Constant	3.95930	1.2356	R^2: 0.939001
RSAL SO(− 1)	0.83872	4.5823	s.e. of regression: 0.912621E–01
RSAL SO(− 2)	− 0.62289	− 4.7528	Sargan: 1.7531316
log(*WPRN7 SO*)	− 4.49570	− 1.6046	
log(*WPRN7 IT*)	5.50860	1.4924	
UM SO	9.91180	1.3874	
UM IT	− 16.72400	− 1.5644	

Table 6.2 (*Cont.*)

Method of estimation: Ordinary Least Squares Dependent variable: *RSAL SE*

Regressors	Estimated coefficient	*t*-statistic	
Constant	− 0.36198	− 0.21068	R^2: 0.909595
RSAL SE(− 1)	0.54744	4.02530	s.e. of regression: 0.109289
log(*WPRN7 SE*)	− 1.01100	− 0.91973	Durbin–H: 0.791567
log(*WPRN7 IT*)	0.93798	0 50429	
UM SE	13.71200	1.82800	
UM IT	− 17.16500	− 2.09960	

Method of estimation: Instrumental variables   Dependent variable: *RSAL SE*
Instrumental variables: *RSAL SE*(− 1), *PROD SE*, *PROD IT*, *UM SE*, *UM IT*,
PROD SE(− 1), log(*WPRN7 IT*) (− 1), log(*WPRN7 SE*) (− 1),
LAMDA SE − LAMDA IT, Constant

Regressors	Estimated coefficient	*t*-statistic	
Constant	− 0.16325	− 0.76887*E*–01	R^2: 0.909319
RSAL SE(− 1)	0.54973	3.71550	s.e. of regression: 0.109462
log(*WPRN7 SE*)	− 1.22500	− 0.86460	Sargan: 1.4539807
log(*WPRN7 IT*)	1.21260	0.60866	
UM SE	13.55000	1.68230	
UM IT	− 17.07300	− 1.99250	

Note: All symbols are explained in the Data Appendix.

rates from each of the six areas towards the remaining five. Each column is therefore obtained by 'pooling' five equations. The coefficients of these five equations are constrained to be the same except for the intercept (which is not reported).

This methodology has the advantage of increasing the degrees of freedom. On the other hand, we are forced to impose a set of restrictions that are not always very appealing: for instance, if we look at the equation for the migration flows from *SO*, it is assumed that the wage differential between *NO* and *SO* has the same effect on the flow from *SO* to *NO* as the wage differential between *SO* and *SE* has on the migration flow between *SO* and *SE*.

These assumptions are testable, in principle; however, as we use this specification to introduce a larger number of variables, given the limited number of time series observations, they become untestable in practice. In a way, we can interpret them as 'identifying' restrictions. Alternative parametrisations can be devised: for instance, one can constrain the coefficients by area of destination rather than by area of origin; or one could even impose that all the coefficients are identical, with the exception of the intercepts.

This discussion should make us cautious[18] in interpreting the results reported in Table 6.3. The variables we consider as determinants of the gross outmigration rates from an area towards another are the male unemployment rate (current and lagged) in the area of origin and destination, the lagged aggregate male unemployment rate in Italy, the log of the private real wage (current and lagged) in the area of origin and destination, the log of the public real wage in the area of origin and destination, the log of housing prices deflated by the lagged nominal wage in the private sector and the lagged dependent variable (with two lags).

The results we obtain are quite variate. In particular, the log of housing prices deflated by the lagged nominal private wage has the expected influence in most cases. The effect of real public sector wages, which are probably a good proxy for reservation wages, seems particularly strong. Real public wages at destination are correctly signed and significant everywhere; real public wages at the origin show the expected sign everywhere (except in *NO*, perhaps because its public sector has a negligible weight), but they are not always very significant. From this point of view, it is interesting to note that current real private wages at the origin have the expected sign everywhere (even in *NO*, where they are significant, with the only exception of *LZ*, perhaps because its private sector has a negligible weight), but they are not always significant. Finally, current real private wages at destination are correctly signed, sometimes significant, with the exception of *SO*, where the (significant) sign of the regressor's coefficient is contrary to the expected one. On the whole, the relevant private wage variables are the lagged ones in the Mezzogiorno, while they are mostly the current ones in the North-Centre; in *LZ* the only private real wage variable with some explanatory power on gross outmigration rates is, understandably, the one at destination.

With regard to the unemployment variables, we notice that the coefficients of the current rates at the origin and at destination are always correctly signed (except for *LZ*, for the well known reasons), but they are not always significantly different from zero. The coefficients of the lagged unemployment rates raise interpretation problems. Finally we would deduce from Table 6.3 that the male (lagged) aggregate unemployment rate does not provide a significant disincentive to migration except in *SE*. One must not, however, forget that this (as other results) could be due to endogeneity and/or multicollinearity problems.

While the equations reported in Table 6.3 provide us with clear insights

Table 6.3. *Pooled regressions on gross outmigration rates in the six geographical areas*

	Dependent variables: REM					
Regressors	NO	NE	CE	LZ	SE	SO
UM^o	0.0222	0.163	0.206	−0.006	0.034	−0.025
	(0.159)	(1.82)	(1.43)	(0.42)	(0.30)	(0.36)
UM^d	−0.084	−0.073	−0.239	−0.143	−0.056	−0.168
	(0.67)	(0.86)	(2.61)	(1.36)	(0.49)	(2.23)
$UMIT_1$	−0.072	−0.121	0.121	0.20	−0.58	−0.224
	(0.24)	(0.456)	(0.47)	(0.98)	(1.96)	(0.84)
$\log(WPRT^o)$	−0.027	−0.116	−0.003	0.0005	−0.0004	−0.001
	(1.81)	(1.21)	(2.38)	(0.38)	(0.60)	(1.20)
$\log(WPRT^d)$	0.003	0.002	0.0001	0.002	0.0005	−0.019
	(3.02)	(2.963)	(0.253)	(2.18)	(0.33)	(2.62)
$\log(PCAB^o/WPR^o_1)$	0.013	0.021	0.023	0.004	0.033	0.021
	(0.88)	(1.887)	(2.41)	(0.44)	(2.40)	(2.84)
$\log(PCAB^d/WPR^d_1)$	−0.008	−0.011	−0.011	−0.001	−0.031	−0.020
	(0.81)	(1.39)	(1.39)	(0.13)	(2.03)	(2.44)
$\log(WPUT^o)$	0.007	−0.052	−0.052	−0.032	−0.007	−0.007
	(0.55)	(3.74)	(3.52)	(1.67)	(0.46)	(0.83)

$\log(WPUT^d)$	0.020	0.051	0.047	0.032	0.029	0.024
	(1.70)	(4.12)	(3.45)	(2.36)	(1.50)	(2.39)
$\log(WPR7^o)_1$	−0.010	0.0147	0.024	−0.004	0.034	0.024
	(0.41)	(1.26)	(2.50)	(0.35)	(2.45)	(3.11)
$\log(WPR7^d)_1$	−0.008	−0.01	−0.010	−0.002	−0.022	−0.018
	(0.88)	(1.27)	(1.34)	(0.16)	(1.48)	(2.22)
UM^o	−0.43	−0.147	−0.33	−0.355	0.114	0.08
	(1.51)	(0.87)	(1.258)	(2.63)	(0.60)	(0.50)
UM^d_1	0.52	0.294	0.196	0.068	0.20	0.064
	(3.79)	(2.86)	(2.13)	(0.577)	(1.43)	(0.71)
REM_1	0.656	0.526	0.445	0.282	0.306	0.318
	(7.67)	(8.57)	(6.56)	(3.49)	(7.87)	(5.79)
REM_2	0.004	0.161	0.263	0.131	0.310	0.30
	(0.05)	(2.72)	(4.11)	(1.71)	(9.13)	(5.29)

Notes: The symbols are explained in the Data Appendix.
t-statistics in absolute value are in parenthesis.

on the importance of some variables (like housing prices, public sector real wages and, to a lesser extent, private sector real wages and unemployment differentials), they partly mask the relevance of others. This is probably due to the fact that a linear specification is not completely satisfactory: a non-linear specification is on the agenda of our future research.

Therefore, at this preliminary stage, we will continue to rely for our interpretation of the migration behaviour on the qualitative description provided by graphs; these hint at the importance for migration decisions of aggregate and differential unemployment levels. In Figure 6.22, we report the net migration rates for *NO*, *CE* and *SO* and the male unemployment rates: the story that emerges is pretty clear. First of all, the net migration rates in *SO* and *NO* are almost symmetrically specular. Furthermore, it is evident that in the first part of the sample the area between these two curves is strictly correlated to the area between the two unemployment curves. In 1965, when the two unemployment curves are closest, so are the two migration balance curves. The picture changes substantially in the second part of the 1970s: even though the gap between the two rates of unemployment widens dramatically, net migration rates remain very small everywhere, the *NO* migration balance becomes positive and that for other regions is far from being as strong as it was in the early 1960s. A possible explanation of this phenomenon is that even though the unemployment differential was large, the unemployment rate was quite high in the North and Centre of Italy, greatly reducing the incentives to migrate.

This is, however, probably only part of the story. In the years after 1986 (which is when our sample ends) preliminary data indicate that there has been a further increase in the gap between Southern and Northern-Central unemployment rates, with the latter at lower levels than before; and this has still apparently not increased gross outmigration rates from the South in a detectable way. Here, the persistence of migration decisions described above and the other factors discussed in the previous sections may provide the most likely explanation.

6   Migration rates and individual characteristics

Migration flows are undoubtedly very different across age groups, sex and labour force status. To the best of our knowledge, the migration data by individual characteristics have never been available in Italy, but in this section we present a preliminary and incomplete analysis of a new data set that disaggregates migration flows by age, sex and working conditions.

The data amount to 500,000 observations[19] gathered from Municipal

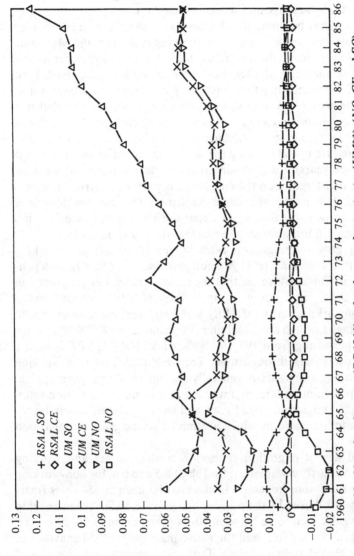

Figure 6.22 Net migration rates (*RSAL**) and male unemployment rates (*UM***): (*NO, CE* and *SO*), 1960–86

Registrars' Offices for the 20 administrative regions since 1969; unfortunately we were unable to find data for the years before 1969. A first glance at the data reveals that there are persistent and strong differences in the migration rates by sex, age and working condition.

This last term may be ambiguous because, according to the methodology utilised in this data set, by 'persons in working condition' the Municipal Registrars' Offices mean those of more than 14 years of age either having a job or being unemployed after previously having been employed. First job seekers, therefore, together with people outside the labour force, belong to the group in a 'non-working condition'. This means that it is impossible to determine if a migrant in a 'working condition' is employed or not. In practice, however, the unemployed who have been previously employed are rare in Italy among the adult population in the central age bracket (20–59 years). Furthermore, it is not clear whether the working condition is registered upon the emigrant's departure or arrival (cancelling or enrollment in the Municipal Registrars' Offices): we think it is made upon arrival, because upon departure most people are first job seekers, at least in the younger age brackets (less or equal to 19).

Examining gross outmigration rates by sex (F or M) and working conditions ('professional' (PR) or 'non-professional' (NPR)), independent of age, in Table 6.4 we see that the main categories of emigrants, in descending order, are: non-working females ($FNPR$), working males (MPR), non-working males ($MNPR$), and lastly working females (FPR). Weights change through areas and time: for instance, $FPR/FNPR$ is lower than 1 but increasing from 1970 to 1985, while $MPR/MNPR$ is higher than 1 but decreasing through time. The weight of females in working condition among emigrants is generally smaller in poorer geographical areas. This is even more evident if we look at within-area migration rates. Finally, the net migration rates by sex and working conditions, independent of age, follow patterns which are similar to the gross outmigration rates.

The modal age of migration changes according to sex and working conditions. As partly documented by Tables 6.5 and 6.6, for non-working females, the maximum frequency is observed between 20–24 years (marriageable age), followed by the primary age (less than 15). As for working females, the peak used to be between 20–24 years, rising to 25–29 years[20] in the 1980s, as if they followed the active male emigrants' behaviour in the most developed Italian regions. The most frequent migration age of non-working males is, as expected, that of boys under 15, followed by men over 60 (return migration). The modal age of working male outmigrants is between 25 and 29 in the most developed areas and between 20 and 24 in SE and SO and in LZ since the 1980s. On the contrary, the

Table 6.4. Within-area migration rates *** ; gross outmigration rates (**RE); gross inmigration rates (RE**); and net migration rates (RSAL**), all ages, 1970 and 1985

% values of the population of the area of corresponding age and sex	1970 All ages								
	FPR	FNPR	MPR	MNPR	F	M	PR	NPR	Total
SO–SO	0.25	1.48	0.91	0.74	1.73	1.65	0.58	1.12	1.70
SO–RE	0.24	1.06	0.93	0.53	1.30	1.46	0.58	0.80	1.38
RE–SO	0.06	0.42	0.37	0.22	0.48	0.59	0.21	0.32	0.53
RSAL SO	0.18	0.64	0.56	0.31	0.82	0.87	0.37	0.48	0.85
SE–SE	0.28	1.13	0.69	0.56	1.41	1.25	0.48	0.85	1.33
SE–RE	0.25	1.04	0.90	0.51	1.29	1.41	0.57	0.78	1.35
RE–SE	0.11	0.56	0.45	0.30	0.67	0.75	0.28	0.43	0.71
RSAL SE	0.14	0.48	0.45	0.21	0.62	0.66	0.29	0.35	0.64
LZ–LZ	0.16	1.01	0.68	0.49	1.17	1.17	0.42	0.75	1.17
LZ–RE	0.17	0.70	0.59	0.35	0.87	0.94	0.37	0.53	0.90
RE–LZ	0.27	1.04	0.89	0.50	1.31	1.39	0.57	0.78	1.35
RSAL LZ	− 0.10	− 0.34	− 0.30	− 0.15	− 0.44	− 0.45	− 0.20	− 0.25	− 0.45

Table 6.4 (cont.)

CE-CE	0.46	1.78	1.30	0.84	2.24	2.14	0.87	1.32	2.19
CE-RE	0.12	1.47	0.41	0.23	0.59	0.64	0.26	0.35	0.61
RE-CE	0.14	0.67	0.50	0.33	0.81	0.83	0.31	0.51	0.82
RSAL CE	−0.02	−0.20	−0.09	−0.10	−0.22	−0.19	−0.05	−0.16	−0.21
NE-NE	0.51	1.83	1.27	0.80	2.34	2.07	0.88	1.33	2.21
NE-RE	0.13	0.45	0.39	0.20	0.58	0.59	0.25	0.33	0.58
RE-NE	0.11	0.48	0.44	0.22	0.59	0.66	0.27	0.35	0.62
RSAL NE	0.02	−0.03	−0.05	−0.02	−0.01	−0.07	−0.02	−0.02	−0.04
NO-NO	0.64	1.89	1.54	0.94	2.53	2.48	1.08	1.43	2.51
NO-RE	0.09	0.56	0.47	0.29	0.65	0.76	0.27	0.43	0.70
RE-NO	0.27	1.08	0.99	0.54	1.35	1.53	0.62	0.82	1.44
RSAL NO	−0.18	−0.52	−0.52	−0.25	−0.70	−0.77	−0.35	−0.39	−0.74
Within areas	0.42	1.61	1.15	0.78	2.08	1.93	0.78	1.21	1.99
Between areas	0.16	0.72	0.62	0.36	0.88	0.98	0.39	0.54	0.93

SO–SO	0.35	1.32	0.91	0.72	1.67	1.63	0.63	1.02	1.65
SO–RE	0.11	0.43	0.40	0.24	0.54	0.64	0.25	0.33	0.58
RE–SO	0.06	0.31	0.26	0.19	0.37	0.45	0.16	0.25	0.41
RSAL SO	0.05	0.12	0.14	0.05	0.17	0.19	0.09	0.08	0.17
SE–SE	0.30	0.91	0.62	0.52	1.21	1.12	0.45	0.72	1.17
SE–RE	0.12	0.44	0.41	0.24	0.56	0.65	0.26	0.34	0.60
RE–SE	0.08	0.42	0.29	0.25	0.50	0.54	0.18	0.34	0.52
RSAL SE	0.04	0.02	0.12	−0.01	0.06	0.11	0.08	0.00	0.08
LZ–LZ	0.24	0.86	0.60	0.50	1.10	1.10	0.41	0.69	1.10
LZ–RE	0.10	0.42	0.41	0.23	0.52	0.64	0.25	0.33	0.58
RE–LZ	0.15	0.53	0.44	0.38	0.68	0.82	0.29	0.45	0.74
RSAL LZ	−0.05	−0.11	−0.03	−0.15	−0.16	−0.18	−0.04	−0.12	−0.16

Table 6.4 (*cont.*)

CE–CE	0.55	0.96	0.97	0.56	1.51	1.53	0.75	0.77	1.52
CE–RE	0.07	0.24	0.22	0.15	0.31	0.37	0.15	0.20	0.35
RE–CE	0.11	0.43	0.37	0.24	0.54	0.61	0.24	0.34	0.58
RSAL CE	−0.04	−0.19	−0.15	−0.09	−0.23	−0.24	−0.09	−0.14	−0.23
NE–NE	0.67	0.98	1.01	0.53	1.65	1.54	0.83	0.76	1.59
NE–RE	0.07	0.20	0.19	0.11	0.27	0.30	0.13	0.16	0.29
RE–NE	0.07	0.26	0.24	0.14	0.33	0.38	0.15	0.20	0.35
RSAL NE	−0.00	−0.06	−0.05	−0.03	−0.06	−0.08	−0.02	−0.04	−0.06
NO–NO	0.76	1.24	1.34	0.71	2.00	2.05	1.04	0.99	2.03
NO–RE	0.08	0.38	0.29	0.25	0.46	0.54	0.18	0.32	0.50
RE–NO	0.11	0.33	0.35	0.17	0.44	0.52	0.22	0.25	0.47
RSAL NO	−0.03	0.05	−0.06	0.08	0.02	0.02	−0.04	0.07	0.03
Within areas	0.52	1.12	0.99	0.63	1.64	1.62	0.75	0.88	1.63
Between areas	0.09	0.36	0.32	0.21	0.45	0.53	0.20	0.29	0.49

Table 6.5. Gross outmigration rates by sex, working condition and age (young, ≤19; central, 20–59; old ≥60 years), 1970 and 1985

% values of the population of the area of corresponding age and sex	1970					1985				
	FPR	FNPR	MPR	MNPR	Total	FPR	FNPR	MPR	MNPR	Total
SO–RE										
≤ 19 years	0.15	1.25	0.28	1.08	1.38	0.02	0.44	0.08	0.39	0.46
20–59 years	0.37	1.12	1.69	0.12	1.65	0.20	0.47	0.71	0.13	0.75
≥ 60 years	0.03	0.45	0.09	0.38	0.45	0.01	0.29	0.02	0.22	0.28
SE–RE										
≤ 19 years	0.14	1.17	0.28	1.06	1.33	0.02	0.44	0.09	0.38	0.47
20–59 years	0.40	1.13	1.61	0.13	1.63	0.22	0.49	0.72	0.15	0.79
≥ 60 years	0.04	0.47	0.09	0.35	0.48	0.01	0.31	0.02	0.24	0.29
LZ–RE										
≤ 19 years	0.01	0.42	0.07	0.69	0.75	0.02	0.41	0.06	0.38	0.43
20–59 years	0.22	0.70	1.02	0.11	1.05	0.14	0.42	0.68	0.12	0.69
≥ 60 years	0.07	0.63	0.14	0.46	0.65	0.01	0.45	0.06	0.37	0.45
CE–RE										
≤ 19 years	0.03	0.61	0.06	0.58	0.64	0.01	0.34	0.03	0.32	0.35
20–59 years	0.19	0.48	0.68	0.06	0.70	0.13	0.24	0.38	0.08	0.41
≥ 60 years	0.04	0.26	0.06	0.20	0.28	0.01	0.17	0.02	0.13	0.16

Table 6.5 (*cont.*)

% values of the population of the area of corresponding age and sex	1970					1985				
	FPR	FNPR	MPR	MNPR	Total	FPR	FNPR	MPR	MNPR	Total
NE–RE										
≤ 19 years	0.03	0.48	0.05	0.45	0.51	0.01	0.23	0.02	0.22	0.25
20–59 years	0.21	0.49	0.69	0.06	0.73	0.13	0.20	0.32	0.06	0.35
≥ 60 years	0.03	0.26	0.04	0.19	0.26	0.01	0.15	0.02	0.10	0.14
NO–RE										
≤ 19 years	0.03	0.77	0.09	0.73	0.82	0.02	0.54	0.03	0.50	0.55
20–59 years	0.14	0.54	0.78	0.07	0.77	0.15	0.38	0.48	0.12	0.56
≥ 60 years	0.03	0.29	0.07	0.27	0.33	0.01	0.25	0.03	0.28	0.28
Between areas										
≤ 19 years	0.08	0.90	0.16	0.82	0.98	0.02	0.42	0.05	0.39	0.44
20–59 years	0.25	0.73	1.06	0.09	0.16	0.16	0.37	0.54	0.11	0.59
≥ 60 years	0.03	0.36	0.08	0.28	0.38	0.01	0.25	0.03	0.22	0.25

Table 6.6. *Within-area migration rates* ** **; *gross outmigration rates* (**RE*); *gross inmigration rates* (RE**); *and net migration rates* (RSAL**), *20–29 age group, 1970*

% values of the population of that area of corresponding age and sex	1970 Age 20–24				Age 25–29			
	FPR	FNPR	MPR	MNPR	FPR	FNPR	MPR	MNPR
SO–SO	0.76	3.13	1.85	0.51	0.83	2.52	3.20	0.26
SO–RE	0.95	2.17	3.42	0.29	1.74	2.93	0.15	0.10
RE–SO	0.17	0.77	1.09	0.18	0.20	0.75	1.34	0.05
RSAL SO	0.78	1.40	2.33	0.11	0.44	0.99	1.59	
SE–SE	1.00	2.51	1.39	0.38	0.90	1.85	2.32	0.16
SE–RE	0.99	1.18	3.46	0.33	0.71	1.85	2.66	0.16
RE–SE	0.29	1.04	1.19	0.24	0.34	1.09	1.66	0.13
RSAL SE	0.70	1.24	2.27	0.09	0.37	0.77	1.00	0.03
LZ–LZ	0.58	2.31	1.40	0.31	0.42	1.52	2.04	0.14
LZ–RE	0.42	1.19	1.80	0.30	0.50	1.13	1.93	0.13
RE–LZ	0.80	1.97	2.91	0.42	0.73	1.70	2.58	0.21
RSAL LZ	−0.38	−0.78	−1.11	−0.12	−0.23	−0.57	−0.65	−0.08
CE–CE	2.11	3.72	2.83	0.41	1.33	2.65	3.96	0.19
CE–RE	0.38	0.94	1.24	0.17	0.37	0.88	1.30	0.08
RE–CE	0.46	1.31	1.47	0.22	0.39	1.13	1.42	0.10
RSAL CE	−0.08	−0.37	−0.23	−0.05	−0.02	−0.25	−0.12	−0.02

Table 6.6 (*cont.*)

% values of the population of that area of corresponding age and sex	1970							
	Age 20–24				Age 25–29			
	FPR	FNPR	MPR	MNPR	FPR	FNPR	MPR	MNPR
NE–NE	2.68	4.65	2.73	0.30	1.45	3.40	4.53	0.16
NE–RE	0.47	0.98	1.16	0.14	0.36	0.84	1.32	0.07
RE–NE	0.31	0.77	1.45	0.13	0.33	0.79	1.23	0.05
RSAL NE	0.16	0.21	−0.29	0.01	0.02	0.05	0.09	0.02
NO–NO	3.19	3.07	3.28	3.25	1.79	2.81	4.93	0.15
NO–RE	0.27	0.95	1.22	0.19	0.25	0.87	1.39	0.08
RE–NO	1.22	2.44	3.84	0.27	0.66	1.63	2.77	0.10
RSAL NO	−0.95	−1.49	−2.62	−0.08	−0.41	−0.76	−1.38	−0.02
Within areas	1.85	3.25	2.47	0.40	1.23	2.58	3.82	0.18
Between areas	0.58	1.43	2.09	0.23	0.44	1.19	1.89	0.11

SO–SO	0.80	2.50	1.64	0.56	1.17	2.03	2.84	0.36
SO–RE	0.29	1.02	1.47	0.30	0.42	0.74	1.25	0.20
RE–SO	0.13	0.51	0.61	0.19	0.20	0.47	0.80	0.11
RSAL SO	0.16	0.51	0.86	0.11	0.22	0.27	0.45	0.09
SE–SE	0.90	1.79	1.13	0.44	1.02	1.42	2.05	0.26
SE–RE	0.37	1.04	1.60	0.33	0.45	0.80	1.27	0.22
RE–SE	0.17	0.69	0.60	0.30	0.25	0.61	0.88	0.17
RSAL SE	0.20	0.35	1.00	0.03	0.21	0.19	0.39	0.05
LZ–LZ	0.56	1.65	1.06	0.51	0.79	1.17	1.82	0.34
LZ–RE	0.24	0.72	1.53	0.28	0.33	0.55	1.22	0.15
RE–LZ	0.27	1.12	1.89	0.63	0.47	0.92	1.29	0.50
RSAL LZ	−0.03	−0.40	−0.11	−0.35	−0.14	−0.36	−0.07	−0.35
CE–CE	2.16	1.80	2.28	0.43	2.34	1.33	3.51	0.27
CE–RE	0.20	0.47	0.89	0.20	0.29	0.41	0.78	0.14
RE–CE	0.37	1.01	1.47	0.33	0.42	0.70	1.13	0.20
RSAL CE	−0.17	−0.54	−0.78	−0.13	−0.13	−0.29	−0.35	−0.06

Table 6.6 (*cont.*)

% values of the population of that area of corresponding age and sex	1970							
	Age 20–24				Age 25–29			
	FPR	FNPR	MPR	MNPR	FPR	FNPR	MPR	MNPR
NE–NE	3.11	1.76	2.38	0.32	2.76	1.30	3.73	0.17
NE–RE	0.20	0.36	0.55	0.15	0.26	0.29	0.56	0.09
RE–NE	0.17	0.49	0.86	0.14	0.28	0.33	0.67	0.09
RSAL NE	0.03	− 0.13	− 0.31	0.01	− 0.02	− 0.04	− 0.11	0.00
NO–NO	3.12	1.97	3.02	0.45	3.16	1.45	4.88	0.22
NO–RE	0.22	0.67	0.67	0.26	0.29	0.54	0.87	0.16
RE–NO	0.40	0.88	1.44	0.20	0.48	0.58	1.20	0.10
RSAL NO	− 0.18	− 0.21	− 0.77	− 0.06	− 0.19	− 0.04	− 0.33	− 0.06
Within areas	1.82	2.03	2.12	0.48	1.99	1.55	3.45	0.28
Between areas	0.25	0.75	1.07	0.26	0.34	0.57	0.99	0.16

within-area migration rates of working males register everywhere a maximum in the age bracket 25–29.

The observation of the different peak ages of emigrants, depending on their sex and working condition, leads us to suppose that the migration decision is possibly taken at different maturity and, probably, skill levels by different groups. One might conversely interpret the postponing of the migration age as a sign revealing a desperate condition, when migration is considered the last resort, to be put off as late as possible.

Indeed, the following four facts can be interpreted in different ways:

1. Northern-Central working male emigrants are older than their Southern counterparts, as far as interregional movements are concerned, no distinction arising, between different areas, in the intraregional movements.
2. Working female emigrants (both within and between areas) are older today than in the past.
3. Working females of *SO–SE* migrating out of the Mezzogiorno are older than working males leaving the same areas.
4. Working males of the two Southern areas (and of *LZ* only since the 1980s) are older when migrating within their area than towards the rest of Italy.

An interesting phenomenon is that of return migration – i.e., migration of elderly, currently non-working emigrants, back to their regions of origin. This concerns retired people formerly employed or their spouses (mainly wives who might have been in a non-working condition even before the retirement age). Assuming that all non-working emigrants in age brackets beyond the retirement age are return emigrants, we get the impression from Table 6.5 that the return migration concerns more males than females, although gross outmigration rates of the elderly are higher for *FNPR* than for *MNPR*. In some of our data that we do not report here it appears that female return emigrants are more frequent among those who emigrated within the same area than between areas. The only partial exception to this statement is observed in the case of gross female outmigrations from *SO* and *SE*, in the 1980s only.

There are several reasons justifying the fact that return migration seems more evident among males than females. An important factor is a sort of 'optical illusion', due to the fact that we measure this phenomenon comparing gross outmigration rates of non-working persons in the old age and in the central age brackets. While non-working male emigrants in the 20–59 age brackets are very rare, female emigrants of the same age are very often already in non-working condition.

The following seem most important among the other reasons for the apparently more frequent return migration of males compared to females: the return migration phenomenon in the case of females is distributed over a larger age interval, as in most dependent jobs of the private sector Italian women retire before men – i.e., at 55, rather than 60 (with longer life expectancy); the female return migration, more than the male one, also concerns persons who, before coming back to their region of origin, were in a non-working condition (particularly wives) and were therefore freer to choose the best age to return (possibly before retirement age); many females who emigrated as wives are not bound to return, either because they married a non-emigrant, setting their home far from their region of origin, or because they married an emigrant without changing their residence. This last argument focuses on a well known bias of these data as well as of the aggregate migration data discussed in section 5: people do not always register their migration movements, all the more so if they are in non-working condition; very often, they officially change their residence after finding a job in the region of destination.

Finally, with regards to variations through time of gross migration rates, it would be a mistake to think that all groups, distinguished by age, sex and working condition, register a migration fall, both within and between areas, comparable to that observed in the aggregate. In fact, there is a notable group – working female emigrants within their geographical area – which shows a rising within-area migration rate from 1970 to 1985. All other categories witness a decline in interregional and intraregional gross migration rates, with the following characteristics. Working male and non-working female emigrants register a sharp fall between 1970 and 1985 in all age brackets and all regions of migration both within and between areas. Non-working male emigrants experience a decrease only in the younger age brackets (younger than 19) and older ones (older than 60). Excluding these age brackets, non-working male emigrants both within and between areas, show an increase through the years in all regions, except *NE*; this suggests that the male emigrant's condition in the central age bracket has changed. The female emigrant's condition in the same age bracket has probably changed, too, sometimes in the opposite direction: observing the working females of 20–59 years migrating between areas, we see that their gross outmigration rate decreased everywhere from 1970 to 1985, with the exception of *NO* where it increased: according to Mincer's argument (1978) referred to above, it is perhaps no accident that this is the most developed Italian area.

7 Conclusions

In this study we have looked at possible determinants of migration rates within Italy. The analysis was mainly a descriptive one and was based on a new data set.

Our main tentative conclusions are:

1. After a period (1960s and early 1970s) characterised by fairly strong migration flows from the South to the North-Centre of Italy, these flows have been steadily declining.
2. The decrease in interregional mobility has been matched by a reduction in intraregional mobility.
3. Not all groups have borne the same patterns; these appear to depend on individual characteristics such as age, sex and working condition.
4. Some geographical areas (*CE* and *NE*) switched from a positive to a negative migration balance. *CE* has become the largest recipient of immigrants from other parts of Italy. The North-Western (*NO*) regions, which traditionally were the largest recipients of immigrants, now have a positive net migration rate.
5. Gross outmigration rates appeared to be strongly correlated with unemployment differentials. However, since the mid-1970s, this link seems to have been broken; we think that this might be partly due to the increase in the level of aggregate unemployment.
6. We also think that three other factors constitute important explanations; these include:

   (a) A strong decrease in interregional net real wage differentials coupled with an increase in the net real wage of the South-West (*SO*) relative to the Northern areas. This pattern has been caused by a reduction in nominal wage differentials, a shift in cost of living differentials in favour of the Mezzogiorno and possibly also by an increase in income taxation progressivity to the detriment of the North-Centre.
   (b) A rise of various forms of Government transfers to the Southern regions, which can take the form of more frequent disability pensions, a higher number of tenured public sector jobs and better pay relative to the private sector: these factors, together with the presence of strong familiar networks, can strongly reduce the incentives to migrate, while leading to 'wait unemployment', or to employment in the underground sector.
   (c) An increase in the fixed costs involved with the decision to migrate. The typical example here is the housing rental price; the

situation has been aggravated by a rationed housing market, due to rent control regulatons.
7.   Finally, we think that the persistence of long periods of low migration rates, *ceteris paribus*, raises the cost of migrating.

DATA APPENDIX

Note:
**   stands for area. Our area definition is as follows: North-West (*NO*); North-East (*NE*); Centre (*CE*); Lazio (*LZ*); South-West (*SO*); South-East (*SE*); Italy as a whole (*IT*). Where the original data refer to the Italian administrative regions this is explicitly indicated here.

AINVOBL**   Total disability pensions distributed by the *Fondo Pensioni Lavoratori Dipendenti* (Private Employees Pension Fund or FPLD) per administrative region, from 1960 to 1986 (millions of Lire at current prices).
Sources: INPS NS, 1960–71 and 1976–7; INPS AR, 1972–5 and 1978–86. (We gratefully acknowledge the help of Dott. Santini and Dott. Tirelli, INPS.)

DIPAGR**   Number of employees in agriculture per administrative region according to the national accounts, from 1960 to 1986 (thousands of units). For 1985–6 data are constructed using the growth rate of those same regional data derived from the new national accounts.
Sources: ISTAT, 1982; ISTAT ACN, 1986. (We gratefully acknowledge the help of Prof. Siesto, Dott. Giovannuzzi, Dott. Pascarella, Dott.ssa Pedullà and Dott. Ricci, ISTAT.)

DIPPR**   Number of private sector employees per administrative region according to the national accounts from 1960 to 1986 (thousands of units). For 1985–6 see *DIPAGR***.
Sources: ISTAT, 1982; ISTAT ACN, 1986.

DIPPU**   Number of public sector employees per administrative region according to the national accounts, from 1960 to 1986 (thousands of units). For 1985–6 see *DIPAGR***.
Sources: ISTAT, 1982; ISTAT ACN, 1986.

DIPTO**   Total number of employees per administrative region, from 1960 to 1986 (thousands of units). *DIPTO*** = *DIPPU*** + *DPPR***. For 1985–6 see *DIPAGR***.
Sources: ISTAT, 1982; ISTAT ACN, 1986.

DISF**   Number of unemployed females per administrative region according to the labour force survey, from 1960 to 1987 (thousands of units). We have at our disposal the ISTAT Italian unemployed females new series data (ISTAT SL, 1986), the regional unemployed females old series data (ISTAT SL, 1970) and the Italian unemployed females old series data (ISTAT SL, 1970). We apply the regional distribution of the old series to the

new Italian series to obtain the 1960–6 data. From 1967 to 1976 the data per administrative regions are provided by the Veneto Region (see also Masarotto and Trivellato, 1984) and are reproportioned to the ISTAT national data.
Sources: ISTAT SL, 1986, from 1977 to 1984; ISTAT RFL, 1985–7, from 1985 to 1987. (We gratefully acknoweldge the help of Dott. Cananzi and Dott.ssa Schenkel.)
Sources: see *DISF***.

DIST**   Total number of unemployed per administrative region according to the labour force survey, from 1960 to 1987 (thousands of units).
Sources: see *DISF***.

EM**   Emigrants from the area ** to the six Italian areas (*NO, NE, CE, LZ, SE, SO*), from 1960 to 1986 (absolute values).
Sources: ISTAT PMA, 1976–81, from 1960 to 1980; ISTAT ASD, 1981–7, from 1981 to 1986.

EMIN**   Emigrants from area ** within the same area, from 1960 to 1986 (absolute values). Within-area migration rates equal *EMIN**/PREST***.
Sources: see *EM***

FLP**   Female labour force per administrative region, from 1960 to 1986 (thousands of units). $FLF^{**} = DISF^{**} + OCCF^{**}$.
Sources: see *DISF***.

FLM**   Male labour force per administrative region, from 1960 to 1986 (thousands of units). $FLM^{**} = DISM^{**} + OCCM^{**}$.
Sources: see *DISF***.

FLT**   Total labour force per administrative region, from 1960 to 1986 (thousands of units). $FLT^{**} = DIST^{**} + OCCT^{**}$.
Sources: see *DISF***.

IM**   Immigrants to the area ** from the six Italian areas (*NO, NE, CE, LZ, SE, SO*), from 1960 to 1986 (absolute values). The gross inmigration rates equal *IM**/PREST***.
Sources: see *EM***.

INAIL**   Effective daily wage paid to the injured-at-work employees of industry and agriculture per administrative region, from 1960 to 1985 (thousands of Lire at current prices).
Source: INAIL NS. (We gratefully acknowledge the help of Dott. Nachmijas, IRI.)

IND**   Self-employed per administrative region according to the national accounts, from 1960 to 1986 (thousands of units).
Sources: ISTAT, 1982; ISTAT ACN, 1986.

INDIPAGR**   Self-employed in agriculture, fishing and forestry per administrative region according to the national accounts, from 1960 to 1986 (thousands of units).
Sources: ISTAT, 1982; ISTAT ACN, 1986.

INDTAX**   Indirect taxes net of subsidies paid per administrative region, from 1960 to 1984 (billions of Lire at current prices). *INDTAX-** = TIND** × VACF**.*
Sources: see *TIND** and VACF**.*

INVW**   Ratio between average disability pensions and the wage rate in the private sector per administrative region, from 1960 to 1986. Sources: see *AINVOBL**, NINVOBL** and WPR**.*

IRPEF1**   Personal income taxes per administrative region, from 1960 to 1986 (millions of Lire at current prices). Before the Fiscal Reform (1960–73), the data are constructed by summing employees' and self-employed supplementary income taxes with taxes on moveable property, both on an accruals basis, inclusive of residual revenues (assessment values). After the 1973 Fiscal Reform, the full personal income tax (*(Imposta sul Reddito delle Persone Fisiche* or IRPEF) is introduced. Data from 1974 to 1976 are reconstructed by applying the regional distribution of income taxes of 1976 employees only (MF ADR) to the Italian 1974–6 total amount. From 1977 to 1984 regional data (MF ADR) are reproportioned to the Italian total. The 1985–6 data are constructed by applying to the 1984 datum the regional growth rates (provided by *Ragioneria Generale dello Stato*). The datum is comprehensive of residual revenues on an accruals basis (assessment values).
Sources: MF ASF, 1965, 1973, 1976; MF ADR, various years. (We gratefully acknowledge the help of Dott.ssa Herr, SOGEI; Dott. Ruggeri, *Ragioneria Generale dello Stato*; Dott. Saggese, Ministero delle Finanze.

LAMDA**   Proxy for direct tax rates per geographical area, from 1960 to 1986. It is estimated as *LAMDA** = IRPEF1**/VACF**.*
Sources: see *IRPEF1** and VACF**.*

NATI**   Live births per administrative region, from 1960 to 1986 (absolute values).
Sources: ISTAT, 1960; ISTAT PMA, 1961–71; ISTAT PBD, 1972–80; ISTAT ASD, 1981–4; ISTAT SD, 1985–6. (We gratefully ackowledge the help of Dott.ssa Veltri, ISTAT.

NINVOBL**   Total number of disability pensions per administrative region, from 1960 to 1986 (absolute values).
Sources: INPS NS, 1960–71 and 1976–7; INPS AR, 1972–5 and 1978–86.

OCCAGR**   Number of unemployed in agriculture per administrative region according to the national accounts, from 1960 to 1986 (thousands of units). *OCCAGR** = DIPAGR** + INDIPAGR**.*
Sources: ISTAT, 1982; ISTAT ACN, 1986.

OCCCN**   Total number of employed per administrative region according to the national accounts, from 1960 to 1987 (thousands of units). *OCCCN** = DIPTO** + IND**.*
Sources: ISTAT, 1982; ISTAT ACN, 1986.

$OCCF^{**}$	Number of female employed per administrative region according to the labour force survey, from 1960 to 1987 (thousands of units). The corresponding employment rates are equal to $OCCF^{**}/PRESF^{**}$. *Sources*: see $DISF^{**}$.
$OCCM^{**}$	Number of male employed per administrative region according to the labour force survey, from 1960 to 1987 (thousands of units). The corresponding employment rates are equal to $OCCM^{**}/PRESM^{**}$. *Sources*: see $DISF^{**}$
$OCCT^{**}$	Total number of employed per administrative region according to the labour force survey, from 1960 to 1987 (thousands of units). The corresponding employment rates are equal to $OCCT^{**}/PREST^{**}$. *Sources*: see $DISF^{**}$.
$ONSOC^{**}$	Social security contributions paid by employers per administrative region, from 1961 to 1986 (billions of Lire at current prices). $ONSOC^{**} = RLD^{**} \times (S^{**}/1 + S^{**})$. *Sources*: see RLD^{**} and S^{**}.
P^{**}	Proxy for product prices index per administrative region, from 1961 to 1986. From 1970 to 1984 the data series is observed (ISTAT ACN, 1986); we have used this series, plus PC^{**}, plus RLD^{**} and $DIPTO^{**}$ (all these series are known) to compute the coefficients of regression, imposing the condition that the sum of the coefficients be equal to unity. Through these coefficients we have constructed the data from 1961 to 1969 and 1985–6. *Sources*: see PC^{**}, RLD^{**}, $DIPTO^{**}$; ISTAT ACN, 1986.
PC^{**}	Consumer price index of employees households per administrative region, from 1960 to 1986. We take the general index relative to the regional capital of each region. This index is constructed considering five expenditure items and therefore five base price indexes ($PCAB^{**}$ = housing rental price index, $PCABB^{**}$ = clothing price index, $PCALE^{**}$ = foodstuff price index, $PCELC^{**}$ = electricity and fuel price index, $PCSVA^{**}$ = other foods and services price index). Each regional capital shows five weights assigned to the five items of their consumption basket. These weights are then utilised in the six areas (WAB^{**}, $WABB^{**}$, $WALE^{**}$, $WELC^{**}$, $WSVA^{**}$), assuming, as done by ISTAT, that within each area the weight system coincides with that of the corresponding regional capitals. According to ISTAT, the weights of the regional capitals belonging to the same ISTAT geographical partitions are identical and change when ISTAT changes the base year (i.e., 1961, 1966, 1970, 1976, 1980, 1985). to obtain the area (general) consumer price index, the (general) consumer price indexes of the regional capitals are weighted with weights equalling the RLD ratio of the region compared to the one of the area. *Sources*: ISTAT ASI, various years.

PCAB**   Housing rental price index of employees households per administrative region, from 1960 to 1986.
            Sources: ISTAT ASI, various years.

PRESF**   Resident female population per administrative region, from 1960 to 1987 (thousands of units).
            Sources: USR, 1960–72; ISTAT PBD, 1973–81; ISTAT PR, 1982–5; ISTAT SD, 1986–7.

PRESM**   Resident male population per administrative region, from 1960 to 1976 (thousands of units).
            Sources: see *PRESF***.

PREST**   Total resident population per administrative region, from 1960 to 1987 (thousands of units).
            Sources: see *PRESF***.

PROD**   Real productivity per administrative region, from 1961 to 1986 (millions of Lire at 1970 prices). $PROD^{**} = (VACF^{**}/P^{**})/OCCCN^{**}$.
            Sources: see $VACF^{**}$, $P^{*}8$ and $OCCCN^{**}$.

RE**   Gross inmigration rates by sex and working condition from the rest of Italy towards the geographical area **, from 1969 to 1986 (absolute values).
            Sources: see **RE*.

REM**   Gross oumigration rates from the geographical area **, from 1960 to 1986. $REM^{**} = EM^{**}/PREST^{**}$.
            Sources: see EM^{**} and $PREST^{**}$.

RLD**   Compensation of employees, inclusive of social security contributions, per administrative region, from 1961 to 1986 (billions of Lire at current prices). There are two regional series: 1961–73 and 1970–84. In the four years in which the two series overlap (i.e., 1970–4) we measure the constant correlation index and use it to reconstruct backwards the 1961–9 series consistent with that of 1970–84 derived from ISTAT ACN, 1986. The 1985–6 data series are estimated by applying the growth rate observed in the new national account series to the old series ending in 1984.
            Sources: ISTAT ACN, 1974; ISTAT ACN, 1986.

RLDPR**   Compensation of private sector employees, inclusive of social security contributions, per administrative region, from 1961 to 1986 (billions of Lire at current prices). We have two regional series, one for 1961–70 and one for 1970–84; they are not homogeneous, as the 1970 data confirm. We therefore use the growth rate of the 1961–70 data to reconstruct backwards the 1961–9 data consistent with the 1970–84 data. For 1985–6, the data are constructed using the ratio between *RLDPR*** and *RLD*** observed in 1984, applying this to the *RLD*** values for 1985 and 1986.
            Sources: ISTAT ACN, 1974; ISTAT ACN, 1986.

*RLDPU***   Compensation of public sector employees, inclusive of social security contributions, per administrative region, from 1961 to 1986 (billions of Lire at current prices). *RLDPU*** = *RLD*** − *RLDPR***.
Sources: see *RLD*** and *RLDPR***.

*RSAL***   Balance between emigrants and immigrants relative to the population of the geographical area ** or net migration rates in the area **, from 1960 to 1986. *RSAL*** = (*EM*** − *Im***)/*PREST***.
Sources: see *EM*** and *PREST***.

*Sx***   Estimated social security tax rates paid by employers per administrative region, from 1961 to 1986. These are constructed at regional evel as a weighted average of the social security tax rates paid by the public sector and by the private sector. The former (*SPU***) is, in any given year, supposed to be equal to the Italian observed data. The latter (*SPR***) is derived from three known series: the regional data on the private employers' contributions paid to the FPLD of INPS; the Italian social security tax rates of private employers and the Italian tax rates of the private employers' contributions paid to the FPLD of INPS. We assume that the ratio between the regional social security tax rates of private employers' contributions and the regional tax rates of private employers' contributions to the FPLD of INPS only is, in a given year, the same in every administrative region and is equal to the ratio between the same variables at the national level, which are observed.
Sources: INPS data in INPS, NS and INPS AR; social security contributions data in ISTAT ACN, 1986 and ISTAT, CEN.

*TIND***   Indirect tax rates per administrative region, from 1960 to 1984. From 1960–9 data are reconstructed as the ratio between indirect taxes net of subsidies and the value added at factor cost per area, contained in ISTAT ACN, 1974. Areas as defined by ISTAT differ from those defined by us: we consider for each administrative region the indirect tax rates of the ISTAT area which includes this region; from 1970 to 1984, *TIND*** = *INDTAX***/*VACF***.
Sources: ISTAT ACN, 1974; ISTAT ACN, 1986.

*TNAT***   Birth rate per administrative region, from 1960 to 1986 (births per thousand residents).
Sources: see *NATI*** and *PREST***.

*UF***   Female unemloyment rates per administrative region, from 1960 to 1986. *UF*** = *DISF***/*FLF***.
Sources: see *DISF*** and *FLF***.

*ULC***   Unit labour cost per administrative region, from 1961 to 1986. *ULC*** = *RLD***/*VACF***.
Sources: see *RLD*** and *VACF***.

UM^{**} Male unemloyment rates per administrative region, from 1960 to 1986. $UM^{**} = DISM^{**}/FLM^{**}$. UM^o are male unemployment rates in the areas of origin, while UM^d are male unemployment rates in the areas of destination of emigrants. The superscripts o and d indicate origin and destination of other variables, too (for example, $\log(WPR7^o)$ indicates the logarithm of the private sector real wage in the origin area of the emigrant).
Sources: see $DISM^{**}$ and FLM^{**}.

UT^{**} Total unemployment rates per administrative region, from 1960 to 1986. $UT^{**} = DIST^{**}/FLT^{**}$.
Sources: see $DIST^{**}$ and FLT^{**}.

$VACF^{**}$ Value added at factor cost per administrative region, from 1960 to 1986 (billions of Lire at current prices). We have at our disposition two series, one for 1970–84 (ISTAT ACN, 1986) and one for 1960–74 (Tagliacarne, 1962, 1963, 1972, 1975a, 1975b). This latter does not follow the SEC classification; we therefore calculate the regression for the common years and we apply them so as to reconstruct a 1960–9 series homogenous with that for 1970–84. The 1985–6 data are observed (SVIMEZ).
Sources: Tagliacarne, 1962, 1963, 1972, 1975a, 1975b; ISTAT ACN, 1986; SVIMEZ. (We gratefully acknowledge the help of Prof. Cafiero, Dott. Padovani, SVIMEZ; Dott. Esposito, Istituto Tagliacarne.)

$VACF\ AGR^{**}$ Value added at factor cost in the agricultural, fishing and forestry sector per administrative region, from 1960 to 1986 (billions of Lire at current prices).
Source: ISTAT VAGGR. (We gratefully acknowledge the help of Dott.ssa Benedetti, ISTAT.)

$VACF7\ AGR^{**}$ Real value added at factor cost in the agricultural, fishing and forestry sector per administrative region, from 1960 to 1986 (billions of Lire at 1970 prices, where ISTAT uses a direct method of price evaluation for marketable goods and an indirect method for intermediate consumption – particularly for consumption of one's own products).
Sources: ISTAT VAAGR.

$VAPC7^{**}$ *Per capita* value added per administrative region, from 1961 to 1986 (millions of Lire at 1970 prices). $VAPC7^{**} = VACF^{**}/(PREST^{**} \times P^{**})$.
Sources: see $VACF^{**}$.

WPR^{**} Private sector nominal wage per employee per administrative region, from 1960 to 1986 (millions of Lire at current prices). The 1960 data are reconstructed using the dynamics of $INAIL^{**}$. $WPR^{**} = RLDPR^{**}/(DIPPER^{**} \times (1 + SPR^{**}))$.
Sources: see $RLDPR^{**}$, $DIPPR^{**}$ and SPR^{**}.

$WPR7^{**}$ Private sector real wage per employee per administrative region,

from 1960 to 1986 (millions of Lire at 1970 prices). $WPR7^{**} = WPR^{**}/PC^{**}$.
Sources: see WPR^{**} and PC^{**}.

WPU^{**} Public sector nominal wage per employee per administrative region, from 1960 to 1986 (millions of Lire at current prices). The 1960 data are reconstructed by using the dynamics of $INAIL^{**}$. $WPU^{**} = RLDPU^{**}/(DIPPU^{**} \times (1 + SPU^{**}))$.
Sources: see $RLDPU^{**}$, $DIPPU^{**}$ and SPU^{**}.

$WPU7^{**}$ Public sector real wage per employee per administrative region, from 1960 to 1986 (millions of Lire at 1970 prices). $WPU7^{**} = WPU^{**}/PC^{**}$.
Sources: see WPU^{**} and PC^{**}.

WTO^{**} Total nominal wage per employee per administrative region, from 1960 to 1986 (millions of Lire at current prices). The 1960 data are reconstructed by using the dynamics of $INAIL^{**}$. $WTO^{**} = RLD^{**}/(DIPTO^{**} \times (1 + S^{**}))$.
Sources: see RLD^{**}. $DIPTO^{**}$ and S^{**}.

$WPRN^{**}$ Private sector nominal wage net of income taxes per employee per geographical area, from 1960 to 1986 (millions of Lire at current prices). $WPRN^{**} = WPR^{**} \times (1 - LAMDA^{**})$.
Sources: see WPR^{**} and $LAMDA^{**}$.

$WPUN^{**}$ Public sector nominal wage net of income taxes per employee per geographical area, from 1960 to 1986 (millions of Lire at current prices). $WPUN^{**} = WPU^{**} \times (1 - LAMDA^{**})$.
Sources: see WPU^{**} and $LAMDA^{**}$.

$WTON^{**}$ Total nominal wage net of income taxes per employee per geographical area, from 1960 to 1986 (millions of Lire at current prices). $WTON^{**} = WTO^{**} \times (1 - LAMDA^{**})$.
Sources: see WTO^{**} and $LAMDA^{**}$.

$WPRN7^{**}$ Private sector net real wage per employee per geographical area, from 1961 to 1986 (millions of Lire at 1970 prices). $WPRN7^{**} = WPRN^{**}/PC^{**}$.
Sources: see $WPRN^{**}$ and PC^{**}.

$WPUN7^{**}$ Public sector net real wage per employee per geographical area, from 1961 to 1986 (millions of Lire at 1970 prices). $WPUN7^{**} = WPUN^{**}/PC^{**}$.
Sources: see $WPUn^{**}$ and PC^{**}.

$WTON7^{**}$ Total net real wage (net of income taxes) per employee per geographical area, from 1961 to 1986 (millions of Lire at 1970 prices). $WTON7^{**} = WTON^{**}/PC^{**}$.
Sources: $WTON^{**}$ and PC^{**}.

$^{**}RE$ Gross outmigration rates by sex, age and working condition from the geographical area ** towards the rest of Italy, from 1969 to 1986.
Sources: unpublished ISTAT data consistent with those of

ISTAT PMA and ISTAT ASD. (We gratefully acknowledge the help of Dott. Cingolani, Dott. Esposito and Dott. Manese, ISTAT.)

_**   Migration rates by sex, age and working condition within the geographical area **, from 1969 to 1986 (absolute values). *Sources*: see **RE.

Abbreviations for Sources

INAIL NS   *Istituto Nazionale per l'Assicurazione contro gli Infortuni sul Lavoro (INAIL), Notiziario Statistico (October–December, various years).*

INPS AR   *Istituto Nazionale della Previdenza Sociale, Allegati Statistici ai Rendiconti* (various years).

INPS NS   Istituto Nazionale della Previdenza Sociale, *Notizie Statistiche* (various years).

ISTAT 1960   Istituto Centrale di Statistica, *Popolazione e Circoscrizioni Amministrative dei Comuni* (1060).

ISTAT 1979   Istituto Centrale di Statistica, 'Una Metodologia di Raccordo per le Serie Statistiche sulle Forze di Lavoro', *Note e Relazioni*, **n. 56** (July 1979).

ISTAT 1982   Istituto Centrale di Statistica, 'Occupati per ramo di attività economica e regione 1960–1970', *Collana d'Informazioni*, **anno IV**, n. 3 (1982).

ISTAT 1983   Istituto Centrale di Statistica, *Contabilità Nazionale, Fonti e Metodi*, Annali di Statistica, **Serie IX, Vol. 4** (1983).

ISTAT ACN 1974   Istituto Centrale di Statistica, *Annuario di Contabilità Nazionale*, **Vol. 4, Tomo 2** (1974).

ISTAT ACN 1986   Istituto Centrale di Statistica, *Annuario di Contabilità Nazionale*, **Vol.14, Tomo 2** (1986).

ISTAT ASD   Istituto Centrale di Statistica, *Annuario Statistico Demografico* (various years).

ISTAT ASI   Istituto Centrale di Statistica, *Annuario Statistico Italiano* (various years).

ISTAT CEN   Istituto Centrale di Statistica, 'Conti Economici Nazionali, 1983–1987', *Collana d'Informazioni*, **n. 19** (1988).

ISTAT PBD   Istituto Centrale di Statistica, 'Popolazione e Bilancii Demografici per Sesso, Età e per Regione', *Supplemento al Bollettino Mensile di Statistica*, **n. 14** (1985).

ISTAT PMA	Istituto Centrale di Statistica, *Popolazione e Movimento Anagrafico dei Comuni* (various years).
ISTAT PR	Istituto Centrale di Statistica, 'Popolazione Residente per Sesso, Età e Regione', *Supplemento al Bollettino Mensile di Statistica*, **n. 21** (1985).
ISTAT RFL	Istituto Centrale di Statistica, 'Rilevazione delle Forze di Lavoro', *Supplemento al Bollettino Mensile di Statistica* (various years).
ISTAT SD	Istituto Centrale di Statistica, *Statistiche Demografiche* (various years).
ISTAT SG	Istituto Centrale di Statistica, *Statistiche Giudiziarie*, **Vol. 34** (1988).
ISTAT SL	Istituto Centrale di Statistica, *Statistiche del Lavoro* (various years).
ISTAT VAAGR	Istituto Centrale di Statistica, 'Il Valore Aggiunto dell'Agricoltura per Regione', *Collana d'Informazioni*, (1/79); (1/84); (1/85).
MF ADR	Ministero delle Finanze, *Analisi delle Dichiarazioni dei Redditi delle Persone Fisiche* (Rome) (various years).
MF ASF	Ministero delle Finanze, *Annuario Statistico*, **Serie 1** (various years).
SVIMEZ	Svimez – Associazione per lo Sviluppo dell'Industria nel Mezzogiorno (a cura di), *Rapporto 1987 sull'Economia del Mezzogiorno*, Bologna: Il Mulino, 1988.
USR**	Università degli Studi di Roma, Dipartimento di Scienze Demografiche, 'Ricostruzione della Popolazione Residente per Sesso, Età e Regione' anni 1952–72, *Fonti e Strumenti*, **n. 1** (1983).

NOTES

1 The construction of the data set used in this study would have been almost impossible without the skilful assistance of Simone Borra and Chiara Rossi: their help and enthusiasm have been invaluable.

Many people belonging to different institutions provided us with useful data and information during the painstaking construction of our data set. They are recalled with gratitude in the Data Appendix. Among them, we are particularly grateful to Professor Guido Rey, Presidente of the Istituto Centrale di Statistica (ISTAT).

We also wish to thank Sally Anne Dickinson, Paola Felli and Angelica Tudini for their competent collaboration. Any remaining errors are the authors' alone.

2 Let us stress the fact that in this study we do not consider gross and net migration rates between Italy and the rest of the world. This important

phenomenon is often illegal and therefore is hardly described by official statistics. The latter tell us that, while up to the beginning of the 1970s, Italian outmigrations abroad exceeded inmigrations, later the sign of the migration balance has been reversed giving rise to a net inmigration flow from the rest of the world into Italy (44,000 people in the period 1972–85, according to Table 6N.1.

Table 6N.1. *Resident population growth, 1951–85, thousand units*

Geographical partitions	1951–72	Of which			1951–85
		1951–60	1960–72	1972–85	
(a) Total variation					
Natural growth					
Mezzogiorno[a]	5,435.1	2,436.9	2.998.2	2,040.4	7,475.5
North–Centre	3,698.0	1,347.8	2,350.2	161.6	3,859.6
Italy	9,133.1	3,784.7	5,348.4	2,202.0	11,335.1
Migration balance					
Mezzogiorno[a]	− 3,951.2	1,566.0	2,365.2	− 497.2	4,448.4
North–Centre	2,258.9	657.5	1,601.4	541.2	2,800.1
Italy	− 1,692.3	− 928.5	− 763.8	44.0	− 1.648.3
Effective growth					
Mezzogiorno[a]	1,483.9	850.9	633.0	1,543.2	3,027.1
North–Centre	5,956.9	2,005.3	3,951.6	702.8	6,659.7
Italy	7,440.7	2,856.2	4,584.6	2,246.0	9,686.8
(b) Annual average variation					
Natural growth					
Mezzogiorno[a]	256.4	264.9	249.9	157.0	218.6
North–Centre	174.4	146.5	195.8	12.4	112.8
Italy	430.8	411.4	445.7	169.4	331.4
Migration balance					
Mezzogiorno[a]	186.4	172.4	− 197.1	− 38.2	130.1
North–Centre	106.6	71.5	133.5	41.6	81.9
Italy	79.8	100.9	63.6	3.4	48.2
Effective growth					
Mezzogiorno[a]	70.0	92.5	52.8	118.7	88.5
North–Centre	281.0	218.0	329.3	54.1	194.7
Italy	351.0	310.5	382.1	172.8	283.2

Note:
a   Corresponds to *SE* + *SO*.

Source: SVIMEZ (1986).

Another 'migratory' phenomenon ignored in this study is the labour mobility limited to such a narrow geographical area that it can be satisfied by commuting rather than by a residence change. This kind of mobility has strongly increased in Italy over the past thirty years.

3 In particular, the figures for each region can be seen from Table 6N.2.

Table 6N.2. *Crime rates in the Italian regions, 1986*

PI	VA	LO	TA	VE	FV	LI	ER	TO	UM
International crimes									
Resident population × 100									
0.979	—	0.529	1.251	0.252	0.328	0.791	0.305	0.336	0.490
Organised crimes									
International crimes × 100									
—	—	2.130	—	—	—	—	—	—	—

MA	LZ	AB	MO	CA	PU	BA	CL	SI	SA
International crimes									
Resident population × 100									
0.631	0.882	0.560	1.497	2.184	1.224	0.808	7.039	3.659	2.436
Organised crimes									
International crimes × 100									
—	2,220	—	—	50.31	—	—	37.33	31.72	—

Sources: ISTAT SD, 1986; ISTAT SG, 1988. The crimes are those reported to the Judicial Authorities from the State Police, the Carabinieri and the Guardia di Finanza. Organised crimes are those committed by the Mafia, Camorra and 'Ndrangheta. The symbols indicating the 20 administrative regions are described in the map of Italy. in Figure 6.1

4 To verify whether regional unemployment and employment differentials correspond to excess labour demand in some markets and excess labour supply in others, we would need some information on vacancies which is lacking in Italy both at national and regional levels. Only recently have attempts been made in Italy indirectly to estimate the aggregate number of unfilled vacancies: through new evidence on media advertising (Sestito, 1988), through business surveys on the firms' constraints due to lack of labour force (Padoa Schippa,

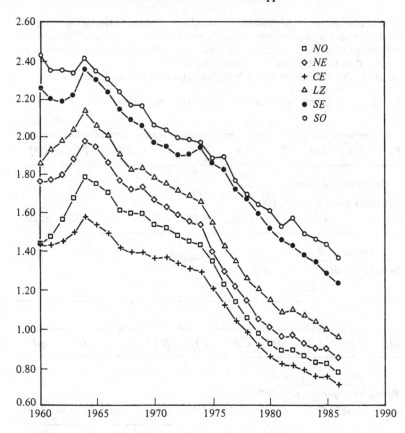

Figure 6.N1   Birth rate $[TNAT^{**} = NATI^{**}/(PREST^{**} \times 10)]$, 1960–86
Sources: See $NATI^{**}$ and $PREST^{**}$.

1990a, 1990b), or finally through flow data on the birth and death of firms (Contini and Revelli, 1990).

5 Let us take $U^d = u^d b^d + (1 - u^d)w^d$; $U^o = u^o b^o + (1 - u^o)w^o$, where superscripts d indicate the variables of the region of destination and superscripts o those of origin; U = expected utility; b = reservation wage, u = unemployment rate, w = real wage. Net migration rates are positively related to the difference $U^d - U^o$, and hence to the expression $(w^d - w^o) + (u^o - u^d)(w^d - b^d) - u^o[(w^d - b^d) - (w^o - b^o)]$. As the only certain sign in this expression is $(w^d - b^d) > 0$, one might conclude that the net migration rates grow with the unemployment rate differential $(u^o - u^d)$, for a given net real wage differential, for a given aggregate unemployment rate and for a given reservation wage differential.

6 It is sufficient to recall Toniolo's point of view (1988, 233): 'There are, schematically, two fields of opinion on the origins of the gap between the North and South of Italy. The first of these comes into being immediately after the unification and attributes to the unification process and to the policies of

Table 6N.3. *Dynamics of employment by status, 1980–7*

| | Employment growth with 1980 = 100 | | | | | | | | % in |
	1980	1981	1982	1983	1984	1985	1986	1987	1987
Total	100.0	100.0	100.5	101.2	101.6	102.5	103.4	101.8	100.0
Regular	100.0	100.0	100.3	99.0	99.6	100.7	101.1	101.0	76.9
Non-regular	100.0	100.1	101.5	106.0	109.1	109.1	111.9	113.8	23.1
Employed undeclared	100.0	91.5	82.1	90.6	98.1	89.6	87.0	82.0	2.1
Non-resident foreign	100.0	117.2	141.8	158.8	169.7	180.7	191.6	204.3	2.5
Second employment	100.0	103.4	107.8	117.4	122.4	122.7	128.0	133.0	8.1
Dependent workers	100.0	99.3	99.5	98.7	98.6	100.0	100.4	100.6	100.0
Regular	100.0	99.2	99.1	97.7	96.9	98.3	98.5	98.4	82.9
Non-regular	100.0	99.7	101.7	104.5	107.7	109.3	111.0	112.7	17.1
Irregular	100.0	97.4	96.7	94.6	92.3	94.8	96.5	98.0	9.3
Employed undeclared	100.0	93.1	85.8	88.3	115.1	105.9	101.5	95.7	1.7
Non-resident foreign	100.0	117.2	141.8	158.8	169.7	180.7	191.6	204.3	3.6
Second employment	100.0	100.7	103.6	116.3	118.7	117.4	116.4	116.2	2.5
Independent workers	100.0	101.6	102.9	106.9	108.6	108.3	110.4	111.2	100.0
Regular	100.0	102.1	103.7	106.5	107.5	108.0	109.1	109.2	64.3
Non-regular	100.0	100.6	101.3	107.6	110.6	108.9	112.8	114.8	35.7
Irregular	100.0	99.9	99.8	101.0	104.7	103.0	103.9	102.7	12.6
Employed undeclared	100.0	90.1	79.0	92.4	83.9	74.1	74.8	70.6	3.0
Non-resident foreign	—	—	—	—	—	—	—	—	—
Second employment	100.0	104.2	109.1	117.8	123.5	124.3	131.6	138.3	20.1

Source: Pedullà (1987).

Piemonte the poverty of Mezzogiorno compared to the rest of the country. The more radical theory talks of colonial exploitation of a prosperous South by the North, whose only merit was to find itself on the winning side of the 1859 Franco–Austrian war. This theory has found very few advocates. Very important, vice-versa, is the opinion dating back to Nitti, according to whom the unity was followed by a net drainage of resources out of Mezzogiorno towards the North, through fiscal policies and the role of banks. Opposed to this opinion is that of Fortunato, according to whom "everyone believed that the promised land, the ultimate of heavenly gifts, to which the weakness of the inhabitants was a poor response, was indeed Mezzogiorno"; whilst it is necessary to convince ourselves that we are dealing with an area "which by its geography and history was condemned to misery: economic and moral misery, the latter being gloomier, from which only political unity, moved by the feeling of common defence, can redeem it". Today's most widely-held opinion seems to be closer to that of Fortunato, even though we lack a summarising study on the causes of the economic divide between the North and the South in the 1850's. On the other hand, many scholars disagree with the opinion of Saraceno according to whom "it must be recognised that the unification did not fail to trigger immediately some forms of economic progress in Mezzogiorno"'.

7 A peak in the postwar birth rate, calculated as the ratio between new-born babies and population by the end of the previous year, was registered in 1964,

Table 6N.4. *Weights on the consumer basket of different items in the six geographical areas*

Areas	Years	Foodstuffs	Clothing	Electricity and fuel	Housing	Other goods and services
NO	Mid-1960s	0.413	0.177	0.071	0.084	0.255
	Mid-1980s	0.286	0.071	0.053	0.100	0.490
SO	Mid-1960s	0.497	0.149	0.051	0.084	0.219
	Mid-1980s	0.304	0.049	0.052	0.019	0.576
CE	Mid-1960s	0.502	0.046	0.022	0.056	0.375
	Mid-1980s	0.400	0.046	0.037	0.034	0.483
SE	Mid-1960s	0.519	0.125	0.055	0.124	0.177
	Mid-1980s	0.313	0.071	0.049	0.035	0.531
NE	Mid-1960s	0.448	0.118	0.086	0.101	0.248
	Mid-1980s	0.323	0.048	0.044	0.045	0.541
LZ	Mid-1960s	0.481	0.103	0.068	0.098	0.250
	Mid-1980s	0.332	0.098	0.054	0.051	0.465

Note: For the construction of the weights see *PC*** in the Data Appendix.

Source: ISTAT ASI (various years).

in the 'baby-boom' era. This rate has decreased everywhere ever since, remaining constantly higher in *SO*, followed by *SE* and *LZ*, and lower in *CE*, preceded by *NO* and *NE*. The death rate does not vary through areas (see Figure 6N.1).

8 Unemployment rates by age and sex are available starting from 1977 for the two main regional partitions – i.e., North-Centre and the Mezzogiorno.

9 These data report effective (not contractual) wages of the private sector, being derived from the national accounts. They therefore represent the factual situation, inclusive of irregular and illegal cases of employment, except for cases of totally underground employment (for example, working for the Mafia, etc.): we must not forget, in fact, that not all the black labour is completely underground. Recently, new evidence on the black labour market at national level has officially emerged, as Table 6N.3 illustrates.

10 'Under the thrust of the affirmation of the principle of equal wage for equivalent labour performances, the Interunion Agreement (*Accordo Interconfederale*) of 18 March 1969 officialised this trend. It envisaged the gradual imposing of a single minimum wage level and the unification of the wage indexation at national level' (Siracusano, Tresoldi and Zen, 1986, 83). According to the rule of the *gabbie salariali*, a previous Agreement reached in 1961 had already reduced to a maximum of 20% the interregional differences in the

contractual wages. However, Lutz (1961, 426) recalled that 'the wage level of Italian Southern provinces will however only be by 13–15% lower than the wages of most of the Northern provinces, as the wages fixed for these last are in most cases by 5–8% lower than the maximum level'.

11 As indeed has the Italian income taxation system become since the Fiscal Reform of 1973–4.

12 The regional differences in the weights assigned to the different items of the consumption basket have been decreasing during the years observed, as shown by the data in Table 6N.4.

13 There are many types of social security detaxations according to sex, qualification or sector which the worker belongs to, beyond the firm's geographical position. Some detaxations are exclusively adopted for Southern firms (see Padoa Schioppa, 1990c).

14 The ratio between the average invalidity pension and the average wage rate in the private sector, presented in Figure 6N.2 has not always increased, not even in the South.

15 For this reason, it has been rightly observed that, 'if there are other family incomes, unemployment does not necessarily mean poverty; people's willingness to work is often conditioned by the social and professional quality of the available jobs and their compatibility with other commitments, such as family, study or leisure time. This helps to explain why the high unemployment rate of the Mezzogiorno is compatible with the difficulties met in finding labour force in certain areas and for certain jobs, as well as with the incredible spread of double-employed workers and the huge presence of foreign workers covering the less-desirable jobs. It also contributes to explaining how a high unemployment rate – even though this is accompanied by serious forms of social discontent and unrest – does not ultimately threaten the social equilibria, as would happen if unemployment hit family heads or the categories better represented both at political and at union levels, and is therefore not considered as a major political problem' (Cafiero, 1987, 217).

16 Note however, that the causation might be reversed: a decrease in interregional migration could have been responsible for the rise in the aggregate unemployment level.

17 Almost the entire movement within areas is in fact a movement within more limited administrative regions. The ratio between the latter and the former is above 90% everywhere and higher in the two Southern areas than elsewhere.

18 From a statistical point of view, a further warning is in order. If the residual of our equations exhibits autocorrelation, the reported standard errors are inconsistent; indeed, the equations did exhibit some autocorrelation. No attempt was made to correct the standard errors.

19 From 1969 to 1986 there exist 18 matrixes. For each year, independent of the age bracket, there exist four matrixes by sex and working condition, each formed by 20 rows and 20 columns, corresponding to the administrative regions of origin and destination. This information is provided by five-year age brackets, starting with 0–5 and ending with 80 years or more, which is why there are more than 500,000 basic data.

20 For working female emigrants the only case in which the peak age does not shift to 25–29 years concerns gross migrations within *NE*.

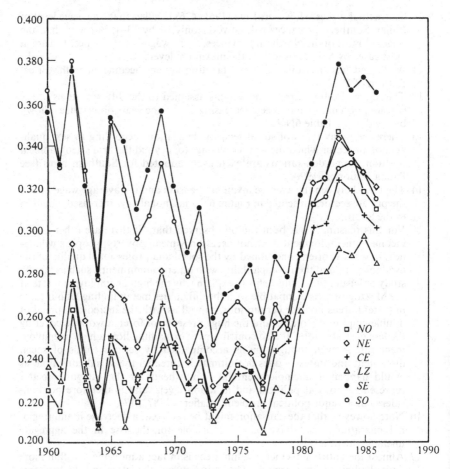

Figure 6.N2   Ratio between average disability pensions and the wage rate in the private sector

$$INVW^* = \frac{(AINVOBL^{**}/NINVOBL^{**})}{WPR^{**}}, \text{ 1960–86.}$$

Sources: See *AINVOBL***, *NINVOBL*** and *WPR***.

REFERENCES

Bentolila, S. and G. Bertola (1990). 'Firing Costs and Labour Demand: How Bad Is Eurosclerosis?', *Review of Economic Studies* (forthcoming).

Bentolila, S. and O. J. Blanchard (1990). 'Spanish Unemployment', *Economic Policy*, **10**.

Bertola, G. (1990). 'Vincoli Istituzionali ai Licenziamenti e Domanda di Lavoro in Italia', in F. Padoa Schioppa (ed.), *Squilibri e Rigidità nel Mercato del Lavoro Italiano: Rilevanza Quantitativa e Proposte Correttive*, Milano: Franco Angeli.

Blanchard, O. J. and P. Diamond (1990). 'The Beveridge Curve', *Brookings Papers on Economic Activity*, **1**, 1–74.

Bodo, G. and P. Sestito (1989). 'Disoccupazione e Dualismo Territoriale', *Temi di Discussione*, **123** (August) Servizio Studi Banca d'Italia.

Cafiero, S. (1987). 'Sviluppo e Occupazione tra Passato e Avvenire', *Studi Svimez*, **2, XL** (March–April) 211–32.

—— (1989). *Tradizione e Attualità del Meridionalismo*, Bologna: Il Mulino, SVIMEZ series.

Contini, B. and R. Revelli (1990). 'Creazione dei Posti di Lavoro e Mobilità della Forza lavoro: Un Modello di Catene di Posti Vacanti Applicato al Piemonte', in F. Padoa Schioppa (ed.), *Squilibri e Rigidità nel Mercato del Lavoro Italiano: Rilevanza Quantitativa e Proposte Correttive*, Milano: Franco Angeli.

Fuà, G. (1983). 'L'Industrializzazione nel Nord e nel Centro', in G. Fuà and C. Zacchia (eds), *Industrializzazione Senza Fratture*, Bologna: Il Mulino, 7–46.

Greenwood, M. J. (1975). 'Research on Internal Migration in the United States', *Journal of Economic Literature*, **13 (2)** (June) 397–433.

Harris, J. R. and M. P. Todaro (1970). 'Migration, Unemployment and Development: A Two-Sector Analysis', *American Economic Review*, **60 (1)**, 126–42.

Instituto Centrale di Statistica (1981). 'Numeri Indici dei Prezzi', *Metodi e Norme*, **Serie A, 20** (December).

Jackman, R. and S. Roper (1987). 'Structural Unemployment', *Oxford Bulletin of Economics and Statistics*, **49 (1)**, 9–37.

Katseli, L. T. and N. P. Glytsos (1986). 'Theoretical and Empirical Determinants of International Labour Mobility: Greek–German Perspective', Centre for Economic Policy Research, discussion paper, **148** (October).

Lutz, V. (1960). 'Italy as a Study in Development', *Lloyds Bank Review*, **58** (October) 31–45.

—— (1961). 'Alcuni Aspetti Strutturali del Problema del Mezzogiorno: la Complementarietà dell'Emigrazione e dell'Industrializzazione', *Moneta e Credito*, **XIV (56)** (December) 407–44.

Masarotto, G. and U. Trivellato (1984). 'Un Metodo di Raccordo delle Serie Regionali sulle Forze di Lavoro senza Informazioni Estranee', *Politica e Economia*, **2 (15) Third Series** (February) 67–77.

McCormik, B. (1983). 'Housing and Unemployment in Great Britain', *Oxford Economic Papers*, **35** (Supplement) (November) 283–305.

Mincer, J. (1978). 'Family Migration Decisions', *Journal of Political Economy*, **86 (5)**, 749–73.

Modigliani, F., F. Padoa Schioppa and N. Rossi (1986). 'Aggregate Unemployment in Italy, 1960–1983', *Economica*, **53** (Supplement) 245–73.

Muellbauer, J. and A. Murphy (1988). 'U.K. House Prices and Migration: Economic and Investment Implications', Discussion Paper (November) Shearson Lehman Hutton Securities, London.

Padoa Schioppa, F. (1990a). 'A Discussion of Italian Employment in the Private Sector, 1961–1984, Combining Traditional Concepts and Disequilibrium Macroeconomics' in C. Bean and J. Drèze (eds), *Europe's Unemployment*, Cambridge, MA: MIT Press.

—— (1990b). 'Classical, Keynesian and Mismatch Unemployment in Italy', *European Economic Review*, **34 (2/3)**, 434–42.

—— (1990c). 'Union Wage Setting and Taxation', *Oxford Bulletin of Economics and Statistics*, **52 (2)**.

(1990d). *Aspetti Strutturali del Problema del Deficit Pubblico*. Bologna: Il Mulino.

Pedullà, G. (1988). 'L'Occupazione nei Conti Nazionali. Concetti, Definizioni e Metodi di Calcolo', in Ministero del Lavoro e della Previdenza Sociale (ed.), *Rapporto '88: Lavoro e Politiche dell'Occupazione in Italia*, Rome: Fondazione Giacomo Brodolini and Centro Europa Ricerche, 57–93.

Pissarides, C. A. (1989). 'The Beveridge Curve in the Growing Economy', London School of Economics, Centre for Labour Economics, discussion paper, **1150**.

Pissarides, C. A. and I. McMaster (1988). 'Regional Migration, Wages and Unemployment: Empirical Evidence and Implications for Policy', London School of Economics, Centre for Labour Economics, discussion paper, preliminary draft.

Pissarides, C. A. and J. Wadsworth (1987). 'Unemployment and the Inter-Regional Mobility of Labour', London ((1989) *Economic Journal*, **99**, 739–55). School of Economics, Centre for Labour Economics, discussion paper, **296**.

Salvemini, G. (1958). 'Riforma Elettorale e Questione Meridionale', in G. Salvemini, *Scritti sulla Questione Meridionale (1896–1955)*, Turin: Giulio Einaudi Editore.

Sarcinelli, M. (1989). 'The Mezzogiorno and the Single European Market: Complementary or Conflicting Aims?', *Banca Nazionale del Lavoro Quarterly Review*, **169** (June) 129–64.

Sestito, P. (1988). 'Esiste una Curva di Beveridge per l'Italia?', *Temi di Discussione*, **101** (March) Servizio Studi Banca d'Italia.

(1989). 'Offerta di Lavoro, Migrazioni e Tensioni Cicliche des Mercato del Lavoro', Discussion Paper, preliminary draft, (March) Servizio Studi Banca d'Italia.

Siracusano, F., C. Tresoldi and G. Zen (1986). 'Domanda di Lavoro e trasformazione dell'Economia del Mezzogiorno', *Temi di Discussione*, **83** (December) Servizio Studi Banca d'Italia.

SVIMEZ (ed.) (1986). *La Questione Meridionale nel Quarantennale della Svimez*, Rome.

Tagliacarne, G. (1962). 'Calcolo del Reddito Prodotto dal Settore Privato e dalla Pubblica Amministrazione nelle Province e Regioni d'Italia nel 1961 e Confronto con gli Anni 1960 e 1951', *Moneta e Credito*, **59** (September) 1–83.

(1963). 'Calcolo del Reddito Prodotto dal Settore Privato e dalla Pubblica Amministrazione nelle Province e Regioni d'Italia nel 1961 e Confronto con gli Anni 1962 e Confronto con il 1961', *Moneta e Credito*, **63** (September) 1–83.

(1972). *Il Reddito Prodotto nelle Province Italiane, 1963–1970*, Milano: Franco Angeli.

(1975a). 'I Conti Provinciali', *Moneta e Credito*, **71** (September) 1–83.

(1975b). *Il Reddito Prodotto nelle Province Italiane nel 1974*, Milano: Franco Angeli.

Toniolo G. (1988). *Storia Economica dell'Italia Liberale. 1850–1918*, Bologna: Il Mulino.

Discussion

GIUSEPPE BERTOLA

I find this informative study quite refreshing, because it does not attempt to give decisive answers to extremely complex questions. The study would have been better, however, if some questions (however complex) had been more clearly posed. The authors choose instead to state at various points what is *not* their purpose: not to address normative issues, not even to provide a positive interpretation of an impressive amount of information in terms of economic models, but simply to describe some facts. These comments summarise what the study does accomplish, focusing on some particularly striking features of the data which would indeed deserve a more careful analysis, and speculate briefly on how more formal structural work – admittedly outside of the scope of the study – might help interpret these features.

The study provides a huge mass of information. The authors, their research assistants, and their sources deserve a lot of credit for their hard work: perusal of the Data Appendix reveals that virtually none of the reported data series actually exist as such. The thorough description of the Italian internal migration phenomenon is more interesting to foreigners than to this discussant; it is extremely important for researchers to be acquainted with the complex internal dynamics of countries different from their own. A careful analysis of *internal* heterogeneity, of the economic phenomena triggered by regional disparities, and of the various (more or less successful) intervention policies will hopefully make it possible to achieve a smooth transition towards Europewide economic integration. This volume as a whole should prove to be a valuable source of comparative information.

While I find some of the reported facts unsurprising, others are not consistent with many Italians' standard view of regional imbalances. The authors choose to report data for six economic regions, and argue that these regions are, in fact, different from each other. Unfortunately, it is not easy to spot a clear pattern of sharp regional differences; it would perhaps be useful to work on more finely disaggregated information, and allow the data to suggest a (possibly different) clustering pattern.

The evidence suggests that the take-home real wages have been increasing faster in 'poor' regions – those experiencing outmigration – than in 'rich' ones. This is interesting and, to some extent, not surprising. I am vaguely aware of much sociological work on migration in Italy, but the study by Attanasio and Padoa Schioppa is the first attempt to interpret the phenomenon in economic terms. In any economic model, migration should be *triggered* by differences in economic opportunities, and should endogenously *cause* difference in wage dynamics by affecting the size and composition of regional labour supplies. As more plentiful and less expensive labour becomes available in 'rich' regions, we would expect lower equilibrium wages there, while 'poor' regions should symmetrically experience relatively fast wage growth. Such simplistic economic mechanisms would provide a solution for the mild puzzle posed by declining labour mobility in the 1970s and 1980s, in spite of a slight increase in unemployment dispersion.

There is more in the data, however. It is quite interesting to find that productivity differentials and tax wedges tend to *reverse* the dynamic pattern when unit labour costs are considered, and that the dynamics of relative real wages have been determined by sharply different behaviour of consumer price indexes in the six regions. The former fact suggests that policy interventions have had an important role (for better or for worse) in shaping regional developments, without however achieving full equalisation of economic opportunities and of productivity. A careful study of regional price indexes would probably deserve a separate – and quite interesting – study of their own, and the evidence should be kept in mind by future structural students of the Italian migration experience.

Before sketching how such an analysis might proceed, I would like to commit briefly on other aspects of the descriptive work in this study. The study makes a first, tentative, pass on a new set of migration data by origin and destination. Given the size of the phenomenon in the 1950s and 1960s, this is a potentially invaluable source of information, and it is truly a pity that earlier data are not available. It is not clear that much can be learned from the partial correlations reported in Tables 6.2 and 6.3; earning opportunities must be the main *economic* determinant of migration decisions: it is not surprising to find that unemployment and wage rates are correlated to migration flows. In the absence of a structural model, of course, no conclusions can be drawn as to causal relationships and to endogenous responses to policy interventions. Even for purely descriptive purposes, however, a more focused and better structured approach to the available data might have been useful. In particular, the study does not attempt to estimate the reduced form relationship as a system, and the statistical results may be misleading. Important unobserved factors certainly affect several regions simultaneously: in Figures 6.20 and 6.21, net migration flows display are almost perfectly pairwise specular. I would expect the disturbances of the pooled regresson equation of Table 6.3 to be cross-sectionally as well as serially correlated: generalised least squares estimation methods would be advisable. The interpretation of the data in terms of 'persistence' is somewhat weak from the empirical point of view (unobserved region effects are highly serially correlated), and perhaps not very interesting; after all, persistence makes it all the more urgent to understand which structural factors trigger migration in the first place.

I conclude with some freewheeling suggestions for future, more structural work. A careful treatment of uncertainty would greatly improve the usefulness of economic models of migration as intepretive tools. I am cited in the study as saying that formal models of this type do not provide quantitative insights; what I think I wrote is that these models do not *yet* provide a framework for formal empirical work. The Harris–Todaro (1970) expected income model of footnote 4 is a useful starting point. An extended model of this type could help interpret some of the most striking facts uncovered by the study: suppose that the market for (say) manufacturing goods is integrated across regions, while the market for services and some non-traded goods is spatially separated, and let the nominal wage paid by manufacturing firms be constrained to be equal across different regions. As the study points out, the latter has – by and large – been the case in Italy since the early 1970s. The price of manufactured goods will then be uniform across regions but, if productivity in that sector is (by historical accident) higher in the North than in the South, then the price of non-tradables will be lower in the South than in the North. It is then very attractive to work for maufacturing firms in the South, where plenty of non-tradable goods can be purchased with a manufacturing sector nominal wage; not many such jobs are available, however, because productivity is higher in the North. If it is not possible to work in non-traded goods production when searching for a manufacturing job, the equilibrium should be characterised by wait unemployment as well as by labour force and capital stock adjustments.

It is unlikely, however, that a model along these lines would help interpret the data tackled by this study. An extended Harris–Todaro model would apply to the very long run: if the 'period' is a lifetime, then the decision to migrate (or to stay in wait unemployment) might be meaningfully modelled in terms of a static comparison of expected incomes. In reality, however, employment uncertainty has a very different role. Over 10- or 15-year cycles, earning opportunities in different regions are highly serially correlated, and the decision to move must be influenced by the value of the option *not* to move.

We know this option is more valuable in turbulent times (the 1970s and 1980s), and this may help explain why migration dried up. In this context, it would be extremely interesting to do more formal work on the migration data by origin and destination, and to use the (probably very limited) information on occupational mobility jointly with that on regional mobility. The cost of migration is by and large fixed, whether the move being considered would take the migrant from the countryside into a nearby town, or all the way to a town in the North or to Australia. Data on the direction of migration will probably need to be used jointly with data on all the other dimensions of real-life problems – down to the family level – before they become useful for posing and answering interesting macroeconomic questions.

7 Skill Shortages and Structural Unemployment in Britain: A (Mis)matching Approach[1]

CHARLES R. BEAN and
CHRISTOPHER A. PISSARIDES

1 Some broad facts about the structure of British unemployment

Media discussion of British unemployment often focuses on the low level of training and vocational skills of the British workforce compared to that of Britain's main industrial competitors. In a world increasingly dominated by the use of robots and other electronic aids to production, traditional manual jobs are harder to come by. It is hardly surprising, so the argument goes, that 1980s' unemployment has been heavily concentrated amongst the unskilled and untrained, while those with computer skills and the like have been in heavy demand – there is, in other words, a growing mismatch between the supply of, and the demand for, different types of labour. Yet academic research on the nature of Britain's unemployment has generally failed to lend support to the idea that technological change has been a significant factor (for example, Layard and Nickell, 1986). Inadequate skills may have much to do with low productivity and low wages, but relatively little to do with high unemployment. Is the casual empiricism misguided, or has academic research missed the point? The purpose of this study is to have another look at the question, invoking microeconomic evidence.

Before plunging into detail, however, it is useful first to set the scene by describing some broad features of the structure of British unemployment in the years 1970–90. Table 7.1 begins by presenting data on the composition of unemployment at selected dates; this reveals marked divergences in unemployment rates by age, sex, region and occupation. The relative importance of different categories appears, however, to remain relatively stable over time; all categories experienced roughly a doubling of unemployment rates between 1979 and 1986 (unfortunately the government ceased publishing an occupational breakdown in 1982). The corollary of this is that the burden of high unemployment was borne primarily by those who had already tended to experience some unemployment – the

325

Table 7.1. *Composition of the unemployed, selected years, % of working population*

	1972	1979	1986	1989[b]
Male	5.0	6.7	13.7	8.0
Female	1.6	4.3	9.1	4.4
South East	2.2	3.7	8.6	4.0
North	6.4	8.7	16.3	6.3
Total	3.8	5.7	11.8	6.5
Of which:				
Manual (%)	76.4[a]	69.9	NA	NA
Under 24 (%)	27.1	37.9	35.4	28.7
Over 45 (%)	39.8	29.5	25.3	28.6

Notes:
a March 1973 figure.
b Estimates.
NA = not available.

Source: Department of Employment *Gazette.*

young, manual workers, workers in the North and West. There is nothing here to disprove the notion that technical change has a part to play.

Tables 7.2 (age, race and sex), 7.3 (skill) and 7.4 (region) provide some more detailed information. Unemployment can rise either because more people become unemployed (the inflow rate rises), or because the same number of unemployed workers take longer to find a job (duration rises). Tables 7.2–7.4 therefore split observed unemployment rates separately into the (monthly) inflow rate into unemployment (separations as a proportion of the workforce for skills, all new entrants into unemployment for demographic group and region) and average duration (the ratio of the stock of unemployed to new inflows). Both unemployment duration and flows differ sharply by age, race and sex: inflow rates fall with age while the average length of unemployment spells tends to increase. A similar pattern holds for the difference between males and females – inflow is higher and duration lower for women. By contrast both inflow and duration are lower for whites than for non-whites.

How can one explain these demographic differences? Certainly human capital considerations are likely to play a significant part. Many of the jobs held by younger workers and at least some women are likely to be casual or part-time in nature, and there is usually a considerable amount of 'job-shopping' at the start of the working life cycle. Older workers, on the other hand, will have accumulated more occupation-specific human

Table 7.2. *Unemployment by demographic group, 1984*

	Inflow rate (months) (1)	Average duration (months) (2)	Unemployment rate (3)
Aged 16–19	3.33	8.5	28.4
Aged 20–24	1.33	15.3	20.4
Aged 25–54	0.74	13.1	9.7
Aged 55–64	0.47	19.2	9.1
White	0.92	12.6	11.6
Non-white	1.43	17.6	25.2
Male	0.78	16.1	12.6
Female	1.17	9.7	11.4

Source: Jackman *et al.* (1991).

capital. Firms will thus be less likely to lay them off – especially during temporary recessions – and such workers will also be both less likely to quit and be more likely to spend longer searching whilst unemployed in order to find a good job match. The pattern of unemployment experience by race, however, is not consistent with this.

The picture by skill (Table 7.3) also does not seem to be entirely consistent with such a human capital explanation. The pattern of inflow rates by skill is as predicted – trained and skilled workers have a lower probability of experiencing unemployment than their unskilled counterparts – but the length of unemployment spells is relatively uniform (being, if anything, higher rather than lower for manual than for non-manual workers). This suggests that other forces may also be at work. One

Table 7.3. *Unemployment by skill, 1984*

	Inflow rate (% per month) (1)	Average duration (months) (2)	Unemployment rate (3)
Professional and managerial	0.50	11.2	5.6
Clerical	0.88	10.1	8.7
Other non-manual	1.14	11.8	13.9
Skilled manual	1.02	14.2	14.4
Other manual	1.32	14.1	18.4

Source: Jackman *et al.* (1991).

Table 7.4. *Unemployment by region, 1988*

	Inflow rate (% per month) (1)	Average duration (months) (2)	Unemployment rate (3)
East Anglia	0.83	4.7	4.9
South East	0.80	5.7	5.3
South West	1.03	5.0	6.2
East Midlands	0.97	6.4	7.5
West Midlands	0.97	7.6	9.0
Yorkshire	1.20	6.8	9.7
Wales	1.40	6.2	10.6
North West	1.30	7.2	10.9
Scotland	1.50	6.9	11.7
North	1.47	7.0	12.2

Source: Jackman *et al.* (1991).

obvious candidate is the exercise of union power by manual workers, leading to the rationing of manual jobs. We pursue this line of argument in our formal model below.

The structure by region (Table 7.4) is also revealing. While both inflow rates and duration tend to rise as one moves from low unemployment to high unemployment regions, about three-quarters of the variation in unemployment rates is due to variation in inflow rates and only a quarter to differences in duration. Now the demographic structure and skill composition of the workforce should be largely – although not entirely – uniform across sufficiently large regions, so that the regional pattern of unemployment rates is likely to be related to the associated regional distribution of industry (together, perhaps, with persistence effects stemming from the history of unemployment in the region: see, for example, Layard and Bean, 1989). In particular the regions experiencing the highest unemployment rates are those traditionally associated with heavy industries such as shipbuilding and steel. This is consistent both with explanations that emphasise shifts in the pattern of demand (either cyclical or long-term) as well as supply-side explanations focusing on technical change.

2   Some preliminary evidence on skill mismatch

Let us now return to the main theme of the study – namely, whether a significant part of the rise in unemployment in the 1980s was technologi-

Table 7.5. *Total factor productivity growth by industry, selected years, % per annum*

	1969–73	1973–9	1979–82	1982–6
Agriculture	3.2	0.2	7.5	2.8
Coal	− 0.9	− 0.6	1.8	5.6
Oil and natural gas	22.6	71.8	− 16.7	11.8
Oil processing	− 5.8	− 4.1	− 0.6	− 0.7
Electricity, gas and water	7.4	2.5	1.2	3.9
Manufacturing industries:				
Metal manufacture	2.4	3.0	13.9	6.0
Other mineral products	6.6	1.5	2.0	4.2
Chemicals	5.8	1.1	3.1	5.5
Other metal products	1.2	− 0.8	1.0	0.5
Mechanical engineering	3.3	0.7	3.5	2.4
Electrical engineering	7.8	3.8	5.9	6.5
Motor vehicles	1.3	− 0.9	6.6	4.4
Ships and aircraft	5.7	− 1.9	7.1	5.1
Food	2.5	1.1	4.3	1.9
Drink and tobacco	2.9	0.8	0.9	3.4
Textiles	4.5	1.4	3.3	4.9
Leather, footwear and clothing	3.9	4.9	3.4	7.3
Timber	5.6	− 1.4	0.2	− 0.3
Paper	4.0	1.7	3.3	2.6
Rubber	4.2	3.6	4.0	7.9
Construction	2.8	0.0	1.8	3.9
Distribution	3.2	0.1	1.9	2.7
Transport	6.5	1.3	2.8	4.1
Communications	3.9	3.4	2.6	4.8
Banking	0.6	0.4	2.2	2.7
Other services	− 2.6	− 1.6	1.5	0.3

Source: Bean and Symons (1989).

cally induced, and whether the mix between the demand and supply of skills has worsened. The 1970s were associated with a widely documented slowdown in productivity growth (output per head rose only 1.1% per annum over 1973–9 as opposed to 3.3% over 1967–73) but recovered during the 1980s (averaging 2.2% over 1979–88). These changes were associated primarily with changes in the rate of growth of total factor productivity rather than the investment rate, and were widely distributed throughout the economy, as Table 7.5 attests. There is considerable agreement that this spurt in productivity growth in the 1980s was the result primarily of changes in the efficiency with which labour was utilised, although there is still debate about whether anti-union legislation or the 1979–82 recession was more important in bringing this about (see, for instance, Bean and Symons, 1989; and Layard and Nickell, 1989). Although not exactly the result of technical change, such labour-saving improvements in productivity have very much the character of labour-augmenting technical progress.

Could these changes in productivity growth have produced a rise in unemployment? The direct effect of labour-augmenting technical progress on the demand for labour is twofold: on the one hand it allows the same output with fewer inputs; on the other at unchanged factor prices it lowers the effective cost of unskilled labour and thus raises labour demand. The second effect dominates if and only if the wage elasticity of labour demand exceeds unity. Seemingly, then, a beneficial technology shock could lead to a rise (or a fall) in unemployment. However, this is obviously a rather partial and incomplete answer since it assumes that own-product factor prices remain unchanged, whereas in general equilibrium these will generally alter. A powerful argument that wages will eventually adjust to ensure that productivity growth is completely neutral with respect to the unemployment rate is prompted by the observation that output per head has roughly tripled since the middle of the nineteenth century, yet the average unemployment rate has remained virtually unchanged. For this reason studies such as Bean, Layard and Nickell (1986) and Layard and Nickell (1986) actually impose this constraint in their estimated models (after suitable tests, of course).

But is this argument completely convincing in the short run, and for every occupational group? As soon as one allows for heterogeneous labour, the unemployment rates of particular groups (and, by implication, their aggregate) need not remain unchanged. One contribution of this study is to develop a formal model with heterogeneous labour in which idiosyncratic technical progress which enhances the productivity of only a subset of the labour force leads to a change in equilibrium unemployment. By contrast, a common technology shock which enhances the productivity of all sorts of labour equally has no effect on equilibrium unemployment and leads merely to equiproportionate rises in the real wages of the different types of labour. The key point is thus that *bias* in the direction of technical change can affect the unemployment rate. The details are spelt out in section 3 below.

So what evidence is there to suggest a bias in the direction of technical change in the 1980s? We shall try to address this question more formally in section 4; until then it is worth recording three pieces of evidence which together might point us in the right direction.

First, whatever the longer-run effects of any technology shock, one would expect the impact effect to be manifested mainly in the behaviour

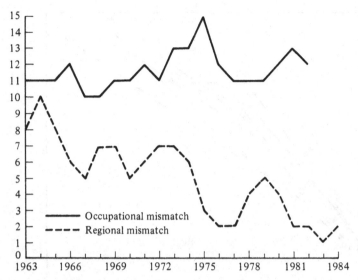

Figure 7.1 Mismatch indices, 1963–84

of quantity variables with increased vacancies for those sorts of labour where demand has risen, and in increased unemployment of those labour types where demand has fallen. In due course, this could be expected to lead to changes in the wages paid to the different types of labour and ultimately to a change in the supplies of different sorts of skills in response to the resultant change in the return to human capital formation in different lines of work. In the short run, at least, one would thus expect to observe an outward shift in the aggregate unemployment/vacancy relation (or Beveridge curve). Such an outward shift during the 1980s is indeed a well-documented phenomenon in both the United Kingdom and the rest of the European Community; this adverse shift is also, however, consistent with other explanations of high unemployment such as outsider disenfranchisement – see, for example, Budd, Levine and Smith (1987).

To get a handle on the role of increased mismatch Jackman and Roper (1987) constructed a variety of indices of mismatch based on the dispersion of unemployment/vacancy ratios across micro markets. One of their indices[2] of occupational mismatch (based on 24 occupational groups until 1972, 18 thereafter) is plotted in Figure 7.1, together with their index of regional mismatch (based on 9 regions) for comparison. Unfortunately, because of data limitations, the series for occupational mismatch ends in 1982, although it is notable that there is no rise in this measure during the 1979–82 recession (and, even more striking, that regional mismatch actually falls during the 1980s).

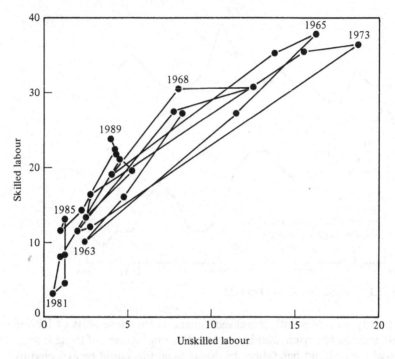

Figure 7.2   Percentage of firms reporting labour shortage, 1965–89
Source: CBI, *Industrial Trends Survey*.

To shed light on behaviour since 1982, and because the occupational categories and vacancy data used to construct the mismatch index are likely to be rather imperfect, we turn to our second bit of evidence: survey evidence from the CBI on the extent of labour shortages. Figure 7.2 details the proportion of firms (all manufacturing) who reported that skilled labour was expected to be a constraint on production in the following four months against the proportion who reported that unskilled labour was expected to be a constraint, from 1961 up to the present. Despite current concerns over skill shortages, it is apparent that reported skill shortages are not especially severe for the current state of the cycle, although those with a keen eye might argue that there has been some slight shift in the relationship during the second half of the 1980s.

There are three possible conclusions that might be drawn from this. One possibility is that technical change has not been biased towards increasing the relative demand for skilled labour. A second possibility is that even with biased technical progress relative wage adjustment reasonably rapidly chokes off any excess demand for skilled labour. A third possi-

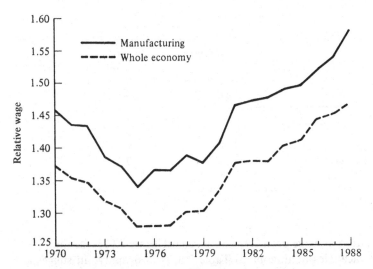

Figure 7.3   Ratio of non-manual to manual wages, 1970–88
Source: Department of Employment, *New Earnings Survey.*

bility is that the supplies of different skills also respond fairly rapidly to
match the evolution of demands. As our third piece of evidence, which
lends at least some support to the second hypothesis, we detail in Figure
7.3 the ratio of non-manual to manual wages, taken from the *New
Earnings Survey*. Interpreted as a proxy for the wage differential between
skilled and unskilled labour, Figure 7.3 strongly suggests that a significant
increase in the relative demand for skilled labour may have occurred, and
been met by increased wage differentials.

As far as the third hypothesis of a significant supply response goes, we
do not at this time have any particularly useful evidence one way or the
other to present. However in the absence of major training initiatives by
government or employers, and in view of the fact that Pissarides (1978)
found that migration between industries was sluggish and Pissarides and
McMaster (1990) and Pissarides and Wadsworth (1989) find that migration between regions is also very slow, we are inclined to believe that this
is not likely to be important over the time frame considered here. A fuller
investigation is, however, deferred to another time and place.

3   An unemployment model with skill differentiation

We have already hinted above that in understanding movements in
relative unemployment rates for skilled and unskilled labour it is necessary to bring together both matching/search considerations and the

Table 7.6. *Vacancies by skill, 1988*

	Engagement rate (% per month) (1)	Duration (months) (2)	Vacancy rate (3)
Managerial and professional	1.0	2.2	2.2
Clerical	2.3	1.5	3.4
Skilled manual	2.8	1.2	3.4
Retail and other services	5.8	0.9	5.1
Unskilled manual	3.8	0.6	2.1

Source: Jackman *et al.* (1991).

determination of wage pressure. In this regard Table 7.6, presenting some data for vacancies analogous to Table 7.3, is informative in suggesting that the duration of vacancies rises with the skill level. This is to be expected since the return to making a good job match between an unfilled post and an unemployed worker is that much greater when there is occupation-specific human capital involved. Matching considerations may consequently be important in determining skilled unemployment, while the level of wage pressure may be more relevant in determining unskilled unemployment. The simple general equilibrium model that follows incorporates this idea.

There are two sorts of labour, skilled and unskilled, denoted by the subscripts s and u respectively. In general, it takes time for unemployed skilled workers to be matched to vacancies for skilled workers. The rate of new hires, $H(V, U_s)$, is increasing in both the number of vacancies, V, and the 'effective' pool of unemployed skilled workers, U_s. We assume that this hiring function is linearly homogenous (see Pissarides, 1986, for empirical evidence), so that hires may be written $H(V, U_s) = U_s h(V/U_s)$ with $h' > 0$. The real cost of a vacancy for a skilled worker is γ. By contrast, in accordance with the evidence presented above, we assume that unskilled workers may be matched to unfilled unskilled jobs instantaneously and costlessly. Finally, we assume that an unemployed skilled worker can always take a temporary job as an unskilled worker while looking for skilled work, without impairing the chances of finding a skilled job. This captures the 'ladder' effect whereby some workers move down the skill ladder during recessions, leading to a concentration of unemployment among the unskilled. We assume that skilled workers always get preference over unskilled workers for an unskilled job, although there is no efficiency difference between them in such a job.

Measured skilled unemployment in this model is thus always identically zero, and U_s instead measures the number of skilled workers in unskilled jobs.

The representative firm possesses a linearly homogenous production technology, $f(A_s N_s, A_u N_u)$, where N_s and N_u are employment of skilled and unskilled workers respectively, and A_s and A_u are the levels of skilled and unskilled labour-augmenting technical progress. The firm has market power in the goods market, facing a constant elasticity demand schedule $DP^{-\eta}$ $(\eta > 1)$, where P is the firm's output price, and D is a shift parameter. The firm is a price taker in factor markets. The programme for the representative firm is then:

$$\max_{\{N_s, N_u, V\}} \int_0^\infty [D^{1/\eta} f(A_s N_s, A_u N_u)^{(\eta-1)/\eta}$$

$$- N_s W_s - N_u W_u - \gamma V] e^{-rt} dt \tag{1}$$

subject to:

$$\dot{N}_s = V h(X)/X - s N_s \tag{2}$$

where W_s and W_u are the wages of skilled and unskilled workers respectively, $X \equiv V/U_s$, s is the (exogenous) separation rate, and r is the discount rate.

The first-order conditions for this problem are

$$\pi P A_s f_1(A_s N_s, A_u N_u) - W_s = (r + s) \gamma X/h(X) - \gamma \mu \dot{X} \tag{3}$$

$$\pi P A_u f_2(A_s N_s, A_u N_u) = W_u \tag{4}$$

where $\pi \equiv (\eta - 1)/\eta$ and $\mu \equiv (1 - Xh'/h)/h$. We assume that the elasticity of the hiring function is less than unity so that $\mu > 0$.

Next we have to characterise the behaviour of wages. The existence of hiring frictions means that skilled workers have natural market power. Following Pissarides (1985) we assume that the firm and the newly employed skilled worker split the marginal surplus according to a Nash bargain. Remembering that an unemployed skilled worker can always work in the unskilled sector, it is easily shown,[3] (see also Pissarides, 1986) that the skilled wage satisfies

$$W_s = W_u + \beta_s[\pi P A_s f_1(A_s N_s, A_u N_u) - W_u + \gamma V/U_s] \tag{5}$$

where β_s and $(1 - \beta_s)$ are respectively the exponents on the worker's share of the surplus and the firm's share of the surplus respectively. Equation (5) simply says that the worker gets his fallback option, W_u, plus a share of the marginal surplus appropriately grossed up for vacancy costs.

Unskilled workers have no inherent market power because of market frictions. However, we shall assume – realistically for the UK – that they are represented by a union which bargains with the firm over wages. For clarity and simplicity we assume that the union cares only about the negotiated wage and not employment – say, because it represents the median voter who because of seniority rules is far from the firing line (cf. Oswald, 1987). The bargain then satisfies

$$\max_{\{W_u\}} (W_u - W_o)\beta_u(\Pi - \Pi_o)^{1-\beta_u} \tag{6}$$

where Π is the firm's profit and an o subscript indicates a fallback option.

The appropriate definition of these fallback positions is open to debate: non-cooperative bargaining theory (see for example, Binmore, Rubinstein and Wolinsky, 1986) would suggest that they should be associated with welfare levels in the event of a delay in reaching agreement – i.e., during a strike/lockout. In such circumstances we assume production ceases, but the firm is still obliged to pay wages to skilled workers, plus vacancy costs, so that

$$\Pi_o = - N_s W_s + \gamma V \tag{7}$$

The fallback position for workers is rather trickier, and will presumably depend amongst other things on strike funds. It will probably also, however, depend on the tightness of the unskilled labour market and the possibility of temporary work. We thus take W_o to be simply the expected income of a typical unskilled worker[4]

$$W_o = W_u(L_u - U)/L_u + \beta_u/L_u \tag{8}$$

where B is the level of benefits and $U(= U_u)$ is measured unemployment.

Substitution of equations (7) and (8) in the first-order condition for equation (6) and use of the identity $U \equiv L_s + L_u - N_s - N_u$, where $L_s(L_u)$ is the supply of skilled (unskilled) labour, then yields:

$$(1 - \rho)(1 - \beta_u)(L_s + L_u - N_s - N_u)/L_u = \beta_u(1 - \pi S_u)/\pi S_u \tag{9}$$

where $\rho = B/W_u$ is the replacement rate for unskilled workers (assumed constant) and $S_u \equiv A_u N_u f_2/f$ is the competitive share of unskilled labour.

Imposing the condition that in a symmetrical general equilibrium of this closed economy $P = 1$, equations (2)–(5) and (9) describe the dynamic evolution of X, N_s, N_u, W_s and W_u. The steady state of this economy then satisfies equation (9) together with

$$\pi(1 - \beta_s)[A_s f_1(A_s N_s, A_u N_u) - A_u f_2(A_s N_s, A_u N_u)]$$
$$= \gamma[\beta_s + (r + s)/h(X)]X \qquad (10)$$

and

$$(L_s - N_s)h(X) = sN_s \qquad (11)$$

What is the effect of a *common* proportionate technology shock ($d(\ln A_s)$ $= d(\ln A_u)$) in this world? If we assume that vacancy costs rise with the level of output so that $\gamma = \gamma_o f$ with γ_o constant,[5] then it is not difficult to show that X, N_s and N_u are all unchanged in the new equilibrium and $d(\ln W_s) = d(\ln W_u) = d(\ln A_s) = d(\ln A_u)$. The model thus has the desirable property that the equilibrium unemployment rate is in the long run neutral with respect to common technology shocks. Furthermore the rather simple dynamic structure (with no lags in wage bargaining, etc.) means that this neutrality holds even in the short run (this need not be so in a more general structure, of course).

The effect of an *asymmetric* technology shock, however, is more interesting. For the sake of argument consider a technology shock which augments unskilled labour alone – i.e., $dA_s = 0$. (Since a common shock is neutral, the effect of a skilled labour-augmenting shock on unemployment will be just the opposite.) It is immediately apparent from equation (9) that steady-state unemployment increases if and only if the competitive share of unskilled labour falls, so that with a Cobb–Douglas technology unemployment would remain constant. However, with more general technologies this need not be the case. Tedious but straightforward algebra establishes the following steady-state results:

$$dN_s/d(\ln A_u) = \delta N_s N_u S_u (NS_s - \alpha N_s)\psi/\Delta \qquad (12)$$

$$dU/d(\ln A_u) = - \alpha N_u[U_s h' \delta(N_u^2 S_s + N_s^2 S_u) + (r + s + \beta_s/\mu)/(s + h)/(1 + \alpha\psi)]\psi/\Delta \qquad (13)$$

where

$$\alpha \equiv \beta_u S_s L_u/(1 - \rho)(1 - \beta_u)\pi S_u N_u > 0$$

$$\delta \equiv \pi(1 - \beta_s)/\gamma_o \mu N_s^2 N_u^2(1 + \alpha\psi)$$

$$\psi \equiv (1/\sigma) - 1$$

Here σ ($\equiv f_1 f_2/ff_{12}$) is the elasticity of substitution in production, $S_s = (1 - S_u)$ is the competitive share of skilled labour, and $\Delta(< 0)$ is the determinant of the transition matrix in equation (14) below. If $\psi > 0$ (the elasticity of substitution is less than unity) then equilibrium unemployment rises in the face of an idiosyncratic unskilled labour-augmenting technology shock, while unemployment of skilled labour may rise or fall,

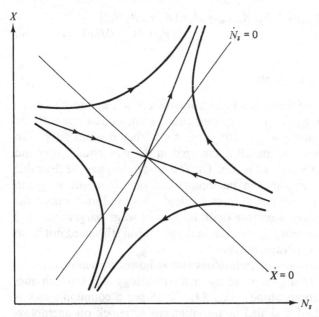

Figure 7.4   Phase-plane diagram

depending on the sign of $(NS_s - \alpha N_s)$. The case of $\psi < 0$ (an elasticity of substitution in excess of unity) is somewhat trickier since $(1 + \alpha\psi)$ could become negative if ψ is large enough in absolute value. However a large elasticity of substitution is also likely to lead to a violation of the stability condition (see below), so that we will henceforth assume that $(1 + \alpha\psi)$ remains positive even when the elasticity of substitution is above unity. In that case an unskilled labour-augmenting technology shock will lead to a fall in unemployment. Recalling that common technology shocks are neutral, it also follows that a beneficial skilled labour-augmenting technology shock must raise unemployment if the elasticity of substitution exceeds unity, and reduces it otherwise.

Turn now to the adjustment path. Linearising equations (2)–(5) and (9) about the equilibrium, further tedious algebra yields the system

$$\begin{bmatrix} \dot{X} \\ \dot{N}_s \end{bmatrix} = \begin{bmatrix} r + s + \beta_s/\mu & \theta \\ U_s h' & -(s+h) \end{bmatrix} \begin{bmatrix} X - X^* \\ N_s - N_s^* \end{bmatrix} \tag{14}$$

where $\theta \equiv [N^2 S_u S_s \psi + N_u^2 S_s + N_s^2 S_u + N_s^2 S_u + \alpha\psi N_u (S_s N_u - S_u S_u N_s)]$ and an asterisk denotes equilibrium values. θ is unambiguously positive when the elasticity of substitution is low.[6] In this case there is a regular saddlepoint. However for high elasticities of substitution, θ can be nega-

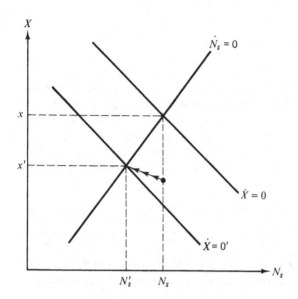

Figure 7.5 **Effect of a technology shock that lowers skilled employment in equilibrium**

tive, and for sufficiently high elasticities even lead to a violation of the condition for saddlepath stability. In our analysis we shall assume that θ remains positive even when the elasticity of substitution exceeds unity.

The associated phase-plane diagram is given in Figure 7.4. A good (bad) unskilled (skilled) labour-augmenting technology shock shifts the X stationary to the right or left, according to whether equation (12) is positive or negative. Figure 7.5 gives the transition path assuming that the shock lowers the equilibrium value of X – i.e., that $(NS_s - \alpha N_s)\psi > 0$. Note that vacancies for skilled labour fall in this scenario: biased technical change is likely to have ambiguous effects on the demand for skilled labour. This may be relevant to understanding the path of vacancies and measures of skill shortage over time. The key to the result that biased technical change can alter equilibrium unemployment, even though neutral technical change does not, lies in the interaction of the firm's technology with the exercise of bargaining power by unskilled workers. Either $\psi = 0$ (unit elasticity of substitution) or $\beta_u = 0$ (unskilled workers extract no surplus) are sufficient to ensure that biased technical change is also neutral. While there is no reason to assume either of these conditions holds in practice, both the sign and size of the effect of biased technical change on unemployment is clearly an empirical matter. We turn next, therefore, to some econometric evidence.

4   Econometric evidence

4.1   The bias in technical change

We begin by investigating the question of whether technical change has been biased in the recent past. This is not something that can be gleaned by examining aggregate or sectoral data on TFP growth. Suppose hourly output, Y, is given by a CRS technology of the form $Y = F(A_s N_s, A_u N_u, A_k K)$ where K is capital, A_k is capital-augmenting technical progress, and other variables are as above. Then, following Hall (1986), TFP growth, $\hat{Z}$, is:

$$\hat{Z} \equiv \hat{Y} - (S_s^*/\pi)\hat{N}_s - (S_u^*/\pi)\hat{N}_u - (1 - S_s^*/\pi - S_u^*/\pi)K \quad (15a)$$

$$= (S_s^*/\pi)\hat{A}_s + (S_u^*/\pi)\hat{A}_u + (1 - S_s^*/\pi - S_u^*/\pi)\hat{A}_k \quad (15b)$$

where a caret denotes a growth rate, π is the ratio of marginal cost to price, and the S_i^* denote *recorded* rather than competitive factor shares.

Clearly even with information on π we cannot disentangle the sources of TFP growth from equation (15b); with industry or firm data, however, there is a chance that we can disentangle them. In particular, suppose that for industry/firm j, $(\hat{A}_{ij} = \bar{A}_i + \tilde{A}_{ij}$ for $i = s, u, k$, where $\bar{A}_i$ is a common economy-wide rate of technical progress for factor i. Then equation (15b) becomes

$$\hat{Z}_j = (S_s^*/\pi)j\bar{A}_s + (S_u^*/\pi)j\bar{A}_u + (1 - S_s^*/\pi - S_u^*/\pi)j\bar{A}_k \quad (16)$$
$$+ (S_s^*/\pi)j\tilde{A}_{sj} + (S_u^*/\pi)j\tilde{A}_{uj} + (1 - S_s^*/\pi - S_u^*/\pi)j\tilde{A}_{kj}$$

Provided the $\tilde{A}_{ij}$ are uncorrelated with the $(S_i/\pi)_j$, consistent estimates of $\bar{A}_i$ can be obtained from a cross-section regression of TFP growth on (S_s^*/π), (S_u^*/π) and $(1 - S_s^*/\pi - S_u^*/\pi)$.

To construct both the dependent and independent variables in this regression we need information on π_j, the inverse of the industry mark-up. Again following Hall (1986), this is obtained from a preliminary set of instrumental variable regressions of the rate of growth of the industry output–capital ratio on the sum of the share-weighted rates of growth of the labour–capital ratios, using the rate of growth of world and domestic output as instruments. To improve precision a Bayesian estimator of π is employed (where the prior distribution of $1/\pi$ is $N(1.33, 0.25)$). The regressions cover the period 1970–86, and relate to 2-digit SIC categories in manufacturing, giving 15 industries in total.[7] In line with the later work in this section the skilled/unskilled distinction is identified with non-manual/manual categories of workers. Finally the regressions also include an hours-based correction for cyclical labour-hoarding. Fuller details of the methodology are given in Bean and Symons (1989).

Armed with estimates of the mark-up by industry $(1/\pi)_j$, we then constructed implied average annual (cyclically-corrected) TFP growth and the average unobserved 'competitive' shares for the 15 industries for the period 1980–6. A cross-section regression of this average TFP growth variable on the 'competitive' shares gave the following result (White t-statistics in parentheses):

$$\hat{Z} = 0.0158(S_u^*/\pi) + 0.0767(S_s^*/\pi) - 0.0264(1 - S_u^*/\pi - S_s^*/\pi)$$
$$(0.79) \qquad\qquad (2.37) \qquad\qquad (1.24)$$

$$\text{s.e.} = 0.0193 \qquad \bar{R}^2 = 0.206 \tag{17}$$

The estimates suggest that technical progress over 1980–6 was primarily skilled labour-augmenting, the coefficients measuring mean unskilled labour- and capital-augmenting technical progress being small and insignificant. (The latter actually suggest capital-augmenting technical regress!) However, the results are not all that precise and we cannot reject the hypothesis that the mean rates of skilled and unskilled labour-augmenting technical progress are identical ($t = 1.17$).

That technical progress appears to have been predominantly skilled labour-augmenting during the 1980s seems rather surprising given the much-discussed shakeout of excess labour during and after the 1979–82 recession which seems likely to have affected manual workers most heavily. By way of comparison we therefore ran the same exercise for the period covering 1970–9. We obtained:

$$\hat{Z} = 0.0023(S_u^*/\pi) + 0.0809(S_s^*/\pi) + 0.0006(1 - S_u^*/\pi - S_s^*/\pi)$$
$$(0.26) \qquad\qquad (5.53) \qquad\qquad (0.05)$$

$$\text{s.e.} = 0.013 \qquad \bar{R}^2 = 0.148 \tag{18}$$

These results are really very similar to those obtained in equation (17) for the 1980–6 period, although the estimates are now somewhat more precise, enabling us to reject the hypothesis that the mean rates of skilled and unskilled labour-augmenting technical progress are the same ($t = 3.49$).

There does thus seem to be evidence in favour of a bias in the direction of technical change, but one that existed prior to the 1980s. Since unemployment started to rise in the 1970s, this is not necessarily incompatible with the facts, although clearly it would be of interest to know whether such a bias existed also in the 1960s. Unfortunately the data required to answer this question is not available.

In any case the existence of a bias in technical change is not sufficient to deliver increased unemployment. As the discussion of section 3 made clear, both the sign and size of the effect depend amongst other things on the nature of the firm's technology. We therefore proceed next to look for evidence of a shift in the relative demand for different sorts of labour over the sample period.

4.2   Relative labour demand

We begin by assuming that the technology can be adequately represented by a CES function with elasticity of substitution σ. Equations (3) and (4) then imply that relative labour demand is given by:[8]

$$ln(N_s/N_u) = \sigma ln(W_u/W_s)$$
$$- \sigma ln\{1 + [(r + s)\gamma X/h(X) - \gamma\mu\dot{X}]/W_s\}$$
$$+ (\sigma - 1)ln(A_s/A_u) \qquad (19)$$

Our aim is to recover estimates of the final term in this regression, $(\sigma - 1)\ln(A_s/A_u)$, which captures the effect of technical change on relative labour demand. We do this by estimating equation (19) on a panel comprising the 15 industries used previously, running from 1971 to 1988, and including industry and time dummies. The latter should then pick up any shifts in relative labour demand due to technical change that are common across industries.

The data on wages come from the *New Earnings Survey* and as above we map skilled and unskilled categories into non-manuals and manuals respectively. Data on the industrial decomposition of employment into skilled and unskilled workers is not, however, readily available. To construct these we take reported total employment in each industry and then pro-rate it according to the sample sizes for the earnings data given in the *New Earnings Survey*. Since these are supposedly random samples this procedure should provide reasonable estimates of manual and non-manual employment by industry.[9]

To proxy the second term on the right-hand side of equation (19), we introduce the CBI survey information on skilled labour shortages by industry, x_s, corresonding to the aggregate data appearing in Figure 7.2. To control for labour-hoarding of skilled labour during recessions we also introduce the proportion of firms in each industry reporting that sales are a constraint, x_d, as an indicator of the cyclical position. Finally to allow for adjustment costs, etc. we introduce additional lags and parameterise the model in error-feedback form. We obtained the following results, where lower-case letters denote logarithms and Δ is the difference operator (industry and time dummies omitted for brevity):

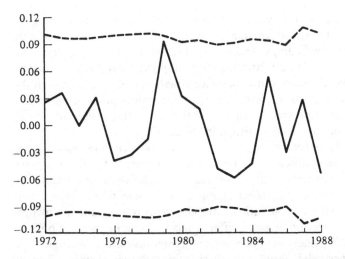

Figure 7.6   Estimated bias in technical change, plus 90% confidence band, 1972–88

$$\Delta(n_s - n_u) = -0.0156(n_s - n_u)_{-1} + 0.231\,\Delta(w_u - w_s)$$
$$(4.03) \qquad\qquad (1.23)$$

$$+\,0.309(w_u - w_s)_{-1} + 0.0022\,\Delta x_d + 0.0057\,x_{d-1}$$
$$(2.27) \qquad\qquad (0.67) \qquad\qquad (1.13)$$

$$-\,0.076\,\Delta x_s - 0.076\,x_{s-1}$$
$$(2.18) \qquad (1.54)$$

s.e. $= 0.079$ (20)

The equation seems moderately sensible, with a short-run elasticity of substitution of 0.23 and a long-run elasticity of 1.97 (with standard error 0.841). Both the shortage variables have the anticipated signs – a shortage of skilled labour reduces skilled employment below desired levels for given wages (see equation (19)), and a high level for the sales constraint variable tends to raise the ratio of skilled to unskilled labour, *ceteris paribus* (hard to replace skilled labour is hoarded during recessions, while unskilled labour which can easily be replaced when demand recovers is laid off). The estimates also suggest a simple partial adjustment relation would be adequate.

Our interest, however, is especially in the time dummies which capture the effect of technical change on relative labour demand. These are plotted in Figure 7.6, together with the associated 90% confidence band. While the year-to-year fluctuations are quite pronounced, one could certainly not reject the hypothesis that the time dummies be replaced by a single constant, and there is no obvious evidence in favour of an exogenous shift towards greater use of skilled labour. This is perfectly consistent with the findings of section 4.1 because the medium-to-long-run elasticity of substitution is around unity, implying that the effect of any bias in technical change is nullified (see equation (19)). Even though the model of section 3 thus suggests that biased technical change could affect equilibrium unemployment, the conditions for the argument to go through do not seem to be satisfied in the data.

This does, however, leave one piece of evidence unexplained, the widening of wage differentials portrayed in Figure 7.3 – for a unitary elasticity of substitution also ensures that relative wages should be unaffected by biased technical change. Now some of the increase in non-manual/manual wage ratio during the 1980s is no doubt an unwinding of the compression of wage differentials wrought by incomes policies during the 1970s, many of which implied tighter restrictions on high wage groups. It nevertheless seems unlikely that this is the whole story. Changes in industrial structure resulting from changes in the pattern of demand – i.e., the movement away from manufacturing towards services – is an obvious candidate. If the expanding industries have a greater need for skilled labour than the contracting ones, the result will be an increase in the relative demand for skilled labour at the aggregate level, even though relative labour demand at the firm or industry level may not have shifted.

4.3   Wages

The theoretical discussion of section 3 suggested that a unit elasticity of substitution is not the only circumstance under which biased technical change is neutral; a competitive labour market for unskilled workers $(\beta_u = 0)$ is also sufficient. In this sub-section we therefore report some econometric results concerning the determinants of industry manual wages. In particular, we are interested in the role played by firm-/industry-specific factors *vis-à-vis* general economic factors. In a competitive market only the latter matter, whereas firm-/industry-specific factors will also matter where bargaining over the division of the surplus is important. Although the ability of skilled workers to extract a share of the rents (β_s) is not crucial in determining the neutrality or otherwise of biased technical change, we also report results for industry non-manual wages, both for comparison purposes and because they are of interest in their own right.

Referring back to section 3 suggests the following general form for our two wage equations

$$w_s = f(w_u, \quad \bar{w}_u, \quad \bar{w}_s, \quad y - n_s, \quad x_s)$$
$$(+) \quad (+) \, (+) \, (+) \quad (+) \tag{21a}$$

$$w_u = f(b, \quad \bar{w}_u, \quad y - n_u, \quad U)$$
$$(+)(+)(+) \quad (-) \tag{21b}$$

where a bar over a variable indicates an economy-wide counterpart.

Skilled (non-manual) wages thus depend on skilled workers' outside options (unskilled work within this firm/industry, unskilled work elsewhere in the economy, and skilled work elsewhere in the economy), their marginal revenue product (assumed to be proportional to their average revenue product), and the level of skill shortages in the firm/industry. The wages of unskilled (manual) workers similarly depend on their fallback options (unemployment benefit or unskilled work elsewhere in the economy), their average revenue product, and a measure of general labour market tightness (we exclude those unemployed for more than a year in our unemployment rate measure to partial out increases in the natural rate due to 'outsider' disenfranchisement).

In practice, we also include as explanatory variables: the unemployment rate in the non-manual wage equation to see if there were any identifiable effects from general, rather than firm-specific, labour market tightness; the non-manual wage in the manual wage equation to pick up any 'comparability' effect; and a measure of firm-/industry-specific labour market tightness in the manual wage equation. With respect to the last of these we initially included the survey measure of unskilled labour shortages, but empirically this was clearly dominated by the skilled labour shortage series, x_s. This is probably a consequence of the imperfectness of our mapping of the skilled/unskilled categories into the non-manual/manual distinction. Finally both equations include an incomes policy dummy (IP) due to Desai, Keil and Wadhwani (1984) which attempts to capture the strength of incomes policies. Our reason for including this is that, as noted above, incomes policies have often had the effect of squeezing wage differentials by permitting larger percentage increases for low-paid workers.

To allow for dynamics, we add a lag of all variables to the right-hand side, and estimate the models in error-correction form. However, the theory suggests both of these equations should be linearly homogenous in the wage, benefit and productivity variables together, and this is imposed as a long-run property in estimation by normalising the manual wage equation on benefits, b, and the non-manual wage equation on economy-wide manual wages, $\bar{w}_u$. Finally we treat $\bar{w}_u$ *and* $\bar{w}_s$ as endogenous when they appear, as well as w_u and w_s, since these will be correlated with any common time-specific components of the error term.[10] A full list of instruments is given at the end of Table 7.7.

Estimates of the manual and non-manual wage equations appear in

Table 7.7. *Manual wage equations: dependent variable $\Delta(w_u - b)$*

	With industry and time dummies[1] (1)	With industry dummies[2] (2)	With industry dummies, restricted[2] (3)
$(w_u - b)_{-1}$	− 0.266 (5.19)	− 0.268 (6.29)	− 0.266 (6.74)
Δx_s	0.037 (2.33)	0.040 (3.53)	0.037 (4.02)
x_{s-1}	0.022 (0.70)	0.035 (1.69)	
$\Delta(y - n_u - b)$	0.035 (1.38)	0.044 (1.88)	0.040 (3.60)
$(y - n_u - b)_{-1}$	0.037 (2.58)	0.042 (2.98)	
$\Delta(w_s - b)$	0.344 (0.55)	0.075 (0.22)	0.142 (3.64)
$(w_s - b)_{-1}$	0.215 (1.03)	0.139 (1.43)	
Δb		− 0.194 (0.81)	− 0.153 (1.62)
ΔU		0.357 (0.97)	0.259 (1.43)
U_{-1}		0.300 (0.79)	
$\Delta(\bar{w}_u - b)$		0.653 (1.72)	0.624 (6.36)
$(\bar{w}_u - b)^{-1}$		− 0.132 (0.89)	− 0.124 (1.51)
ΔIP		0.246 (1.54)	0.227 (2.44)
IP_{-1}		0.224 (1.23)	
Test of overidentifying restrictions $(\chi^2(n))$	1.98 $(n = 3)$	1.65 $(n = 5)$	2.54 $(n = 10)$

Instruments

1 $(w_u - b)_{-1}$, $(w_s - b)_{-1}$, Δx_s, x_{s-1}, Δx_d, x_{d-1}, $\Delta(y - n_u - b)$, $\Delta(y - n_u - b)_{-1}$, $\Delta(y - n_s - b)$, $(y - n_s - b)_{-1}$, plus 17 time dummies and 15 industry dummies.
2 As for 1 but omitting time dummies and including Δb, ΔU, U_{-1}, ΔIP, IP_{-1}, $(\bar{w}_u - b)_{-1}$, $(\bar{w}_s - \bar{w}_u)_{-1}$, $\Delta(\bar{y} - \bar{n}_u - b)$, $\Delta(\bar{y} - \bar{n}_s - b)$ instead.

The test of overidentifying restrictions is a Lagrange Multiplier type test of the orthogonality of the equation error with the instrument set, distributed asymptotically as $\chi^2(n)$.

Table 7.8. *Non-manual wage equations: dependent variable $\Delta(w_s - \bar{w}_u)$*

	With industry and time dummies[1] (1)	With industry dummies[2] (2)	With industry dummies, restricted[2] (3)
$(w_s - \bar{w}_u)_{-1}$	−0.320 (5.32)	−0.315 (5.34)	−0.302 (5.44)
Δx_s	0.018 (0.92)	0.015 (0.84)	0.023 (1.87)
x_{s-1}	0.049 (2.43)	0.042 (2.33)	
$\Delta(y - n_s - \bar{w}_u)$	0.014 (0.69)	0.016 (0.79)	0.027 (1.87)
$(y - n_s - \bar{w}_u)_{-1}$	−0.008 (0.49)	0.004 (0.23)	
$\Delta(w_u - \bar{w}_u)$	0.043 (0.11)	0.091 (0.20)	0.066 (1.04)
$(w_u - \bar{w}_u)_{-1}$	0.040 (0.44)	0.056 (0.65)	
$\Delta \bar{w}_u$		0.263 (1.02)	−0.102 (1.04)
ΔU		0.358 (0.56)	0.645 (3.11)
U_{-1}		0.840 (2.73)	
$\Delta(\bar{w}_s - \bar{w}_u)$		0.494 (1.59)	0.277 (2.71)
$(\bar{w}_s - \bar{w}_u)_{-1}$		0.341 (1.81)	
ΔIP		−0.099 (0.74)	0.064 (0.58)
IP_{-1}		0.393 (1.10)	
Test of overidentifying restrictions ($\chi^2(n)$)	1.82 ($n = 3$)	2.61 ($n = 5$)	14.60 ($n = 11$)

Note: For a list of instruments see Table 7.7.

Tables 7.7 and 7.8 respectively. (Coefficients on industry and, where appropriate, time, dummies are omitted for brevity.) Column (1) in Tables 7.7 and 7.8 reports estimates including time as well as industry dummies (and therefore omitting all economy-wide variables). Consequently all economy-wide influences, from whatever source, are partialled out leaving only cross-section variation over time to be explained. A test of the joint significance of the six independent regressors – i.e., excluding the lagged dependent variable – thus gives an indication of the statistical importance of industry-specific factors in the development of wages over time. In each case these are highly significant ($\chi^2(6) = 26.51$ and 12.47 for manuals and non-manuals respectively), suggesting rejection of the simple competitive model in each case.

Column (2) in Tables 7.7 and 7.8 reports results replacing the time dummies by the economy-wide variables. Since some common time-specific element may remain, we assume a random time effects specification for the error term and employ a suitable Generalised Instrumental Variable estimator. The residual unexplained time-specific effect is relatively small, however; the ratio of the variance of the idiosyncratic error component to the variance of the time-specific error component is of the order of 30 in each case. The estimates for the industry-specific variables are generally fairly similar to those appearing in column (1) (as should, of course, be the case). Finally, since the estimates suggest that most of the difference and lagged level terms in the error-correction can be replaced by current level terms, column (3) in Tables 7.7 and 7.8 reports a restricted version imposing these constraints where they are not obviously rejected by the data. Our discussion of the economic implications of the estimates will generally relate to this final set of results.

The strongest short-run influence on manual wages appears to be manual wages elsewhere in the economy, although the estimated long-run effect is perverse. The estimated long-run elasticities are: 0.15 for productivity; 0.53 for non-manual wages in the industry; – 0.47 for economy-wide manual wages; and 0.78 for benefits. It seems likely that the benefits effect is overestimated and the economy-wide manual wages effect underestimated. Notable is the strong 'comparability' effect coming from non-manual wages in the industry and the significant effect from the skill shortage variable. By contrast, aggregate unemployment appears with a positive rather than a negative coefficient. The perverse long-run effect of economy-wide non-manual wages suggests that one should take this result with a pinch of salt; nevertheless the finding that an industry-specific labour market tightness variable dominates unemployment is an interesting finding. Finally incomes policy appears with a small positive coefficient. (The theoretical impact of this term is ambiguous: on the one hand it should reduce the mark-up of manual wages over benefits; on the other it should raise manual wages relative to better-paid non-manual workers.)

The strongest influence on non-manual wages is the level of non-manual wages elsewhere in the economy. Again, however, there is a slight oddity in the long-run coefficients: 0.09 for productivity; 0.22 for manual wages in the industry; − 0.23 for economy-wide manual wages; and 0.92 for economy-wide non-manual wages. As with the equations for manual wages the industry-specific skilled labour shortage variable is a better indicator of labour market tightness than unemployment, which now enters with a highly significant positive coefficient! Incomes policy plays no significant role − which is not surprising since this equation essentially relates the mark-up of non-manual wages over economy-wide non-manual wages to productivity and a labour-market tightness indicator with no important role for non-manual wages.

Despite some unexplained puzzles meriting further work − especially the perverse effects of aggregate unemployment − the results point toward the following broad conclusions:

1. Both manual and non-manual wages are influenced by firm-/industry-specific factors as well as economy-wide developments.
2. Non-manual wages are determined primarily by the level of non-manual wages elsewhere, modified by productivity and labour market tightness as measured by skilled labour shortages.
3. Manual wages are influenced by the level of non-manual wages in the firm/industry − the 'comparability' effect − as well as the levels of productivity, benefits, and manual wages elsewhere. The presence of this 'comparability' effect means that an idiosyncratic shock that raises the demand for skilled non-manual labour will raise both unskilled/manual wages and unemployment.
4. The skill shortage variable appears to be a better indicator of labour market pressures than the unemployment rate.

5   Summary and some policy considerations

Let us first summarise our findings. We have investigated the thesis that much of the rise in British unemployment during the late 1970s and early 1980s can be attributed to a mismatch between the supply of, and demand for, different types of skills resulting from technological change. We presented a theoretical model in which biased labour-augmenting technical change could alter the equilibrium unemployment rate, even though neutral labour-augmenting technical change did not affect it. However, our examination of the empirical evidence suggested that even though technical change appeared to be biased towards economising on the use of skilled (non-manual) labour in the 1970s and 1980s, a necessary condition for this to be transmitted into a shift in the relative demand for different types of labour – a non-unitary elasticity of substitution between skilled and unskilled labour – was not fulfilled. Any shift in the pattern of demand for different types of labour thus seems to be associated more with shifts in the structure of product demand. We did however, find evidence that both manual and non-manual workers possess a degree of market power and thus that one of our other conditions for biased technical change to affect unemployment – a non-competitive market for unskilled (manual) labour – was at least fulfilled. We also found evidence to suggest that survey-based data on skill shortages may be a better guide to potential wage pressure than aggregate unemployment.

In spite of the lack of compelling evidence that technology-induced skill mismatch is a serious problem, we conclude with a brief and somewhat speculative discussion of the policy implications. It is tempting to see concentration of high unemployment as an argument for selective policy intervention – e.g., subsidising the employment of unskilled labour. There may be good equity arguments in favour of such intervention. From an efficiency standpoint, however, it is not immediately obvious what market failure such intervention is supposed to offset. In the model of section 3 inefficiencies arise because the unskilled union exerts market power. The empirical results suggest that a concern by unskilled workers to maintain relative wages within an industry in the face of shocks may exacerbate matters; in that case, the appropriate first-best policy action would be to reduce union power and discourage wage agreements that seek to maintain wage parity across skills (or regions), not to subsidise unskilled employment.

Yet this may be too hasty an assessment, especially with respect to the subsidisation of retraining. The presence of distinct labour markets by skill arises because of the existence of significant fixed costs of retraining. The private fixed costs of retraining often exceed the social costs; firms may be unwilling to undertake retraining because – in the absence of slavery – they cannot be sure that they, rather than other employers, will reap the returns from the investment in workforce human capital. In principle, this problem of the non-appropriability of returns could be circumvented by having the worker pay for the retraining, but capital market imperfections mean that this is not always a viable option either.

Investment in human capital is also likely to be a potent source of positive externalities, as the recent endogenous growth literature has highlighted (see, for example, Lucas 1988; Romer, 1986). Such investment

frequently benefits not only the parties directly involved in the investment, but often has a wider spin-off. This is especially true of basic human
knowledge, but is also true to some extent of more vocational skills, and
intervention to encourage such skill formation is again justified. A proper
analysis of the extent of such intervention would, however, take us well
beyond the limited ambitions of this study.

DATA APPENDIX

All variables are deflated by the consumer price index unless otherwise stated.

B — Value in April of Supplementary Benefit for a married couple (ordinary rate). *Source*: *Social Security Statistics*, Table 34.01.

$N_s(N_u)$ — Employment of non-manual (manual) workers in industry. Calculated
by pro-rating total industry employment (*Source*: *Annual Abstract of
Statistics*) by sample sizes for respective labour types reported in *New
Earnings Survey*, Part C.

$S_s^*(S_u^*)$ — Share of non-manual (manual) labour in industry value-added. Calculated by appropriately pro-rating total labour share in value added
(*Source*: *Annual Abstract of Statistics*) by relative labour shares and
relative wages (see $N_s(N_u)$ and $W_s(W_u)$ for sources).

$W_s(W_u)$ — Median gross hourly earnings of full-time non-manual (manual) males
on adult rates. *Source*: *New Earnings Survey*, Part C.

$x_s(x_d)$ — Proportion of firms in each industry saying that skilled labour (sales)
are expected to be a constraint over the next four months. In practice
the transformation $x_i = ln[1/(1 - Z_i)]$ is used, where Z_i is the raw
percentage saying factor i is expected to be a constraint. *Source*: *CBI
Industrial Trends Survey* (January).

Y — Hourly value added by industry. Value added data comes from the
Annual Abstract of Statistics, while data on hours worked is drawn
from the Department of Employment *Gazette*.

NOTES

1 Research assistance by Fabio-Cesare Bagliano and Guglielmo Caporale is
gratefully acknowledged, as is the financial assistance of the Department of
Employment.
2 The index is based on the quantity

$$I = 1 - \sum_i \left(\frac{U_i}{U}\right)^{1/2} \left(\frac{V_i}{V}\right)^{1/2}$$

where $U_i(V_i)$ is unemployment (vacancies in region/type i and $U(V)$ is total
unemployment/vacancies. The index takes the value zero when each region/-
type has the same share of vacancies as unemployment – i.e., $(U_i/U) = (V_i/V)$
for all i, and increases towards unity as dispersion increases.

3 Let $\Omega^e(\Omega^u)$ denote the value to a skilled worker to being employed (unemployed). Then it follows that the flow return from being employed is

$$r\Omega^e = W_s + s(\Omega^u - \Omega^e)$$

and the flow return from being unemployed is

$$r\Omega^u = W_u + h(\Omega^e - \Omega^u)$$

Hence the surplus from being employed is

$$\Omega^e - \Omega^u = (W_s - W_u)/(r + s + h)$$

Let $\Delta^e(\Delta^v)$ be the value to the firm of a filled (unfilled) vacancy. A similar argument establishes that the surplus from filling a vacancy is

$$\Delta^e - \Delta^v = (\pi P A_s f_1 - W_s + \gamma)/(r + s + h/X)$$

The Nash bargain then solves

$$\max_{\{W_s\}} (\Omega^e - \Omega^u)\, \beta_s (\Delta^e - \Delta^v)^{1-}\beta_s$$

which together with the steady-state condition for X

$$h/X = (r + s)\,\gamma/(\pi P A_s f_1 - W_s)$$

yields equation (5) in the text.
4 Implicitly we therefore assume that the union cares only about the welfare of unskilled workers and not about the welfare of any skilled workers who currently hold unskilled jobs. This simplifies the algebra somewhat – and is arguably more realistic, too.
5 For instance, this might well be the case if growth is based on increasing specialisation. We assume these costs are imposed by growth *elsewhere* in the economy so that firms continue to treat γ as fixed.
6 Note that $S_s/N_s - S_u/N_u = [W_s - W_u + (r + s)\,\gamma X/h]/\pi f > 0$.

7 They are metal manufacture, other mineral products, chemicals, other metal goods, mechanical engineering, electrical engineering, motor vehicles, other transport equipment, food, drink and tobacco, textiles, clothing and footwear, timber and furniture, paper and publishing, and rubber and other products.
8 Note that this could include capital, or any other inputs for that matter. Equations (3), (4) and thus also equation (19) would still be valid.
9 Both of these items were in fact used earlier to calculate the skilled and unskilled labour shares employed in section 4.1.
10 We have also tried treating the current values of x_s and the productivity terms as endogenous. The results are similar, although inevitably much more imprecise.

REFERENCES

Bean, C., R. Layard and S. Nickell (1986). 'The Rise in Unemployment: A Multi-Country Study', *Economica*, **53** (Supplement) S1–S22.
Bean, C. and J. Symons (1989). 'Ten Years of Mrs T.', *NBER Macroeconomics Annual*, 13–61.

Binmore, K., A. Rubinstein and A. Wolinsky (1986). 'The Nash Bargaining Solution in Economic Modelling', *Rand Journal of Economics*, **17**, 176–88.

Budd, A., P. Levine and P. Smith (1987). 'Long-Term Unemployment and the Shifting U–V curve: A Multi-Country Study', *European Economic Review*, **31**, 296–305.

Desai, M., M. Keil and S. Wadhwani (1984). 'Incomes Policy in a Political Environment: A Structural Model for the UK 1961–80', in A. Hughes Hallet (ed.), *Applied Decision Analysis and Economic Behaviour*, Hingham, MA: Martinus Nijhoff.

Hall, R. E. (1986). 'Market Structure and Macroeconomic Fluctuations', *Brookings Papers on Economic Activity*, **2**, 285–322.

Jackman, R. and S. Roper (1987). 'Structural Unemployment', *Oxford Bulletin of Economics and Statistics*, **49 (1)**, 9–37.

Jackman, R., R. Layard, S. Nickell and S. Wadhwani (1991). *Unemployment* (Oxford: Oxford University Press).

Layard, R. and C. Bean (1989). 'Why Does Unemployment Persist?', *Scandinavian Journal of Economics*, **3**, 371–96.

Layard, R. and S. Nickell (1986). 'Unemployment in Britain', *Economica*, **53** (Supplement) S121–S171.

   (1989). 'The Thatcher Miracle?', *American Economic Review*, **79** (Papers and Proceedings) 215–19.

Lucas, R. E. (1988). 'On the Mechanics of Economic Development', *Journal of Monetary Economics*, **22**, 1–42.

Oswald, A. (1987). 'Efficient Contracts are on the Labour Demand Curve: Theory and Facts', London School of Economics, Centre for Labour Economics, discussion paper, **284**.

Pissarides, C. (1978). 'The Role of Relative Wages and Excess Demand in the Sectoral Flow of Labour', *Review of Economic Studies*, **45**, 453–68.

   (1985). 'Short-run Equilibrium Dynamics of Unemployment, Vacancies and Real Wages', *American Economic Review*, **75**, 676–90.

   (1986). 'Unemployment and Vacancies in Britain', *Economic Policy*, **3**, 500–59.

Pissarides, C. and I. McMaster (1990). 'Regional Migration, Wages and Unemployment', *Oxford Economic Papers* (forthcoming).

Pissarides, C. and J. Wadsworth (1989). 'Unemployment and the Inter-regional Mobility of Labour', *Economic Journal*, **99**, 739–55.

Romer, P. M. (1986). 'Increasing Returns and Long-Run Growth', *Journal of Political Economy*, **94**, 1002–37.

Discussion

UGO TRIVELLATO

I would like to begin the discussion of the study by Charles Bean and Christopher Pissarides by congratulating the authors for a very interesting and stimulating piece of work.

I would also point out from the beginning that I will make only sporadic comments on the study, rather than discussing it systematically. The basic reason for that is that the study is a difficult one to discuss. Bean and Pissarides present a very articulate contribution. Section 1 (and partly section 2) deals (rather briefly, it must be said) with some facts and does some theorising about structural unemployment and mismatch in the United Kingdom; the core of the study (sections 3 and 4) is devoted to the presentation of a very specific model of unemployment with skill differentiation, and to its estimation and use for empirical analyses on British data; the final part (section 5) is concerned with a brief discussion of policy implications. Besides, the various pieces of evidence from the rich set of empirical analyses are not fully consistent with the proposed model; on the whole, they seem to suggest that the questions addressed by Bean and Pissarides are far from being convincingly settled, and that further research is needed to account for observed divergences in unemployment rates by skill.

1 Main points of the study

Before presenting my comments, let me restate very briefly the main points of the study as I perceive them.

(a) For the initial part (facts and theorising about unemployment and mismatch in the United Kingdom):

-   There is a striking overall stability of *relative* unemployment rates – by age, sex, skill, and region – over the last twenty years.
-   Human capital considerations are likely to play a significant part in explaining demographic differences.
-   The pattern of unemployment experience by skill and region is not entirely consistent with a human capital story, and demands different explanations. The hypothesis of a rise in skill mismatch, and unemployment, induced by (largely unskilled) labour-augmenting technical progress is especially well developed.

(b) For the core of the study – an unemployment model with skill differentiation:

–   The model combines matching/search considerations, for skilled workers *only*, with the determination of wage pressure, both for skilled and unskilled workers.

–   The model is a short-run dynamic model (the supply of skilled and unskilled workers is given; technology is given, apart from technology shocks).

–   The model purports to elucidate the quite different impact on unemployment of two types of technological shocks: a *common* proportionate shock, and an *asymmetric* ($\equiv$ idiosyncratic, biased) shock which enhances the productivity of only a sub-set of the labour force. The equilibrium unemployment rate is not neutral with respect to common shocks. On the contrary, it rises in the face of an asymmetric unskilled labour-augmenting technology shock, if $\psi > 0$ (remember that $\psi = 1/\sigma - 1$, where $-$ is the elasticity of substitution between skilled and unskilled labour, so that $\psi > 0$ if and only if $\sigma < 1$). The key to this result depends on the non-competitiveness of the market for unskilled labour. In particular, the rise in the equilibrium unemployment rate will be aggravated if, in the face of a widening of the wage differential, typically associated with this type of shock, the union of unskilled workers cares about relative wages. (Obviously, the model predicts just the opposite in the case of an idiosyncratic skilled labour-augmenting technology shock. This shock will increase unemployment if the elasticity of substitution exceeds unity, and reduce it otherwise.)

–   Empirical evidence from panel data – from 1970 to 1988, with 15 industries – rests on a very ingenious manipulation of various data resources and on a convincing statistical analysis. The results, however, are only partially consistent with the implications of the model.

On the basis of this brief (and hopefully unbiased) summary, I will group my comments on the study under two headings: (1) a discussion of some key explanations advocated by the authors, and of the empirical evidence provided to support them (my sections 2–5); (2) a more general question about the relevance of a mismatch approach to labour market disequilibria (section 6).

2   The basic model

In their section 3, Bean and Pissarides present their basic model, and carry out a sophisticated exercise on the effects on unemployment of an asymmetric technology shock in the context of a labour market with skill differentiation. Although of a somewhat reduced scope with respect to the facts documented in section 1 and the questions stemming from them, the exercise is analytically stimulating and perceptive. I have just a couple of comments about its set-up.

A first remark has to do with an assumption: that an 'unemployed skilled worker can always take a temporary job as an unskilled worker while looking for skilled work, without impairing the chances of finding a skilled job'. My questions are:

(a)   How much is such an assumption tenable in a labour market seg-
       mented into skilled and unskilled workers? In other words, is it
       reasonable to assume that intensity of job search and the stigma
       effect are irrelevant for matching? To me, the assumption does not
       seem fully plausible.
(b)   What are the likely consequences of dropping this assumption for
       the exercise? Or, otherwise stated, is the assumption crucial for
       deriving the main results of the exercise? I am inclined to think that it
       is not, but an analytical argument would clearly be better.

My second point is about the relevance of the model for long-run behaviour. If in the unskilled sector relative wages are too high and union power too strong, it is likely that other mechanisms will come into operation to reduce wages and power. (As an illustration, the growth of the so-called 'underground economy' in Italy in the 1970s can be partly interpreted as a way of escaping from too intense union pressure.) Now, it is precisely the persistence of unemployment differentials in the long run that has to be explained. In this respect, the model does not seem to me fully appropriate, unless one can demonstrate (or is willing to assume) that a sustained sequence of asymmetric technology shocks of the same type occurred.

3   Econometric evidence

As pointed out by the authors at the end of section 3, 'both the sign and size of the effect of biased technical change on unemployment is clearly an empirical matter', in that it depends on the elasticity of substitution between skilled and unskilled labour and on the non-competitiveness of the market for unskilled labour. The econometric evidence presented in section 4 is, therefore, crucial. Empirical results, however, are far from being conclusive, and on the whole do not support the main thesis – i.e., that 'much of the rise in British unemployment during the late 1970s and early 1980s can be attributed to a mismatch between the supply of, and demand for, different types of skills resulting from technological change'.

The fact is patently admitted by the authors: in section 5, before concluding with some policy considerations, they recognise 'the lack of compelling evidence that technology-induced skill mismatch is a serious problem'. Yet, some contradictory empirical evidence is perhaps underestimated in their comments, at least in two respects.

(a)   From preliminary descriptive evidence in sections 1 and 2, Bean and Pissarides draw the tentative thesis that 'labour-saving improvements . . . [in the last decade in Britain] have very much the character of . . . labour-augmenting technical progress'. Presumably such change is largely *unskilled* labour-augmenting, yet the econometric analysis of section 4.1 suggests that technical progress (particularly in the 1970s but probably also in the 1980s) was primarily *skilled* labour-augmenting. They basically argue about the evidence of a bias in technical change, and tend to disregard the fact that the direction of the bias suggested by the estimated model is opposite to the expected one.

(b)   The evidence of non-competitiveness of the labour market for unskilled workers, provided by the results concerning the determinants of industry manual wages (section 4.3) seems to me rather dubious. The problem is not with the relevant coefficient *per se* ('the finding that an industry-specific labour market tightness variable dominates unemployment is [indeed] an interesting finding'), but with 'some unexplained puzzles' concerning other coefficients, which appear with the wrong sign. This suggests that the wage equations are possibly affected by some specification error, and casts obvious doubts on the conclusions one can reasonably draw from them, even for those variables whose coefficients turn out to have the expected signs.

Consequently, I would recommend the authors to be even more cautious than they actually are in discussing (albeit speculatively) some policy implications of their mismatch model.

4   Microeconomic evidence on job search behaviour would help

The partly inconclusive results of the econometric analysis on panel data by industry stimulate a side comment about different data sources, potentially suitable for testing the main thesis advocated by Bean and Pissarides, and for confronting it with alternative explanations of the rise in unemployment paying more attention to individual behaviour (e.g., reduction in search intensity). Particularly, it would be interesting to have microeconomic evidence on the pattern of unemployment duration. Duration (= hazard) models of unemployment have a long and honourable history in the United Kingdom (one can refer to the seminal study by Silcock, 1954, and to the series of innovative studies by Lancaster and Nickell in the late 1970s, such as Lancaster, 1979; Nickell, 1979; Lancaster and Nickell, 1980). It is a pity that such models were not used, or could not be used because of lack of relevant data. In principle, they could document the impact of variables associated with wages and wage differentials at the firm or industry level, with a human capital explanation, with unemployment benefits, and alternatively provide evidence of negative duration dependence.

5   Stability of relative unemployment rates

Taking a broader perspective, indeed the very same one outlined by Bean and Pissarides in the introductory section of their study, it is natural to consider the role of some key explanations advocated by them in explaining the *fact* of the stablity of relative unemployment rates over time.

  Such a stability, incidentally during a period of significant changes in economic and social policies in the United Kingdom, stands as an intellectual challenge for economists and, in my opinion, calls for an integrated set of explanations (albeit at the beginning possibly speculative and/or fragmentary). The economic reasoning should pay attention not only to the functioning of the labour market, but also to other determinants of the behaviour of firms and families, and any plausible explanation should account for the long-term dimension of differences in unemployment. Over twenty years, new generations entered the labour market, new technologies were introduced, new social regulations set. But the relative patterns of unemployment were not dramatically altered.

  In this respect, I found section 1 and partly section 2 of the study rich in interesting evidence and stimulating ideas. At the same time, however, it seems to me that such a line of reasoning is somehow abruptly interrupted. It is as if one were presented with a complex mosaic and were provided with stimulating clues for its explication and then everything is taken away, except for a nice tessera, which is investigated in a fairly sophisticated way. After looking at the results of this ingenious investigation, it seems to me that the effort to shed a penetrating light on the tessera cannot be profitably uncoupled from the broader task of understanding the mosaic as a whole.

6   The term 'mismatch'

My last comment is stimulated by, but only partially related to, Bean and Pissarides's study. It has to do with a sort of interpretative ambiguity that, as far as I can see, still affects the term 'mismatch'. Is 'mismatch' a temporary displacement from some equilibrium? Or does it identify a structural, long-lasting, imbalance?

If tentative evidence seems to be in favour of the second interpretation of the term, at least as far as modern European economies are concerned, then a basic issue arises. To be brief, I will simply phrase the problem in two different ways, which in my opinion are illustrative of two different approaches to it. (1) On the basis of this evidence, can we respond to the argument, lucidly put forward by Heckman and MaCurdy (1988, 235–6), that 'if worker heterogeneity is viewed as empirically relevant, . . . the market-clearing view is an irrefutable tautology, and tests against it have no power'? (2) If evidence in favour of a structural interpretation of mismatch is taken for granted, how appropriate is an analytical framework largely inspired by a neoclassical or equilibrium perspective, and (even more important!) how appropriate are policies derived from it?

REFERENCES

Heckman, J. J. and T. E. MaCurdy (1988). 'Empirical tests of labor-market disequilibrium: an evaluation', in *Carnegie–Rochester Conference Series on Public Policy*, **28**, Amsterdam: North-Holland, 231–58.

Lancaster, T. (1979). 'Econometric methods for the duration of unemployment', *Econometrica*, **47**, 939–56.

Lancaster, T. and S. Nickell (1980). 'The analysis of re-employment probabilities for the unemployed', *Journal of the Royal Statistical Society*, **A**, **143**, 141–65 (with discussion).

Nickell, S. (1979). 'Estimating the probability of leaving unemployment', *Econometrica*, **47**, 1247–66.

Silcock, H. R. (1954). 'The phenomenon of labor turnover', *Journal of the Royal Statistical Society*, **A**, **117**, 429–40.

8 Labour Market Tightness and the Mismatch Between Demand and Supply of Less-Educated Young Men in the United States in the 1980s[1]

RICHARD B. FREEMAN

One of the most disturbing economic developments of the 1980s in the United States was the deterioration in the real and relative earnings of less-educated male workers, particularly younger men (Murphy and Welch, 1990; Blackburn, Bloom and Freeman, 1990; Katz and Revenga, 1989; Bound and Johnson, 1989; Levy, 1988). In 1979 a male high school graduate aged 25–34 working year-round full-time earned $23,440 per year in 1987 dollars, 15% below the earnings of a comparably aged male college graduate. In 1987 the 25–34-year-old male high school graduate earned $21,420 per year – 9% less in real terms than in 1979, and 29% below the earnings of a 25–34-year-old college graduate. Declines of a similar magnitude occurred in the real and relative pay of young male high school dropouts. If one looks at workers with less than five years of work experience, moreover, the rise in the educational earnings differential is even greater: college men with less than five years' experience averaged 0.54 *ln* points more in weekly earnings than high school men with less than five years' experience in 1981–7 compared to 0.35 *ln* points more from 1974 to 1980.[2] Among older less-educated men there were smaller but still noticeable drops in real and relative earnings.[3] After decades in which the real wages of the less skilled trended upward, often rising more rapidly than the wages of the more skilled, the economy seemed to be on another course entirely, with a growing mismatch between the labour market demand and supply for skills.

Did differences in labour utilisation – unemployment or employment–population ratios – by skill also widen in the 1980s in the United States, or did the falling real and relative wages of the less skilled improve their employment prospects? How did young less-educated men fare in local labour markets with relative shortages of labour? Will demographic-based projections of labour market shortages in the 1990s and early 2000s restore the historic pattern of rising real earnings for the less educated and reduce earnings differentials?

In this study I examine these questions using Current Population Survey (CPS) data.[4] To determine how the labour utilisation of less-educated male workers changed from the 1970s to the 1980s, I examine unemployment rates and employment-to-population rates for male workers aged 25–64 and those aged 25–34 from 1973 (when the real earnings of the less educated began to fall) through 1987–8. To see how local area unemployment affected unemployment and earnings, I compare the economic position of more-/less-educated recent male labour market entrants (defined as those schooling was completed within 0–5 years) across the 202 Metropolitan Statistical Areas (MSAs) identified in the 1987 CPS Merged Demographic File. I also contrast the changes in the economic position of these men from 1983 to 1987 in the 45 MSAs (identified in the 1983 and 1987 Merged Demographic Files.

There are three findings:

1. Unemployment rates and employment–population ratios of men with high school or less education have deteriorated relative to those of more-educated men, implying that inward shifts in the demand for the less educated dominated movements down demand curves due to lower wages. The widened structure of unemployment/employment–population rates by education implies that the market for less-educated men is weaker at given levels of aggregate unemployment than in the past. Rising educational pay differentials thus understate the growing mismatch between demand and supply for labour skills in the United States.

2. In local areas with low unemployment rates less-educated young men had markedly higher earnings and employment–population ratios than in areas with high unemployment rates, both absolutely and relative to more-educated young men. This suggests that sluggish economic growth and upward drift in aggregate unemployment contributed to the 1980s' deterioration in the earnings and employment of the less educated. Extrapolating the estimated effects of area unemployment on the earnings of men with 0–5 years of experience to the country as a whole suggests that had the aggregate unemployment rate been 2 percentage points lower in the 1980s the college–high school earnings differential among the less experienced would have risen by some 30% less than the observed 0.19 *ln* points rise; while the college–high school employment–population differential among young men would have risen by about 2 percentage points less than it did from the early 1970s. While the looseness of the labour market contributed to the problems of less-educated young men, the bulk of the growing labour market mismatch for less-experienced men with

differing education is thus due to factors other than aggregate economic conditions.
3. The finding that wages are higher in areas with low unemployment is consistent with the Blanchflower–Oswald (1989) 'Wage Curve' found in other countries but runs counter to the 'Harris–Todaro' (1970) pattern of high unemployment in high wage cities found by Hall (1976), Marston (1980) and Reza (1978) for the United States for the 1970s. The difference in the relation between area unemployment and wages in the United States in the 1980s and in the 1970s highlights the potential instability of the 'reduced form' geographic wage–unemployment locus.

I present the evidence for these claims in three stages. First, I develop a wage adjustment model that relates wages and employment–population rates to their underlying determinants. I show that in such a model the reduced form geographic wage–unemployment loci can be either positively or negatively sloped. Second, I document the falling labour utilisation of less-educated men in the 1970s and 1980s. Third, I compare the employment and earnings of more-/less-educated young men across MSAs with differing rates of local unemployment. I conclude with some speculations about the possible impact of tight labour markets on the economic position of less-skilled men in the next decade or so.

1   Earnings and unemployment

When the earnings of the less skilled fall sharply, as in the 1980s, how ought one to expect their unemployment rate or employment-to-population ratio to change?

Since declines in earnings can reflect declines in labour demand that reduce employment as well as pay and/or movements along demand schedules (due to shifts in supply or changes in wage-setting practices) that raise employment, there is no general answer to this question. In a market-clearing model one has to know the causes of the change in relative earnings to assess the likely reduced form relation between the two endogenous variables. When wages do not clear the market, one also must know something about the speed of wage adjustments. From this perspective the pattern of change in the labour utilisation of less-skilled men from the 1970s to the 1980s provides evidence on whether the reduction in wages reflects primarily shifts in demand or movements along demand schedules, and whether those changes overstate or understate the magnitude of the market twist against the less skilled.

A simple wage adjustment model that links wages and employment–population rates illustrates these points. Let

D' = shift in ln labour demand
S' = shift in ln labour supply
E' = change in ln employment
W' = change in ln wages
h = labour demand elasticity
e = labour supply elasticity.

Then the market clearing change in wages and employment resulting from shifts in the schedules is:

$$W' = (D' - S')/(h + e); \tag{1}$$

$$E' = (eD' + hS')/(h + e) \tag{2}$$

Subtracting S' from equation (2) to obtain the change in the employment–population ratio and rearranging yields:

$$E' - S' = (D' - S')e/(h + e) = eW' \tag{3}$$

Equation (3) shows that in a market-clearing model wages and the employment–production ratio move in the same direction as long as labour supply is upward sloping ($e > 0$).

How might one define a 'mismatch' in such a model? The simplest interpretation of a mismatch is in terms of shifts in the supply and demand schedules that in the long run induce offsetting long-term changes in labour supply, with S' taken as endogenous. For instance, if demand shifts against less-educated workers while the supply of these workers increases (due to decisions made in the past) the effect will be a reduction in their earnings and in their probability of employment as well. These conditions should induce long-run changes in labour supplies to rectify the 'mismatch'. By contrast, changes in earnings and employment that do not induce offsetting changes in long-run supplies of labour can be viewed as indicative of long-term equilibrium adjustments rather than as indicative of market mismatches.

When wages respond to factors other than the current supply–demand balance, such as changes in wage-setting institutions (weakened unionism, falling real minimum wages in the period under study) or past supply–demand imbalances due to sluggish adjustment, wages and employment–population ratios can move in opposite directions. Let $(0 < \phi < 1)$ be an adjustment parameter reflecting the response of wages to current shifts in demand or supply and let W'_o = pressure for changes in wages due to other fctors. Then the natural generalisation of (3) is:

$$W' = \phi(D' - S')/(h + e) + (1 - \phi)W'_o, \tag{4}$$

where observed wage changes are a weighted average of changes due to the current supply–demand balance and other wage determinants.

If employment lies on the demand durve, the change in employment will be $E' = D' - hW'$,[5] giving a change in employment/population of:

$$E' - S' = D' - S' - hW'$$
$$= [(h + e - h\phi)/(h + e)](D' - S') - h(1 - \phi) W'_o \qquad (5)$$

This can be rewritten as a function of wages:

$$E' - S' = [(h + e - h\phi)/\phi] W' - [(h + e)(1 - \phi)/\phi] W'_o \qquad (5')$$

According to equation (5') employment–population ratios will vary directly with wages unless there are sizeable wage determining factors moving in the opposite direction as current shifts in the demand–supply balance. The greater the adjustment parameter ϕ the more likely will shifts in wages and in employment–population ratios be in the same direction.

2   Migration and the area unemployment–wage locus

How should the earnings and labour utilisation of the less skilled be related to area unemployment?

The model in equations (4)–(5'), while useful for examining changes in wages and labour utilisation for workers whose supply (S) is exogenous or pre-determined, must be modified to analyse patterns across areas whose labour supply changes due to migration. If, as in Harris–Todaro models, S is infinitely elastic with respect to expected earnings ($= E/S \times W$), expected earnings will be constant, and changes in wages will generate offsetting changes in the probability of employment. This yields the migration supply curve $S' = E' + W'$.[6] The Appendix shows that introducing this labour migration equation into the model of equations (4)–(5') gives the standard Harris–Todaro prediction of a positive association of wages with high unemployment. This is because changes in demand have no effect on wages or on employment rates when supply is infinitely elastic, making non-market clearing factors (W^o,) the sole determinants of wages and employment. This necessarily produces a positive relation between exogenously determined wages and unemployment rates across areas. If S is less than infinitely elastic with respect to expected wages, however, the relation between wages and area unemployment is quite different. Let the working population depend on expected wages according to

$$S' = k(W' + (E/S)') \qquad (6)$$

where $k > 0$ is the elasticity of supply due to migration to expected wages. Rearranging terms yields:

$$S' = p(E' + W'')$$ (6')

where

$$p = (k/(1 + k)) < 1$$ (6')

The Appendix shows that substituting equation (6') into the model of equations (4)–(5) eliminates the strong prediction that high unemployment and high wages go together. When k is less than infinite shifts in demand once again raise employment–population ratios and wages, inducing a positive relation between those variables, while exogenous changes in wages move wages and employment–population in opposite directions, as in the Harris–Todaro case. In sum, this exercise shows that the shape of the wage/employment–population or unemployment locus cannot be predicted *a priori*, barring infinite elasticity of migrants to expected real earnings. Demand factors tend to produce an inverse relation between area unemployment and wages (Blanchflower and Oswald's (1989) 'Wage Curve') while exogenous wage determining factors tend to produce a positive relation. The former will dominate the locus when wages adjust rapidly to current market conditions and migration elasticities are modest; the latter will dominate under the opposite conditions.

3   Changes in labour utilisation by education, 1970s–1980s

Turning from models to evidence, Table 8.1 gives unemployment and employment–population rates for less- and more-educated men aged 25–64 and 25–34 from 1974 to 1988, as tabulated from March CPS tapes (1974, 1980 and 1988). The tabulations provide an unambiguous answer to the question of whether the 1970s–1980s decline in the real/relative earnings of less-educated workers was accompanied by increasing or decreasing utilisation of these workers: both the unemployment rates and employment–population ratios show a marked deterioration in labour utilisation of the less skilled. Although the US aggregate unemployment rate was virtually the same in 1988 (5.4%) as in 1974 (5.5%), the unemployment rates for 25–34- and 25–64-year old male high school dropouts and graduates were twice as high in 1988 than in 1974. By contrast, the unemployment rate for college graduates remained roughly the same. The employment–population rates in Table 8.1 also exhibit a widening gap between more-educated and less-educated workers, with the proportion employed falling exceptionally sharply for those with less than

Table 8.1. *Unemployment rates and employment/population rates for white male workers, by education and age, 1974–88*

Item	Male workers 25–64			Male workers 24–34		
	1974 (1)	1980 (2)	1988 (3)	1974 (4)	1980 (5)	1988 (6)
Unemployment rates						
< High school	4.4	7.4	9.2	6.2	11.8	12.1
High school grad.	2.7	4.7	5.4	3.6	7.1	6.7
College grad.	1.4	1.5	1.5	2.1	2.2	2.1
Employment–population rates						
< High school	80	73	69	88	80	77
High school grad.	91	85	84	94	89	89
College grad.	95	93	93	94	94	94

Source: Tabulated from March CPS tapes for 1974, 1980, and 1988.

high school education. Finally, Table 8.1 shows that the deterioration in the labour utilisation of the less educated was more severe in the 1970s than in the 1980s. The unemployment rate gap between 25–34-year-old college graduates and high school dropouts rose, for example, by 5.5 percentage points from 1974 to 1980 compared to a 0.4 percentage point rise from 1980 to 1988, while the gap in unemployment rates between college and high school graduates rose between 1974 and 1980 and then fell slightly from 1980 to 1988.

Bureau of Labor Statistics (BLS) tabulations of unemployment rates and employment/population ratios for other CPS samples provide additional evidence that labour utilisation of less-educated men deteriorated in the past two decades. Figure 8.1 depicts BLS estimates from all the monthly CPS surveys of the unemployment rate and employment–population ratio for 25–64-year-old men with less than four years of high school, with four years of high school, and with four or more years of college education. It shows a substantial widening in the gap of labour utilisation between more and less educated male workers comparable to that found in my March CPS tabulations. Table 8.2 gives BLS data on the unemployment and employment–population rates of 16–24-year-old men not enrolled in school and of 16–24-year-old 'recent high school graduates and school dropouts' from the October CPS surveys. It shows a marked upward trend in unemployment rates and downward trend in employment–population rates for high school dropouts and graduates compared to rough stability in rates for college graduates or students. The only differ-

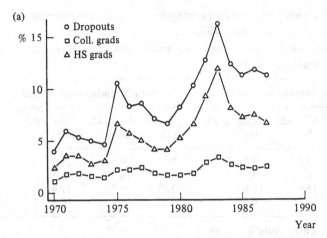

(a)

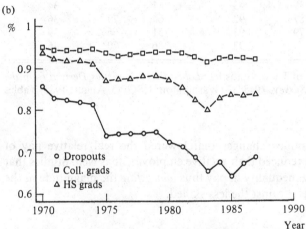

(b)

Figure 8.1   Unemployment rates and unemployment/population ratios for male workers, 25–64, 1970–90
Source: US Bureau of Labor Statistics, *Labor Force Statistics Derived from the Current Population Survey, 1948–87* (Washington, DC: USGPO, August 1988) Tables C-23 and C-24.

a   Unemployment rates by education

b   Employment/population ratios by education

ence between this pattern and that shown in Table 8.1 for 25–34-year-olds is in the timing of the decline in utilisation. Among less-skilled 16–24-year-olds the decline in labour utilisation was greater in the 1980s than in the 1970s.[7]

Table 8.2. *Rates of unemployment and employment/population rates for 16–24-year-old males, by education, 1973–86*

	Rates of unemployment					
	Men not enrolled in school			Recent HS graduates/dropouts		
	< hs (1)	hs grad. (2)	Coll. grad. (3)	< hs (4)	hs. grad. (5)	coll. stud. (6)
1973	12.9	5.6	3.2	24.2	9.6	13.5
1979	16.1	8.1	5.5	19.0	13.9	11.5
1983	26.2	15.0	6.0	32.7	25.6	17.4
1986	21.0	10.2	4.6	22.2	19.4	10.8
	Employment/population ratios					
1973	75	89	93	61	82	34
1979	71	87	92	64	79	36
1983	61	79	93	51	66	39
1986	66	84	93	56	70	46

Source: US Bureau of Labor Statistics, *Labor Force Statistics Derived from the Current Population Survey, 1948–87* (Washington: USGPO, August 1988) Tables C-20 and C-21.

In sum, the economic changes that lowered the real/relative pay of less-educated men reduced their relative employment as well. Studies that focus on the rising inequality in pay thus *understate* the magnitude of the labour market twist against the less skilled.

4   The effect of area unemployment

Did young less-skilled men fare better in areas with tight labour markets than in other areas in the 1980s, suggesting that tighter markets in ensuing decades might moderate, and ultimately reverse the downward trajectory in their employment and earnings?

To answer this question, I relate the employment and earnings of more-/less-educated men who left school within five years to area unemployment rates across the 202 metropolitan areas (MSAs) that the CPS identifies on its Merged Demographic File. I contrast outcomes by area in 1983 and in 1987 to make sure that 1987 cross-section relations do not reflect permanent area differences in unemployment and wages rather than the effects of current local labour market conditions. Unfortunately, extending the analysis back to 1983 limits the sample to 45 MSAs

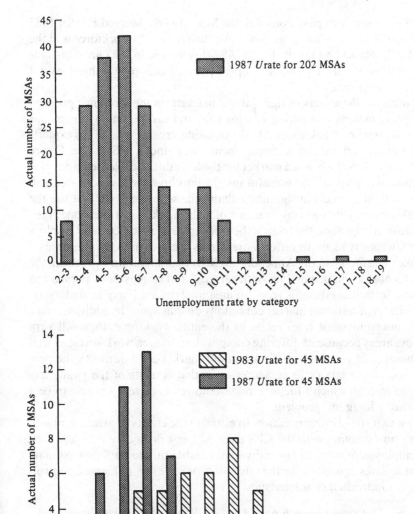

Figure 8.2   Rates of unemployment in 205 MSAs in 1987 and in 48 MSAs in 1983 and 1987

(including sub-groups of consolidated MSAs) as the Merged File for 1983 does not identify other areas. Since over half of the US workforce is in the 45 MSA sample and results for the 45 MSA sample in 1987 are comparable to those for the 202 MSA sample in 1987, I believe that this does not distort the findings.

Estimating the effects of tight labour markets on the economic position of young men by comparing employment and earnings across areas has both virtues and weaknesses. On the plus side, cross-area analysis exploits substantial variation in unemployment rates among MSAs (see Figure 8.2) in the period when the market for the less educated was deteriorating. It thus may provide more useful insight into how the less educated will fare in tight markets in the future than time series analyses that use the 1950s or late 1960s as observations of tight markets. At the same time, because of migration the relation between market conditions and employment/wages is likely to differ more across areas than in the nation as a whole. The model in the Appendix suggests that migration will reduce the effects of shifts in demand on both earnings and employment–population ratios, so that coefficients from an area analysis are likely to understate the effects of national market conditions on outcomes. In addition, since area unemployment rates relate to the entire workforce, they will vary across areas because of differing compositions of area workforces, as well as because of genuinely different labour market conditions. As the proportion of the labour force across areas that consists of the young less skilled men on which I focus is modest, however, there is unlikely to be a serious 'adding up' problem.

I use two statistical procedures to estimate the effects of area unemployment on outcomes with the CPS data. My first procedure is to add area unemployment rates to the individual records on the CPS and estimate least squares equations for the effect of those rates on outcomes, controlling for individual characteristics:

$$\text{Outcome}_{ij} = a + b \text{ Area } Une_j + c \text{ Personal Characteristics}_{ij} + u_{ij}$$

where u_{ij} is the residual.

Because area unemployment rates relate to groups which are likely to have common group components in their residuals, however, the standard errors in these regressions are likely to be biased downward, with the degree of bias depending on the intracorrelation of disturbances and the average number of persons in each area (Moulton, 1988). My second procedure is designed to deal with this problem. I estimate the effects of area unemployment rates using a random effects regression design, in which the error term is modelled as

Table 8.3. *Employment/population rates for men with 0–5 years of potential labour market experience, by education, in areas with different local unemployment rates, 1987*

Area unemployment rate (1)	Men with	
	12 or less years of school (2)	16 or more years of school (3)
< 4%	75	94
4–5%	77	94
5–6%	69	92
6–7%	68	93
> 7%	66	91

Source: Tabulated from the CPS Merged Demographic Files (1987). Statistics based on the ESR variable in the public use file, with all persons whose major activity is in school deleted. Employment is the number working and the number with a job but not working. Area unemployment rates obtained from published aggregate rates in Bureau of Labor Statistics, *Employment and Earnings* (May 1988) for 202 MSAs.

$$u_{ij} = a_i + v_{ij}$$

for area effect a_i and where v_{ij} is a residual with the usual properties.[8] I use a two-stage procedure to fit this model, first estimating the magnitude of the MSA group correlations and then using generalised least squares to fit the model, as in Johnston (1984, 410–15). The results from both analyses are similar.[9]

5 Employment of recent male school leavers

As a starting point for assessing how local labour market tightness affects the employment of recent male school leavers, I tabulated employment–population ratios for recent male school leavers having 12 or fewer years of school completed and for those having 16 or more years of school completed across MSAs with 1987 aggregate unemployment rates of: below 4%; 4–5%; 5–6%; 6–7%; and of 7% or more. The ratios, given in Table 8.3, show a near-monotonic increase in employment/population for the less educated as area unemployment falls but only a slight increase in employment–population ratios as area unemployment falls for the more educated. While this is partly due to the metric used (the 91% employment–population ratio for college graduates in the high unemployment MSAs rules out large absolute increases in

Table 8.4. *Regression estimates (std errors) for the effect of area unemployment on employment of men who left school within 0–5 years, by education, 1987 and 1983*

	12/less years school			16/more years school		
	202 MSAs	45 MSAs		202 MSAs	45 MSAs	
Ind. var.	1987 (1)	1987 (2)	1983 (3)	1987 (4)	1987 (5)	1983 (6)
OLS estimates						
1987 *Une*	− 1.98 (0.26)	− 2.01 (0.68)	1.31 (0.57)	− 0.93 (0.29)	− 0.66 (0.60)	− 1.54 (4.16)
1983 *Une*	—	− 0.50 (0.40)	− 1.47 (0.34)	—	− 0.26 (0.35)	− 0.61 (0.27)
R^2	0.13	0.13	0.09	0.02	0.03	0.01
GLS estimates						
1987 *Une*	− 1.94 (0.34)	− 2.10 (3.61)	1.31 (0.60)	− 1.06 (0.44)	− 2.63 (2.56)	− 0.30 (0.59)
1983 *Une*	—	0.81 (2.20)	− 1.50 (0.36)	—	0.85 (1.52)	− 0.66 (0.37)
N	5357	3085	2712	2260	1471	1436

Note: The area unemployment rate is measured in actual units, not as percentage points, so that a 0.01 change represents a 1 percentage point change in area unemployment. Since the employment–population rate is also in actual units, the coefficients indicate that a 1 percentage point change in area unemployment has an effect on the percentage employed of a similar magnitude.

Source: Calculated from CPS files with additional explanatory variables: age, age-squared, actual grade completed, and a dummy variable for race. GLS estimates based on program provided by Alan Kreuger that uses the model set out in Johnson (1984, 410–16).

employment/population as labour market conditions tighten), it also presumably reflects the fact that the labour market for men with high school or less is more local in scope than that for college graduates. In any case, the difference in employment–population rates between more- and less-educated men is markedly less in areas with low unemployment than in areas with high unemployment.

Table 8.4 takes the analysis a step further by recording the estimated coefficients and standard errors of area unemployment on the 0–1 variable for whether an individual is employed, controlling for the individual's characteristics listed in the Note to Table 8.4. The upper panel of Table 8.4 gives regresson coefficients from OLS regressions.[10] The lower panel gives regression coefficients from GLS regressions. Column (1)'s estimates of the effect of 1987 area unemployment on the probability of employment in 1987 for men with high school or less education confirms the finding that less-educated young men have much greater chances of employment in areas with low aggregate unemployment rates. Here, the GLS coefficients in the bottom panel are similar to the OLS coefficients, and the estimated standard errors are only modestly higher than the OLS estimated standard errors, indicating that the intra-area correlation is modest.

Columns (2) and (3) of Table 8.4 probe the cross-section relation between area unemployment and youth employment for potential permanent omitted area factors that might confound the effect of current market conditions. Column (2) includes 1983 area unemployment as a determinant of 1987 employment while column (3) records the results of regressing 1983 employment on 1987 area unemployment and on 1983 area unemployment. Both are limited to 45 MSAs because the 1983 CPS contains data on only that number of areas. If the estimated effect of 1987 area unemployment represents the influence of current market conditions rather than of some stable omitted area characteristic, the coefficient on 1987 area unemployment should be more negative in the 1987 regression than in the 1983 regression. Similarly, the coefficient on 1983 area unemployment ought to be more negative in the 1983 regression than in the 1987 regression. Put differently, if 1987 local labour market conditions affect the employment of young men, the difference between the coefficients on 1987 unemployment rates in the two regressions ought to remove persistent omitted area factors and isolate the effect of current area unemployment on youth employment. As both the OLS and GLS calculations yield negative coefficients on current area unemployment and positive coefficients on area unemployment in the 'other' year, they support the causal interpretation of the cross-section pattern as reflecting the influence of current local labour market conditions on outcomes. The small number of MSAs in this analysis, however, produces high standard errors in the 1987 GLS calculations.

As for the effect of area unemployment on more-educated young men, the regressions on the right-hand side of Table 8.4 show a much weaker link between area unemployment and youth employment. In the regressions for the 202 MSA sample, the estimated effect of area unemployment on employment is roughly half the estimated effect for the less educated in column (1). The regressions for the smaller 45 MSA sample yield disparate coefficients with generally high standard errors. The conclusion I

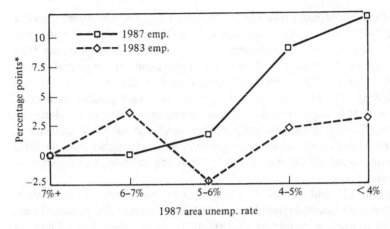

Figure 8.3   Estimated effect of 1987 area unemployment on the probability of employment for less-experienced men with high school or less education, 1987 and 1983

Note:
*Percentage point difference in probability of employment versus probability of employment in areas with > 7% unemployment.

Source:
Estimated from GLS regressions of employment on dummy variables for area rates of unemployment, with age, age squared, years of school completed and race as controls. The GLS takes account of the intra-area correlation of residuals.

reach is that differences in area unemployment rates are a significant factor in the employment–population rate of less-educated young men but not necessarily in that of more educated young men – as indicated in the means in Table 8.3. Roughly a 1 percentage point improvement in area unemployment reduces the employment–population differential among the young by 1 percentage point. Generalising from the cross-section to time series changes, this suggests that the increased unemployment rate from 1970–5 through 1976–87 contributed 2 percentage points to the increased differential in employment probabilities for the more and less educated.[11]

Finally, Figure 8.3 organises the data in a slightly different way to show, perhaps more dramatically, the effect of current area unemployment on the employment chances of less-educated youths. It records the estimated difference on a youth's probability of employment in 1987 and 1983 of being in labour markets with 1987 unemployment rates of < 4%, 4–5%, 5–6%, 6–7% (compared to the deleted group of > 7%). The estimates are obtained from regressions of the 0–1 employment variable on dummies for the area unemployment category and the personal characteristics of the youth. By measuring area unemployment in terms of dummy variables, this analysis captures potential non-linearities in the relation between area unemployment and youth employment. The 1987 figures show clearly the inverse association between 1987 youth employment and 1987 area unemployment among the less educated, while the 1983 figures show the lack of association between 1983 employment and 1987 area unemployment that leads me to conclude that the area unemployment–youth employment relation is a genuine one. The sharp rise in the effect of area unemployment on youth employment after 5–6% unemployment suggests a substantial non-linearity in the relation.

6   Area unemployment and earnings

Are the absolute and relative earnings of young less-educated men also sensitive to the aggregate unemployment rate in their local labour market? If so, are their earnings positively correlated with area unemployment, as Hall (1976) and others found to be true for all workers in the 1970s, or are their earnings negatively correlated with area unemployment, because demand factors dominate local labour markets?

To determine the impact of area unemployment on the earnings of less-educated young men and on their earnings relative to those of more-educated young men, I performed a set of analyses similar to those just described for youth employment. First, I regressed the *ln* of usual hourly earnings (= usual weekly earnings/usual hours worked) on a standard set of personal controls – age, age squared, years of schooling and race – and on the unemployment rate in the MSA in which the youth resided. The results of these calculations for the 202 MSA sample are given in columns (1) and (2) of Table 8.5. They reveal a significant inverse relation between area unemployment and the earnings of young less-educated men. They also show no relation between area unemployment and the earnings of young more-educated men. The difference between the estimated coefficients of area unemployment on the *ln* earnings of the two groups suggest that a 1 percentage point increase (0.01 units) in aggregate area unemployment reduces the earnings differential between the groups by 0.02 (GLS estimates) to 0.03 (OLS estimates) *ln* points. For MSAs with drastically different unemployment rates – for instance Boston and Detroit – this suggests that skill differentials will be some 0.08 to 0.12 *ln* points lower in the low-unemployment area. If changes in national unemployment had a similar effect on the earnings differential between the groups over time, a 2 percentage point lower national unemployment rate in the 1980s (the rate rose from 6.2% in the 1970s to 7.7% in 1981–7 would have produced a 0.04 to 0.06 point lower *ln*

Table 8.5. *Regression estimates (std errors) for the effect of 1987 and 1983 area unemployment on ln earnings of less- and more-educated men with less than 5 years of work experience*

Group*	202 MSAs 1987		45 MSAs 1987		45 MSAs 1983	
	LE12 (1)	GE16 (2)	LE12 (3)	GE16 (4)	LE12 (5)	GE16 (6)
OLS estimates						
Ind var						
1987 *Une*	− 3.20	− 0.10	− 3.54	3.00	1.91	1.42
	(0.28)	(0.64)	(0.71)	(1.27)	(0.65)	(1.07)
1983 *Une*	—	—	− 0.66	− 2.22	− 1.43	− 1.29
			(0.42)	(0.75)	(0.40)	(0.68)
R^2	0.21	0.06	0.22	0.09	0.20	0.07
GLS estimates						
1987 *Une*	− 2.71	− 0.33	− 3.22	3.09	1.83	1.37
	(0.49)	(0.86)	(1.28)	(1.87)	(1.04)	(1.04)
1983 *Une*	—	—	− 1.30	− 2.81	− 1.37	− 1.23
			(0.75)	(1.08)	(0.62)	(0.66)
N	3891	1983	2201	1285	2283	1303

Notes:
LE12 = men with 12 years of schooling or less.
GE16 = men with 16 years of schooling or more.
The area unemployment rate is measured in actual units, not as percentage points, so that a 0.01 change represents a 1 percentage point change in area unemployment.

Source: Calculated from CPS files with additional explanatory variables: age, age-squared, actual grade completed, and a dummy variable for race. GLS estimates based on program provided by Alan Kreuger that uses the model set out in Johnson (1984, 410–16).

earnings differential between the groups – offsetting 15%–20% of the massive rise in differentials in the 1980s.[12]

Probing the relation between area unemployment and youth earnings further, I regressed the *ln* earnings of less- and more-educated young men on 1987 and 1983 area unemployment rates (and other factors) in both 1987 and 1983 in the 45 MSA sample. Columns (3) and (5) of Table 8.5 give the results for the less-educated men. The coefficients on 1987 area unemployment in the 1987 *ln* earnings regression are negative while the coefficients on 1987 area unemployment in the 1983 *ln* earnings regression are positive. This pattern supports the claim that the cross-section regres-

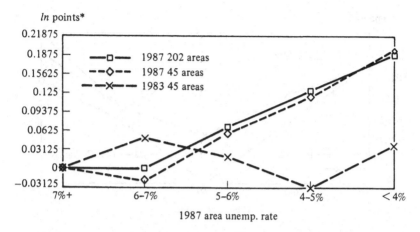

In points*

Figure 8.4 Estimated effect of 1987 area unemployment on *In* earnings for less-experienced men with high school or less education, 1987 and 1983
Note:
**In* point difference in *In* earnings in areas with > 7% unemployment.

Source:
Estimates from GLS regression of *In* earnings on dummy variable for area rates of unemployment, with age, age squared, years of school completed and race as controls. The GLS takes account of the intra-area correlation of residuals.

sions identify the effect of current labour market conditions on youth earnings rather than the effect of an omitted area factor. In fact, since 1987 unemployment rates were associated with higher *In* earnings in 1983, these results suggest that the cross-section estimates may understate rather than overstate the effect of current conditions on earnings. For young men with college education, by contrast, regressions of *In* earnings on 1987 and 1983 area unemployment yielded positive coefficients on 1987 unemployment rates and negative coefficients on 1983 unemployment rates. This is more indicative of an omitted area factor than of any true effect of local labour market conditions on earnings. Given the insignificant negative relation between area unemployment and the earnings of young college graduates in column (2) of Table 8.5, the safest conclusion is that the hourly earnings of college graduates do not depend on area unemployment rates.

As a final piece of CPS-based evidence that the earnings of less-educated recent labour market entrants are increased by tight labour market conditions absolutely and relative to the earnings of more-educated recent entrants, I have made the calculations in Figures 8.4 and 8.5. In Figures 8.4 and 8.5 the lines marked 1987 202 areas show the estimated

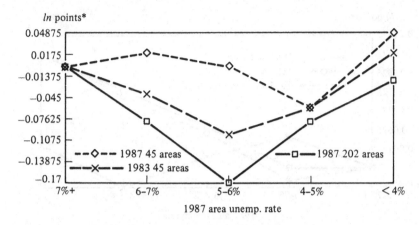

Figure 8.5   Estimated effect of 1987 area unemployment on *ln* earnings for males with college or greater education
Note:
**In* point difference in *ln* earnings in areas with > 7% unemployment.

Source:
Estimated from GLS regression of *ln* earnings on dummy variables for area rates of unemployment, with age, age squared, years of school completed and race as controls. The GLS takes account of the intra-area correlation of residuals.

effects on *ln* earnings of being in MSAs with the specified 1987 area unemployment rate group in the 202 MSA sample. They are obtained from GLS regressions of 1987 *ln* earnings on dummy variables for being in those markets and the workers' personal characteristics, taking account of intra-area correlation of residuals. The lines marked 1987 45 areas are based on comparable regressions of 1987 *ln* earnings for the 45 MSA sample. The lines marked 1983 45 areas are based on comparable regressions of 1983 *ln* earnings for the 45 MSA sample. The pattern in Figure 8.4 is clear: less-educated youths had markedly higher earnings in 1987 in areas with low 1987 unemployment rates but did not have higher earnings in those areas in 1983. Note, however, that for rates of area unemployment below 6–7% the wage curve is relatively linear, suggesting no markedly greater rise in earnings with declines in unemployment at lower than at higher levels. Figure 8.5 shows relatively little relation between the earnings of more educated youths and area unemployment rates.

7   Conclusion

The deterioration in the real and relative earnings of less-educated men in the United States in the 1980s was associated with a worsening of employment prospects for those men that began somewhat earlier. This implies that inward shifts in the demand for the less educated dominated movements down demand curves due to lower wages and that rising educational pay differentials understate the growing mismatch between demand and supply for labour skills in the United States. As less-educated young men had markedly higher earnings and employment–population ratios in local labour market areas with low unemployment rates compared to those with higher unemployment rates, the sluggish economic growth and upward drift in aggregate unemployment would appear to have contributed to the 1980s' deterioration in their earnings and employment. Extrapolating the estimated effects of area unemployment on the earnings and employment of men with 0–5 years of experience to the country as a whole suggests that a 2 percentage point lower aggregate unemployment rate in the 1980s would have eliminated about 15% of the observed rise in college–high school earnings differential and about 36% of the observed rise in the college–high school employment–population differential among those men. While the looseness of the labour market contributed to the problems of less-educated young men, however, the bulk of the growing labour market mismatch for less-experienced men with differing education is thus due to factors other than aggregate economic conditions (such as unionisation, minimum wages, changes in relative labour supplies, etc. – as stressed in Blackburn, Bloom and Freeman, 1990 and Murphy and Katz, 1990). The finding that wages are higher in areas with low unemployment is consistent with the Blanchflower–Oswald (1989) 'Wage Curve' found in other countries but runs counter to the 'Harris–Todaro' pattern of high unemployment in high wage cities found for the United States in the 1970s. This highlights the potential instability of the 'reduced form' geographic wage–unemployment locus, particularly in periods of structural economic changes.

In terms of future economic prospects, the finding that the economic position of less-educated young men is affected by the state of the local labour market suggests that if demographic changes produce the aggregate labour market shortages that many expect by the year 2000, the employment and earnings of young less-educated male labour market entrants will improve markedly. Such changes are, however, unlikely to do much for the lifetime incomes of those cohorts whose real earnings and employment deteriorated so greatly from the 1970s to the 1980s.

APPENDIX

The labour market model with migration consists of three equations:

Wage adjustment:
$$W' = \phi(D' - S')/(h + e) + (1 - \phi) W_o', \text{ with } 1 > \phi > 0 \tag{A1}$$

Migration: $S' = p(W' + E')$, with $p < = 1$, as derived in the text.   (A2)

Demand: $E' = D' - hW'$ (A3)

Solving yields:

$$W' = 1/V[\phi(1 - p)D' + (h + e)(1 - \phi)W'_o]$$ (A4)

$$E' - S' = 1/V[(1 - p)(e + h(1 - p\phi))D' \\ - (1 - \phi)(h + e)(p + (1 - p)h))W'_o]$$ (A5)

where $V = h(1 - p\phi) + e + p\phi > 0$

When migration has an infinite elasticity, $p = 1$ and the terms relating D' to W and to $E' - S'$ disappear. The only cause of differences in W and E/S are hence differences in W_o, which have opposite effects on wages and on employment–population.

When migration has a less than infinite elasticity, both demand and exogeneous wage-determining factors influence wages and employment–population rates, giving a locus whose shape depends on whether demand or exogenous wage shocks dominate the market.

NOTES

1 Bill Rodgers and Alida Castillo provided invaluable research assistance.

2 Calculated from Katz and Murphy (1990).

3 The magnitude of these changes depends modestly on the deflator used to translate money into real earnings. The figures in the text use the consumption deflator for GNP.

4 The Current Population Survey (CPS) is the basic household survey in the United States. It is a monthly sample of some 50–60,000 households and provides the basic information on employment and earnings of individuals used in government reports and academic studies.

5 I assume employment is on the demand curve for ease of analysis. While this is likely to be correct empirically, it is possible to modify the analysis to allow for other disequilibrium relations.

6 Since $(E/S)W$ is constant, $E' - S' + W' = 0$, which gives the expression $S' = W' + E'$ in the text.

7 For instance, among all 16–24-year-old male high school dropouts, the proportion working dropped from 71% to 66% from 1979 to 1987 and the proportion unemployed rose from 16% to 21%, after changing relatively moderately from 1973 to 1979. The data for recent high school graduates/dropouts show an actual rise in employment–population rates for dropouts and graduates who did not go to college from 1973 to 1979, followed by drops of 8–10 points from 1979 to 1986.

8 To do this I make use of a program written by Alan Kreuger that handles the unbalanced design of the data, with differing numbers of people in the different MSA cells.

9 In addition I estimated the effects of area unemployment on outcomes using a two-stage procedure in which I estimated area effects by adding area dummies to the individual outcome regressions and then regressed the coefficients on the dummies on the area unemployment rates. These results are similar to those reported in the study.

10 I also estimated comparable models using a logit specification and obtained analagous results. I report the linear model results for ease of presentation.

11 Unemployment averaged 5.4% from 1970–5 compared to 7.5% from 1976 to 1987, a 2.1 point differential. Multiplied by the near 1 point difference in the coefficients of area unemployment in the linear probability analysis, this difference implies an approximate 2 point increase in decadal employment-population rate differentials due to the weaker labour market of the 1980s. Note that the rise in the employment–population differential shown in Table 8.1 follows this time path, with the rise occurring between the early and late 1970s.

12 In the 1970s the earnings differential between college and high school men with 0–5 years of experience averaged 0.33 *ln* points, whereas by 1987 the differential was 0.63 *ln* points. See Katz and Murphy (1990). The figures in the text are obtained by dividing 0.04 and 0.06 by the 0.30 change in this period.

REFERENCES

Blackburn, McKinley, David Bloom and Richard Freeman (1990). 'The Declining Economic Position of Less-Skilled American Males', in G. Burtless (ed.) *A Future of Lousy Jobs?*, Washington: Brookings Institution.

Blanchflower, David and Andrew Oswald (1989). 'The Wage Curve', NBER Working Paper, **3181** (November).

Bound, John and George Johnson (1989). 'Changes in the Structure of Wages During the 1980s: An Evaluation of Alternative Explanations', NBER Working Paper, **2983** (May).

Hall, Robert (1976). 'Turnover in the Labor Force', *Brookings Papers on Economic Activity*, **3**, 709–64.

Harris, John R. and Michael P. Todaro (1970). 'Migration, Unemployment and Development: A Two-Sector Analysis', *American Economic Review*, **60**, 126–42.

Johnston, J. (1984). *Econometric Methods*, New York: McGraw-Hill, 3rd edn.

Katz, Larry and Kevin Murphy (1990). 'Changes in Relative Wages, 1963–87: Supply and Demand Factors' NBER Summer Workshop (August).

Katz, Larry and Ana L. Revenga, (1989). 'Changes in the Structure of Wages: The United States vs Japan', *Journal of the Japanese and International Economics*, **3** (**4**), 522–53.

Levy, Frank (1988). *Dollars and Dreams*, New York: Norton.

Marston, Stephen (1980). 'Anatomy of Persistent Local Unemployment', paper for the National Commission for Employment Policy Conference, Washington (October).

Moulton, Brent (1988). 'An illustration of a Pitfall in Estimating the Effects of Aggregate Variables on Micro Units', BLS Working Paper, **181**, Washington (April).

Murphy, Kevin and Finis Welch (1988). 'Wage Differentials in the 1980s: the role of international trade', paper presented at Mont Pelerin Society Meeting.

Reza, Ali (1978). 'Geographic Differences in Earnings and Unemployment Rates', *Review of Economics and Statistics*, **60**, 201–8.

Schwartzman, David (1989). 'Unemployment Among the Unskilled', New School for Social Research (November).

Discussion

M. BURDA

This study is a notable contribution to a growing literature on pay inequality in the United States, in that it confirms a deterioration of relative pay for less-skilled young males, as opposed to the college-educated, in the 1980s. Freeman's central conclusions are (1) adverse shifts to labour demand for low-skilled males, rather than the reduction of the real minimum wage, deregulation or union busting are responsible; (2) lower migration characterises the less-educated as opposed to the more skilled group; and (3) a generalised tightening of labour markets due to demographic changes forecast for the coming decade should improve the lot of the less skilled.

To my knowledge this study represents one of the first estimates of Blanchflower and Oswald's (1990) 'wage curve' with US data. As the Current Population Survey CPS data are arguably the best around, the potential value added of this effort is considerable. Implicit in the inclusion of a North American study in a largely European conference is the 'benchmark' value of the US experience. Despite its relatively stationary aggregate unemployment rate, the United States has also suffered its share of terms-of-trade shocks in low-tech manufacturing sectors, which if anything were worse due to their relatively high foreign exposure. The drop in relative wages recorded in the United States may have at least attenuated the decline in utilisation rates (rise in unemployment rates) compared with the Federal Republic of Germany, where relative wage dispersion at the 1-digit industry level has fallen since the mid-1970s (Burda and Sachs, 1988). One of the factors maintaining wage compression in the latter, or its absence in the former, may be the slopes of the respective supply curves.

The general interest of the findings does not, however, exonerate the study from the faults of the wage curve approach. One of the key differences of this study from that of Blanchflower and Oswald (1990) is that for the latter unemployment actually *causes* wage levels in an economic model; high local unemployment reduces the fallback of unions negotiating over wages with management, and thus reduces the Nash-bargained outcome. By contrast, unemployment and wages are both endogenously determined in Freeman's model. Why would local unemployment itself influence wage outcomes? That local unemployment is exogenous from an individual perspective does not eliminate the 'adding-up' constraint, or the possibility that a region-specific element of wages common to all individuals may be correlated with local unemployment.

Let me elaborate this point by setting out Freeman's estimating equation:

$$\text{Outcome}_i = \text{constant} + X_i\beta + \alpha U_j + a_j + \epsilon_i[+ FRC_j] \qquad (1)$$

where outcome$_i$ is either the dichotomous employment status or earnings of individual i, X_i is a vector of individual is' characteristics (age, age squared, years of schooling and race), β is the coefficient vector, a_j is a set of stochastic regional effects in region j where individual i resides, and FRC is an optional control for regional fixed effects.

Here I decompose the disturbance into a regional (a_j) and an individual ϵ_i) component. While Freeman attempts to control for fixed regional effects, he neglects the potential for trouble present in the stochastic region-specific component a_j.

Since the wage equation is in reduced form, the error term a_j is really a mixture of all unobservable characteristics of the jth region, and is likely to be correlated with the local unemployment rate unless the list of controls X is very large; this means omitted variable bias. I can think of several interpretations of the disturbance that will imply such a correlation. For instance, a_j might represent a regional labour demand shock: shifts in the regional terms of trade or aggregate demand, for example, which in many sensible models of wage determination would raise wages; it would also reduce local unemployment. In this case, the bias $\alpha - E\alpha$ given by $\alpha\text{cov}(a_j, u_j)$ is positive, so Freeman underestimates the actual effect. On the other hand, suppose that a_j is a shock to the local price level (recall that the left-hand side variable is the nominal wage) and is *positively* correlated with the unemployment rate. Here the resulting bias is negative, so the effect of local unemployment is overestimated.

Now consider a third possibility: a_j represents an aggregate demand shock. It raises the attractiveness of outside prospects relative to the local area and hence the net migration to other areas. This aggregate shock should *increase* the local wage at any local jobless rate. In this case, the bias is unclear, as it will be determined by the correlation of the aggregate shock with local unemployment.[1] Note that all three of these interpretations – and possibly others – could be operative at the same time, or with varying intensities.

The problem would be less severe if the sign of the correlation and the implied bias were unambiguous or bounded. The problem is that we have little guidance from theory. At best Freeman's wage equation is a semireduced form, with the 'effect' of local unemployment on wages in fact a mongrel parameter. In the parsimonious form that Freeman estimates, it is probably not stable over time either, given the various sources of omitted area shocks.[2] The lack of clear differentiation of shocks in a theoretical model of wage formation makes interpretation of the reduced form difficult, and I am somewhat sceptical – as is Freeman himself – about the confidence one can place in the estimates in predicting future outcomes.

I imagine that not all researchers will share my misgivings about the 'wage curve' and what we can learn from it. In addition to my remarks above, I have some general suggestions that might have improved the cogency of the study's results:

1. *Industry wage effects*   The work of Krueger and Summers (1988) has demonstrated a significant and robust industry effect on wages in the CPS data. The addition of industry dummies would eliminate, in my view, one of the most likely sources of omitted variable bias discussed above. If a high-wage industry is growing rapidly in a local area and contributing to a reduction of unemployment, then the omitted variable will be negatively correlated with a lower local unemployment rate and bias the estimated unemployment effect upwards; if the high-wage industry is contracting, then the correlation may be positive, leading to a negative bias on $\hat{\alpha}$.

2. *Women*   Freeman documents that utilisation rates are down for unskilled men and unchanged for skilled men, while aggregate unemployment is constant. The 'adding-up' constraint implies that other groups must have done better than average, and this leaves only skilled and unskilled *women*. It is a pity that women – whose labour force participation in the United States has risen dramatically since 1970 – were left out of the analysis. Indeed, unemployment rates for both black and white women aged 16–19 in the United States have fallen faster than those of their male counterparts since 1980. The adverse demand shift inferred for low-skilled men might be partly attributable to a steeper drop in unskilled women's real wages (which presumably enter the demand function for male workers with positive sign) or from increased willingness of employers to hire women, and low-skilled women in particular.

3. *Heteroscedasticity*   This is surely present in the error of the dichotomous employment outcome regressions, and the significance of this should be checked, by either employing more robust standard errors or examining comparable logit or probit estimates.

4. *Stability of the wage equation*   Since the evidence of Hall (1976) and others seemed to support the competing Harris–Todaro model during the 1970s, it would have been useful to conduct the same analysis for

a pair of representative years in the 1970s. A test for sub-sample stability on a pooled sample would be even more convincing than simply comparing estimates in each year. The stability of the fixed regional effect might also be tested, and I suspect that it would be rejected. Finally, the contention that the local unemployment effect is stronger for the less educated could be buttressed statistically by simply adding an interaction term between the local unemployment rate and a college dummy. Why these tests were not performed is, for me at least, somewhat puzzling.

5. *Marital status of workers* Here I am thinking of the labour force status of the spouse. Following Freeman's interpretation of his wage equations, the employment/wage outcome should be 'worse' for those with working spouses, since their better half could help absorb the shock and allow postponement of migration. Since the less educated tend to marry earlier, this may even explain part of the differential effect of local unemployment on wage outcomes. As some of the discussion at the January 1990 conference revealed, this issue has important implications for European migration, or the lack of it, and given the high quality of the US data merits further investigation.

Although I learned much from the study and appreciate its contribution to the inequality debate in the US, its fruit is not yet ripe for picking: I would be reticent to draw broad policy conclusions from the results.

NOTES

1 In addition, this raises an interesting issue of *interregional* (spatial) correlation in the regressions, which may affect the standard errors and thereby statistical inference. This should be distinguished from the intraregional correlations, for which Freeman corrects.

2 Incidentally, the existence of a stable wage equation is relevant for other studies in this volume which employ a measure of mismatch based on the presumption of a stable wage equation (e.g., Jackman, Layard and Savouri, Chapter 2 in this volume).

REFERENCES

Blanchflower, D. and A. Oswald (1990). 'The Wage Curve', *Scandinavian Journal of Economics* (forthcoming).

Burda, M. and J. Sachs (1988). 'Assessing High Unemployment in West Germany', *The World Economy*, **11**.

Hall, R. (1976). 'Turnover in the Labor Force', *Brookings Papers on Economic Activity*, **3**, 709–64.

Harris, J. and M. Todaro (1970). 'Migration, Unemployment and Development: A Two-Sector Analysis', *American Economic Review*, **60**, 126–142.

Krueger, A. and Summers, L. (1988). 'Efficiency Wages and the Interindustry Wage Structure', *Econometrica*, **56**.

9 Skill Mismatch, Training Systems and Equilibrium Unemployment: A Comparative Institutional Analysis[1]

DAVID SOSKICE

1 Introduction

Considerable work has now been done on the incorporation of comparative industrial relations institutions into the explanation of wage bargain outcomes and hence into macroeconomic models, as in Calmfors and Driffill (1988) and Jackman, Layard, Nickell and Wadhwani (1991) (hereafter JLNW). There is virtually no comparable work on the comparative role of education and training (ET) systems. This study is a preliminary attempt to see how the relations between ET systems, mismatch and equilibrium unemployment might fit into a simple version of the open economy model in Chapter 8 of JLNW.

The study draws first on the now substantial literature on comparative national ET systems (Sorge and Warner, 1980; Dore, 1987; Finegold and Soskice, 1988; Maurice, Sellier and Silvestre, 1986). To replicate as far as possible the country study chapters in this volume, section 3 looks at Germany, Japan, Sweden, the United Kingdom and the United States. The focus, as in much of the ET literature, is on the initial/further/and re/training of workers up to the technical level, thus leaving higher education aside. The consensus view in the literature is that Germany, Japan and Sweden have effective ET systems, while the United Kingdom and the United States do not. The literature on ET systems does not define 'effectiveness' clearly, but two criteria are implicitly used: first, the reduction of skills mismatch; and second, reflecting the preoccupation of policymakers with international competitiveness, the increased provision of skills needed for export success, and more generally a labour force which is well educated and trained. Attention has been shifting from the first to the second criterion; the ranking of cross-country effectiveness above refers to the provision of a well-educated labour force as much – as if not more than – to the reduction of mismatch. This is consistent with the limited aggregate national statistics on skill mismatch available. Some case can be made out for an inverse correlation between the consensus ordering of the effectiveness of national ET systems in the 1970s, but it is noticeably weaker in the 1980s.

The relation between the effectiveness of ET systems and equilibrium unemployment is only touched upon in the study by Jackman, Layard and Savouri (1990) (Chapter 2 in this volume, hereafter JLS). The implicit relation is that improved training reduces mismatch, and the reduction in mismatch – by lowering the bargained real wage at any given rate of aggregate unemployment – leads to a decline in the equilibrium rate of unemployment. The argument is developed in the context of a closed economy.

This study looks at the open economy. It adopts the framework set out in Chapter 8 of JLNW, where the minimum sustainable rate of unemployment is determined by the current balance of payments equilibrium condition as well as by real wage bargaining.

What is the relation between the effectiveness of ET systems and the balance of payments constraint? A considerable literature now argues that the key to the success in world (and domestic) markets of countries such as Germany, Japan and Sweden in the 1980s has been their ability to innovate rapidly in the production of high-quality and/or customised goods (see OECD, 1988 for a general survey and other references). It has been only as a result of the microprocessor that this has become possible across most industries, including what have traditionally been thought of as medium and low-tech; and across different sizes of firms. This ability has depended on cooperative forms of work organisation, often described as flexible specialisation, and in turn on a high skill level throughout most of the workforce in manufacturing. The maintenance of a competitive position in these markets has required considerable retraining as new or changing skills have been necessary. The ET systems of these countries provide a high level of secondary education for most of the population, publically and/or privately good initial vocational training and subsequent further training to meet changing skill needs. Abstracting from mismatch, these 'good' ET systems can thus be seen as reducing equilibrium (or minimal sustainable) unemployment through their role in easing the balance of payments constraints.

In what ways do ET systems affect mismatch, and what is the net overall effect on equilibrium unemployment? In two important ways, ET systems as in Germany, Japan and Sweden (hereafter GJS) improve mismatch, but in two other ways they make it worse. Mismatch is improved in these systems first, because they match closely the initial training with the skills requirements of companies. Second, GJS companies devote resources to retraining existing employees rather than hiring externally to meet changing skill requirements, and thus reduce the mismatch which occurs when the main resort is to external labour markets (at least, if wages are not fully flexible).

By contrast, however, these systems are prone to increase mismatch in two ways as a consequence both of the generally high level of skills provided and of the incentives which support the systems. First, the success of these systems in providing the labour forces for effective competition in world markets for high-quality goods has led to the need for more and more highly-qualified technicians and professionals, and this can frequently not be met by internal retraining. Whether or not the failure of GJS ET systems to meet these needs is contingent, it represents an important source of mismatch.

Second, if the unemployment rate for unskilled workers is high, it is difficult for these systems to reduce it. This is primarily because wages are insufficiently flexible, and that in turn reflects the needs of these systems to set up wage systems which reduce poaching. Thus in Germany and Sweden the fact that wages are collectively bargained across companies both reduces the ability of individual companies to offer inducements to skilled outsiders, and also limits the flexibility between skilled and unskilled wages across companies and regions. A contrast will, however, be drawn between these two systems and that of the Japanese, which permits greater flexibility at this point.

The relation between effectiveness of the ET system and mismatch has thus operated in a threefold way. (1) Increased effectiveness enables companies to operate in high-quality, innovative markets. (2) At a given level of innovation, increased effectiveness reduces mismatch, so long as the unskilled worker problem is not too acute. (3) But at a given level of effectiveness, there is greater mismatch the higher the level of innovation, as a result of the increased range of skills required. In consequence, the net relation between effectiveness and mismatch can go either way. The effect on equilibrium (or minimum sustainable) unemployment then depends on the balance of two effects: on mismatch and on the external balance. If, as many believe, these systems reduce mismatch, both effects go in the same direction and equilibrium unemployment is reduced; but they may go in different directions. This is set out in a simple development of the Layard–Nickell model in section 2. Section 3 sketches out the structure of incentives and institutions which support these systems and which do not exist in the United Kingdom and in the United States.

2   Mismatch, effectiveness of ET systems and equilibrium unemployment in a simple Layard–Nickell open economy framework

In this section a simple model is used to provide a framework for the main arguments of the study. We start by considering the relation between the effectiveness, e, of a training system, and the degree of mismatch, m. (Think at this stage of an increase in e as simply representing a move towards a GJS type of ET system.) Define by k the level of sophistication of products, or the degree of product innovation. Assume that given e, companies choose a level of k, so that $k = k(e)$ with $dk/de > 0$; this summarises the idea that companies need an effective ET system to engage in innovative markets. Next, assume that holding k constant, an increase in e will reduce mismatch, m; this arises both through the relation between the system of secondary education and of vocational training and of the skill requirements of employers and because the development of in-company training systems enables companies to retrain workers to meet their changing skill requirements. Finally, assume that the higher is k, the more advanced are the skills which companies foresee they will need to remain competitive and the greater their reliance on external labour markets to meet these needs; given e, the rise in k increases mismatch. Hence

$$m = m(e, k(e)) \tag{1}$$

with $m_e < 0$, $m_k > 0$ and $k_e > 0$ (where i_j is the partial derivative of i with respect to j).

So the net effect on mismatch of an improvement in e is unclear, and may go either way. A more effective training system enables companies to move up-market. This appears (in the 1980s) associated with an increased variance of skill requirements, and leads to increased mismatch, but the more effective system reduces the mismatch for any given variance.

In the closed economy model of Chapter 5 of JLNW the effect of increased efficiency of training on equilibrium unemployment operates via the effect on mismatch. Equilibrium unemployment equates the bargained real wage wb to the real wage determined by pricing behaviour, wp. wb depends on the aggregate unemployment rate u negatively and the rate of mismatch m positively; taking wp as constant, equilibrium unemployment u solves:

$$wp = wb(u, m) \tag{2}$$

Hence du/de has the same sign as dm/de: if an increase in training efficiency decreases net mismatch, equilibrium unemployment falls – since a lower rate of unemployment is needed to equate the bargained real wage with wp; but if net mismatch rises, then so too does the equilibrium rate of unemployment.

There are two ways to modify the model to escape this conclusion: one, which will not be followed in this study, is to make wb depend inversely on the quality of output, k. The alternative is to move to the open economy model in Chapter 8 of JLNW.

In the open economy model in its simplest form, the feasible real wage, wb, depends on the real exchange rate or price competitiveness, cp; (where the real wage is deflated by final expenditure prices):

$$wp(cp) = wb(\hat{u}, m) \tag{3}$$

This states that for a given level of price competitiveness there is a unique equilibrium rate of unemployment associated with a constant rate of inflation. Lower price competitiveness – a lower real cost of imports – increases the feasible consumption real wage, and hence permits a lower equilibrium unemployment rate.

The model is either closed, or a minimum constraint is put on equilibrium unemployment, by a condition relating to the external performance of the economy. The form which this constraint takes is a matter of debate, partly because it involves political perceptions as well as those of financial markets. Here we follow the suggestion of JLNW and suppose it to be the requirement that the current balance is in equilibrium,

$$B(cp, y(\hat{u}), y^*) = 0 \tag{4}$$

where B is the current balance, y is GDP and y^* is world GDP; $y(\hat{u})$ collapses the employment demand function and the definition of u.

It may be plausible alternatively to think of B as an inequality constraint,

$$B(cp, y(\hat{u}), y^*) > 0 \tag{5}$$

The interpretation of $\hat{u}$ which solves for $B = 0$ is then the minimum equilibrium rate of unemployment consistent with external equilibrium and a constant rate of inflation, as opposed to the unique equilibrium rate. This interpretation is more useful than the unique NAIRU in discussing countries like Germany and Japan.

Implicitly what is assumed by this interpretation is that (1) no countries can avoid inflationary pressure as a result of depreciation if they run prolonged external current deficits unless they have access to stable long-run sources of finance; and (2) countries can maintain a stable rate of inflation with a current account surplus for prolonged periods of time.

With this minimum equilibrium unemployment rate interpretation of $\hat{u}$, let us rewrite this simple version of the Layard–Nickell model to examine the relation between the effectiveness of training systems, e, and the minimum equilibrium rate of unemployment, $\hat{u}$. There is now a three-equation system with as before:

$$wp(cp) = wb(\hat{u}, m) \tag{3}$$

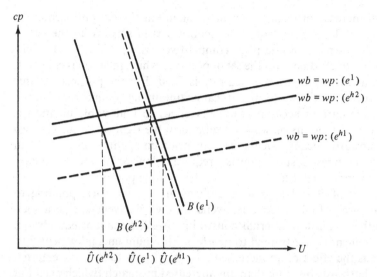

Figure 9.1   *B* and *wp* = *wb* schedules

and

$$m = m(e, k(e)) \tag{1}$$

In addition the external constraint now includes k as a measure of non-price competitiveness. Much work now points to non-price competitiveness as the key to understanding the successful export behaviour of countries like GSJ in the 1980s, reflecting their superior ability to innovate rapidly and/or produce differentiated, customised goods. Hence:

$$B(cp, k(e), y(\hat{u}), y^*) = 0 \tag{6}$$

In this three-equation system, an increase in training effectiveness will always reduce the minimum equilibrium unemployment rate if it reduces mismatch. For then it both improves price competitiveness, given u, from equation (3), and it directly improves non-price competitiveness, k. $\hat{u}$ also falls, even if mismatch increases, so long as the consequent worsening of price competitiveness does not offset the improvement to the external balance as a result of improved non-price competitiveness. Only when that condition fails does an improvement in training systems increase minimum sustainable unemployment.

This argument can be usefully put in a diagrammatic framework (Figure 9.1). The real exchange rate is measured on the vertical axis and unemployment on the horizontal. The external balance schedule, $B = 0$, is downward sloping – a fall in price competitiveness needing compensation from an increase in unemployment to maintain the current account in equilibrium. To the right of B the economy is in surplus, to the left in deficit. An increase in non-price competitiveness, k, shifts B to the left. The $wp = wb$ schedule gives the set of points at which inflation is constant, so long as the nominal exchange rate is fixed. For the purposes of this study, we assume that governments can maintain the nominal rate fixed so long as the current account is not in deficit; so that stable inflation is associated with points on $wp = wb$ on and to the right of $B = 0$. $wp = wb$ slopes upward because an increase in price competitiveness – i.e., an increase in the real cost of imports – requires a lower real wage and hence higher unemployment to reduce union bargaining power.

Three sets of B and $wp = wb$ schedules are drawn, corresponding to different levels of ET system effectiveness. Low effectiveness, e^1, is associated with the tightest external constraint, $B(e^1)$; minimum equilibrium unemployment is constrained to be $\hat{u}(e^1)$. Minimum unemployment falls so long as the effect of an increased e – e.g., e^{h2} – is to shift the external balance leftwards by more than any increased mismatch (which need not of course occur) shifts the $wb = wp$ schedule to the right. Only in a case like e^{h1} does the minimum equilibrium unemployment rise.

3   Comparative education and training systems

This section looks at the ET systems of five countries: Germany, Japan, Sweden, the United Kingdom and the United States. It is pretty much the consensus view of ET experts that, if higher education is set aside, the GJS ET systems are more effective than those in the United Kingdom and the United States. At a formal level the GJS systems are very different: it will be argued that their effectiveness results from their functioning in somewhat similar ways, and that they function in similar ways for broadly similar reasons. An analogous argument will be made for the British and American systems. The discussion will be at a general level, identifying a broad GJS model and a broad UK/US model. It will be argued here first that the structures of incentives both for companies and for workers have important similarities within each model, and suggested, second, that an understanding of these incentive-structure similarities lies in the power (or lack of it) of employer coordination and employer–government links, and to a lesser extent in the role of unions and of financial institutions.

An ET system for non-managerial and non-professional workers can be broken down, usefully if arbitrarily, into three components. (1) Initial education and training including secondary education to the age of 16 or 18 and subsequent initial vocational training, whether formal or informal and public- or company-based. (2) Formal or informal company-related retraining and/or further training while employed (whether or not it takes place within the company). (3) Non-company-related post-initial training designed to enable the recipient to move to other employment, particularly when redundancy is threatened or has taken place. Although it is customary to think of the latter as the centrepiece of at least the Swedish model, this emphasis is misplaced, and this study concentrates on the first two components.

3.1 Initial education and training

The incentives for individuals start in secondary school. In marked contrast to the United Kingdom and the United States, GJS all show relatively high scores on a range of subjects for the bottom two-thirds of the age group at age 16 and 18 (with Japan and Germany more successful than Sweden). Length of educational and initial training experience cannot by itself account for this: in Germany most young people stay at school until 16, then embark on a three- or four-year apprenticeship (about 10% of the age group drop out); in Japan about 95% of the age group stay in secondary school until 18, with a third in vocational secondary high schools, and then move on to employment with a major training content within companies; the Swedish system is in a process of change: currently 90% + stay in a comprehensive school until 18 or 19 with a large proportion doing vocational courses, closely linked to subsequent employment with further initial training. However in the American system also most young people stay in high school until 18 – even if in the United Kingdom 60% leave school at 16 and have little further effective training.

Many factors explain the difference in performance in these different systems. This study focuses on the role of long-term incentives to young people, as this is often underplayed. To understand the differences in performance it is necessary to appreciate the difference in incentives for young people between the two types of systems. In the GJS type, adequate performance in school is necessary and sufficient to gain access to broad-based training and (usually) long-term employment as a skilled worker. Links between schools and business are designed to give a large proportion of young people a clear bridge between the two, rather than one which relies on the uncertainties of the market. It is true for the majority of schoolchildren that a sustained improvement of individual performance is likely to lead to somewhat better training and employment prospects, to being accepted on a better training course and by a more prestigious company.

By contrast, in Britain and America, few employers open to young people the prospect of training followed by long-term skilled employment. Adequate performance at school is not seen as necessary to gain an unskilled or semi-skilled job. And, critically, individual improvements in performance for the majority of schoolchildren do not result in improved prospects for training and employment, unless the improvement gives access to higher education. (Of course other factors will enter into a full explanation of the failure of UK and US systems to provide an adequate education for those who do not go on to enter higher level occupations.)

Why do companies behave so differently in the two systems? There are four main reasons.

1. The larger the proportion of companies who have, and want to maintain, a predominantly skilled workforce, the greater will be the concern of companies to examine school credentials in order to hire the best-educated young people available; hence marginal improvement in school performance will marginally raise the quality of training and work on offer. In addition, the number of openings for training and subsequent skilled employment will increase; and where, as in GJS, the number is large, adequate performance in school will be likely to be rewarded. There is a strong incentive for companies to cultivate close relations with schools to ensure that they have good information about pupils.

   In the UK/US-type system, these incentives exist for a smaller proportion of companies. Where a company does want a skilled workforce, it is seldom a large enough employer in a local labour markt to give an adequate incentive to schoolchildren. With a large proportion of companies producing standardised goods and services, few are concerned with school credentials.

2. The benefits *less* the costs of training depend to a great extent on how good secondary education has been, on its seriousness and relevance. Hence there is a virtuous or vicious circle: where the secondary education system is good, employers have a strong incentive to train and maintain a highly-skilled workforce; in turn they have incentives to build close links with the educational system and thus provide the right incentives to schoolchildren to work hard and effectively at school. The circle works virtuously in the GJS-type systems and viciously in the UK/US-type.

3. Employer organisations or information coordination between employers (and to a much lesser extent between unions) play a critical role in GJS. Initial training in Germany – the dual apprenticeship system – provides certificated marketable skills, and Japanese initial training in companies (albeit technical on the job) generates quasi-marketable skills especially in large and medium-sized companies.

The Swedish case is slightly different since much of the initial training takes place at school: employer organisations are involved in curriculum development, but are not involved in directly pressuring or policing companies. In Germany, employer organisations play the leading role in the dual system, both in its development and in its policing; in particular at local level chambers of commerce pressure companies into taking enough apprentices to meet local educational needs (though there is some concern that this has led to a lowering of standards). In Japan large companies and zaibatsu play functionally similar roles: ensuring that the training is broad, and that enough new trainees get taken on. It is interesting that Matsushita, the one large Japanese company to adopt decentralised profit centres, retained control of training and personnel development as a central function.

Coordinated employers in GJS also make poaching difficult. The role played by payment systems in this respect has not been adequately appreciated. In Germany and Sweden, wages are determined by collective bargaining; this limits the ability of companies to offer inducements to poach workers with particular skills away from other employers. In Japan employers set tenure-related pay scales, although skills are taken into account: the incentive for workers to transfer is therefore limited. Neither type of system is in the interest of any individual employer, if others conform to these systems. Such payments systems thus require coordination among employers or powerful unions.

None of these arrangements hold in the United Kingdom or the United States, reflecting the inability of employers in these countries to give up power to representative bodies. In particular UK and US employers have much greater freedom to use wage incentives to bid skilled workers away from other companies.

4. For reasons which will be discussed at length below, GJS companies can credibly offer employment security, while UK/US companies cannot. Moreover, GJS companies are unlikely to offer subsequent possibilities for training and skilled employment, for corresponding reasons. There is thus a strong incentive for young people to move into employment at this stage in GJS economies. (As mentioned above, and as will be set out below, this leads to skill mismatch, since those who failed at school find it hard to get trained subsequently and hard to find unskilled work.) But these considerations do not apply to UK/US companies; even IBM and Kodak now find it difficult to offer employment security, and most companies are organised around increased numerical flexibility.

3.2   Further training in companies

We turn next to the incentive for employers in GJS economies to retrain workers in response to the need for new skills, rather than hiring new workers with appropriate skills and making existing workers redundant. There are two main reasons why GJS employers usually behave in this way.

1. First there is a straightforward profit-maximising reason. Where there is a high percentage of skilled workers, flexible systems of work organisation in the production of high-quality goods and services become possible and existing employees develop critical company-specific skills in work reorganisation. Moreover, so long as the new skills are related to existing skills, the cost of retraining well-educated workers may not be great. Reinforcing these considerations, the cost of finding workers with the needed skills may be high, particularly if poaching is ruled out by inability to offer appropriate inducements. The company will also wish to maintain a reputation for employment security to enable it to get good recruits.

2. Second, even if the balance of the above considerations comes out differently, there are complex institutional pressures against redundancies. Both coordinated employers and unions in GJS play a role in these pressures. Employment security is a public good in this type of system, since it reinforces educational incentives; more important, making redundancies costly reduces excess demand for skilled labour and the reduction of this excess demand is also a public good. There is, of course, a cost to making redundancies costly: necessary restructuring may be deterred. Institutional pressures in GJS-type systems take account of these conflicting aims, however imperfectly. In Germany the Works Council legislation requires agreement by the Works Council to a social plan in the event of threatened redundancies; national unions, to whom works councils are generally closely linked, can use this to put substantial costs on companies which they feel are not playing by the rules. Despite a decade in CDU government in the 1980s, the employer organisations have not sought seriously to change these provisions. In Sweden, the union movement changed its position on employment security in the early 1970s, from the 'right to manage' clause which had governed company level industrial relations since the Basic Agreement of the late 1930s, to being able to bargain over redundancies; this was reflected in legislation in 1974, modified slightly in 1982 (partly a symbolic gesture by the Social Democrats to reassure companies that it was not intended to prevent necessary restructuring). With over 90% unionisation and

virtually full employment the main blue-collar union has in principle great power as a result, but the power is used more to ensure that companies behave as 'good citizens' than to prevent redundancies in any blanket fashion. In both Germany and Sweden, the unions play their role normally in coordination with employer organisations at national, regional and local levels; indeed, without powerful employer organisations to reassure companies that unions will not abuse their position, it is difficult to see this sort of system working.

Japan operates somewhat differently. The importance attached to employment security stems from the largest companies and company groups. The public good incentives are similar, but internalised. Restructuring can take place within company groups, without too much disruption of a group reputation for employment security. But individual companies within a group would be liable to sanctions if they were seen to be refusing to retrain where it was feasible to do so and instead were trying to hire on the external market. Even outside groups, the cooperative links between large companies are such that not behaving as a good citizen – refusing to play one's part in retraining – would be a risky strategy.

By contrast in the United Kingdom and the United States few companies are constrained by the need to provide employment security, and in the 1980s the operation of UK and US financial markets has led many companies to adopt strategies of greater employment flexibility so as to minimise the potential damage to profits caused by adverse product market fluctuations.

4   Conclusions: problems of mismatch in GJS

GJS systems have the structure of incentives to provide a well-educated and continuously retrained labour force. As argued in section 2, this has enabled these countries to compete effectively in the world markets of the 1980s and thus to have low minimum sustainable unemployment rates. In the process, mismatch is reduced both in the bridge from school to employment and in the retraining of skilled workers within companies to meet changing skill needs.

But there are two problems of mismatch which do arise. First, the success of these countries in providing generally high-quality goods and services has exposed them to competition in product innovation, where preservation of market share requires increasing technical, technological and scientific skills; companies find themselves at the limits of their abilities to train up their own workforces to meet these needs. How this problem (of success) is resolved rests with the relation between companies and the higher educational system, rather than with the systems of training that have been described above.

The second problem of mismatch which may arise is that of high relative rates of unemployment among unskilled or less-skilled workers. With fixed skill wage differentials it is reasonable to suppose that the relative underlying demand for skilled labour rises over time; whether the implied increase in unskilled unemployment is avoided depends on three main factors, leaving aside measures to persuade the unemployed to leave the labour force:

1. The possibility of widening the skilled–unskilled wage differential.
2. The possibility of subsidising the employment of the unskilled, either by job creation in the public sector or by tax subsidies in the private.
3. The possibility of retraining the unskilled unemployed.

Retraining the unskilled unemployed is a costly option for several reasons. It generally requires basic education as well as vocational training. In addition, taking place later in life than initial education and training, it has a lower return. And there is a basic problem of system design: GJS-type systems rely on a strong incentive structure to perform well in school; an alternative easy route into good employment via later education and vocational training reduces those incentives.

To what extent can the skilled–unskilled wage differential be reduced in response to an increase in the relative unemployment rate of unskilled workers? There is a major difference between the external national union-based collective bargaining systems of Germany and Sweden and that of Japan. The wage systems in all three countries are highly coordinated, and fulfil two public good functions. The first, described above, is to reduce the incentive for the individual company to bid away skilled labour from other employers. The second is better known: to provide overall wage restraint for the economy in the interests of maintaining international competitiveness.

All three systems fulfil, at least partially, these two functions; while the Japanese operates primarily through coordination between large employers, the German and Swedish work via coordination by national unions as well as by employer organisations. Coordination across national unions causes great problems of securing consent, especially when both more- and less-skilled workers are recruited. It is for this reason that unions in both countries lay stress on some form of egalitarianism. This may take the form – as it still tenuously does in Sweden – of a wages policy geared to a reduction of differentials, or of a tacit agreement between unions that percentage wage increases will be roughly equal across industries, as in Germany. Thus in Sweden and Germany, widening of skill differentials is held back by union policies, themselves important for the maintenance of wage systems which support the functions of restraint and effective training.

In Japan, despite the more limited role played by external unions, there is still a need to gain a wide consensus for wage restraint. Company unions representing skilled workers in large, profitable companies are less weak than is often made out; wage increases are typically less than could be achieved if large company unions were to bargain unrestrictedly. An important element of the consensus is that percentage increases are very similar across large companies – where the bargaining power lies. But because the consensus does not need to include less-skilled workers, there is more potential flexibility in the wage differential between skilled and unskilled workers.

Japan appears less constrained than Germany and Sweden in dealing with this source of mismatch via wage flexibility. This perhaps explains why Germany, and particularly Sweden, has had more resort to public sector job creation and subsidisation to deal with the unemployed unskilled. Why Sweden more than Germany? Part of the answer in the 1980s is political: there was a conservative government in Germany but not in Sweden for most of the decade. But there is also an institutional argument. Ultimately the unions have to pay with additional wage restraint for the resources devoted to job creation. Swedish unions have a stronger interest in agreeing to such restraint, in the Swedish case, the single encompassing blue-collar union stands to gain as members unemployed unskilled workers who become employed in the public sector, an argument reinforced by the high rate of unionisation in Sweden. By contrast in Germany, individual industrial unions have much more limited incentives – in particular, since there is a much lower unionisation rate. And in both countries a slow growth of (pre-restraint) real wages makes wage restraint in the interest of the unemployed harder to sell to members. For all these reasons the German–Swedish version of the GJS-type system may be prey to high rates of unemployment among the skilled as a potential source of mismatch.

NOTE

1 I am indebted for helpful comments to Katherine Abraham, Fiorella Padoa Schioppa, Ronald Schetkatt and to the participants at the January 1990 conference.

REFERENCES

Calmfors, L. and J. Driffill (1988). 'Bargaining Structure, Corporatism and Macroeconomic Performance', *Economic Policy*, 6.

Dore, R. (1987). *Taking Japan Seriously*, London: Athlone Press.
Finegold, D. and D. Soskice (1988). 'The Failure of Training in Britain. Analysis and Prescription', *Oxford Review of Economic Policy*, **4(3)** (November).
Jackman, R., R. Layard and S. Savouri (1990). 'Mismatch: A Framework for Thought' (Chapter 2 in this volume).
Jackman, R., R. Layard, S. Nickell and S. Wadwhani (1991). *Unemployment*, Oxford: Oxford University Press.
Maurice, M., F. Sellier and J. J. Silvestre (1986). *The Social Foundation of Economic Power*, Cambridge, Mass.: MIT Press.
OECD (1988). *New Technologies in the 1990s* (Report of a Group of Experts on the Social Aspects of New Technologies), Paris: OECD.
Sorge, A. and M. Warner (1980). 'Manpower Training, Manufacturing Organization and Workplace Relations in Great Britain and West Germany', *British Journal of Industrial Relations*, **18**.

Discussion[1]

LEONARDO FELLI

David Soskice's study highlights some interesting ideas on employment and training (ET) programmes and their effect on mismatch. I will begin by considering the structure of Soskice's presentation.

The first half of the study makes a methodological point. It suggests that, in an open economy framework, an *effective* ET programme may have an ambiguous influence on the level of skill mismatch of the economy. This because an effective ET programme, on the one hand, increases workers' skills, reducing mismatch but, on the other, may induce firms to move to product markets that require workers with higher skills, in this way increasing mismatch. In spite of this result, effective ET programmes have an uncontroversial negative effect on the equilibrium level of unemployment. Soskice suggests this last variable as the key indicator of the effectiveness of an ET programme.

The second part of the study presents an analysis of the interaction between the institutional structure of ET programmes and their effectiveness. Soskice's analysis suggests that ET programmes can be structured in two ways. Programmes may be offered by the government to prospective workers before their entrance in the job market, in the form of secondary or professional education. Alternatively, they may be offered by each firm according to its needs with some, or no, subsidies from the central authority.

Soskice argues that, according to his definition of effectiveness, the best ET programmes are the ones of the first type. Such programmes exist in countries like Germany, Japan or Sweden (GJS). In contrast, the ET programmes observed in countries like the United Kingdom or the United States (UKUS) have the characteristics of the second class of programme described above, and seem to be less effective in reducing the equilibrium rate of unemployment.

In the final section of the study, Soskice argues that an effective pre-job education is always accompanied by good retraining of employees. Therefore, to the extent that ET programmes are effective, they are characterised by low labour mobility.

Soskice's study is certainly quite interesting as an analysis of the effectiveness of ET programmes in reducing the equilibrium rate of unemployment. However, it fails to give a general and systematic analysis of the role of ET programme and their interaction with the phenomenon of mismatch and so leaves a number of questions unanswered, and sometimes not even posed.

1   A missing question

I think that the primary concern of a research project aimed at analysing the impact of training programmes on mismatch should be to test whether ET programmes are the right instrument to reduce the low level of mismatch in the economy. The natural starting point for an answer to such a question is a definition of mismatch: as has been highlighted in Padoa Schioppa (1990) (Chapter 1 in this volume) and Jackman, Layard and Savouri (Chapter 2 in this volume), this is a relevant problem that does not have an exhaustive treatment in the existing literature. A second step in this project – once a definition of mismatch has been chosen – would be to analyse the effect of ET programmes on this variable. With reference to Soskice's model, this would imply a justification of the existence of the mismatch function $m(k, e)$ and an explanation of the economic factors that are imbedded in the variable e (effectiveness of ET programmes) which determines both the function $m(.,.)$ and the degree of product innovation $k(e)$. In a closed economy framework, a sketch of an analysis, in line with the research project just presented, can be found in section 5 of Jackman, Layard and Savouri (1990) (Chapter 2 in this volume).

2   A screening interpretation

Suppose now that we accept the idea that an ET programme can help to reduce the level of mismatch in the economy; the next problem is then how to implement such a programme. I will follow Soskice's classification of ET programmes; on one side, there are GJS programmes that stress the crucial importance of the role of secondary (and, in general, pre-job) education. On the other, there are UKUS programmes that are privately offered by each firm according to its own needs. Different institutional and incentive structures are associated with different types of programmes. Soskice argues that GJS programmes are characterised by higher incentives for prospective workers to perform well in their pre-job education, and by a stronger incentive for firms to keep close ties with the educational system. The implications are higher average job tenure, low number of quits or layoffs and a limited possibility for individuals that perform well in the training period to have a new chance to improve their situation later, during their job. On the other hand, UKUS systems are characterised by no incentive for prospective workers to perform well in their secondary education (unless their objective is college education) and by no firms' interest in the schooling or pre-job training of prospective workers. Here the implications are higher job turnover, higher level of mismatch, the existence of poaching of workers from other firms and, in general, a higher level of equilibrium unemployment.

I think that the interaction between the institutional characteristics of the two kinds of ET systems previously described and the functioning of the labour market deserves a more systematic analysis. I will present below an alternative, but observationally equivalent, interpretation of such a link. Let us assume that the main purpose of ET programmes is to help firms to screen the unobservable individual productivity of workers. In reality, the ET programmes also help to increase the workers' firm-specific or general human capital, but it may be simpler to leave aside this second aspect and concentrate completely on the implications of the first.

The main characteristic of ET programmes offered in countries such as GJS is that this screening activity is done mainly in the pre-job education, so that the schooling system supplies good information on the productivity of the prospective workers when they enter the job market. In other words, labour is closer to an *inspection good* – to use Jovanovic's (1979) terminology – and the quality of the match between the firm and the worker may be correctly foreseen by looking at the school performance of the worker. If we add to these characteristics of the pre-job training a good information network on the vacancies that firms offer, then job security, low turnover, no poaching and similar facts are no surprise. Both firms and workers can concentrate the search activity for the best match to the pre-job market period and leave the workers' activity unaffected by the learning process on the quality of the firm/worker match. In particular, it is clear why companies here will be unlikely to revise their information on workers' productivity if they have failed to be selected by the schooling system.

This is not true for the UKUS ET system. In this case, a firm cannot count on pre-job training to get useful information on workers' productivity, but it has to use its own (or eventually other firms') screening procedures, that may well be represented by a privately supplied ET programme. Job security cannot be guaranteed by firms and poaching activity is an efficient way in which a firm can try to use other firms' screening devices. A firm can try to hire a worker that has already been selected by a different firm ET programme and whose ability is better known. Labour is then an *experience good*: the only way to know the quality of a particular match is to try it.

This screening interpretation of ET programmes is clearly partial, but it can account for the basic implications described by Soskice and for the fact that GJS programmes seem to be more effective than UKUS programmes. In fact, if we accept the interpretation I have just presented, information about workers' productivity is made readily available, in the GJS system, by the pre-job training and can be easily accessed by each interested firm. On the contrary, in the UKUS system information is privately produced by each firm; this implies a slower learning process, a duplication of learning activity by firms – and, most of all, a higher level of mismatch and equilibrium unemployment.

It is natural at this point to wonder how the suggested screening interpretation extends to the case in which we assume that training – and especially retraining – programmes increase the workers' human capital. In this case, the effects previously described coexist with a higher incentive for firms to retrain skilled workers rather than poaching them from other firms. In fact if, to accumulate firm-specific human capital, a worker has to exert some form of unobservable effort, then the only way to induce him to exert such an effort will be through job tenure and low labour mobility; otherwise any incentive for the worker to invest on the match with the firm in which he is employed disappears.

3   Cooperative vs. non-cooperative institutions

The final step in any analysis of ET programmes and their effect on mismatch needs to account for the reason why there are such different institutional characteristics – pre-job training or retraining programmes – in the two groups of countries mentioned in section 2.

Soskice's thesis suggests that the rationale of different training programmes should be found in the fact that in one group of countries (GJS) there is a cooperative behaviour of firms and unions, while in the other the behaviour is non-cooperative.

In my opinion, this is still not a satisfactory explanation, since it leaves open the problem of why in GJS countries the outcome of firms'/unions' behaviour is cooperative while this is not true for UKUS countries. A satisfactory answer to this primary question requires us to model the labour market institutions of these two groups of countries.

4   Conclusion

I conclude with two additional observations. I think that a study that makes such strong claims on the characteristics of different countries' ET programmes should provide some supporting empirical evidence: the screening interpretation presented in this Discussion could offer an interesting empirical test.

A final econometric comment: Soskice's definition of effectiveness, though interesting, does not seem to be a useful empirical measure. In fact, I think it is difficult to capture, ina data set, the contribution of ET programmes to the reduction of the equilibrium level of unemployment. A test of the effect of an ET programme on the level of mismatch, controlling for job skills, seems to me a feasible econometric test that takes care of the possible effects of an ET programme on the firm's production decision.

NOTE

1 I am indebted to Giuseppe Bertola, Andrea Ichino and Fiorella Padoa Schioppa for helpful comments and discussions.

REFERENCES

Jovanovic, B. (1979). 'Job Matching and the Theory of Turnover', *Journal of Political Economy*, **87**, 972–90.
Jackman, R., R. Layard and S. Savouri (1990). 'Mismatch: A Framework for Thought' (Chapter 2 in this volume).
Padoa Schioppa, F. (1990). 'A Cross-country Comparison of Sectoral Mismatch in the 1980s' (Chapter 1 in this volume).

10 Unemployment, Vacancies and Labour Market Programmes: Swedish Evidence[1]

PER-ANDERS EDIN and
BERTIL HOLMLUND

1 Introduction

Research on European unemployment over the past two decades has frequently claimed that European labour markets have become less 'flexible'. Evidence of more severe labour market rigidities is often revealed by outward shifts of the Beveridge curve – i.e., the relationship between unemployment and vacancy rates (the u/v curve). The British experience of a huge increase in unemployment at given vacancy rates is especially striking, but outward shifts of the Beveridge curve have been typical rather than exceptional in Europe since the early 1970s. As a broad generalisation, it seems as if labour markets with substantial increases in unemployment have experienced outward u/v shifts as well. In contrast to what has happened in most other European countries, the u/v curve in Sweden has proved to be a relatively stable relationship since the late 1960s.

The interpretations of u/v shifts have been diverse and often tentative; hypotheses of increasing sectoral imbalances across industries, regions, or occupations ('mismatch') have been launched, but found only limited support (Jackman and Roper, 1987). Other researchers have paid attention to declining search effort and the role of long-term unemployment (Budd, Levine and Smith, 1988; Jackman, Layard and Pissarides, 1989).

This study focuses on the role of labour market programmes in the process of matching workers and jobs in the Swedish labour market; labour market policies come in many guises, but it is useful for our purposes to ignore the differences and focus on the common features. The programmes are arrangements whereby the government attempts to cushion labour market shocks, and they may also involve training in order to facilitate future employment prospects; the Swedish temporary public jobs ('relief jobs') and manpower training programmes are obvious examples. Such programmes may be thought of as representing a particular labour market state, in addition to the usual classifications of workers as either employed, unemployed, or out of the labour force. Workers in relief jobs are classified as 'employed' in Sweden, whereas participants in training programmes are considered as 'out of the labour force'; the distinction between workers in relief jobs and the unemployed is not sharp, however. Relief jobs have limited duration (less than 6 months), and are conceived as stepping stones to regular employment; relief workers are supposed to be available for placements in regular jobs, and engaged in active search for such jobs.

How, then, does government intervention in the form of labour market programmes affect labour market transitions? The programmes influence the matching of workers and jobs via many different routes, and we can illustrate only a few here. First, there is the obvious direct effect on unemployment outflow: new (temporary) jobs or training opportunities reduce the duration of unemployment analogous to the effects of a general labour market improvement. A number of other effects may potentially offset – or reinforce – the outflow effect. The temporary nature of the programmes may involve a substantial risk of re-entry into unemployment. The mirror image of this re-entry risk is the probability of a successful transition from a programme to regular employment. Programme-to-employment transition probabilities are increased by search effort while in programmes, and by any skill-enhancing training that the programmes may provide. Whether or not programme participation facilitates transitions to regular employment is *a priori* unclear, however, and has to be resolved by empirical analysis. Our study is an attempt to offer evidence on this matter.

The first issue we address is whether workers in relief jobs can be regarded as perfect substitutes for the unemployed concerning job search and transitions to regular jobs. Do workers in relief jobs enter regular employment at the same pace as workers in unemployment? The relevance of this issue is obvious from a Swedish perspective: Swedish labour market policy has clearly stated objectives to facilitate job search and job placements among workers in relief jobs; such jobs are not provided with the intention of enhancing workers' skills.

Manpower training programmes are different in this respect, however; the primary objective here is skill improvement – i.e., to provide training so as to improve *future* labour market prospects. The study's second main issue concerns this question: does programme participation in the past facilitate an unemployed worker's re-employment?

Although relief jobs and manpower training programmes have different stated objectives, the differences should not be exaggerated. It is conceivable that relief jobs provide some useful training, thereby improving a participant's future labour market career; it is also conceivable that training programmes offer little more than a temporary escape from unemployment. Whether or not relief jobs and training programmes have different effects is, therefore, ultimately an empirical issue. Despite the importance of these programmes in Swedish labour market policy, available evidence regarding the effects of the programmes is surprisingly scant. In a recent survey, Björklund (1990) concludes that available research provides no conclusive evidence on the relationship between the Swedish labour market policy and unemployment.

We begin in section 2 with a brief review of some facts of relevance, including an investigation of the Swedish Beveridge curve. Section 3 proceeds to time series analyses of labour market 'matching' in Sweden, the key issue being whether programme participants can be regarded as perfect substitutes for the unemployed as job searchers. We first outline a simple framework in which search efforts among programme participants influence the equilibrium unemployment rate. The next step involves estimation of matching functions, relating new hires to the number of vacancies and the number of unemployed (and other measures of the pool of job searchers). Matching functions are estimated for the aggregate labour market and for manufacturing. The results indicate that workers in relief jobs do not contribute to the flow of hirings to the same extent as workers in open unemployment.

Section 4 turns to microevidence, using two different longitudinal data sets. A number of duration equations are estimated, explaining transitions to regular employment. The issue in focus is whether it is useful to think of programme participation – and relief jobs in particular – as a behaviourally distinct labour force state. Our findings are largely consistent with the time series evidence: relief workers appear to enter regular employment at a slower pace than the unemployed. These behavioural differences may reflect the fact that relief workers are less active searchers than the unemployed – indeed, available evidence on workers' search effort in the two states show that relief workers search less intensively than the unemployed.

Section 4 also includes attempts to examine the programmes' effects on the participants' *future* labour market prospects. By and large, the results suggest that past programme participation is conducive to future employment prospects.

2   Background

2.1   Unemployment and labour market programmes

The Swedish unemployment rate, as measured by labour force surveys, has fluctuated in a narrow band between 1 and 3.5% since the early 1960s (Figure 10.1). There is a slight trend increase in unemployment, however;

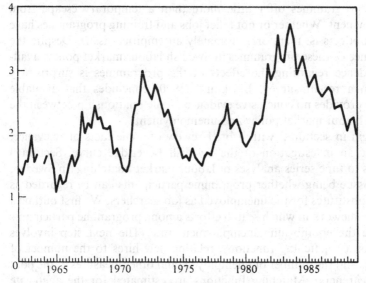

Figure 10.1   The Swedish unemployment rate, %, 1962–88
Note: Data is seasonally adjusted.

Sources: See Appendix.

the cyclical peaks in the 1970s involved lower unemployment than the peaks in the 1980s, and the same holds for the slumps. Seemingly minor changes in measurements techniques from 1987 and onwards have reduced recorded unemployment figures by roughly 0.5 percentage points. (The unemployment series in Figure 10.1 is adjusted so that it confirms to the old definition.)

The weak trend increase in the unemployment rate is driven by an increase in unemployment duration, whereas unemployment inflow has displayed a trend decline from the mid-1960s to the late 1970s, with some reversal of this trend in the 1980s. The average duration of completed unemployment spells was around 7 weeks in the late 1960s, whereas it approached 15 weeks in the mid-1980s. The share of long-term unemployment, measured by the ratio between the number of people unemployed more than 6 months and total unemployment, has increased from 6% in 1965 to 27% in 1985. The fraction of unemployed individuals with more than a year's unemployment experience has not exceeded 10%, however, and this is an exceptionally low number by comparison with some unemployment-ridden European countries.

The modest increase in open unemployment since the early 1960s is accompanied by an increase in the number of persons in various labour

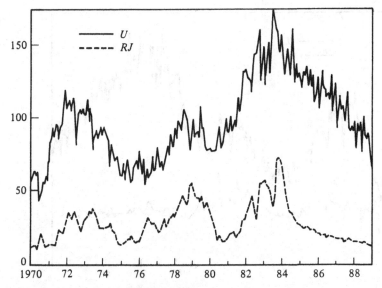

Figure 10.2   Workers unemployed (U) and in relief jobs (RJ), thousands, 1970–88
Note: Data is seasonally adjusted.

Sources: See Appendix.

market programmes. The programmes vary in scope and objectives, some attempting primarily to facilitate matching and labour mobility, others designed to provide employment opportunities for handicapped people. Two of the oldest and most comprehensive programmes are *temporary public jobs* (relief jobs) and *manpower training*, respectively. Figure 10.2 confirms a marked cyclical pattern in the number of relief jobs, whereas the cyclical pattern is less clear for manpower training in Figure 10.3. The government has used temporary public employment as a main counter-cyclical device, attempting to adjust to the ups and downs of the business cycle. Most relief jobs are in the public sector, but a system of recruitment subsidies to the private sector has many features in common with temporary public jobs. The workers engaged in relief jobs are paid market wages.

Manpower training courses typically last less than 6 months, and the eligibility criterion is that the person is unemployed, or is at risk of becoming unemployed. Participants in training programmes receive a stipend corresonding to the unemployment benefit level. (Persons not qualified for regular unemployment insurance receive lower amounts.)

Relief jobs respond to movements in the economy-wide unemployment rate, whereas the counter-cyclical pattern is very weak for training

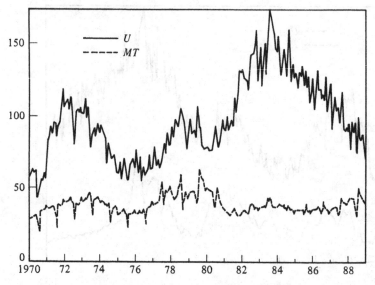

Figure 10.3 Workers unemployed (*U*) and in training programmes (*MT*), thousands, 1970–88
Note: Data is seasonally adjusted.

Sources: See Appendix.

programmes. Table 10.1 presents results of regressons where the number of participants in each programme is explained by lagged unemployment and a time trend. The long-run response of relief jobs to unemployment is close to 0.5; an increase in the number of unemployed by 10,000 persons is thus associated with a rise in the number of relief jobs by 5000.[2] Manpower training, by contrast, does not exhibit much responsiveness to movements in unemployment.

Relief jobs typically last for 6 months, but workers in such jobs are supposed to be 'available' for regular employment; the programmes can be abolished when the labour market improves, and workers are supposed to be engaged in search for regular jobs. Not much is known about the extent and intensity of search among relief workers; Table 10.2 gives some information from a small sample of (initially) unemployed youth in the Stockholm area in the early 1980s. The unemployed spend on average 7 hours on active search, whereas workers in relief jobs search less than an hour. There is also a clear difference between the groups with respect to the number of search methods used.

Labour market programmes appear to be an important 'destination' for exits out of unemployment. Table 10.3 shows a decomposition of

Table 10.1. *Unemployment and labour market programmes: Sweden, 1970–88; dependent variables RJ$_t$ (workers in relief jobs and MT$_t$ (participants in training)*

	RJ_t			MT_t		
	(1)	(2)	(3)	(4)	(5)	(6)
U_{t-1}	0.342	0.045	0.091	−0.017	0.003	0.046
	(9.891)	(4.089)	(6.391)	(0.969)	(0.263)	(2.408)
RJ_{t-1}		1.432	1.314			
		(24.691)	(24.068)			
RJ_{t-2}		−0.519	−0.488			
		(9.083)	(9.195)			
MT_{t-1}					0.541	1.016
					(8.228)	(16.614)
MT_{t-2}					0.300	−0.394
					(4.597)	(6.360)
Time	−0.059	−0.010	−0.019	0.010	−0.0007	−0.008
	(4.117)	(2.591)	(3.229)	(1.360)	(0.157)	(0.985)
Long-run effect of unemployment		0.47	0.52		0.02	0.12
Seasonal dummies	Yes	Yes	No	Yes	Yes	No
R^2	0.465	0.961	0.908	0.715	0.899	0.630
s.e.	11.828	3.220	4.797	6.158	3.676	6.871
DW	0.21	1.95	2.05	0.45	2.06	2.00
LM(6)	151.08	3.01	3.39	65.95	3.85	3.17

Notes: Absolute values of t-ratios in parentheses. The sample period is 1970: 3–1988: 12. LM(6) is the F-form of a Lagrange multiplier test for autocorrelation up to the 6th order.

unemployment outflow based on the registered unemployment pool at the employment exchange offices. Relief jobs and manpower training programmes have accounted for 26% and 23% of the outflow during 1987 and 1988, respectively (when the unemployment rate has been unusually low).

2.2 On vacancies

Sweden has had compulsory notification of vacancies to the public employment exchange offices since the late 1970s; jobs of very short duration are excluded. Compulsory notification was regarded as a way of

Table 10.2. *Search effort among unemployed, programme participants and employed*

	Hours of search per week	Number of search methods used
Unemployed (*n* = 900)	7.2	3.1
Relief workers (*n* = 76)	0.7	0.6
Training participants (*n* = 31)	0.6	0.5
Employed (*n* = 647)	0.8	0.4

Source: Own computations from the Stockholm Youth Survey (Holmlund and Kashefi, 1987).

facilitating job search and improving job matching; it is an open question, however, whether the legislation on compulsory notification has had much effect on actual notification behaviour. An early evaluation (SOU, 1978: 60) indicated a substantial increase in notification, but comparisons of different series of labour shortages, vacancies and new hires do not indicate any changes in notification behaviour, at least in the manufacturing sector (Holmlund, 1986).

An investigation in the mid-1970s (UPI, 1974) found that approximately 60% of the total number of vacancies were notified to the employment exchange offices. More recent investigations arrive at similar estimates (Lundin and Larhed, 1985). The emloyment exchange offices' coverage of vacancies advertised in newspapers is higher, however; estimates for 1987

Table 10.3. *Unemployment outflow, by destination, %, 1984–8*

	1984	1985	1986	1987	1988
Re-employed (incl. recalls)	36.7	40.5	41.8	43.8	47.2
Training and relief jobs	35.4	28.6	26.9	26.3	23.3
Other reasons	17.1	19.4	19.7	18.7	17.6
Attrition	10.8	11.5	11.6	11.2	11.9

Source: Own computations from the National Labour Market Board unemployment register.

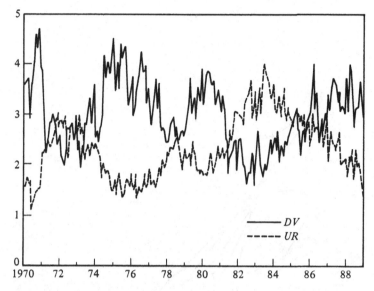

Figure 10.4   The duration of vacancies (*DV*, weeks), and the rate of unemployment (*UR*, %), thousands, 1970–88
Note: Data is seasonally adjusted.
Sources: See Appendix.

suggest that the coverage is 90% on average, and close to 100% in regions outside the three biggest cities (Farm, 1989).

Most registered vacancies expire through a job–worker match – i.e., there are relatively few 'discouraged vacancies'. Only 10% of the posted vacancies are withdrawn because of failure to find a suitable applicant (Farm, 1989). The average duration of registered vacancies has varied in a range around 2 to 4 weeks since the mid-1960s. Figure 10.4 gives a stylised picture of fluctuations over time in the duration of vacancies. We have used monthly data and computed the ratio between unfilled and new vacancies (with the flow expressed on a weekly basis). The cyclical pattern is marked, with the stock/flow ratio increasing when unemployment falls. In Sweden, as in other countries, the average duration of vacancies is much shorter than the average duration of unemployment (cf. Abraham, 1983, who reports evidence from Canada and the United States of vacancy durations somewhere between 5 and 15 days).

2.3   The Beveridge curve

The Swedish unemployment rate has not increased since the late 1960s if we control for movements in the vacancy rate.[3] This is confirmed by

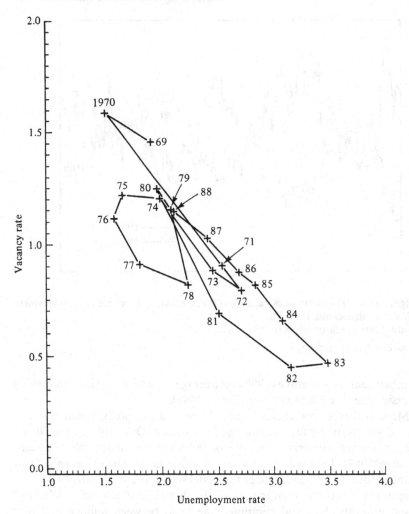

Figure 10.5   The Swedish Beveridge curve, 1969–88

visual inspection of Figure 10.5, and by regression results in Table 10.4. We use seasonally unadjusted quarterly data, choose a log-linear functional form, and allow for some dynamics. The aggregate unemployment rate (u) as well as the (registered) aggregate vacancy rate (v) are defined in terms of the labour force. A trend term is included to test for structural shifts over time.

The trend term is insignificantly different from zero, and we also note that the lagged dependent variable is highly significant. Lagged adjust-

Table 10.4. *The Swedish Beveridge curve; estimation period 70: 2–86: 4; dependent variable:* $\ln u_t$

	OLS		TSLS ($\ln v_t$ endogenous)	
	(1)	(2)	(3)	(4)
Constant	0.068	0.070	0.065	0.063
	(1.398)	(1.279)	(1.318)	(1.141)
$\ln u_{t-1}$	0.796	0.797	0.816	0.814
	(11.871)	(11.497)	(11.588)	(11.297)
$\ln v_t$	− 0.261	− 0.261	− 0.204	− 0.208
	(6.070)	(5.981)	(3.043)	(3.053)
$\ln v_{t-1}$	0.125	0.125	0.092	0.095
	(2.431)	(2.404)	(1.535)	(1.577)
Trend		$- 0.5 \times 10^{-4}$		$- 0.5 \times 10^{-4}$
		(0.077)		(0.075)
Long-run elasticity w.r.t. the vacancy rate	− 0.67	− 0.67	− 0.61	− 0.61
R^2	0.927	0.927		
s.e.	0.076	0.077	0.077	0.078
DW	2.062	2.066	1.963	1.967
LM(5)	0.79	0.79	0.64	0.68

Notes: Absolute values of t-ratios in parentheses. Three seasonal dummies are included; the intercept refers to the fourth quarter. LM(5) is a Lagrange multiplier test (F-form) for serial correlation up to the 5th order. The instruments used in TSLS are: $\ln v_{t-2}$, $\ln v_{t-3}$, $\ln v_{t-4}$, $\ln u_{t-2}$, $\ln u_{t-3}$, $\ln u_{t-4}$.

ment implies loops in the u/v space, as suggested in the early model by Phelps (1971) as well as in later contributions by, for example, Pissarides (1985). It is noteworthy that the estimated steady-state elasticity of the unemployment rate with respect to the vacancy rate is close to the estimates for the UK reported by Budd, Levine and Smith (1988).

The estimates in Table 10.4 allows us to calculate the unemployment rate at which the vacancy rate equals the unemployment rate. Using the estimates from column (1) or (3) of Table 10.4, allowing for the seasonal dummies, and assuming a notification rate of 60%, we arrive at 1.9% as the annual average unemployment rate at which the vacancy rate is equal to the unemployment rate. By comparison, Abraham (1983) draws on available US sources and concludes that an unemployment-to-vacancy ratio of unity corresponds to an unemployment rate of 3% in the United States. Both calculations are subject to substantial uncertainty, but taken at face values the numbers suggest that frictional/structural unemployment (as conventionally measured) is somewhat higher in the United States than in Sweden.

The Beveridge curve bears a close relationship to the aggregate hiring function, as has been noted by, *inter alia*, Blanchard and Diamond (1989). We proceed by presenting a simple model of vacancies and hirings, along the lines of Johnson and Layard (1986). The model offers an example of how temporary public jobs, and search effort among programme participants, may influence equilibrium unemployment. The effect operates via the hiring function.

3   Macroevidence on matching

3.1   A framework

We consider an economy where firms set wages and can influence quits and new hires by the choice of (relative) wages. Flow equilibrium at the level of the ith firm requires that quits are balanced by new hires – i.e.,

$$q_i N_i = h_i N_i \tag{1}$$

where q_i is the quit rate, h_i is the new hire rate, and N_i is employment. The quit rate is taken to be decreasing in the firm's relative wage and in the ratio between the aggregate number of unemployed and vacancies. Hence,

$$q_i = q(R_i, U/V) \quad q_1, q_2 < 0 \tag{2}$$

where $R_i \equiv w_i/w$ is the relative wage, w the average wage, and U and V are the number of unemployed and vacancies, respectively.

The firm's new hire rate depends on its vacancy rate (V_i/N_i) and on the probability of filling a vacancy (θ). The latter is taken to depend positively on the relative wage as well as the ratio between the aggregate number of searchers (S) and the number of vacancies – i.e.,

$$h_i = \theta(R_i, S/V) \frac{V_i}{N_i} \quad \theta_1, \theta_2 > 0 \tag{3}$$

The number of searchers includes a proportion (c_1) of the unemployed and a proportion (c_2) of workers in temporary public jobs (P), so we have $S = c_1 U + c_2 P$.

The firm's profit per worker is given by

$$\pi_i/N_i = \gamma - R_i w(1 + t) - \phi(1 + V_i/N_i), \tag{4}$$

where γ is the (constant) marginal product of labour, t is the payroll tax rate, and ϕ is the capital cost per workplace. Expression (4) can be rewritten as

$$\pi_i/N_i = \gamma - R_i w(1 + t) - \phi[1 + q_i(\cdot)/\theta_i(\cdot)] \tag{5}$$

and the first-order condition for the firm's profit-maximising wage takes the form

$$w(1 + t) = \phi[q_i(\cdot)/\theta_i(\cdot)] \eta \tag{6}$$

where η is the sum of the absolute elasticities of q and θ with respect to the relative wage.

In a symmetric general equilibrium we have zero profits with $R_i = R = 1$ and $V_i/N_i = V/N$. Using equation (6) together with the zero-profit condition and the flow equilibrium constraint ($qN = \theta V$) yields

$$\gamma = \phi[1 + (\eta + 1)(V/N)] \tag{7}$$

Equation (7) determines the vacancy rate if we assume η to be constant. To determine unemployment we make use of the aggregate flow equilibrium constraint

$$q(1, U/V) = \theta[1, (c_1 U + c_2 P)/V](V/N). \tag{8}$$

By dividing through by N we obtain a relationship between U/N and P/N, given the vacancy rate. The higher is P/N, the smaller is U/N so long as programme participants are engaged in active search – i.e.,

$$U/N = g(P/N) \qquad g'(\cdot) \le 0 \quad \text{as} \quad c_2 \ge 0 \tag{9}$$

The labour force is fixed and the labour force identity is given as

$$L \equiv N + U + P \tag{10}$$

which can be written as

$$L \equiv N + Ng(P/N) + P \tag{11}$$

The effect of programmes on private sector employment is thus given by

$$\frac{\partial N}{\partial P} = -\frac{1 + g'(\cdot)}{1 + (U/N) - (P/N)g'(\cdot)} \tag{12}$$

which is approximately -1 when unemployment is low and programme participants don't search – i.e., when $g'(\cdot) = 0$. This special case thus corresponds to complete crowding out; an increase in public employment reduces private employment by the same order of magnitude. The effect on unemployment is given by

$$\frac{\partial U}{\partial P} = -\frac{\partial N}{\partial P} - 1 \tag{13}$$

The higher is search effort among programme participants, the less crowding out of private sector employment and the greater the impact of the programmes on equilibrium unemployment. The tax increase needed to finance temporary public employment does not affect unemployment; it is clear from the zero-profit condition that labour cost, $w(1 + t)$, is determined once the vacancy rate is determined. Any tax increase is fully offset by a corresponding fall in the wage rate.

3.2   Empirical matching functions

Our empirical work focuses on how the flow of new hires is affected by unemployment and other components of the pool of searchers, such as workers in labour market programmes. Data on registered stocks and flows of vacancies are used to calculate the aggregate outflow of vacancies. We use the identity

$$V_t - V_{t-1} \equiv IV_t - OV_t, \tag{14}$$

where IV_t is the inflow and OV_t is the outflow of vacancies.

The Labour Market Board (AMS) provides series on stocks and inflow of vacancies, and the outflow is calculated by using the identity above (see Appendix for details on the data). As already noted, the available evidence indicates that the major part of the outflow of vacancies is associated with hirings. For manufacturing there is a series on new hires of blue-collar workers available on a monthly basis. This series is based on surveys to employers. We will examine movements in the aggregate outflow of vacancies (OV) as well as the number of new hires (H) in manufacturing.

Table 10.5 and Table 10.6 present estimates of basic matching functions, using the stock of vacancies (beginning of month) and the stock of unemployment (middle of the previous month) as explanatory variables.[4] For manufacturing we consider two alternative measures of unemployment – unemployment in manufacturing occupations according to the labour force surveys, and unemployment among insured blue-collar workers.

Turning to Table 10.5 first, we note that both vacancies and unemployment matters for hirings; there is a significant trend decline in hirings,

Table 10.5. *Estimates of aggregate matching functions: Sweden, 1970–88; dependent variable: ln OV$_t$*

	1970: 2–1986: 12		1970: 2–1988: 12	
	(1)	(2)	(3)	(4)
ln V_t	0.528	0.556	0.516	0.558
	(20.725)	(23.229)	(22.139)	(23.516)
ln U_{t-1}	0.148	0.268	0.131	0.234
	(4.818)	(7.963)	(4.515)	(6.758)
Time		-0.71×10^{-3}		-0.49×10^{-3}
		(5.903)		(4.907)
R^2	0.900	0.916	0.898	0.908
s.e.	0.080	0.073	0.081	0.077
DW	1.29	1.55	1.33	1.48

Notes: Absolute values of *t*-ratios in parentheses. Seasonal dummies are included.

holding vacancies and unemployment constant. Some moderate experimentation with the dynamic specification did not indicate that important lags were omitted. The estimates suggested that the matching function was characterised by decreasing rather than constant returns to scale in vacancies and unemployment.

In the hiring equations for manufacturing we must allow for lagged adjustment in order to avoid substantial autocorrelation in the residuals. Returns to scale is close to unity in the *long* run in these dynamic specifications. There are no interesting differences across equations with different measures of unemployment. Again, there is a trend decline in hirings, holding constant the number of vacancies and the number of unemployed.

Some British studies have argued that the long-term unemployed may expend little search effort, and the Beveridge curve may thus be influenced by the duration structure of unemployment. We have captured long-term unemployment by the number of unemployed more than 27 weeks, whereas the usual British practice is to focus on the group with more than a year of unemployment. Our attempts to test for unemployment composition effects (not reported) have been largely unsuccessful, however. We have not been able to pin down the coefficient on long-term unemployment with any precision.

Table 10.7 presents estimates of specification which allow the pool of searchers to include participants in labour market programmes. The estimated equation is of the form

Table 10.6. *Hirings in Swedish manufacturing, 1969–87; dependent variable: ln H_t (new hires, blue-collar workers)*

	1969: 3–1986: 12			1969: 3–1987: 12		
	(1)	(2)	(3)	(4)	(5)	(6)
ln V_{t-1}^m	0.644	0.542	0.196	0.664	0.544	0.204
	(32.601)	(18.446)	(4.553)	(24.071)	(20.747)	(4.908)
ln U_{t-1}^m	0.472	0.377	0.154			
	(9.227)	(7.086)	(3.129)			
ln U_{t-1}^{ui}				0.328	0.401	0.161
				(5.244)	(7.557)	(3.218)
Time		− 0.001	− 0.0004		− 0.002	− 0.0008
		(4.516)	(1.560)		(9.581)	(3.128)
ln H_{t-1}			0.504			0.507
			(6.963)			(7.180)
ln H_{t-2}			0.135			0.122
			(1.891)			(1.748)
Long-run elasticities:						
$\partial \ln H / \partial \ln V$			0.54			0.55
$\partial \ln H / \partial \ln U$			0.43			0.43
R^2	0.912	0.920	0.947	0.888	0.922	0.947
s.e.	0.179	0.171	0.140	0.199	0.166	0.138
DW	1.03	1.04	2.05	0.72	1.01	2.03
LM(6)	11.25	11.13	1.94	26.79	12.07	2.23

Notes: Absolute values of t-ratios in parentheses. Seasonal dummies are included. V^m is vacancies in manufacturing industry, U^m is unemployment insurance funds for blue-collar workers in mining and manufacturing. LM(6) is a Lagrange multiplier test (F-form) for autocorrelation up to the 6th order.

$$\ln OV_t = \alpha_0 + \alpha_1 \ln V_{t-1} + \alpha_2 \ln\{\beta_U U_{t-1} + \beta_T MT_{t-1} + \beta_R RJ_{t-1}\} + \gamma \text{Time} + \epsilon_t \tag{15}$$

with $\beta_U = 1$ imposed. The estimation displayed in column (1) of Table 10.7 imposes the assumption that the unemployed are perfect substitutes for workers in training programmes and relief jobs, a restriction that is relaxed in the estimations shown in the other columns. The message from column (2), where the maintained hypothesis is $\beta_T = \beta_R$, is that workers in programmes are imperfect substitutes for the unemployed; a larger pool of programme participants contribute to a somewhat larger flow of hirings, but the effect is only one-half of the effect arising from the unemployed. Column (3) contains the most general specification, allowing the two types of programmes to have different effects. We cannot reject that workers in training programmes are perfect substitutes for the

Table 10.7. *Matching and labour market programmes: Sweden, 1970–88;*
dependent variables $\ln OV_t$ *(outflow of vacancies)*

	(1)	(2)	(3)	(4)
$\hat{\alpha}_1$	0.558	0.568	0.566	0.571
(Vacancies)	(23.516)	(24.061)	(23.354)	(23.818)
$\hat{\alpha}_2$	0.234	0.282	0.290	0.249
(Unemployment +	(6.758)	(7.461)	(6.503)	(7.169)
Programmes)				
β_U	1^c	1^c	1^c	1^c
(Unemployment)				
β_T	1^c	0.450	0.570	0^c
(Training		(2.406)	(1.437)	
programmes)		[2.941]	[1.086]	
β_R	1^c	0.450	0.391	0.528
(Relief jobs)		(2.406)	(1.491)	(2.109)
		[2.941]	[2.324]	[1.888]
$\hat{\gamma}$	-0.49×10^{-3}	-0.48×10^{-3}	-0.48×10^{-3}	-0.46×10^{-3}
(Time)	(4.907)	(4.784)	(4.749)	(4.608)
R^2	0.908	0.912	0.912	0.907
s.e.	0.077	0.075	0.075	0.076
DW	1.48	1.53	1.53	1.51

Notes: The estimated model is given by equation (15). Seasonal dummies are included. Superscript c denotes a constrained coefficient. The restriction $\beta_T = \beta_R$ is imposed in column (2). Absolute values of t-ratios in parentheses and brackets; tests for coefficients equal to unity in brackets. The sample period is 70: 2–88: 12.

unemployed, but we can reject that relief workers are perfect substitutes for the unemployed.

The interpretation of these results is not entirely straightforward. Perfect substitutability between unemployed workers and workers in training programmes may reflect active job search among programme participants and a high propensity to quit the programmes as job offers arrive. Another hypothesis – perhaps more plausible – is that the link between the flow of hirings and the number of persons in training programmes operates through the regular outflow of newly trained workers (with completed training courses). The larger the number of persons in training programmes, the larger in general the number of trainees that complete their courses during any given month.

One plausible explanation of the trend decline in hirings is unemployment compensation; another is employment protection legislation. There has been a trend increase in replacement ratios since the mid-1960s, presumably with some effects on unemployment duration (see the investigation by Björklund and Holmlund, 1989). The Employment Protection Act from 1974 (LAS, Lagen om anställningsskydd) requires 'just cause' (saklig grund) for dismissals, thereby raising the explicit or implicit costs of firing workers. Employers are likely to respond by becoming more selective in their recruitment decisions, and studies from the late 1970s indicate that employment protection did indeed reduce hirings at a given level of vacancies and unemployment (Holmlund, 1978a). The legislation was revised in 1982, however, making it generally more easy for employers to hire and fire. Uncertainty about a job applicant's productivity can be reduced by making use of a 6-month probationary contract.

We have experimented with two variables capturing employment protection legislation and unemployment compensation: a dummy for the period 1974:7–1982:3 (when the stricter version of the employment protection law was in operation), and series on replacement ratios for workers covered by unemployment insurance. Both variables entered with negative coefficients as would be expected, although only the employment protection dummy was significant. A specification where both these variables are replaced with a single time trend is however clearly superior (in terms of the equation's standard error). We are thus unable to produce precise estimates of the effects of employment protection and more generous unemployment benefits, but some induced decline in the flow of hirings has almost certainly occurred. It is notable that the negative trend coefficient in the hiring equation does not translate into an outward shift of the Beveridge curve. The reason seems to be the decline in unemployment inflow, which has offset outward shifts due to increases in unemployment duration.

This concludes our examination of the aggregate evidence. The results indicate that workers in relief jobs are imperfect substitutes for workers in open unemployment as far as hirings are concerned. Although relief jobs reduce regular employment, there is not complete crowding out. A larger pool of programme participants increases the flow of hirings into regular jobs which, according to our theoretical framework, implies that relief jobs contribute to a lower equilibrium unemployment rate.

4   Microevidence on labour market transitions

In this section we analyse transitions between employment, unemployment and labour market programmes in two different longitudinal data sets. The key issue in this analysis is whether it is reasonable to treat relief jobs as a behaviourally distinct labour market state; this emphasis on relief jobs is dictated by the very small number of transitions to other labour market programmes in our data sets. Finally, we will report some preliminary evidence on the existence of 'occurrence effects' of labour market programmes (and unemployment). Does previous participation in relief jobs and training programmes have any effect on the future reemployment probabilities of the unemployed? This question is central in any attempt to evaluate Swedish labour market policy.

4.1 The data

The two data sets utilised in this section both contain detailed information on individual labour market histories for more than four years, but the nature of the samples are widely different. The first data set (the 'Stockholm youth sample') is based on interviews with about 900 youths (age 16–24) registered as unemployed with the employment exchange offices in the county of Stockholm at the end of January 1981. Interviews were carried out twice in 1981, once in 1982, and a fourth interview was conducted in 1985; for further details, see Holmlund and Kashefi (1987). The second data set (the 'Displaced worker sample') is based on register data covering about 300 workers displaced due to the closing of a pulp plant in a small town in the north of Sweden in 1977. The register data, obtained from the local employment exchange office, was used to construct continuous time labour market histories for the time from the advance notification of the plant closure in early 1976 to late 1981; see Edin (1988). These two samples thus include individuals in very different situations in the labour market. The main advantage with the samples is that both groups show a high mobility in the labour market, and in particular that they are two groups which are extensively involved in various public labour market programmes.

The very different situations of the two samples are illustrated by Table 10.8, which reports some descriptive statistics. The Stockholm youth sample consists of young (21 years) individuals with less than two years' work experience on average. The average individual in the displaced worker sample, on the other hand, is middle-aged (39 years) and had almost 12 years of tenure before displacement. Another difference is that while the youth sample is equally distributed by gender, only 12% of the displaced workers are females. The proportion of foreign citizens is also much higher in the youth sample – 22% compared to 6% among the displaced workers.

In the bottom lines of Table 10.9 we find some information on the unemployment and relief job spells recorded in the data. The Stockholm youth sample contains 1451 unemployment spells and 262 relief job spells; the corresponding figures for the displaced worker sample are 578 unemployment spells and 167 relief job spells. The mean unemployment

Table 10.8. *Characteristics of the sample*

| | Stockholm youth | | Displaced workers | |
	Mean	Std dev.	Mean	Std dev.
Age	20.74	2.51	38.62	15.86
Female[a]	0.52		0.12	
Foreign citizen[a]	0.22		0.06	
Months of experience	23.55	21.20	—	
Gymnasium[a] (Senior High School)	0.33		0.33	
University[a]	0.05		—	
Cash benefits[a]	0.14		—	
Unemployment benefits[a]	0.07		—	
Non-labour income[a]	0.48		—	
Dependents[a]	0.30		—	
Married[a]	—		0.55	
Children[a]	—		0.29	
Health problem[a]	—		0.13	
Pre-displacement seniority (years)	—		11.89	14.90
ln (pre-displacement wage) (weekly)	—		6.91	0.37
No. of individuals	830		307	

Notes: Time varying variables refer to first interview and date of displacement, respectively. Superscript *a* denotes dummy variables. Unemployment benefits refer to regular unemployment insurance benefits (with a replacement ratio up to 0.9). Individuals not eligible for regular benefits may receive Cash Benefits (kontant arbetsmarknadsstöd, KAS), a much lower amount than regular benefits. Dependents indicate that other persons (mostly the spouse or children) depend financially on the survey respondent. Non-labour income refers to individuals whose main source of income is spouse or parents.

duration is almost identical (around 15 weeks) in the two samples. Turning to the mean duration of relief jobs we find that mean duration is much shorter in the displaced worker sample (16 weeks) than in the youth sample (27 weeks); this latter figure is actually longer than the stipulated maximum duration for relief jobs. The explanation for this large figure is threefold: first, we are not able to distinguish one long spell from two shorter spells; second, some temporary relief jobs may actually be longer than 6 months; and third, some spells of (permanent) sheltered jobs are classified as temporary relief jobs in the youth sample. The first two points apply to both samples, implying that we overestimate relief job duration, while the third point is unique to the Stockholm youth sample, and may

Table 10.9. *Recorded transitions out of unemployment and out of relief jobs, by destination, %*

Origin	Sample Stockholm youth unemployment	Relief job	Displaced workers unemployment	Relief job
Destination:				
Employment	62.1	26.7	47.9	10.8
Permanent	21.2	7.6	27.0	4.2
Temporary	40.9	19.1	20.9	6.6
Relief job	13.5	—	27.5	—
Training	5.0	5.0	7.9	5.4
Unemployment	—	38.5	—	68.9
Out of labour force	12.8	20.9	10.0	6.6
Censored	6.5	8.8	6.6	8.4
Σ	99.9	99.9	99.9	100.1
No. of spells	1451	262	578	167
Duration (weeks)	15.40	27.29	14.90	16.33

thus be part of the explanation of the large differences in relief job duration between the samples.

Even though the mean duration of unemployment is similar in the two samples, Table 10.9 shows that the pattern of exits from unemployment differs substantially between the samples. The youth unemployment spells are terminated through transitions to employment to a much larger extent (62%) than displaced worker unemployment spells (48%). This difference is due to transitions to temporary employment being twice as common in the youth sample. This low proportion of transitions to employment among the displaced workers is 'compensated' by the proportion of transitions to labour market programmes being twice as high: actually, more than a third of the unemployment spells in the displaced worker sample are terminated through transitions to programmes.

Turning to exits out of relief jobs, we find that only a small proportion of spells end with a transition to employment: 27% of the youth relief job spells and 11% of the displaced worker spells. Instead, the bulk of exits from relief jobs is to unemployment: more than one-third of all relief job spells in the youth sample and two-thirds in the displaced worker sample end with a transition to unemployment. We also find that a fairly large number (21%) of relief job spells among youth end in withdrawals from the labour force.

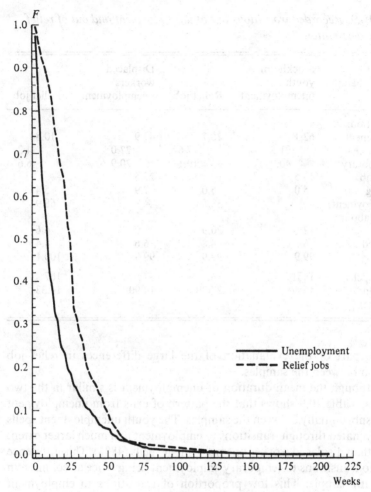

Figure 10.6   Kaplan–Meier survivor function estimate: Stockholm youth sample

To provide some information on the sample distributions of the duration of spells in unemployment and relief jobs, Figure 10.6 reports the Kaplan–Meier survivor function estimate in the Stockholm youth sample. (See, for example, Kalbfleisch and Prentice, 1980, 13.) The figure reveals much lower exit rates from relief jobs than from unemployment. Such a difference is not present in Figure 10.7 which shows the corresonding estimates for the displaced worker sample. Comparing the estimated unemployment survivor functions for the two samples, we find they track each other extremely well.

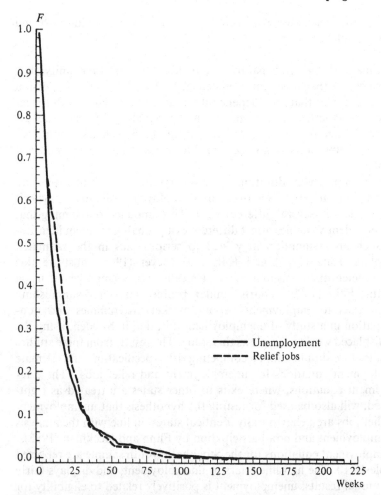

Figure 10.7   Kaplan–Meier survivor function estimate: displaced worker sample

4.2   Are unemployment and relief jobs behaviourally distinct states?

To investigate the determinants of unemployment duration and relief job duration in both of our samples, we report estimates of standard reduced form duration models.[5] We estimate the location-scale version of the familiar Weibull duration model – i.e.:

$$ln\, T = \beta'X + \sigma W \tag{16}$$

where $\sigma = 1/\alpha$ and $\beta = -\sigma\beta^*$. W has an extreme value distribution, α is the standard Weibull hazard function duration dependence parameter, and β^* is the 'regression parameter' (see, for example, Kalbfleisch and Prentice, 1980, 33).

An estimate of the scale parameter, σ, less (greater) than unity thus implies positive (negative) duration dependence, and a positive regression coefficient implies that an independent variable is associated with longer duration. As independent variables in the estimated equations we include personal characteristics,[6] and also a measure of labour market tightness, the ratio between the number of vacancies and the number of unemployed.

Many unemployment duration equations reported in the literature are estimated ignoring the fact that an unemployed individual may exit unemployment in several different ways. This amounts to assuming that the independent variables affect different exit probabilities in an identical way. Such an assumption may lead to serious bias in the estimated parameters. Katz (1986) and Katz and Meyer (1988) illustrate this problem when distinguishing between recalls and re-employment using US data. Edin (1989) reports similar problems when distinguishing between exits to employment, labour market programmes and non-participation in a study of unemployment duration in Sweden, using the same displaced worker sample as this study. The results from these studies suggest that we should adopt a competing risks specification, and estimate re-employment equations for unemployment and relief jobs.[7] These re-employment equations, where exits to other states are treated as right-censored, will also be used for testing the hypothesis that unemployment and relief jobs are behaviourally identical states, in line with the analysis of unemployment and non-participation by Flinn and Heckman (1983).

Re-employment equations for the Stockholm youth sample are reported in Table 10.10. The first line refers to unemployment, and displays fairly conventional results: unemployment is positively related to eligibility for unemployment benefits and the age of the individual, and is negatively related to work experience, education and the vacancy–unemployment ratio. Somewhat less intuitive is the finding that there is a tendency for youths with cash benefits to have shorter spells of unemployment (compared to those without any benefits at all). The scale parameter, σ, shows a slight tendency towards negative duration dependence, but this effect is not significant to conventional levels.

Turning to the estimates of relief job duration, we find that the parameters are estimated with less precision, probably due to the small number (54) of non-censored spells. The only significant effect is that youth entitled to cash benefits have a higher re-employment probability than youth with no benefits. (Note that this variable does not capture

Table 10.10. *Weibull estimates of re-employment equations for unemployed and relief workers: Stockholm youth sample*

Dep. var.	$\ln T^U$ (1)	$\ln T^R$ (2)	Joint ($\ln T^U$ and $\ln T^R$) (3)
σ	1.0411	0.5548***	1.0195
	(0.0269)	(0.0554)	(0.0255)
Intercept	2.2071***	3.0346***	2.1497***
	(0.4029)	(0.8789)	(0.3810)
Age	0.0898***	0.0598	0.0890***
	(0.0189)	(0.0414)	(0.0179)
Female	− 0.1533**	− 0.2394	− 0.1600**
	(0.0750)	(0.1739)	(0.0710)
Foreign citizen	0.1978*	0.1720	0.1960**
	(0.1035)	(0.2322)	(0.0982)
Experience	− 0.0080***	− 0.0060	− 0.0083***
	(0.0023)	(0.0056)	(0.0022)
Gymnasium	− 0.7253***	− 0.1328	− 0.6964***
	(0.0844)	(0.1980)	(0.0802)
University	− 1.2532***	—[a]	− 1.2156***
	(0.1854)		(0.1804)
Cash benefits	− 0.2006*	− 0.9161***	− 0.2244**
	(0.1109)	(0.3042)	(0.1084)
Unemployment benefits	0.3070**	− 0.3832	0.2913*
	(0.1566)	(0.5800)	(0.1529)
V/U	− 0.6325***	0.2516	− 0.5477***
	(0.0816)	(0.1633)	(0.0760)
Non-labour income	0.1180	0.0206	0.1077
	(0.0824)	(0.1851)	(0.0783)
Dependents	0.0983	0.1048	0.0831
	(0.0842)	(0.1643)	(0.0791)
Relief job	—	—	1.5909***
			(0.1553)
(Relief job) × (Cash benefits)	—	—	− 1.3612**
			(0.5309)
(Relief job) × (Unemployment benefits)	—	—	− 0.9661 (1.0328)
Non-censored	806	54	860
Censored	471	163	634
Log likelihood	− 1646.64	− 118.36	− 1788.77
Likelihood Ratio Test (9 d.f.)	—	—	47.54***

Notes: Standard errors in parentheses. Asterisks denote statistical significance at the 10% (*), 5% (**), and 1% (***) level, respectively.
The test regarding the scale parameter (σ) refers to H_0: $\sigma = 1$. All tests are based on chi-square statistics. Superscript *a* denotes parameters which are not identified.

income when in a relief job, but rather reflects income if returning to unemployment.) Finally, we note that the estimate of the scale parameter implies *positive* duration dependence in the relief job equation. This may in part be due to the legal limits on the duration of relief jobs, a question which we will return to below.

Column (3) of Table 10.10 reports a test of the hypothesis that unemployment and relief jobs are behaviourally identical states with respect to job search. This test is obtained by concatenating the two samples – unemployment spells and relief job spells – estimating a joint model, and testing this restricted model against the two individual models using a likelihood ratio test. The test rejects the null hypothesis that the independent variables have the same coefficients in the two states, even though we allow for a separate intercept for relief jobs and separate benefit effects.

The interpretation of the tests performed above is complicated by the problems associated with measuring the duration of relief jobs. Observe that these measurement problems will be increasing in duration: spells consisting of multiple spells and permanent sheltered jobs will be more heavily concentrated among long spells. To investigate the sensitivity of our results to these measurement problems, we re-estimated our re-employment equations, treating spells longer than 20 weeks as censored. The choice of 20 weeks is arbitrary, but the limit is lower than the legal restriction on duration for the typical relief job, which is 26 weeks. The results obtained for the separate re-employment equations (reported in Table 10A.2 in the Appendix) are similar to those obtained using the original samples. The re-employment probability is still significantly lower in relief jobs, and cash benefits have a positive effect on the re-employment probability for individuals in relief jobs. Except for these two differences, we cannot reject the null hypothesis that relief jobs and unemployment are behaviourally identical states, possibly due to the very small number of non-censored relief job spells.

Re-employment equations for the displaced worker sample are reported in Table 10.11. The estimated parameters for the unemployed are similar to those obtained in the youth sample. The exceptions are that females now have a significantly lower re-employment probability, and that the scale parameter implies significant *positive* duration dependence.[8] This sample contains very few transitions from relief jobs to employment, which is reflected by the low precision in the estimates of the re-employment equation for individuals in relief jobs. Turning to the joint model we find, once again, that the exit rate from relief jobs to employment is significantly lower than the exit rate from unemployment to employment; we cannot, however, reject that the other coefficients are the same.

Table 10.11. *Weibull estimates of re-employment equations for unemployed and relief workers: displaced worker sample*

Dep. var.	$ln\,T^U$ (1)	$ln\,T^R$ (2)	Joint ($ln\,T^U$ and $ln\,T^R$) (3)
σ	0.9051**	1.2236	0.9263*
	(0.0403)	(0.2425)	(0.0402)
Intercept	6.0913***	(13.9023***	6.2328***
	(0.8059)	(4.7848)	(0.8079)
Age	0.0405***	0.0139	0.0391***
	(0.0080)	(0.0419)	(0.0079)
Female	0.3411**	0.2914	0.3506**
	(0.1691)	(1.3436)	(0.1710)
Foreign	− 0.3481	− 1.5504*	− 0.4193*
citizen	(0.2248)	(0.8936)	(0.2158)
Gymnasium	− 0.3696***	− 0.4801	− 0.3771***
	(0.1331)	(0.6774)	(0.1316)
V/U	− 0.7569***	0.6236	− 0.7457***
	(0.2095)	(1.1358)	(0.2037)
Married	− 0.5384***	− 0.1830	− 0.5113***
	(0.1657)	(0.9984)	(0.1654)
Children	0.0100	− 0.6830	− 0.0133
	(0.1613)	(0.8865)	(0.1595)
Health	0.6658***	0.6101	0.6517***
problem	(0.1890)	(1.3287)	(0.1899)
Pre-displacement	0.0007	0.0277	0.0013
seniority	(0.0086)	(0.0537)	(0.0086)
ln (pre-displacement	− 0.2009*	− 0.8912	− 0.2154**
wage)	(0.1085)	(0.6445)	(0.1089)
Relief job	—	—	1.7019***
			(0.2399)
Non-censored	271	17	288
Censored	302	148	450
Log likelihood	− 572.9	− 66.78	− 643.18
Likelihood ratio	—	—	7.22
Test (11 d.f.)			

Notes: Standard errors in parentheses. Asterisks denote statistical significance at the 10% (*), 5% (**), and 1% (***) level, respectively.
The test regarding the scale parameter (σ) refers to H_0: $\sigma = 1$. All tests are based on chi-square statistics.

The evidence presented so far ignores potential problems associated with unobserved heterogeneity and selection into programmes; the selection rule for programme participation may depend on unobserved variables, and this will affect the estimated duration equations. In this case, we

Table 10.12. *Weibull estimates of re-employment equations for unemployed with controls for previous programme participation: Stockholm youth sample*

Dep. var.	$\ln T^U$ (1)	$\ln T^U$ (2)	$\ln T^U$ (3)	$\ln T^U$ (4)
σ	1.0340	1.0333	1.0214	1.0180
	(0.0267)	(0.0267)	(0.0263)	(0.0261)
Intercept	1.9252***	1.9860***	1.6444***	1.8080***
	(0.4095)	(0.4232)	(0.4160)	(0.4169)
Age	0.0844***	0.0832***	0.0955***	0.0840***
	(0.0193)	(0.0194)	(0.0192)	(0.0193)
Female	− 0.1129	− 0.1199	− 0.0403	− 0.0307
	(0.0752)	(0.0762)	(0.0754)	(0.0752)
Foreign citizen	0.2290**	0.2256**	0.1768*	0.1907*
	(0.1034)	(0.1035)	(0.1019)	(0.1020)
Experience	− 0.0066***	− 0.0067	− 0.0055***	− 0.0045*
	(0.0024)	(0.0024)	(0.0023)	(0.0023)
Gymnasium	− 0.6832***	− 0.6843***	− 0.6758***	− 0.6331***
	(0.0850)	(0.0849)	(0.0854)	(0.0857)
University	− 1.1825***	− 1.1806***	− 1.0555***	− 0.9562***
	(0.1863)	(0.1863)	(0.1849)	(0.1861)
Cash benefits	− 0.1708	− 0.1683	− 0.2254**	− 0.2215**
	(0.1105)	(0.1106)	(0.1085)	(0.1079)
Unemployment benefits	0.3377**	0.3348**	0.2967*	0.2475
	(0.1558)	(0.1557)	(0.1540)	(0.1544)
V/U	− 0.4609***	− 0.4582***	− 0.3958***	− 0.3656***
	(0.0997)	(0.0997)	(0.0984)	(0.1008)
Non-labour income	0.1473	0.1501*	0.1396*	0.1181
	(0.0826)	(0.0827)	(0.0823)	(0.0820)
Dependents	0.1481*	0.1522*	0.1712	0.1780**
	(0.0854)	(0.0856)	(0.0848)	(0.0848)

cannot judge whether the observed differences in re-employment rates in unemployment and relief jobs, respectively, depend on sample selection or 'true' behavioural differences. For example, the estimates in Table 10.10 and Table 10.11 indicate that the re-employment rate is significantly lower in relief jobs, a result which is consistent with individuals with unobserved negative characteristics being selected into relief jobs.

To investigate the sensitivity of our estimates to sample selection, we re-estimated our duration equations using only spells of individuals who had *both* unemployment and relief job spells during the sample period. This is a way of reducing the difference in unobserved heterogeneity between the unemployment and the relief job samples, at least as long as

Table 10.12. (*cont.*)

Dep. var.	$\ln T^U$ (1)	$\ln T^U$ (2)	$\ln T^U$ (3)	$\ln T^U$ (4)
Number of previous spells:				
Unemployment	0.0926*	0.1098*	0.0380***	0.1445**
	(0.0497)	(0.0581)	(0.0603)	(0.0685)
Relief job	0.2570***	0.2566***	− 0.6212***	− 0.7032***
	(0.0986)	(0.0986)	(0.1389)	(0.2029)
Training	− 0.0694	− 0.0685	− 0.6142***	− 0.4207*
	(0.1371)	(0.1370)	(0.1727)	(0.2246)
Total number of spells:				
Unemployment	—	− 0.0177	− 0.1821***	− 0.1768***
		(0.0312)	(0.0336)	(0.0334)
Relief job	—	—	0.8302***	0.8387***
			(0.0949)	(0.0948)
Training	—	—	0.4674***	0.4754***
			(0.1050)	(0.1046)
Total previous duration:				
Unemployment	—	—	—	0.0135***
				(0.0033)
Relief job	—	—	—	0.0010
				(0.0060)
Training	—	—	—	− 0.0114**
				(0.0053)
Non-censored	806	806	806	806
Censored	471	471	471	471
Log likelihood	− 1638.79	− 1638.73	− 1576.08	− 1563.80

Notes: Standard errors in parentheses. Asterisks denote statistical significance at the 10% (*), 5% (**), and 1% (***) level, respectively.
The test regarding the scale parameter (σ) refers to H_0: $\sigma = 1$. All tests are based on chi-square statistics.

the unobserved variables are time invariant or temporally correlated.[9] The estimates, reported in Table A3 and A4 in the Appendix, do not lead to any dramatic revisions of the conclusions regarding the differences in re-employment probabilities between the two states. The parameter estimates in the separate equations for unemployed and relief workers display some instability, but the tests for behavioural differences in the two states lead to almost the same results. We thus conclude that it seems unlikely that the observed difference in re-employment rates between unemployed and relief workers are entirely due to sample selection.

The evidence reported here suggests that we cannot treat unemployment and relief jobs as behaviourally identical states.[10] The re-employment rate is significantly lower in relief jobs than in unemployment. The difference in re-employment probabilities between unemployed and individuals in relief jobs may be due to different compensation levels in the two states, which in turn influence the choice of search effort and reservation wages; as shown in Table 10.2, there are indeed striking differences in search effort between workers in relief jobs and the unemployed. There may also be differences in 'search environment' between the two states: relief jobs presumably entail some restrictions on individual time allocation on the job, which may reduce the likelihood of finding regular employment.

4.3   Do programmes affect future employment prospects?

We now turn to the question whether participation in relief jobs and manpower training affect the participants' *future* labour market prospects. Such effects are the main motivation for the training programmes, with an explicit objective to upgrade the skills of workers who are unemployed (or at risk of becoming unemployed). Also, relief jobs may provide useful skills by 'on-the-job training', thereby improving future employment prospects of participants.

In Table 10.12 we report re-employment equations for unemployed in the Stockholm youth sample. These equations are augmented with variables for individual labour market histories, including programme participation. The empirical strategy used in this analysis is to add the number of *previous* spells in unemployment, relief jobs and training programmes to the duration equation to check for evidence of occurrence effects. This specification allows for two kinds of occurrence effects: a 'pure' occurrence effect due to past spells of unemployment affecting present unemployment duration, and a 'treatment' effect of programme participation.

A discussion of how to estimate occurrence dependence using complete – i.e., non-censored – duration data is found in Heckman and Borjas (1980). Their test for occurrence dependence is a test of whether the effects of time invariant variables have different coefficients across adjacent completed spells. Our strategy of including the number of previous unemployment spells may be viewed as a simple test for occurrence dependence, where we restrict occurrence dependence to changes in the intercept across unemployment spells.

If participation in a programme affects subsequent re-employment probabilities, we should find (ignoring unobserved heterogeneity for the moment) that post-programme unemployment spells are shorter than pre-programme spells. In principle, this problem is very similar to the problem of evaluating the impact of interventions on earnings (see, for example, Heckman and Robb, 1985).

In column (1) of Table 10.12 we report estimates where we include the number of previous spells in unemployment, relief jobs and training. This is a very simple specification which ignores unobserved heterogeneity; participation in programmes and unemployment occurrence are treated as random events. The estimated parameters reveal no striking differences compared to the original estimates in Table 10.10. The number of previous unemployment spells and relief job spells both enter with positive signs, the latter strongly significant, while the number of previous training spells has a negative sign and is insignificant.

This simple specification thus indicates that participation in relief jobs has a *negative* effect on subsequent re-employment probabilities. It is, however, difficult to accept a specification which completely ignores the potential problems of unobserved heterogeneity. The positive association between unemployment duration and past participation may well be due to workers with low re-employment probabilities being selected into relief jobs. Consequently, we interpret the estimated coefficients as a net effect of sample selection and a 'true' occurrence effect. In the following we make a crude attempt at reducing the impact of sample selection by introducing additional explanatory variables. We do not claim to solve the selection problem, but we think that at least some of the bias may be eliminated, thus producing more reliable estimates.

The problem at issue is that unobserved heterogeneity in the duration equation may be correlated with the selection rule for programme participation.[11] Here we try to limit the consequences of such correlations by including variables that are correlated with probability of selection into programmes. In column (2) of Table 10.12 we introduce the *total* number of unemployment spells during the sample period as a control for unobserved heterogeneity.[12] In columns (3) and (4) we also introduce the total number of spells in relief jobs and training. If selection into programmes is influenced by time-invariant omitted variables, we would expect these variables to be correlated with the total number of programme spells (note that the estimated occurrence and treatment effects now are conditional on the total number of occurrences and treatments).

When the total number of unemployment spells are introduced in column (2) of Table 10.12, we find that the coefficient of this variable is close to zero and insignificant. Furthermore, there are almost no differences in the estimated parameters compared to column (1). Introducing the total number of spells in relief jobs and training, however, produces some drastic changes in the estimated occurrence effects. All three occurrence effects are now highly significant. The estimates show that past unemployment spells are *negatively* associated with current re-employment probabilities. Both treatment effects, previous spells in relief jobs and training, are strongly *positive*. This suggests that treatment is positively associated with the re-employment probability.

Turning to the total number of spells variables, introduced to control for unobserved heterogeneity, we find that these are strongly significant. The re-employment probability is increasing in the total number of unemployment spells, and decreasing in the total number of spells in relief jobs and manpower training. We interpret these estimates as evidence of negative selection into programmes; workers with low re-employment probabilities are more likely to enter training programmes and relief jobs. The unemployment effect is more difficult to interpret because of its closer connection to the dependent variable, unemployment duration, but in a fixed sample period we expect a large number of unemployment spells to be associated with a short average duration of unemployment.

In column (4) of Table 10.12 we introduce previous duration in unemployment and programmes as additional regressors. This is a simplistic attempt to discriminate between occurrence dependence and lagged duration dependence. The procedure is problematic, since lagged duration is endogenous if unobserved heterogeneity is temporally correlated. The instrumental variable approach discussed by Heckman and Borjas (1980) is, however, not feasible in our case. Lagged exogenous variables that change across spells can be used as instruments for lagged duration, but we are short of time-varying exogenous variables (only the unemployment–vacancy ratio shows variation worth mentioning); we therefore proceed and estimate the model, bearing in mind that any heterogeneity that is not controlled for will affect the estimated lagged duration parameters. The results suggest that occurrence dependence dominates the relief job effect, while the training effect seems to be a combination of both occurrence and lagged duration dependence. For unemployment, we find significant positive coefficients for both the occurrence and the lagged duration variable.

The results reported here do not contradict the position held by the Swedish labour market authorities; unemployment 'causes' future unemployment, and manpower training and relief jobs are measures that counteract these negative effects. We must nevertheless underline the preliminary nature of our results: ideally we would like to use fully-fledged longitudinal methods to come to grips with the unobserved heterogeneity problem. It is also worth stressing that the sample used (Stockholm youth) is not representative of the Swedish labour market as a whole.

5 Concluding remarks

Our investigation of job matching in Sweden has focused on the role of two kinds of labour market programmes – manpower training and, in particular, relief jobs. One role of these programmes is to cushion the labour market consequences of recessions or sectoral shocks. It seems clear that the programmes work in this respect; exits to the programmes account for a significant fraction of total unemployment outflow, and employment in relief jobs has tracked the business cycle quite well.

To what extent do the programmes also work as stepping stones to regular employment? Do workers in programmes enter employment at the same pace as workers in open unemployment? The time series evidence suggests that relief jobs contribute less to the flow of aggregate hirings than open unemployment. This finding is largely consistent with the evidence from microdata. The transition rate to regular employment is higher for workers in unemployment than for workers in relief jobs, holding constant a number of observable characteristics of the individual. Placing unemployed workers in relief jobs thus seems to involve a cost in terms of a reduced number of hirings in regular jobs.

These costs are possibly counteracted by the 'long-run' effects of upgrading the skills of unemployed workers. Our findings are consistent with the view that current unemployment has negative effects on the re-employment probabilities in future unemployment spells, but that relief jobs and training programmes counteract these effects.

These results should be regarded as preliminary and in need of further investigations. One caveat relates to the possible influence of unobservables; we have tried to control for heterogeneity across individuals in the different states by including a reasonably large number of covariates, capturing the individuals' demographic, economic, and human capital characteristics as well as the labour market situation. We have made only crude attempts to control for unobserved heterogeneity, however: it is conceivable that individuals with unfavourable employment prospects are disproportionately selected into relief jobs, in which case the differences in transition rates between workers in unemployment and relief jobs may reflect the selection rules rather than features of the states *per se*. Similar selectivity problems are also encountered when we estimate the impact of the previous labour market history on re-employment rates.

Our research casts some light on findings from recent investigations of wage determination in the Nordic countries. Studies from Sweden (Calmfors and Forslund, 1990; Holmlund, 1990) and Finland (Eriksson, Suvanto and Vartia, 1990) indicate that it is open unemployment that is conducive to wage moderation. A transfer of workers from unemployment to labour market programmes brings about a wage increase, and this increase is of the same order of magnitude as if the workers had been placed in regular employment. The results from these studies suggest that programme participants are not very effective as job seekers, an hypothesis that is consistent with the findings of this study.

The investigations in this study by no means attempt to provide a comprehensive picture of how labour market programmes influence worker–job matching in the Swedish labour market; the effects of the programmes operate through a number of routes, with intricate effects on regular employment and unemployment. Abolishing relief jobs would almost certainly increase open unemployment, but there is little reason to expect an increase of the same magnitude as the prevailing volume of relief jobs.

APPENDIX: DATA DESCRIPTION AND SOME ADDITIONAL ESTIMATES

(for abbreviations used, see below)

Time series data:

U the number of unemployed according to the labour force surveys (AKU). The ratio for 1986 between the number of unemployed according to new and old measurement techniques is used to adjust the series for 1987–8 so that it corresponds to the old definition.

u unemployment rate (AKU), adjusted for 1987–8 so that it conforms to the old definition (+ 0.5 percentage points).

U^m the number of unemployed blue-collar workers in mining and manufacturing calculated from $U^m = [u^m/(1 - u^m)]N$, where u^m is the unemployment rate among workers in manufacturing occupations (AKU), and N is the number of employed blue-collar workers (SCB).

U^{ui} the number of unemployed blue-collar workers in mining and manufacturing calculated from $U^{ui} = [u^{ui}/(1 - u^{ui})]N$, where u^{ui} is the unemployment rate among members of unemployment insurance funds for workers in mining and manufacturing (industrikassor) (AMS).

V the number of unfilled vacancies (AMS) (no adjustment for compulsory notification of vacancies from the late 1970s).

V^m the number of unfilled vacancies in manufacturing industry (AMS) (no adjustment for compulsory vacancies from the late 1970s).

H the number of new hires of blue-collar workers in mining and manufacturing calculated from $H = hN$, where h is the new hire rate and N is the number of blue-collar workers in mining and manufacturing (SCB).

OV the (monthly) outflow of vacancies calculated from the identity $V - V_{-1} \equiv IV - OV$, where IV is the flow of new (registered) vacancies (AMS).

RJ the number of workers in relief jobs (beredskapsarbeten); the series is based on the register of job searchers at the employment exchange offices. For the period 1970–8 a different data source is available ('system B').

A period with observations from both sources (1978: 1–1985: 6) gives a ratio (0.96) between the new and the old series; this ratio is applied to the data from system B for the period 1970–8 (AMS).

MT the number of workers in training programmes (excluding training of workers facing layoff risks); a new series, excluding some courses, is available from 1979 onwards.

The ratio between the new and the old series in 1979 (0.94) is applied to the old series for 1970–8 (AMS).

Abbreviations:

AKU The labour force surveys (arbetskraftsundersökningarna), conducted by SCB.

AMS The National Labour Market Board (Arbetsmarknadsstyrelsen).

SCB Statistics Sweden (Statistiska Centralbyrån).

Table 10A.1. *Weibull estimates of unemployment and relief job duration*

Sample	Stockholm Youth		Displaced workers	
Dep. var.	$\ln T^U$	$\ln T^R$	$\ln T^U$	$\ln T^R$
σ	0.9787	0.5782***	0.9398**	0.8491***
	(0.0202)	(0.0304)	(0.0297)	(0.0515)
Intercept	1.4403***	2.1829***	5.2276***	8.7339***
	(0.3052)	(0.4906)	(0.6101)	(1.7731)
Age	0.0953***	0.0561**	0.0304***	− 0.0080
	(0.0144)	(0.0234)	(0.0052)	(0.0090)
Female	− 0.1233**	0.1515*	0.4174***	− 0.4354
	(0.0580)	(0.0884)	(0.1279)	(0.2720)
Foreign	0.0706	0.0326	− 0.499	− 0.2481
citizen	(0.0773)	(0.1119)	(0.1845)	(0.3294)
Experience	− 0.0072***	0.0016	—	—
	(0.0018)	(0.0032)		
Gymnasium	− 0.5403***	0.0129	0.0101	− 0.2046
	(0.0666)	(0.1138)	(0.1006)	(0.1928)
University	− 1.0192***	− 0.3375	—	—
	(0.1526)	(0.4228)		
Cash	− 0.1715*	− 0.5367**	—	—
benefits	(0.0891)	(0.2126)		
Unemployment	0.2578**	− 0.2380	—	—
benefits	(0.1230)	(0.4195)		
V/U	− 0.4623***	− 0.0270	− 0.7303***	− 0.0288
	(0.0612)	(0.0838)	(0.1556)	(0.2684)
Non-labour	0.0900	− 0.1289	—	—
income	(0.0636)	(0.0931)		
Dependents	0.0578	0.2894***	—	—
	(0.0642)	(0.0893)		
Married	—	—	− 0.5485***	0.1176
			(0.1212)	(0.2158)
Children	—	—	0.0870	− 0.1159
			(0.1201)	(0.2133)
Health	—	—	0.1330	− 0.3821*
problem			(0.1138)	(0.1983)
Pre-displacement	—	—	0.0079	0.0113
seniority			(0.0054)	(0.0094)
$\ln$ (pre-displacement	—	—	− 0.1503*	− 0.5081**
wage)			(0.0842)	(0.2552)
Non-censored	1198	202	529	151
Censored	79	15	44	14
Log likelihood	− 1850.78	− 212.61	− 807.21	− 213.98

Notes: Standard errors in parentheses. Asterisks denote statistical significance at the 10% (*), 5% (**), and 1% (***) level, respectively.
The test regarding the scale parameter (σ) refers to H_0: $\sigma = 1$. All tests are based on chi-square statistics.

Table 10A.2. *Weibull estimates of re-employment equations for unemployed and relief workers: Stockholm youth sample, spells longer than 20 weeks treated as censored*

Dep. var.	$\ln T^U$	$\ln T^R$	Joint
σ	0.8498***	0.5261***	0.8451***
	(0.0269)	(0.1303)	(0.0265)
Intercept	2.3093***	3.8375**	2.3062***
	(0.3636)	(1.5442)	(0.3575)
Age	0.0730***	0.0486	0.0725***
	(0.0172)	(0.0733)	(0.0170)
Female	− 0.1610**	− 0.2675	− 0.1645**
	(0.0663)	(0.3140)	(0.0653)
Foreign	0.1906**	0.5670	0.1985**
citizen	(0.0930)	(0.5742)	(0.0920)
Experience	− 0.0068***	− 0.0136	− 0.0071***
	(0.0021)	(0.0097)	(0.0021)
Gymnasium	− 0.5667***	0.0491	− 0.5560***
	(0.0756)	(0.3810)	(0.0743)
University	− 0.9131***	—[a]	− 0.9025***
	(0.1630)		(0.1616)
Cash	− 0.1177	− 1.2857***	− 0.1212
benefits	(0.0953)	(0.4474)	(0.0947)
Unemployment	0.2970**	—[a]	0.2969**
benefits	(0.1379)		(0.1370)
V/U	− 0.6763***	− 0.0789	− 0.6592***
	(0.0768)	(0.2738)	(0.0751)
Non-labour	0.1310*	− 0.4103	0.1160
income	(0.0768)	(0.3153)	(0.0716)
Dependents	0.1053	0.2773	0.1095
	(0.0764)	(0.3551)	(0.0752)
Relief job	—	—	2.3958***
			(0.2658)
(Relief job) ×	—	—	− 2.0065***
(Cash benefits)			(0.5532)
Non-censored	674	14	688
Censored	603	203	806
Log likelihood	− 1429.33	− 49.36	− 1483.60
Likelihood Ratio	—	—	9.82
Test (9 d.f.)			

Notes: Standard errors in parentheses. Asterisks denote statistical significance at the 10% (*), 5% (**), and 1% (***) level, respectively.
The test regarding the scale parameter (σ) refers to H_0: $\sigma = 1$. All tests are based on chi-square statistics. Superscript a denotes parameters which are not identified.

Table 10A.3. *Weibull estimates of re-employment equations for unemployed and relief workers: Stockholm youth sample, restricted to spells of individuals with both unemployment and relief job spells*

Dep. var.	$\ln T^U$	$\ln T^R$	Joint
σ	1.0055	0.5320***	0.9166**
	(0.0562)	(0.0537)	(0.0450)
Intercept	2.5336***	2.8886***	2.3713***
	(0.7849)	(0.8438)	(0.6326)
Age	0.0749**	0.0611	0.0755**
	(0.0370)	(0.0400)	(0.0299)
Female	0.1095	− 0.2600	− 0.0131
	(0.1644)	(0.1728)	(0.1286)
Foreign	0.3825	0.1045	0.3505*
citizen	(0.2390)	(0.2336)	(0.1893)
Experience	− 0.0032	− 0.0028	− 0.0035
	(0.0052)	(0.0058)	(0.0042)
Gymnasium	− 0.5001***	− 0.0870	− 0.4378***
	(0.1849)	(0.1916)	(0.1478)
University	− 0.8150	—[a]	− 0.6681
	(0.7718)		(0.6874)
Cash	− 0.3068	− 0.9007***	− 0.3312
benefits	(0.2484)	(0.2911)	(0.2236)
Unemployment	0.4282	− 0.3484	0.3778
benefits	(0.4310)	(0.5580)	(0.3398)
V/U	− 0.3606**	0.2947*	− 0.1722
	(0.1584)	(0.1593)	(0.1251)
Non-labour	0.1242*	0.0029	0.0760
income	(0.1676)	(0.1781)	(0.1355)
Dependents	− 0.0894	0.1635	− 0.0551
	(0.1718)	0.1604)	(0.1338)
Relief job	—	—	0.8958***
			(0.1599)
(Relief job) ×	—	—	− 0.8268
(Cash benefits)			(0.5338)
(Relief job) ×	—	—	− 1.0408
(Unemployment			(1.0139)
benefits)			
Non-censored	186	52	238
Censored	273	156	429
Log likelihood	− 463.54	− 110.14	− 591.48
Likelihood Ratio	—	—	35.60***
Test (9 d.f.)			

Notes: Standard errors in parentheses. Asterisks denote statistical significance at the 10% (*), 5% (**), and 1% (***) level, respectively.
The test regarding the scale parameter (σ) refers to H_0: $\sigma = 1$. All tests are based on chi-square statistics. Superscipt a denotes parameters which are not identified.

Table 10A.4. *Weibull estimates of re-employment equations for unemployed and relief workers: displaced worker sample, restricted to spells of individuals with both unemployment and relief job spells*

Dep. var.	$\ln T^U$	$\ln T^R$	Joint
σ	0.8474***	1.2480	0.9019*
	(0.0568)	(0.2559)	(0.0572)
Intercept	6.8361***	14.3467***	7.0141***
	(1.0723)	(4.7981)	(1.0736)
Age	0.0171	0.0205	0.0176**
	(0.0138)	(0.0443)	(0.0133)
Female	0.0130***	0.3733	0.9585**
	(0.3524)	(1.3783)	(0.3590)
Foreign	0.5180*	− 1.6943*	− 0.6031**
citizen	(0.2824)	(0.9334)	(0.2702)
Gymnasium	− 0.4726***	− 0.3255	− 0.4818**
	(0.2077)	(0.7129)	(0.2015)
V/U	− 1.1951***	− 0.7034	− 1.1154***
	(0.3087)	(1.1916)	(0.3039)
Married	− 0.1981	− 0.4330	− 0.1858
	(0.2967)	(1.0672)	(0.2880)
Children	− 0.2388	− 0.6844	− 0.2785
	(0.2696)	(0.9104)	(0.2607)
Health	1.3458***	0.52262	1.2476***
problem	(0.3646)	(1.3530)	(0.3604)
Pre-displacement	0.0035	0.0233	0.0036
seniority	(0.0143)	(0.0551)	(0.0141)
$\ln$ (pre-displacement	− 0.1682	− 0.9388	− 0.1946
wage)	(0.1268)	(0.6364)	(0.1303)
Relief job	—	—	1.6266***
			(0.2511)
Non-censored	126	16	142
Censored	223	476	370
Log likelihood	− 285.55	− 63.80	− 354.14
Likelihood Ratio	—	—	9.58
Test (11 d.f.)			

Notes: Standard errors in parentheses. Asterisks denote statistical significance at the 10% (*), 5% (**), and 1% (***) level, respectively.
The test regarding the scale parameter (σ) refers to H_0: $\sigma = 1$. All tests are based on chi-square statistics.

Table 10A.5. *Weibull estimates of transitions from temporary and relief jobs to unemployment: Stockholm youth sample*

Dep. var.	$\ln T^E$	$\ln T^R$	Joint
σ	1.2493***	0.6382***	1.1385***
	(0.0550)	(0.0532)	(0.0445)
Intercept	2.8832***	2.6882***	2.7756***
	(0.7498)	(0.89412)	(0.6176)
Age	0.0733**	0.0431	0.0695**
	(0.0344)	(0.0400)	(0.0283)
Female	0.6522***	0.5635***	0.6383***
	(0.1414)	(0.1584)	(0.1160)
Foreign citizen	0.2868	− 0.0251	0.2105
	(0.1966)	(0.1900)	(0.1575)
Experience	0.0108**	0.0091	0.0100***
	(0.0046)	(0.0059)	(0.0039)
Gymnasium	0.3386**	0.1428	0.2863**
	(0.1631)	(0.2017)	(0.1355)
University	0.5349	− 0.0917	0.4873
	(0.3819)	(0.6762)	(0.3322)
Cash benefits	− 1.3164***	− 0.0929	− 1.1195***
	(0.2330)	(0.4652)	(0.2022)
Unemployment benefits	− 0.6842**	− 0.3553	− 0.6366**
	(0.3474)	(0.6572)	(0.3030)
V/U	− 0.4993***	− 0.0943	− 0.3963***
	(0.1400)	(0.1406)	(0.1124)
Non-labour income	− 0.7080***	− 0.1696	− 0.6023***
	(0.1542)	(0.1532)	(0.1233)
Dependents	0.2835*	0.3875**	0.3208***
	(0.1491)	(0.1534)	(0.1203)
Relief job	—	—	0.0660
			(0.1415)
Non-censored	332	87	419
Censored	661	130	791
Log likelihood	− 972.91	− 175.36	− 1173.58
Likelihood Ratio Test (11 d.f.)	—	—	50.62***

Notes: Standard errors in parentheses. Asterisks denote statistical significance at the 10% (*), 5% (**), and 1% (***) level, respectively.
The test regarding the scale parameter (σ) refers to H_0: $\sigma = 1$. All tests are based on chi-square statistics.

Table 10A.6. *Weibull estimates of transitions from temporary and relief jobs to unemployment: displaced worker sample*

Dep. var.	$\ln T^E$	$\ln T^R$	Joint
σ	0.6672***	0.8002***	0.7753***
	(0.0467)	(0.0551)	(0.0375)
Intercept	3.1094**	9.0833***	5.3231***
	(1.5525)	(2.0646)	(1.1261)
Age	0.0334***	− 0.0122	0.0060
	(0.0082)	(0.0100)	(0.0065)
Female	− 0.5423**	− 0.5742**	− 0.3554*
	(0.2404)	(0.2887)	(0.1880)
Foreign	− 0.0690	− 0.0188	0.0838
citizen	(0.2194)	(0.4299)	(0.2122)
Gymnasium	0.1347	− 0.2615	− 0.0268
	(0.1377)	(0.2214)	(0.1235)
V/U	0.2740	0.0914	0.0929
	(0.2450)	(0.2930)	(0.1908)
Married	− 0.8471***	0.0484	− 0.2202
	(0.2244)	(0.2348)	(0.1821)
Children	0.8185***	0.0475	0.3322**
	(0.2020)	(0.2372)	(0.1622)
Health	0.0436	− 0.3880*	− 0.3034*
problem	(0.2504)	(0.2101)	(0.1592)
Pre-displacement	− 0.0350***	0.0098	− 0.0052
seniority	(0.0099)	(0.0098)	(0.0072)
$\ln$ (pre-displacement	0.1192	− 0.5050*	− 0.1003
wage)	(0.2218)	(0.2972)	(0.1581)
Relief job	—	—	0.4302***
			(0.1081)
Non-censored	129	114	243
Censored	31	51	82
Log likelihood	− 178.55	− 180.85	− 371.91
Likelihood Ratio	—	—	25.02***
Test (11 d.f.)			

Notes: Standard errors in parentheses. Asterisks denote statistical significance at the 10% (*), 5% (**), and 1% (***) level, respectively.
The test regarding the scale parameter (σ) refers to H_0: $\sigma = 1$. All tests are based on chi-square statistics.

NOTES

1 We are grateful to Anders Björklund and the January 1990 conference participants for useful comments, and to HSFR for financial support. Susanne
  Ackum provided excellent research assistance.

2 Ohlsson (1990) estimates reaction functions for the government's grants to
  relief jobs, and confirms that the grants respond to movements in the
  unemployment rate.

3 There is some evidence of an outward u/v shift in the late 1960s, however; as is
  documented in Holmlund (1978b).

4 Matching functions for the Swedish labour market have previously been
  estimated by Holmlund (1980).

5 Albrecht, Holmlund and Lang (1989) outline a structural approach to the
  analysis of unemployment duration, using the Stockholm youth sample.

6 Note that we do not have complete information on the time variation of some
  of the explanatory variables – i.e., eligibility for benefits, in the Stockholm
  youth sample. In such cases we use information from the interview which is
  closest in time to the starting date of the spell in question. This will introduce
  some errors in the independent variables.

7 Single-risk equations for unemployment and relief job duration are reported in
  Table 10A.1 in the Appendix for comparison.

8 Available Swedish research, cited in Edin (1989), finds no evidence of negative
  duration dependence. This is the case even when unobserved heterogeneity,
  which produces a bias towards negative duration dependence, is *not* accounted
  for.

9 Alternatively, we can use longitudinal data to eliminate time–invariant
  omitted variables, using methods for duration data discussed by Chamberlain
  (1985). However, these methods are developed for multiple completed spells, a
  restriction that would reduce our sample drastically.

10 Given these results, it seem reasonable to consider the reversed hypothesis: do
  individuals in relief jobs behave as if they were employed in an ordinary
  (temporary) job? In Table 10A.5 and 10A.6 in the Appendix, we report some
  evidence on the determinants of transitions from relief jobs and temporary
  employment to unemployment. The Stockholm youth sample contains information on 1131 spells of temporary employment (as defined by the survey
  respondent). The displaced worker sample contains 160 spells of temporary
  employment (as defined by the employment agency). The average duration of
  temporary employment is much shorter in this sample, only 14 weeks or about
  half the mean duration in the youth sample.

  The tests for the hypothesis that temporary employment and public relief jobs
  are behaviourally identical states produce similar results. The intercept shift
  term for relief jobs is close to zero, but the Likelihood Ratio Test statistic
  rejects that the states are behaviourally identical. A closer examination reveals
  that the most notable difference between the two states concerns the Weibull
  duration dependence parameter. As a matter of fact, restricting the scale
  parameter to unity, the exponential model, leads to test statistics which are no
  longer significant at conventional levels. The main difference between the exit
  rates to unemployment from temporary employment and relief jobs is thus
  associated with different time patterns of the exist rates.

11 In the standard linear model we can try to account for this correlation by using
  longitudinal data to eliminate time–invariant omitted variables (fixed effects).

Similar methods for duration data require multiple completed spells, a restriction that would reduce our sample considerably (cf. note 9 above).
12 Ridder (1986) uses similar methods – i.e., he includes dummy variables for frequent spells of unemployment and long spells of unemployment, to control for unobserved heterogeneity in an analysis of labour market programmes in the Dutch labour market.

REFERENCES

Abraham, K. (1983). 'Structural/Frictional vs. Deficient Demand Unemployment: Some New Evidence', *American Economic Review*, **73**, 708–23.
    (1987). 'Help-Wanted Advertising, Job Vacancies, and Unemployment', *Brookings Papers on Economic Activity*, **1**, 207–48.
Albrecht, J., B. Holmlund and H. Lang (1989). 'Job Search and Youth Unemployment: Analysis of Swedish Data', *European Economic Review*, **33** (Papers and Proceedings), 416–25.
Björklund, A. and B. Holmlund (1989). 'Effects of Extended Unemployment Compensation in Sweden', in B. Gustafsson and A. Klevmarken (eds), *The Political Economy of Social Security*, Amsterdam: North-Holland.
Björklund, A. (1990). 'Why is the Swedish Unemployment Rate so Low?', in *Issues in Industrial Economics – celebrating 50 years of research*, Stockholm: IUI.
Blanchard, O. J. and P. Diamond (1989). 'The Beveridge Curve', *Brookings Papers on Economic Activity*, **1**, p. 1–60.
Budd, A., P. Levine and P. Smith (1988). 'Unemployment, Vacancies and the Long-Term Unemployed', *Economic Journal*, **98**, 1071–91.
Calmfors, L. and A. Forslund (1990). 'Wage Setting in Sweden', in L. Calmfors (ed.), *Wage Formation and Macroeconomic Policy in the Nordic Countries*, Oxford: SNS and Oxford University Press.
Chamberlain, G. (1985). 'Heterogeneity, Omitted Variable Bias, and Duration Dependence', in J. J. Heckman and B. Singer (eds), *Longitudinal Analysis of Labor Market Data*, Cambridge: Cambridge University Press.
Edin, P. A. (1988). 'Individual Consequences of Plant Closures', Ph.D. dissertation, Department of Economics, Uppsala University.
    (1989). 'Unemployment Duration and Competing Risks: Evidence from Sweden', *Scandinavian Journal of Economics*, **91**, 639–53.
Eriksson, T., A. Suvanto and P. Vartia (1990). 'Wage Setting in Finland', in L. Calmfors (ed.), *Wage Formation and Macroeconomic Policy in the Nordic Countries*, Oxford: SNS and Oxford University Press.
Farm, A. (1989). 'Arbetsmarknad och arbetsförmedling' (Labour Markets and Employment Services), SOFI, University of Stockholm (mimeo).
Flinn, C. J. and J. J. Heckman (1983). 'Are Unemployment and Out of the Labor Force Behaviorally Distinct Labor Force States?', *Journal of Labor Economics*, **1**, 28–42.
Heckman, J. J. and G. J. Borjas (1980). 'Does Unemployment Cause Future Unemployment? Definitions, Questions and Answers from a Continuous Time Model of Heterogeneity and State Dependence', *Economica*, **47**, 247–83.
Heckman, J. J. and R. Robb, Jr (1985). 'Alternative Methods for Evaluating the Impact of Interventions', in J. J. Heckman and B. Singer (eds), *Longitudinal Analysis of Labor Market Data*, Cambridge: Cambridge University Press.

448   Per-Anders Edin and Bertil Holmlund

Holmlund, B. (1978a). 'Erfarenheter av Åman-lagarna' (Experiences of the Employment Security Act), *Ekonomisk Debatt*, 6, 236–46.

(1978b). 'Arbetslöshet och lönebildning i ett regionalt perspektiv' (Unemployment and Wage Formation in a Regional Perspective), in SOU, 1978: 60, *Arbetsmarknadspolitik i förändring*, Stockholm: Almänna Förlaget.

(1980). 'A Simulation Model of Employment, Unemployment and Labor Turnover', *Scandinavian Journal of Economics*, 82, 273–90.

(1986). 'A New Look at Vacancies and Labour Turnover in Swedish Industry', FIEF, Stockholm (June) (mimeo).

(1990). *Svensk lönebildning – teori, empiri, politik* (Wage Formation in Sweden – Theory, Evidence, Policy), Stockholm: Almänna Förlaget.

Holmlund, B. and B. Kashefi (1987). 'Frågeformulär och variabelförteckning för undersökningen om arbetslösa ungdomar i Stockholm' (The Stockholm Youth Survey: Questionnaire and List of Variables), FIEF, Stockholm (August) (mimeo).

Jackman, R. and S. Roper (1987). 'Structural Unemployment', *Oxford Bulletin of Economics and Statistics*, 49, 9–37.

Jackman, R., R. Layard and C. Pissarides (1989). 'On Vacancies', *Oxford Bulletin of Economics and Statistics*, 51, 377–84.

Johnson, G. E. and P. R. G. Layard (1986). 'The Natural Rate of Unemployment: Explanation and Policy', in O. Ashenfelter and R. Layard (eds), *The Handbook of Labor Economics*, vol. 2, Amsterdam: North-Holland.

Kalbfleisch, J. D. and R. L. Prentice (1980). *The Statistical Analysis of Failure Time Data*, London: John Wiley.

Katz, L. F. (1986). 'Layoffs, Recall and the Duration of Unemployment', Working Paper, 1825, Cambridge: National Bureau of Economic Research.

Katz, L. F. and B. D. Meyer (1988). 'Unemployment Insurance, Recall Expectations and Unemployment Outcomes', Working Paper, 2594, Cambridge: National Bureau of Economic Research.

Lundin, U. and T. Larhed (1985). 'Arbetsförmedlingens andel av de lediga platserna' (The Public Employment Exchange's Share of Vacancies), AMS (mimeo).

Ohlsson, H. (1990). 'Job Creation Measures as Activist Fiscal Policy', working paper, 1990: 7, Department of Economics, Uppsala University.

Phelps, E. S. (1971). 'Money Wage Dynamics and Labor Market Equilibrium', in E. S. Phelps (ed.), *Microeconomic Foundations of Employment and Inflation Theory*, New York: Norton.

Pissarides, C. (1985). 'Short-Run Equilibrium Dynamicss of Unemployment, Vacancies and Real Wages', *American Economic Review*, 75, 676–90.

Ridder, G. (1986). 'An Event History Approach to the Evaluation of Training, Recruitment and Employment Programmes', *Journal of Applied Econometrics*, 1, 109–26.

SOU (1978: 60). *Arbetsmarknadspolitik i förändring* (Labor Market Policy in Transition), Stockholm: Allmänna Förlaget.

UPI (1974). *Utredningen om förbättrad platsinformation* (The Investigation on Improved Information on Vacancies), Stockholm: AMS.

Discussion

DENNIS J. SNOWER

One of the standard comments that discussants of conference papers are wont to make is that the study under consideration looks exciting, but that further reflection reveals the approach to be nothing new. The study by Edin and Holmlund merits the opposite assessment: the study is not exciting, but further reflection reveals matters of importance. In this discussion, I will not quibble about the appropriateness of the authors' data and econometric tests; rather, I will concentrate on two significant issues raised by their study.

The first concerns the authors' classification of labour market states. It is very common in the theory of labour markets (and in much of the empirical work in this area as well) to distinguish only between two states: employment (E) and unemployment (U): in other words, workers who are not employed are assumed to be unemployed. There is, however, a growing body of evidence suggesting that this twofold classification overlooks some important alternatives:

(a) The state of being 'out of the labour force' (OLF) is important in the sense that the flows between OLF and E, and between OLF and U, often are of the same order of magnitude as the flows between E and U.

(b) The employment state (E) is far from homogeneous. As an initial step, it is often useful to distinguish between 'primary' and 'second-ary' employment, with the former characterised by comparatively higher wages and more job security than the latter. The difference between the present value of income from the primary and second-ary sectors is often greater than the difference between the present value of income from secondary employment and unemployment. Similarly, it is also useful to distinguish between full-time and part-time employment.

For these reasons it is refreshing to see that the analysis of Swedish labour market programmes by Edin and Holmlund explicitly considers three labour market states: employment, unemployment, and 'out of the labour force'. Furthermore, the authors sub-divide the employment state into 'temporary', 'permanent', and 'relief' jobs, and they sub-divide the 'out of the labour force' state into a 'regular' one and 'training pro-grammes'.

This is the context in which they investigate the impact of relief jobs and training programmes. In particular, they examine

(a)   the importance of flows from the unemployment state to relief jobs (they find these flows to be significant),
(b)   the comparative importance of the flows from relief jobs, from training programmes, and from unemployment to the employment state (they find the flows from the relief jobs to be comparatively small, *ceteris paribus*), and
(c)   the comparative importance of the flows from relief jobs and unemployment to the 'out of the labour force' state (they find the flows from the relief jobs to be comparatively large).

Clearly, this investigation is a far cry from providing us with a complete Markov matrix of transition probabilities among the states above, but it is certainly a welcome step in this direction.

The second issue I wish to address is the one empirical result which the authors apparently consider surprising: namely, 'that workers in relief jobs do not contribute to the flow of hiring to the same extent as workers in open unemployment'. To my mind, this result is less surprising than it may appear at first sight, but the underlying reasons are potentially interesting; they certainly deserve some attention in the authors' research programmes.

Let me illustrate this point by means of a particularly simple model of job search by two types of workers: unemployed workers (u) and workers on relief jobs (r). For simplicity, let the workers in each group be homogeneous, and let both have a two-period time horizon. Let Y_u and Y_r be the present values of income for an unemployed worker and a relief worker, respectively. Let S_u and S_r represent the search intensities of these two types of workers. For simplicity, let the workers' utility function be given by

$$V[u] = V(Y_u, S_u) \text{ and } V[r] = V(Y_r, S_r) \tag{1}$$

where $V_1 > 0$, $V_2 < 0$, V_{11}, $V_{22} < 0$, and $V_{12} = 0$

Furthermore, let B stand for the unemployment benefit, W the market wage, and ρ_u and ρ_r the employment probabilities of an unemployed worker and a relief worker, respectively. Assume, plausibly enough, that the employment probabilities depend on the search intensities as follows:

$$\rho_u = \rho_u(S_u), \qquad \rho_u' > 0, \quad \rho_u'' < 0 \tag{2a}$$

$$\rho_r = \rho_r(S_r), \qquad \rho_r' > 0, \quad \rho_r'' < 0 \tag{2b}$$

(Of course, ρ_u also depends on S_r, and ρ_r also depends on S_u, but these relations are not relevant for what is to follow.) Let δ be the workers' rate of time discount. Then we may express the present values of income for an unemployed worker and a relief worker as follows:

$$Y_u = B + \delta \cdot [\rho_u \cdot W + (1 - \rho_u) \cdot B] \qquad (3a)$$

(i.e., in the first period, an unemployed worker receives the unemployment benefit B; in the second period, he receives the wage W with probability ρ_u and the unemployment benefit B with probability $(1 - \rho_u)$), and

$$Y_r = W + \delta \cdot [\rho_r \cdot W + (1 - \rho_r) \cdot B] \qquad (3b)$$

(where, as the authors note, the relief worker receives the market wage).

Substituting equations (2a, 2b) and (3a, 3b) into equation (1) and differentiating with respect to S, we may derive the first-order conditions characterising the optimal search intensities:

$$\frac{dV_{[u]}}{dS_u} = V_1(Y_u) \cdot \delta \cdot \rho_{u'} \cdot (W - B) + V_2(S_u) = 0 \qquad \Rightarrow \quad S_u = S_u^* (4a)$$

$$\frac{dV_{[r]}}{dS_r} = V_1(Y_r) \cdot \delta \cdot \rho_{r'} \cdot (W - B) + V_2(S_r) = 0 \qquad \Rightarrow \quad S_r = S_r^* \quad (4b)$$

Letting $\zeta_u = (dV_u/dS_u)$ and $\zeta_r = (dV_r/dS_r)$, we find that

$$\frac{d\xi_i}{dS_i} = \frac{V_i}{S_i} \delta \cdot (W - B) \cdot \rho_{i'} \cdot (\epsilon_i + \eta_i) + V_{22}(S_i) < 0 \qquad i = u, r \quad (5)$$

where $-\epsilon_i = (\partial V_1/\partial S_i)/(S_i/V_1) < 0$ is the elasticity of the marginal utility of income with respect to the search intensity and η_i is the elasticity of the marginal employment probability with respect to the search intensity. Intuitively, ϵ_i may be viewed as a measure of the 'income effect of job search intensity', and η_i as the 'marginal employment effect of job search'.

This simple analytical set-up allows us to gain some insight into what determines the comparative search intensities of relief workers and unemployed workers. Given that the wages of relief workers (W) exceed the unemployment benefit (B), equation (5) implies that the relative magnitudes of S_u and S_r depend crucially on the sum of the income effect and marginal employment effect of search.

It is important to emphasise that the model above is merely illustrative. Yet it does indicate the importance of moving beyond the authors' empirical results towards an understanding of the underlying channels whereby labour market programmes can affect flows into the employment pool.

11 Mismatch and Labour Mobility: Some Final Remarks[1]

KATHARINE G. ABRAHAM

1 Introduction

One of the things that struck me most in reading the studies prepared for this volume – as it had in listening to the discussion at the conference at which the papers were originally presented – was the lack of consensus among their authors concerning the appropriate orientation for an investigation of labour market mismatch. In their overview study (Chapter 2 in this volume), Jackman, Layard and Savouri (hereafter JLS) argue that researchers interested in mismatch ought to direct their efforts toward understanding the persistent differences in the unemployment rate across skill groups and regions. This orientation leads them to focus on labour market equilibrium, and the factors that affect it, with rather little attention given to labour market dynamics. In contrast, most of the individual country studies are concerned more directly with the question of whether, and how, labour market adjustment problems have contributed to the increases in those countries' unemployment rates during the 1970s and early 1980s. This latter orientation leads these authors to focus on a variety of issues related to changes in the labour market and the dynamics of labour market adjustment.

While both sets of issues are clearly important, I cannot say that the existence of persistent cross-group unemployment rate differentials strikes me as especially surprising. Differences in unemployment rates across skill groups, for example, are easily rationalised in terms of differential rates of investment in firm-specific human capital that produce different degrees of attachment to particular jobs. Similarly, persistent differences in unemployment rates across regions can be explained in terms of differences in industrial structure and in local amenities.

In contrast to the persistent differences in the rate of unemployment across skill groups and region – which I suspect most economists would explain in much the same way, though perhaps not so elegantly as JLS have done – the causes of the rise in unemployment experienced by the developed economies in the 1970s and early 1980s remain a subject of considerable debate. In many countries, the increase in unemployment through the mid-1980s was very large indeed. The OECD-standardised unemployment rate in Germany, for example, rose from an average of 1.1% over the 1967–74 period to 8.6% in 1984. Comparable numbers show an increase in unemployment in the United Kingdom from 3.4% to 13.2%; in Italy from 5.6% to 10.2%; and in Spain from 2.7% to 20.1%. Smaller, but still significant, increases in unemployment were experienced in the United States, Sweden and Japan over the same period (Bean, Layard and Nickell, 1986).

A long list of potential explanations for these increases can be put forward. These include: insufficiently aggressive macroeconomic policy; sluggish adjustment of the real wage level following the OPEC oil shocks; increased turbulence in the economic environment, which might have taken the form of shocks to the allocation of jobs across sectors, shocks to the distribution of labour supply across sectors, or simply higher job or worker turnover rates; decreased responsiveness of workers to shifts in relative demand; decreased responsiveness of employers to shifts in relative supply; a deterioration in the work ethic that has lead unemployed persons to be less vigorous in their search for work; and greater caution in hiring on the part of employers. Several of these possible sources of increased unemployment seem likely, should they be found to have been important, to have been associated with increases in labour market mismatch. No clear consensus concerning the relative importance of the various potential underlying contributors to the increase in unemployment observed in so many of the developed economies has yet been reached.

In discussing what I think we have learned from the studies included in this volume, my primary concern will be with what they tell us about the contribution of labour market adjustment problems, and associated increases in labour market mismatch to observed increases in unemployment and with the related issue of how the developed economies have responded to labour market imbalance. As will quickly become clear, I have not sought to summarise the specific results of the individual studies in any detailed or systematic fashion. Instead, I have attempted, undoubtedly with only partial success, to place those results within the broader context of ongoing research on labour market mismatch and the dynamics of labour market adjustment. My aim has been not only to highlight selected aspects of the results reported, but also to offer my thoughts about why the findings on certain issues are weak or ambiguous and to suggest directions for future research. Measurement and data quality issues – a major topic of discussion during the conference – figure prominently in my comments.

Section 2 begins with the subject of why growing mismatch has seemed a natural candidate for explaining at least a part of the increase in unemployment observed in the developed economies during the 1970s and early 1980s. These were turbulent years; in addition, in many countries both job turnover rates and geographic mobility were lower than they had been in earlier decades, and the job vacancy rate associated with given unemployment rose. These facts suggested that growing mismatch might have contributed to the rise in unemployment.

Section 3 discusses a variety of issues related to the measurement of mismatch and section 4 summarises existing evidence on mismatch trends. A number of labour market mismatch indicators have been proposed in the literature; I review the conceptual underpinnings of those used in this volume's studies. Attaching a structural interpretation to any of these measures requires the imposition of some rather strong assumptions concerning the job matching and wage determination processes. Probably more important, it is critical that the skill or geographic categories used in the measures' construction correspond to actual labour market contours. In practice, the occupational categories used in reporting unemployment and vacancy data may do a poor job of capturing relevant skill groupings; geographic categories are presumably less problematic. The volume's studies report very mixed results concerning trends in skill mismatch. While these findings could be taken as reason to reject the hypothesis that growing mismatch offers a general explanation for rising unemployment, the ambiguity of the skill mismatch evidence might also reflect conceptual and data limitations of the measures used. The studies' findings lend little support to the view that there has been a general increase in geographic mismatch.

Section 5 considers the roles of skill acquisition and geographic mobility in labour market adjustment. Differences in countries' employment and training systems seem likely to be associated with important differences in how their labour markets respond to skill imbalance, but the potential diversity of functional institutional structures should also be recognised. Evidence reported in two of the volume's studies suggests that workers' location decisions respond to regional imbalance, but that this process can take many years. The question of how employers respond to labour market imbalance is a major issue that receives little attention in the volume's studies.

Section 6 offers a few concluding thoughts and observations, emphasising future research needs.

2   Mismatch as a suspect in the case of the rising unemployment rate

Given the largely negative findings reported in the studies prepared for this volume, it may be useful to recollect why anyone should ever have thought that labour market adjustment problems and associated increases in mismatch might have contributed to the rise in unemployment in the developed economies during the 1970s and early 1980s. One good reason to have suspected that growing mismatch might have been important was that these economies were subjected to a series of major shocks during this period, including the movement from a fixed to a flexible exchange rate regime and the two OPEC oil shocks. These shocks are widely believed to have caused significant shifts in the pattern of employment worldwide. In addition, there is considerable anecdotal evidence that the introduction of microelectronic technologies into the workplace during these years has altered job requirements in important ways. It would not be surprising if these developments had in fact lead to an increased pace of job reallocation across skill groups and increased skill mismatch. To the extent that employment in particular sectors tends to be geographically concentrated, the same developments might also have produced increased disparities in regional growth rates and increased geographic mismatch.[2]

Somewhat surprisingly, given the important developments just cited, available evidence on the intensity of job reallocation shocks – measured using data on changes in the composition of employment or differences in employment growth rates by industry or by region – does not show a clear pattern of increased turbulence during the 1970s and 1980s. Among the countries represented in this volume, industrial turbulence, measured using employment data for broad industrial sectors, has risen only in the United Kingdom and the United States, and even there the level of turbulence is still far below levels experienced during the interwar period. Regional turbulence has risen in several countries; though, except in the United States, these increases did not occur until the 1980s.[3]

One problem with turbulence measures of the usual sort is that they are computed using realised, rather than desired, changes in employment; if mismatch were a sufficiently serious problem, measures based on actual employment changes might fail to capture important reallocation shocks. A second, and probably more important, problem is that these measures are likely not to capture the effects that the introduction of new technology has had on the skill mix of labour demand. Different industries do employ different sorts of workers, but important changes in skill mix may occur within an industry without necessarily affecting the industry's share of total employment.[4] While the absence of clear trends in measured turbulence must temper one's enthusiasm for the view that reallocation shocks have become more intense than they were in the 1960s, it does not constitute definitive evidence for the opposite view, particularly not with respect to shocks that might have affected the skill distribution of labour demand.

A second reason to have suspected that labour market mismatch might have become more important is that there have been significant declines in labour market turnover and geographic mobility in most of the developed economies for which data are available.[5] This has led to speculation that labour markets, particularly European labour markets, have become less responsive than they used to be, thereby contributing to increased mismatch. A significant problem here is the difficulty of identifying cause and effect: has decreased mobility contributed to high unemployment, or is high unemployment responsible for decreased mobility? I return to this issue below.

A third (and perhaps the best) reason to have believed that the mismatch explanation for growing unemployment deserved serious consideration was the outward shift in the relationship between the unemployment rate and the job vacancy rate, commonly referred to as the Beveridge curve, observed in many of the developed economies by the late 1970s. Increases in unemployment may result either from factors that cause the economy to move to the right along a given Beveridge curve, such as slower than expected growth of the money supply or an excessive real wage level, or from factors that cause an outward shift in the Beveridge curve, such as developments that lead to worsening mismatch or to changes in search behaviour. While growing labour market mismatch is not the only possible explanation for outward shifts in the Beveridge curve, it must have appeared, at least initially, high on most analysts' lists of likely culprits.

Among the countries represented in the studies prepared for this conference, data on both unemployment and job vacancies exist for Germany, Japan, the United Kingdom and Sweden. Outward shifts in the relationship between the unemployment rate and the job vacancy rate over the period since the early 1970s have been reported for three of these four countries: Germany, Japan and the United Kingdom (see Franz, Brunello, and Bean and Pissarides, Chapters 3, 4 and 7 in this volume). While job vacancy data for the United States are not available, examination of data on unemployment and the volume of 'help wanted' advertising, a proxy for the level of job vacancies, suggests that the US Beveridge curve also shifted outward during the 1970s (Abraham, 1987), though much of that outward shift has been reversed since 1985 (Blanchard and Diamond, 1990). In all four of these countries, a significant fraction of the observed increase in unemployment can be attributed to outward shifts in the Beveridge curve rather than to movements along it (or, more accurately, to factors that have shifted the Beveridge curve rather than to factors that have caused movements along it).

Sweden is the only country represented in the individual country studies prepared for this volume for which job vacancy data are available and in which there apepars to have been no outward shift in the unemployment/vacancy relationship. Even in Sweden, there is reason to believe that, in the absence of offsetting favourable developments, the Beveridge curve would have shifted outward. In their study (Chapter 10 in this volume), Edin and Holmlund estimate an aggregate matching function, in which outflows of job vacancies (corresponding to new hires) are related to the stock of unemployed persons and the stock of vacant jobs.[6] They find evidence of a strong negative time trend in this relationship, implying that given stocks of unemployed persons and vacant jobs are associated with fewer matches than would have been true in the past. One possible explanation for this finding – though not the explanation that Edin and Holmlund argue for – is a growing mismatch between the unemployed population and the stock of vacant jobs. Only the fact that there has been a trend decline in the rate of inflows into unemployment has prevented the Swedish Beveridge curve from shifting outward.

One thing made clear by this volume's discussions of the data series used to trace movements in individual countries' Beveridge curves is the importance of paying careful attention to the underlying sources of information, particularly the sources of information on job vacancies. In most countries that report job vacancy statistics, the numbers reported are derived from administrative records rather than from surveys designed for statistical purposes; this means that institutional changes can have an important effect on the job vacancy numbers. In Germany, for example, analyses using the official unemployment and job vacancy data show little if any outward shift in the unemployment/vacancy relationship since 1970.[7] Between 1970 and 1985, however, the share of all new hires mediated by the labour office fell from about 45% to under 25%.[8] Under the assumption that the average duration of job vacancies filled through the labour office is equal to the average duration of job vacancies filled in other ways, this implies that the true level of vacancies was somewhat more than twice as large as the official level in 1970, but roughly four times as large by 1985. In contrast to the relationship based on unadjusted German data, the Beveridge curve constructed using vacancy data adjusted for the changing percentage of hiring done through the labour office shows a substantial outward shift since 1974 (see Franz, Chapter 3 in this volume).

In the United Kingdom, it turns out that working with unadjusted vacancy data would have lead to the opposite error; since the share of job vacancies registered with the employment service has risen, the outward shift in the unadjusted unemployment/vacancy relationship has been larger than the outward shift in the adjusted curve (see Jackman, Layard and Pissarides, 1984). Analysts who have worked with unadjusted 'help wanted' index data as a proxy for US job vacancies have probably also exaggerated the outward shift of the Beveridge curve, since institutional developments have almost certainly raised the value of 'help wanted' advertising relative to the number of job vacancies. Changes in the occupational composition of employment and equal employment opportunity pressures appear to have raised the share of job vacancies that employers choose to advertise. Even more important, the demise of competing newspapers in many cities appears to have raised the volume of advertising garnered by the one newspaper per city represented in the ad counts used to construct the index. Correcting the 'help wanted' series for these problems reduces the magnitude of the outward shift in the US Beveridge curve between 1970 and 1985, although it remains substantial (see Abraham, 1987). These data issues underscore the difficulties faced by those who seek to undertake comparative cross-national research, and the value of involving in any such study researchers who are knowledgeable concerning each individual country's institutions and data collection procedures.

Neither evidence of an outward shift in the Beveridge curve nor evidence of a deterioration in the aggregate hiring function, however, constitutes proof of worsening mismatch. The most often cited alternative explanation for these developments is reduced intensity of search by unemployed workers, such as might have been induced by changes in labour force demographics or changes in government transfer policy. Increased employer choosiness in hiring – such as one might expect if, for example, legislation governing layoffs and dismissals had raised the costs associated with a poor hiring decision – could have produced the same result. While these possibilities deserve to be taken seriously, there is little *a priori* basis for preferring either of them to some variant of the mismatch explanation. Direct evidence on changes in search behaviour is very difficult to come by; those who have reached the conclusion that such changes must have been important have invariably arrived at that conclusion through a process of elimination. Given that there are serious difficulties associated with the measurement of mismatch, the importance of changes in search behaviour may well have been exaggerated. Before concluding that growing mismatch had contributed to the outward shifts in the Beveridge curve and the associated increase in unemployment between the early 1970s and the early 1980s, one nonetheless would like to have at least some direct evidence that mismatch had, in fact, increased.

3   Measurement issues

Any effort to construct an empirical measure of mismatch presupposes that both workers and jobs can be differentiated along one or more dimensions, most especially the skill and the geographic dimensions. Skill mismatch may arise if workers cannot readily learn new skills, or are unwilling to accept jobs that do not utilise their existing skills, and jobs cannot readily be redesigned to be performed by persons with a different set of qualifications than were initially envisioned; geographic mismatch may arise if neither workers nor jobs are fully mobile. In either case, mismatch arises because moving either workers or jobs across categories is costly, so that disproportionate numbers of unemployed persons in some sectors may coexist with disproportionate numbers of job vacancies in others. Provided there is significant convexity in the sectoral unemployment/vacancy relationships, this will imply aggregate levels of unemployment and vacancies that are higher than their theoretical minimum flow equilibrium values, given aggregate labour demand and aggregate labour supply.

3.1   Measures that use data on unemployment and vacancies

Various empirical measures of mismatch that make use of data on the distribution of unemployed people and job vacancies across labour market categories, such as occupation and region, have been proposed. One such measure, used by both Franz and Brunello (Chapters 3 and 4), is:

$$M_1 = \tfrac{1}{2} \sum_i |u_i - v_i| \tag{1}$$

where u_i is the share of unemployed persons, and v_i the share of job vacancies, in category i.

This measure varies from a minimum of zero (when the distribution of unemployment and vacancies across categories is identical), to a maximum of 1 (when there is no category containing both unemployed persons and vacant jobs). It has a straightforward interpretation: it equals the fraction of unemployed persons (or, equivalently, the fraction of job vacancies) that would have to be moved to make the proportion of unemployed persons in each category equal to the proportion of job vacancies in the category.

The JLS and Bean and Pissarides studies (Chapters 2 and 7) make use of a similar mismatch indicator, computed as:

$$M_2 = 1 - \sum_i (u_i v_i)^{1/2} \tag{2}$$

where u_i and v_i are as defined above.

Like M_1, M_2 varies from a minimum of zero (when the shares of unemployment and vacancies across sectors are identical), to a maximum of 1 (when there is no sector in which unemployment and vacancies coexist). Under plausible assumptions, this measure can be given an appealing structural interpretation: it represents the proportion by which aggregate unemployment and aggregate vacancies could be reduced if aggregate labour demand and aggregate labour supply were redistributed so that u_i equalled v_i in all sectors, holding the relative distribution of employment across sectors constant.

Suppose that the hiring function in any individual sector can be represented as:

$$H_i = \beta_i U_i^{\alpha_i} V_i^{1-\alpha_i} \tag{3}$$

where H_i represents the number of new hires, U_i the number of unemployed persons and V_i the number of job vacancies in sector i, and β_i and α_i are the parameters of the hiring function.

In steady state, inflows to unemployment must be just balanced by outflows. Ignoring flows into and out of the labour force and taking the rate of separation from employment as given, the hiring function can thus be represented as:

$$(s_i/\beta_i) = (U_i/N_i)^{\alpha_i}(V_i/N_i)^{1-\alpha_i} \tag{4}$$

where N_i is employment in sector i, U_i/N_i is the sectoral unemployment rate, V_i/N_i is the sectoral vacancy rate, s_i is the (exogenously given) separation rate, and α_i and β_i are as above.

Equation (4) implicitly defines the unemployment/vacancy relationship for a particular sector.

To proceed further, additional restrictions must be imposed. The key additional assumption is that α equals $\frac{1}{2}$ in all sectors, so that all of the sectoral Beveridge curves can be represented as rectangular hyperbolas (see JLS in Chapter 2 for evidence on this point). Rewrite the right-hand side of equation (4) by first multiplying and then dividing by $(U/N * V/N)^{1/2}$, where U, V and N are aggregate unemployment, vacancies and employment, respectively, and then take the weighted sum of the resulting expression across sectors, using the sectoral employment shares as weights. After some manipulation, this yields:

$$\sum_i (N_i/N)(s_i/\beta_i) = [(U/N)(V/N)]^{1/2} \sum_i (u_i v_i)^{1/2} \qquad (5)$$

where U/N is the aggregate unemployment rate, V/N is the aggregate vacancy rate, and u_i and v_i are, as before, the shares of unemployment and vacancies in sector i.

Equation (5) implicitly defines the aggregate unemployment/vacancy relationship.

Note that the term on the right-hand side of equation (5) containing the u_is and v_is is just equal to $1 - M_2$. In this formulation, decreases in mismatch permit reductions in the aggregate unemployment rate and/or the aggregate vacancy rate. To see this more clearly, rewrite equation (5) with $1 - M_2$ substituted for the term in brackets, take the logarithm of both sides of the equation, and make use of the approximation that the logarithm of $1 - x$, where x is a small number, is approximately equal to x. This yields:

$$C = \tfrac{1}{2} ln(U/N) + \tfrac{1}{2} ln(V/N) - M_2 \qquad (6)$$

where C is the logarithm of the left-hand side of equation (5) and depends only upon the employment-share-weighted values of the (exogenously given) s_i/β_i ratios.

With C given, a 0.01 decrease in M_2 would permit an (approximately) 1% reduction in both U/N and V/N.[9]

Given the availability of both unemployment and vacancy data, an alternative approach to assessing the contribution of mismatch to shifts in the aggregate unemployment/vacancy relationship would be to begin by estimating the sectoral unemployment/vacancy relationships directly. If any observed outward shift in the aggregate unemployment/vacancy relationship reflects growing mismatch rather than other causes, one should find that the corresponding sectoral relationships have been stable over time. In contrast, if these aggregate outward shifts reflect factors other than mismatch, one should find that the corresponding sectoral relationships have exhibited generally similar outward shifts. In intermediate cases, it should be possible to decompose the aggregate shift in the relationship of interest into a part attributable to movements along the relevant sectoral curves and a part attributable to shifts in those curves. This approach has the advantage that no particular restrictions concerning the shapes of the sectoral hiring functions are required. The only additional data required to implement this approach, beyond that required for construction of either M_1 or M_2, is data on employment by sector (i.e., by occupation or region). While this approach strikes me as an attractive alternative to the construction of mismatch measures of the sort just discussed, it is not an approach adopted in any of the studies included in this volume.[10]

3.2 Unemployment rate dispersion and mismatch

Any of these approaches to the measurement of mismatch requires disaggregated job vacancy data, which for many countries is unavailable. An alternative strategy for measuring the extent of mismatch is to make use of information on the dispersion of sectoral unemployment rates. This is an old idea that can be traced back to work by Lipsey and Solow in the early 1960s (see Lipsey, 1960 and Solow, 1964). The studies by JLS; Brunello; Bentolila and Dolado; and Attanasio and Padoa Schioppa (Chapters 2, 4, 5 and 6) all make use of a mismatch indicator based upon the relative dispersion of sectoral unemployment rates:

$$M_3 = \text{var} \left(\frac{U_i/N_i}{U/N} \right), \tag{7}$$

where U_i/N_i is the sectoral unemployment rate and U/N is the aggregate unemployment rate.[11]

One issue that provoked considerable discussion at the conference was whether the *relative* dispersion of sectoral unemployment rates, $\text{var}[(u_i/N_i)/(U/N)]$, is in fact a more meaningful mismatch proxy than the *absolute* dispersion in sectoral unemployment rates, $\text{var}(U_i/N_i)$. If the aggregate unemployment rate had been relatively stable over time, these measures would track one another quite closely, so that the measure one chose would be relatively unimportant. Because aggregate unemployment in many countries has risen markedly, however, it has been possible for relative and absolute dispersion measures to behave quite differently; in Spain, for example, the relative dispersion of unemployment rates across regions fell markedly between 1976 and 1989, even though the absolute dispersion was rising (Bentolila and Dolado, Chapter 5 in this volume). The choice of measure is thus of some practical significance.

One approach to making this choice is to think about the relationship between unemployment rate dispersion measures and mismatch measures like M_1 and M_2. When sectors have very different hiring functions, a given sectoral unemployment rate may imply quite different sectoral vacancy rates, leading to unemployment and vacancy shares that diverge substantially from one another. In this situation, an increase in the dispersion of unemployment rates across sectors, holding mean unemployment constant, might either raise or lower the value of mismatch measures like M_1 and M_2, so that neither the relative nor the absolute dispersion in unemployment rates is necessarily a very good mismatch proxy. In the case where all sectors have the same hiring function, measures like M_1 and M_2 can be shown to depend upon the dispersion of sectoral unemployment rates relative to their mean, not their absolute dispersion.

This can be illustrated simply in the case where the economy consists of two sectors of equal size. Suppose, as before, that the sectoral unemployment/vacancy relationship is of the form:

$$s/\beta = (U_i/N_i)^{1/2}(V_i/N_i)^{1/2} \tag{8}$$

where all terms are as defined above and s and β are assumed to be equal across sectors.

Whatever the mean unemployment rate, so long as the two sectors have identical hiring functions, both M_1 and M_2 will equal zero. Now suppose that the dispersion of unemployment across the two sectors changes, so that the first sector has an unemployment rate that is Δ above the mean and the second sector an unemployment rate that is Δ below the mean. It is straightforward to show that, in this situation, the value of M_1 rises to $2\Delta/(U/N)$ and the value of M_2 rises to $1 - (1 - (\Delta/(U/N))^2)^{1/2}$, where U/N is the mean unemployment rate. Both M_1 and M_2 clearly depend upon the size of the gap between the unemployment rates in the two sectors relative to the mean unemployment rate, not upon the absolute difference between the two rates. This result can be generalised, and provides some basis for preferring the relative, rather than the absolute, dispersion of unemployment rates as a mismatch proxy.

One implication to be noted here is that M_3 will be a better proxy for the degree of mismatch between unemployment and job vacancies across sectors when those sectors have similar hiring functions and, as a result, similar sectoral Beveridge curves. If hiring functions are more similar across regions than across skill groups, for example, the relative dispersion of unemployment rates across regions may be a reasonable proxy for the degree of geographic mismatch, while the relative dispersion of unemployment rates across skill groups may be a poor proxy for the degree of skill mismatch.

My discussion thus far has conceptualised 'mismatch' in terms of discrepancies between the distribution of unemployment and vacancies across sectors that lead to aggregate unemployment and aggregate vacancies in excess of their theoretical flow minimum values, taking as given aggregate labour demand, aggregate labour supply, the shares of employment accounted for by each sector and the turnover and matching processes in individual sectors. An alternative rationale for the use of relative unemployment dispersion as a mismatch proxy is proffered by JLS (in Chapter 2), who define labour market mismatch with references to the NAIRU. They observe that, under particular assumptions concerning the wage and price determination process, the aggregate unemployment rate consistent with the absence of inflationary pressure exceeds its theoretical minimum value by a proportion equal to one-half the relative dispersion of unemployment rates (that is, by $\frac{1}{2} * M_3$). The key assumptions required to generate this result are that the logarithm of the wage rate in a sector is linearly related to the logarithm of the sectoral unemployment rate and that the wage/employment elasticity is the same in all sectors. Note that, in addition to being restrictive with respect to functional form and with respect to the exclusive role of local conditions in determining local wage growth (issues that provoked some discussion at the conference), this specification excludes job vacancies from the wage determination process. If all sectors have the same hiring function, unemployment and vacancies have a unique inverse relationship with one another, and the inclusion of either of the two variables in the wage equation should suffice. If different sectors have different hiring functions, however, the exclusion of vacancies from the wage function could be an important omission, and M_3 might be a poor indicator of the degree to which the NAIRU exceeds its theoretical 'no-mismatch' minimum value.

Insofar as it explicitly incorporates the behaviour of wages, the JLS conceptualisation of 'mismatch unemployment' differs from mine. It seems to lead, however, to the same basic conclusion concerning the use of sectoral unemployment dispersion measures as mismatch proxies: unemployment rate dispersion measures may not be very good mismatch proxies, but relative dispersion measures are probably better than absolute dispersion measures.[12]

3.3   Drawing labour market boundaries

All of the mismatch measures that I have described presume that the labour market categories into which unemployment (and, if applicable, vacancies) have been divided correspond in some meaningful way to distinct labour markets. The development of a valid mismatch indicator requires a decision about which identifiable categories best correspond to these labour markets. The mismatch statistics reported in this volume's studies generally use data categorised either by occupation, as a proxy for skill groups, or by region.[13]

If the set of classifications used to categorise unemployment (and vacancies) is too fine – in the sense that groups of workers who in fact compete for the same jobs, or groups of jobs that are filled from the same pool of workers, are assigned to different categories – the degree of mismatch may be exaggerated. If, as is perhaps more likely, the set of classifications used to categorise unemployment (and vacancies) is too coarse, mismatch may be significantly understated. The degree of aggregation can make a considerable difference to the level of measured mismatch. Results for Germany reported by Franz (Chapter 3), for example, indicate that the value of M_1 computed using data for two occupational categories equalled 0.05 in 1976, while the value of the same measure in the same year computed using data for 327 occupations equalled 0.37. JLS (Chapter 2) report that, in Britain, M_3 equalled 0.05 in 1985 when computed using data for 10 regions, while in the same year the dispersion of relative unemployment rates across 322 travel-to-work areas equalled 0.24.

If one is interested in assessing trends in mismatch rather than the level of mismatch, one might suppose that these problems were not terribly worrisome. A potential concern, however, is that the degree of heterogeneity within classifications, at least along the skill dimension, may have risen in recent years. For example, factory operatives might once have been largely interchangeable, but today there may be an important distinction between factory operatives who have education or training that prepares them to work with computerised technologies and those who do not. If it is true more generally that workers and jobs within what were once fairly homogeneous groupings have become increasingly differentiated over time, standard measures of occupational mismatch may fail to capture even a significant deterioration in the 'fit' between the skills of unemployed workers and the requirements of vacant jobs. The trend in measures of geographic mismatch is presumably less likely to be affected by this problem.

A related problem is that individuals cannot easily be assigned to a single occupational, or even a single geographic, category. Any one individual's previous experience might have prepared him or her for employment in a number of occupations. Indeed, it is well known that a substantial number of job changers also report changes in occupation. Similarly, depending upon other factors, the potential pool of applicants for a particular job vacancy might include persons living outside the geographic region in which the employer's place of business is located. A conceptually preferable measure of mismatch might capture not simply discrepancies between the distributions of unemployment and vacancies across occupational or geographic categories, but rather the 'distance' between the available labour supply and available jobs. Constructing such a measure would admittedly be a daunting task. A natural strategy would be to weight excess unemployment and excess vacancies in particular sectors by some measure of the 'distance' between their current occupational or geographic location and those occupational or geographic locations with relative shortfalls. Two categories might be considered far apart if movement between them is unusual and close if it is relatively common.[14] Again, this issue is almost certainly more important for measures of skill mismatch than for measures of regional mismatch.

3.4   The behaviour of wages

I have thus far paid almost no attention to the behaviour of wages. This is clearly an important omission. If relative wages are rigid in the short to medium run, shifts in either demand or supply will translate fully into quantity changes and there will be no loss in focusing on movements in unemployment and vacancies to the exclusion of wages. In general, however, demand and supply shocks may affect not only quantities but also prices. Increases in the relative demand for workers in a particular skill category, for example, might produce not only an increase in the share of vacancies and a decrease in the share of unemployment accounted for by that skill category, but also an increase in the relative wages of workers in the group. Again speaking somewhat loosely, the more responsive are wages to shifts in the balance between labour demand and labour supply, the less likely are such shifts to cause increases in measured mismatch. A full understanding of the evolution of labour market mismatch, even in the flow equilibrium sense in which I have been using that term, clearly requires some consideration of wage behaviour.

4   What have we learned about trends in mismatch?

One of the important contributions of the studies prepared for this volume is to present evidence on a variety of measures of skill and geographic mismatch. As noted earlier, most of the measures of *skill* mismatch make use of information on unemployment and, where available, job vacancies, categorised by occupation.

Table 11.1 summarises the evidence on occupational mismatch reported by the authors of the individual country studies and by JLS in their overview study (Chapter 2). For the sake of completeness – at least with respect to the countries represented in the individual country studies – selected occupational mismatch series reported by Jackman and Roper (1987) are also included. Taken as a whole, the information summarised

Table 11.1. *Evidence concerning the trend in skill mismatch, selected OECD countries*

Country and study	Measure	Labour market categories and time period	Trend
Germany: Franz (Chapter 3)[1]	M_1	'Unskilled' versus 'skilled' workers, where 'unskilled' is defined as the absence of a complete vocational education (1976–88)	Mismatch much higher since 1981 than during the 1976–80 period
Germany: Jackman and Roper (1987)	M_1	40 occupations (1969–83)	Average level of mismatch lower over the 1976–83 period than in earlier years
Germany: Franz (Chapter 3)	M_1	327 occupations (1976–88)	Mismatch lower over 1983–8 period than during earlier years
Germany: JLS (Chapter 2)	M_3	6 occupations (1976; 1978; 1980; 1982; 1984; 1985)	Mismatch substantially higher in 1982 and later years than in earlier years
United Kingdom: Jackman and Roper (1987)	M_1	24 occupations (1963–72; 1973–82)	No trend in mismatch
United Kingdom: Bean and Pissarides (Chapter 7)	M_2	24 occupations (1963–72; 1973–82)	No trend in mismatch
United Kingdom: JLS (Chapter 2)	M_2	6 occupations (1974–85)	No trend in mismatch

Sweden: Jackman and Roper (1987)	M_1	7 occupations (1970–82, with break in series in 1977)	Substantial increases in mismatch in 1971–2 and 1981–2, but no obvious trend
Sweden: JLS	M_3	8 occupations (1973–84)	Mismatch higher since 1976 than in earlier years
United States: JLS (Chapter 2)	M_3	6 occupations (1973–87, with break in series in 1983)	Increase in mismatch during the early 1980s, but this increase partially reversed between 1983 and 1987
Spain: Bentolila and Dolado (Chapter 5)	M_3	4 occupations (1977–89)	Mismatch stable through 1985 and higher thereafter
Spain: JLS (Chapter 2)	M_3	7 occupations (1977–89)	Increase in mismatch through 1983, followed by a sharp decline to below its 1977 level

Notes:
1. All chapters in this volume unless otherwise stated.
2. The mismatch measures M_1, M_2 and M_3 are defined in the text. M_1 and M_2 make use of data on the shares of unemployment and job vacancies by sector; M_3 is a measure of the relative dispersion of sectoral unemployment rates.

provides only very weak evidence of increases in skill mismatch. In several countries (Germany, Sweden, the United States and Spain), the level of at least one occupational mismatch indicator was higher by the mid-1980s than it had been in the mid-1970s. All of the series that show increases in skill mismatch, however, begin in 1973 or later. This means that it is not possible to compare the level of skill mismatch during the 1970s and 1980s with that during the 1950s and 1960s. In addition, the timing of the reported increases in skill mismatch varies a good deal across countries.

The disturbing feature of the results summarised in Table 11.1 is that trends in measured skill mismatch within individual countries appear to be sensitive both to the measure used and to the occupational groupings employed in their construction. The M_1 mismatch measure for Sweden reported by Jackman and Roper (1987), for example, shows no clear trend over the 1970–82 period. In contrast, the M_3 measure for Sweden reported by JLS in Chapter 2, calculated for the 1973–84 period using what appears to be a similar level of occupational detail, jumps upward and remains higher after 1976. Differences in the occupational groupings used in constructing the various mismatch series appear to produce even more dramatically different results. Three different M_1 series are available for Germany, one based on a simple unskilled/skilled breakdown, one based upon a 40-occupation classification and one based upon a 327-occupation classification. The first series suggests that occupational mismatch has been much larger since 1981 than during the late 1970s; the second shows no significant changes in mismatch between 1976 and 1983; and the third indicates that mismatch has been substantially lower over the 1983–8 period than during the late 1970s. One can clearly draw no conclusion concerning trends in occupational mismatch in the German labour market without first resolving the question of which groups of workers in fact compete with one another for which jobs! Only for the United Kingdom, among the four countries for which multiple skill mismatch indicators are available, do all of the reported measures move in a consistent fashion.

The geographic mismatch measures summarised in Table 11.2 appear to be somewhat more robust, in the sense that the movements in different mismatch measures for a particular country seem generally to be similar. They certainly do not support the conclusion that there has been any general increase in regional mismatch. All of the measures for Germany and for Japan agree that regional mismatch was higher by the mid-1980s than it had been in 1975, though there is some disagreement among the measures for both countries concerning the time path of mismatch over the intervening years. In Germany, however, this recent increase appears to represent only a return to pre-1970 mismatch levels. In Italy regional mismatch, based upon the relative dispersion of unemployment rates, has been higher during the 1970s and 1980s than it was during the 1960s. There is also some evidence of increased regional mismatch in the United States, though the time period covered is relatively short. In Spain, where M_3 is again the only reported mismatch measure, the absolute dispersion of unemployment rates across regions increased, but mean unemployment also increased and M_3 has fallen fairly steadily since the early 1960s. Two separate regional mismatch measures are reported for Sweden; neither shows any clear trend. Three separate regional mismatch measures are reported for the United Kingdom; all show that the level of mismatch has actually been lower since 1975 than before.[15] In short, while there have been increases in geographic mismatch in some countries, this has not been a universal phenomenon.

While the reported evidence provides strong support neither for the conclusion that there have been general increases in skill mismatch nor for the conclusion that there have been general increases in geographic mismatch, the skill mismatch results, in particular, are so fragile that it is difficult to place much confidence in them. Given the discussion in section 3, the lack of consistency exhibited by the various skill mismatch measures is perhaps not surprising. First, the choice of mismatch measure is apt to make more of a difference when there are important differences in the hiring function across sectors, and it seems likely that different skill groups have quite different hiring functions. Second – and probably more important – errors in the grouping of workers and jobs into categories can invalidate any mismatch measure, and the identification of appropriate skill groups poses very serious problems. For these reasons, I am reluctant to move from the available evidence to any positive assertion that skill mismatch has not worsened.

One question that might naturally be raised at this point is whether data on the behaviour of wages can tell us anything about trends in skill mismatch. In the United States, but not to my knowledge in other developed countries for which data are available, there has been a very significant widening of skill-related wage differentials.[16] Trends in the relative supplies of more- and less-educated workers cannot account for the widening gap between the earnings of more- and less-educated workers in the United States. The most obvious interpretation of these widening wage differentials is that there has been a larger than anticipated rightward shift in the demand curve for relatively skilled labour. While it is difficult to identify the precise technological or other developments that have produced this rightward shift, one might guess that similar forces have affected other developed economies. Skill-related wage differentials, however, appear to have been relatively stable. This apparent stability in the face of what one can infer have been large rightward shifts in the demand curve for more

Table 11.2. *Evidence concerning the trend in geographical mismatch, selected OECD countries*

Country and study	Measure	Labour market categories and time period	Trend
Germany: Jackman and Roper (1987)	M_1	9 regions (1967–83)	Decline in mismatch over the 1970–5 period, followed by an increase to near pre-1970 levels by 1982
Germany: Franz (Chapter 3)[1]	M_1	141 regions (1976–88)	Mismatch higher since 1978 than earlier
Germany: JLS (Chapter 2)	M_3	11 regions (1978–86)	Mismatch lower in 1977, and higher in 1985 and 1986, than in other years, but no clear trend during the intervening period
United Kingdom: Jackman and Roper (1987)	M_1	9 regions (1963–84)	Mismatch higher before 1975 than afterwards
United Kingdom: Bean and Pissarides and JLS (Chapters 7 and 2)	M_2	9 regions (1963–84)	Mismatch higher before 1975 than afterwards
United Kingdom: JLS (Chapter 2)	M_3	10 regions (1967–87)	Mismatch higher before 1975 than afterwards
Sweden: Jackman and Roper (1987)	M_1	24 regions (1970–83)	No clear trend in mismatch
Sweden: JLS (Chapter 2)	M_3	24 regions (1976–87)	No clear trend in mismatch

Japan: Brunello (Chapter 4)	M_1	10 regions (1975–87)	After standard adjustment for changes in the share of notified vacancies by region, mismatch increased between 1975 and 1979, fairly steady thereafter
Japan: Brunello (Chapter 4)	M_3	10 regions (1975–87)	Mismatch higher since 1977 than in 1975 and 1976
Japan: JLS (Chapter 2)	M_3	20 regions (1974–87)	Mismatch highest in 1974 and lowest in 1975 and 1976, with no clear trend since 1977
United States: JLS (Chapter 2)	M	51 regions (1976–87)	Mismatch generally higher since 1980 than during 1976–9 period
Spain: Bentolila and Dolado (Chapter 5)	M_3	17 regions (1962–89)	Steady and pronounced downward trend in mismatch through 1985, with a very slight upturn since then
Italy: Attanasio and Padoa Schioppa (Chapter 6)	M_3	6 regions (1960–86)	Mismatch higher in the 1970s and 1980s than during the 1960s

Notes:
1. All chapters in this volume unless otherwise stated.
2. The mismatch measures M_1, M_2 and M_3 are defined in the text. M_1 and M_2 make use of data on the shares of unemployment and job vacancies by sector; M_3 is a measure of the relative dispersion of sectoral unemployment rates.

highly skilled labour might reasonably be expected to have been associated with worsening skill mismatch.

An alternative explanation of the available data on the behaviour of relative wages in Europe and Japan is, of course, that European and Japanese employment and training systems are more responsive than the US system, so that increased demand for more highly skilled labour has been met more effectively there than in the United States. This possibility is considered in section 5, in the context of the broader topic of labour market responsiveness.

5   Mobility and labour market adjustment

To the extent that labour market mismatch along either the skill or the geographic dimension has worsened – an issue on which available evidence is unfortunately less than fully conclusive – a logical next question is how the labour market has responded to these imbalances. Adjustment might take a variety of forms. One would expect, for example, that an increase in the relative demand for workers of a particular skill type would lead eventually to an outward shift in the relative supply curve for labour of that type, either because of changes in the education and training decisions of new entrants or through occupational mobility on the part of the existing work force. Similarly, increases in the relative demand for labour in particular regions should eventually produce greater net mobility to the regions where relative demand has risen. The behaviour of measured mismatch will depend critically upon the speed with which these adjustments occur.

A similar argument can be made concerning employers' responses to labour market imbalance. Excess relative supplies of workers of given skill types are likely to lead eventually to jobs being redesigned so that the relative demand curve for those types of labour shifts outward. Similarly, excess relative supplies of workers in particular locations may lead to changes in the location of jobs. There is anecdotal evidence of both sorts of employer response. In the fast food industry, for example, the difficulty of attracting workers with adequate basic skills and the relative abundance of unskilled workers has led to the development of cash registers that can be operated even by persons who cannot read, add or subtract. There are also well-publicised cases in which banks and insurance companies that have experienced difficulty in attracting low-level clerical personnel to central city headquarters have relocated back office operations to suburban locations that are more convenient for people with home responsibilities who might be unwilling to travel to a more distant site.

The literature on labour market mobility has considered both occupational mobility (the movement of workers across skill boundaries) and geographic mobility (the movement of workers across locational boundaries). In principle, one might also think about two other sorts of mobility: the movement of jobs across skill boundaries (changes in the skill mix of workers employed) and the movement of jobs across locational boundaries (movement of a plant or facility to a new site). These movements cannot be studied in quite the same way as the occupational and geographic mobility of workers, but it would certainly be appropriate to incorporate employers' work design and business location decisions into the analysis of labour market adjustment.[17]

5.1 Skill adjustment

With respect to the issue of skill mobility, Soskice (Chapter 9 in this volume) argues that there may be important differences in the effectiveness of different countries' employment and training systems that influence whether, and how, workers acquire new skills. In particular, Soskice suggests that students in the United States and the United Kingdom may have less incentive to take their education seriously, and that employers in those countries have weaker incentives to make investments in the skills of their workforce, than do their counterparts in Germany, Japan or Sweden. Soskice stresses the fact that the association between the strength of these incentives and labour market mismatch is complex; because employers in countries with stronger employment and training systems may opt to make more use of innovative technologies and to produce less standardised products, labour market mismatch there may be no lower than elsewhere. Differences in investment incentives nonetheless may have an important effect on the ability of different countries' labour markets to respond to shocks that generate skill imbalances.

The first weakness of the US and UK systems that Soskice identifies is the absence of standardised educational credentials, which he argues undermines the incentives for students to work hard in school and makes it more difficult for employers to evaluate the likely productivity of potential employees, thereby undermining their incentive to invest in the human capital of those they hire. One caveat I would note here is that, at least in the United States, it is relatively easy for employers to dismiss workers who prove to be unsatisfactory. Even though US students may have less of an incentive to take particular courses or to earn high marks in school, there is arguably good reason for them to acquire skills that will make them valuable employees. On the employer side, a probationary period may serve, in part, the same screening role that formal educational credentials play in other systems.

Soskice is also concerned about the shorter average tenures of US and UK workers, which he argues discourage investment in skills by employers. Most of the difference in average worker tenures across countries, however, reflects higher turnover rates in the first year or two on the job; beyond that period, expected tenures differ little across countries.

One feature of the US system that is seldom stressed is the relatively strong incentive that I suspect it provides for adult workers to invest in their own skills. In an employment and training system like that of the United States, where internal labour markets tend to be relatively open and where relative wages appear to be relatively flexible, there is the potential for workers who invest in skills that are in high demand significantly to improve their own economic position. US colleges, particularly community colleges, increasingly cater to adult learners, many of whom are employed full time and are taking job-related courses on their own initiative. Ongoing training and retraining may thus be worker-driven to a larger extent in the United States than is true elsewhere.

Unfortunately, there is very little empirical evidence on the responsiveness of skill acquisition among experienced workers to changing labour market conditions. JLS in Chapter 2 cite some evidence concerning the elasticity of new enrolments with respect to wage differentials, but none of the studies present evidence on the occupational mobility and training activities of experienced workers. Further study, not only of the behaviour of young persons but also of career transitions by older workers in the context of different employment and training systems, could prove extremely valuable.

None of the volume's studies directly addresses the question of how job structures respond to labour market imbalance. The Freeman study (Chapter 7 in this volume) contains one tantalising bit of related evidence. He finds that less-educated young men fare much better, not only absolutely but also relatively, in tight local labour markets than in local labour markets where aggregate unemployment is higher. Further evidence on the factors that influence employers' hiring patterns would certainly be welcome.

5.2   Locational adjustment

Two of the volume's studies examine geographic mobility. The study by Bentolila and Dolado (Chapter 5) looks at regional mobility in Spain; that by Attanasio and Padoa Schioppa (Chapter 6) examines regional mobility in Italy. Both sets of authors begin by commenting on the pronounced decline in interregional mobility over the period studied, from 1962 through 1986 in Spain and from 1961 through 1986 in Italy. In Spain, for example, Bentolila and Dolado report that interregional migration flows, as a percentage of population, averaged 0.65% between 1962 and 1969, but fell to 0.36% for the 1976–86 period. Attanasio and Padoa Schioppa report that net outmigration from southern Italy averaged in excess of 1% per year during the 1960s, but had fallen to somewhere in the neighbourhood of 0.10 or 0.20% per year by the late 1970s.

In both Spain and Italy, these declines in interregional mobility have been accompanied by increases in the absolute dispersion of unemployment rates across regions. One might have expected increased unemployment rate dispersion to have been accompanied by rising, not falling, interregional mobility;[18] it is thus an interesting question why it has not been. Chapters 5 and 6 consider several possible explanations. One contributing factor has almost certainly been the decline in interregional real wage differentials observed in both countries. Given the relatively low responsiveness of migration flows to observed wage differentials, however, this cannot be the whole story. The authors of both Chapters 5 and 6 conclude that the increase in the overall unemployment rate was probably the key factor in producing the observed decline in mobility. In the first instance, high unemployment rates are likely to reduce mobility simply by reducing the number of potential employment opportunities.[19] Attanasio and Padoa Schioppa in Chapter 6 suggest the interesting possibility that there may also be an hysteresis effect that depresses mobility subsequent to a period of high mobility: if few people from a given region have moved over some period of time, the probability of future migration may be reduced because potential migrants do not have a network of other recent migrants who can help them make the transition from one location to another. As was noted by several people at the 1990 conference, the fact that geographic mobility has been relatively stable in the United States and Sweden (two of the countries represented in the volume with the smallest increases in unemployment), whereas geographic mobility has fallen dramatically elsewhere, is supportive of the view that high aggregate unemployment depresses mobility.

In evaluating the results of Bentolila and Dolado in Chapter 5 and Attanasio and Padoa Schioppa in Chapter 6, data issues are again of some importance. For both Spain and Italy, available migration data refer to the entire population, rather than just to the active labour force. It would be of interest to know more about the migration behaviour of labour force members, and particularly the unemployed. One specific issue that participants at the conference felt merited investigation was the extent to which migrants who were attached to the labour force cared about the unemployment rate in the region to which they were moving. If most migrants had jobs at the time they moved, this might be something that, for most migrants, was of relatively little importance.

  None of the studies included in the volume directly addresses the issue of why capital has not flowed to high unemployment areas. In the Italian context, for example, several conference participants wondered why job growth in the south has not been more rapid; this would be an interesting subject for another study. Bentolila and Dolado's assessment of the Spanish situation leads them to suggest that efforts to move jobs to people, rather than people to jobs, might be warranted. The question why such flows have not been larger in the absence of active policy intervention merits study.

6   Conclusions

Although there were good reasons to believe that skill mismatch (and perhaps also regional mismatch) might have worsened in the developed economies during the 1970s and 1980s, efforts to measure trends in mismatch have failed to produce consistent evidence of worsening problems. These negative findings have lead some analysts to conclude that growing mismatch does not offer a general explanation for rising unemployment. At least with respect to assessing the trends in skill mismatch, however, available measures are so fragile that it is difficult to place much confidence in them. One set of questions concerning the measurement of both skill and geographic mismatch has to do with the choice of a conceptually appropriate mismatch indicator. The more serious problem with existing measures of skill mismatch, however, is not that mismatch indicators have been defined in a conceptually inappropriate way, but that the occupational categories that underlie existing implementations of these indicators do not correspond in any clear way to distinct labour markets. Given all of the problems that stand in the way of constructing a believable skill mismatch indicator I am unwilling, in spite of the lack of positive evidence, to conclude that skill mismatch has in fact not worsened. The evidence concerning geographic mismatch, on the other hand, seems less ambiguous: while there have been increases in geographic mismatch in certain countries, increasing geographic mismatch does not seem to have been a general phenomenon.

  Whether or not labour market mismatch has worsened – though perhaps particularly if it has – the question of how the labour market responds to skill and geographic imbalances is both interesting and important. The volume's studies provide some insight into the adjustment process, but leave many questions unanswered. While neither skill mobility nor geographic mobility are fully understood, we know much less about how and why workers (particularly adult workers) make career transitions than we do about interregional mobility. We also know far less about employers' decisions concerning how work will be organised – and thus what sorts of workers will be utilised – and concerning the location of their plants and facilities than we do about workers' skill investment and locational decisions. These latter issues are not addressed at all in this volume's studies; these seem to me to be particularly important issues for future research.

NOTES

1 I am grateful to the German Marshall Fund of the United States for a travel grant that permitted me to attend the conference at which this volume's studies were originally presented.
2 Shocks to the distribution of labour supply across sectors are another possible source of mismatch, but there is no obvious reason to believe that such shocks have caused worsening problems. This is not to say that labour supply shocks are never important: the recent influx of immigrants from East Germany to West Germany is a case in point.
3 Evidence on industrial and regional turbulence is summarised by JLS (Chapter 2 in this volume). See also the evidence reported by Franz, Brunello and Bentolila and Dolado (Chapters 3, 4 and 5 in this volume).
4 An additional problem is that turbulence measures constructed using data on employment shares are likely to be affected by cyclical fluctuations (see Abraham and Katz, 1986, on this point). This suggests the use of moving average rather than annual data to examine trends in turbulence.
5 The United States stands out as an exception to this generalisation. During the conference, it was also noted that geographic mobility had declined very little in Sweden.
6 This specification implicitly assumes that the total stock of job seekers is proportional to the number of unemployed persons.
7 Franz (Chapter 3 in this volume) reports that econometric analysis using the unadjusted job vacancy data reveals that the unemployment/vacancy relationship has shifted outward, but this outward shift is not obvious from his plot of the raw data.
8 These estimates come from data on total inflows on to the job vacancy register compared to the total number of new hires captured by social security records compiled by the Bundesanstalt für Arbeit, the same data as used by Franz to construct his adjusted vacancy series.
9 This discussion follows JLS (Chapter 2 in this volume). Jackman and Roper (1987) demonstrate that M_2 can be interpreted as a measure of the proportional outward shift in the aggregate unemployment/vacancy relationship for the special case in which hiring functions are identical across sectors.
10 See Abraham (1987) and Jackman and Roper (1987) for analyses that examine whether regional Beveridge curves in the United States and Britain have shifted outward by as much as those countries' aggregate Beveridge curves. Abraham's results lend support to the view that growing regional mismatch has been important in the United States, while Jackman and Roper's results suggest that it has not been important in Britain.

11 Employment or labour force weights should presumably be used in constructing this measure. Attanasio and Padoa Schioppa (Chapter 6 in this volume) report data on the coefficient of variation of regional unemployment rates, but this just equals the square root of M_3.

12 Still another approach to assessing the contribution of mismatch to aggregate unemployment, based upon estimation of a disequilibrium macroeconomic model, is tried in the studies by Franz and by Bentolila and Dolado (Chapters 3 and 5 in this volume). In contrast to the results of more standard mismatch analyses, this approach implies that there have been very large increases in mismatch in both Germany and Spain. A reconciliation of these conflicting results is beyond the scope of the present discussion.

13 Occupation-by-region cells might correspond more closely to actual labour markets, but none of the volume's studies use data categorised in this way.

14 Kathryn Shaw (1984, 1989) has implemented an approach in much this spirit in the context of measuring individuals' investments in occupation- and industry-specific human capital.

15 The results reported for the United States and the United Kingdom are also consistent with the work by Abraham (1987) and Jackman and Roper (1987) cited above.

16 Freeman (Chapter 8 in this volume) cites some of the evidence on the behaviour of skill-related wage differences in the United States. JLS (Chapter 2) summarise trends in manual/non-manual wage ratios in a number of other countries.

17 There is a large literature on the design of work and a smaller, but still sizeable, literature on business location decisions, but neither is oriented toward understanding these decisions as part of the labour market adjustment process.

18 This is what one would expect if, for example, individuals cared about the expected value of their wages, defined as $W(1 - UR)$, where W is the wage and UR is the unemployment rate.

19 As noted by several people at the conference, the reasoning here is exactly the same as that leading to the expectation that quit rates should fall when the unemployment rate rises.

REFERENCES

Abraham, Katharine G. (1987). 'Help-Wanted Advertising, Job Vacancies and Unemployment', *Brookings Papers on Economic Activity*, 1, 207–48.

Abraham, Katharine G. and Lawrence F. Katz (1986). 'Cyclical Unemployment: Sectoral Shifts or Aggregate Disturbances?', *Journal of Political Economy*, 94, 507–22.

Attanasio, Orazio P. and Fiorella Padoa Schioppa (1990). 'Regional Inequalities, Migration and Mismatch in Italy, 1960–86' (Chapter 6 in this volume).

Bean, Charles R., Richard Layard and Stephen J. Nickell (1986). 'The Rise in Unemployment: A Multi-Country Study', *Economica*, 53 (Supplement) S1–S22.

Bean, Charles R. and Christopher Pissarides (1990). 'Skill Shortages and Structural Unemployment in Britain: A (Mis)matching Approach' (Chapter 7 in this volume).

Bentolila, Samuel and Juan J. Dolado (1990). 'Mismatch and Internal Migration in Spain, 1962–86' (Chapter 5 in this volume).

Blanchard, Olivier and Peter Diamond (1990). 'The Beveridge Curve', *Brookings Papers on Economic Activity*, 1, 1–74.

Brunello, Giorgio (1990). 'Mismatch in Japan' (Chapter 4 in this volume).

Edin, Per-Anders and Bertil Holmlund (1990). 'Unemployment, Vacancies and Labour Market Programmes: Swedish Evidence' (Chapter 10 in this volume).

Franz, Wolfgang (1990). 'Match and Mismatch on the German Labour Market' (Chapter 3 in this volume).

Jackman, R. and S. Roper (1987). 'Structural Unemployment', *Oxford Bulletin of Economics and Statistics*, **49** (February) 9–37.

Jackman, Richard, Richard Layard and Christopher Pissarides (1984). 'On Vacancies', London School of Economics, Centre for Labour Economics discussion paper, **165** (revised).

Jackman, Richard, Richard Layard and Savvas Savouri (1990). 'Mismatch: A Framework for Thought' (Chapter 2 in this volume).

Lilien, David (1982). 'Sectoral Shocks and Cyclical Unemployment, *Journal of Political Economy*, **90**, 771–93.

Lipsey, R. (1960). 'The Relation Between Unemployment and the Rate of Change in Money Wage Rates in the United Kingdom, 1862–1957: A Further Analysis', *Economica*, **27** (February) 1–31.

Medoff, James L. and Katharine G. Abraham (1982). 'Unemployment, Unsatisfied Demand for Labor and Compensation Growth, 1956–1980', in Martin N. Baily (ed.), *Workers, Jobs and Inflation*, Washington, DC: Brookings Institution.

Shaw, Kathryn L. (1984). 'A Formulation of the Earnings Function Using the Concept of Occupational Investment', *Journal of Human Resources*, **19** (Summer) 319–40.

Shaw, Kathryn L. (1989). 'Investment in Job-Specific Skills: Implications for Wage Growth and Worker Displacement', working paper, Carnegie Mellon University, Graduate School of Industrial Administration.

Solow, Robert (1964). *The Nature and Sources of Unemployment in the United States*, Stockholm: Almquist and Wiksell.

S. J. NICKELL

1   Introduction

The notion of 'mismatch' is by no means an easy one to pin down. Despite the fact that authors of this volume were invited to write on mismatch in a variety of different countries, the individual country chapters have addressed a number of apparently different topics. For example, the Italian study (Chapter 6) is about long-run regional differences in unemployment whereas the Swedish study (Chapter 10) is concerned with the effectiveness of labour market policies and the Japanese study (Chapter 4) deals mainly with short-run adjustment problems.

Overall, it is clear that we must distinguish between short- and long-run considerations. In the short run, mismatch is associated with sector specific shocks and is, essentially, a temporary phenomenon. In the long run, we know that there are large and persistent regional and occupational differences in unemployment rates. Whether or not we should refer to this state of affairs as one of 'mismatch' is, then, a moot point. In my own view it is probably better to use some other term – such as 'unemployment dispersion' – to describe this situation. However, it is clear that this view is not shared by Jackman, Layard and Savouri (hereafter JLS) who, in their Chapter 2 describe such unemployment dispersion as essentially a mismatch problem.

Leaving aside questions of nomenclature, we shall now expand on the two aspects of the mismatch issue described above: in the short and in the long run.

2   Short-run mismatch and turbulence

Suppose there is a demand or productivity shock which is differentiated across sectors. Overall, such shocks may balance out, as in the case of purely intersectoral demand shifts; then some industries will expand and others will contract. If the supply of labour to the expanding industries is relatively inelastic in the short run – because of some impediment to intersectoral labour mobility, for example – then employment may initially fall by more in the contracting industries than it rises in the expanding ones. Unemployment will then rise and such a rise will be associated with a mismatch problem – that is, there is a temporary excess demand for labour in the expanding industries along with a temporary excess supply in the contracting ones. Such mismatch is readily measured by one of the standard sectoral unemployment/vacancy discrepancy indices, and it is typically also associated with a rise in the index of interindustry turbulence. This latter, popularised by Lilien (1982), is defined as the standard deviation of proportional employment changes across sectors.

An obvious policy to deal with this type of unemployment is to speed up the process of adjustment by reducing the impediments to intersectoral labour mobility. There are, however, two points worth noting about such intersectoral disturbances. First, it is generally the case that such sectoral shocks are, in fact, consequent on aggregate shocks (such as the oil shock) rather than genuinely autonomous (see Abraham and Katz, 1986, for example). Second, such turbulence has exhibited no secular upward trend in the postwar period in most countries, although it appears to have been somewhat higher in the interwar period. As a consequence, this issue is not taken to be very important by most European economists who are searching for explanations of the secular rise in unemployment over the last two decades. It has, however, attracted the attention of devotees of real business cycle theory in the United States, because of the apparently cyclical nature of the turbulence measure. One further point is important. It is clear that this form of mismatch is endogenous and so cannot be said to *explain* unemployment in a direct sense. As a result of certain shocks mismatch and unemployment may both rise, and the latter may rise by more than it otherwise would have done because of the impediments to mobility which generate mismatch. It is in this sense that the notion of mismatch 'causing' unemployment must be interpreted.

3   Long-run mismatch or dispersion

Here we are concerned with what is, perhaps, a more interesting question, that of understanding why it is that unemployment rates differ widely and persistently across both occupations and regions in many countries. In this regard, the study by JLS (Chapter 2) provides a very elegant theory. In its simplest form, the long-run elasticity of migration across sectoral boundaries is infinite so that, in long-run equilibrium, expected wages (wages × the employment rate) adjusted for amenities specific to the sector, are equalised. In the regional context, this might be termed a Harris–Todaro (1970) condition whereas in the occupational context it is a simple extension of the standard human capital model. The extension arises because, for some reason or other, wage differentials may not match the (flow) cost of moving from one sector to another (i.e., a lower to a higher occupation). Unemployment rates must then adjust so that expected wage differentials are matched to the relevant flow cost of migration. For example, suppose skill differentials (adjusted for the non-pecuniary attributes of jobs) are not big enough to cover the cost of skill acquisition, then in long-run equilibrium, the unskilled must have higher unemployment than the skilled in order to make it worthwhile to incur the cost of becoming skilled. This model has the very important consequence that demand shifts have no impact on unemployment differentials in the long run, which offers an explanation for the extraordinary stability of some of these differentials. Of course, it remains to be explained why the wage differentials are not big enough, and here there are any number of possibilities. On the skill front, the wages of the unskilled are supported by the benefit floor; on the region front, wage differentials may be squeezed by national bargaining or comparability considerations. Where these are absent – in the United States, for example – regional unemployment differentials do not exhibit any of the stability to be found in Europe.

What are the consequences of the unemployment dispersion for the overall level of unemployment? Here JLS present the interesting result that if wages within each sector are a convex function of sectoral unemployment rates, then any policy which tends to reduce unemployment dispersion will also reduce the aggregate equilibrium unemployment rate. This arises because the convexity means that the rise in wage pressure due to the reduction of unemployment in the high unemployment sector is *more than offset* by the fall in wage pressure due to the rise in unemployment in the low unemployment sector. This enables the economy to be run at a higher level of activity without rising inflation.

This analysis may be extended along the lines discussed by Soskice (in Chapter 9). Suppose wage differentials with regard to skill are 'too low'. Then a reduction in unemployment dispersion may be induced by subsidising the acquisition of skills. If we further suppose that a rise in the overall skill level enables firms to compete more effectively in world markets, such a policy will reduce overall unemployment in equilibrium, not only because of the reduction in unemployment dispersion but also by reducing the trade deficit or increasing the trade surplus at any given level of unemployment with stable inflation. This relaxes the trade balance constraint on the level of economic activity. Soskice argues convincingly that this is precisely the policy followed with such success in West Germany and Japan.

Does this mean that policies to subsidise mobility between sectors to reduce unemployment dispersion and the overall unemployment rate should always be pursued? The results of JLS indicate that the answer is 'no'. Such policies should be associated only with well-defined externalities of the standard kind. One such, which is particularly relevant, is the case where there is some kind of leading-sector problem in wage bargaining – that is, there is some connection between wages in the low-unemployment sector and those in the remaining sectors (because of comparability or national bargaining, for example). Some intervention to enhance intersectoral mobility may then be justified, although the alternative of directly attacking the mechanism by which wage differentials are attenuated is also a possibility.

4   Summary and conclusions

To summarise, 'mismatch' in this volume is used to refer to two distinct phenomena. The first is associated with the temporary consequences of intersectoral shocks. Here mismatch arises because the workers released from the contracting sectors are, for some reason, not immediately available or suitable for work in the expanding sectors. The impediments to mobility can take many forms from problems with the housing marker to absence of appropriate facilities for retraining.

The second mismatch phenomenon is the large and more or less permanent difference in unemployment rates across regions or skill groups. This is a fundamentally different phenomenon from that described above, in the sense that it arises essentially from the supply side and tends to be immune to shifts in demand. I am doubtful that 'mismatch' is a suitable word to describe it although, in most respects, it is a phenomenon that is more interesting and more worthy of study than the mismatch associated merely with short-run turbulence. In the light of this, it must be hoped that this volume will encourage further investigation into the apparently intractable problems posed by regional and occupational differences in unemployment.

REFERENCES

Abraham, K. and L. Katz (1986). 'Cyclical Unemployment: Sectoral Shifts or Aggregate Disturbances?', *Journal of Political Economy*, **94**, 507–22.

Harris, J. and M. Todaro (1970). 'Migration, Unemployment and Development. A Two-Sector Analysis', *American Economic Review*, **60**, 126–42.

Lilien, D. M. (1982). 'Sectoral Shifts and Cyclical Unemployment', *Journal of Political Economy*, **90**, 777–93.

Index